IGNATIUS OF LOYOLA AND THE FOUNDING OF THE SOCIETY OF JESUS

ANDRÉ RAVIER, S.J.

IGNATIUS OF LOYOLA AND THE FOUNDING OF THE SOCIETY OF JESUS

Translated by Maura Daly,
Joan Daly and Carson Daly

IGNATIUS PRESS   SAN FRANCISCO

Title of the French original:
*Ignace de Loyola fonde
la Compagnie de Jésus*
© 1973 Bellarmin, Desclée de Brouwer
Paris, France

Cover by Roxanne Mei Lum

With ecclesiastical approval
© 1987 Ignatius Press, San Francisco
All rights reserved
ISBN 0-89870-036-1
Library of Congress catalogue number 86-83262
Printed in the United States of America

CONTENTS

PART TWO

THE GRADUAL DEVELOPMENT INTO A MISSIONARY SOCIETY

PART FOUR

THE "ARS GUBERNANDI" OF IGNATIUS OF LOYOLA

INTRODUCTION

THE INTERPRETATION AND
MISINTERPRETATION OF OUR TITLE

I. THE MISINTERPRETATION

The title of this book[1] would have made Bobadilla roar—and the other *primi Patres* as well—with softer, but nonetheless steady, voices! Of course, it would have affected Simón Rodríguez this way, but also the humble Favre and even Xavier, Ignatius' friend. Moreover, Ignatius himself would have protested against it.

The reason for this is that in the eyes of everyone the Society of Jesus was the work of Christ himself—much more than that of men. Its sudden birth in history was of a charismatic nature rather than that of an ordinary project or apostolic plan. The Society carried the name of Jesus and to him it owed its origin, spirit and life. The members had the impression, if not of experiencing a new Pentecost, at least of having rediscovered the vitality, the fervor, the joy and the effectiveness of the earliest apostolic times, of the "primitive Church".

If it is necessary to speak of a founder in the human sense of the word, the early members of the Society considered themselves as all co-founders. This entire group was with the Society from its inception: first, the seven of them, and later, the others had made their vow at Montmartre; together they had offered themselves to Pope Paul III in 1538; together they had decided in 1539 to make themselves into a religious order and to select a superior: the Superior General had been elected by all of the members of the Society both those present and absent.

Bobadilla even occasionally referred to his title of co-founder. More-over, what made the crisis concerning Simón Rodríguez most painful was that Ignatius as Superior General had to deal severely with one of the *primi Patres*: the Superior General against one of the co-founders. We shall see that even in his severity, Ignatius will take great pains to respect in Rodríguez his companion of the early days.

In fact, Ignatius always treated his earliest companions with special consideration. In many cases, he entrusted them with important respon-sibilities and missions; if he did not make superiors of them, he strove

[1] The French title is *Ignace de Loyola Fonde la Compagnie de Jésus*, literally "Ignatius of Loyola *Founds* the Society of Jesus".

13

not to make them submit to any authority which post-dated the foundation of the Society. Thus, they were subordinate only to the Pope, to Ignatius himself or, if the need arose, to one of the other *primi Patres*.

Ignatius' attitude in this respect should be emphasized from the very beginning of this study because it both clarifies and determines much of the Superior General's conduct.

II. THE INTERPRETATION

Why, then, have we chosen the word "found" in order to signify the role that Ignatius played in the origin of the Society of Jesus?

The Two Meanings of "To Found"

Founding, when it is a question of an order, especially of a missionary order, assumes a much greater significance than that accorded the word in common usage. To found, then, is not only to institute, to provide the original basis or even structure, but it is also to launch and to communicate a new creative spirit. These nuances are present in the expressions "to found a political party", "to found a religion", or "to found a movement".

If one is allowed to make a play on words concerning such a serious matter (and in Latin, no less!), one could say that "to found", when it concerns the Society of Jesus, partakes of the meaning of *fundare* (to establish or provide a basis) and also of the meaning of *fundere* (to spread out or to diffuse). To these meanings we could add the comparison of the English terms *"foundation"* and *"fundement"*.

The Meaning of Our Title

Be this as it may, our problem is clear: is the Society of Jesus more indebted to Ignatius for its vitality, structure, spirit, dynamism and way of life than to the other *primi Patres*? I hesitated a long time myself before adopting the title of this book. Before condemning the title, let the reader be willing to follow minutely the details of this work and to take into account our explanations. Finally, however, our claim will be clear and categorical: humanly speaking, it is definitely Ignatius who founded and *is still founding* the Society of Jesus. In this work, he was the privileged instrument of the Holy Spirit: somewhat as he had used the apostle Peter to found his Church, God used him as the cornerstone.

To Which Society of Jesus Are We Referring?

At this point, it is necessary to make an essential distinction so that the reader does not mistake our intention. We are very much concerned with the foundation of the Society of Jesus as a religious missionary order and not only with the gathering together of several companions, something which Ignatius had attempted three times and which succeeded only at the college of Sainte-Barbe from 1529 on (and there, only after five years of effort). The difference between the two is crucial. In the case of a loosely knit group, there is no constituted "authority"; there is only an exchange between souls. There is no communal life except that of companionship, and there is neither structure nor framework. Each person follows his own path depending upon his own motivation. Companions are united merely by a spiritual affinity, and thus, the smallest thing can dissociate a member from the group. In such a case, one could not speak of a "founding" but rather of an "encounter": was it by chance or providence? In such a group, each brings what he has, and each receives from the others what they have. One receives more, another less. As a result of his age, his experience, his great virtue and, above all, as a result of his charity, Ignatius was incontestably the center: it was around him and because of him that the group was founded. These qualities sufficed. His six companions thought of him as a father or as an older brother—not at all as a "Founder" and still less as a legislator. Moreover, among themselves, there was no organizational framework whatsoever. Within the group itself, Ignatius voluntarily took a back seat to Pierre Favre because the latter was the only priest among them. His priestly character, combined with his gifts of empathy, kindness and a definite spiritual radiance, earned him the deference and the respect of the six others including Ignatius himself. When, in 1535, Ignatius left Paris to go to Spain, it was Favre who assumed responsibility for the group; but Favre too was like an older brother.

Thus, the question that we are addressing here is entirely different: it is a question of the founding of the Society of Jesus as such, as a religious order destined to work all over the world in an integrated manner, authorized to recruit members and destined to grow in numbers.

III. THE TIMELINESS OF THIS STUDY

Circumstances oblige us to assert very clearly that this study, even if its "hour has come" in this time of *aggiornamento*, is not a polemical work; this study is perhaps timely, but not of an opportunistic nature. Undoubtedly, this work will be able to aid contemporary research. Having heard several "masters of spirituality" discuss "what the nature of the Society of Jesus was" over a period of many years, I was astonished at the diversity of their views—not to say amazed at the divergences among their interpretations—and therefore I searched for a way of resolving these contradictions.

Everyone will realize that if a consensus had been established on the sixteen "Ignatian" years of the order, our current research would be much clearer as a result. Consequently, the problems (concerning details) that we have to consider acquire their true interest and cannot receive an honest solution unless they are placed once again in the *total* context of the Ignatian mentality: his attitude toward poverty, the steps of spiritual growth, priesthood, lay religious, etc., and obedience itself.

What can one do, then, except work, certainly not alone, but linked by friendship with other scholars, notably with the writers of the Historical Institute of the Society of Jesus and the Fathers of the Institute of Spirituality at the Gregorian University, and also with other solitary researchers. Knowing in advance that this study will undoubtedly not achieve the completeness or the breadth which such a subject demands, we can only hope to contribute one stone to the edifice which will inevitably someday be erected.

This study then is only a modest attempt, undoubtedly too personal, and therefore inevitably biased: it is certainly open to criticism.

Aware of this vulnerability, I have decided to divide the results of my research into two separate works: in the first, the documents, and in the second, an attempt at synthesis. In the first volume, I give a "chronicle" of the first seventeen years of the Society of Jesus.[2] The facts are categorized, assembled and presented on the documentary level, in their stark objectivity. In the second volume, I give an analysis along with this chronicle, in other words, an interpretation: this comprises the present volume.

Some people may say that this book is too late. Perhaps others will say that it is too early, because current events—what everyone has agreed to call "the crisis"—have given rise and continue to give rise to numerous studies both inside and outside the Society of Jesus. There are many noteworthy studies among these which throw new light on numerous problems. Furthermore, at the highest levels of the order, intense research work and exchanges of ideas are being carried out, in keeping with the evolution of the Church itself, which should directly or indirectly clarify this essential privileged period of sixteen years during which Ignatius of Loyola governed the young and turbulent Society of Jesus.

IV. THE GOOD FORTUNE AND DIFFICULTIES
CONNECTED WITH THIS STUDY

Even in this attempted synthesis, we have tried to remain as faithful as possible to the original documents—convinced that it was in them and

---

[2] Cf. *Les Chroniques saint Ignace de Loyola*, available at the magazine *Christus*.

them alone that we would be able to capture the real Ignatian mentality, along with that of his followers, and to perceive at least something about the ambience in which they lived.

Good Fortune

In this project, we enjoyed much good fortune. Although one might wish that the *Chronicon* of Polanco—the fundamental document—might soon be redone in an improved edition, the present edition already is a first-rate source. Undoubtedly, Polanco, the Secretary of the Society, was involved to a certain extent in the inevitable brouhahas that shook the entire Jesuit world, especially after 1560. It is also indubitable that, despite his efforts at objectivity and impartiality, the chronicler allowed some of his sympathies and antipathies to show. He even displays a kind of dry irony which is not lacking in cruelty—for example, in regard to Simón Rodríguez and Bobadilla. Finally, it cannot be doubted that his account sometimes (although rarely) lacks precision concerning details and poses some problems; the fact remains that the *Chronicon* constitutes a truly remarkable monument—it is the work of a great annalist and its more than five thousand pages are an invaluable mine of information.

We have also made great use of the correspondence, or rather the correspondences: that of Ignatius, taking account of some letters *ex commissione* written by the secretaries, but under the inspiration and responsibility of Ignatius; those also of the *primi Patres*, without neglecting those of some of Ignatius' closest collaborators which can be found in the *Epistolae Mixtae*, the *Epistolae Quadrimestres* or in such individual collections as those of Borgia, Nadal, Ribadeneyra, etc. These correspondences were one of Polanco's sources for the *Chronicon*, but they act simultaneously as a "control" for it and, in a way, the best commentary on it—that is to say, they actually provide an indispensable complement to it.

Thus, almost all of the volumes of the *Monumenta Historica Societatis Jesu* (MHSJ) with their texts and commentaries, have served as the basis for our documentation. What good luck for the would-be historian to have at his disposal—to cite only a few of the volumes—such editions as those of the *Spiritual Exercises* of Fathers J. Calveras and C. de Dalmases, the edition of *Constitutions and Rules* by Father Codina and his associates, and that of *Fontes narrativi* which gives us so many texts which would be hard to obtain otherwise. To the MHSJ it is also necessary to add its valuable complementary volume *Archivum Historicum Societatis Iesu* (AHSI).

There was still another stroke of good luck which makes one want to smile. The taste, at times naive, of certain of the first members of the Society for autobiography, spiritual diaries or other confessions has been invaluable. This literary genre can, not without reason, annoy its readers, but it is nonetheless necessary to do justice to these documents: they often disclose invaluable secrets. Among these works, two are particularly important: the *Autobiography* that Luis Gonçalves da Câmara coaxed out of Ignatius at the end of his life and the *Memorial* by the same author which allows us to enter into the daily atmosphere of the community at Rome, indeed, into an intimacy with Ignatius, the Superior General.

In France, we have at our disposal, thanks to the "Christus" collection, translations of the majority of the important texts that either originated with Ignatius or concern him.

Difficulties

Side by side with this good fortune, which is indisputably rare for the historian, it is also necessary to mention certain difficulties, some of which are very important. These difficulties can be divided into three primary groups:

1. Discrepancies—in quantity and in quality—between the studies which concern Ignatius before the foundation of the Society of Jesus (up until 1539) and those which concern the founding and governing of the Society by Ignatius and his companions (1539–1556). The *"caballero"*, the "pilgrim", the "student" of Alcalá, of Salamanca, of Paris, has been the subject of assiduous research, and putting aside certain secondary considerations, one can be sure that nothing has been left obscure, and that general agreement concerning most points has been established. The *Spiritual Exercises* are and will always be the object of new readings, in connection with the development of exegesis or of theology, and with the appearance of certain philosophical and psychological systems.

Since scholars have been able to deduce the dates of certain occurrences as a result of their proximity to other events, the text itself has been established as very reliable. If in this first part of the life of Ignatius, some advances in understanding can be made, they will probably be due to developments or changes in the science of history itself: as a result of more attention paid to economic facts, to social classes (including the religious milieu), or to the contemporary mentality accompanying them.

Unfortunately, one cannot say as much for the second part of Ignatius' life as Superior General. It seems as if the recent biographers of Ignatius have run up against some extreme difficulties in coming to grips with this new phase of his life and have hesitated to get their bearings in this labyrinth of various actions, directives, initiatives and behavior. To mention only two of them, the Irish writer, Father James Brodrick, will never give us the second volume of his *Saint Ignatius of Loyola*. As for Father Robert Rouquette, death interrupted his work and it was a major blow for Ignatian studies; he was gifted and well equipped to complete successfully this arduous task. Fortunately, I was able to consult most of the notes which he had assembled. In these notes, the first part of Ignatius' life is almost completed; but much of the second part is merely in rough draft. It is not that biographies of St. Ignatius are lacking in libraries—as the collection of Father Iparraguirre certainly demonstrates.[3] However, all those to which I had access seem to suffer from the same "distortion" between the two parts of the life of Ignatius. This is such a characteristic fact of Ignatian studies that comprehensive dictionaries are even in the habit of distinguishing between the two: those of Ignatius' personal life, even at the time when he was Superior General (filed under *Ignatius* or *Loyola*), and those concerning his life as Superior General (filed under the rubric *Jesuits*). This procedure is convenient, but one cannot help wondering whether it favors a true knowledge of the subject.

2. What is the source of these difficulties? They derive from several sources. Nonetheless, it seems that one can specify two particularly important ones, but they certainly are not unrelated.

First, the breadth of the subject. Whether he wanted to or not, Ignatius found himself, as Superior General, coming to grips with the most acute problems of his era, political and economic as well as social and religious. It was not only a question of the enormous problem of Catholic Reform with its doctrinal, disciplinary and diplomatic aspects. However, how is it possible to write definitively of the oppositions that the young Society of Jesus encountered in Flanders or France or even Spain? Has, for example, the Simón Rodríguez affair, which shook Portugal so violently, even now been clarified? Concerning this issue, we are still today confronted with a Portuguese and a Spanish theory which do not agree perfectly. The recruitment of the order during these early years, the training of the candidates and of novices according to different regions, sometimes according to different houses, the confusing business of exits and returns pose confusing, if not contradictory, questions. What of Ignatius' "callings" to a deepening spiritual involvement, indeed, to holy orders? What of his relations with the Pope, with princes, with other religious communities—some of which were just newly founded? The fact that Ignatian literature in recent years, and notably doctoral theses, displays particular interest in these questions reveals the degree of obscurity that still envelops the mentality of Ignatius as Superior General.

The second source of difficulties which it is necessary to mention is the

---

[3] *Orientaciones bibliográficas sobre San Ignacio de Loyola* (2nd ed. published IHSI, Rome, 1965), pp. 16–26, nn. 63–103.

rapid evolution of the historical method and the new orientations it brings with it, one could say its new philosophy. This is not, however, the place to embark on that subject. It suffices to say that in order to satisfy the present exigencies of historical science, it would be necessary to bring to bear on each contested point an exhaustive inventory of the subject. We have not yet arrived at that point!

3. If one were to try to proceed in such a manner, all efforts at synthesis would be doomed to failure if there were not already extremely serious studies written with all due scientific rigor, be they on certain aspects of the early Society, or on certain facts and figures connected with it. We will cite some characteristic examples. In publishing his history of the Italian contribution to the Jesuits, *Storia della Compagnia di Gesù in Italia*,[4] Father Pietro Tacchi Venturi was forced to address many problems which pertained to the entire Society, and he did so with his habitual mastery and competence: in particular, he describes Ignatius' life in Rome at length. Another historian of great merit, Father Mario Scaduto, took up where Tacchi Venturi left off, with *L'Epoca di Giacomo Laynez*.[5] Numerous passages of this work illuminate retrospectively the generalcy of Ignatius, his actions and the people in his entourage. For many of the facts of Ignatius' life, it suffices to cite the names of Leturia and Hugo Rahner and to mention the *Fontes narrativi* and the *Archivum Historicum S.J.* in order to measure the progress made over some years. The real story of the missions is enriched by the noteworthy works of the Fathers who contributed to the *Monumenta Historica*. It is not possible to mention them all, but at least we must not fail to mention the name of Father Georg Schurhammer, who died in November 1971, and his monumental work *Franz Xaver, sein Leben und seine Zeit*.[6] We must also cite Father Otto Braunsberger's exemplary publication, *Beati Petri Canisii S.J. epistulae et acta*.[7] With such authors, the historian feels himself perfectly secure—especially since all of these works are equipped with notes, references and indices which permit the reader, if he wishes, to consult certain records.

From this superabundance, however, arises yet another difficulty. Don't these brilliantly studied areas, facts and figures, however, deepen the shadow that still covers other areas, facts and figures? This objection is not negligible. We must remember, however, that the books cited above are mentioned only as examples: to mention only the history of

[4] Four volumes in octavo.
[5] Two volumes in octavo.
[6] Four volumes in octavo.
[7] Eight volumes.

the Assistancies[8], we would have at our disposal six additional works (the reader will find a list of these in our bibliography). On the other hand, however, one can regret the fact that the biographies of Juan Alonso de Polanco and of Simón Rodríguez have not yet tempted some great writer. These are the lacunae that create real voids.

Is our work, then, imprudent?

We weighed this consideration well before bringing the project to fulfillment, and it seems to us that we were able to overcome these worries for the following reasons:

—First, today there are enough published documents and serious studies that it is already possible to distinguish the general outlines of Ignatius' administration, and his "mentality" as Superior General, and thus, to support the synthesis that we propose: humanly speaking, Ignatius founded and today is still founding the Society of Jesus.

—Next, this is an essay open to criticism and correction—and not a study that pretends to be exhaustive or definitive.

—Finally, our field is deliberately and conscientiously limited to information that is definitely established. Nonetheless, some obscure points remain and will be pointed out with all possible objectivity as they arise.

---

[8] Assistancies are administrative divisions in the Society of Jesus, grouping several provinces together (Tr.).

PART ONE

FROM AN INFORMAL COMPANIONSHIP
TO AN APOSTOLIC BODY

CHAPTER I

NOVEMBER 1538: TEN COMPANIONS, "PRIESTS OF REFORM", OFFER THEMSELVES TO THE POPE FOR ANY MISSION THROUGHOUT THE WORLD

We are in Rome at the end of the summer of 1538. Ten men that the Roman crowd call the "pilgrim priests" live together in poverty, prayer and charity. They still live in the small house where, according to Nadal, they had moved in April in order to be closer to the center of the City: or had they already moved into the "haunted house" that Antonio Frangipani had put at their disposal? The second of these hypotheses seems more likely.[1]

I. A FIRST FAVORABLE WELCOME BY PAUL III (APRIL 1537)

Their reassembly in the Eternal City had really just occurred. Toward the middle of Lent in 1537, they were already doing missionary work in Venice and its environs; but Ignatius had then sent them to Rome in groups of three:[2] they had to present themselves to Pope Paul III, solicit

---

[1] Ignatius and his group of companions occupied five houses in succession in Rome. (1) On their arrival, they took shelter in a house set on the slope of the hill of the Trintà dei Monti that had been put at their disposal by Quirino Garzoni (November 1537–April 1538), today number 11 on Via Sebastianello. (2) This residence was too far out of the way; they moved into the area near the Bridge of Sixtus (according to Nadal) (April–November 1538). (3) In November 1538, they moved into a house that Antonio Frangipani had put at their disposal: people said that it was "haunted"; it was situated close to the Tower of Melangolo, where the palace built by Mario Delfini near the middle of the sixteenth century stands (today number 16 on the Via Delfini). It is there, according to Simón Rodríguez and Polanco, that they welcomed, nourished and assisted a great many poor people during the course of the terrible winter of 1538–1539. The companions lived there until February of 1541. (4) In February of 1541, Ignatius and his companions moved into the house of Camillo Astalli, which was situated on the site of the choir loft of the present-day church of the Gesù. (5) Finally, in September of 1544, Ignatius and his community moved into the southern part of what is today the scholasticate at number 54 of the Piazza del Gesù. Cf. *Vestigia Sanctorum Societatis Jesu in Urbe Roma*, ALDAMA. 1953, and TACCHI VENTURI.: *Le case abitate in Roma da san Ignazio di Loyola.*

[2] Cf. *Epist. Mixt.* I, pp. 11–14. Father Schurhammer has restored the integral text of the letter (*Franz Xaver*, I, 348–50). The two additional companions were Arias, a Spanish priest endowed with a certain number of vices, and Landivar, one of Xavier's former domestics in Paris who had tried to assassinate Ignatius when Xavier converted. Both of these recruits "dropped out" in the course of the voyage!

His Holiness's authorization to go to Jerusalem, inform him of their apostolic plans, and request the right to receive Holy Orders, because, for the most part, they were not yet priests. Ignatius did not accompany them; he was afraid that his presence might interfere with the success of this step because both Cardinal Carafa (the Theatine), whose institute and manner of living Ignatius had recently criticized, and Dr. Ortiz, Charles V's ambassador to Rome (who, Ignatius thought, had suspected him of illuminism and of heresy) were then living in Rome.

This step by the companions succeeded beyond their fondest hopes, thanks to Dr. Ortiz, who himself introduced them to Paul III. On April 3 (Easter Tuesday), the pontiff put their theological knowledge to the test: he made them debate in his presence and in that of cardinals, bishops and theologians; he even intervened in the debate himself. Satisfied with their mastery of doctrine and with the ideal they supported, the Pope, who favored reform in the Church,[3] gave them everything that they sought: the freedom to go to Palestine and to live there as long as they wished; the priestly power to preach and to hear confessions throughout the world (and without recourse to the bishops of each place); permission to those who were not yet priests to have themselves ordained under whatever title they wished, at whatever time of the liturgical year, and by the bishop of their choice. To all these favors, the Pope had added a purse of thirty three gold coins to finance their voyage to the Holy Land; with the bestowal of gifts by other ecclesiastical dignitaries, the sum was raised to more than one-hundred fifty ducats: the companions sent this money to Venice by letters of credit that some merchants made out for them free of charge.[4]

II. THE ORDINATIONS OF VENICE (JUNE 1537)

They came back then to Venice. All either professed or renewed their vow of perpetual poverty, according to the spirit of Montmartre,[5] into the hands of Jerome Virallo, the legate at Venice; and a few days later, all those who were not priests were ordained by Vincent Negusanti, the

---

[3] The Pope had received the *consilium aureum* in the final days of March of 1537, at the end of the work of the commission for reform in the Church; this commission named by Paul III was presided over by Cardinal Contarini.

[4] *Autobiog.* R.P., n. 93.

[5] The vow of poverty made at Montmartre contained, as Simón Rodríguez points out, a restrictive clause ("*De Origine et progressu Societatis Jesu*", *Epist. Broëti*, p. 457): "Immediately, the Fathers specified that they were not bound by their vow of poverty while they were busy with their studies in Paris, and that they could accept money (*une viatique*) for the pilgrimage to Jerusalem."

bishop of Arbe (on the Dalmatian coast); thus, they received minor orders on June 10, the subdiaconate on the fifteenth, the diaconate on the seventeenth, and the priesthood on June 24, the Feast of St. John the Baptist. As the letters from Rome allowed, they chose to be ordained "in the name of voluntary poverty and of sufficient knowledge."[6] Only Salmeron, who was not yet twenty-three, had to put his ordination off until later.

In order to prepare themselves for their first Mass, the companions decided to withdraw into solitude for three months to give themselves over to contemplation and penance. On July 25, they dispersed, two by two or three by three, and went to the small towns in the seignory of Venice: Ignatius, Favre and Laynez chose an abandoned house at the gates of Venice "which had neither door nor window"—San Pietro-in-Vivarolo.

However, before the three months were up (at the end of September 1537), Ignatius reunited all of the companions at Vicenza. With the exception of Rodríguez[7] and of Ignatius who "had determined to wait a year without saying Mass in order to prepare himself and to pray to the Virgin to keep him with her Son";[8] the recently ordained priests (five in all) celebrated their first Mass. What was the reason for this premature call to reunite? An explanation based on political events alone does not seem sufficient. Since June 3, 1536, Venetians and Turks had certainly been involved in overt hostilities, but, according to Bobadilla,[9] it was still possible to think that they would soon be reconciled: "for the Turks cannot live without Venice, nor Venice without the Turks": the plan for the pilgrimage to Jerusalem remained intact. In any case, the time allotted for the departure to the Holy Land in the vows taken at Mont-martre fell due at the earliest[10] in December 1537. The companions could legitimately hope to leave for the Holy Land in spring 1538.

---

[6] Did they renew their vow of perpetual chastity? The question is debated by the historians. In a letter to Verdolay (*Epist. ign.* 1, p. 120) Ignatius only speaks of a vow of perpetual poverty. The meaning of this vow and of the terms of ordination is admirably specified by a letter that Claude Jay sent to his other companions, from his retreat at Bassano on September 5, 1537 (cf. T. VENTURI, *Storia* 2, pp. 43–44 (incomplete text), and SCHURHAMMER, lib. cit. 1, pp. 339–40 (complete text): On San Pietro-in-Vivarolo, cf. *Autob.* R.P., n. 94.

[7] Rodríguez celebrated his first Mass a short time later in Ferrara and Ignatius celebrated his on Christmas Day 1538 on the altar of the Nativity of St. Mary Major.

[8] These are Ignatius' own words. Cf. "*Acta*", n. 96, in *Scripta* 1 or *Font. narr.* 1 (cf. T. VENTURI, op. cit., 3, p. 88).

[9] *Bobad. Mon.*, p. 616, n. 9.

[10] "At the earliest", for the experts disagree on this point: Tacchi Venturi is in favor of December 1537, and Leturia (AHSI, vol. 9 [1940] favors 1538).

III. MISSIONS BY GROUPS IN THE UNIVERSITIES OF NORTHERN ITALY

In order to fill up the months of waiting, the companions decided, after having "deliberated" together, to separate once again into groups of two or three, but no longer in solitude: on the contrary, they divided themselves among the closest universities and took up once again their Parisian habit of living an evangelical life among the youth, with the hope that some recruits would join them. Codure and Hozes left for Padua, Xavier and Bobadilla for Bologna, Jay and Rodríguez for Ferrara, and Salmeron and Broët for Siena. Ignatius, Laynez and Favre went toward Rome. In spite of the hope that they all kept of realizing the dream of a pilgrimage to the Holy Land, it was necessary to prepare everything in case the war between Venice and the Turks continued— and hence that they remain where they could offer themselves to the Pope for any mission.

All of these decisions were unanimous, as "among friends in Christ", according to Ignatius' expression. Before separating, they established some rules for practical conduct that all of the groups would observe in order to manifest their community of spirit. One of these rules, among others, was that in each group, taking weekly turns, one companion would be responsible for decisions, although the entire group would still deliberate concerning them. Above all, they agreed, "after long deliberation", on what they would answer to those who asked them what they were: "Seeing", wrote Polanco in 1547,[11] "that there was no head man among them, no superior other than Jesus Christ whom they wanted to serve to the exclusion of all others, it seemed good to them to take the name of him whom they had as their master and to call themselves the Society of Jesus. . . ."[12] If one believes Polanco, who relies on the testimonies of the first companions, this name was confirmed by God to Ignatius in many divine illuminations which permitted him firmly to maintain this name against all opposition that later arose against it.[13]

---

[11] *Summarium hispanicum.* Cf. *Font. narr.* I, pp. 203-204.

[12] In order to make a good judgment concerning the event, it is indispensable to take account of Ignatius' letter to his nephew Beltran, of [24] September 1539. Cf. Saint Ignace, *Letters* (coll. "Christus"), p. 69; cf. SCHURHAMMER, *Franz Xaver*, I, p. 475.

[13] If the name "Society [*Compagnie*] of Jesus" aroused some opposition, the word *Compagnie* itself, at least in French, suggests the opposite meaning. Here, we must be on our guard not to look at the question with too modern an approach. It is clear that by the word "company", the first members did not mean to consider themselves only as "soldiers". But that there was in the word no reference to the obedience that one owes to a "leader", and to an absolute leader, seems questionable; even the fact that the word *compagnie* (society) was added to the name of "Jesus" gives it its true sense: faith, fidelity, devotion, service, total self-giving and obedience. It was Jesus, after all, who first declared

IV. IGNATIUS, LAYNEZ AND FAVRE AT ROME (OCTOBER 1537)

Toward the middle of October, Ignatius, Favre and Laynez left Venice. About fifteen miles from Rome, at an intersection of the Claudian and Cassian Ways called La Storta, the three travelers entered a chapel. Ignatius then had a vision: God the Father appeared with Christ carrying his Cross. "I want", said the Father to Christ, "you to take this man [Ignatius] as your servant." Christ then said, "I want you to be my servant." The Father added, "I will be watching over you in Rome." Depicted in its essential details, this is the vision of La Storta.[14]

At the end of the month of October 1537, the three companions entered Rome by the Flamian Gate. They took shelter in a small house that Quirino Garzoni had lent them. Soon, Ignatius was going to put his companions totally at the Pope's disposal. The Pope left Ignatius free in his apostolate to attend to his spiritual interviews and to the Spiritual Exercises, which were his personal spiritual gift [charisme personnel]. As for Laynez and Favre, Paul III conferred on them two chairs at the Sapientia, the theological school that Clement VII had closed after the devastating sack of Rome by Charles V's soldiers and which Paul III had reopened scarcely three years earlier. Favre taught positive theology, that is to say, Holy Scripture; Laynez, scholasticism. Laynez confides that, at the beginning, he satisfied neither himself nor his auditors,[15] and that it took him a little time to adjust and to get under way.

Sensing the auspicious atmosphere, Ignatius reunited at Rome all the companions who had been spread throughout all the university towns of northern Italy. Sometime after Easter 1538 (April 21), they were all reunited once again: the only person missing at this reunion was the novice Diego Hozes, the first recruit that Ignatius had made in Italy. Sent

---

himself "King". The real question lies elsewhere: what will become of this obedience, which is legitimate in regard to Jesus, on the day that Ignatius and his companions "offer themselves" to the Vicar of Jesus Christ and even more, on the day that they organize themselves into a hierarchy within the Society of Jesus? We will strive to discover what Ignatius and the first Fathers thought on this major point.

[14] Cf. infra, p. 425. This vision has gained a considerable importance in the Jesuit tradition. Ignatius' intimates have given us several different versions of it: Gonçalves da Câmara, Laynez, Nadal (4 accounts), Polanco, Ribadeneyra (2 accounts), Canisius. In fact, there are only three sources concerning this event: an allusion in the *Spiritual Diary*, a short account made by Ignatius himself in the *Autobiography*, and immediate confidences made by Ignatius to Laynez who was present. Laynez who often mentions this fact, puts it in a lecture given to all the Fathers at Rome in 1559. If one wants to gauge the fact properly, one must have recourse to Laynez. But beyond that this vision raises the whole question of "visions" in general and of other external phenomena of mysticism, notably the words heard by St. Ignatius. Cf. the fifth part of the present study.

[15] *Lainii Mon.* 1, p. 550.

to Padua with Jean Codure when the companions dispersed, Diego Hozes remained there working with admirable zeal. However, one day, after having preached out of doors on the Gospel injunction to "watch and pray" he was taken ill and barely an hour later he died at a public hospital for the poor.[16]

V. THE COMPANIONS REASSEMBLE IN ROME

At this point, there were ten companions reassembled. Paul III was not in Rome, but in Nice where he was trying to reconcile Charles V and Francis I, because the "Turkish danger" had become severe: since October the Turks had occupied Syros, Patmos, Paros and Naxos: in October they fought at Goritzia near Dakovo with the armies of the King of the Romans[17] and they were beginning to exert pressure on the Hungarian borders. It was crucial to form a holy alliance against the threat posed by the crescent of Islam. At this time, there was no question of going "to offer oneself to the Pope" according to the vow sworn at Montmartre: and then, wasn't there still some hope of achieving the pilgrimage to the Holy Land? At this time, a treaty, a peace, was very quickly signed. The companions continued to hope. Whatever the situation, it was necessary to remain in Rome while awaiting the Pope's return. Cardinal John Vincent Carafa, the "Neapolitan Cardinal",[18] was governing the city in the Pope's absence. The companions addressed themselves to him in order to obtain the necessary powers for the exercise of their ministry. On May 3, 1538, the Cardinal allowed them the right to preach and to hear confessions without any territorial limitations. They were also allowed to say Mass, to distribute the Eucharist, and to administer the other sacraments—but only with the consent of the local pastors and only without interfering with the latters' rights.[19] The companions set to work immediately.[20]

Even before this permission had been accorded to the group, a violent wave of calumny crashed down upon them concerning Agostino Mainardi, the heretical preacher whom certain members of the Curia at the

---

[16] Cf. T. VENTURI, Storia 3, pp. 111, 112, 113.

[17] The King of the Romans is the person designated by the Emperor of the Holy Roman Empire to be his successor.

[18] Cousin of Cardinal Gian Pietro Carafa, the Theatine cardinal.

[19] The text concerning their "powers" can be found in Scripta, 1, pp. 548–49.

[20] On all these facts, we benefited from a very valuable document: the long letter that Ignatius wrote to Isabel Roser on December 19, 1538 (cf. Font. narr. 1, 6–14, translation in RAHNER, Ignace de Loyola et les femmes de son temps, 2, pp. 34–39).

Vatican were protecting. There is no need to recount here the various aspects of this crisis since all the historians report them in great detail.[21] But one thing is certain: this entire affair illustrated Ignatius' calmness and faith in the face of the strongest of storms and demonstrated his clearness of thought and his tenacity in totally and correctly resolving the difficulties that faced him. On November 18, 1538, the crisis was ended by a decision in due form that cleared the companions of any suspicion of heresy.[22]

VI. THE OBLATION OF NOVEMBER 1538

It is at this point that Ignatius and his companions took a major step. The exact date is not known, but it was between the eighteenth and the twenty-third of November.[23] Undoubtedly, it would have taken place at the time of the companions' reunion in Rome, but the absence of the Pope and then the Mainardi affair delayed it. Whatever the case may have been, at that time, the amount of time decided upon in the vows of Montmartre for the pilgrimage to the Holy Land had surely already been overextended. According to the alternative stipulated in the vow, the group had, in conscience, to put themselves totally and unconditionally at the disposal of the "Vicar of Christ in order to be sent wherever it seemed appropriate to him to send them and on whatever mission he chose". In the meanwhile, if the route to Jerusalem was reopened, the group would be advised of it.

It is noteworthy that Ignatius' letter of December 19, 1538, to Isabel Roser does not mention this "offering" that marked an important step in the life of the companions.[24] This is especially remarkable since this letter is long and goes into minute detail. In his *Autobiography*, Bobadilla does not go into this matter any more than does Ignatius. Consequently, Favre's letter to Diego de Gouvea takes on greater importance and heightened meaning. Let us first clarify a mistaken expression here: we say "Favre's letter to Gouvea", but we should say "the companions'

[21] Notably T. VENTURI, *Storia* 3, pp. 139–64.

[22] The text is in *Scripta*, 1, pp. 627–29.

[23] The eighteenth of November is the date of the "judgment", and as early as the twenty-third, Favre announced the "offering to the Pope" in a letter to Diego de Gouvea, the former "principal" of the college of Sainte-Barbe. Cf. *Fabri Mon.*, p. 14, and especially, *Epist. ign.* 1, pp. 132–34. Would it be possible, as some wish to believe certain, to put this "offering" before the eighteenth of November? It does not seem possible because of Favre's expression in his *Memorial* (*Font. narr.* 1, p. 43, n. 18): "*post habitam sententiam nostrae purificationis*" which seems to leave no room for doubt.

[24] RAHNER, *Ignace de Loyola et les femmes de son temps*, 2, p. 34.

letter to Gouvea" since it is signed to that effect: *Petrus Faber et ceteri ejus socii ac fratres*: these are all the companions who, in fact, signed the letter that Favre composed. And, above all, it is the theme of the letter that is important: Gouvea informed his friends that the Emperor was looking for missionaries to go to the Spanish Indies, and he invited them to go with the expedition. The plan was very tempting to the companions:

> We would like to be able to satisfy your request; but two things prevent us from doing so: all of us, insofar as we are what we are—tied to one another (*as invicem colligati*) in this society—are devoted (*devovimus nosmetipsos*) to the Supreme Pontiff because he is the master of the universal harvest of Christ, and by this self-offering [oblation] we have signified to him that we are ready for anything that he would decide to do with us in Christ. If then, he sends us where you have called us, we will go there with joy. Why have we undertaken to submit ourselves to the will and judgment of the Pontiff? It is because we know that he is best able to recognize what is most suitable for universal Christianity.

Gouvea was not the first to think of the companions as good candidates to go to the Indies; there were even some steps to effect this before the Pope; but the Emperor's ambassador quickly realized that "the Pope's will was that we not leave here because even in Rome the harvest is abundant. It is not the distances that scare us or the learning of a new language that disturbs us, but what matters to us is that we do that which is most pleasing to Christ."

In his *Memorial*,[25] Favre will speak again of this "oblation" to the Pope: and one can easily see that, in his eyes, in 1542, the oblation had lost none of its importance. On the contrary, "It was", he says, "a grace worth remembering and, in some respects, was the foundation of the entire Society (*quasi totius Societatis fundamentum*) when we offered ourselves (*nos ipsos praesentaremus in holocaustum*) to the Pope", and God permitted him "to accept us and to approve our projects heartily". Favre exclaims, "I and all my companions with me will always be bound to render thanks to the master of the harvest of the entire Catholic Church, that is to say, to Jesus Christ our Lord who has deigned to declare by the voice of his Vicar on earth (which is the clearest vocation), who has deigned, I say, to indicate that he is willing that we serve him and that he always wants to make use of us." This text of the *Memorial*, however lyrical it may be, corresponds very well to the letter to Gouvea. The point of view espoused therein is fundamental.

This stage in the evolution of the plans of the companions was of major importance. It allows us to see already that the Society of Jesus did

---

[25] *Font. narr.* I, p. 42.

not arise from an awareness, inspired though it may have been, taken up with a plan for Catholic Reform: the attitude today is in line with the occurrences of yesterday and remains open to the events of tomorrow. For the moment, the companions stayed away from any idea of an organized congregation; one may even suppose that they did not stop hoping that they might still achieve their objective of going on a pilgrimage to the Holy Land together. But because the official amount of time foreseen by the vow of Montmartre had already elapsed, and they were still in Rome, they returned to Paul III the purse that he had bestowed on them in 1537. . . .

How did they go about "offering" themselves to the Pope? We do not know anything about it. Certain historians would like to attribute to this occasion Paul III's celebrated remark, "Why do you want to go to Jerusalem? Italy is a good and true Jerusalem, if you want to make the Church of God fruitful. . . ." The source of this anecdote is the *Autobiography* of Bobadilla;[26] this text does not specify in the least at which of the numerous meetings with Paul III that these words were pronounced. ("The more numerous meetings are, the more content I shall be with them.") In any case, it seems that the Pope's original intention was to keep these "priests of reform", whom God had sent him, in Italy, and even in Rome itself.

It was in their faith that the companions found the explanation for what had happened to them. We can see their attitude clearly set forth in the letter from Ignatius to Isabel Roser:[27]

> Since we began (here, in Rome), until now, there have always been two or three sermons on each feast day and also two scriptural lessons each day. The others (companions) have been busy with confessions and with the Spiritual Exercises. Since the verdict (in the Mainardi affair) has been handed down, we hope to do more with our sermons[28] and also with teaching catechism to children. Since the ground is so sterile and dry [Ignatius is speaking here of Rome!] and the opposition that we have experienced is so strong, we can truly say that we have not lacked work and that our Lord God has accomplished more than our knowledge and intelligence alone could possibly have obtained.

---

[26] *Bobad. Mon.*, p. 616, n. 11.

[27] RAHNER, op. cit., 2, p. 59.

[28] These sermons, given in a language that the companions did not know very well, were more of an exercise in mortification for them than a source of conversions. However, as a result of their desire to preach the true and pure Christian doctrine, they affirmed this and it is a fact that these sermons were accompanied by long sessions in the confessional and by "spiritual colloquies".

From this time on we notice the appearance of an argument that Ignatius and the first generation of his sons would often use: the argument concerning the "disproportion" between their own strength and the apostolic results that they effected as a sign of the divine favor bestowed on the Society of Jesus. In the postscript to this letter, another sign of God's will is mentioned in connection with the preceding one, the order of the Pope: "While I was writing this letter, the Pope ordered the governor to direct the city to group together schools for small children whom we shall instruct in Christian doctrine as we had already begun to do. May it be pleasing to our Lord God; it is *because it is his work*[29] that he wants to give us strength for his greater service and glory."

Thus, even *before* the Society of Jesus became a religious order, its ideal and the mystique attached to it were already very clearly defined. According to an attitude that we will have the opportunity to mention many times, the structures of the society were, for Ignatius, "secondary" in comparison with its spirit. This "offering" of November 1538 is an important event because in it the companions had offered their obedience to the Pope in the fullest sense. In this act of obedience, they believed that they would find the sure discovery of God's will as a fecund apostolic source, the necessity of a universal apostolate, and total self-abnegation in the service of Jesus Christ through his Vicar—all this was included in the action of the first companions. Furthermore, their fundamental condition appeared: in order to respond fully to pontifical missions, even if it were teaching catechism to children, it was necessary to be priests who were truly reformed.

God continued to show them his will by the events that occurred. What happened in the winter of 1538–1539 provides a perfect example. Precisely because this winter was so bitter, the poor were hungry and cold; in fact, they were dying in the streets. The companions devoted themselves wholeheartedly to these victims. The companions nourished them from the proceeds of their collections; cared for them with their own hands, assisted those who were dying and buried the dead.[30]

As soon as they had offered themselves to the Pope for any mission whatsoever, the companions felt that their stay together in Rome would not last long—especially since they were already being called on from all sides, and already people were asking the Pope for their services. Furthermore, there were recruits who were presenting themselves and whom the companions could not accept since it would cause "grief

---

[29] The emphasis is mine.

[30] Polanco (*Font. narr.* 1, 199, and 2, 587), Rodríguez (*Epist. Broëti*, 499, 500), Ridbadeneyra (*Font. narr.* 4, pp. 296–97), Laynez (*Font. narr.* 1, 126), etc. speak, occasionally not without exaggeration, of this charitable effort.

among the others . . . to receive candidates and to make an order or a congregation without the authorization of the Holy See."[31]

While the companions were waiting for God to show them the way they were to follow, they preached, catechized children, heard confessions and begged for their bread and that of the poor. Four of them at that time were teaching at the Sapientia and debating theological questions from time to time in the presence of Paul III. One clearly perceives here at its source the apostolic dynamism of these ten men, who were at this point no more for each other than companions.

---

[31] Ignatius to Isabel Roser, RAHNER, op. cit., 1, p. 38.

CHAPTER II

VARIOUS ASPECTS OF CHRISTIANITY
IN THE TIME OF PAUL III

The enterprise attempted by Ignatius of Loyola and his companions between 1538 and 1556 can be understood only in the context of the years which were decisive for the reform of the Church. Moreover, the Church itself was caught up in the enormous political, social and economic change which had begun at the end of the thirteenth century and had continued up to the beginning of the seventeenth century: according to common usage, we call this period the Renaissance.

It is evident that we cannot here trace out in its entirety a vivid picture of this tumultuous and, in some respects, outrageous era. Among the excellent studies which have been made of this period during recent years, I remember with pleasure that of Jean Delumeau:

> Rarely during any period in history has the best been so closely juxtaposed with the worst as in the time of Savonarola and the Borgias, of Saint Ignatius and of Aretino. Thus, the Renaissance itself appears like an ocean of contradictions, a concert, albeit sometimes grating, of diverse aspirations, a problem-ridden combination of the desire for power and fascination with the beginning of science, a desire for beauty and an unhealthy appetite for the horrible, a combination of simplicity and complexity, of purity and sensuality, of charity and hate.

And this "civilization marks the institutions, the enterprises and even the men."[1]

Our study of this period must necessarily be brief: it will mention only that which clarifies, or sometimes explains, the mentality and actions of Ignatius as the Superior General of the Society of Jesus; it was into this strange, seductive yet perilous world of the Renaissance that he and his companions first had to integrate themselves, and then work and preach the gospel. These poor, reformed pilgrims, in love with the Cross and the glory of Jesus Christ, found themselves confronting all these ambiguous changes in western civilization. In order to evaluate their actions fairly, it is necessary that we keep in mind (as much as possible) the background of the Renaissance against which they occurred.

---

[1] *La Civilisation de la Renaissance* (Paris: Arthaud, 1967), p. 21.

I. ROME, THE POPE AND THE CURIA OF CARDINALS

Today, we little realize what the Pope used to be: first, the spiritual head of all Christendom, but also the head of a temporal state; and thus, upon occasion, in wartime, the supreme military commander as well. The criteria according to which he was chosen and finally judged were not the same as those according to which popes are chosen in modern times. Moreover, this was as true of the Pope as of the curia of cardinals who surrounded, counseled, represented and sometimes opposed him— whether discreetly or flamboyantly.

> The sacred college recruited people whose lineage was illustrious; who enjoyed the special favor of princes or other temporal lords; who were related or otherwise closely connected with the reigning pontiff; who had exceptional talents in managing public affairs or even the art of war; or who were distinguished for their general culture and their taste in the *beaux-arts*. From Nicholas V to Paul III, those who selected the Pope did not attach appropriate importance to doctrine, to the sacred sciences, or to the integrity of the candidate's life.[2]

In this regard, Father Tacchi Venturi cites the example of Ippolito de' Medici, the cousin of Clement VII:

> He wore a knight's sword, spent the greater part of his days fencing, never wore his ecclesiastical habit unless he was obliged to attend the consistory or some public ceremony. He was seen more often at the races, hunting, and at the theatre than in his office or in churches. At night, he was sometimes seen walking around Rome with people who lived erratic or even lax lives.[3]

"It was not considered infamous", Tacchi Venturi adds, "that the pope had bastards and that he tried by every possible means to procure fortunes and titles for them; on the contrary, this was considered a proof of prudence and of ability in the case of pontiffs who aspired to temporal greatness."[4] At the death of Clement VII, the move for Catholic Reform

---

[2] VENTURI, op. cit., I, p. 8. This entire volume (I) is devoted to religious life in Italy during "the beginning of the Society of Jesus". This study is particularly valuable in relation to the question which concerns us: it would be wonderful to have analogous studies of all the countries in which the young Society of Jesus had its beginnings. In that way, one would be better able to measure the original impact of the "missions" of the first companions. The reading of PASTOR, *Histoire des papes*, especially in volumes 9 to 14 (of the French edition), is indispensable in aiding one to appreciate the atmosphere during this time period.

[3] Ibid., pp. 10–11.

[4] Ibid., p. 12.

had at least been outlined by both Adrian VI (January 1522 to September 1533) and by Clement himself (1523–1534); but these attempts had not resulted in any appreciable improvement, often because of the opposition of certain cardinals or of their families.

Paul III himself had not been brought up "adhering rigidly to holy principles. Unfortunately, he came out of that group of cardinals who, in youth, had followed an entirely different star."[5] But these youthful faults were countered by a great "integrity of life in older age". In this regard, we believe the excellent historian of the Italian Assistancy. But he is a little bothered when he has to mention that one of the first acts of this "reforming Pope" was to elevate solemnly to the purple (on October 18, 1534) two of his young nephews: one fourteen years old and the other seventeen. This was a bad way to initiate the reform of the Church in general and of the Roman curia in particular. Fortunately, Paul III very soon gave less controversial proof of the interest he had in Catholic Reform. On May 26, 1535, he created some new cardinals, and this time he chose them from among men of well-known virtue and solid doctrinal beliefs. This action was motivated not only by a desire to silence the critics who blamed him for the promotion of his nephews: he was already preparing valuable representatives for the council that he dreamed of creating. In this second group one finds names like Nicholas Schönberg, Jean du Bellay, Jerome Ghinucci, James Simonetti, John Fisher, the courageous bishop of Rochester and future martyr, and Gaspar Contarini. Ignatius would work with several of them. A third group soon added ten names of unquestioned value to the sacred college: Gian Pietro Carafa, James Sadoleto, Rodolfo Pio di Carpi, Reginald Pole, Marcello Cervini, John Morone, Otto Truchsess, etc. This gave hope to Catholics eager for true reform in the Church, And this was truly the beginning of such a renewal: Paul III's four successors, who were chosen from among these cardinals, inaugurated the series of popes that history books call (using too general a term) "the Popes of the Catholic Reformation". If not all of them were "saints", at least they had at heart the desire to give the Church a new image that was less unworthy of Christ.

As early as the end of 1535, Paul III had appointed a certain number of expert advisors to consider the serious question of doctrinal and spiritual reform. At this point, they did not yet all have, and some of them would never have, the honor of being cardinals. In response to the Pope's formal order, this group drafted one of the most extraordinary official documents that we possess concerning the state of the Church on the eve of the Council of Trent (from the end of 1536 to the beginning of 1537),

[5] Ibid., p. 14.

the document known to historians as "The Council of the Cardinals and Other Prelates Concerning the Reform to Be Implemented in the Church, etc.".[6]

Once thanks had been given to God for this pontifical project, the *consilium* immediately began to analyze the Church's most pressing problems: the afflictions besetting the papacy itself. This was attacking the evil at its root, and this root was the abuse of the property of the Church by the pope. Some jurists upheld the idea that the pope was the absolute master of all "benefices"; he could, then, without incurring the stigma of simony, dispose freely of whatever was considered his— distributing, selling or exchanging it. His will, whatever that might be, became the only rule and created the law. "As a result of this, most holy Father, like the Trojan horse, scores of evils and abuses are unleashed in the Church of God, driving us to such a state as to make us despair of the Church's salvation. This situation is well known even among infidels and for this reason they deride our religion and the name of Christ is dishonored."

The experts very quickly seized upon what they considered the most baleful abuse: the promotion of ignorant and totally unworthy men to holy orders. From this practice, innumerable scandals and suspicion of the ecclesiastic state resulted as well as a certain distrust of any religious sect.

This fundamental abuse involved another with it: the dispensation of benefices based on "considerations regarding the individual candidates" and not on the welfare of the souls for whom the benefices had been instituted. The system of benefices was indeed an "abcess" in the body of the Church, and an abcess which the patient either did not want to cure, or perhaps could not immediately cure. This was in part because benefices already played such an integral part in the structure even of civil society. Thus, it was in vain that the councils and canon law had tried to suppress this abuse. Be that as it may, the experts had had quite a time enumerating the lamentable consequences: illegitimate advowsons; more or less fraudulent or even simoniac operations; transfers of properties by wills; dispensations given to illegitimate sons of priests, to the detriment of candidates who deserved them; plurality of incompatible benefices or even bishoprics; and sly combinations of these benefices in order to avoid, by the appearance of regularity, the ban on holding several

---

[6] *Consilium delectorum cardinalium et aliorum praelatorum de emendanda Ecclesia, etc.*, edited for the first time in Rome by Blado in 1538, then redone more or less completely by various editors. Cf. PASTOR op. cit. 5, p. 113. In this analysis, we will follow closely T. VENTURI, I, pp. 19 and sqq., who himself follows the *Monumentorum ad historiam Concilii Tridentini illustrandam . . . collectio* (Louvain, 1781) by Judocus LE PLAT, 2, pp. 596–605.

benefices simultaneously. On this subject, many cardinals were not above reproach, for they had conferred episcopal revenues on themselves. Whence the request of the experts: that one distinguish between the functions of cardinals and those of bishops, emphasizing that cardinals were created in order to aid the pope in the administration of the universal Church, whereas the bishops were consecrated to tend their flocks, and therefore should always be present among their people. This distinction already stipulated the famous "obligatory residence requirement" that the Council of Trent would uphold so strongly. This difficulty concerning "the absence of pastors" afflicted the ecclesiastical hierarchy from top to bottom: the ones who were supposed to be responsible for the bishoprics, the parishes and the benefices entrusted their flocks to poorly paid mercenaries, and then went elsewhere to live themselves. They were assured of impunity in buying rescripts from the Penitentiary and the Datary.[7] At least the reasons for this scourge, the system of benefices, so odious in any Church, and above all in the Church of Christ, who was both just and poor, becomes clear when one remembers that the Pope was also a temporal prince trying to attract men to his cause by giving them favors and money.

The *consilium* was particularly severe regarding the regular priests, and the council's criticism explains Ignatius' hesitation, or even repugnance, and that of his companions to form themselves into a religious order. "Many regular priests", declared the experts, "are so corrupt that they really scandalize the laity and gravely hurt the Church by their example." They even proposed that conventual orders be suppressed little by little: these orders would not be allowed to admit new novices and those who had not yet taken their final vows would be sent home. For the time being, those who had professed their vows and had obtained a license to preach and hear confessions were subjected to an examination by the bishops. Monasteries of nuns were relieved of obedience to conventual orders because their state had become "abominable": *in plerisque monasteriis funt publica sacrilegia, cum maximo omnium scandulo.*[8] We should note, however, that the experts were far from opposing the clerical state itself, and that they recognized implicitly that there still existed religious who remained faithful to their vows.

This discouraging picture of religious life ended with a strong warning to the Pope because in all of these abuses dispensations of all sorts

---

[7] The Penitentiary was an ecclesiastical tribunal which met in Rome on cases in which only the Pope could give absolution. The Datary was the building in Vatican City in which the fiscal affairs of the Vatican were transacted (Tr.).

[8] Cf. Judocus LE PLAT, op cit., 2., p. 602.

bestowed by the departments of the curia in the name of the pope played an important role: permission not to wear the ecclesiastical habit; exemption from the jurisdiction of one's superiors; trafficking amongst the "almsgivers of the Holy Spirit and of Saint Anthony"; and other abuses deceiving well-meaning souls with a thousand superstitions. Among other irregularities were those of allowing those who had received holy orders to contract marriages; of giving dispensations for marriage between closely related parties; of authorizing absolution and revalidation of titles obtained through simony; of giving clerics freedom to make wills disposing of the Church's goods; of overlooking abuses of the system of indulgences; of excessive ease in the commutation of personal or religious vows or in the modification of wills.

It was not surprising, however, that matters should have arrived at such a sorry state of disintegration, when we consider that professors in the schools and universities were teaching "impious doctrines" and that the printing house was freely distributing "depraved books" that even children could read.

This was certainly harsh criticism, but constructive: the nine experts wanted to remedy the evils that they had diagnosed. The appeal to the Pope to reform the Church (even of Rome, of which he was bishop) was written with rare liberty of language:

> Blessed Father, all foreigners are scandalized when they enter St. Peter's to see Mass celebrated there by ignorant priests in filthy liturgical vestments. It is essential that the Most Reverend High Priest and the *Pénitencerie* put an end to these abuses. This also applies to the other churches. Courtesans travel around the city like respectable "matrons": they circulate in mule-drawn coaches, escorted in the plain light of day by nobles who are the familiar associates of cardinals and clerics. In no other city can one see such instances of improper behavior. . . . All of this needs to be corrected. In Rome there are many hostilities and hatreds. Since appeasing these is the role of the bishop, wouldn't it be appropriate for some cardinals who have the gift of peace-making to concern themselves with this issue? The hospitals, the orphanages, the widows also require your solicitude. By using some cardinals with integrity as go-betweens, your Holiness would easily be able to attend to so many necessities.

The document ended with a pathetic hope:

> You have chosen the name Paul. We believe that you will imitate Paul's charity. He was elected by God's choice to carry Christ's name to the Gentiles: we hope that you have been elected to restore in our hearts and our works the name of Christ that has been forgotten by the people and by us the clergy, in order to heal our ills, to bring the sheep of Christ together

again into one flock, to shield us from Christ's anger and the merited retribution which already hangs over our heads.[9]

Even if this *consilium* reflects an excessive severity in regard to the pontiffs who had immediately preceded Paul III, and even if the chaff has always mixed with the good grain in the Church, one cannot argue that this analysis was not sadly true. Contemporary documents abound confirming the accuracy of these accounts.

All of this information clarifies tremendously the feelings and attitudes of the companions for us: their choice of ministry and service, their relations, and their conduct. Henceforth, we note that as Superior General Ignatius was involved with four popes: Paul III (October 1534–November 1549), Julius III (February 1550–March 1555), Marcellus II (April 10–April 30, 1555), and Paul IV (May 1555–August 1559). Four popes—and what different temperaments and attitudes they had regarding Ignatius and the Society of Jesus! As far as Ignatius was concerned, these differences had little importance. In his eyes, they were all "Vicars of Christ on earth", and they all seriously wanted to promote reform in the Church.

Quite soon, in 1545, Paul III opened the Council of Trent. In this arduous enterprise, as prickly a diplomatic venture as can be imagined, and one which dragged on until 1563 with a thousand dangerous issues, the Pope used some of the companions: in them the papacy found solid theologians, but also "priests of reform" who sought to present before the eyes of the world the image of the poverty, the humility, the charity of Jesus Christ.

II. TEMPORAL PRINCES

It seems that at least one trait characteristic of the early days of the Society of Jesus, from 1539 to 1556, should be mentioned and even emphasized. In the great majority of countries where the Society took root and sometimes developed rapidly, the companions were constantly involved with political heads of state: Charles V, Ferdinand the King of the Romans, Philip II, John III, Juan de Vega, etc.

Ignatius was not directly involved with *Charles V*[10] who was elected emperor in 1519, and who, as a result of the actions of members of

---

[9] Ibid., 2, pp. 604 sq.

[10] He was the son of archduke Philip the Handsome and Joanna the Mad; he married Isabel of Portugal.

Charles's family, abdicated as master of the Golden Fleece and sovereign of the Burgundian lands in favor of Philip II in October, 1555. In January of 1556, Charles V renounced the Spanish crowns and those of their dependencies in Italy and in America in favor of the same Philip. In September of the same year Charles had to renounce the imperial crown in favor of his brother Ferdinand, who would not be emperor in fact until 1558. Charles would die in 1558, at San Yuste in Estremadura.

Charles's brother, *Ferdinand I*, was king of Austria (1521) and of Bohemia and Hungary (1526). He was also called the "King of the Romans" (this was the title given to the designated successor of the reigning emperor in the German empire). In 1558, after his ratification by the Grand Electors, Ferdinand actually assumed the imperial crown.

Philip II, the son of Charles V and regent of "the Spains" in the name of his father, became their king in 1556 upon the abdication of Charles V. Philip married (in succession) Mary of Portugal (d. 1545), Mary Tudor of England (d. 1558), Elizabeth of Valois (d. 1568) and Anne Hapsburg (d. 1580). It was mainly with him that Ignatius had to deal in Spain, in the viceroyalty of Naples, and even in Flanders. During the period when Philip II was King of England as a result of his marriage to Mary Tudor, "the Spains" had as their "Governess" (in Philip's name) *Princess Juana of Austria*, the sister of Philip II and the widow of the prince of Portugal.

Another daughter of Charles V, *Mary of Austria*, married Maximilian II, the son and future succesor of the King of the Romans. "Queen Mary" would be very favorable to Ignatius' plans. It is necessary, however, not to confuse her with Philip's aunt, *Mary of Austria*, the sister of Charles V who was the "Governess" of Flanders for the Emperor and who had formerly been the Queen of Hungary.

Maximilian II, the son of Ferdinand I, the King of Bohemia and of the Romans, who became the emperor of Germany in 1578, was the husband of Queen Mary. Only at the end of Ignatius' life did he have to deal with Maximilian II.

John III, the King of Portugal (b. 1502; king from 1521 to 1557) was a great admirer and friend of Ignatius[11] and Francis Xavier, as well as a distinguished benefactor of the Society of Jesus. His attitude was the determining factor in the crisis involving Simón Rodríguez. Thanks to John III and the other Infantas Henry (his brother, archbishop of Evora, Cardinal and Supreme Inquisitor), John (d. 2 January 1544; husband of the Princess Juana) and Louis (d. November 1555), the "province" of Portugal was one of the Society of Jesus' most flourishing areas. This was all the more true because the King of Portugal had in his charge part of the

---

[11] Ignatius was his candidate for the Holy See in 1555.

Indies, Brazil and the Congo; and he was in contact (more or less close depending upon the period of time) with the Negus of Ethiopia. At the time, Lisbon was one of the great ports of Europe and the most important port for sailings to the Indies.

At this point, it is necessary to note that in Ignatius' time Sardinia belonged to the kingdom of Aragon and that the "kingdom" of Naples belonged to the kingdom of Castile. As for Sicily, a possession long disputed among the German emperors, the House of Anjou and the papacy, in Ignatius' time this island belonged to Spain (after 1479). If the Society of Jesus developed with great vigor in Sicily, it was owing to the presence of a viceroy who put all his authority—which was sometimes more than energetic—at the service of the Christianization of his realm. It was only in 1547 that Juan de Vega, the emperor's former ambassador to Rome, became the viceroy of Sicily, but from the moment that he took power, things went very well for the Society. It is also true that two other circumstances facilitated the work of the companions. First, Juan de Vega was encouraged in this devotion to the Society by his wife, Eleanor Osorio; by his daughter Elizabeth, who became the Countess of Luna and Duchess of Bivona; by his brothers Ferdinand and Anthony (the abbot of the monastery of Itala); by his sons, Ferdinand, Alvaro (who took the name Ferdinand when his elder brother died), and Suero—all of whom occupied high positions in the kingdom. One of Juan de Vega's nephews, Ferdinand, even belonged to the Society of Jesus for a little while. The Society's second stroke of luck was that during these nine years of apostolic and charitable activity (1547–1556), Juan de Vega dealt mainly with excellent members of the Society. Chief among these were Nadal and Jerónimo Doménech: in fact, people even reproached Ignatius with paying particular attention to the province of Sicily and with sending the most brilliant members of the order there.

In Italy, also, there were princes who helped the development of the Society of Jesus in their states: Ercole II d'Este, Duke of Ferrara and of Modena (the husband of Renée of France who was well disposed toward "new ideas"); and Duke Cosimo I of Florence (a Medici). Then in Germany, there were the dukes of Bavaria: William IV, his son Albert V and his grandson William V. Even so, in Ignatius' relations with temporal princes, there were some stormy times and some tempests!

Aside from these "reigning" personages, it is necessary to name the various "friends", the "benefactors", who, for the most part, belonged to that propertied and powerful class[12] without whose support it would

---

[12] There were also benefactors and benefactresses of modest means, who did not have great authority in the state or in the city. For example, one was Andrea Lippomani, the prior

have been practically impossible to attempt anything, given the socio-economic structures of sixteenth-century Europe.

Between the lifetimes of most of these personages and the superior generalship of Ignatius there existed a sort of coincidence which was very auspicious for the activities of the young Society of Jesus. Whether one regrets the assistance of these powerful individuals, or exults in it, their favor was an indispensable element in the reform of the Church in Ignatius' time. Politics was so inextricably mixed with religion: the *cujus regio, ejus religio* was then, if not a principle of law, nonetheless a fact. The religious state of a country was closely related to the politico-religious choices of the prince and on those of the people who surrounded him: whether it was a question of Lutheranism, nascent Calvinism, of the Jews or the Hussites, or above all, of Islam—the rule was the same. This can be seen clearly in England of the period. Under Henry VIII (1509–1547), the independence of the state church of England was asserted and confirmed, notably by the Act of Supremacy (1534); but when in 1553 Mary Tudor ascends the throne, we see the overthrow of political policies and religious trends—an overthrow so violent that Mary Tudor would be called "Bloody Mary", even though official visits and festivities celebrated "the return of England to the Catholic faith".[13]

This façade should not, however, hide from us the real drama that was unfolding. The worldly power of the papacy, like that of great political powers such as the German Empire,, was beginning to crack. That national consciousnesses were awakening was obvious in the development of the various languages and even of language in general: Latin was receding in importance and national literatures were being born. But, at the same time, tensions between the various countries of Europe were erupting, sometimes necessitating alliances that were, from a religious standpoint, monstrous. On the frontiers of Europe, the "great Turk" lay in wait for this Christianity which was already prey to internal disintegration. Indeed, some writers at the end of the sixteenth century or at the beginning of the seventeenth, like Francis de Sales, would try to alert these princes-turned-enemy-brothers, and to revive a European Christian conscience.

Up to this point we have looked only at Europe. So that our picture will not be incomplete, it is also necessary to say something concerning

---

of Holy Trinity at Venice. Ignatius was all the more grateful and faithful to them since their generosity was more evangelical; in the case of Lippomani, Ignatius was not even afraid (as we shall see) to ask of the companions sent to Venice or Padua to express a degree of docility which was almost heroic.

[13] We should not forget here the "testament" of Isabella the Catholic, even though this document antedates the periods with which we are concerned.

the "Portuguese and Spanish missionary expansion in the fifteenth and sixteenth centuries".[14] These two countries were in the midst of the exploration of the New World. And the caravels that left for the Indies, Brazil, the Congo and the Americas each time took some "missionaries" of the Dominican, Franciscan and Augustinian orders. After 1541, at least in Portuguese explorations, Jesuit missionaries were also added to their number. Although these two countries were at peace on the Iberian peninsula, they did not hesitate to clash with each other at sea, In 1481, a line was drawn between the Portuguese and Spanish possessions in Africa by the bull *Aeterni Regis*. But from 1493 on, after the first of Christopher Columbus' voyages to the Bahamas and to the Antilles, the rivalry between Portugal and Spain reached such a point that a new decision had to be handed down:

> The arbitration of Pope Alexander VI was necessary, if not to put an end to it, at least to put it in a legal context. The papal bull of May 4–June 28, 1493 (*Inter coetera*), often called "the bull of demarcation", separated the Portuguese and Spanish domains by an imaginary line, which was, to tell the truth, very imprecise, and was situated at 100 leagues to the west and south of the Azores and the isles of Cape Verde. This decision was changed by the Hispano-Portuguese treaty of *Tordesillas* (June 7, 1494) which moved the line of demarcation 270 leagues more to the west and caused Brazil to fall in the Portuguese zone. Widely separated on the Atlantic seaboard, the two empires overlapped in the Pacific ocean, and this situation caused quarrels and fights about the Sunda archipelago.[15]

The papal arbitration specifically clarified the missionary enterprises of the first Society of Jesus: it was only under Portuguese colors that the Fathers and Brothers were sent out as missionaries. Whenever Xavier or one of his successors ventured outside his domain, John III—or his viceroy in the Indies—would balk at approving the expedition and at supporting it financially.

III. THE "PEOPLE" IN SIXTEENTH-CENTURY CHRISTIANITY

This is a subject which is still being researched, but already many things have become clear. An author like Jean Delumeau writes:

> Renaissance Europe was less pagan and de-Christianized than was commonly believed for a long time. . . . We have not sufficiently insisted on the

[14] This is the title of the synthetic commentary that Professor Ricard gives in the *Histoire Universelle des Missions Catholiques*, vol. 1, chapter 9, pp. 223–6. This article illuminates the plans, difficulties, successes and failures of the first Society of Jesus.

[15] Robert RICARD, art. cit. p. 225.

fact that the Renaissance subjected Christianity to a re-thinking. This was true not only in reforming its structures and in clarifying its theology, but also in introducing into the heart of Christian civilization values that had been considered with suspicion up until that time.[16]

Here we must retrace at least the main lines of discovery in that research effort. We especially emphasize that there were three principal sources of the "misery" of the populace, three sources deriving in reality from the same origin: the widening of the social gap between the "patricians" and the "plebians".

1. *Money*. There was the discovery and the development of new lands, accompanied by considerable technical progress (in transportation, textiles, war equipment, mining, metallurgy, printing, glass-working, etc.), advances in creature comforts, especially in the cities—creating business developments which especially helped the rich but did much less for the poor. "In the course of the sixteenth century, the rich became richer, and the poor became poorer. The latter were the victims of the rise in prices and of the enormous increase in taxes. The rich, on the contrary, saw their revenues growing as a result of the extension of commerce and banking because their landed properties were bringing them greater profits."[17] It was at this time that the great firms or companies with worldwide influence were organized, and also the great banks.

Just to cite two examples: the *Medicis* were bankers who appeared in Florence in the thirteenth century. The history of this house is full of the most contradictory adventures: sometimes philanthropists and sometimes bankrupts; sometimes the undisputed masters, other times banished or even assassinated: Lorenzo I called "the Magnificent", and two Popes, Leo X and Clement VII (the predecessor of Paul III); later on, Catherine de Medici and Marie de Medici—all belonged to this family.[18] From the fifteenth century on, the Medici firm was organized according to the structures of a modern holding company. Its power was considerable: the firm made loans to princes and to large companies and invested in important business deals, ready to risk bankruptcy with all of its social consequences; the firm sold fabrics, spices, horses, alum (the production of which the company controlled); the firm also did business in Flemish tapestries, etc. The Medici company also put its fortune at the service of the arts and the humanities and thus developed the prestige of the city.

The *Fuggers*, a family from Augsburg who became involved in high

---

[16] Op. cit., pp. 466–67.
[17] DELUMEAU, op. cit., p. 323.
[18] Cf. Maurice ANDRIEUX, *Les Médicis* (Paris: Plon, 1958).

finance toward the end of the fifteenth century, reigned over a large part
of Europe during all of the sixteenth century until their decline after
1607. Their situation characterized that of the period: they exerted their
influence upon princes and even upon the Pope himself. Jacob Fugger,
Jacob II, called "the Rich" (1459–1525) lent money to the Tyrolean
government; he speculated in fabrics, jewels and pepper. In the Tyrol,
Hungary and Slovakia, he worked copper and silver mines. He was the
creditor of Maximilian and of Charles V (whose imperial election Fugger
assured in 1519) and then of the Spanish sovereigns. He was also the
papacy's agent for collecting indulgences and was in possession of the
leases of the Roman mints [ateliers monetaires]. In view of all this, the
sixteenth century would be called the "century of the Fuggers". Despite
this, however, they would fade into the background—partially ruined by
the successive bankruptcies of the Spanish monarchy. One figure can
clearly suggest their power: at the death of Jacob Fugger in 1525, his
capital, and that of his four nephews who had been associated with him,
attained (after debts had been deducted) a total of 1,602, 319 Rhenish
florins. Leon Schick has made the following calculations concerning this
amount: invested at a regular rate of interest, this fortune would have
made 100,000 florins per year, assuring each of the partners of 20,000
florins. During this same period, the annual salary of an unskilled laborer
was 15 florins (1,333 times less) and that of a skilled worker was 33
florins (606 times less). Evidently, the Fuggers' case represents the
extreme point of the enormous division between the rich and the poor.
However, the advent of monetary powers side by side with governmen-
tal and noble powers profoundly changed social relations.

The situation had redoubtable consequences for the people. This is
made perfectly clear in Polanco's Chronicon: everything was for sale—
alliances, posts, ecclesiastical positions and honors, benefices, indulgences and exemptions. Courtesans were everywhere and one even
distinguised among them, calling some "honest courtesans" (that is, the
rich ones), and others "candlelight courtesans" (those located in the
backs of stores). Converting them to respectability was a very delicate
matter: in order to marry them off, one had to procure a dowry for them,
and in order to wean them from their vice, it was necessary to assure
them of an amount on which they could live, clothe and lodge themselves. In order to do this, some of the first companions undertook the
charitable action of founding the "Houses of St. Martha" and of supporting them. The prisons, and even the holds of galleys, were full of
insolvent people whose freedom would have been a hopeless cause if the
companions had not begged alms in order to pay the debts of these
people, organized pawnshops, etc. Money, a redoubtable evil and the

means of living, would be one of the torments of Ignatius the Poor. If one wants to get an idea of how true this is, one can count the number of letters in which money problems are mentioned in one form or another.

2. *Culture.* Another problem that broadened the gap between the "nobles" and the "plebians" was the difference in their degree of education. The sons of the rich had access to culture and science; the poor were practically excluded from both, because one had to pay for instruction. Tutors and *"ludimagistri"* (to use a term that is not entirely exact) and professors demanded recompense, and books were expensive. For poor families, children's studies, at least after the age when they could be placed with a "patron", were totally neglected, and when a child or an adolescent came from a rural area, it was necessary for him to find the means to support himself and to pay rent in the city. According to the statistics furnished by Jean Delumeau, "there were certainly more cultivated people in the sixteenth and seventeenth centuries than between 1200 and 1400. If fewer children of modest means gained access to a relatively high level of education,[19] on the other hand, there was an almost massive rise in instruction in the higher classes of society: the nobility and the bourgeoisie."[20] However, many people of small means, especially in England and France, deprived themselves, even bled themselves dry, in order to educate their sons. The parents dreamed of freeing their sons from their social rank and of making it possible for them to achieve "the long gown" of a judge, a doctor, a government worker or a clerk. But this fact does not change the proportions, and it remains true that

> the Renaissance gave rise to a quantitative revolution in the domain of education because the spread of teaching today classified as "secondary" also grew considerably. But this pertained to the wealthy classes—a nobility which renewed itself from the bottom and a bourgeoisie becoming ever more important—which profited more than anyone else from this enlarged distribution of knowledge.[21]

The gap between the rich and the poor grew ever larger, because knowledge, for the man of the time, led to "wisdom". One of Erasmus' books, entitled *Declamatio de pueris . . .* , gives advice of a simplicity that today astonishes us, but illustrates a concern with making schooling a complete upbringing. In France, Rabelais (c. 1494–1553) with *Gargantua,*

---

[19] The medieval school sytem, which depended most often on abbeys or churches, favored the child of plebian origin. Of course, the nobles tended to be more interested in the art of war than in education.

[20] Op. cit., p. 424.

[21] Ibid., p. 430.

and then Montaigne (1533–1592) with his famous *Essai* (I, 26) "On the Instruction of Children", and the Englishman Thomas Elyot with *The Boke Named the Gouvernour* (1531)—all favored an integral education of man; it is sufficient to read these books if one wants to gauge the distance that separated the aristocratic child from the plebian one. The seventeenth century would give society *l'honnête homme*; the sixteenth century produced *le gentilhomme*.

There were no schools for girls, apart from rare exceptions; for example, Alcalá. The Ursulines did not establish the first French-speaking college[22] at Avignon until 1574. Hence cultivated women were instructed at home. Some of them were even erudite, as the sixteenth century shows. Whence came their culture, their learning? From masters and tutors whom the parents hired to teach at home. These lessons were very expensive. Although women were playing a more important role in society, it was only the rich women with leisure, those liberated from domestic chores, who fit into this category. The poor women were still busy with housework, on the farm, or taking care of the children. Unless, of course, in an effort to enrich themselves they had joined the ranks of the numerous prostitutes who swarmed throughout Rome; it is necessary to say *particularly* in Rome. Lorenzo the Magnificent called Rome "the trysting place of all the vices", not excluding homosexuality.

3. *Insufficient Catechetical Training.* These divergences between the poor and the rich had a baleful influence on religious life. Although there were brilliant universities, the people themselves were either poorly or not at all catechized. Their practice of religion was encumbered by superstition—magic, sorcery and diabolism—so much more so because the sculptures, the paintings and the windows which they saw in holy places like the churches, chapels and tombs easily mixed holy subjects with the most pagan mythology. In this respect, "The cathedral is the poor man's Bible" merits an explanation: the statement expressed well the mingling of the best and the worst elements (from a religious, not necessarily an aesthetic point of view) which characterized the period. The feasts of the Church sometimes turned into the most disorderly festivals; the processions ended in masquerades, the liturgy, in theater. Who then took the responsibility of teaching the people, of instructing them in real religion, of insuring their education concerning the sacraments? It was not that priests or other religious were lacking in number. But ignorance, when it is not a kind of moral disorder, does not prevent anyone from achieving holy orders, or even the episcopacy or cardinalate.

---

[22] This word is used in the French sense—meaning secondary school, usually for boarders, but not meaning university as it does in English.

There were some holy priests and faithful religious, but it is a fact frequently stated in Polanco's *Chronicon* that the companions in their ministries or missions kept running into the ignorance of the clergy and its absence of sacramental education; some priests mumbled any old formula for absolution on consecration and some did not even know how to read a missal;[23] the "Catholic reclamation" of such a region or city, consisted first in teaching the priests how to administer confession and the Eucharist properly and then how to say the liturgy correctly. Finally, the priests who had not been properly instructed needed to be taught the most elementary rules of morality. It was not unusual of some of the priests to be living with concubines in full view and with the full knowledge of their flocks. "Sons of priests" abounded. We should repeat, however, that despite these abuses, there were many fervent and charitable priests.

If the testimonies of contemporaries were not so numerous and so formally set down, one would not be able to believe that such a "degeneration" of the priestly state was possible. It is in this light, however, that it is necessary to consider the first ministries of the companions: the readings of Holy Scripture, the "cases of conscience" (or elements of moral theology), even the presence of priests in grammar classes, the "examinations" for priests who were candidates for certain benefices. We would have a hard time envisaging such anarchy if the documents were not irrefutable on these points. Anyone who would like to get an idea of the situation has only to read in studies like that of Tacchi Venturi on Italy, the sections about "preaching": there one may see to what a great degree decadence, vulgarity, extra-vagances and trivialities had successfully passed as holy eloquence. Moreover, what Tacchi Venturi says of Italy can also be said of Germany, of Flanders and of France. Considering such preaching and such preachers, it is not astonishing that heresy was spreading. It was, in fact, for opposing Mainardi, the most fashionable orator in Rome itself, that the companions weathered their first storm.

If the pastors were in this state, imagine what the ignorance of the people must have been! We understand why one of the first ministries of the young Society of Jesus was "to teach Christian doctrine to children and to ignorant people". Even of the diocese of Milan—the diocese of St. Ambrose and of Charles Borromeo—before 1566, see what can be asserted by the historian J. P. Giussani: "The people had almost no knowledge of the basis and principles of the Catholic faith; they didn't know how to recite either the Our Father or the Hail Mary; they could

---

[23] T. VENTURI, op. cit., 1, p. 52.

barely make the sign of the Cross. Even less did they know the articles of the Creed and God's Commandments."[24] Unfortunately, neither Milan nor Italy alone had a monopoly on these miserable conditions. How could there be any question of a parish life or of teaching catechism under such conditions? The commonest laws of the Church were often ignored. One region (among all those in Italy) was particularly lax: that around Abruzzi, Apulia and Calabria. This was a veritable spiritual wasteland: in their "familiar colloquies" as in their correspondence, the companions whose missions were in these areas called them "the Italian Indies". Even in the regions around Modena and Bologna, there were savage vendettas which often ended in shameless murders.

It was this religious ignorance which also caused another dangerous problem, superstition. In certain classes of the population, it achieved an incredible virulence: miracles of all sorts were invented or fabricated, false prophecies, visions, etc. were only minor examples of this difficulty. But magic, sorcery, sacrilegious practices and diabolism of all sorts were mixed in with these distortions of religious sentiment. To the great profit of entrepreneurs in this area, witch hunts were keeping the Inquisitors very busy.[25]

What could one do to oppose such a situation? Only one tactic would be effective: to start the work of evangelization from the very beginning, to emphasize the elementary essentials of Christian faith and practices. The movement had begun in Italy at the end of the fifteenth century with St. Anthony's excellent *Libretto della dottrina cristiana* published in Florence in 1473; this was written in Italian and adapted to the level of children and of simple people; however, it had only a regional success. Nonetheless, the movement was launched. Three-quarters of a century later it would intensify. The Fifth Lateran Council in its ninth session gave schoolmasters the serious duty of teaching catechism to children. However, the decree remained ineffectual. It was necessary to wait for the advent of Paul III for children to be properly catechized—at least those children who went to school. This explains the first ministry Pope Paul entrusted to the companions: the teaching of catechism to the children in all the schools of Rome. In this light, we can also understand the individual preaching to adults of which Polanco speaks so often in his *Chronicon*: "the lessons of Christian doctrine" for which the companions most often used the First Week of the Spiritual Exercises and which

---

[24] T. VENTURI, op. cit., I, p. 323.

[25] One of Father Tacchi VENTURI's sources when he studied these strange phenomena was the *Anatomia delli vitti*, published in 1550 by Lorenzo Davidico, which confirms the accounts in the *Confessionaires* of the time, in particular that of St. Anthony, the Bishop of Florence in the fifteenth century.

neglected neither the great theologians nor the *"concionatores"* (orators or preachers): these lessons in Christian doctrine were very often followed by confessions; many of the "sinners" of this time were, in fact, no more than baptized but uneducated persons.

The picture that we have just painted is very cursory and very incomplete. It does, however, permit us to understand in what kind of world Ignatius and his companions began their ministries as "reformed priests". It is necessary, however, if we are not to mistake the nature of their actions, to remember that they were not the only or the first to work for the reform of the Church. The majority of religious orders, despite the disrepute which crippled them, had tried to improve themselves well before the Council of Trent. The Augustinians of Germany, the Dominicans of the Congregation of Holland and the Poor Clares of St. Colette had returned to the old rule even before 1517. Spain, in general, thanks to Cisneros, gave an example of courageous faithfulness to the Catholic faith; as early as 1526, the Hermits of St. Francis of Assisi, who would soon be called the Capuchins, began to preach; new religious foundations were laid: Barnabites, Somaschi, Theatines, the Oratory of Divine Love, etc. All of these attempts bore witness to the vitality of the faith despite the disorders. Even more significant was the "hunger for the Word" which was evident in simple Christian people; Lucien Febvre quite rightly emphasizes Luther's farsightedness in relating the religious problems of his epoch to the Church's insufficient pastoral adaptation to the religious needs of the mass of the Christian population. Catholics, as well as Protestants, had to try to remedy this insufficiency through their catechisms and through informal meetings of the clergy with the laity. *"Monachatus non est pietas"* was the cruel remark that Erasmus aimed against the monks. This was, however, compensated for by the lay people's desire to live an authentically Christian life in their professions and in the married state. Doubtless this situation inclined souls toward religious individualism. St. Thomas à Kempis' *The Imitation of Christ* (1420–30) was the most-read book of the fifteenth century; Gerson's *devotio moderna* would favor the ecclesiastical or communal life (in the monastic sense of the word) less than one's personal relationship with God. This individualism cannot be denied. On the other hand, we must acknowledge its influence on Ignatius' *Spiritual Exercises* and in preparing for the magnificent mystical explosion of which Teresa of Ávila and St. John of the Cross were the most illustrious, but not the only, examples.

Before our eyes, as a back-drop in the course of our study, we must keep the tableau of this Christendom, with its greatness and wretchedness, its strengths and weaknesses, its "best" and its "worst". If we fail to do so, we risk misunderstanding Ignatius' efforts and those of his companions, as well as misconstruing their whole mentality. Even if their wish was to recognize in their personal and apostolic experiences something of "the early Church",[26] their attempts to do so were made in a particular time and were rooted in a specific kind of Christianity into which the young Society of Jesus plunged its "cosmic and natural roots".[27]

[26] The phrase is found quite frequently in the correspondence of the members of the society and in the *Chronicon* of Polanco.

[27] The expression is taken from the end of the study *Le Milieu Mystique* (1917) by Teilhard de Chardin.

CHAPTER III

WHO WERE THESE COMPANIONS?

Who were these ten companions who, in November 1538, introduced and offered themselves to Pope Paul III to serve in whatever capacity he might confer on them, to aid a Christianity which was devitalized and threatened, but nevertheless burgeoning with hope?

I. THE PARISIAN GROUP

IGNATIUS OF LOYOLA

First of all, we must consider Ignatius, not because he was the leader or the superior, nor even the founder, but because he was the very soul of the group, the "father", according to the companions.

In 1538 Inigo of Loyola (1491–1556) was forty-seven years old. First a page in the service of Juan Velasquez de Cuellar (Treasurer General under King Ferdinand the Catholic (1506?–1517), then a nobleman at the court of Antonio Manrique (viceroy of Navarre), he had led the life which Polanco described in these restrained and suggestive words: "Like all the young men who live at court and dream of military exploits, he was rather free in affairs of the heart, in games of chance and in matters of honor." Wounded in combat at Pamplona, May 20, 1521, he received first aid from the French, his conquerors, then was taken by them back to the chateau of Loyola. There Inigo was converted. There, he had his first spiritual experience, which was, nonetheless, a very important one, for it involved visions, interior revelations of great inner impact, initiation into the interplay of "spirits" and a state in which human dreams and calls from God were inextricably mingled.[1] Once cured, Inigo quickly set forth on his way, as a pilgrim, a mendicant—a pilgrimage which led to Montserrat, to Manresa with its decisive illuminations (1522), to Rome and Jerusalem (1523), Venice, Genoa, Barcelona (1524), Barcelona once again, to his first studies and the first companions: Calixto de Sa, Juan de

---

[1] Cf. *Autobiography*. All that we will say here was inspired by Ignatius' confidences to Gonçalves da Câmara: it would be pointlessly punctilious to give all references to this "classic" concerning Ignatius' biography. Cf. infra, pp. 396 sqq., especially the "hypothesis" indicated on p. 398.

Arteaga, Lope de Cáceres,[2] and the fourth, a Frenchman, Jean Raynal.

Alcalá (March 1526–June 1527): a time of study "of the arts", but especially a time in prison with three interrogations before the Inquisition: it all ended with the favorable testimony of Juan Rodríguez de Figueroa. The four companions from Barcelona went with Inigo to Alcalá. There was an astonishing coincidence: among the young men who frequented the University of Alcalá at that time there were several students who would later be companions: Diego de Eguía, Martín Olave, Alonzo Salmeron, Diego Laynez, Nicolas Bobadilla, Manuel Miona, Jerónimo Nadal, Diego de Ledesma:[3] for the moment, they were only university comrades who may not even have yet met Ignatius. In June 1527, Inigo and his four companions went from Alcalá to Salamanca; but there Inigo was soon again imprisoned and in trouble with the Inquisition. Once again, his judge (the vicar general Martín Frías) handed down a sentence totally favorable to Inigo. However, the judge forbade him to discuss theological questions until he had finished his studies. Inigo then decided to leave for Paris; Jean Raynal had already left him to enter the religious life; as for the three others, they would wait until Inigo sent word from Paris for them to join him. Actually, they would never join him.

On February 2, 1528, Inigo at the age of thirty-seven, entered the gates of Paris. Why did he choose the University of Paris? If one compares the different and varying explanations given by Laynez,[4] Polanco[5] and Nadal,[6] two apparently contradictory motives emerge: Frías' sentence, after the experience at Salamanca, had deprived Inigo of spiritual contacts through which he had aided souls (Nadal, Polanco); but most of all, Inigo realized that it was better for him to separate himself from the Spanish universities where he was divided between his desire to pursue and complete his studies and his attraction to continue with his apostolate (Laynez). It seems that there is an element of truth in each of these explanations, but one must also add another, simpler reason which accurately corresponds with Inigo's human and spiritual realism. Since Alcalá and Salamanca were practically closed to him, Paris was, in the

---

[2] Lope de Cáceres should not be confused with Diego de Cáceres who will become associated with the group in Paris during the years 1538–1539, and will leave the order shortly thereafter. Cf. *Chronicon* 1, 33–34; *Font. narr.*, 2, 544, pp. 566–567; SCHURHAMMER, op. cit., 1,228, n. 6.

[3] Cf. RIBADENEYRA, *Font. narr.* 4, pp. 176–187; *Nadal Mon.* 1, p. 1

[4] Letter of 1547, *Font. narr.* 1, p. 99, n. 27.

[5] "Vita Patris Ignatii", *Font. narr.* 2, p. 553, n. 48.

[6] "Apologia contra censuram". Ibid., 2, p. 75, n. 65. "Dialogi pro Societate". Ibid., 2, p. 249, n. 15.

last analysis, the most convenient university for him in which to try to attain the goal which he had set for himself: to complete university degrees and to take holy orders while doing spiritual works and hoping to gain a few new companions for his way of life. Moreover, perhaps it would be easier midway between Spain and Flanders to secure the necessities for the life and studies of the group, if the need arose. Whatever the reason, this is what happened.

From February 1528 to September 1529, he was enrolled as a *martinet* (day pupil) at the celebrated "college" of Montaigu[7] in order to resume basic Latin studies. Next, Inigo entered the faculty of "arts" because the degree of master of arts was required for entrance into any one of the three other colleges,[8] including the school of theology which this elder student perhaps aspired to enter. But this is what hampered his plan: before leaving Barcelona some friends had given Inigo a bill of exchange for twenty five gold coins to pay the cost of room and living expenses in Paris for one year. Desirous of leading a life of poverty, Inigo had entrusted his gold to one of the other Spanish students who shared his lodging. In April 1528, however, the student absconded and Inigo found himself on the streets of Paris; he went to lodge in the Hospital of S.-Jacques, a night shelter on the other bank of the Seine. A good half league (four kilometers) separated S.-Jacques and the Latin Quarter where the college of Montaigu was located, and the hours there of opening and closing (dawn to dusk) did not coincide with the times of the courses at Montaigu (4:30 A.M.–7:30 P.M.); moreover, S.-Jacques lodged its guests but did not feed them, so Ignatius had to beg for his bread. Finally, on the advice of a friend, he decided to devote a few weeks each year to begging from the rich Spanish merchants in Flanders the wherewithal to live for one year. He did this for two years in a row.[9] Then the merchants

[7] In those days the University of Paris was a sort of corporation or federation of independent "colleges" (*Universitas magistrorum et scolasticorum parisiensium*). Cf. Charles THUROT, *De l'organisation de l'enseignement dans l'Université de Paris, au Moyen Age* Paris: Dezobry, E. Magdeleine et Cie, 1850. Cf. also *Journal d'un Bourgeois de Paris sous le règne de François Ier* (*1515-1536*), new edition, published with an introduction and notes by V.-L. BOURRILLY (collection of texts for the study of history no. 43 [Paris: Alphonse Picard, 1910]).

[8] There were four faculties at the University of Paris: arts (which was the equivalent of philosophy); law (canon law; civil law was taught at Bourges and at Orléans); medicine; and finally theology, which one should not confuse with that of the Sorbonne. In order to be admitted to "the arts," it was necessary to have a good knowledge of Latin; and Latin was taught within the colleges.

[9] It was during his first voyage to Flanders that Ignatius met Luis Vives. The two men did not get along. It seems, however, that there were other reasons that explain the suspicion that Ignatius demonstrated concerning the works of Vives.

freed him from this necessity and waste of time by giving him a bill of exchange each year, but time was passing, and it became obvious that Inigo would never be a perfect Latinist.

At the beginning of the school year in October 1530, he was enrolled in faculty of arts. Flemish charity[10] allowed him to pay board and room to the college of Sainte-Barbe; he was entered there as a "portionniste". He shared the room of the "regent", Master Juan Peña, with a Savoyard student, Pierre Favre, and an aristocratic scholar from Navarre, Francisco de Xavier y Jassu. This circumstance would have unexpected consequences for Inigo's fate. It is safe to say that Inigo applied himself seriously to these studies in the college of arts, no matter what some historians have written. In 1533, he obtained his licentiate in arts although he had requested, according to Nadal, to be rigorously examined, despite his age;[11] he did honorably, ranking thirtieth out of a group of at least a hundred students;[12] (Favre, an excellent student, had been twenty-fourth in 1530, and Xavier twenty-second).[13] Inigo did not, however, hurry to take his master's degree; was it concern for poverty? Perhaps he did not feel the need of the M.A. since he intended to be neither a professor nor a teaching fellow. It was not until March 14, 1535, that he decided to receive that degree[14]—officially, at least, for if

---

[10] At that time the annual rate for pensioners was thirty gold coins (about two hundred francs in 1913). This is one of the rare points on which Schurhammer made an error or made a slip of the pen: he speaks of thirty *sols tournois* or thirty ducats (*Franz Xaver*, 1, pp. 75 and 107).

[11] "Adhortatio Complutensis" (1561, *Font. narr.* 2, p. 196).

[12] This rank is given by Petau (in the letter of July 28, 1635, with extracts from registers that have today been lost from the Abbey of Ste. Geneviève: the translation is in the *Acta Sanctorum*, 7, pp. 441–42).

[13] Wrongly, Brodrick doubts that Xavier had not gotten his licentiate as some authors say, but a Master of Arts. In order to receive the M.A. the person who had already earned a licentiate did not have to pass a new exam, but had to pay new fees and to give a banquet for his friends and teachers. Schurhammer has found Xavier's name in the *Acta rectoria* listed among the names of those students who had gone through their *Incipientes*, that is, the first lesson, after which those with licentiates were declared "masters"—during the time that Pierre Avril was rector (from December 15, 1525 until March 24, 1530); Schurhammer concludes from this that Xavier received his licentiate and M.A. during the same month— March 1530 (cf. SCHURHAMMER, *Franz Xaver*, 1, p. 137 and n. 8; James BRODRICK, *Saint François Xavier*, [Paris: Spes, 1954], p. 41). As for Pierre Favre, he took his master's degree later.

[14] Cf. the rectorial registers of the University of Paris (kept at the Bibliothèque Nationale): Ignatius received his M.A. during the rectorship of Florentin Jacquart (December 15, 1534–March 24, 1535); see Ignatius' letter to Inès Pascual on June 13, 1533 in which he tells his benefactress "during Lent, he received his M.A.", which must include the licentiate as well, which was the only "exam" necessary in order to obtain an M.A. We should note that Father Larrañaga (*Obras Completas* 1, p. 365) makes an error in giving the

one is to believe Schurhammer[15] the *Acta Rectoria* gave Inigo the title of "Magister Ignatius" in 1532.

Although his studies were nearing their conclusion, Inigo did not lose sight of his plan for a group of spiritual companions. The companions from Alcalá and Salamanca had disappointed him: the group had disbanded. Jean Raynal had become a monk near Salamanca, even before Inigo had left there. Cáceres had returned to Segovia, his native city, and lived as if he had never even dreamed of either poverty or of any kind of apostolate; Arteaga had entered military orders, become a commander and bishop in Mexico and died of accidental poisoning. As for Calixto de Sa, Inigo had procured for him, through the efforts of Leonor Mascarenhas, a scholarship at Sainte-Barbe and a mule; he took the money and the mule but fled to Portugal, made two trips to the Indies and returned to Salamanca loaded with gold.[16] The first attempt at apostolic companionship had ended in failure.

A second attempt was no more successful, but for very different reasons, and for ones that reflect more honorably on the new candidates. Upon his return from the first trip to Flanders (1528), Inigo resumed (though still cautiously) his activity trying to make apostolic contacts: it ranged from "spiritual colloquies" to the Exercises themselves, more or less long (doubtless) and more or less complete—adapted to the situations of the candidates and to their individual study programs. Among those who took this retreat there were three Spaniards already well advanced in their studies:[17] Castro who had already completed ten years of theology (the complete course consisted of thirteen or fourteen years) and who would later gain the doctorate; Peralta who already held the M.A. degree; and Amador who lived at the college of Sainte-Barbe. Three generous souls, taking very seriously the demands of the Christian life—especially true evangelical poverty—these men gave all they possessed to the poor, even down to their books. They left their rooms, which were provided for regents and pensioners, to go to live at the Hospital of St. Jacques where Ignatius had taken refuge the year before, and like him, they begged for their bread. On their account, there was a great uproar in the Spanish colony of the Latin Quarter and particularly at Sainte-Barbe. In an armed group, the friends of our mendicants came to get them out of the Hospital of S.-Jacques. It all ended in a sort of pact: Castro, Peralta and Amador would finish their studies; then each

---

date of Ignatius' M.A. as May 14, 1534 (the degree is on file in Rome). Cf. SCHURHAMMER, op. cit. 1, p. 231 and n. 4).

[15] Ibid.

[16] On Ignatius' first four companions, see the *Autobiography* R. P. n. 80.

[17] Ibid., n. 77–78.

would be free to follow whatever way of life seemed best to him. This was simply wise. But the crisis (and its solution) must have given Inigo pause for thought: had he not himself formerly known and practiced the zealous excesses of these young Spaniards? Furthermore, had he not adopted for himself and his friends the solution which was finally imposed upon them? On the day of the vows at Montmartre, when the seven companions would take the vow of evangelical poverty, might they not postpone the full import of this vow until after they had completed their studies? The great choices and challenges that Ignatius would have to face as Superior General of the Society of Jesus (responsible for the drafting of the *Constitutions*) were already involved in these first experiences of companionship.

Moreover, this affair of Castro, Peralta and Amador almost turned out badly for Inigo. After all, who was really responsible for these excesses? The Spiritual Exercises and hence Inigo. On him, therefore, anger had fallen. Diego de Gouvea, principal of the college of Sainte-Barbe, accused Inigo of having driven Amador mad and declared that if Inigo came near his college, he would impose the correction called *de la salle* on him: this consisted of being made to pass (stripped to the waist) between two rows of masters armed with rulers in a crowded refectory in the presence of all the students at Sainte-Barbe. The threat was formidable. Nevertheless, a few months later Inigo entered Sainte-Barbe as a *portionniste*. What had happened? How did this change of feeling on the part of Gouvea come to pass? Ribadeneyra offers us the account of an interview which supposedly took place between Inigo and Gouvea and which presumably ended in an honorable and public apology by the principal. This, however, smacks a bit too much of the "edifying life"; moreover, it concerns an unwritten recollection that Ribadeneyra would have gathered in Paris in 1542, fourteen years after the event. Furthermore, Ribadeneyra was at that time a mere youth of sixteen, a jolly fellow fond of escapades and amusing stories, especially if the adventures befell Father Ignatius to whom he was a source of both amusement and torment. Historians are not in agreement regarding Ribadeneyra's version of this event, and those who accept it are not agreed on how much to accept or reject in the account.[18] Certainly there must have been a reconciliation between Gouvea and Inigo or the latter would not have been admitted to Sainte-Barbe. If there was a reconciliation, there was an

---

[18] See RIBADENEYRA. *De Actis P. N. Ignatii (Font. narr.* 2, pp. 382–83, n. 90). DUDON, lib. cit., p. 202; SCHURHAMMER, lib. cit., 1, p. 132 and n. 3: SCHURHAMMER holds to this account (even though he softens it somewhat) because of the parallel accounts that occur in Laynez, Salmeron and Polanco. See references in the Schurhammer note.

interview, because Inigo was not one to explain himself through a third party. And it is probable that the interview had a stormy beginning, but how the return to peace was achieved remains a mystery for posterity.

What had to upset Inigo even more was that at the time of this affair (we do not know on what count of indictment) he was denounced to the Inquisitor of Paris.[19] He must have wondered whether the affairs of Alcalá and Salamanca were going to begin all over again. Fortunately, the Inquisition in France was less touchy than in Spain, and the faculty of theology saw to it that it was not deprived of its proper rights in the matter of judgments of faith. Inigo was not the object of any inquest nor the victim of any punitive action.

When Inigo entered Sainte-Barbe everything seemed to have returned to a state of calm. He himself was undoubtedly more discreet and careful in his relations with other *portionnistes*. Did he keep contact with Castro, Peralta and Amador? We do not know. None of the three, in any case, was a part of the third group which was soon to form, man by man, around Inigo.[20]

Let us sum up briefly. Inigo's, first two attempts to attract companions who would adopt his "way of life" were apparently failures. Three facts, however, should be pointed out concerning these attempts: first, the diversity of the characters and the situations of the candidates: all were students—that was the only thing they had in common, but the rest of their existence, as much as we know of it, reveals very diverse temperaments and talents.

On the whole, Inigo was not selective—not selective enough— according to some; he excluded no one; he had no preliminary reluctance regarding anyone, provided that the desire to serve God in poverty and charity motivated that soul. His judgments were not "closed", but open to the workings of the Holy Spirit. The second fact derives from the first: Inigo did not rush; he took his time, or rather he followed God's timetable; since it was God who called, since this type of life depends on grace, the role of Inigo was clear: it was his job to exemplify this evangelical "way of life". Then, if any soul was attracted by it, Inigo should accept this companion, to help him in his personal progress in relation to God—to the point that, if by chance this companion should reject this way of life, he would still remain a friend. For example, in 1535, on his voyage to Spain, Inigo would make a detour to see Reynal in

---

[19] On this subject, we should mention that Ignatius must have made a mistake here in identifying this Inquisitor with Mathieu Ory, who was not, it seems, the Grand Inquisitor until after 1536.

[20] Castro, at least, would one day enter the Carthusian community at Valencia and would there live a saintly life.

his Carthusian monastery. Thus (and this is the third fact), Inigo never let himself be discouraged by these failures. "He had the type of temperament which", according to psychologists, "bounces back under difficulties." Perhaps, but Inigo especially possessed an authentic spirituality in which all his views, judgments and actions became, so far as possible, manifestations of God's will. It was thus that he was to form the third group of companions which, this time, would not be dissolved except by death, and he would found, despite a thousand vicissitudes, the Society of Jesus.

PIERRE FAVRE

At Sainte-Barbe (September 1529) Ignatius shared the room of the "regent" Master Juan Peña along with Pierre Favre and Francis Xavier.

Pierre Favre was from Savoy, born in 1506 at Easter-time in Villaret, a small village in the valley of the Grand Bornand. As a member of a peasant family, the child Pierre tended the livestock in the fields and was destined when he grew older to work the land like his father. Pierre, however, had other ideas.[21] At

> about the age of ten, I felt a desire to study, but being a shepherd and destined by my father to remain in the world, I would not be comforted and I cried, because I had a great desire to pursue learning; so strong was this desire that my parents were forced, against their will, to let me start. Observing the benefits which I derived from these studies, they did not know whether they could prevent me from continuing my studies; especially since God had not allowed anyone to discover in me any aptitude whatsoever for life in the world.

A pious priest who lived at Thônes, a neighboring town, came for two years to teach Pierre Latin until 1516 when he would enter the well-known school of La Roche, nine kilometers from Villaret. Pierre Velliard, who was the director of the school at that time, was a born educator: Pierre Favre made rapid progress—as much in his studies as in his religious formation. During his vacation in 1518, Pierre, who was tending a flock of sheep, felt the inward necessity of making a vow of chastity to Jesus Christ. He remained at the school of La Roche for nine years; in September 1525, upon the advice and with the aid of his uncle,

---

[21] We will be citing this work, the *Memorial* by Favre, quite frequently. *Fabri Mon.* 490 sqq. (*Font. narr.* 1, pp. 28–49). This jewel of mystical literature is too little known. It is true that it is not easy to translate because the work is lyrical and contains many nuances of expression. In France at the present time, however, we can make use of Michel de Certeau's excellent translation in the "Christus" collection.

Claude Perissin, the prior of the Carthusian monastery of Reposoir, he went to study at the University of Paris. Being of a gentle, sensitive temperament and given to introspection, Pierre experienced painful onslaughts of scrupulosity: however, far from conquering him, the experience strengthened him.

Pierre Favre was preparing himself to become a master of arts when Inigo de Loyola came to Sainte-Barbe. Thirteen years later Pierre wrote:

> Blessed be Providence who utilized all this for the good and the salvation of my soul. Having been ordered by Peña to teach this holy man, I profited first of all from his general conversation and then from our private talks. We lived together in the same room, ate at the same table and shared the same purse. He was my master in spiritual things and showed me the way to grow in the knowledge of the will of God. Thus, we finally became one in our resolve to choose the life of all those who live at present or who have lived in the Society of which I am not worthy.[22]

Despite Pierre's fervor, Inigo made no haste to introduce him to the Spiritual Exercises. He first worked at releasing him (Pierre) little by little from his scrupulosity, by teaching him to distinguish between what one actually wills and what one is subject to, by advising him also to prepare to make a general confession of all the sins of his whole life which would mark a clear break between the past and the future. Thus, he encouraged Pierre to take the sacraments of penance and Holy Eucharist once a week and to make an examination of conscience every day. That was all—but on these basic principles, Pierre built a spiritual life of very high quality. For almost two years there was no question of following Inigo. Pierre did not even know whether he would marry, whether he would be a medical doctor or a jurist, whether a doctor of theology or whether, without academic degrees, he would enter the ecclesiastical life or a monastery. Favre hesitated; Inigo waited. Toward the end of 1531, Favre finally decided on his own to follow the path of Inigo. It was Inigo's turn not to rush and he did not change anything in the spiritual rhythm of Favre's life. In July 1533, Favre even returned to his native Villaret and stayed there seven months.

It was upon his return from Savoy, before the end of the winter of 1534, that Favre finally made the Spiritual Exercises. He had known Inigo for four years; it had been more than two years since he had decided to adopt his "way of life"; for a long time, Favre had been seeking the grace to do so. He was without doubt the first person who did the "long" Exercises. His "Manresa" was a house in the Faubourg Saint Jacques: there he became acquainted with the fervor and also the saintly

---

[22] *Font. narr.* 1, p. 32, n. 8.

zeal of Inigo at Manresa; but more fortunate than Inigo, Favre had near him an experienced master. Nevertheless, he passed six full days without eating or drinking—except for the Host at daily Communion and the sip of unconsecrated wine which the rubric prescribed for those who had just received Communion. The winter was cold, the Seine frozen, but Favre lighted no fire; he even went sometimes (for more penance) to meditate in the courtyard in the snow. In the course of these exercises, Pierre Favre confirmed his decision to be a companion and to receive major orders as soon as possible. On February 28, he was made subdeacon; on April 4, deacon; and on May 30, 1534, he received the priesthood, which was conferred upon him by Jean du Bellay, the Bishop of Paris. For almost two months he prepared to celebrate his first Mass. He did so on July 22, the feast of St. Mary Magdalen. It was he who, on August 15, 1534, in the crypt of Montmartre, would celebrate Mass, surrounded by Inigo and the five other companions. Soon Favre would resume his theological studies; he obtained his master of arts after Easter in 1536. However, let us not anticipate anything about the life of the group in 1535 and 1536.

FRANCIS XAVIER

Inigo's other roommate at Sainte-Barbe was of different mettle than the shepherd of Savoy. Francis Xavier was of noble birth. Through his father, Don Jean Jassu (or Jasu) and his mother, Doña Maria de Azpilcueta, he belonged to the first families of Navarre in the fifteenth century. Don Jean, doctor *in decretis* was treasurer of Navarre, under John III d'Albret and Catherine de Foix, president of the royal council, alcade and judge of the court. Francis was born April 7, 1506, and at first enjoyed a delightful childhood enveloped by his parents with a somewhat delicate tenderness. But he was not yet ten when suffering entered his life. In 1515, his father died; two years later he witnessed the dismantling of the ancestral castle, as well as the fortress of Navarre by the powerful Viceroy Ximenes; he saw his family ruined, two of his brothers imprisoned for their political views and condemned to death, their possessions confiscated; they were subsequently pardoned by Charles V. Despite these misfortunes, it was at the Xavier chateau that Francis received his education and his first instruction from 1512 to 1521; it seems that he also attended (at some time) the very good school of Sanguessa where Latin was taught.[23]

---

[23] Cf. SCHURHAMMER, lib. cit., 1, p. 26 which goes back to the "Documents" of Cros. T. VENTURI, op. cit., 3, p. 124.

Toward the first of October 1525, he left for Paris: he stayed there for eleven years. He took a room at the college of Sainte-Barbe where he arrived exactly the same year as Pierre Favre: the two young men were the same age. Francis followed the regular course of studies for the licentiate. He was named regent (lecturer in philosophy) at the college of Beauvais, part of the University of Paris. Francis was at that time a typical young hidalgo—ambitious, easily offended, lively, exuberant and the university champion of the high jump. All that he desired was to obtain the grades which would permit him to have a brilliant career in the ecclesiastical world, that is, to be a qualified candidate for the beneficed clergy—why not a bishopric with big revenues?—because, after all, as a result of his aristocratic birth, he was destined for the Church. As an aristocrat, even one dedicated to ecclesiastical affairs, he had complete freedom of movement. He would declare one day that he had "leaped over the wall" many times with one of his masters and several of his comrades, to roam the Latin Quarter where the youth were wont to amuse themselves. However, in 1546, he confided to a priest at Goa that he had "never in his life been intimate with a woman"; but that was less from virtue than from fear of the diseases which had affected certain of his comrades.

The summer of 1525 marked a major threshold in his life. First of all, his mother Maria de Azpilcueta, to whom he had remained profoundly attached, died on July 25. Moreover, at the opening of school the following year a new student came to live in the room which he shared with Juan Peña and Pierre Favre: it was Inigo of Loyola. This belated and devout student at first barely interested Francis, except as a target for teasing and gibes—and also,[24] was there not an unhappy memory between them? At Pamplona in 1521 Xavier's brothers had fought on the side of the French. Inigo himself had defended the citadel; this did not help to diminish the reciprocal antipathy between the Navarrans and the Basques.

If at the time Xavier was incapable of surmounting these very natural feelings, Inigo himself saw in Xavier only a man who would be fine and good to gain for Jesus Christ. How could he manage it? The conversion of Francis Xavier remains a secret between him and Inigo. In any case, it was not by dinning into the ears of the ambitious youth, as is rumored, the famous "What does it serve a man to gain the whole world if he loses his soul?"[25] We know only that Ignatius rescued Xavier several times

[24] Contrary to what several biographers say, Francis was not under Ignatius' supervision but under that of Juan Peña. Furthermore, he was not Favre's tutor.

[25] SCHURHAMMER, lib. cit., I, p. 167, n. 4.

from poverty when the latter was without funds and procured for him lucrative private lessons. The best account at our disposal is that furnished by Edmond Auger, a Frenchman, who, having entered the Society of Jesus in 1550, had known Francis for several years and had gathered a few reminiscences from and about him. "I've heard it said," Polanco supposedly told him,

> that the young Francis Xavier was the toughest material that Ignatius, our great molder of men, ever had to handle. However, God used Francis more than any other person of our times . . . to take possession of almost a quarter of the world for the Cross of His Son. He was a young, gallant Biscayan nobleman: having been educated in philosophy, he did not think much of Ignatius' accomplishments and of his state in life, for at that time Ignatius was struggling to keep body and soul together through the mercy of others so as not to have to interrupt his course in theology. Francis could scarcely encounter Ignatius without making fun of his plans and aiming a few words of mockery at Laynez and Salmeron who had come from Alcalá to Paris to find Ignatius because of their devotion to him—based upon the combination of Ignatius' rare virtues and spiritual perfection. Ignatius knew Francis so well and treated him with such persuasive and gentle skill that he won Francis over and made him the immortal apostle of the Indies. In this Ignatius made himself no less known than Alexander the Great, that excellent horseman, who tamed his fierce Bucephalus. . . .[26]

Leaving Bucephalus to his epic galloping, we should remember from this text that Francis Xavier's conversion and then Inigo's victory over him were not accomplished in one day. Was there a conversion first and then a separate decision to accompany Inigo in the steps of the impoverished Christ? We do not know; nor do we know exactly what date this metamorphosis was accomplished. The authorities disagree on this point: we are inclined to accept Schurhammer's suggestion that Xavier was "converted" between December 1532 and June 1533.[27] What is certain, is that Xavier was at Montmartre on August 15, 1534, and that he took his vows there with Inigo and five other companions. It was not until after Montmartre, in 1535, that Xavier made the Exercises with a

[26] Cited by Ferdinand TOURNIER, "Saint François Xavier, d'après un manuscrit inédit du P. Auger" which, unfortunately, has not been found, where Father Auger presents his memories under the form of a *Dialogue* (*Etudes*, vol. 109, 1906, pp. 662–63). Cf. SCHURHAMMER, op cit., I, p. 162, n. 2.

[27] See his long discussion in *Franz Xaver*, I, p. 176, n. 2. If we only knew the date of Landivar's grotesque assassination attempt on Ignatius. Landivar, Xavier's servant, went crazy when his master converted to total poverty and decided to dispense with Landivar's services. Landivar announced that he was going to assassinate Ignatius who was responsible for his dismissal; but he fell on his knees and asked his pardon. Landivar even wanted to enter the Society of Jesus at a later date.

generosity which nearly killed him. Subsequently, he went back to studying theology, until he left for Venice on November 15, 1536.

SIMÓN RODRIGUEZ de AZEVEDO

In what order did Inigo encounter and enter into relationships with the other companions who participated in the offering at Montmartre on August 15, 1534? The answer is not certain. When Simón Rodríguez in his *De origine et progressu Societatis Jesu* enumerated the companions in order of their appearance on the scene, he assigned himself the fourth place (after Inigo, Favre and Xavier, but before Laynez). "The fourth place", he says, "was held by a Portuguese who, because of his unworthiness, does not deserve to be numbered among these servers of God who were of such excellence and such perfection."[28] This "Portuguese" was Rodríguez himself. But can we rely upon his memory? His commentary, *De origine*, dates from July 1577. Born in 1509 or 1510 at Vouzela (in the north of Portugal) in the diocese of Viseu, Simón Rodríguez wrote this nearly forty years after the events, and he insists that his relationship with Inigo was of a very intimate nature, but one also wonders whether his memory was accurate. "[I][29] was pushed from above to change the type of life I had previously led into total oblation to God. I shall add that I had never dealt previously with Father Ignatius, but that his reputation for very great sanctity had reached me and I decided to confide my intimate thoughts and feelings to him. I did not know anything at all of the plan the three companions had of going to Jerusalem to consecrate themselves and their lives to the salvation of others." In his *Vita Sancti Ignatii*, Polanco, on the contrary, puts Rodríguez in place as the last arrival among the companions.[30] All in all, the "hierarchy" which Simón Rodríguez gives seems the more likely.[31] But let us leave these petty debates aside!

Simón Rodríguez de Azevedo was of noble lineage; his father, Egide

---

[28] *Epist. Broëti*, p. 455.

[29] We put in the first person this confidence that Rodríguez puts in the third person in his account—he presents himself as "a Portuguese".

[30] *Chron.* 1, p. 49: "Magister S. Rodericus, post quinque vel sex prius enumeratos, Ignatio adhaesit." We should not overemphasize this little discussion, but it seems to illustrate the post-Ignation friction that sprang up among certain of Ignatius' earliest collaborators: in 1572, Ribadeneyra published his *Vita Ignatii Loiolae*; 1574, Polanco (who was not much in favor of this biography) finished his *Vita Patris Ignatii* begun in 1548; in 1577 Rogríguez wrote his *De Origine*. It is often in these small details that the real history reveals itself. And I've cited here only three biographies which concern themselves with the point that we are discussing.

[31] Cf. SCHURHAMMER, op. cit., 1, p. 179, n. 8.

Gonçalves, and his mother, Catherine de Azevedo, were numbered among the rich families of the country. Simón was raised at Lisbon under the tutelage of the dean of the royal chapel, Diego Ortiz de Vilhegas. It was perhaps to this protector that he owed the receipt of one of the fifty scholarships that King John III of Portugal had just founded at the college of Sainte-Barbe. It was in June 1527 that Simón arrived in Paris, but he did not join the companions until 1533; he participated in the vows at Montmartre in 1534. In March 1536, he presented himself as a candidate for the licentiate in arts and received the degree. After Easter he got his master of arts. It seems that it was Rodríguez and not Inigo who took the initiative for their meeting.

DIEGO LAYNEZ

The fifth and sixth companions were two friends: Diego Laynez and Alonzo Salmeron. They had studied together at Alcalá when Inigo had studied there himself. But about them, historians seem to differ. Some maintain that the two friends came to Paris to find Ignatius whose sanctity had so impressed them at Alcalá. Others say that they came to Paris to study philosophy more deeply and to begin their theological studies and that by chance on the first day they had the good fortune to meet Inigo. Another point on which the experts disagree is whether the two friends decided together or separately to join the Ignatian group. Some say that they decided to join together, but others, interpreting one of Rodríguez's sentences[32] too literally, say that although they were both placed under Ignatius' direction, each was unaware of the other's plan and decided on his own to renounce the world, to leave for Jerusalem and to embrace the same kind of life as the first four companions.

Diego Laynez was born in 1512 at Almazán, a large city of old Castile in the diocese of Siguenza. His father, Juan Laynez, and his mother, Isabel Gomez de León, were noteworthy and comfortable citizens, but the family bore a taint which in Spain was more infamous than illegitimacy: Diego's parents—at least his father—were descended from those called "the new Christians", that is, from converted Jews.[33] However, because of their piety, Diego, and his parents, grandparents and even great-great-grandparents enjoyed the high regard of Christians of old stock.

---

[32] "De Origine," *Epist. Broëti*, p. 455 " . . . cum alter alterius consilia ignoraret, uterque decrevit, etc."

[33] One should judge this "infamy" keeping in mind that Ribadeneyra, Laynez's first biographer, says nothing of this supposed Jewish origin; and when Tacchini finally dared to talk about it, it caused quite a bit of astonishment in Spain. Cf. T. VENTURI., op. cit., 3, p. 99, n. 4, and pp. 380–85.

Diego Laynez was a brilliant student at Soria and then at Siguenza. Later, he entered the University of Alcalá, where because of his very keen intelligence, his conscientious temperament, his diligent study habits and his courteous and affable manner, he enjoyed a very fine reputation among his teachers and fellow students alike. On October 26, 1532, at the age of twenty, he received his master of arts degree.

ALONZO SALMERON

Alonzo Salmeron was three years younger than Laynez. He was born at Toledo on September 2, 1515, and bore the same Christian name as his father; his mother was called Martina Diaz Olias y Mayan. Despite their poverty, they arranged for the studies of young Alonzo who was avid for learning, afterward sending him (we don't know the exact date) to the University of Alcalá to perfect his Latin and Greek and to devote himself to philosophy. It was there that he met Diego Laynez and that they became inseparable friends. Together they went to Paris in 1533, joined Inigo's group and participated in the vows at Montmartre. Afterward, Salmeron took courses in theology for eighteen months, until his departure for Venice. Previously, in the spring of 1536, he had received his master of arts degree.

NICOLAS BOBADILLA

The seventh recruit to the Montmartre group is known to history by the name of Nicolas Bobadilla. Actually, this appellation is comprised of his Christian name to which the name of the village in which Nicolas was born has been added. We know, nevertheless, that his father was called Francisco Alonso and his mother, Catherine Perez, and that he was born in in 1508 or at the beginning of 1509 in the village of Bobadilla del Camino in the diocese of Palencia. It would be both easy and amusing to make a caricature of Nicolas' character. Almost all the historians have shot a few barbs in his direction! One must state that alone among all the first companions, only Rodríguez rivaled Bobadilla in the worries which he created for Ignatius. But Ignatius was not mistaken about Bobadilla. Bobadilla was valuable; his snap judgments were almost always accurate, and as an apostle, he was indefatigable. Nicolas studied grammar "in his country" (no more specifics are given), rhetoric and logic at Valladolid; philosophy at Alcalá with the regent Diego Naveros, and won the title of master of arts. At the same time, he began his studies in theology; later he continued them at Valladolid under the Dominican Diego de Astudillo. For four years he remained there, teaching logic in the public schools of the town. Desirous of advancing his knowledge of Latin, Greek and Hebrew, he departed for Paris no later than the autumn of 1533 (we don't know the exact date). At the beginning of 1534, he was conquered by Inigo. The latter was worried to see Nicolas among the students of the "three languages", for this young group furnished the best and the most numerous recruits for the "heretics": "to Grecianize" had become synonomous with "to Lutheranize". Inigo patiently turned Nicolas away from his [the latter's] first intention and urged him to deepen his knowledge of scholastic and positive theology. Nicolas then became the disciple of the Dominicans of Saint Jacques and of the famous Franciscan Pierre de Cornibus. On August 15, 1534, Bobadilla made his vows with the six companions at Montmartre.

II. THE VOWS AT MONTMARTRE

Montmartre provides one of the high points from which one must contemplate the landscape of Ignatius' achievements for a long time, if one wishes to see fairly and to give each detail its proper value.

Here then we have seven companions who share a common spirit: first of all, a mission for which God (at least, if we believe Simón Rodríguez)[34] had inspired each one personally, which consisted of going on a pilgrimage to Jerusalem and of dedicating their lives to further the salvation of their fellow men; and this plan was defined in the "way of life" of their eldest member, Inigo de Loyola:[35] particularly by his absolute evangelical poverty. We should note that at this time in 1534, the companions had not all done the Spiritual Exercises, but that they had all had very frequent spiritual conversations with Inigo and among themselves. Furthermore, they practiced a prayer life which reinforced their spiritual desires. They had no intention of fulfilling this mission by entering an existing religious order—not even an order which they might found themselves. The idea of founding an order was totally foreign to them, but not the idea of recruiting other companions to join them.[36] And what then?

Then they took their time. . . . Their first decision was that they would give themselves three years to continue their theological studies, during that time changing nothing in their external manner of living.

[34] *Epist. Broëti*, p. 455.

[35] In 1534, Ignatius was 43 years old; Favre 28; Xavier 27; Bobadilla 25; Rodríguez 24; Laynez 22; Salmeron 19.

[36] Simón RODRÍGUEZ, ibid., p. 456. Our analysis will follow Rodríguez's account, pp. 457 and 458. He agrees with POLANCO, *Summarium hispanicum* and above all the *Summarium italicum*, *Font. narr.* i, pp. 185, n. 56 and 264, n. 7.

Their second decision concerned the question of their mission, which "seemed to them so serious and so arduous, of such difficulty and of such weight that it would be necessary for them, before resolving it, to turn it over to God for some time" in order to further fortify their hearts to go on, to surmount obstacles, to prepare for all the dangers which ordinarily confront such projects.

Having given themselves this respite and having set up these arrangements, they engaged in long deliberations: *Deinde longam post disputationem ad majorem rei firmitatem statutum est ut sese omnes voto obstringerent.* . . . It is very necessary to follow the order of events: the vows of Montmartre were merely the confirmation, the crystallization, so to speak, of a spiritual state with which the companions were already inspired.

> *Later*, after a *long* discussion intended to better assess their plan, it was decided that they would all bind themselves together by a vow of poverty, of chastity, and of making a pilgrimage to Jerusalem, and, upon their return, with God's help, to work with all their might for the salvation of their fellow men—the unfaithful as well as the faithful—to preach the word of God to all, to administer the sacraments of penance and Eucharist freely.

To this matter of vows, the companions immediately added qualifications: the vow of poverty would not be fully operative until the completion of their studies and the expenses necessary for the trip to Jerusalem would not fall under the vow; if the journey to Jerusalem should prove impossible the year after they finished their studies, or if after the pilgrimage they should decide to come back to Europe, they were resolved as of that moment and without the necessity of further deliberation, to turn to the sovereign pontiff to determine what kind of apostolic life they should lead, and what kind of ministerial activities they would undertake and in which countries they would work: for to him who receives his mission from the Pope "no determination is necessary": the Pope knows God's intention, as a result of the very position which he has attained.

On all of these points, agreement was unanimous among the seven companions. However, in the course of the discussion, one point remained obscure and resisted unanimity:[37] several would have liked to decide right then that "they would carry the light of truth to the infidels"; and the group deliberated on this question. But already, all,

---

[37] The question itself does not even come up in the same way in Rodríguez's account (op. cit., pp. 457, 458) and in Polanco's account (op. cit., pp. 185 and 264): Polanco only envisages this preaching to the pagans and probable martyrdom in the Holy Land in Jerusalem. According to Rodríguez, it seems that the companions considered the question in a more total, more universal sense. This was a nuance, but not one that was unimportant.

with an admirable spiritual alacrity, had taken a clear stance: if the need arose, they would steadfastly give their whole lives for whatever might be conducive to the greater service and honor of God. Then they came to this unanimous agreement; their vow to propagate the faith of Christ was thus interpreted: all would depart by sea for Jerusalem and there they would have a new election, asking for enlightenment from the Lord. If, at that time, a majority agreed that they should work among the infidels, they would seize every opportunity that the Lord offered them to do so; for what better and more favorable opportunity would there be? And if a majority disagreed, all together, without any disagreement, they would return to Venice.

It is necessary to read and reread these accounts of the deliberations and the content of the vows at Montmartre. Despite this, however, it is impossible to fathom all of their meaning. It is a marvel of generosity and wisdom, of unity and balance. It is remarkable that in these texts which have come down to us, one can distinguish neither the opinion nor the role of any one individual, not even of Inigo; and it is even more remarkable to see in its pure state, so to speak, the original plan of the seven companions, of seven men so different in age, character, nationality, social origin, even indeed in apostolic and spiritual experience. Their group was already international and combined diverse social backgrounds: one Basque, one from Navarre, two Castilians, a Toledan (so much for Spain), a Savoyard and a Portuguese. Nobles and peasants, rich and poor, merchants and shepherds, Christians of old stock and those of Jewish blood: their common point was their meeting place, the Latin Quarter of the University of Paris. As students, they all had enthusiasm, an exuberance, a sense of camaraderie and a taste for adventure.

On August 15, 1534, the seven men climbed to Montmartre, the mountain where according to tradition the martyrdom of St. Denis and his companions had taken place. There, a chapel with a crypt had been dedicated to the martyrs. The companions stopped there. The dawn rose over Paris. The place was deserted and at a distance from the city; here and there the arms of a few mills with rounded towers waved in the wind. Favre was the only priest in the group, having been recently ordained (on May 30). He celebrated the Mass. At the moment of Communion, each pronounced his vows—so carefully studied and perfected. Favre gave the Eucharist to his six companions. As they left the chapel, pure joy inundated the hearts of these men: the joy of having given a purpose to their lives for all time; the joy of belonging unreservedly to Christ; the joy of participating henceforth in the great work of redemption, without limits, without boundaries, without reserve;

finally, the joy of a fraternal community of faith, hope and charity. They spent the rest of the day in prayer and in "spiritual colloquies" in the deserted countryside.

III. AN ATTEMPT AT CONQUEST WHICH FAILS: JERÓNIMO NADAL

Since they had decided to allocate three more years for their classical studies, the companions stayed in Paris. They did not change anything about their "way of life". At this point—in 1535—we have a very interesting testimony concerning the manner in which Inigo recruited companions. Among the students who used to keep Inigo company there that year was one Jerónimo Nadal, born at Palma de Mallorca in 1507; he was twenty seven years old when he registered at the University of Paris. He had known Laynez, Salmeron and Bobadilla at Alcalá, and had even met Inigo. "I had seen him, but I did not know him."[38] In Paris Nadal fell ill and, when he was cured, met Inigo (at Faubourg St. Jacques), and confided to him the danger that he had been in and the fear that he had felt of death: "Poor fellow," answered Inigo, "of what were you afraid?" "What?" answered Nadal, "You don't fear death? Christ was even afraid of it!" "For fifteen years," said Inigo, "I have not feared death." "Some time later," says Nadal, "I began to confess my sins to Father Miona[39] and started to attend the Sunday Mass of the Carthusians with the companions."

It was Laynez who began to siege for Nadal's soul: "One day, Laynez came to my house to stimulate me in my spiritual growth. We talked about the mystical knowledge of the Scriptures because he had found me in the process of reading Theophilactus. *Nihil me movit, nihil intellexi* (If you feel nought, you understand nought). The second assault in the campaign to enlist Nadal was assigned to Pierre Favre: "Favre ran into me at Escobar's;[40] we talked about spirituality, but made no progress." The tactics shifted: the assault changed to a slow encompassment. Then Miona intervened: "Miona, my confessor, also tried to push me toward Inigo, but I answered him, 'And you—you're not one of Inigo's followers; why do you wish me to be one?' Inigo, suspecting that Nadal was prejudiced against him and his views—remember the Spanish difficulties

---

[38] This entire paragraph on Nadal relies on the text of the *Chronicon Natalis* published in *Nadal Mon.* 1, pp. 1–3.

[39] He was a Portuguese priest whom Ignatius had known at Alcalá and who had been his confessor from that time on. He entered the Society of Jesus in 1544 and was admitted to his solemn profession in 1549.

[40] Was this the great Francis de Escobar from Barcelona who was celebrated for his knowledge of Latin and Greek?

—tried first of all to work out how best to approach Nadal, "Inigo continued to act in the same way. He told me near the gate of S.-Jacques about his persecution at Salamanca, the investigations which he had undergone, etc. I think that he was doing this because he suspected that I was contemptuous of him because of these incidents. He was far off the mark." Ignatius exposed himself further. "He also took me to the little old church which is near the convent of the Dominicans;[41] near the baptismal fonts, he read me a long letter which he had written to one of his nephews in Spain; it was entirely devoted to calling him from the things of this world to the spiritual perfection of life."[42] This time Inigo scored points, but he was not alone in his longing to conquer Nadal.

> Then, the devil perceived the effect which Inigo's letter had upon me; violently, he made the spirit which attracted me seem something odious. We left, we paused in the square before the door of the church, and I said to Inigo: "As for me, it is this book which I wish to follow (I held in my hand a copy of the New Testament); you—I don't know where you are going; speak no more to me about this question; don't meddle any more in my affairs." Inwardly, this was my feeling: I don't want to join these men: who knew whether they would not all one day or another fall into the hands of the Inquisitors. I think that what turned me away from Inigo was the fear that a Franciscan monk, Panadesius, my compatriot and my friend whose authority was not negligible, would write distressing things about me in my country. In Rome I saw no more of Inigo or of his followers.

Ignatius had lost the battle, but not the war. Jerónimo Nadal entered the Society of Jesus in 1545. Later, he would be the Vicar General twice and the inspector visitor of the order through all of Europe. Ignatius would confer on him the mission of "declaring the *Constitutions*" in several countries.

IV. IGNATIUS DEPARTS ALONE FOR SPAIN, THEN VENICE

The group consisted of but seven members when Inigo left for Spain around March 25, 1535, probably on the thirtieth (Easter Tuesday). His health demanded that he attempt a "cure of native air", for all the care and the remedies tried had been powerless against his profound fatigue and his stomach ailments. Furthermore, he had to put the affairs of his original Spanish companions in order concerning the vow of poverty, visit their families and explain to them the new situation, and also to set right in his own country, Azpeitia, the bad example which he had formerly given there. It is also fair to conclude that, in leaving Paris,

---

[41] Ignatius gladly went there to pray.
[42] Unfortunately, this letter has never been found.

Inigo wanted to protect the companions from trouble with the Inquisition: had not he and his Exercises just been denounced by Mathieu Ory? He had escaped with honor and had even obtained a certificate—one more—which testified to the rectitude of his teaching and the purity of his morals. But who knew what might happen? It was important that his companions be able to study theology in peace in order to complete the work for their degrees, if they had not already done so, and to proceed calmly toward their ordination. Is it necessary to mention again that Inigo was not averse to testing the solidarity of the group? Christ alone was to gather the companions; no one was to put any obstacles between the companions and the Lord; the Holy Spirit was to guide the group. Favre, the priest and first companion, would play the role which up until now had been played by Inigo. Inigo put everything in God's hands. "He mounted a little horse which his companions had bought for him and he departed alone for his own country: he felt better in the course of the journey."[43]

We will not follow Inigo on his visit to Spain: he remained at Azpeitia for about three months (from about the end of April to the end of July 1535), then carried out his missions to the families of the companions and left for Genoa in November. One fact on this visit to Azpeitia, however, is related to our subject: on all of these trips and visits, Inigo instinctively resumed his life as a pilgrim: the route itself was his great light, the source of his apostolate, his place of prayer. His ministries—*he was not a priest*—were those to which his first companions would always devote themselves, with or without the priesthood. From Genoa he went on foot to Bologna: on the way, he got lost and almost died; he said in his *Autobiography*: "This was the worst fatigue and greatest danger that I ever had to bear; but in the end I escaped from it."[44]

Why had he chosen Bologna to await the end of the three-year period, and the arrival of his Parisian companions? The University of Bologna had no faculty of theology. Moreover, there he was overtaken with "his stomach ailments"[45] which he attributed to the dampness on the plain of Emilia. On December 27 or 28, he left for Venice where there was not even a university. Padua, however, which was nearby, had a university and a faculty of theology. Perhaps he thought that from there he could provide better for the departure of the group to the Holy Land.

Whatever the reason, he stayed alone in Venice for the entire year of 1536. He studied theology on his own;[46] he gave himself over to his

[43] *Autobiographie* R. P., n. 87.

[44] Ibid., n. 91.

[45] This is how he refers to them. At the time of his death, the physicians' examination discovered another reason for these sicknesses.

[46] Cf. *Epist. ign.* 1, 95–96.

customary penances and prayers; he gave the Exercises and bound himself by his spiritual conversations to several important people in the city. He did not lack apostolic opportunities: Venice, like all the big cities of Italy, was ravaged by a moral disintegration which made light of heresy. It was in Venice, in 1536, that he met the bachelor Diego Hozes from Málaga; to this Andalusian priest, "swarthy and of fearsome aspect, but with a heart full of enthusiasm for working in the vineyard of the Lord",[47] Inigo gave the Spiritual Exercises,[48] and made him a companion before the arrival of the Parisian group. Hozes would share in the life of the group until his death, in March 1538.

It was also in Venice, at the end of 1534, that the two brothers Esteban and Diego de Eguía met Inigo. Esteban was a widower, Diego a priest. These two rich Spaniards, whose family was related to that of Xavier, were passing through Venice on their return from a pilgrimage to the Holy Land. Inigo had them do the Exercises, and they decided to give themselves totally to Jesus Christ. They could not join his group immediately: first they had to set their affairs in order, but both would soon enter the Society. Diego, whom Inigo sometimes made his confessor, had Inigo's entire confidence: at the end of April, 1540, when a small group of companions would be sent from Rome to Paris to study there, it was Diego who would be responsible for them.[49]

From that same year of 1536 dates another of Inigo's memorable meetings: the one with Gian Pietro Carafa who would one day become Pope Paul VI. Gian Pietro Carafa was bishop of Chieti where he had received into his diocese a congregation of regular clergy called Theatines,[50] in whose founding he had assisted, hence his name "the Theatine bishop". He would soon be elevated to the cardinal's purple in the same year (1536). Inigo and Carafa began by getting along well, and they maintained friendly relations, but it all ended in a kind of breach. The reason for this misunderstanding, which would have far-reaching consequences in Inigo's life and work, was part of the history of his plan for a religious order: it concerned a letter which Inigo had written to Carafa in 1536 (the exact date is not known). Inigo stated that the

---

[47] SCHURHAMMER, op. cit., I, p. 288.

[48] *Autobiographie* R.P., n. 92, and POLANCO, *Vita*, p. 55, recounts the early scorn of Hozes regarding Ignatius. This contempt was dissipated to such a point in the course of the Exercises that Hozes asked his director to accept him as a companion.

[49] Cf. SCHURHAMMER, op. cit., I, passim, but above all 289–91, and 629.

[50] The Theatines (Theatinus was the adjective formed from the Latin name for the town of Chieti) were only one of the many new congregations which were cropping up in the Church to work for its reform. There were also the Somaschi, the Barnabites, etc. The Theatines had been founded in 1524 by Cajetan de Thiene.

"Society"[51] of Theatines had not expanded, whereas if it were more numerous it could better serve and praise the Lord. He wondered why. For this lack of growth he had discovered two causes: Carafa lived in the comfort of a bishop and not as a religious, that is, according to the spirit "of Saint Francis, Saint Dominic and many others [founders]".[52] The second cause was the manner of living of the Theatines which, so far as poverty was concerned, seemed to Inigo unadapted "to the necessities of [religious] life" for three reasons. "The first was that they did not beg for the bare necessities and did not have enough to live on; the second was that they did not preach; and the third was that they did not even devote themselves to the works of corporal mercy, like burying the dead, saying Masses for them, etc." Thus, the faithful scarcely knew them. If they did some of the things Inigo mentioned, "Our Lord God would be better served, the faithful would be more impelled to provide for their priestly needs with greater charity, other clergy who lived with little regard to Christian poverty would be more inclined to improve themselves, and finally, those who lived justly would be more encouraged to persevere and to make progress." Inigo suggested that one should look at the example of St. Francis and the other blessed saints.

> They all waited with a tremendous confidence in our Lord God, but without ever neglecting the most suitable ways to save and develop their religious families for greater service to and greater praise of this Divine Majesty. Otherwise, they would have believed that they tempted the Lord whom they served instead of following the way that must be taken in order to serve him.

The reprimand was severe. But the text raises some questions for the historian. First of all, was this letter ever sent? Certain scholars, like Father Rouquette,[53] wonder whether it was even meant for Carafa.[54] It certainly seems that one must consider the objection that this text is only the rough draft of a letter which was perhaps never sent; but it also seems difficult to deny that Inigo's position was known to Carafa: the quasi-break between the two men, and what followed it, is hard to explain

[51] This is Ignatius' word.

[52] We take our quotations from the translation of Gervais DUMEIGE, SAINT IGNACE, *Lettres* (coll. "Christus", pp. 59–63). A study of this letter has been presented by Father Georges Bottereau at the Ignatian days in Chantilly in 1973; one hopes that one day this will be published.

[53] MS unedited, chap. 13, p. 5.

[54] The absence of ordinary phrases of respect like "Vuestra Merced" should not astonish us. At this time, Ignatius deliberately did not address important people by the titles by which they were addressed in polite usage. It was only in 1540 that he concerned himself with using the usual titles with each cardinal, bishop and prince.

without that. The second question arises in relation to the occasion for this letter: how and why was Inigo meddling, all of a sudden, with the Theatines' way of life? Could there have previously been a vague plan for them to merge with the companions? (We know that such a proposal was made twice during Ignatius' lifetime). If Inigo had spontaneously taken the initiative in this criticism, one would feel a kind of embarrassment about this letter—as about an indiscretion—an unwarranted but daring interference in the affairs of others. Recognizing this, it is necessary to note that this text is extremely valuable to us because it touches on the heart of Ignatian plan, that is, the poverty of an apostolic group.

V. THREE COMPANIONS JOIN THE GROUP IN PARIS

While Ignatius was working in this manner in Venice, the six companions, remaining in Paris under the spiritual authority of Favre, pursued their theological studies; their way of life and their conversations attracted a few new companions to them.

CLAUDE JAY

The first among these was the Savoyard Claude Jay.[55] Jay was born between 1500 and 1504 at Mieussy, a large parish of upper Savoy, about 30 kilometers to the north of Villaret, from where Favre hailed: his parents were simple but honest farmers. Like Favre, he studied at the college of La Roche, under the master Pierre Velliard, but in a higher class. He was ordained a priest on March 23, 1523, in Geneva. In the autumn of 1534, at the suggestion of Favre who, in 1533, had returned for a little while to Villaret, Claude Jay went to Paris to improve his knowledge of theology. It was then that Favre gave Claude the Spiritual Exercises: the effect was such that when the companions renewed their vows on August 15, 1535, Jay joined them. The following year, after Easter, Claude received his master of arts. St. Francis de Sales would be able to rejoice that there had been two Savoyards among Ignatius' first eight companions. . . .

---

[55] It would perhaps be better to call him Jay than Le Jay. An old woman, who was about a hundred years old "remembered very well having seen the formerly mentioned Father Claude when he was approximately 18 years old; she maintained that at that time he was corpulent and of average height, with a thin face, gray eyes, blond eyebrows; his general appearance being more blond than otherwise." (*Fabri mon.*, p. 846). Cf. also Jean-Marie PRAT, *Le Père Claude Le Jay* (Briday, Lyon, 1874) and Henri TAVERNIER, "Father Claude Jay, sa patrie et sa famille", *Revue Savoisienne*, t. 35 (1894), pp. 79–94.

PASCHASE BROËT

At Montmartre, in 1536, the group was increased by another two new recruits; Paschase Broët and Jean Codure.

Paschase Broët was from a village in Picardy, Bertrancourt, about five kilometers from the outskirts of Amiens. His date of birth is thought to be around 1500. His father, Ferry, or Frédéric de Brouay, was a comfortable peasant of the area. Paschase began his studies in his own village and then went to Amiens. He received holy orders in the Bishop's chapel from the abbot of the convent of Prém'ontrés. He was given a patrimony of twenty four pounds [ducats] guaranteed by his family. It was not until 1534 that he went to Paris to complete his intellectual background. On March 14 of that year, the same day as Rodríguez and Codure, he received his M.A. degree. He made (we don't know how) the acquaintance of Favre and chose him as his spiritual guide. We don't know on what date he decided to join the group; but he was at Montmartre on August 15, 1535.

JEAN CODURE

The last Parisian recruit was Jean Codure from Dauphiné. He was born in the little town of Seyne in the diocese of Embrun on June 24, 1508 or 1509. Not much is known of his childhood. He had already begun theological studies when he went to Paris. There he lived at the college of Lisieux or de Torcy, very near the college of Sainte-Barbe. How did he join the other companions? No one knows. It must have been after Inigo's departure for Spain. In any case, it was Favre who worked with him and gave him the Spiritual Exercises. On August 15, 1536, he was a part of the group. Formerly, on March 14, he had received his licentiate and on April 16, his master of arts.

Thus, at the end of 1536 the group consisted of eleven companions: nine were in Paris; Ignatius and Hozes were in Venice. Four were priests; the others were studying theology with the intention of becoming priests.

The deadline established in 1534 was approaching: the companions in Paris had to set out January 25, 1537. But in June 1536, Charles V declared war on Francis I in connection with the succession of the duchy of Milan. In July and August imperial troops invaded Picardy and Provence. Thus, it was necessary for the travelers to hasten their departure from Paris: they fixed on the fifteenth of November, 1536, as the date for departure. To avoid Provence, they took the route through Lorraine, Germany, Switzerland, Vorarlberg and the Tyrol. They made

their way on foot, evidently among troops on the move and through
some countries which had already passed into heresy. For the majority of
them this was their first experience of the "way of poverty and prayer"
and to what an extent it brings spiritual vigor. After a thousand adventures, about which we know in detail from Simón Rodríguez's
accounts,[56] they all arrived safe and sound in Venice on January 8, 1537:
Inigo and Hozes were awaiting them.

Venice, for them, was only a stop on the way to Rome. They stayed at
two huge hospitals in the city, five at the Incurables and five at the
hospital of Saints John and Paul. Inigo stayed alone in another house.
They spent two months in performing works of charity among the
impoverished, sick people. It was then that Xavier, in order to conquer
his disgust, repeated the gesture of the saints: he kissed the wounds of a
leper. Theirs was not an apostolate in the true sense of the word; they
were not priests, and they did not know Italian; only Favre and Hozes
sometimes heard confessions.

The delay in departure provided them with some very realistic experiences of human misery. This assistance to the poor, to the peasants and
to the plague-stricken would always be a part of the "particular ministry" of the companion of Jesus.

On the tenth or twelfth of March, ten of the companions set out for
Rome. Inigo remained alone in Venice. The pilgrims passed through
Loreto (March 25 and Holy Week). They went to seek authorization
from the Pope to make a pilgrimage to the Holy Land and the permission
to receive Holy Orders. We already know what happened. Their trip
met with success; ordinations took place in Venice; they were divided
into groups in the universities of upper Italy; Inigo arrived in Rome as
did Favre and Laynez; they were all regrouped in Rome in September
1537; and finally, they offered themselves to the Pope's service in
November 1538.[57]

---

[56] "De Origine", *Epist. Broëti*, pp. 461 to 467. Cf. also the *Memorial* of FAVRE, *Font. narr.*
I, pp. 39 sqq., and LAYNEZ, ibid., pp. 102 sqq.
[57] Cf. supra, pp. 25 sqq.

CHAPTER IV

AFTER OFFERING THEMSELVES TO THE POPE, THE DELIBERATIONS OF 1539 (MARCH–MID-JUNE)

November 1538: Having favorably accepted the companions' offer of themselves, Paul III gave them as their first apostolate the city of Rome itself.[1] For these men, enamored of evangelical expeditions to all parts of the earth, this task must have been somewhat of a test; moreover, it was the first time—it would also be the only one—that they would all live together, under the same roof. They graciously submitted to all of these duties. After all, Jerusalem, like the Indies, is everywhere! It is the heart that counts. In June 1539, before dispersing, they would discover that, even in Rome, had they had four times as many members, they would not have had enough for the work demanded for them.

They sensed that this situation would not last long. In his letter of December 19, 1538, to Isabel Roser,[2] Inigo wrote: "We are already overrun by a number of prelates who want to go, if the Lord allows it, to bear fruit in their own lands. We are remaining calm, biding our time and awaiting a better opportunity." This better opportunity could be only by order of the Pope.

This is the way that events affected the little group: pressures were brought to bear upon the Pope. Charles V wanted them to go to the Spanish Indies, John III wanted them in the Portuguese Indies,[3] the bishops and princes of northern Italy who had witnessed the group's behavior in their first apostolates, wanted them to return to them. It was evident that the group was about to split apart; then, some new companions presented themselves.

Would this then be the end of the beautiful, informal, spiritual friendship which for five, seven and, in certain cases, ten years had gathered them around Christ?

Since an important question had arisen, the companions undertook, as was their custom, a general deliberation.

I. REASONS, GOAL AND PROCEDURE

From these deliberations which began in March 1539, at the home of

---

[1] At the time, Rome was a city of fifty thousand inhabitants. (SCHURHAMMER, *Franz Xaver*, 1, p. 312).

[2] *Epist. ign.* 1, p. 141.

[3] Letter from Favre to Diego de Gouvea, *Epist. ign.* 1, pp. 132–33.

Antonio Frangipani, near the Tower of Melangolo,[4] and which would not end until June 24, the Feast of St. John the Baptist, we have rather precise accounts[5] which trace the spiritual stages through which the participants passed before arriving at *some* decisions. This is fortunate for us, because the step which was going to be taken in the history of the group, although it was in the usual style of the companions, is nonetheless surprising, and in a certain sense, dramatic; a superficial glance would lead one to think that the companions, by the decisions that they were going to make, had turned their backs on the past and were beginning anew. On the contrary: their chief concern was to maintain their uncontaminated spiritual experience of the past in the new framework of the present. Just as Manresa and Jerusalem had dominated the life of the group in Paris, so Paris, Venice and Rome of 1538 were to remain alive and present for all the companions, spread out "all over the world": the Holy Spirit marked once and for all each of the hearts of these men.

The Fathers decided first upon the regularity of their meetings. They were so involved in their ministries that there was no question of interrupting them; souls might be lost, and would there not be a chance of resurgence of the recent gossip concerning the Mainardi incident? Thus, they would dedicate evenings to deliberations. Before the meeting, the point to be discussed would be chosen by the most competent members of the group. During the day, they would ask for divine enlightenment: each one, especially during Mass, would consider carefully and sincerely the pros and cons of each solution. And then, they would take their time, as generously as circumstances would permit: "*Per multos . . . dies*": "We decided to assemble for a number of days before separating in order to consider together our vocation and our way of life." For what purpose? "To arrive more quickly (*citius*) at the end which we had determined in advance for ourselves, and about which we were thinking."

They made a sincere avowal of their differences and kept a balance sheet of divergent opinions, "*Scindebamur*": "We differed in our sentiments

---

[4] Concerning the year of these "deliberations", see the discussion of it in *Const.* 1. pp. XXXV and XXXVI. For an eye witness account: cf. T. Venturi, *Le case abitate in Roma da S. Ignacio di Loyola*, op. cit., pp. 297–301.

[5] The text of the "Deliberatio primorum Patrum" seems written by Codure, but the draft is not in his writing (cf. *Const.* 1, pp. XXXVII–XXXVIII). On the other hand, the "Determinationes Societatis" are certainly in Favre's handwriting (loc. cit., p. XLVI). According to Schurhammer, the scribe was Antonio de Strada (*Franz Xaver*, 1, p. 435, n. 14). Let us mention in passing that Father Rouquette thought that he recognized Favre's style in the writing (*Notes manuscrites*, ch. XVI, p. 5, note). I think that it is indeed necessary for us to resign ourselves to uncertainty concerning the identity of the writer and the technical expertise of his penmanship.

and opinions regarding the state of life which was to be ours." What was surprising about this *pluralitas sentiendi*? "We were French, Spanish, Savoyard, Cantabrais . . . weak and frail men . . . and the princes and pillars of the church, and even many saintly persons have divergent opinions and upon occasion have even opposed each other." Such was their avowal, and here is the balance sheet: On one point all the companions were unanimous (*una omnium nostrum et communis mens et voluntas*), that was "to seek the perfect will of God as he is pleased to reveal it to us, according to the aims of our vocation". It was on the question of "the means of proceeding so that our activities might be freer and more efficacious for us and for those we were serving, that there was a plurality of opinions."

This fact established, "we desired to find a way of resolving this plurality. By means of care and attention, it was necessary to find a way out of this dead end (*aliquam viam plene apertam*) so that we might offer ourselves as a holocaust (*in holocaustum offerremus*) for the praise, honor and glory of God, for whom we would give up all that belonged to us." Such was the atmosphere of the undertaking.

A first decision about which all were in agreement was that these deliberations would be above all a sincere and loyal questioning of God. The conditions were first to reenforce their habitual fervor (*ferventius solito instare*) in prayer, penance and meditation; then, to do all we could to succeed; as for the rest, to cast upon the Lord all our thoughts, "all this in the firm hope that he who is so good and generous that he does not refuse the good spirit to those who ask it of him with humility and simplicity of heart without reproaching anyone, he would not abandon us; instead, he would assist us, more abundantly according to his benevolence, than we would have requested or could understand." It is necessary to weigh all the words of this heavy text. But how? Throughout this entire verbal process of deliberation every word is heavy with meaning.[6]

One must begin by considering one by one the "doubts" (*dubia*).

II. FIRST DOUBT: MUST WE STAY TOGETHER?

At their first evening meeting, the "dubium" which was proposed evoked, one might say, a prior question: basically, in offering and dedicating themselves and all their lives to Christ Our Lord and to his

---

[6] A simple comment: all of this text is written in the comparative because the companions were aware of making a choice: a choice between "good" and "better". Their spiritual freedom was involved.

"true and legitimate" Vicar on earth, so that the latter might dispose of them and send them wherever he deemed that their work would bear the most fruit, whether it would be in the land of the Turks, in the Indies, with the heretics—no matter where, with the faithful or with infidels,— had they not implicitly agreed to split up their group? Then at present, would it be better to be bound into one body (*corpus*) so much "one" that no cleavage within the body,[7] no matter how severe, could separate them? A specific case presented itself: the sovereign Pontiff was sending two of the companions to Siena.[8] "Must we then be concerned with those who are going to leave, and they with us, and keep exchanging news with them, or not bother with them any more than with those who are not of the Society?" The answer was "ultimately"[9] affirmative. The two arguments which won the day are noteworthy: one was the argument of Providence:

> God in his mercy graciously willed to assemble and to unite us, although we were weak and strangers to each other by virtue of nationality and mind. It is not up to us to break up that which God has united, but we must rather affirm and stabilize this unity by drawing closer into a single body, each having responsibility and understanding of the other; for courage itself when it is concentrated has more vigor and strength to accomplish all sorts of good but difficult deeds than when it is divided.[10]

And the companions further added: "in all that we have said and will say, we understand: we will take absolutely nothing from our own minds, but will rely only on that, whatever it may be, which God will have inspired and which the apostolic See will confirm and approve."

What exigencies, yet what spiritual freedom! All of that would be written in the *Constitutions* on "Body of the Society of Jesus" was already here in embryonic form.

III. SECOND DOUBT: MUST WE ALL OBEY ONE AMONG US?

Having resolved the first "doubt", they proceeded to a more difficult settlement which merited no less consideration nor fewer appeals to

---

[7] The repeated use of the word [*corpus*] is intentional in the Latin text and we are keeping the repetition.

[8] Paschase Broët and Simon Rodríguez.

[9] "*Tandem*" in Latin, which indicates that the Yes was not immediate. Nothing indicates that agreement was reached in only one day, as SCHURHAMMER supposes (*Franz Xaver*, I, pp. 436–37).

[10] It is unwieldy to portray here the density of the original text. The abstraction which Latin allows, lets many double meanings abound in the text which French obliges one to eliminate.

God. "To the vows of perpetual chastity and poverty which we had uttered under the hands of the papal apostolic nuncio at Venice was it fitting to add a third—that of obeying one of us?" We should note that however involved this question may have been with the preceding question, it was still legitimately distinct from it: the bond of chastity does not necessarily include the bond of obedience as well. Moreover, the motivation for it is different; and—an important point—the motivation is written into the question itself: "In order that we might be able, with more sincerity and merit, to achieve during all of our lives the will of our Lord God, and to follow the wishes and orders of His Holiness to whom we have freely offered all that is ours: will, intelligence, strength, etc." Decidedly, these ten men left no aspect of the problem unconsidered.

Regarding this second doubt, an impasse arose. It was not, let us note, that there was disagreement between different companions. *Nihil occurreret quod impleret animos nostros*, that is to say, "After several days of prayers and reflections nothing (no solution) fully satisfied us in spirit." Thus there was not sufficient enlightenment and that applied to all without exception. Hence, the companions reverted to their habitual method in similar situations: to wait, but actively. They were confident in God (*in Domino sperantes*). They were going to take measures to *better* resolve this doubt. Enough of words and discussions—it was time for prayer and penance. Was it necessary for this supplication that they all withdraw for thirty or forty days of solitude or should they select three or four companions, in the name of all, to go to the desert? Or should they divide the days in two parts: the first part for prayer and penances, the second part for their usual ministries? But wouldn't all that make talk in Rome? And also, could they reduce the ministries when each of them already had to do the work of four!

It was necessary to find a solution. Someone proposed that they all follow three spiritual steps:

1. That each one go about prayer, penance and meditation in such a way as to strive to find peace and joy in the Holy Spirit in regard to obedience, working his hardest to want to obey more than to command, equally for the glory of God and for the praise of his Majesty.

2. That no one speak to anyone of this matter, that the companion not question it so that he would not undergo any pressure nor be influenced to obey rather than not to obey—nor the reverse; that each seek only in prayer and meditation what would be best.

3. That each should imagine that he did not belong to the group, even that he would never belong to it, so that by this device, he might not be influenced to judge according to his own emotions, but that he might be

freed of them so as to express his opinion before the group on obedience or nonobedience and that he might be able to support his ideas on the manner in which he believed the service of God would be the greatest and which would best assure the future of the Society.

Anyone who is familiar with the "Three Times of Election" of the Spiritual Exercises will easily orient himself to this spiritual method of proceeding. However, it was not a single person who was involved in deliberation but a whole group. Therefore, it was necessary that, after each personal choice had been made, there be an exchange of motivations and ideas. For this exchange, two times were set aside: a first day, when each would bring arguments against obedience, the disadvantages, reasons, thoughts which would have come to him during reflection, meditation and prayer.[11] The following day, there would be all the arguments in favor of obedience.

The verbal proceedings give examples (but not an exhaustive catalog) of the cons which were brought up. They are very interesting.

Someone said, "The very name of religious order or of obedience is odious to the ears of Christian people because of our weakness and our sins."

Another said: "If we wish to live under obedience, we can be led by the sovereign pontiff under an already existing rule. Whence it would happen that no longer having either the opportunity or the place to work for the salvation of souls (which is our sole purpose) after our own salvation, all these desires which we have nourished with the help of the Lord our God would be thwarted."

Still another said: "If we vow obedience to a Superior, there will be fewer recruits for our group to work in faith in the vineyard of the Lord; already, although the harvest is great, one finds few real workers and many, such is the weakness and fragility of humans, seek their own interest and their own will rather than the will of Jesus Christ and the total abnegation of self."

And so it went: the fourth, the fifth, etc., explained the arguments against obedience.

The next day the content of the discussion was reversed: each explained to the others the advantages and the fruits of obedience as they had discovered them in prayer and meditation. The arguments, says the chronicler, were of two types: some demonstrated (*deductio ad absurdum et impossibile*), that is, showed what great drawbacks would result from the rejection of obedience; the others consisted of simple and direct affirmations of obedience.

---

[11] The order of priorities in this list is important.

For example: Experience has shown us that no one really takes charge of "making decisions", whether spiritual or temporal; each person depends on others to make them. Without obedience, there is anarchy.

Furthermore: Our first intention is to assure the permanence of our Society and nothing preserves a society like obedience. And more especially, we have made a vow of poverty and given ourselves up to spiritual and temporal work of an absorbing and diverse nature; this was not done to preserve a society. Without obedience there's no chance of our surviving.

Another said: He who lives under a vow of obedience is quick to execute orders, even the most difficult ones, . . . even the most humbling."

Another said: Nothing is more contrary to pride than obedience. Pride makes us follow our own judgment and will, to the scorn of others. Obedience makes us follow the judgment and will of another and to submit in all: it is the partner of humility. Here, we must translate the argument word for word; "And although we have given total obedience to the Sovereign Pontiff and Pastor (both individual and general), nevertheless it is not possible for him to be concerned with the innumerable personal affairs that occur and even if it were possible, it would not be fitting."

The delineation and the discussion of these arguments for and against obedience went on for many days (*multis diebus*); they weighed the most important reasons and above all everyone prayed, meditated and reflected.

Finally, with the Lord's help, with unanimity and not a plurality of voices they concluded: "It is better for us, it is necessary to promise obedience to one of our group" and this will serve a triple purpose: "That we might be able to realize better and in a more exact fashion our primary purpose of accomplishing (by our every action) the will of God; then, that the Society might be more reliably preserved and, finally, so that everything might be correctly provided for whatever might happen to each one—be it temporal or spiritual." The ministries, the body of the Society, the personal contact of the Superior with each of the members, were the three goals to which the ten early Fathers sacrificed the dear, relished, fruitful liberty of the earlier companionship. It was a historic moment.

Two points here demand attention if one does not wish to misinterpret this decision. The first is this one: "It is *better for us.* . . ."[12] This comparative, to which the numerous comparatives of this text correspond,

---

[12] In order to understand the meaning of these obscure words, it is necessary to

signifies that there was a choice—that to sustain and to adopt the contrary option would have been possible, that there would have been good reasons and, finally, that they did not repudiate in any way the liberty and equality of the early group. Moreover, we shall see, that a big effort will be made by Ignatius in his administration and in his *Constitutions* to safeguard (as much as possible) from within the structures of obedience, liberty and spiritual equality. The decision of 1539 was not, then, a break with the past; it was a *clarification* of it which demanded more attention under the new conditions of the existence of the Society of Jesus. The second observation is no less important; "obedience to one among us" was located *within the context* of obedience to the Pope and was a consequence of it: this later obedience would evidently be the object of a vow and not merely an offering, and it would envelope, legitimize and require obedience to the Superior "who would be one among us". We shall return to these two cardinal ideas.

On April 15, 1539, during Mass, before Communion, the companions took the solemn pledge to make the vow of obedience, if the Pope would authorize them to do so. Pierre Favre drafted the text with his own hand; each of the companions signed it:

> I [name], the undersigned, attest before the all-powerful God, the blessed Virgin Mary and all the heavenly court that after having prayed to God and weighed the matter thoroughly, I have decided of my own accord that in my judgment it is more to the glory of God and to the perpetuation of the Society that we vow obedience; of my free choice, I have offered myself without this being a vow or its implying any obligation[12] to enter this same Company if it is confirmed by the Pope, the Lord so willing. In memory of this decision (wherein I recognize a gift of God) I go forward with it now, although very unworthy, to Holy Communion. Tuesday, April 15, 1539.

At the bottom of the document, were eleven signatures: ten that we would expect, (and) that also of an eleventh person whom we have not yet met, Caçres—i.e., Diego de Cáceres. Not having yet taken any vows (of chastity and poverty), he did not yet belong to the group, but he lived with the companions whom he had known in Paris. He was a master of arts, but he was not yet a priest. He had never belonged, it seems, to the order, at least in the strict sense of the word. He had never taken vows,

---

remember that the Society was not yet a religious order: the companions therefore could only make a hypothetical offering, and this offering could be neither a vow nor a binding promise. It is a shame that we do not have the original document, but only copies of it, and, as is the case with many documents of that time, several of the signatures are reproduced in calligraphy: Cf. *Const.* 1, p. 8, n. 1.

but he became a priest in 1541, or 1542, and broke definitively with the Society in 1542. Soon he began a very adventurous career as a secret agent in the service of Francis I, then King of Navarre. In his unpublished *Dialogues* of 1591, Ribadeneyra claims that he died as a result of the "questioning" to which the French subjected him because they suspected him of being a double agent. Despite the eleven signatures, history titles the deliberation of 1539 that of the "ten fathers". But it was not perhaps without providential significance that Diego de Cáceres took part in this initial deliberation.[13]

IV. FOLLOWING THE DELIBERATIONS (APRIL 15–JUNE 24, 1539)

The deliberation of the first Fathers was prolonged beyond April 15. It would last two months more until June 24.

The verbal proceedings of the *Deliberatio primorum Patrem* gives only six or seven lines to this period—which signifies that for the author of the document the essential points had already been decided. This brevity is, however, a little disconcerting when one knows the details, however summarily, of what happened: "We kept the same regulation for discussion and the same method of procedure for all the other questions: alternate examination of the pros and the cons. . . . The day that we finished [the Feast of St. John the Baptist], all was completed smoothly and harmoniously. Many late vigils, prayers, reflective efforts and much physical fatigue[14] were necessary in order to deliberate and to conclude everything." In fact, the questions which were considered during this period were important. The work progressed in three stages: the first ended May 4, the "Feast of the Holy Cross" and "the following Sunday",[15] the second ended May 23, and the third, June 11.

From the end of May, however, there were only eight companions: Bröet and Rodríguez had left for Siena on the Pope's orders (with Francisco Strada, a candidate who would soon play an important role in Portugal and Spain) to reform the monastery of Saint Prosper and Saint Agnes; as for Xavier, it is generally believed that he was involved in a ministry outside of Rome, but Tacchi Venturi[16] believes that Xavier was

[13] Concerning Diego de Cáceres see SCHURHAMMER, *Franz Xaver*, 1, p. 228, n. 6 and *Const.* 1, p. XLV.

[14] *Const.* 1, p. 7.

[15] Ibid., p. 9; concerning this date Favre has indubitably made a mistake: the Feast of the Holy Cross was May 3 and the following Sunday of that year was May 4. Cf. T. VENTURI., op. cit., 3, p. 178, n. 1. These dates are given by the *Actes*, that the *Const.* 1, pp. 9 and sqq., call "Conclusiones septem Patrum".

[16] T. VENTURI, op. cit., 3, p. 180, n. 2. To our great surprise SCHURHAMMER does not bring up Xavier's absence (*Franz Xaver*, 1, p. 440).

sick (*infermita non lievi*): he would have had to have been seriously ill in order not to participate in such a debate.

The First Group of Determinations

Accordingly, from May 3–5 these points were unanimously approved. We quote them despite their super-subtle style (which we'll try to clarify): it is of a totally different style from that of the "Deliberatio"![17]

1. Whoever asks to enter the Society is expected to take the vow of obedience to the person of the Pope. He must agree to go into no matter what province or region to minister to the faithful as well as to infidels; it is understood that this pertains only to those who have sufficient gifts to aid the souls to whom they will be sent. This vow will be made to the Sovereign Pontiff through the Superior General or through the Society and not to the Sovereign Pontiff himself except in a special case—regarding which the Superior General or the Society would decide.

2. Candidates of lesser capabilities may be admitted to the Congregation, but they must be motivated by the same spirit as the others. They would also have to take a vow of obedience to the Sovereign Pontiff. If he wanted to send them to the pagans, even if they knew only how to say to them "Christ is the Savior", or among the faithful, even if they knew only how to teach them the Our Father and the Commandments of God, public or private, according to the mandate of the Superior or to the Pope's personal wish, they would go.

3. They would explain the Commandments to children and to everyone else.

4. It would be necessary to determine the time when they could teach the Commandments and the rudiments in an established order and according to the proper manner.

5. For forty days each year, they would teach these rudiments. In these forty days, they would include, or not include, as they chose, Sundays and feast days. To avoid any qualms, it was understood that these forty days would be interpreted loosely, give or take two or three days, or even more.

6. It is for the Superior General of the Society to decide whether the person sent to some particular place must teach the Commandments, preach, or do this or that.

7. If someone in the Company wanted to go to one province rather than

---

[17] The text is such that it seems to have discouraged translators: SCHURHAMMER for example (*Franz Xaver*, I, pp. 440–41) presents it, but totally transforms its style and eliminates many details; T. VENTURI, op. cit., 3, pp. 178 sq., skipping a paragraph here and there and summarizing others; ROUQUETTE (*Notes manuscrites*, chap. XVI) abandons analysis and returns to the elaboration of the constitutions. It seems to us that it is necessary to have the courage to stick closely to the original text: the companions had difficulty clarifying their project, and doesn't the very mediocrity of the text suggest the problems of converting the "deliberation" into written form? Are not the copies only an edited version of the lost verbal discussions?

another, whether it was to the faithful or to the pagans, that person would not be able in any manner, either directly or indirectly, nor by himself nor by an intermediary, have recourse to the Sovereign Pontiff with the idea that the latter would send him there; but the individual should submit to the Society or its Superior General, to whom he would reveal his wish and his point of view, while remaining disposed to do what would be expected of him.

Second Group of Determinations: Bobadilla Refuses to Sign

Here, the writer specifies a precise date: on the Saturday before the fourth Sunday after Easter,[18] he says, they concluded their deliberations and the following Sunday, they confirmed points eight and nine as follows:

8. That children be taught for one hour—but without scrupulously keeping to the sixty minutes exactly—according to the judgment of the person teaching.

9. The candidates who are accepted will spend three months, before their probationary year, in doing the Spiritual Exercises, in going on pilgrimages, in serving the poor in hospitals or elsewhere; the way that these three months is divided up is left to the judgment of the Superior General, or to that of the whole Society. For example: whether the candidates should spend two entire months on pilgrimage, or in the service of hospitals, or a month in each of these ministries, etc. The candidate also had to be actually poor before being admitted on probation.

These two points having been established, the text adds others.

10. Everyone, however, was agreed on this point: that it was necessary to leave a "loophole" on the subject of three months in the case of a candidate who might be of such high rank, for example, of the nobility or of powerful parents or relations, that there would be danger in sending him on a pilgrimage or to service in the hospitals, and in this case the Superior could excuse him from these two ministries.

11. It was also decided unanimously that if someone manifested to the Superior, or to the Society, the desire to go to a pagan land, and that the Sovereign Pontiff left the decision to their judgment, the candidate would have to spend ten days in Spiritual Exercises so that one might judge by what motives he was led to this desire. "Test the spirits to see if they are from God . . ." (1 Jn 4:1). The candidate would be sent only after this time, if that seemed good to the Superior General or to the Society.

12. The Friday before Pentecost,[19] all, with the exception of Bobadilla, concluded and decided that the above article which is concerned with the

---

[18] In 1539, Easter Sunday fell on April 6. The Saturday before the fourth Sunday after Easter therefore fell on May 4.

[19] Consequently, May 23.

teaching of children for forty days and for one hour each day, would fall under a formal vow, obliging the member under pain of mortal sin, exactly like the vow of obedience to the Superior General and to the Sovereign Pontiff, and not to have recourse directly to the Pope when one wanted to be sent to pagan lands.

With the exception of Bobadilla . . ." This is the first time that Bobadilla shows his character and spirit of opposition. It is also the first break in unanimity. The circumstances may seem slight, but the effect was serious. The first consequence was the necessity of changing the rule for making decisions. But wasn't the very principle of "deliberation" somewhat weakened by this dissent? However that may be, here is what was decided the same day:

> 13. It was clarified and decided that in all these discussions of business, whatever their importance, that the opinion of the majority would be binding; however, as they had done up to the present, they would take three days for the more important questions and they would not decide anything until the third day when they would adopt the opinion of the majority; those signing this new rule made it clear that, in their opinion, it would not be right for someone who differed with the others to lose his right to vote.[20]

Seven signatures followed (six companions and Cáceres). The only ones missing were Broët and Rodríguez, who, as we have said, were in Siena; Xavier, who was ill; and Bobadilla, who was not in agreement on one point.

It is necessary to elaborate briefly on this point. Bobadilla was never an easy companion to get along with; to canonize Ignatius, one wit said, it would have been sufficient to consider by itself his patience with Bobadilla! Obviously, the latter's opposition on May 23 was serious. But was it a reason to indict him as certain people did? Could he not have opposed the inclusion of additional vows in good faith, even if it entailed his submitting to a pontifical decision that went against his own opinion? This point might well be argued. In Bobadilla's life there were even more suprising instances, to cite only one example: it was necessary in 1541 to force him to make his solemn profession. Some even accused him of wanting to leave the order.[21] Everything went on with him as if he were

---

[20] How could Nadal (*Nadal Mon.* 2, p. 52 and "Apologia", n. 111 *Font. narr.* 2, pp. 98–99, n. 138) have been able to believe that if someone's ideas differed from those of the others, he would no longer be allowed "in tractatione rerum"? This view is guilty of two mistakes: Nadal thinks that the dissenter would lose not only his right to vote, but even the right to take part in the discussion of business. It is true that this note of Nadal is in his account of daily events for the year 1557 and is directly followed by his terrible description of Bobadilla (*Nadal Mon.*, 2, p. 53). Cf. *Const.* 1, pp. XLIX, LI, and note 15.

[21] It is necessary to read carefully, and without prejudice, the texts of Nadal (*Font. narr.*

still a part of the companionship of Paris, of Venice and of the first months in Rome. If our hypothesis is correct, Bobadilla's opposition emphasized once again (as if there were need of it), the dramatic character of the deliberation of 1539.

One notices, moreover, with what care, from the first "constitutions", the two poles of authority were separated: the *societas* and the *praelatus*.

The Third Group of Determinations

Let us return to the "determinations of the seven Fathers". For the deliberations continued: the eve of the octave of Corpus Christi (June 11) the three following points were approved without being definitely confirmed:

14. There will be a sole Superior for the entire Company, he will be elected for life, taking into account exceptional cases to be determined.

15. If the Society receives churches or houses for habitation it will be necessary that the legal document not confer proprietary rights, so that the benefactors may take back their property at their own will without any opposition from us. Moreover, we have no right to bring suit, regardless of the legal manner in which they have put this property at our disposal, even if someone were to try to take it from us unjustly.

16. Concerning the reception and rejection of novices, the Superior will be bound to take the advice of some of the other members of the Society who appear to him to be able to give the most exact information about the candidate; then he will have recourse to God and will finally make the decision which appears to him to be the best for the glory of God and for the progress of the community. He alone will judge whether there will be an admission or a rejection.

17. In three cases, however, he will not be able to decide, nor even have the right to vote: first, if the candidate is one of his family or relations; second, if he is from his native country or from a neighboring country, so close that one might suspect the Superior of being influenced by this circumstance; third, if the candidate is the spiritual protégé of the Superior, or if the Superior has given him the Exercises, or if he is his confessor. In these three cases, the decision to admit or refuse the candidate will belong to the majority of the community.

What happened between June 11 and June 24? We don't know. If we

---

2, p. 104, par. 122, and n. 161) and Ribadeneyra's "De Actis" (ibid., p. 393, par. 21), and to refer to the exact words of the *Mémorial* (n. 210): if one believes Câmara, Bobadilla hesitated in professing his vows, but Câmara does not say that Bobadilla wanted to leave the Society. In 1541, there was a difference between the two positions. Nadal himself, in 1557, went so far as drawing a very uncompromising portrait of Bobadilla (cf. *Nadal Mon.* 2, pp. 52–53). Ignatius was more Christian regarding his turbulent companion.

believe Schurhammer,[22] Laynez raised the question of founding colleges in universities on the model of those in Paris, for the recruits of the order, but the proposal was rejected in the name of poverty: they then envisioned renting houses for those who were studying. They also considered the questions of a choir, of music, of mandatory fasts and penances.

One might be perhaps surprised that these first determinations made no allusion to the name of the order. That was because there was no reason, just the opposite, to abandon the name which had been chosen at Venice and which the vision of La Storta had confirmed: the group of companions had been called the "Society of Jesus" since 1537,[23] and the religious order founded by the companions would continue to be called the "Society of Jesus". In their fidelity to this name, there was a sign of their fidelity to a particular spirit.[24]

V. IN 1537, HAD INIGO PLANNED TO CREATE A RELIGIOUS ORDER?

The study of this chapter undoubtedly permits us to ask the following question and helps us to resolve it: When Inigo entered Rome in 1537, did he have the firm intention, or simply the idea, of founding a religious order?

Let us deliberately put aside the old belief that at Manresa Inigo had had a revelation on his work concerning the framework of the Society of Jesus; this belief seems definitely discredited by the discovery of the documents concerning the origins and the development of the *Constitutions*. Everything hinges on Inigo's arrival in Rome in 1537.

If, at this particular time, Inigo had secretly carried the project within him, and even the blueprint for the Society of Jesus, what would have been the purpose of these hesitations, meetings, deliberations, gropings, prayers and penances which we have just witnessed? This would have been a rather cruel and brilliantly executed comedy.

And would he have lied to so many friends? To Jean de Verdolay, to whom he wrote from Venice on July 24, 1537, that he could barely see how the Lord would make use of him? To Isabel Roser to whom he said on December 19, 1538, "Four or five have decided to enter the Society"?

---

[22] Cf. SCHURHAMMER, *Franz Xaver*, p. 442 and n. 7. Cf. *Font narr.* 1, p. 610, Câmara's *Mémorial*, n. 138. Since Laynez left Rome as early as June 20, 1539, and consequently before the end of the deliberation, it was then that the institution of the "collegia" must have been proposed, discussed, and accepted. Cf. Laynez's 1547 letter to Polanco (*Font. narr.*, 1, p. 128).

[23] Cf. POLANCO, *Font. narr.* 1, pp. 203–4.

[24] Cf. DUDON, lib. cit., pp. 622–25. T. VENTURI, op. cit., 3, pp. 182 sq. See, however, SCHURHAMMER, lib. cit., 1, p. 200, n. 8.

"It has been many days and many months that they have persevered in this decision. We don't dare admit them because that would cause one more complaint among others already among us of receiving subjects and forming a congregation or an order without the authorization of the Holy See."

What advantage would there have been in continuing to lie once the Society was launched in the world? Father Francis Palmio, in July 1553, submitted to him a work intended to inform the public on the origin, nature and works of the Society of Jesus. The manuscript arrived in Rome on the twenty-second of July. On the twenty-ninth, Polanco answered Palmio (at Bologna):

> Y. R. did his best. You will be able to add that the first companions our Father Ignatius had gathered around him in Paris did not go to Italy to form a religious order, but to go to Jerusalem in order to preach and to die among the pagans; but then since they could not travel to the Holy Land (something never before experienced in our times except for that particular year, because of the war between Venice and the Turks), they had to remain in Italy. The Pope used them for works of service to God and to the Apostolic See; then they agreed to form a body (*di far un corpo*); and this Company was confirmed by Popes Paul and Julius, etc., and enriched with privileges and great favors in order to help souls.[25]

In their account of the beginning of the order the first companions do not speak differently from Ignatius. This is true of Laynez in his famous letter about Ignatius,[26] of Bobadilla in his letter to Aquaviva on August 15, 1589,[27] and of Rodríguez in his *Commentary* (1577); Rodríguez even dates the actual foundation of the Society from the first vows of Montmartre in 1534, as if the constitution of an order was only the additional clarification of a fundamental act; in 1577, Rodríguez undoubtedly had reasons other than historic ones to support this point of view, but his statement expressed no less the feeling of the other companions.[28] Polanco, the faithful interpreter of Ignatius' numerous memoirs, never stops affirming in his writings and in his correspondence that when Ignatius and his companions went to Rome, "They had no plan to form a congregation, nor any other form of religious order, but they wanted to dedicate themselves to the service of God and to that of the Apostolic See, from the moment that they discovered that they could not go to Jerusalem."[29]

[25] *Epis. ign.* 5, p. 259.
[26] *Font. narr.* I, p. 111, n. 36.
[27] *Bobad. mon.*, p. 602.
[28] *Epist. Broëti*, pp. 457, 498, 508 sq.
[29] POLANCO, *Summarium hispanicum*, n. 86. *Font. narr.* I, p. 204.

However, between Manresa and Montmartre and between Montmartre and Rome, there was a mysterious continuum. What God taught Inigo during his retreat at Manresa was the secret of his ways. He taught him the indispensable frame of mind that one must have in order to be receptive to God's calls, to recognize his Spirit, to achieve step by step God's plan for him. It was not Inigo who knew that one day with nine companions he would found the Society of Jesus—it was God. God needed a man whose heart would be in tune with him, who would perfectly accomplish his will. By giving Inigo this experience of the discernment of spirits, this wisdom of choice that was simultaneously mystical and human; in leading Inigo to this point of personal abnegation wherein the human heart finally breathes in the universe of God, beats to the rhythm of the heart of God, regards the world with the eyes of God; from the time of Manresa, God was preparing the instrument which would serve him in founding in Rome the Society of Jesus. The deliberation of 1539 was no more than the experience of Manresa, lived by a group and in new circumstances.

A word dear to Ignatius and to his companions summarizes and symbolizes the Ignatian mentality: pilgrimage. They were essentially pilgrims, they always marched towards one Jerusalem or another, first the terrestrial one and then the celestial one. They went on the Way according to the will of God, in his footsteps. . . . The Way consisted of all the roads of the world—of Spain, of France, of Lorraine, of Germany, of Italy—all the ways which brought them together and then led them to Rome. However, it was still more the way of mystery and light that the Lord made them follow in the course of these long earthly marches. On the pilgrims' route there was also self-abnegation, poverty, sometimes hunger and thirst, the capriciousness of the seasons and the uncertainty of the future.

There was also a freedom of the spirit, the infinity of the horizons without limit or constraint, the overflowing joy of adoration, of offering oneself and of acts of grace.

There was the meeting of "faithful and pagan", of companions who "went along the route" for a while or who remained faithful, friends who helped them, enemies who lay in wait for them, thieves who robbed them; the rich who gave them alms, the poor who shared their bread.

The Way beckoned to them each day, each minute, but the Goal to which it lead, though often veiled, was nonetheless certain. When we look back, however, we perceive that the itinerary was truly marvelous, that the experience transformed them, that they were "purer", freer, truer . . . in short, that God who is at the end of the Way was already traveling with them.

The Ignatian deliberation, this communal and personal election, is the most important element for staying "on the right track". It is the stop, the momentary halt, either alone or in a group that pushes one ahead, by which one becomes oriented, by which one chooses. The Ignatian deliberations were accomplished in accordance with only the most tangible realities, the truest situation, the weighing of opportunities and defeats, but above all, in invoking the Lord who called himself the Way, "*Ego sum via*" (Jn 14:6).

The Ignatian deliberation was the act of a "wise man": "*sedebit solitarius . . . tacebit . . . et levavit super se*" (Lam 3:28). It was wise to stop for solitude, silence, serious reflection, and to commune with God, in order to make sure that one was progressing well according to God's itinerary.

CHAPTER V

THE FIRST SEPARATIONS; THE "PRIMA SUMMA INSTITUTI"; IGNATIUS, SUPERIOR GENERAL

I. THE FIRST PONTIFICAL MISSIONS

Broët and Rodríguez in Siena

The deliberations of 1539 were not terminated before four of the first companions had already left Rome by order of the Pope. The Archbishop of Siena and other notables of the city (through the intercession of Cardinal Gian Pietro Carafa) had succeeded in getting Pope Paul III to order Paschase Broët (by virtue of his holy obedience) to report to Siena with one of his companions. Francisco Strada, a young man of twenty who lived with the companions, was designated to accompany him. Simón Rodríguez joined them later. Broët and Strada departed at the end of April or in early May, with very broad powers. Their assignment was to bring back the religious of the monastery of Saint Prosper and Saint Agnes to the keeping of the monastic rule. The zeal of the missionaries did not end with the reform of the monastery: they worked in the city and more particularly among the student youth of the great university. Soon, Strada was installed at Montepulciano. In November, 1539, exhausted from his labors and austerities, Rodríguez fell ill; it was then that John III of Portugal asked (through his ambassador at Rome, Don Pedro de Mascarenhas) that several companions be sent to the Portuguese Indies; for this mission, Ignatius and his companions selected Bobadilla and Rodríguez who had returned to Rome during the first days of 1540.

Favre and Laynez at Parma and Placenza

Parma and Placenza, two cities which remained attached to the Papal States, were governed by a cardinal. At the beginning of 1539, this "legate" (the title of the governor) was Cardinal John Mary del Monte, the future successor of Paul III. On April 21, he was replaced by Cardinal Filonardi (of the title Sant'Angelo). The latter soon requested two companions for his territory. For this mission, the companions elected Pierre Favre and Diego Laynez. The two missionaries left Rome on June 20 and arrived at Parma by way of Loreto during the first days of July. There they found a very critical religious and moral situation: "This city", wrote Gian Angelo de Medici, "has for many months been worse than a bacchanalian woods: so many murders, robberies, and other sins have been committed here."[1] Through their preaching, and especially through the Spiritual Exercises that they themselves gave and that those to whom they had given them, gave in their turn a wave of conversions (slow and bristling with difficulty) resulted. It was then that Jerónimo Doménech (a priest for twenty-four years and a canon, from Valencia in Spain) met Favre and Laynez, made the Exercises and decided to join the group of companions, as did Paul de Achillis, Elpide Ugoletto, John Baptist Viola, Antonio Criminali and the two brothers, Francesco and Benedetto Palmio—all names which would often recur in the history of the first years of the Company. The laity, men and women, collaborated in the activity of the two missionaries, even to the point of going from house to house to instruct at home the children and women who could not get to church.

All this activity was not accomplished without some acrimony and opposition: certain preachers hardly appreciated the companions' fervent recommendation that the faithful participate once a week in the sacraments of penance and Holy Eucharist.

It was not until May of 1540[2] that Laynez began working at Placenza. Soon his preaching and his example produced happy results among the population. But about August 20, 1540, rumor had it that the Pope was going to send Laynez to France and Favre to Spain. The Parmesans intervened at Rome to prevent his departure, but in September, Favre was designated to accompany Dr. Ortiz to Worms in the capacity of theologian. As for Laynez, Cardinal Marcello Cervini had obtained his services from the Pope for the reform of the monasteries and of the city of Reggio, in Emilia. Soon, however, Ignatius asked the Pope (in December 1540) to recall Laynez to Rome. The Society of Jesus had been approved two months previously, and it was now necessary to proceed with the election of the Superior General.

Bobadilla at Naples

At the beginning of autumn 1539, Nicolas Bobadilla left Rome for Naples. A private and particularly delicate mission had been conferred upon him. Don Ascanio Colonna and Joan of Aragon, after more than twenty years of marriage, were about to separate—to the great scandal of their people. As early as July 4, this mission had been discussed in the small community of the companions in Rome as imminent.[3] In fact,

---

[1] *Carteggio Farnesiano* (1540), cited by T. VENTURI., op. cit., 3, p. 222.
[2] Undoubtedly because of Favre's long illness and his arrival in mid-July 1539.
[3] Letter of Bobadilla to Hercules II, Duke of Ferrara. *Bobad. Mon.*, p. 16.

Bobadilla did not leave until the end of September for Ischia where Ascanio lived. In his *Autobiography*, speaking of himself in the third person, Bobadilla recounts his voyage and his arrival:

> [From Mola] he went by sea to the island of Ischia, but during the voyage, he was taken ill with a malevolent fever, the "pecoria" which is usually fatal. Having disembarked on the island, extremely ill, he was not able to stay there because there was no hospital. He was, therefore, taken to Naples, to the Annunziata where they took a sample of his blood and gave him a purgative. He often heard the doctor say to the nurse: "He's going to the tomb . . ." but God had pity on him. Bobadilla got better. Two months later, he returned to the island of Ischia and lived there until Easter of 1540: he completed the mission which he had received from Doña Juana, succeeded to the satisfaction of the Sovereign Pontiff and of Don Ascanio Colonna; then he returned to Rome barely cured of his long illness.[4]

Actually, he was not cured, and he had not succeeded in his mission so well as he had thought, but at least the rupture between the wedded Colonnas was deferred. Ignatius, thirteen years later, would try in his turn to reconcile them, and he would fail like Bobadilla.

In the first days of March 1540, Bobadilla returned to Rome. Ignatius recalled him because they thought of sending him with Rodríguez to Lisbon, and from there to the Indies in accordance with the proposal of John III of Portugal. But scarcely was he at Rome, when the fever which in fact had never left him mounted anew. They could not wait. Don Pedro de Mascarenhas was ready to leave. It was then that Bobadilla was replaced by Xavier—Xavier who would then serve as secretary for the group and would be responsible for correspondence with the scattered companions.[5] God continued to do things in his own way. Bobadilla, almost cured, resumed his mission in southern Italy. At Bisignano in Calabria (autumn 1540), he visited the entire diocese, preached, heard confessions, reformed monasteries and clergy, battled against Lutheranism—not without a certain amount of brutal vigor. In the spring of 1541, the Pope recalled him to Rome at Ignatius' request. There, he participated in the election of the Superior General of the Society of Jesus.

---

[4] *Bobad. Mon.*, p. 618, n. 15.

[5] The companions had promised to write to each other every week, or at least every month. It was the beginning of this correspondence of the period which, despite its copiousness, presents, at least in so far as what concerns the companions of Ignatius, regrettable and, one must say, astonishing gaps. Let's point out that the post in those times was neither reliable nor rapid: cf. Mario Scaduto, "*La Corrispondenza dei primi Gesuiti e le poste italiane*", AHSI, vol. 19 (1950), pp. 236–54.

Jay at Bagnoregio and Brescia

Another companion, Claude Jay, was finally given a mission lasting for several months. As early as March 22, 1540, Bobadilla was able to announce the departure of Claude to Duke Ercole II of Ferrara:[6] he was sent into the region of Bagnoregio. Despite a hostile reception, Claude remained firm and ended by winning the hearts of the people and by doing much good. In the fall, he went to Brescia where the young and ardent Francisco Strada had preceded him. The reception there was much more cordial although Brescia was one of the first cities where heresy had sprung up. Strada and Jay worked together in the city until the spring of 1541. Then, like the other companions, Jay was recalled to Rome for the election of the Superior General.

As for Strada, he rejoined the group of student candidates in Paris over whom Diego de Eguía presided and from among whom the first nucleus had left Rome at the end of April 1540.

II. THE "PRIMA SOCIETATIS JESU INSTITUTI SUMMA"

The result of the long deliberation of 1539 had no canonical efficacy as long as the Pope had not officially approved it. Therefore it was first necessary to draft a more comprehensive and better-organized document which could be presented to the Pope. How, and by whom was this "First Summary of the institution of the Society of Jesus"[7] written in five chapters? We do not know.[8] The date is not affixed to the document, but it is certain that it was finished in August, for it was presented to Paul III for approval by Cardinal Gasparo Contarini on September 3.[9] Tacchi Venturi, an expert on the subject,[10] has declared: "Anyone who wants to have an exact knowledge of the Society of Jesus as the founder conceived and presented it to the Vicar of Christ for approval, need only examine this document." It is noteworthy that the text would be reproduced almost in its entirety in the bull of the institution of the Society *Regimini*

---

[6] *Bobad. Mon.*, p. 22.

[7] *"Prima Societatis Jesu Instituti Summa"*: This title was invented by the editors of the Monumenta (*Const.* 1, p. 14): it is entirely suitable for this type of document.

[8] T. VENTURI., op. cit., 3, p. 268, sees there the "mark" of Ignatius. That is probable. In any case, all the companions then present in Rome continued collaborating until its completion.

[9] Cf. Contarini's letter of September 3, 1539, to Ignatius. *Const.* 1, p. 21. Cardinal Contarini had already conversed with Paul III about the Society at the end of June or the beginning of July in 1539 and had begged him to receive favorably the formula which he would soon present to him.

[10] T. VENTURI., op. cit., 3, p. 271.

militantis in 1540, and the intervening variations are very instructive on the origin and progressive development of the Society's organization.

We must therefore analyze this document in a precise fashion. We cannot cite it in its entirety, but one should read it as a whole and carefully weigh all its words.

In a prologue, independent of the text, the Pope[11] placed in context the act which he was going to promulgate. He knew the ten companions, named them, observed that they came from many diverse geographical areas. He also knew their works, their titles, their motivations, and he had been informed of the "deliberation" which they had just made and the decisions at which they had arrived under the inspiration of the Holy Spirit. The Master of the Sacred Palace, Thomas Badia, had studied the project and found it most worthy. The "*Summa*" is comprised of five chapters.[12]

First Chapter

This first chapter is fundamental. What is the Society that we wish to designate by the name of Jesus? What can one find therein? Such is the question that above all else must be resolved.

Before considering the Society, it is necessary that the candidate have the desire to "fight under the standard of Christ" and "to devote himself only to God and to his Vicar on earth". This intention was an indispensable prerequisite for any candidacy.

If he really was so disposed, then the candidate, having made the vow of perpetual chastity, could ask to join the group of companions: for it was precisely this "desire" which had already united them in Paris and Venice.

But each candidate should know that from among the forms of service to God, the Society had chosen certain ones in preference to others: to help souls "to progress in Christian life and doctrine, to propagate the faith by ministry of the Word, the Spiritual Exercises,[13] and works of charity, notably through Christian instruction of children and of ordinary people."

What essential attitude did the candidate have to adopt if he was admitted? "To have his eyes always on God first of all." God is the purpose, the unique purpose, and the form of this organization is merely a means (*via quaedom*) of arriving at God, but this "way" has been personally proposed by God himself to the candidate. In itself the "way"

---

[11] The Pope: for the "Summa" is a sort of rough draft for the bull which the Pope would have drawn up and would sign.

[12] From whence its other name: "The Five Chapters".

[13] The meaning here goes beyond the truly Ignatian *Spiritual Exercises*.

is not the purpose; the form of the organization is "secondary" (deinde) in relation to the service of God. But for him who is called, the service of God blends with the form of the organization. He must therefore pursue the goals of the Society with all his might.

With all his might? Yes, but each has his own vocation within the universal vocation of the Society. First, the grace of the Holy Spirit varies in form and intensity according to individuals and then among the companions not all were skilled or destined for all tasks.

Let there be no intemperate zeal or slipshod work (ne quis forte zelo utatur sed non secundum scientiam), but let everything be as it should be. The matter of judging each one, of discerning and distributing the duties, should be the sole responsibility of the Superior General who should be elected by the companions so that everything might be correctly ordered: for order is essential if a community is to be solid in its foundations.

This authority of the Superior General is not absolute. The element of the "companionship" enters in to temper it: The Superior will have authority to make the Constitutions so as to implement the work which we have proposed as a group"; but three conditions balance and check this right: this authority is to be exercised "in council", the Superior will hear "the opinions of the brothers", the decision will take into consideration the "right" according to the majority of the voters. What is this council? It is that portion of the Society which the Superior will easily (commode) be able to assemble:[14] he will not do it except for matters of the greatest importance and which would have a lasting effect on the Society; for less important and more temporary matters, he will assemble all those who are located at the place where he himself is residing. On the other hand, the Superior General will have unrestricted power to give orders and to see that they are executed. In conclusion, the Superior General does not have exclusive legislative power, even over minor matters, but in contrast, he does have total executive power.

It is indispensable to understand all of the nuances of this first chapter of the "Summa". Immediately, it established the relationship between the members and the different directive elements which make up the originality of the Society of Jesus.

Second Chapter

It is totally devoted to the obedience of the entire Society and of each of the companions to the currently reigning Pope. It is very clear and very eloquent:

Let all the companions know and may they remember, not only in the

[14] This text was drafted in the context of still scanty manpower.

early days of their profession, but every day, so long as they may live, that
this entire Society and all of its members fight the battle of God in faithful
obedience to our most Holy Father Paul III and to his successors and that
they have submitted themselves to the authority of the Vicar of Christ and
to his power of divine right, not only by virtue of the common obedience of
all the clerics but also by the bond of a vow: in such a way that everything
that His Holiness may order us to do for the good of souls and the
propagation of the faith, we are bound to implement immediately without
tergiversation or excuse and with all of our strength, whether he sends us to
the Turks, to the new worlds, to the Lutherans[15], or to no matter what
others—faithful or pagan.

The first Fathers knew through reflection and experience that this commitment was of a redoubtable exigency and that they thereby were
risking their lives in its execution. We have seen that martyrdom held no
terror for them; but they loyally warned prospective candidates about it.

> May those who aspire to join us, before taking such a burden upon their
> shoulders, meditate long and deeply to ascertain whether they have enough
> spiritual reserves to lead to fruition, in accordance with the guidance of the
> Lord, such a grand undertaking, that is to say, if the Holy Spirit which
> encourages them promises them sufficient graces to carry, with his help, the
> weight of this vocation.

Obviously, the companions did not gild either the present reality or the
future: it was the "All" of God which expressed itself in their vocation;
they emphasized his transcendance, his absoluteness . . . and, more
specifically, the example of Christ who saved the world by his sufferings,
his humiliations and his Cross. If the "evaluation" of the candidate was
positive (in regard to the aforementioned criteria), then, under the
inspiration of the Holy Spirit, he would have given himself to this
Society of Jesus Christ, and he would have to remain prepared and ready,
both by day and night, to fulfill such an extraordinary commitment. The
end of the chapter cautions that no one, not even the Superior General,
must make any attempt to obtain from the Pope a mission of his own
choice.

Third Chapter

This chapter is concerned with obedience to the Superior[16] of the
Society. This is based on a vow from one person to another: *singuli*, as

---

[15] Let us note this unique, or at least very rare, precision in the official texts of the first
Society of Jesus.

[16] In this text, the word "Superior" is always singular: in the circumstances of the
Society, it was a question of only one superior. The hierarchy of superiors would be
introduced later on.

the text says. Let each one make the vow of obedience to the Superior General in all that concerns the observance of this rule. For his part, the Superior General will order what he considers opportune for the accomplishment[17] of the objective which God and the Society have proposed to him: and that in the exercise of authority, he will always remember the benignity, the bounty, the charity of Christ, and the examples of Peter and Paul. He must see to it that he and his council conform to this norm. It is in this chapter on obedience and authority that the companions, aggressively and insistently, return to the fundamental obligation to catechize children and ordinary people by adopting themselves "to the diverse circumstances of people, places and times":

> It is particularly necessary that the Superior General watch diligently concerning this point: first, because faith cannot flourish in souls without a solid foundation; and [second reason] because, on the part of the companions, there is a danger that the more scholarly a person is, the more he seeks to avoid this ministry which appears less brilliant: but in reality, there is none which is more efficacious, be it aiding one's neighbor or giving opportunity to members of the Society to exercise, as they must, charity and humility.[18]

This point covered, the text continues to exhort all the companions to be obedient "in all that concerns the body of the Society". There are two reasons for this insistence: this obedience "has immense (*ingentes*) advantages for the order; it is a continual exercise in humility,—that virtue which one cannot praise enough". The mystery of this obedience? To recognize Christ as present in the person of the Superior. May they venerate him then, as is fitting.

Fourth Chapter

How, after these two chapters, can certain historians claim that "the document emphasizes poverty above all"? That is to confuse lyricism with a hierarchy of values. What is true is that the fourth chapter begins with a sort of hymn to poverty, where all the memories of the first companions are reviewed and, for Ignatius, all the joys of being a pilgrim[19] are recalled.

---

[17] The Latin words "*constructio finis*" are used here for the second time by the authors of the "Summa". How can we translate this expression? What words would include the nuance that the "end" is achieved only by a "harmonious assemblage of diverse elements pursued methodically"? Schurhammer utilizes the German word "*Erreichung*"; Tacchi Venturi uses the Italian word "*raggiungere*".

[18] It is difficult not to see here an echo of divergences of views with Bobadilla. In July August, 1539, he was still in Rome; but had he participated in the wording of the text?

[19] Evangelical poverty "sang" in their hearts. Apostolic companionship also. If after a

We have experienced the fact that no life is more joyous, more pure, more apt to enlighten one's neighbor than that which is the most removed from the blight known as the love of money and which seeks instead to be as close as possible to evangelical poverty. We know that our Lord Jesus Christ will provide the food and clothing to those who seek only the kingdom of God. So, therefore, each one and all together must make a vow of perpetual poverty, declaring that for themselves and even for the community, for the maintenance and the needs of the Society, they will renounce all civil right to dispose of fixed property, of revenues or of rents. They will be happy to have only bare necessities at the will of benefactors and to receive alms and letters of credit to buy necessities.

From lyricism one returns to the down-to-earth realities, the experience of Paris:

However, in order to join to their group a few very gifted students and to mould them in the universities, especially in the sacred sciences, the companions may be able to acquire by law the rights to stable income or revenues; that is to say, for the maintenance of these scholars who want to progress in spiritual and academic life and to be received subsequently into our Society, their studies to be completed after their probation.

Fifth Chapter

The fifth chapter appears at first to concern a sort of practical set of rules: recitation of the Divine Office, each in his own way and no required ceremonies: neither choir, nor organs nor chanting. In fact, this principle is based on an experience: in all that "we have found grave inconveniences; according to our vocation, in addition to other obligations, we must pass a great part of our days and sometimes of our nights in helping the spiritually sick, when it is not a question of nursing them."

There follows a sort of conclusion. This "Summa" corresponds to the Holy Father's wish for a document detailing the organization of the Society:

We have drafted it also to inform, at least summarily, those who question us on our manner of living and to inform those who, if it please God, would like to imitate us; we know from experience that our life is not without numerous and grave difficulties; we consider it opportune to warn those who would wish to follow us of these things, for fear that, under the pretext of good, they go aground on these reefs which we ourselves have avoided. The first danger would be to impose upon the companions under pain of

---

long debate they were resolute about obedience "to one among us", it was precisely for "better achieving their primary objectives" (*prima desideria*) for deprivation, spiritual friendship, efficacy and apostolic universality.

mortal sin fasts, disciplines, bared feet and head, special clothing, special diets, penances, hairshirts and other corporal mortifications: all that, we do not forbid because we condemn it—on the contrary, we praise and exalt it for those who practice it—but do not follow these practices ourselves, only because we do not want our brothers to be overwhelmed by so many accumulated burdens that they find therein some excuse for divorcing themselves from the purpose which we have established for ourselves. Moreover, each will be able, if the Superior does not forbid him, to indulge piously in these things to the extent that he will have recognized in them a necessity or utility for himself. The second danger would be to accept into the Society someone who would not have been tested over a long period and with care; it is not until he will have proved his prudence in Christ and his doctrinal and spiritual quality, that he will be admitted into the Society of Jesus Christ. May this same Jesus Christ be favorable to that which we have undertaken in weakness, for the glory of God the Father, to whom only be honor and glory forever. Amen.

The document ends with a total and enthusiastic approbation of Paul III. The Pope accorded the companions the authorization to draft among themselves (inter vos) the constitutions: "As for the work, much loved sons of Christ; follow your vocation according to the guidance of the Holy Spirit, then work indefatigably like good laborers, in the vineyard of the Lord, under the protection of the Holy See, and with the grace of our Lord Jesus Christ."

This joy of the Pope was not solely for appearance's sake. From the time that he first had knowledge of the "Summa", Paul III had agreed that the bull or letter (whichever seemed better) be drafted, "on the advice of the Master of the sacred palace, to whom His Holiness had had me transmit the order to examine the matter and to give him his reaction."[20] It is reported that after reading the document, Paul III said, "Herein is the Spirit of God", or, "Here is the finger of God."[21]

The same day, Cardinal Contarini informed Ignatius of the happy outcome of his preliminary steps and informed him that as soon as he returned to Rome with the Pope, two days later, he would give the order to the Most Reverend Ghinucci, to draft the official document of approval.

III. THE DIFFICULT OFFICIAL APPROVAL

All seemed near conclusion.[22] Jerome Ghinucci was well versed in

[20] These last bits of information were added by Cardinal Contarini to the document. It was Contarini himself who read this *Summa* to Paul III in Tivoli.

[21] Cf. T. VENTURI., op. cit., 3, p. 275.

[22] The principal source of our information on the very great difficulties (*laboriosi trattati,*

curial affairs. Secretary in charge of signature of letters for many years under the pontificates of Julius II and Leo X, created Cardinal of the Consistory on May 22, 1535, he was frequently consulted by Paul III on affairs of the curia. According to a letter of September 28, from Lattanzio Tolomei to Contarini, then in Loreto, Ghinucci had examined the document in depth. For three chapters (the first, third and fourth), he had demanded only a few corrections of form or terminology. But for the second and the fifth, such was not the case: in the fifth, Ghinucci had eliminated everything that concerned organs, sacred chant, corporal austerities, etc., so as not to give heretics the opportunity to claim that they had won. These deletions would not raise any difficulty, for the companions had accepted them. The criticisms addressed to chapter two were more serious; the vow of obedience to the Pope had seemed superficial to the Cardinal: was not obedience to the Pope the duty of all Christians and particularly of all clerics? But after having heard the explanations of some companions, Ghinucci agreed to pass over this difficulty. For their part, the companions declared themselves ready to accept the proposed corrections, provided that the organization of the Society of Jesus would be approved. They felt this way so strongly that on September 24, Ignatius and Salmeron could write to Spain that they considered the approval assured.

It seems that Contarini took his own wishes to be reality. In order to judge, one would have to have the precise time when the Pope declared himself in favor of the document of the "Five Chapters" and on which Ghinucci had written his own opinion. Unfortunately, we don't have it. What is sure is that Paul III, informed of the objections of Ghinucci, entrusted the arbitration between Contarini and Ghinucci to another Cardinal, Guidiccioni.[23]

Cardinal Guidiccioni was an eminent canonist who did not make a judgment until after he had accumulated all the information possible. "An upright pastor, zealous for his flock, a wise canonist, tenacious in his convictions, disposed to argue rather than concede": thus Tacchi Venturi describes him. Now, Guidiccioni had his own ideas about religious orders, it was necessary to reduce the existing orders to four: Domini-

---

says Tacchi Venturi) which the approval of the Society of Jesus encountered is a letter from Master Lattanzio Tolomei which was not published until the end of the nineteenth century (Franz DITTRICH, *Regesten und Briefe des Cardinals Gasporo Contarini.*, J.-A. WICHERT, Braunsberg, 1881). Cf. T. VENTURI., op. cit., 3, pp. 276 sq.

[23] Contrary to the affirmations of the historians of the sixteenth century no cardinal commission, in the strict sense of the word, was created to examine the "Five Chapters": only Contarini, Ghinucci and Guidiccioni intervened in this matter, the last-named serving as arbiter between the two others. Cf. T. VENTURI., op. cit., 3, p. 281.

cans, Franciscans, Cistercians, and Benedictines! He maintained this
thesis in public and defended it in several unpublished works: he
brought, in support of his opinion, decisions of the fourth Lateran
Council and of the Council of Lyon of 1274: a great portion of the
disorders in the Church came from the multiplication of religious orders,
from their privileges and their dissensions. What hope could the companions have of seeing their organization approved? What was going to
become of the frail "Summa" in the hands of such an arbiter? The
companions sensed the danger. They turned first to God and promised to
celebrate three thousand Masses in the event of success for their request.
They then strove to find, especially in the cities where they had served as
missionaries or where their companions were serving, allies, support
among persons and towns which, having seen the companions at work,
could witness to the purity of their lives and the efficacy of their labors:
we recognize here Ignatius' favorite method that he used in his difficulties
with the Inquisition and which he applied during his whole term as
Superior General.[24] Ercole II and his brother Cardinal Ippolito d'Este,
the magistrates of Parma, the archbishop of Siena, Francesco Bandini,
the Cardinal legate of Bologna, Bonifacio Ferreri, John III of Portugal,
who attempted to add to his own supplication, Charles V and the
King of France, and even Costanza Farnese, the daughter of the Pope,
married to Count Bosio de Santafiore[25] all used their influence on
Ignatius' behalf.

The Cardinal's citadel was rife with factionalism.[26] In the face of
testimony, requests and supplications from so many illustrious protec-
tors, Guidiccioni made "a strategic retreat". The matter, he said, did not
depend upon him but on Contarini and Ghinucci; as for himself, he had
made the report demanded of him; he had acknowledged therein that the
"Five Chapters" were correct and of a deep spirituality; he was not even
opposed to the new organization's being approved in a more solemn
form than the *viva voce* of Paul III, nor of the companions' inaugurating a
new and original order, provided that nothing be contrary to the sacred
canons; he even went so far as to recognize the good results already
achieved by the Society of Jesus. The decision was at a stalemate and it
was already February 1540.

However, within a month the situation resolved itself: an intervention
by Duke Ercole II and by his brother, Cardinal d'Este, "obtained",
according to the expression of Bobadilla in a letter to the Duke, "What

---

[24] In particular from the time of the Decree of the faculty of theology of Paris.

[25] Regarding this step which astounds us today, cf. T. VENTURI, op. cit., 2, p. 198.

[26] In this account, we are inspired by Tacchi Venturi, who was well situated to "sense"
this atmosphere. Op. cit., 3, pp. 286 sq.

many others had not succeeded in obtaining."[27] A letter from Ignatius, after the events of 1540, confirmed the testimony of Bobadilla: after having reminded the Duke of another successful intervention in favor of the Company in 1538, "and since", continued Ignatius,

> we found ourselves facing another opposition, no less severe in conse-quences, when after having confirmed (*viva voce*) our little Society, His Holiness found, in several Cardinals, members of his council, a certain hesitancy concerning us. Thanks to the intervention of Your Excellency and his mediator, the Most Reverend and Illustrious Cardinal of Ferrara, his brother, our cause was won, for which we give you thanks, acknowledging the perpetual gratitude which we owe you.[28]

Time passed, however, and no decision was made. Abruptly it arrived in the beginning of September 1540. In a letter to the Archbishop of Siena, Monsignor Bandini, Ignatius himself recounted that Cardinals Contarini, Carpi and Guidiccioni had given the Pope a definitive opin-ion, after which Paul III had ordered the final conclusion of this matter.[29]

Guidiccioni in this "skirmish of honor" had found a middle position which permitted him neither to contradict himself nor to renounce his principles. His was a position of really fine diplomacy: he recalled that, from the beginning, he had recognized the deeply spiritual quality of the "Five Chapters", that he had been the witness (always the best informed party) to the virtues and the labors of the companions, that he had observed the esteem in which the Pope held Ignatius and his group; for example, at the time of an audience granted by Paul III to the ambassador from Portugal, Pedro de Mascarenhas. Guidiccioni was therefore in agreement that the young Society of the number of professed members (and here it is necessary to take the common sense meaning of the word "professed", i.e., trained religious, those already dedicated to the re-ligious life) be limited to sixty. Hence, the outcome was postponed: according to the circumstances, this group could become an order, or be eliminated without an uproar. Was it necessary to accept the statement of Ribadeneyra[30] according to which the Cardinal would have attested to having experienced the momentary influence of the Holy Spirit so that all objection vanished in him? The first Jesuit historians have had a tendency

---

[27] *Bobad. Mon.*, p. 22.

[28] *Epist. ign.* 1, pp. 275 sq, undated, but one can place it in the first months of 1543.

[29] *Epist. ign.* 1, pp. 159 sq. Is the name of Capri a misprint? See the discussion in note 5 on page 290 in T. VENTURI, op. cit., 3. If I may add my opinion to that of so many eminent historians I would lean toward the accuracy of the text: Capri will be the first (and the only) "cardinal protector" of the young society.

[30] *Vita, Font. narr.* 4, pp. 308–309.

to interpret according to the influence of spirits what simple psychology or even, as here, diplomatic subtlety would suffice to explain. Whatever the case may be, the solution satisfied everyone. Guidiccioni withdrew, with his honor intact, from a thorny situation; Contarini saw his efforts finally come to fruition; friends of the young Society rejoiced at the success of their interventions.[31] Paul III could finally give a logical follow-up to his *viva voce* approval of September 3, 1539. The happiest, of all, obviously, were the companions.

Paul III then signed the bull *Regimini militantis* on September 27, 1540, at the Palace of St. Mark: the Society of Jesus was canonically established.

Between the "*Prima Summa Instituti*" and the bull, a few modifications were introduced. The prologue was abridged and certain formulas were rewritten in curial style. In the conclusion, two clauses were inserted, of which one, derogatory in nature, responded to the objection of Guidiccioni, taken from the second Council of Lyon and from the *Decretal*; the other, restrictive in emphasis, limited to sixty the number of professed religious.[32] In the final draft of the "Five Chapters", one finds again a trace of the criticisms of Ghinucci, to which are added a few minor changes, mostly of a stylistic order.

The bull *Regimini militantis* (or *Apostolic Letters*), one must emphasize, did not constitute a *Rule*, but a *formula*, as they said at the time. Today, we would say an outline, a sort of legal framework. Paul III, moreover, gave therein the authorization to the companions to "make the constitutions", and to establish laws. It is therefore inexact to call this document the "Rule of Saint Ignatius, approved and confirmed by Paul III".[33] We are certain that no distinct "rules" existed in the "Five Chapters" at that time. On the contrary, this bull *Regimini militantis*, or better still, the *Formula instituti* established, for the Society of Jesus, the point of reference essential for knowing the spirit and plan of the first Fathers and for

[31] The enemies of the Society claimed that the Society owed its approval to the intercession of certain noted ladies with Paul III, particularly Madame Margaret of Austria, illegitimate daughter of Charles V and wife of Ottavio Farnese, the nephew of the Pope. This rumor was formally denied by Ignatius, three months before his death: "To say that the Society was approved through the intervention of women, and especially of Madame, is false. We were then actually having business relations with Madame's house; but her support was not solicited for either the first confirmation or the second in 1543, when the same Pope, officially, again confirmed the Society, without limitation of numbers, because of the happy result that God was giving to his work, as much in our regions as in the Indies." Cf. letter of May 1556, addressed to Bartolomé de Torres in *Epist. ign.* 12, p. 277.

[32] This restrictive clause would be omitted in 1544.

[33] This unfortunate expression can be read even in the *Apostolic Letters* of Pius VII (March 7, 1801), to whom the Society of Jesus owed its resurgence.

living by it through the changes of mentality and vicissitudes of history. It is a text for unceasing meditation, for weighing one's conduct before God, for interiorizing. By this document we gain access to the experiences of Ignatius himself and of the first companions. We travel again with them the long journey which was dolorous and rugged, reasonable and mystical, by which they traveled together . . . already we catch a glimpse of the fundamental question which we shall try to treat in our fifth part. Did Ignatius, the Superior General of the Society, succeed in transposing the spiritual experience of Manresa, Paris, Venice and Rome into language and into universal structures? The whole future of the Society hangs on the response that one gives to that question.

When Paul III thus approved the organization of the Society of Jesus, only Ignatius, Salmeron and Codure were present in Rome. Xavier and Rodríguez were awaiting their departure for the Indies. Favre was already, without doubt, en route to Worms where he was to serve as theologian to Dr. Pedro Ortiz. Laynez, Jay, Bobadilla and Bröet were missionaries at Placenza, Brescia, Bisignano and Siena.

IV. IGNATIUS AS SUPERIOR GENERAL

The first matter of urgency was to elect one of the ten companions as Superior General so that he might "construct" the constitutions, with a council and with the agreement of the nine other companions. Ignatius, therefore, recalled to Rome the four companions scattered throughout Italy. As for Xavier and Rodríguez, they had wisely left their votes (folded and under seal) before leaving Rome, and Favre had sent his from Germany on December 27, 1540. At the beginning of Lent, which in 1541 began on March 4, Laynez, Jay and Bröet rejoined the three Romans. Only Bobadilla was missing, because the Pope had not given him authorization to leave Bisignano, where he was working with great success. It was feared that the Pope would again rapidly disperse the group of seven.[34] So it was decided to proceed as soon as possible to the election of the Superior General.

"The Forty-nine Points of Rule"

First, however, a task had to be undertaken. On March 4, 1540, the dispersion having begun, and long-awaited approval having been granted, the six companions still present in Rome[35] had drafted and

---

[34] The mission of nunciature in Ireland had already been decided since March 5, 1540; but it would not be realized until September, 1541.

[35] Ignatius, Rodríguez, Jay, Codure, Salmeron and Xavier. (*Const.* 1, p. 24.)

personally signed an act, to which the absentees subsequently adhered: they had decided that in whatever related to the constitutions, they would agree with the judgment of the Fathers sojourning in Italy. Exactly one year later all those who lived in Italy, except one whom the Pope kept on a mission, were reunited in Rome. It was important, therefore, that before proceeding to the election, these few men, in full equality of power and votes, would outline a schema for the governing rules according to which the future Superior General would govern. On March 4, 1541, Ignatius, Codure, Jay, Salmeron, Laynez and Broët met in council: they decided that the last-named four would undertake the ministries, while Ignatius and Codure would prepare a certain number of constitutions in the spirit of the "Five Chapters" and of the bull *Regimini*; they would subsequently argue about it, vote on this new document, and then submit it to the authority of the Pope.

The work of Ignatius and Codure[36] began on March 10. Of these "forty-nine points of rule", as they called it, half were devoted to questions of poverty; the others dealt with the habit, the teaching of Christian doctrine to children, and the founding of houses and schools within the order. The document reflected a certain haste and some overlapping of questions. Thus it was that the fourteenth point, so brief for such an important question, "the Superior, one among all of them chosen for life", appears abruptly after the article concerning visits to important personages. We do not know when or where the companions signed: it was very probably at the end of March or the beginning of April,[37] because the ceremony of the solemn vows at St. Paul Outside the Walls would take place on the twenty-second of April. Between the signing of the document and the ceremony at St. Paul's the election of Ignatius as Superior General would take place.

A Dramatic Election

This election was long and dramatic, following a pattern which would be maintained for all the generals succeeding Ignatius; it was conducted in this way:[38]

The companions first gave themselves three days of solitude, reflection

---

[36] To tell the truth, Ignatius was the principal architect: one recognizes in it his manner of reflecting and his experiences.

[37] It is necessary to rectify the very hazy affirmation of Polanco at the beginning of his chronicles for the year 1541 (*Chron.* I, p. 92): "As the principal constitutions had been prepared by Ignatius, he called the companions, scattered in Italy, to sign them and to elect a General."

[38] Ignatius himself informs us about it down to the last detail in "*Forma de la Compañia y oblación*" (*Font. narr.* I, pp. 16–22. Cf. T. VENTURI., op. cit., 4, p. 7, n. 1).

and prayer. Then they met and each presented his vote written in his own hand. To these ballots were added the votes of the absentees: Xavier, Rodríguez and Favre. They locked up all of these ballots in a strong box where they remained for three more days. On April 8, Passion Wednesday, they opened the ballots: eight of the ten electors had chosen Ignatius. Bobadilla, detained at Naples, had not sent his ballot, or or if he had sent it, the letter had not arrived.[40] The tenth was Ignatius'. So as not to give preference to any one of his companions, he had voted for the one who would receive the most votes, whoever it might be, with the exclusion, however, of himself.

Since the electors were not constrained to vote according to a uniform formula (they had so decided) several expressed reasons for their choice. Salmeron, the youngest of the group, chose Ignatius "because", he said, "it was he who gave all of us birth in Christ, nourished us with milk during our spiritual infancy, and guided us, sustaining our strength through obedience, in the lush and fertile pastures of Paradise and at the fountain of life."[41] Codure claimed to having in view only the greatest service to God and the greatest good of the Society: he gave his vote to Ignatius, because, he said, "I have always observed in him a very ardent zeal for the honor of God and the salvation of souls: he was made to command others because he has always made himself the least important of all and always made himself our servant." He even stipulated that he would vote thus even at the hour of his death.[42]

The vote of Xavier (Rome, March 15, 1540) is of a moving sincerity:

The one who must be chosen for superior of our Society, to whom we all owe obedience, this Superior must be, it seems to me—I say it according to my conscience—our old and true friend, Father Don Ignatius. It was he who assembled us, not without great difficulty; and he would know better still, not certainly without new difficulty, how to keep us together, to govern us, to help us progress from good to better, for it is he who knows each of us most intimately.[43]

---

[39] We preserve several (not all) of the printed formulas of these votes. Cf. the indications given by *Font. narr.* I, p. 17, n. 5.

[40] He rightly says in his *Autobiography* that he had given his voice to Master Ignatius (*Bobad. Mon.*, p. 619, n. 18). But since he was not very explicit (that's the least one might say) about these difficulties with Ignatius and the group of companions, and that the *Autobiography* dates from 1589, there is every reason for regarding this statement with a certain amount of reserve.

[41] *Epist. Salm.* I, p. 1.

[42] *Epist. Broëti*, pp. 418 sq.

[43] SCHURHAMMER, *Franz Xaver*, I, p. 533.

Ignatius refused his election.

Four of the electors, Codure, Xavier, Rodríguez and Favre had thought it advisable to designate another companion in case Ignatius should die. Codure, Xavier and Rodríguez chose Favre. Favre chose Xavier. Prudence, in this case, showed itself to be imprudence, for Ignatius saw therein an important indication: in his absence, Favre would have been elected. Moreover, the honest Codure specified that Favre was endowed with just as great virtues as Ignatius. In the presence of all, Ignatius affirmed that he felt more inclination to be governed than to govern: incapable of governing himself, he was even more unable to govern others. He declared his former sins, his bad conduct past and present, his faults and his miserableness. He declared and affirmed that they should not permit him to assume the heavy burden that they were imposing upon him unless it was still more evident that such was the will of God.[44] He therefore begged his companions in the Lord to agree to another three or four days of surcease during which they would implore God for new light in order to choose with more certitude the one who would be the best Superior General.

Moved by this refusal, the companions set a new election for April 13, Wednesday of Holy Week. One need not be a prophet to guess what the result would be: Ignatius was again elected. Again, he refused. Then, Diego Laynez rose and declared in a serious tone that if the elected person persisted in evading the responsibility which, from all the evidence, the Lord imposed upon him, then Laynez too would withdraw from the Society of Jesus, for he did not feel disposed to obey a superior who was not selected by God.[45] Laynez's tactic succeeded. Ignatius, fearing to disobey the divine will by persisting in opposing the vote of his companions, answered that to avoid the worst and for his own greater peace of mind, he would submit the decision to his confessor, Fra Theodosio da Lodi, a Franciscan of San Pietro-in-Montorio. Against their wish, but with unanimity, the companions accepted this new delay.

On Wednesday evening, the thirteenth of April, Ignatius presented himself at the convent of San Pietro-in-Montorio. There he spent the three last days of Holy Week in prayer. He made a general confession of his entire life to Fra Theodosio. On Easter Sunday, April 17, he asked his confessor whether or not he was to accept the election as Superior General. Fra Theodosio told him explicitly that to struggle further would be to resist the Holy Spirit. Ignatius still did not capitulate: he begged Fra Theodosio to examine further this matter before God. He himself would

[44] Cf. for all this account, "*Forma de la compañia y oblación*", *Font. narr.* i, pp. 18 sq.

[45] Cf. ORLANDINI, *Historia Societatis Jesu pas prima, seu Ignatius*, p. 74, n. 8.

return to the house of the Astalli, near the church of La Strada where, since January 1541, the group had been quartered, and he would await a definitive response there.

Previously, he had written out his own vote, sealed it and set it to the companions.

Two days later, on Easter Tuesday, April 19, the response from Fra Theodosio reached Ignatius. It confirmed to him what Fra Theodosio had already told him orally. Ignatius accepted the vote of the companions. He was henceforth the Superior General of the Society.

These hesitations of Ignatius caused much comment, especially among the historians less favorable to Ignatius. Some saw it as a worldly deviousness, a Machiavellian stratagem in the grand style: could Ignatius for a single instant think that this companions would change their vote? He had made them force his hand so as to be even more absolute in his governing. This opinion overlooks his whole past, the serenity of Ignatius confronted with the defections of the companions of Alcalá, of Salamanca and of the beginnings in Paris, his long absence in Azpeitia and Venice by which he wished, so to speak, to prove to the companions that he was not indispensable to the group. It also overlooks his acute feeling about the sins of his youth, of his unworthiness before God; "Inigo poor in goodness" he signed his letters. It also overlooks his wish for an active apostolate. It entirely overlooks his state of health.

The Solemn Professions of the Ten Companions

Once Ignatius had accepted the generalship, things began to happen; on Wednesday, April 22, 1541, the six companions present in Rome made a pilgrimage to the seven basilicas. At St. Paul Outside the Walls, they confessed to each other; then Ignatius celebrated Mass in the Chapel of the Virgin,[46] his companions surrounding him. At the moment of Communion, Ignatius turned around holding in his hand the paten on which reposed the body of the Lord and in the other a piece of paper on which he had written his profession in Latin:

> I, Ignatius of Loyola, promise to God Almighty and to the sovereign Pontiff, his Vicar on earth, in the presence of the Virgin Mother and of all the celestial Court, in the presence of the Society, perpetual poverty, chastity and obedience, according to the way of life contained in the Bull of the Society of our Lord Jesus and in its Constitutions, already declared or to be declared. I promise, moreover, a special obedience to the sovereign

---

[46] This chapel is located on the right: a mosaic, dating from the period of Honorius III, represented Our Lady carrying the Infant Jesus in her arms.

Pontiff in matters relating to missions as is incribed in the Bull. I further promise to work so that children may be instructed in the fundamentals of faith, in conformity with the said Bull and the Constitutions.[47]

Having thus made his profession, Ignatius received Communion himself, then he put on the paten five consecrated hosts and taking one of them between his fingers, he turned again to his companions who also were very moved. Each of them, Codure the first, made an irrevocable promise to God, to the sovereign Pontiff, and to Ignatius, then received the Eucharist.[48]

The Holy Sacrifice completed, each went to meditate before one or another altar in the basilica. Then they met once again around the Altar of Confession; and there, near the tomb of the apostle Paul, they made a vow of filial homage to Ignatius, their first Superior and Father, received from him the kiss of peace and embraced each other.

Before leaving St. Paul's, they established the verbal formula of the ceremony and the events which had preceded it.[49] In a joyful mood, they left St. Paul Outside the Walls and continued their pilgrimage to the seven basilicas. On the way, Codure sang. . . . Four months later, on August 29, he entered into the joy of his Lord.

Letters soon went out to the four absent companions to inform them of the election of Ignatius and of his profession. Favre was then at Ratisbon: on the Octave day of the Visitation (July 9), he went to the church of Our Lady, said his prayers there, and celebrated the Holy Sacrifice. Before taking Communion, he made his profession according to the formula of St. Paul Outside the Walls which they had sent him from Rome; and on the following day he sent his profession in his own handwriting to Ignatius. The second of the four absentees to make his profession was Bobadilla, but not without a new incident arising. In September or October, he passed through Rome because Paul III had recalled him from Calabria and sent him to Germany; was not this the opportunity to pronounce his vows like his companions? He refused to do so. A commission, composed of Doctors Michael de Torres and Inigo Lopez, and the licensed Cristobal de Madrid, studied his objections and his situation; they concluded that it was necessary that he make his profession. Bobadilla accepted the decision and made, in his turn, his profession at St. Paul's into the hands of Ignatius.[50] As for Francis

[47] *Epist. ign.* 1, pp. 67 sq.

[48] "Forma . . . , etc.," *Font. narr.* 1, p. 21.

[49] Cf. *Font. narr.* 1, pp. 16–22 *AA. SS.* VII, n. 367 and *Epist. ign.* 2, pp. 8 sq. Cf. also SCHURHAMMER, "Anfänge des römischen Archivs der Gesellschaft Jesu", in AHSI, vol. 12 (1943), pp. 99 sq.

[50] Cf. *Bobad. Mon.*, p. 620, n. 21; *Chron.* 1, p. 97, n. 36 and *Font. narr.* 1, p. 651, note 5.

Xavier, on leaving for the Indies on March 15, 1540, he had bound himself to God by simple vows, and it was not until December 1543 in Goa that he made his solemn profession in accordance with the formula of St. Paul Outside the Walls which had been sent to him from Rome.[51] The last of the first Fathers to make his profession was Simón Rodríguez, at Évora on December 25, 1544; his formula was original and did not resemble that of St. Paul Outside the Walls except in essentials; a rather brief letter, actually a rather chatty one, accompanied the sending of the document to Rome on December 26. It announced that he had made this profession at the first Mass of midnight just before saying, "Domine non sum dignus"; he had satisfied his conscience, he said, but this gesture did not make any great change in his life. It seems that he had made this profession in silence and secrecy.[52]

As Superior General, Ignatius lived with his companions in his fourth lodging,[53] i.e., in the house which Camillo Astalli had rented to them for a nominal price near the church of Santa Maria della Strada which, contrary to persistent legend, was modest, run-down and of small dimensions; it was there, however, that Ignatius and the companions celebrated Mass, preached and heard confessions.

Through a succession of happy circumstances, this chapel and even some neighboring houses were given to them: this spot became the seat of the Society of Jesus in Rome. Today, there stands on this spot the Gesù, a school with a residence. One can worship there in the "little room" where Ignatius lived, trained the first recruits over a period of fifteen years, wrote the *Constitutions*, and died on July 31, 1556.[54] This providential location is due to the first Italian who officially entered the Society of Jesus, Pietro Codacio.

Santa Maria della Strada, Our Lady of the Way . . . the name of the

---

It is regrettable that Bobadilla in his autobiography did not make the least allusion to these difficulties. Cf. Câmara, *Mémorial*, p. 164, n. 210.

[51] SCHURHAMMER, *Franz Xaver*, 2, pp. 379 and 380.

[52] Cf. *Epist. Broëti*, pp. 535 and 536. In his letter of December 26, Rodríguez declares: "Master Favre is at this moment in Coimbran." This is inaccurate but he could have been mistaken: illness had kept Favre in Flanders; he would not arrive in Portugal until the very end of December, if not even in the beginning of January: cf. *Fabri. Mon.*, pp. 298–99.

[53] Let us recall which were the first three residences of the companions in Rome: a poor house (lent through charity) in the vineyard of Quirino Garzoni on the slopes of the Trintà dei Monti; a second (rented) of which we do not know the exact location; the third in the "haunted" house of Frangipani, near the Tower of Melangolo. Cf. T. VENTURI., *Le Case*, op. cit.

[54] See in this "little history" the excellent pages of T. VENTURI., *Storia*, op. cit., 4, pp. 19 to 26.

church must not have been displeasing to Ignatius, the pilgrim. In fact, he would scarcely ever leave this place during the fifteen years of his generalship, but from the heart of his little room, he would follow the flight of his sons on the roads of the world, he would inspire them in their missionary zeal, sustain them in their battles. There, success and failure, sorrows and joys, good news and bad would blend; hundreds of companions would pass through there to be trained or to work. "La Strada" was for many years the heart of the Society of Jesus. Let us install ourselves in this lodging with Ignatius; let us follow with him the progress and reversals of his sons on the map of the world; let's observe him, among so many cares, undertaking disputes, drafting little by little the *Constitutions* of the Society of Jesus. Let us try, through these facts, to grasp something of his mysterious personality, mysterious with the mystery of God.

PART TWO

THE GRADUAL DEVELOPMENT INTO
A MISSIONARY SOCIETY

"ANYWHERE IN THE WORLD WHERE THE VICAR OF CHRIST MAY SEND US"

This motto, by itself, would serve to discourage those who make Ignatius out to be a planner, a strategist, who chose his means of action. We shall see that the facts are even more eloquent. Looking over Ignatius' shoulder, let us be carried along with him as if by an unexpected and overwhelming wave. Ignatius, the Superior General, dispatched his companions on the roads indicated to him by the Pope or by circumstances, these infallible interpreters of the will of God; but he weighed all these missions in a very intimate contact with God, and, having weighed them, he, for whom the will of God was an absolute command, pursued their realization with energy, tenacity and perseverance.

Our plan in this chapter is not to reconstitute a history of these fifteen years of the generalship of Ignatius. That would be a monumental work for which the cornerstones are still lacking.[1] The fundamental work is without doubt the *Chronicon* of Polanco. Polanco, who was very intelligent and possessed a clear, methodical mind, was the first to organize and utilize the original documents. A friend of Ignatius and the first Fathers, he was able to retrace the events with the Ignatian perspective; he was informed about and on everything. Perhaps he made a few errors on dates, or involuntarily displaced certain details; he had likes and dislikes, but his information was generally correct. Moreover, he was sincere; he hid nothing, although he spoke, when it was fitting, with certain vagueness. We have followed him in our work *Chroniques saint Ignace de Loyola*. Here, we will not go into this story in detail. What interests us here is the mentality of Ignatius, the Superior General, his psychology, his tendencies, his directives, his personal style: in other words, the man himself. Our perspective is, therefore, different from that of Polanco. Nevertheless, Polanco will be very helpful to us: throughout his work, objective as he strives to be, he was unable to avoid explaining things in a particular way, and as a perfect secretary and collaborator he saw them as Ignatius saw them. Even in his style, he reflected the mentality of Ignatius himself and those of the companions who were closest to the Ignatian spirit. Year by year, we are going to see

---

[1] Cf. our bibliography of the monographs of the Assistancies. It also lacks important biographies. However, the number of interesting studies is already considerable.

the formation, the growth and the development of the Society of Jesus up to 1556. We have said what happened in 1540. Let us therefore begin with 1541.[2]

1541

In Rome, Ignatius, Codure and Salmeron—and the three companions, who had returned there for a short time to approve the "forty-nine points of rule" and to elect the superior—gave themselves to what one would soon call the "*ministeria assueta*" (or *consueta*): spiritual exercises (in a variety of forms), sermons, "informal conservations", confessions, teaching of Christian doctrine, assistance to the ill and dying, aid to the poor, visiting prisoners or those condemned to death, conversion of public sinners, reconciliations. . . . The house of La Strada, where a dozen novices, some of whom were priests, were being trained under the supervision of Ignatius, was the very active center of these ministries.

Bobadilla continued as a missionary, on the personal order of the Pope: recalled from Bisignano, he was sent by Paul III to Viterbo, but he was destined to accompany Cardinal Morone to Germany.

Favre was in Worms in January, then at Ratisbon, where alone he made his profession on July 9. But since the Pope had given him the mission to accompany Dr. Ortiz and the doctor, as foreseen, had gone to Spain, Favre followed him. This was the first and very fortuitous contact of the Society with Spain. He would remain in Spain until March 1542. Actually in 1541, another companion, a novice who was not yet a priest, also made the young Society of Jesus known there, at least in certain areas. He was Antonio de Araoz, a nephew of Ignatius who returned for a short time to his native country to take care of family affairs. A man on whom Ignatius depended, he would make his solemn profession as early as February 19, 1542, six years before Borgia, scarcely two years after his entrance into the order.

When Favre left Germany, Jay, by order of the Pope, replaced him.

In Portugal, an important question arose. Rodríguez and Xavier, awaiting their departure for India, were doing missionary work in Lisbon and its environs. Their apostolic success was such that John III thought of keeping the two missionaries for Portugal and establishing colleges for recruits to the Society. Ignatius submitted the matter to the Pope for decision. The Pope left the decision to the King. Ignatius proposed that one of the companions depart for India and that the other

---

[2] We have omitted, without exception, references for this chapter: Our sources are the *Chronicon* of Polanco and the correspondences.

remain in Lisbon.[3] The King accepted this decision and so Xavier departed with three recruits; Rodríguez remained behind. What might have been merely an incident without consequence resulted in the establishment of a most fecund and active province—also, alas, the most turbulent in the Ignatian Society. John III would remain a very good friend of the Society, both in Portugal and in India. In Lisbon the first "house"[4] of the order was set up, and in October, the group of Portuguese already recruited there was augmented by several more "students" whom Ignatius had sent from Paris or Rome.

Paris, on the other hand, was the site favored by Ignatius. In the spring of 1540, he sent a first group there under the leadership of Diego de Eguía, then in the fall, another group under the leadership of Jerónimo Doménech: they were all students. One can guess Ignatius' plan: to establish a college near the University of Paris, where he and the first companions had been educated, had met each other, had bound themselves into a *societas* of free companionship; where they had made their first vows. Paris, the first site selected by Ignatius . . . at his death the Society would still not be recognized there; it would be opposed by the famous Decree of the faculty of theology which would do the Society so much harm in France and beyond her borders as well.

Another typical mission presented itself also: on July 3, Paul III named as nuncios to Ireland Paschase Broët and Salmeron. It was as if they were being sent to their deaths. They departed at the beginning of September. Before their departure, Ignatius gave them an instruction in two parts which inaugurated the long list of *instructions*, the study of which would be so important for the understanding of the Ignatian mentality.[5]

However, among the scattered companions, a very fraternal correspondence was exchanged. Anything that one was doing was not unknown to the others. Not only did the companions write to Rome, they also wrote to each other; in every way possible Rome shared the news received there. These are the letters offering an "overview of the world", invaluable for the historian, provided that he knows how to read between the lines, for they were destined as much to encourage and to inspire with enthusiasm as to inform. Let us point out right away, in

---

[3] Here a problem difficult to resolve presents itself. In this year of 1540, Ignatius seems indeed to act as Superior, the choices seem to come from him alone. There was undoubtedly preliminary consultation, and Ignatius spoke in the name of all. However, the matter is not clear.

[4] The vocabulary of the various dwellings of the order is far from being fixed. At the stage where we are, it seems sufficient to distinguish the *domus* (houses) and the *collegia* (colleges). See the words in the index of our *Chroniques saint Ignace de Loyola*.

[5] *Epist. ign.* I, pp. 174–81.

order not to come back to it, to utilize this correspondence correctly, it would be necessary for us to know not only the exact date the letters were sent but the date of their arrival. These dates are very variable depending upon the opportunities to send letters, the distances, the circumstances (war and peace), and the postal system of those times. Certain dramas would not have occurred, if the letters had arrived on time, or simply if they had arrived. We have seen an example of this in the "vote" of Bobadilla. There will be many other examples.

1542

ROME: The companions developed the *ministeria assueta*; Ignatius, with his companions, collaborated actively in these pious ministries. Notably, he obtained the letter *Cupientes* from Paul III in favor of Jewish converts, the brief *Dudum per nos* in which the Pope, after having forbidden begging in Rome, organized a service for the poor. But already, toward May 18, a crisis of health obliged him to assign the signature of certain letters to collaborators. That would happen again. On December 15, by his apostolic letter *Alias postquam*, the parish churches of Sant' Andrea della Fratte, of St. Nicolas and of Sts. Vincent and Athanasius were united with the church of Our Lady of La Strada.

ITALY: There was the opening of the first Italian college of the Society of Jesus at Padua. This gesture of Ignatius was an act of gratitude to Andrea Lippomani, the prior of the Trinity: Lippomani was a man of extreme charity, sometimes excessive. Had he welcomed, as they say, Ignatius and his companions when they traveled in 1537 from Paris to Venice to embark for the Holy Land? Whatever the case, in 1542, it was at his home that Laynez stayed, and Lippomani offered to shelter students who came to take courses at the celebrated University of Padua; he even promised to equip them with a good library. André Frusius and Juan de Polanco were among these first students at Padua.

By order of the Pope, Laynez was serving as a missionary at Venice where heresies thrived. There too Lippomani wanted to establish a college.

PORTUGAL: Thanks to the generosity of John III, the college of Coimbra was created and another college planned at Evora. Ignatius continued to support the Rodríguez group. However, between the two men a certain tension was already perceptible, made even more delicate because at the moment Paul III and John III were at odds and Ignatius was trying to reconcile them. In June, Ignatius promised Prince

Henry of Portugal, Cardinal and Grand Inquisitor, to aid "the Holy Inquisition". Ethiopia renewed relations with Portugal: this soon gave birth to the plan for the Ethiopian missions.

INDIA: Xavier arrived at Goa on May 6; he worked as a missionary with his three companions; and already the problem of colleges for the non-Jesuit student arose: companions were asked to collaborate at the college of Sainte-Foy in Goa where a native elite was being trained; Xavier was inclined to accept.

SPAIN: Ignatius called Araoz to his solemn profession; the ceremony took place on February 19 in Rome. Araoz was sent by Ignatius to Barcelona where he served as a missionary with Diego de Eguía who had returned from Paris; then Araoz came back to Rome at the end of the year. Favre also left Spain in March or April and reached Speyer: he felt himself "drawn by the Spirit to work in Germany rather than in Spain". In November-December, he was in Mainz; the Prince-elect and the Cardinal of Trent chose him for the next council.

GERMANY AND EASTERN EUROPE: Favre spend the second half of the year there. Bobadilla was doing missionary work at Innsbruck, then Vienna. There was a question of his being given the post of chaplain to the armies. Jay was working at Ratisbon.

PARIS: A group of sixteen students took courses at the University. They lived under the supervision of Jerónimo Doménech.

LOUVAIN: Since Francis I had renewed his war with Charles V, an edict of July expelled from the kingdom within eight days all the subjects of the emperor. Doménech then left Paris for Flanders and finally installed himself at Louvain: it was the very propitious beginning of the college of Louvain.

THE MISSION OF IRELAND: From February through April it was a total failure because of the anti-papist persecution. Soon, Broët and Salmeron had to pass through France, again, waiting in Paris for orders from Rome. The Pope, informed of the situation, recalled them to Italy.

The epistolary exchanges continued, and in the same fraternal manner. A letter (December 10) which Ignatius addressed to Favre, encouraging him to write, shows us how much these letters meant to him. Three points should be noted: problems of obedience began to arise; the companions truly had an apostolic technique: the *ministeria assueta*; they traveled on foot, as pilgrims; they served as missionaries "by order of the Pope". In this correspondence, one perceives also the direction in which the apostolic orientations of Ignatius and his companions were going: for them, the most urgent problem of Christianity was heresy but also of concern was the reform of the clergy, the conversion of Jews, the Islamic peril (from which not even Barcelona was safe), and the "Holy Inquisition". These concerns remained with them in the ensuing years.

1543

ROME: La Strada[6] became a more and more important apostolic center in Rome. The *ministeria instituto nostro germana* was defined: the house was strongly oriented toward the conversion of Jews (they sheltered them, fed them and instructed them), toward charity for the new converts, toward the salvation and welfare of fallen women and toward hospitals. Ignatius obtained three important documents from Paul III: a bull of March 16 which established the society of St. Martha (for converted women sinners); an authorized bull of March 19 which founded a college for catechumens converted from Judaism; the renewal on May 30 of the decree of Innocent III, *Cum infirmitas corporalis*, which forbade physicians to care for the sick before they had received the sacraments of the Church. While he was working on the Constitutions, he brought together the Fathers who were in Rome to consult them, questioned the Fathers who were passing through Rome concerning their projects, and reminded all of them (even if it was Laynez) of their obligation to teach catechism to children.

On the land belonging to the abandoned church of Sant' Andrea della Fratte and given by Paul III to the Society, Codacio started to build a new house for the companions.

ITALY: The group of students by now installed in Padua was in very great poverty. Laynez was doing missionary work in Padua and Venice; Broët and Salmeron were doing the same at Foligno, Montepulciano and Modena. The difficulties raised by the invading heresies were such that Paul III instituted "for the salvation of Italy" the tribunal of the Inquisition: Ignatius was among the people who signed the official request.

---

[6] We shall use this abridged form to designate the enclave (church and house) where the Roman companions lived. When the meaning demands it, we shall specify whether it is a matter of the church or the house.

PORTUGAL: As early as January, Rodríguez announced to Ignatius that thanks to John III the Society could perhaps enter Castile, for there were plans of marriage between the children of the King and those of Charles V, specifically, between his daughter María and "Philip, Prince of Spain". Thus, even in Spain it was a political factor which facilitated the acceptance of the Society. However, for this mission, the King wanted one of the "first Fathers", particularly Favre. In Rome unfavorable rumors were circulating about John III and Simón Rodríguez. Rodríguez asked Ignatius not to believe any of them. Coimbra prospered: novices presented themselves and were trained according to three specifications; pilgrimage, menial domestic services (for humility) and *meditationes spirituales consuetae*. The King planned to construct a college for one hundred students.

INDIA: Xavier worked indefatigably throughout the whole country. The companions participated more and more in the life of the college of St. Foy in Goa. There was one symbolic initiative of Ignatius: he wished that the companions might work also in the Indies which were under the crown of Spain: this desire was not achieved in his lifetime.

SPAIN: Araoz and five companions were sent into Spain again at the end of the year.

GERMANY AND EASTERN EUROPE: Favre, who had been delivered from any invitation to the Council, received in September/October an order to depart for Portugal. Bad sea conditions and illness detained him in Antwerp; he returned to Louvain and asked Ignatius whether he was to remain in Germany or to depart for Lisbon. In the course of the year, the relations of the companions with Gerhard Kalckbrenner, the prior of the Carthusian monastery of Cologne, became very friendly: the prior wanted the installation of the Society in Cologne; for the companions he would be a friend through thick and thin. He would send abundant alms to Ignatius and in every way aid the gradual establishment of the college of Cologne.

As for Jay, he was expelled from Ratisbon in February-March. He served as a missionary in Ingolstadt and in Nuremberg where Bobadilla was also working.

LOUVAIN: A little group continued to live there and kept recruiting. Since the danger of war had been avoided, the exiled companions could have returned to Paris. Ignatius conducted a poll[7] for which we do not know the motive: he asked them whether they were ready to stay in

---

[7] See this word in the index of the *Chroniques saint Ignace de Loyola*. Several times

Paris, even if it meant begging or to go to Portugal or to Rome under obedience? All the answers were positive.

The year 1543 also belongs to what one could call the "Era of the first Fathers": their apostolic activity corresponded to what it would have been if, after the oblation of 1537, the Society had not been established as a religious order: there were great availability and mobility. All the mission assignments were given by the Pope. At this time, the new recruits were little by little coming to the forefront, and the "houses" would multiply: these developments would raise some unexpected questions concerning obedience. For the time being, however, the correspondence still exuded an atmosphere of freedom of personal action, of spiritual detachment and of missionary inspiration. The misunderstandings between Ignatius and Rodríguez, and Ignatius and Bobadilla, were still dormant. One sees certain signs that Ignatius was not without anxiety concerning the perfect obedience of certain companions.

1544

ROME: Ignatius worked actively on the *Constitutions*: several important points were decided. The *Spiritual Diary*[8] is the very precious testimony to Ignatius' reflection. In this document true "personal deliberation" blends with the questioning of God in prayer and penance: This testimony is also important because we discover Ignatius taking therein a strong position on poverty—a solution which goes against the position unanimously accepted by the companions some time previously (the revenues from the "sacristies" of our churches). Undoubtedly to be more at ease in his legislative work, he recalled Jerónimo Doménech to Rome in January and made him Secretary General of Correspondence: Doménech filled this office from 1544 to 1545.

However, the apostolic influence of La Strada developed. It was in 1544 that Ignatius opened the "House of Saint Martha" (for "errant women", who could not be admitted among the *mulieres conversae*. On March 15, once again upon the request of Ignatius, Paul II promulgated the letter *Ad monasteria* in favor of the confraternity of catechumens.

In September the new construction of La Strada was sufficiently advanced for Ignatius and his companions to live there.

Ignatius utilized this procedure to become acquainted with the spiritual dispositions of the companions, especially so far as the qualities of obedience and missionary desire were concerned.

[8] The fragment which we possess begins on February 2, 1544, and ends on February 27, 1545. See the French translation in the "Christus" collection.

ITALY: Laynez continued as a missionary in Padua, Brescia and Venice. Salmeron returned to Rome, but Broët, after having continued his work for some time at Montepulciano, was sent in May to "reform" a monastery of Poor Clares at Reggio (near Modena); in September he then went to Faenza.

PORTUGAL: The nuncio Poggio ordered Favre to remain in Germany; Favre returned to Cologne while his twelve companions departed with the Archbishop of Compostella. However, at the end of the year (at the latest, in November), Ignatius sent him again the order to leave for Portugal. He worked there, particularly at Évora. What exactly was his "mission"? It seems that it was internal within the Society, a fact-finding mission intended to enlighten Ignatius on the exact situation of the Society in Portugal; whatever the case may be, Favre addressed to the companions in Coimbra (among whom were numerous recruits) an important letter on the conditions of perfect obedience and on the "spirit" to be maintained in religious life: was Ignatius already worried?

SPAIN: It was the insistence of Duke Francis Borgia that Ignatius decided to found the first college in Spain: this would be Valencia. In July, Diego Miron, rector of Coimbra, left his post in Portugal and came to found the college which Gerónimo Doménech's father was supporting financially.

Moreover, Araoz and a few companions left from Rome for Portugal at the beginning of the year; en route they served as missionaries in Barcelona, Valencia and Gandia. At the end of the year, Araoz went to Castile in accordance with John III's plan.

LOUVAIN: The group reaped conversions and vocations especially thanks to Favre.

GERMANY AND EASTERN EUROPE: Favre worked very effectively as a missionary in Cologne. He had a clear understanding of the religious danger with which Germany was struggling and he alerted Ignatius; he wanted the Society to establish itself in a "stable manner" in Germany. Six companions, among whom was Peter Canisius (he entered the Society in 1543), lived with Favre in Cologne; they were sustained by the charity of the Carthusians and of two benefactresses. Favre sought a house in which to install the college. When he left Cologne for Portugal, he left Canisius at the head of the little community. Shortly afterward, a persecution was triggered by the Senate of Cologne: the companions were obliged to disperse.

Jay began the year at Ingolstadt where he was offered a chair and the title of doctor, but he soon received the order to accompany the Bishop

of Augsburg to the Provincial Council of Salzburg, merely as a counselor
(his "mission" not including "that he discuss matters of faith in public").
The Council ended, he served as a missionary at Dillingen. He advised
several bishops of the region to found colleges in order to resist heresy.
The bishop of Augsburg wanted him to be present at the Diet of Worms.

Bobadilla began the year at Passau. The Bishop of Passau wanted to
send him to Speyer. At first Bobadilla refused: "It is not in the mission
which I received from the Pope." Then on the order of Cardinal Farnese,
Bobadilla went there. In June he returned to Passau, then to Vienna. In
December he left for Prague and finally arrived at Worms where the
nuncio had summoned him.

PARIS: With new rumors of war, the foreigners once again went into
exile: but the majority of them soon succeeded in regrouping in Paris.

INDIA: Two companions left this year from Lisbon, but a storm brought
the fleet back to port. From January to December, Xavier covered a
tremendous amount of ground in India. Thanks to his correspondence,
we can follow his labors, his hopes, his discouragements, his suffering
and also his marvelous rapport with his companions in Europe. What
warmth and friendship among the "first Fathers", what a sense of Corpus
Societatis! Paradoxically, yet quite understandably, it was the solitary
one, lost at the other end of world, who remained the most faithful to the
spirit of companionship and who lived it with the greatest fervor.

In the correspondence—much too scarce—which we have saved from
the year 1544, certain characteristics become more and more clearly
apparent: the universal character of the apostolic activity (they worked as
much among the primarii as the plabeii, among "free men" as much as
among prisoners or slaves, among noble ladies as much as among "errant
women"); the primacy of spiritual means in the search for efficacy:
prayers, penances, sacraments, spiritual exercises, informal conversations; clarity in the analysis of the sociological conditioning of faith; the
concern of remaining in close communion with the Pope (the idea of
"mission" was preeminent) as well as with the Superior General. They
took special care to choose novices and to train them well: certain
unfortunate experiences demanded it.

1545

ROME: Ignatius worked actively on the Constitutions. The Spiritual Diary
continued until February 27. From several indications, one perceives that
Ignatius wanted to meet with the primi Patres, except Xavier, of course.
What was his intention? What were his motives? He did not reveal them.
Laynez and Salmeron were often in Rome. Broët was not far away and

could rejoin him easily; Bobadilla too, but it does not seem that Ignatius called him; he recalled Jay on December 12. All year, he insisted (without success, however) that John III allow Rodríguez to come to Rome.

Ignatius was very much in favor with the Pope. He discussed serious matters with him concerning Spain and Portugal and attempted to effect a reconciliation between John III and Paul III, between whom the affair of the Cardinal of Viseu had created ill will. On June 3, 1545, Paul III granted the Society very broad powers in whatever concerned the administration of sacraments. Ignatius, being prudent, shared them discreetly and only with reliable men. It was in December that Paul III asked that some companions be sent to the Council of Trent, not as official "theologians" of the Pope, as is often maintained, according to Ribadeneyra, and of Orlandini, but simply as "reformed priests"; Laynez and Salmeron were chosen; they arrived in Trent only in time for Session V. At first, they participated in the Council only in conversations and special consultations; later in comments at the meetings of the commission of theologians called "minor theologians".

However, little by little, prelates responsible for with reports or talks sought out the two companions. When, on March 12, the Council moved to Bologna, Laynez and Salmeron went there, as did Peter Canisius whom Cardinal Truchsess had sent to Trent to help Jay, his "representative" as early as the end of February.[9]

In the house of La Strada, apostolic activity was intense: the *ministeria assueta*, was, to be sure, the basis of the activity, but Ignatius took a personal interest in the house of St. Martha (nevertheless, he strove to transfer the responsibility for it to laymen). The community of La Strada consisted of about thirty people, for the most part novices whom Ignatius trained *tam domi quam in peregrinationibus et hospitalium ministerio*; some groups of companions departed for different establishments. After Lent at Bassano, Laynez came back to Rome where he met Salmeron again and preached and gave lessons in Holy Scripture. At the end of the year, Doménech abandoned his task as Secretary of the Society: in the last days of November, Bartolomo Ferrão replaced him. It was at this time that a man entered the society who had formerly resisted Ignatius[10] and who would play a primary role in the development of the order: Jerónimo Nadal.

An event occurred this year which took much time and gave Ignatius[10] much worry: Isabel Roser, a former benefactress of Ignatius in the Barcelona period, trying to overturn his refusal, obtained permission

[9] Cf. T. VENTURI, op. cit., 4, pp. 501 and sq.
[10] Cf. supra, pp. 73–74.

from the Pope to come to Rome with a few companions and to live there under obedience to Ignatius. What was to be done? Since the Pope wished it, Ignatius obeyed. On December 24, Isabel Roser gave up her possessions to the Society and on the 25th she made her profession, as did her companions. (The adventure would result in failure as early as October 1546.)

The first letter of spiritual direction written by Ignatius to Duke Francis Borgia dates from the end of 1549.

ITALY: Until Lent, Laynez remained in Venice and Padua. Andrea Lippomani pursued little by little the realization of his plans. For the first time, a companion, Laynez, was seriously threatened by the episcopate: the bishop of Laybach wanted him as coadjutor with the right of succession. The plan dragged on for a long time. Laynez celebrated Lent at Bassano, then returned to Rome. Broët was a missionary at Faenza, where he initiated several charities and taught catechism, particularly in seven schools. In his preaching, he came up against the formidable Franciscan apostate, Bernard Ochino, whom Ignatius had not and would not succeed in reconciling with the Church.

PORTUGAL: Favre and Araoz lived there in January and February. In a letter of January 9 to Ignatius, Favre made allusion to the malaise which reigned in Portugal among the companions: he remained, however, optimistic, but Araoz, he said, was less satisfied. Certain subsequent letters, written by companions to Favre, give us some insight into the cause of the malaise: many evinced an excessive taste for humiliations, spectacular penances and theatrical sermons which astonished the general populace; rumors circulated against the Society. Nevertheless, novices were abundant—a few of whom would become famous: Gonçalves da Câmara, John Nuñez, the future patriarch of Ethiopia, Emmanuel de Nobrega, one of the founders and the first provincial of the mission of Brazil.

At Coimbra sixty scholars lived lives devoted to studies and some ministries. Rodríguez created a "ruling" for them and "rules of offices" upon which Ignatius would draw at a later date. Seven companions even resided at the court of the king.

INDIA: There were three departures from Lisbon, among which was that of Antonio Criminali, who would be the first martyr of the Society of Jesus. Still, Xavier sent anguished requests to Europe. He appealed for real missionaries; he even hoped that Rodríguez would rejoin him. His letters, which were circulated in Portugal and in Spain, aroused much enthusiasm.

SPAIN: On March 4, Favre and Araoz finally received authorization from John III to go into Castile. On March 25, they were at Valladolid: they received a warm welcome from Philip II, the bishops from Cartagena and Calahorra and even from the Inquisitor. There was also, however, Favre tells us, a certain reserve and even a certain amount of suspicion. Soon the two companions began to preach and to hear confessions. Favre remained more at Valladolid; Araoz traveled from city to city in a missionary capacity. Soon many plans for colleges sprang up (Salamanca, Alcalá, Barcelona, Toledo, etc.). Actually, Ignatius became involved only in the college of Gandia. Oviedo would go there on November 16 and establish in effect "the spiritual college"; the actual college would not be established until 1546. The young college of Valencia developed in a regular fashion.

From Madrid whence he had followed the court, Favre could write to Rodríguez that numerous candidates were coming forward. The companions were aided in their projects by important and faithful benefactors, such as Eleanor de Mascarenhas, who had been governess to Philip II and was now governess of Prince Charles.

GERMANY AND EASTERN EUROPE: At the beginning of the year, Jay was at Worms, and he pushed the bishops who were present to create in their dioceses "colleges for poor students", to facilitate access to orders for worthwhile candidates with solid doctrinal background. At Worms he preached during Lent: Ferdinand I, King of the Romans, frequently attended his sermons; on the Feast of the Holy Trinity, he would even bring his brother, Charles V. In September, we find Jay at Dillingen: he was preparing himself to participate in the Council of Trent as "proxy for the Cardinal of Augsburg"; he was actually there on December 16. Favre, Laynez and Salmeron would also have to go to Trent, but not in the capacity of theologians; the latter two would not arrive until May 18, 1546. In December, Ignatius would wish to recall Jay to Rome but he gave precedence to the "mission" which Jay had received from the Cardinal of Augsburg.

Bobadilla, too, was at Worms in January. Then he went to Brussels and returned to Worms where he became involved in the outlandish affair regarding the escape of Cardinal Farnese (June 27); finally, he was named chaplain "to the armies of the King" which fought against the heretical princes. Meanwhile, he wrote books which he distributed among the princes, bishops and theologians.

In Cologne, the situation was dramatic, for the bishop was more than favorable to the new doctrines; if Cologne fell, there was the danger of the entire region's fall into schism. Persecution against the companions was virulent: to such a point, that Canisius favored sending students to Louvain. Favre, from Spain, followed these events with intense interest.

LOUVAIN AND PARIS: In Louvain and Paris, the situation was normal; the companions, who were not numerous, fulfilled their studies and some ministries. In Paris, the group, for lack of a house, lived at the college of the Lombards.

In short, the year of 1545 was rich in important events. The actual presence or proximity of four companions at the Council of Trent would have serious consequences: it would introduce the companions into the world of theologians and it would reveal the existence of the Society of Jesus to the bishops present at the Council. On this occasion, Jay, Laynez, Salmeron and Canisius would establish personal relationships with many of the participants who were bishops, but also princes, religious and even Lutherans, and these relationships would considerably influence the development of the order. It was definitely world events and Church circumstances, let us say God himself by his Providence— and not Ignatius—which directed the fate of the young Society of Jesus. Ignatius' particular role consisted in assuring that these "missions" be implemented in a certain spirit, the *mens et modus Societatis*. In the first months of 1546, he addressed a brief instruction to Laynez and Salmeron which was significant, because of its excess of minute detail concerning the manner in which Ignatius wanted his companions to perform their missionary duties.

1546

ROME: The year 1546 was burdensome for Ignatius. The first difficulty came to him on the occasion of the Council of Trent. In May, Jay,[11] Laynez and Salmeron had arrived in Trent, but Favre was unable to leave Spain. Although sick, he took the route for Rome on July 17; he arrived there exhausted and died on August 1. This death was a very hard blow for the young Society, for Favre had held an unobtrusive, but eminent, position among the *primi Patres*. From the beginning of the new session of the Council, the three companions had maintained a low profile— that is to say, at least they lived there as truly "reformed priests". Thus, they revealed to all present the true face of the Society: they won for it the sympathy of numerous bishops, particularly that of the Spanish bishops, who had not at first been favorable to it. Several bishops

---

[11] Jay was in Trent as early as December 1545, that is to say, from the time of the first session.

proposed colleges in their dioceses; the Bishop of Clermont, Guillaume du Prat, wanted to establish two foundations: one in Paris where he would give the companions the use of a house on "rue de la Lyre", and the other in his diocese in Auvergne.

Ignatius realized that the apostolic appeals exceeded the number of companions and thought of admitting into the Society "spiritual and temporal coadjutors who could be elevated to sacred orders". The letter of Paul III, *Exponi nobis*, of June 5, conferred this right on the Society.

Among the constitutions which Ignatius drafted that year, one was destined for the students at the college of Padua (end of 1546).

On October 1, the Roser experiment came to an end: Isabel Roser and her companions were relieved of their vows and of all obedience to the Society. Through a constitution, *De foeminis in Societatam non admittendis*, Ignatius definitively closed the door on any similar experiment, and his legendary tenacity would be required so that door not be reopened.

Ignatius was more and more absorbed by the *ministerium gubernationis*, especially since his health was not improving and the training of novices demanded all his attention. The number of expulsions and departures from the order bothered him; therefore, he focused on "the impediments to entrance into the Society", which would henceforth be a part of the "Examen" of the candidate. The document would be enriched little by little and would become a sort of important preface to the *Constitutions*.

ITALY: It seems then that it was Ignatius' intention to create some colleges in northern Italy: Padua was stabilized. A college at Venice was in the planning stage. Ignatius would have liked Laynez to explore the ground in Florence and Pisa: the Council of Trent allowed Laynez only to outline the steps. The college of Bologna was strengthened and put in order: Bröet even left Faenza from time to time to back up Doménech who was experiencing difficulties. Parma remained dear to the heart of the *primi Patres* in memory of 1537; Salmeron preached during Lent there en route to Trent: but would they be able to install a college there which would have some chance of lasting?

SICILY: For the first time, this year a companion served as a missionary in Sicily. It was the Cardinal Carpi, the "protector" of the Society, who had requested this; he gave the permission to visit his diocese and to reform several monasteries.

PORTUGAL: The position of the Society there was very strong; Rodríguez was the tutor and confessor of the heir apparent. Vocations were abundant; the King guaranteed the financing of the college of

Coimbra (eighty students, plus fifteen companions "in the service of the house" and more than fifteen "confessors"). On October 25, Ignatius established the province of Portugal: Simón Rodríguez was its first provincial.

INDIA: In 1546, Rodríguez sent ten companions to India. Many more of them were needed! Xavier called for them and wanted them to be of "solid virtue". The companions' existence there was essentially of a missionary character: Xavier especially was always full of apostolic zeal. Two houses, however, appeared, Goa and Comorin, and Xavier wondered if it they should not increase the number of schools like the college of St. Foy. One of his concerns was to adapt methods of evangelization to the conditions of the country, because the Catholic faith was contaminated in certain regions by its contact with Islam, by the disastrous example of many Portuguese colonists, by heresies imported from Europe, and even by the ignorance and immorality of many European priests. This was true to such an extent that Xavier asked King John III to introduce the "Holy Inquisition" into India. Other problems—spiritual, psychological, and even those simply concerned with health—arose; in several of his letters one senses an anxiety which comes through: how to cope with an authentic evangelization? how to implant truly the Church of Jesus Christ? was the gravity of the situation understood in Europe?

SPAIN: When Favre had to leave Spain to go to Rome, and from there to Trent, it was Araoz whom he called to Philip's court. Araoz left Valencia towards April, did missionary work en route, fell sick twice, and finally arrived at the Court.

One event would exercise a decisive influence on the development of the Society in Spain: Duke Francis Borgia, having become a widower, sought admission into the Society. Favre, before leaving Spain, was able to arrange the delicate matter with Ignatius. It was on October 9 that Borgia, very secretly, entered the Society of Jesus. For the outside world, he remained the Duke. He continued to work on the progress of the order in Spain. Gandia was henceforth an active mission center. On September 10, Ignatius sent from Rome to Araoz a companion who was going to play an important role in the history of the beginning of the order in Spain and Portugal, Doctor Michael de Torres. The instructions which Ignatius gave him before his departure and which established his mission en route and in Spain constituted a typically Ignatian document.[12] Everything indicated a great development of the Society in Spain.

[12] *Epist. ign.* I, pp. 415–24.

GERMANY AND EASTERN EUROPE: Bobadilla covered the main roads of Germany, Flanders, Cologne, Liège, Ratisbon; the armies of the Emperor and of the Pope (he was wounded, taken prisoner, and escaped) accepted him each in turn. He played the role of intermediary between the Pope and the Emperor, openly criticized the politics of both of them, refused the bishopric of Trieste, printed his book on the Christian conscience, gave it to important personages, particularly to the Queen of Bohemia, and sent bulletins of victory to Rome. With what attitude could Ignatius read these self-praising documents? Undoubtedly, with the humility, affection and humor with which his letters of 1543 to Bobadilla were filled.[13]

Canisius worked effectively in Cologne, but under dramatic conditions: the Archbishop had gone over to heresy. In Louvain, the companions could hardly grow for they were not "recognized" by the law. It was not much better in Paris: in fact, the future of the Society in France was being decided at this moment in Trent where Guillaume du Prat laid out plans for the future with Laynez and Salmeron.

ETHIOPIA: The plan of John III for a Portuguese legation in Ethiopia developed. Much correspondence was exchanged between the King and Ignatius to the effect that the legation be connected with a missionary group. John III wanted the future patriarch to be a member of the Society (Ignatius and his counselors thought of Bröet).[14] If they could find no one for this perilous mission, Ignatius proposed that he himself assume it.

The correspondence of 1546 takes on a new interest: a rather voluminous dossier of letters from Favre informs us about Portugal, Spain, and even Germany and Flanders, with which he had kept in contact. The letters of Jay, Salmeron and Laynez enlighten us on the Council of Trent; the letters of Xavier, on the gravity of the situation of the Church in India. One feels that the law of distances and numbers comes into play; undoubtedly the *primi Patres* were in the forefront; but other personalities began to emerge; and the "missions" were so demanding and absorbing that each was already experiencing difficulty in recognizing and following the works of the other companions in the regions which were not his own.

---

[13] SAINT IGNACE, *Lettres* (French translation), pp. 94 sq.
[14] Rodríguez is thinking of Bobadilla.

1547

ROME: The ministries, the formation of novices, the concern of administration, everything continued and weighed more heavily. The year was, however, marked by a vigorous effort in administration, or if one prefers, in organization: in March, Polanco was named Secretary of the Society (as well as Procurer General). Juan Alonso de Polanco was without doubt the most remarkable "administrator" the Society ever had. The more one uncovers his activities and his influence, the more his role appears fundamental: he could have handled the most important duties, yet he assumed the most unobtrusive, but very effective, role as Secretary. In a period when everything was to be formulated, at least to be organized and brought to completion, he applied his remarkable intelligence, his knowledge, his methodical mind and his heart to the service of Ignatius and his successors in the Society. "Polanco", said Father Oliverio Manareo, was "very close to the Saint [Ignatius], he had been educated by the Founder, and trained according to his heart."[15] And Ribadeneyra says: "He seemed to bear on his shoulders the entire Society."[16] Such was the man whom Ignatius called to him in March 1547, and whose activity would be closely associated in many ways with that of Ignatius without ever losing its own identity. Polanco, barely appointed, reorganized the normal operation of correspondence between Rome and the companions throughout the world;[17] the completion of this reorganization would take many years. Above all, Polanco began, in close collaboration with Ignatius, to prepare the codex of the *Constitutions*: He first emptied the entire file, already voluminous with what had been done up to that time, classified the subjects already considered or to be considered and noted the unsettled problems. These tasks would last until 1549 and would be completed in 1550 in the first text of the *Constitutions*. Polanco would render another service to the emergent Society: the assembling of the documents for the archives. Undoubtedly, the archives, as we possess them today, present some regrettable omissions, some of them astonishing,[18] but the whole is remarkable and valuable. From the archives, Polanco drew the *Chronicon*, which despite its defects remains the fundamental document on the Ignatian years of the Society.

In 1547, one of the concerns of Ignatius was certainly the evolution of

---

[15] MANAREO, *De rebus Societatis Jesu commentarius*, p. 129.

[16] *Illustrium scriptorium religionis Societatis Jesu catalogus*, Plantin, Anvers 1613, p. 154.

[17] Letter of July 27, *Epist. ign.* 1, pp. 536 sq. n. 179 and 180.

[18] I think here of certain parcels of letters of S. Rodríguez during his great crisis or those of P. Broët in Paris during the time of the Decree of the faculty of theology. It seems that certain archives disappeared in the time of P. Vitelleschi.

the Council of Trent. At the seventh session which took place in Bologna (March 1547), four companions were present among the theologians: Jay (still the proxy of the Cardinal of Augsburg); Salmeron; Laynez; and Canisius, called from Cologne. At the eighth session (March 11) Laynez, Salmeron and Jay were absent. However, at the wish of the Cardinal of St. Croix, Laynez rejoined the Council on April 12; Salmeron, sick in Padua, did not rejoin them until later (between mid-June and early July); Jay also rejoined them in turn, but Ignatius, in the middle of June, recalled Laynez and Canisius. Laynez was sent to Florence; Canisius had to make his novitiate in Rome, under the supervision of Ignatius. At the end of the year, the Council dissolved. It did not resume until 1550, by the will of Julius III.

Problems of obedience also continued to preoccupy Ignatius. Several important documents on this subject date from 1547: a letter of May 7 to the companions of Coimbra, a letter of July 29 to the companions of Gandia and Valencia, as well as frequent allusions to the subject of obedience in many personal letters. In many ways linked to the problem of obedience were the problems of recruitment, choice of candidates and their training. The admission standards were not sufficiently strict, hence the too numerous departures and expulsions. Also, the novices were sent to Rome too easily. Henceforth, they would first have to ask authorization from Ignatius. In addition, where there was a novitiate, for example, at Coimbra, the house must be separate from the college. Ignatius regretted not being able to do that in Rome.

The system of professions and of vows of spiritual coadjutors still remained undefined: a letter of November 20 to Lancillotto[19] is one of the most curious of those remaining to us on this question. The "habit of the Society", at that time, was to admit as spiritual coadjutors "and hence participants in the privileges of the Society" certain Fathers whom the Superior could later call to profession which, at that time, could be made only in Rome. It seems, moreover, that Ignatius did not consider the time ripe for "calling" the companions to profession—with the sole exception of Araoz (1542). Ignatius would also call Borgia on February 2, 1548, but it was not until 1549 that he would really begin to have solemn professions made and he would not multiply them.[20]

In 1547 (or 1548?), Ignatius wrote to Charles V an account of the founding of the Society of Jesus. The report, despite its brevity, or perhaps because of it, revealed many points which Ignatius considered innovative or the most essential for the life of the companions.[21]

---

[19] *Epist. ign.* 1, pp. 638–41.
[20] Cf. infra, pp. 346 sqq.
[21] *Const.* 1, pp. CLVII–CLXI and 240–44.

ITALY: Because of the presence of the Council, Bologna became famous that year. Broët preached there during Lent and then remained. Consequently, the four *primi Patres* found themselves once again frequently reunited that year. Canisius, who had formerly met Favre and Bobadilla and soon was going to make his novitiate in Rome under Ignatius, would thus have known six of the *primi Patres*. Laynez spent some time in Florence and gave the support of his authority to the still distant establishment of a college in that city. In Ferrara the situation was delicate: Duke Ercole II was definitely a great friend of the *primi Patres*. He had proved it already and now he was looking for a spiritual advisor. However, his wife, Renée of France, favored the "novelties of Geneva". A friend of the Duke arranged for Jay, despite his obligations to the Council, to put himself at the disposal of the Duke. Actually, it soon became apparent to Jay that the Duke's Friend had taken his own desires for those of the Prince. This brief encounter, however, would not have negligible results.

SICILY: The Society of Jesus began activity there which would soon gain a considerable and totally unexpected expansion. Father Lhoost continued to do missionary work in the diocese of Agrigento, but, at the request of Juan de Vega, the Viceroy, Ignatius quickly sent Fr. Jerónimo Doménech. Immediately, the two men, who had a marvelous rapport, conceived the plan of a series of charitable works to create or to reform. Toward the end of June or July, it was even question of a "college-university"[22] at Messina. The official request for one would go to Ignatius on December 18, a date by which Doménech would already have left the big island for a while. The Sicilian plans were such that Ignatius had to remind them of the scarcity of men in the young Society.

PORTUGAL: Here, everything developed magnificently. There was talk of sending four missionaries to the "Congo": all the companions at Coimbra volunteered. The regional missions increased. There were dangers in this rapid expansion: they did not examine the candidates rigorously enough, and Ignatius asked Rodríguez to be more demanding.

INDIA AND JAPAN: While one group of companions worked at Goa, Xavier continued his apostolic travels with some other fathers and brothers. Passing through Malacca he heard mentioned for the first time

---

[22] Here a change in the meaning of the word college takes place in our early documents. Sometimes it will signify, as formerly, a group of students of the Society; sometimes a teaching establishment for day students; sometimes an establishment where scholastics and day students were mingled.

the recently discovered islands of Japan where there would be serious hopes of evangelization. On November 20, Ignatius asked that one of the missionaries be chosen to come to inform him and King John III of the situation of the Society in India.

SPAIN: Two facts dominated the rapid development of the Society in Spain. First, the considerable support which Borgia gave it: he obtained from the Pope the building of a university at Gandia (November 4—it would be the first university of the Society); the official approval of the *Spiritual Exercises* (in their two Latin versions); Prince Philip hoped to make Borgia his *major domus*, but because of his vows, Borgia convinced Philip to renounce the plan. The second event was the establishing of Spain as a province with Araoz as the first provincial (September 1). Araoz was a well-known personality in Spain; his sermons, particularly in Madrid, had a huge audience. Actually, the companions were still not very numerous; but candidates presented themselves. Unfortunately, because of a lack of financial resources, not all could be admitted. They had to invent what one could call "the stratagem of the congregatiunculae" in the five cities where they were established (Alcalá, Valladolid, Valencia, Gandia and Barcelona), they lived in small groups of three, four, eight or ten at the most. If Portugal, well supplied by the King, had helped Spain, there would have been a solution to the problem, but John III and Rodríguez turned a deaf ear. They even refused Ignatius' request that Father Strada, an excellent preacher, leave Portugal for Spain—even for a brief period.

GERMANY AND EASTERN EUROPE: Bobadilla increased his trips, his interference, his outbursts and his criticisms. He participated in the Diet of Augsburg. He gave advice to Paul III, to Cardinal Farnese, to Duke Ercole d'Este. His activity was effective because he had a very clear perception of situations, a single-minded zeal and dauntless courage: he refused to despair and shared his hope with others. Polanco himself one day sent glowing praise of Bobadilla to all the communities.

COLOGNE: The heretical Archbishop was excommunicated. His replacement delegated Canisius to serve the Emperor.

LOUVAIN: The group was in a badly defined canonical situation; they hoped for the return as Superior of Father Lhoost who was still detained in Italy. He would get under way in August. While waiting, Ignatius, from Rome, advised the companions to elect a "prefect" whom they would obey, and he also approved their giving themselves regulations until such time as they would receive the Rules.

PARIS: The group led a student life under the leadership of Paul de Achillis.

1548

ROME: The activity of the companions of La Strada developed favorably. Ignatius, absorbed by the cares of the general administration of the Society, left more and more responsibility for his Roman "works" to intermediaries, reserving to himself only the "graviores": "It would take too long", said Polanco, "to enumerate the charitable works in which Ignatius was interested and for which he worked." In the first months of 1548 was Ignatius thinking of resigning, as a letter of Laynez hinted?[23] It was not an impossibility. His state of health would have sufficed to explain such a desire.

Whatever the case may be, Ignatius' relationship with the entire Society was astonishing. Undoubtedly, because of distances and postal delays, certain things escaped him, but even in these cases he instinctively grasped the situation. One after the other he established the indispensable canonical structures—too slowly for the wishes of some people. He encouraged those responsible to provide better training of recruits and called some Fathers or Brothers to him in Rome to complete their first novitiate which had been too summary. He was concerned about the quality of obedience: as he had done with the companions in Paris, he tested the obedience of the companions in Rome upon the occasion of the upcoming departure of ten among them to Sicily; published several documents on perfect obedience; he stopped using almost contradictory variations in the exercise of his authority because he took into account the mental or physical health of individuals. Certain of his contemporaries were themselves disconcerted by this.

On July 31, Paul III, at the request of Borgia, praised the Spiritual Exercises and recommended them in the brief *Pastoralis officii*. The printing of the book began with an introduction by Polanco. On September 20, Ignatius suggested to Borgia that on the occasion of the presentation of the work to Paul III, they ask the Pope to grant the Society "powers" commonly called *mare magnum*, in other words, extremely broad powers that the Holy See had thus far granted only to a few large mendicant orders.

In 1548, one of Ignatius' prevalent attitudes appeared more clearly—that of considering the "first Fathers" of Paris-Venice as true cofounders of the Society and of consulting them on problems which involved its

---

[23] *Epist. ign.* 12, p. 228, n. 9. The authenticity of this letter is contested. Cf. also *Scripta* 1, p. 666.

fate. Two events clearly characterized this attitude. First, in the course of the year, perhaps even as early as January, he addressed a questionnaire to the four *primi Patres* on missions in Italy: Laynez, Salmeron, Broët and Jay.[24] Since the death of Codure, in 1542, Ignatius had worked alone. Consequently, it seemed only fitting to him to tie up all the loose ends at the time when, thanks to the presence of Polanco, the codex of the constitutions had arrived at its final draft. We do not know the exact tenor of Ignatius' questionnaire, but here are the responses of the four companions: (1) They were of the opinion that the constitutions should not be obligatory under pain of sin. (2) They approved of all that Ignatius had obtained from the Holy See up to the present and gave him carte blanche for all that he would obtain in the future; they approved of the constitutions which he had already written and those which he would write in the future. (3) They accepted the idea that those who lived *at the time* in the Society (there was no mention of the future) who would fall under one of the categories of impediments (written down some time before by Ignatius) would be received into the Society, unless one of the professed thought that he must oppose such an admission. (4) They designated ten companions, who in their opinion, could make their profession without supplementary probation, even without any further study than what they had already completed up to that point. They were: Francisco Strada, Diego Miron, Andrés de Oviedo, Pietro Codacio, Miona, Nadal, Jacques Lhoost (who would die that summer in Bologna, en route to Louvain), André Frusius, Jerónimo Doménech and Juan de Polanco.[25] The second event was the unveiling of a plan that Ignatius had nurtured to bring about a reunion of the companions in Rome during the jubilee year of 1550, motivated by his desire to have all the surviving "first Fathers" participate in that reunion. For this purpose, he asked John III to authorize Xavier's return from India and Rodríguez's leave of absence from Portugal. John III refused during the entire year of 1548.

We should note that in June of this year, Pietro Codacio completed the new living quarters at La Strada; the house consisted at the time of forty bedrooms, but it was already too small.

ITALY: All the companions worked effectively in northern Italy. However, in Padua, serious difficulties began with Andrea Lippomani whose

---

[24] *Const.* 1, pp. LVI and 244 sq.

[25] Miona, Polanco, Oviedo and Miron will indeed make their profession in 1549, Frusius in 1550, Strada in 1551, Nadal in 1552, Doménech in 1555. Codacio will die suddenly in Rome in 1549, but as "spiritual coadjutor"; he will have refused solemn profession because of humility. In this study we have deliberately kept the Latin name of André des Freux, Frusius, the name by which he is best known. The same is true for Canisius, etc.

charity was greater than his resources—difficulties which would last a long time, to the great detriment of the health, studies and even the perseverance of the companions. Laynez became an indispensable advisor to the Duchess of Florence. His departure for Sicily at the end of December (where Ignatius had appointed him to visit) was not without opposition. Jay still remained in Ferrara with Duke Ercole, but with no more success than formerly: happily, in May, he went back to Germany. As for Broët, he was a missionary in the region of Bologna and Faenza; the Council had adjourned in September because of the systematic opposition of Charles V.

SICILY: Sicily undoubtedly represented one of the most typical cases of the apostolic tactics of Ignatius. Since the big island had an urgent need of reform and evangelization, and since the Viceroy, seconded by his daughter and his sons, was very well disposed, Ignatius made a very strong effort to send men of great worth to Sicily: ten companions went there from Rome that year, and among them Nadal, Canisius (whom Ignatius would reproach for his being too nostalgic for Germany), Frusius, du Coudret, Benedetto Palmio, etc. He chose them from five different nationalities to show the universal character of the Society. Three points particularly commanded his attention: "the academy" of Messina which would soon become a "college-university" and would be devoted in part to the teaching of the companions; the "orphanage" for which he especially dispatched Baroello; finally, the reform of the monasteries of religious, not to mention the itinerant missions. The departure from Rome of the ten companions on March 18 would be done in the way Ignatius would favor for the rest of his life: the group would present itself to the Pope, and Paul III would bless them; all this would be done so as to show that it was truly a pontifical mission. The reception at Messina was overwhelming, especially since the academy of Catania viewed with a jaundiced eye the birth of this academy for which, in the name of the Viceroy, extravagant publicity was being made throughout the whole region. Messina, however, was of such importance that in March Ignatius asked all the regions of Europe to send "masters" of great worth there. Rodríguez, in a rather lively answer, called Ignatius' attention to the fact that masters of value, if there were any of them, would be better utilized in the universities which were more developed than Messina. In any case, the inauguration of the university in the beginning of October was lavish, to the point that Ignatius had to suggest more discretion to the companions. Messina would henceforth serve from then on as a support center for numerous missions and domestic charities. Doménech, who curiously shared with Nadal the authority over the companions according to a typically Ignatian schema,[26] showed himself to be extremely active: with the poor, the sick, the prisoners, the galley slaves, the "errant women", the orphans, the children to be catechised, etc.—no sector escaped his zeal. The Viceroy had been thinking for quite some time of entrusting the reform of all Sicily to the Society. In the meantime, several cities clamored for colleges like that of Messina, and vocations increased.

Things were such that Ignatius designated Laynez as visitor; the latter would not be able to leave until the end of December (business at Padua having detained him a long time). Doménech would then return to Italy, but he fell ill and remained in Sicily for the entire year of 1549.

PORTUGAL: Simón Rodríguez, tutor and confessor of the young prince, lived at the court with a few companions. Domestic missions increased; Coimbra continued to flourish: there were ninety companions, not counting "those who served"; an atmosphere of great missionary fervor reigned among these youths. Five great apostolic avenues opened before them: first of all, India to which twelve companions (five of whom were priests) departed on March 17; the Congo for which four companions departed on February 18; Brazil, where members of the Society were being requested; Ethiopia, where King John wanted to send an important team to further his diplomatic relations with the Negus; finally, "Mauritania", actually Ceuta, where two companions were going to work with Christian captives. Simón Rodríguez volunteered to Ignatius and to King John. This missionary zeal drew many vocations—perhaps too much sought-after, and in the opinion of Ignatius, too quickly approved.[27]

INDIA: From the letters which Xavier sent at the beginning of the year to John III, to the "companions in Rome", to Ignatius and to Rodríguez, one realizes the considerable achievement of the missionaries. Nonetheless, obstacles and miseries were not lacking: the Portuguese colonists gave a negative example of Christianity and Xavier asked that the Viceroy and governors who had not embraced evangelization be punished upon their return to Portugal. There were also confrontations with other religions: with Islam and especially with Judaism. India was

[26] We shall study further these overlappings of responsibilities and obediences to which Ignatius had willing recourse.

[27] The correspondence between the companions of Portugal and the "procurator" of the province in Rome, Father de Santa Cruz, teaches us much about the situation. Ignatius was not very satisfied with the manner in which Father de Santa Cruz managed matters. Moreover, inasmuch as the procurator was to be very much involved in litigations, and even matters of money, Ignatius did not want him to live at La Strada. Santa Cruz died at the end of the year, having, said Polanco, "detested his mistakes". (Chron. 1, p. 327.)

definitely far from Europe. Among the twelve companions who arrived from Lisbon that year, there was Anthony Gomez to whom Rodríguez, believing Xavier absent from Goa for a long time, entrusted the responsibility of the college of Goa and authority over all the companions in India. Soon, serious differences of opinion arose between Xavier and Gomez, especially concerning the native students of the college. A crisis finally occurred between the two men. However, Xavier was preparing to leave for Japan.

In December Ignatius wrote to John III and to Rodríguez so that Xavier could return from India and participate in the *conventus priorum Patrum* which was scheduled for 1550. In any case, it was important that if he could not come in person, he delegate a Father who would inform the King, Rodríguez and Ignatius of the true situation of the mission.

THE CONGO. It was on February 18, that Father Viaz left with four companions for the Congo. Already, in the time of King Emmanuel, Portugal had attempted to begin to evangelize: there had been conversions, as well as baptisms, and they had constructed a few churches. The companions arrived at Pinda on March 17, and in the capital on April 20, where the native King welcomed them lavishly. One brother created a school for six hundred children; the companions labored as missionaries and performed baptisms. The euphoria would be short-lived: the king was a maniac.

ETHIOPIA: Political negotiations continued between the emperor of Ethiopia and Portugal. The Negus played a subtle game balancing between Islam which threatened him and Portugal from which he wanted protection—just enough to keep Islam's respect. The choice of the Patriarch provoked some tension between Ignatius and John III: John III set aside the candidacy of Broët and demanded that a Portuguese be selected.

MAURITANIA: *(Ceuta)*. In mid-August John Nuñez and Louis Gonzales departed. This was a very perilous but fertile apostolate among captive Christians confronted by Islam and Judaism. Louis Gonzales was soon obliged to return to Portugal. Nuñez remained alone; he was an apostle of great spiritual influence.

SPAIN: Borgia made his profession of the four vows on February 2. It remained a secret, for a pontifical indult authorized him to keep the administration of the duchy and his possessions for three years. As for Araoz, Borgia and Torres (whose attachment to the Society was not officially declared either), they were the instigators of the vigorous growth of the Society in 1548. At Valladolid, Valencia, Saragossa and Barcelona, things developed at a normal pace; but at Gandia and its environs, there was an evangelical explosion. The regular presence of Duke Francis did much to bring it about; he financed, built and also intervened in the disputes. On May 9, eve of the Ascension, the companions entered the college which he had built for them; the rector of the college was Andrés de Oviedo, who was also rector of the University. This nomination was characteristic of the manner in which Ignatius treated certain men: Oviedo was a fervent priest, but one who dreamed of living a hermit's life with long periods of contemplation and rigorous penances. With Father Onfroy, he asked Ignatius on February 8 to allow him to withdraw for seven years of solitude. Gently, patiently, as he had formerly done with Borgia himself, Ignatius curbed these excesses, balanced them, insisted on obedience, this "badge" of the Society of Jesus, and finally led these men whose only fault was excessive fervor, back to the authentic spirit of the order. It was not only in Gandia that the Duke performed great services for Ignatius, but also in Rome. Having considerable influence at the court of Paul III, the Duke intervened in order to obtain great favors for Ignatius.

This does not mean that things in Spain went smoothly. At Salamanca, Melchoir Cano unleashed a furor against the Society; neither the intervention of the nuncio, nor that of the Superior would calm the irascible Dominican: to the end of his life, he remained one of the most fierce adversaries of the Society. In his struggle he would be abetted and supported by the Archbishop of Toledo, Siliceo.

At the end of March, Araoz was named Visitor to Spain *cum amplissima potestate*. An indefatigable worker, he too was inclined toward rigorous poverty and external mortification; however, his health was delicate.

The relations of the companions with the "Master of Ávila" date from 1548. Juan of Ávila exerted at that time an extraordinary spiritual influence. He dreamed of founding an organization which would strongly resemble the Society of Jesus. When he became acquainted with it, he abandoned his own project. Even better, he directed several of his disciples, some of whom possessed great humanitarian and spiritual qualities, to the Society.

GERMANY AND EASTERN EUROPE: Bobadilla continued his brilliant and effective missionary work here. However, he repeatedly requested that Ignatius allow him to leave Germany; he considered the Germans "too slow". By yet another audacious act, he was going to get, without willing it, what he desired: he boldly opposed the *Interim* which Charles

V had just decided and that the Pope had approved: the Emperor expelled Bobadilla.[28] On June 20, the exile was in Rome, where it seemed that Ignatius prudently did not give him asylum at La Strada. In June the Pope appointed Bobadilla to accompany a bishop who was desirous of reforming his diocese in the kingdom of Naples.

In Cologne, a group of seven companions worked under the authority of Leonard Kessel. They lived in extreme poverty. The prior of the Carthusian monastery, Gerard Kalckbrenner, helped them with alms. He even sent money to Ignatius, who was in the clutches of debt.

LOUVAIN: A group devoted themselves to "studies and to the edification of our neighbor". Polanco tells us that Ignatius followed the progress of this little community with particular interest.

PARIS: The group lived in a precarious situation and in a semi-clandestine manner: they lived in the midst of the students, at the college of the Lombards. Viola, the one responsible for the group, had even been elected "Superior" by the Italians. Obviously, the situation could not last. Guillaume du Prat had made a sizeable gift, but the companions did not find a house that they could buy. Moreover, it would then be necessary to obtain French "naturalization", in order to be able to possess property and fixed revenues. Serious concerns loomed on the horizon for the years ahead!

1549

ROME: A folder marked "very urgent" was on Ignatius' desk: it was imperative that the constitutions be ready for the *conventus* to be held the following year: Ignatius and Polanco worked on them diligently, especially during the spring and summer months. Ignatius willingly consulted the Fathers passing through Rome or wrote to others. Correspondence from the provinces more and more frequently brought him questions—sometimes very serious ones—on vows, powers, ministries, obedience and poverty. It was urgent that the companions have at their disposal a common text, even if it was not yet approved officially. From different sides, Ignatius could feel the impatience of the companions who wanted to know to what document they could refer for guidance. This situation was made even more serious by the bull *Licet*

---

[28] It is regrettable that the correspondence of this time has been preserved only in part and in the form of a summary of expeditions. Bobadilla does not speak of his expulsions in his autobiography.

debitum, in which Paul III had granted the Society numerous new and important privileges on October 18.

They did not yet know who was to participate in the *conventus* of 1550, nor exactly when it would be held. On November 10, the death of Paul III occurred but the Jubilee was held as was the *conventus*.

This work on the constitutions did not prevent Ignatius from following the evolution of the whole Society. Everywhere, in Rome or out of Rome, the companions' intense activity was evident.

In Rome itself, the novitiate, the *domus probationis* remained full: a total of one hundred twenty companions departed in the course of the year, but as soon as one group left the house, another replaced it. About fifty people lived at La Strada. A very hard blow struck the community on December 7 with the sudden death of Father Codacio, the procurator of the house in Rome. Ignatius honored him, for good reason, with the title of "Benefactor of the Society" (it owed him, among other things, the house in La Strada), but he left debts of nearly one thousand ducats and no one was up to date on the financial matters. A Frenchman, Father Cogordan, succeeded him.

Circumstances imposed heavy expenses. In April the church of La Strada, finally freed by Paul III from all curial responsibility (*cura animarum*) was supposed to be enlarged, and it was already necessary to think about its reconstruction. In June, Ignatius talked for the first time of creating a Roman college. Cautiously, Ignatius warned Borgia, who was going to come to Rome for the jubilee year, not to renounce his property until he had seen "things in Rome" with his own eyes. The inauguration of a house of the Society in Tivoli (five leagues from Rome) took place on September 8. This house would remain closely linked to the Roman houses.

Outside Rome, Ignatius' activity was just as intense. There were four hundred sixty letters which left La Strada for different regions, and some of these concerned important matters. In return, Ignatius demanded that certain companions write each month, and in certain cases, every week. Ignatius felt that the Society was entering a crisis of growth; spiritual or apostolic deviations were developing (Borgia, Oviedo, Araoz, etc.); it was necessary to weed these out as soon as they appeared. From the exchanges of correspondence, an exuberance of life gushes forth; letters of missionaries on the native mentalities, creativity, adaptations of methods of evangelization, confrontations with Islam, Judaism, "heresy", the world of colonists, of captives, of usurers. One understands why, in good times and in bad, Ignatius insisted on obedience and presented it as the distinctive sign of the companions. Monetary problems always became more and more acute as the houses and missions developed. The canonical lack of precision on the questions of vows, professions and training was no longer tolerable in light of the number of departures, returns, unusual vocations and even frauds. Obliged to deal with temporal powers, the Society was subject to their sway. Inevitably, since the companions, after all, were human, there arose frictions, misunderstandings, rivalries, in a confused mixture, through which emerged, without always being untouched by them, a few marvelous apostles: Xavier, Laynez, Lancillotto, Doménech, Araoz and still others. What did these difficulties matter since the "Right hand of the Most High" ("Dextera Excelsi") wanted to use the "least Society of Jesus" (*minima Societas*) in the Church to advance its glory?

ITALY AND NAPLES: Broët remained all year in Bologna; Salmeron in Venice-Padua, and Jay in Ferrara, until, in September, Ignatius sent them to Ingolstadt. In the wake of these veterans, more recent companions did missionary work.

Bobadilla, exiled from Germany, arrived in Naples on January 18. For the whole year, he worked freely as a missionary in the region, but he was forbidden to cross the borders of the kingdom, and he had to send by way of La Strada letters which he wanted to send to the Emperor or any personage of the court.

SICILY: Laynez, appointed Visitor, debarked there on January 18. Doménech was there, but ill. All prospered under the faithful supervision of Juan de Vega. In September, Ignatius sent nine companions who would found the college of Palermo, on November 24. As for the college of Messina, it was Nadal who presided over its organization.

PORTUGAL: The apostolic success there remained spectacular. But the Rodríguez crisis was festering under the success. Ignatius was uneasy, Laynez severe; it seems that from that time on, Ignatius had thought of replacing Rodríguez with Doménech. "With Doménech," wrote Laynez, "the Portuguese matters would go better and would be more unified at the top."[29] However, Doménech was detained in Sicily, and the Viceroy did not look favorably upon his departure. Thus, Rodríguez remained in Portugal where, moreover, the entrance into the Society of the extravagant Don Theotonio, brother of the Duke of Braganza, one of the first personages of the kingdom, would soon complicate matters further. During this time, Coimbra prospered, the regional missions bore good fruit, and four missionaries left Lisbon for Brazil.

[29] *Lainii mon* I, p. 106, n. 43.

INDIA: The central event was the departure of Xavier for Japan (in April) while on November 10, Ignatius named India a province and Xavier provincial . . . all the while striving to make him come to Europe in 1550. Thirty companions worked at that time in India, some in an atmosphere of heroism, even sometimes of martyrdom: it was the "primitive church": Antonio Criminali was cut down on February 7, thus inaugurating the martyrology of the Society. The divergence of views between Anthony Gomez, the rector of Goa, and Xavier had become insoluble. That year there was an interesting advance: Xavier installed a companion at Hormuz, a key citadel, which commanded the Persian Gulf and the Gulf of Oman and was a month's trip by road from Jerusalem, a great marketplace where races and religions blended as did the Orient with the Occident.

BRAZIL: The first of February, three missionaries under the leadership of Father de Nobrega, departed from Lisbon. Fifty-six days later, the fleet arrived at the Bahia do Todos os Santos. Immediately, the Portuguese built a city (Bahia São Salvador) and the companions worked as missionaries. The country was admirable, the customs abominable.

Whether it was a matter of India or Brazil, they began to be aware of a problem which appeared to be insoluble: how were they to maintain continuity in their missions? For a long time henceforth one could not hope to have sufficient native recruitment; on the other hand, could Europe, or more specifically Portugal, supply men of value for these missions in full development? This was a serious concern for Ignatius, Xavier and Nobrega.

CEUTA: Although he was alone, Father Nuñez accomplished considerable work there; he also worked as a missionary at Tétuan.

SPAIN: The labors and business of the Society were progressing well. Gandia remained the strongest point of implantation; the Duke, in keeping with Ignatius' orders, studied theology in his own university. As for Oviedo, the double rectorate was too heavy for this conscientious man; in July, he was relieved of the responsibility of the college. In Salamanca, Cano made less commotion than the year before. At Alcalá, on the contrary, the campaign of defamation by Archbishop Siliceo developed to the point that Villanova deemed it useful to go to Juan d'Ávila whom they believed shaken. This did not prevent Ignatius from thinking of founding a college in Toledo, the home of Siliceo! In Barcelona, a group of Poor Clares, supported by Araoz and Queralt, wanted to place themselves under the obedience of the Society. Ignatius firmly resisted these advances. One vocation created a sensation: that of Anthony de Córdoba, son of the Marchioness of Pliego, and brother of the count of Feria. He would play an important role in years to come. Anthony de Córdoba, after Araoz, Borgia . . . it was a characteristic that marked the expansion of the Society in Spain: it recruited at all levels, but the entrance into the Society of some of the aristocrats of Spain contributed not a little to revealing it to the public and to drawing it to the attention of princes and bishops.

GERMANY AND EASTERN EUROPE: The major event was the sending of three companions: Jay, Canisius and Salmeron to the University of Ingolstadt. It was the Duke of Bavaria, William IV, who with the Bishop's agreement took the initiative of calling them; he also obtained the support of the Pope for his request.

The negotiations began in February, and it was at first a matter of only a temporary mission. The departure of the companions, set for August 10, was delayed: it was not easy, even for Ignatius, to wrest Jay from Duke Ercole d'Este, Salmeron from Venice, and Canisius from Nadal! They finally arrived at Ingolstadt, not without having, in passing Bologna, taken the title of doctor. On November 24 and 29, Canisius and Salmeron gave their first lesson: Jay would not give his until the beginning of 1550.

LOUVAIN: Little by little, the group took form, under the "presidency" of Adrianus Adriani,[30] who had been trained for several months in Rome under Ignatius.

PARIS: Would they be able to obtain the "naturalization" of the Society? A campaign was begun just at that time which would restrain even the best friends of the Society, and even Guillaume du Prat. He advised Ignatius to send a professed member of the order to Paris to handle the negotiations in his name and to meet the French cardinals who would be in Rome for the conclave. Despite the situation, the group lacked neither quality nor fervor; they bore the new persecution easily. Ignatius authorized Viola to make his vows as spiritual coadjutor; he even envisaged having Jean Pelletier and Everard Mercurian[31] do so as well; the day before the Feast of the Presentation, they went up to the chapel of

---

[30] We keep the Latin form of this name. The original name is Adriaenssens, which means the "son of Adrian" or the "son of the son of Adrian".

[31] These three "spiritual coadjutors" will later make their solemn profession. One of them, Mercurian, will even be General of the Society.

Montmartre to "renew their vows" (what vows?). Paris interested Ignatius greatly; the opening of the college for day students, of which Messina was the prototype, created a need for competent "instructors" with degrees, and Ignatius hoped that many would train in Paris, according to the *modus parisiensis*.[32]

The year of 1549 opened new horizons for the Society: wasn't there talk of England's possible return to Catholicism? There was also a question of a college in Poland, and of another in Mexico. Another more modest project, although very important for Italy, was the request of the Cardinal of Burgos, John Alvarez of Toledo, to Ignatius for some "visitors" of Corsica. The holy and fiery Landino departed for that island on November 16.

1550

ROME: Let us summarize, because 1550 marked a point of transition in the development of the Society of Jesus. At the beginning of this year, there existed twenty-five established residences, but this number needs qualification because among the nine residences in India (not including Goa), and the three in Portugal, for example, there was little more than name in common. Even in Europe, the types, or if you will, the "levels" of the houses were different: groups, colleges of companions, colleges for day students; "houses of the professed"[33] constituted rather different situations. As for the three "Provinces" (Portugal, Spain, India), each one had its own personality. Moreover, the activity of the Society was deployed in many other regions and in many different ways: the University of Ingolstadt, the apostolate among captive Christians in North Africa, Brazil, the reform in Corsica, etc.: what a lot of variety! There was, however, one single point in common: all these activities wanted, above all, to be missionary in character. However, it became more and more urgent to give the order an institutional charter if they did not want this diversity to turn into little more than disconnected efforts. To this end Ignatius expended considerable effort in 1550.

The work on the constitutions progressed. It was an edited draft that Ignatius would present to a certain number of companions at the end of this year, but he presented it to them to be criticized, corrected and revised according to their observations. This text would not moreover be put into final form until the beginning of September.

---

[32] Cf. DAINVILLE, *La naissance de l'humanisme moderne*, Beauchesne, Paris, 1940.

[33] The expression "domus professorum" is repeated several times in the *Chronicon* of Polanco. See in particular a good definition in *Chron.* 2, p. 135. Cf. ibid., 3, pp. 391, 400, 406, etc.

This *conventus priorum Patrum* was not a general reunion of delegates, a congress or an assembly, although the participants had been called together "for autumn". It would be held, according to circumstances, possibilities of travel for each group, sometimes for each person. The goals of this consultation were precise: to submit to the judgment of the companions the constitutions already completed, to inform each other of the situation of the Society in different countries, to consider "everything that might involve the organization of the Society".

At this assembly, Ignatius would have liked to have present all the "first Fathers" who were still living. Xavier, however, would not be there, nor even a qualified representative from India. Rodríguez finally arrived, through the request of Ignatius and of Rodríguez himself to John III: he would not leave until December 1550, and would not reach Rome until February 8, 1551. Salmeron would not come until January 1551, and Jay would not be there either. On May 31, Ignatius recalled him from Ingolstadt, and sent him to Augsburg, to join Cardinal Truchsess who wanted him for the Diet, which Charles V and Ferdinand, the King of the Romans, attended. Broët seems not to have gone (and therein lies an historical enigma, because he was still at Bologna although he had been invited). Bobadilla was finally expected in Rome in December: in fact, it seems that he did not arrive until March 1551. His position on the document called *Observata Patrum* was clearly different from that of Salmeron, Laynez and Araoz. As far as one can judge, the notes of these three companions date from January through the beginning of February 1551, and those of Bobadilla from March–April; at this time, he spent a few days in Rome.[34] Among the other companions who were called together, Araoz and Torres came from Spain; Nadal, from Sicily. Among the others there were Francisco Strada, Diego Miron, Andrés de Oviedo, Francis de Rojas (who was to leave the community a few years later) and Emmanuel de Sa who was not yet a priest. One notices that Portugal was not represented before the arrival of Rodríguez and that the Spanish participation was on the contrary considerable, especially if one includes therein, as one should, Laynez and Polanco, who then resided in Rome. Moreover, Duke Francis Borgia himself arrived: officially, he came to Rome on business; in fact, it was also to participate in the assembly as a professed (though secret) member of the order. It was even "in his entourage" that the Spanish group traveled. During his stay in Rome, Borgia stayed with all his people at La Strada; he lived there, as much as possible, as a simple religious. He had long and frequent conversations with Ignatius.

[34] Cf. *Const.* I, pp. LXXVII–XC and 390–96.

A dramatic touch: on January 30, 1551, Ignatius profited from the presence in Rome of the *priores Patres* to submit his resignation. All, unanimously, except for the overly obedient Oviedo, kept him in charge.[35]

Another very important event marked this year of 1550: Cardinal del Monte was elected Pope on February 8, under the name of Julius III. It didn't take long to see his benevolence regarding the Society: on June 21 he published the bull *Exposcit debitum* by which he confirmed the Society of Jesus, and renewed all its privileges, even extending them.

About five people lived at La Strada, but the financial situation was serious and it would deteriorate during the ensuing years. During the conclave, Ignatius begged from the cardinals, and on certain days the companions begged in the streets of Rome. When Julius III was elected Pope, he asked Ignatius, under an obligation of obedience, to appraise him if "material resources" were lacking: but he had old debts. Ignatius appealed to Juan de Vega, to John III, and to Borgia. The last-named financed the project of the Roman college and the new church of La Strada (which very fortunately would not be completed).

ITALY AND NAPLES: Broët was still a missionary in Bologna. Coming from Spain to Rome, Borgia encouraged the zeal of Duke Ercole so that he would finally establish the college of Ferrara: the decision was made at the end of the year. He also insisted to the same end with Duke Cosimo de Medici (Florence). At Padua the companions continued to live in a disquieting penury; however, Ignatius decided nothing without the agreement of Andrea Lippomani. As for Bobadilla, he worked courageously in the region of Rosano; several bishops clamored for his help.

SICILY: At Messina, there were thirty companions; twenty at Palermo. The principal work was to teach, but they did missionary work also and kept busy with "pious works"—there were many fine ones. In June the fleet of the army from Africa readied itself: Laynez presented his "conscientious objections" to Juan de Vega who wanted him as chaplain; but Ignatius ordered him to accept. He departed therefore, and worked with success, especially among the sailors and soldiers and among the wounded, the sick and the prisoners. Back in Sicily, he departed for Rome: Ignatius wanted his presence at the assembly in December. The first novitiate of the Society of Jesus not attached to another house had been created at Messina at the beginning of the year; another attempt at Palermo failed at first, but it would be begun again later.

[35] Cf. infra, p. 233.

Two deaths this year befell the family of Juan de Vega: the Viceroy's wife Eleanor died on March 29, then Ferdinand, one of his three sons, in September.

PORTUGAL: At the center of relations between Ignatius and Portugal there was the voyage of Rodríguez to Rome. There was alternate hope and refusal. Finally, in December, the King gave his authorization.

One hundred fifty scholars lived at Coimbra: it was necessary to send a certain number of them to St. Felix nearby. As for Lisbon, the college, through its ministries and its way of life, resembled more and more a "house of the professed".

This year, three companions departed for India (but two departures failed); six for Tètuan, Ceuta and Mazagan [Al-Jadida] where Nuñez with a companion continued to work with the captive Christians under ever more perilous conditions.

SPAIN: Borgia remained the great architect of the developments of the Society. It was at the end of August that he left Gandia for Rome, not without having received his doctorate at the University. At Gandia, the college prospered: there were numerous theologians and solid studies. Everywhere else, the same works and the same opposition as in 1549. The lack of men, and of trained men, made itself felt: at Alcalá, the rector was still a novice; the community of Valladolid was composed almost entirely of novices: they were pauci, it is true, and they organized themselves religiously while awaiting the Constitutions and the Rules.

GERMANY AND EASTERN EUROPE: Canisius, Jay and Salmeron did remarkable work at the University of Ingolstadt. Their teaching was appreciated. However, they realized that if the young Germans were scarcely motivated toward theological studies, it was because their preceding literary and philosophical studies had been very mediocre. Whence the plan of Ignatius to create a college there for day students, where they would teach arts and letters. The death of Duke William obstructed the plan. On May 31, Ignatius sent Jay to the Diet of Augsburg and recalled Salmeron to Rome; Goudanus, a brilliant but depressed individual, replaced them.

COLOGNE: Kessel did all he could to keep this little community alive "according to the beneplacitum" of Ignatius. Nonetheless, difficulties assailed it from all sides, and they were very poor.

LOUVAIN: Because of the opposition of Queen Mary, sister of Charles V, they did not obtain from the Emperor the "naturalization" of the Society, which provided the right to possess and have revenues.

PARIS: There was slight progress: a few of the companions finally entered the house of Guillaume de Prat, called the "House of Clermont"; the "scholarship students" remained at the college of the Lombards. Cardinal de Guise (at the time Cardinal of Lorraine) half-promised Ignatius, at the time of the conclave, "to protect" the Society in France; in effect, upon his return he obtained from King Henry II letters of naturalization, but the legal confirmation of the Parliament, which would give the letters of the King their full effect, did not follow. The group lived in fervor and observed the rules which they had given themselves, with the approval of Ignatius, while awaiting the constitutions from Rome.

Thanks to the progress—although still insufficient—of the correspondence between Rome and the regions of the Society, we are better and better informed of the events, and through them, of the character of Ignatius. His personality provoked the highest admiration: he attracted and edified, but at the same time he astonished and disconcerted; in him extremes met. As the Society developed and had more and more to do with the world, the problem of relationships and finances became more acute. With these developments, the human aspect of Ignatius became more and more sharply defined. The confrontation with earthly interests became more difficult, sometimes violent. However, there emanated from him such a feeling of evangelical mission, such goodness, such total abnegation of self, such an ardent passion for Jesus Christ and his kingdom that even those who suffered his firm authority were obliged to recognize the sincerity of his character and the rectitude of his faith.

1551

ROME: Ignatius, who, as we have said, tried to resign in January of 1551, was maintained in his position.

The year 1551 marked a second wind, or more exactly, an intensification of apostolic zeal in the Society of Jesus. It was the fruit of the assembly of December 1550–February 1551. (Borgia and Laynez did not leave Rome until February 4 and Rodríguez did not arrive there until February 8: the two groups met at Viterbo.)

It seemed in particular that Ignatius had taken a firmer position in favor of "colleges for day students". It was that year that he composed the first rules of the Roman college, which alms left by Borgia had allowed them to launch.

Julius III showed great benevolence toward the Society of Jesus. He increased his favors and privileges to them. Salmeron enjoyed the Pope's personal esteem; he chose Salmeron as well as Laynez, as "theologians of the Pope", for the Council of Trent, which, in accord with Charles V, he wished to reopen in May (in fact, in September). The Pope received before their departure the "colonies" (groups) which Ignatius had sent to Vienna, then to Naples, to found colleges there. Was it this favor of the Pope that pushed Ignatius to plan in November to get the Society of Jesus approved by the Council of Trent? He had spoken about it to Laynez and Salmeron who dissuaded him from it, after having "sounded out" the idea with some prelate friends.[36] These two theologians of the Pope would accomplish work in the thirteenth and fourteenth sessions of the Council, which treated the Eucharist, penance and extreme unction.

In December 1551, Ignatius made an important decision: these *Constitutions* which he had submitted to the Fathers and which he had corrected according to their suggestions, he was going to "declare" (as well as the Rules, so far as they existed), in the different countries. For this task, he chose Nadal.

It was in February that the courses in the humanities (Greek, Latin and Hebrew) were inaugurated at the Roman college: the rector was Jean Pelletier. The developments were rapid despite the poverty of the house and the jealousies of the *ludimagistri*. Soon they even had to move into a more suitable location (from the Via Capitolina they moved close to Santa Maria sopra Minerva). Indefatigable, Ignatius, from the first of August, planned to create a German college. The rumor was circulating in Rome that Borgia had left Ignatius considerable sums and the Romans showed themselves less generous in alms. Ignatius had taken care to separate the finances of the Roman college and those of the house: the scarcity of food and the debts of La Strada were aggravated by this unfortunate reduction of alms.

In 1551, Ignatius addressed more than eight hundred letters to the companions outside Rome. One feels him astonishingly present on all fronts of the Society. On December 5, he created the province of Italy (Rome and Naples not included), and named Paschase Broët provincial. At the end of the year the Portuguese crisis erupted: Rodríguez came to Rome in February and March. At the beginning of April, he departed for Portugal, confirmed by Ignatius in his role of provincial; he arrived there on June 28. In July, Ignatius gave the order to Diego Miron (Rector of Valencia) to go to Portugal and on August 18, named him rector of

---

[36] This approval will be obtained by Laynez at the twenty-fifth session, of December 3, 1563.

Coimbra where he "introduced", says Polanco, "Roman customs".

What happened there then? The Portuguese and Spanish historians are not in agreement. It is nonetheless indisputable that abruptly, on December 31, Ignatius named Miron provincial of Portugal, and on January 1 dismissed Rodríguez from that position. It was undoubtedly the most serious crisis, along with the now imminent one in India that the Ignatian Society ever experienced: both would last until the death of Ignatius and even beyond it.

ITALY AND NAPLES: Several important plans were begun or were completed. At Ferrara, Duke Ercole II kept the promise he had made to Borgia: on June 5, seven companions arrived under the direction of Pelletier (taken from the Roman college) to open the college. At Bologna *scholae* (classes) began in October. In Venice, things gradually improved though Lippomani scarcely cared any more about sustaining the companions who worked there. On February 22, André Frusius, with a few companions, came there to prepare the opening of the college (after Easter). In Padua, the companions were still less numerous this year. In Florence and in Pisa, things were more uncertain: Ignatius wanted to open a college for day students in one of the two cities—preferably in Florence. All during the year Ignatius had numerous discussions with the ducal couple, who equivocated. Even Laynez who stayed at Pisa from February 4 until his departure for Trent (in July), obtained only evasive answers. In October Ignatius decided to put an end to all this beating around the bush. Depending upon the very vague promises of the Duke and the Duchess and the blessing of the Pope, Ignatius sent to Florence a "colony" of twelve companions under the leadership of Louis du Coudret. Florence was a city peopled with humanists and scholars, where the twelve "masters" cut an unimpressive figure. The college began in humility.

Naples, which did not want the return of Bobadilla, requested Laynez and Salmeron. It was Bobadilla, however, who departed in December with a group of twelve, not without first having received the pontifical blessing. Classes would open at the beginning of 1552. The group represented an organization which characterized well the attitude of Ignatius regarding the "first Fathers": Bobadilla was not the rector of the college, it was Oviedo; but Bobadilla did not come under the jurisdiction of Oviedo.

SICILY: The death of the Viceroy's wife, the current events (the Turkish threat) and the departure of some companions of great value (Nadal, Canisius, Frusius, etc.) modified the activity of the companions, but scarcely slowed it down.

Doménech returned to Spain on March 30.

To liberate Sicily, Apulia and Calabria from the incessant pressure of the Turkish fleet, the Viceroy decided upon an expedition into North Africa. With the agreement of Ignatius, Nadal volunteered to accompany him and "to exercise the habitual ministries of the Society"; he even thought of installing two companions in Africa after the conquest of the citadel. On September 19, Ignatius asked him to return to Sicily and on December 19, to return to Rome. Ignatius counted on him to "declare" the *Constitutions* in his name. Ignatius then called him to the solemn profession of his vows.

The two colleges, Messina and Palermo, were going well. The novitiate of Messina was flourishing; as for that of Palermo, after an inauspicious beginning, it had regained life. Works and missions continued, but the Sicilian populace, facing the Turkish threat, earthquakes (Reggio) and famine, returned willingly to ancestral magic and to superstition: the apostolate became more difficult. For Monreale, a plan for a college crystallized. The "Arab college", on the other hand, conceived and financed by the viceroy, failed.

PORTUGAL: The Rodríguez crisis did not yet seem to have touched the companions. One hundred forty students lived at Coimbra, forty of whom were theologians: when Diego Miron arrived there as rector, he was heartily welcomed and his decisions were readily accepted. Domestic missions were active. Prince-cardinal Henry created a college in September at Évora. Nonetheless, whether at the court (where Rodríguez lived with some companions) or in certain houses, one perceived a malaise.

INDIA, JAPAN, BRAZIL: A group of six companions departed in March from Portugal for *India*; there were with them ten "young orphans", raised by the abbé, Pierre Doménech, eventual candidates for the Society, and five "spiritual men", three of whom had been admitted into the Society and would complete their novitiate at sea. The group arrived at Goa on September 5.

Goa, where chaos regarding jurisdictions broke out: who was the rector at Goa? Paul de Camerino, designated by Xavier before his departure for Japan? Anthony Gomez, sent by Rodríguez as Superior two years previously, but who had strained relations with Xavier? or Melchior Nuñez who debarked and had been designated in Portugal as rector? While awaiting the return of Xavier, de Camerino took charge.

Combination post-residences were not lacking in the immense territory covered by Xavier in the last ten years: Goa, Baçaim, Cochin, Chaulan,

São Tomé, Malacca and the Moluccas. For the time being, he had given the order to Barzée to return from Hormuz (where companion would replace him) and to join Xavier in Japan. Everywhere work was over-abundant, everywhere their health was at the breaking point, every-where enormous difficulties, and even danger of death, rose up before the missionaries. Father Melchior Gonzales, who had finally been desig-nated, in the absence of Xavier, to go to inform the authorities of Portugal and Rome, died in Baçaim.

In *Japan*, Xavier continued his mission of exploration during the beginning of 1551: Kagoshima, Hirado and Amanguchi. The chief of Amanguchi gave him authorization to preach the new religion and granted him a monastery where he could live and teach. The King of Bungo called him; during an absence of Xavier, Amanguchi was devas-tated and pillaged. The King of Bungo became the head of it and continued support of Xavier. Toward the end of the year, Xavier returned to India "full of white hair", but in good health and filled with joy. Many things disappointed him in the situation that he found upon his return; he decided upon a few "dismissals". Already, he was preparing his departure for China in 1552.

In *Brazil*, the companions were "itinerants": there were no real com-munities; the "posts" were scarcely more than rest stops for the apostolic trips: Bahia São Salvador, where Emmanuel de Nobrega (who played the role of provincial without the title) worked most often, São Vicente, Porto Seguro, Espírito Santo, Pernambuco and Santo Amaro. The evan-gelization was very difficult because of the customs of the natives; the companions catechized, but rarely baptized. One particular difficulty was the presence of European priests who had been sent to Brazil because they were undesirables in Europe, "demons rather than priests". The more the missionaries went into the interior of the areas, in other words, the farther they went from the places inhabited by the Portuguese colonists, the more the native tribes they met were closer to "the natural law" (this was not always so).

The missionaries had had to withdraw from the *Congo* because the extravagances and the mores of the King left no hope of evangelization.

SPAIN: Ignatius confirmed Araoz in his post as provincial; he even increased his powers. Borgia, on his return from Rome, visited Azpeitia and Loyola, then went to Oñate where a house had been given to the Society. He renounced his title of Duke, and in June received holy orders; he could still not make his solemn profession in public because of the papal indult which authorized him to keep the management of his goods. He resided principally in his hermitage of St. Madeleine, but in fact they called him from all over. On August 1, he celebrated his first Mass at Loyola. From the correspondence one can imagine the "shock" which these first Masses and first sermons of the former Duke of Gandia produced on the population.

Valladolid, Salamanca, Alcalá, Gandia, Valencia, Saragossa, Barcelona developed well. However, at Alcalá the Archbishop of Toledo, Siliceo, fomented trouble against the companions. As for Melchoir Cano, he did not become less virulent. A colony came from Salamanca to establish Medina del Campo. Many vocations appeared, especially in the university cities; but because of the lack of resources, admissions were limited.

Trinity Sunday, May 25, the oldest son of Borgia, the Marquis of Lomba, became the Duke of Gandia. Ignatius soon perceived that relations with the new Duke would not be the same as with Duke Francis.

GERMANY AND EASTERN EUROPE: It was Vienna which was the center of interest that year with the founding of the college for day students. A colony of eleven companions left Rome on April 24, after having presented themselves to the Pope and received his blessing. The welcome of the King of the Romans in Vienna on May 27 was warm. The courses began immediately under very difficult conditions concerning work, food and lodging. This founding of the college of Vienna was typical of the Ignatian tactics for resisting Protestantism: no Catholic reform without reform of the theological studies at the University; but no serious theological studies without a solid basis of literary and philosophical studies. It was the responsibility of the college to assure this first training. At the same time, Ignatius counseled the immediate replacement of *all* the professors of the university who were more or less tainted by the new ideas. Ferdinand I and his counselors opted for a less rigid method. In fact, the companions, by their teaching, their ministries, and the style of their relationships, would little by little win the sympathy of a population which was at first hostile, and even of the professors and students at the university. Vienna, moreover, was far from presenting a homogeneous appearance: if there were a lot of "Germans", one also met Spaniards and Italians. It was a stronghold where troops gathered because the Turkish threat weighed more and more heavily upon Europe, after the victories of Suleiman in Hungary.

A diplomatic game was in progress between Ferdinand I and Albert, Duke of Bavaria. Ferdinand wanted to have Canisius and Goudanus come from Ingolstadt to Vienna, but Jay and Canisius were advocates of a single vigorous college rather than two mediocre colleges. For the time being, the matter was held in abeyance; it was not decided.

COLOGNE: Seventeen companions were reunited under the authority of Kessel who himself was continuing his own studies; they lived in extreme poverty, which the abbess of the monastery of the Eleven Thousand Virgin Martyrs and the prior of the Carthusians alleviated as much as they could. For the moment there was no hope of obtaining legal recognition.

LOUVAIN: The situation was similar to that of Cologne. Without legal recognition, the companions risked expulsion and confiscation of their goods from one day to the next. Charles V and the authorities of Louvain did not seem disposed to accord naturalization: in Flanders religious and colleges were already too abundant. Moreover, false rumors coming from Spain (Siliceo, Cano) were circulating against the Society, and finally, the *votum simplex*[37] of the Society puzzled, in the absence of the Constitutions, the legal advisors of the Emperor.

PARIS: The Parliament still refused to grant the letters of legal recognition, despite the authorization of the King and the agreement of the privy council. The group of companions (an average of fourteen, although two groups of novices had been sent to Rome) lived only by the charity of Guillaume du Prat and the few scholarships of the college of the Lombards; despite the uncertainty of the days ahead, studies and ministries continued to be pursued.

Thus, 1551 appeared like a particularly important year for the young Society. This impression is confirmed by the abundant correspondence: as stated earlier, there were more than eight hundred letters from Ignatius and forty quadrimestrial letters. The small number of letters or documents coming from the *primi Patres* or from other important early collaborators of Ignatius is astonishing, especially since Polanco had divided the Society into three zones of correspondence: Italy (once a week); outside Italy (every month except in personal cases); outside Europe (once a year). This correspondence, moreover, was to be utilized with certain prudence: the distinction between "open" letters and confidential letters was maintained; the "open" letter was an edifying letter,

---

[37] A type of vow which, the novitiate ended, scholastics and temporal coadjutors pronounced, and which was not a solemn vow, even though it was perpetual. The General had the power to release them from it.

one could say, a letter for publicity purposes; nothing that was reported therein was false, but there were silences which are very annoying for the historian. These archives are, nonetheless, valuable as they are. As the administration took a more active role in the governing of the Society, and became involved with more delicate matters, Ignatius' character became more sharply defined. He was indisputably a man of great gifts, but one who also had limits, idiosyncratic reactions and his own temperament: he appeared more and more like someone who carried within him, in the manner of St. Paul, even in his infirmities a certain "power of God". The "reading" of such a complex individual reveals itself to be difficult in many situations.

1552

ROME: In 1552, the Society experienced a sort of growth crisis, one could say, of outlook. The *Constitutions* began to be known in certain regions, and a certain "selection process" operated among the companions. The majority entered fully into the spirit of this charter, but in other areas, Ignatius was obliged to intervene to recall some to obedience, to poverty and to community life: he did so with lucidity and tenacity.

One important point must, however, be noted: although Ignatius already hoped to have them printed, the *Constitutions* of 1550 did not have the force of law; they remained experimental. They would surely need revisions, amendments and corrections. Moreover, the *observata quatuor patrum*[38] demanded them, and Ignatius continued to work on the *Constitutions*. But already the *Constitutions* lent some unity to the scattered companions, and that was urgent. Once printed, the *Constitutions* would not be "sent". Nadal would go to declare them locally in each spot; and, as much as circumstances would permit, he would put them into practice.[39] He began in Sicily, which proved to be an auspicious place to start.

---

[38] *Const.* 1, pp. 390–96.

[39] A very clear example of the clarifications is given by the Constitutions: Whoever has tried to specify the different categories of "vows" which up to that point the candidates could make before their entrance, during their novitiate, and after their novitiate, has experienced the feeling of maneuvering in a virgin forest. It was not entirely like that from 1551 on. The letter which on February 9, Polanco addressed in the name of Ignatius to Father Adriani is of such clarity that it leaves nothing to be desired: the three types of vows are therein perfectly defined and distinguished. Impossible to confuse them with "the vow to enter the Society" made prior to entry: a vow of pure devotion, a private vow, of which the Society as such had no need of knowledge (cf. *Epist. ign.* 12, p. 306, n. 48).

Ignatius closely followed the progress of the Council of Trent, where Laynez and Salmeron were being noticed because of their position as "the Pope's theologians". The fourteenth session was hardly finished, when they began active preparation for the fifteenth. Everything seemed ready for this session to be held on January 25, when an unexpected incident occurred to trouble and finally to interrupt the Council. The Protestant theologians, invited to the January 24 discussion, declared that the Council was "neither free, nor universal, nor Christian". Consequently, the fifteenth session was postponed in order to resolve this dispute. During this time however, the elector Maurice of Saxony, supported by France, had revolted against Charles V, beaten the imperial army and seized Innsbruck. The Fathers of the Council, feeling threatened, began to leave Trent. On April 15, Julius III once again suspended the Council. On June 11, Ignatius named Laynez provincial of Italy, as a replacement for Broët who took charge of the group and the work in Paris. Salmeron came back to Florence, but in October he replaced Bobadilla in Naples.

The *Spiritual Exercises* gained wider and wider circulation. They were truly the primary tool of the apostolate and, consequently, of recruitment. Ignatius sent copies of them to friends and to benefactors. Any candidate for the Society was to do them either before, or a few months after, being admitted.

Despite exterior contradictions and interior crises, the Society had such renown (*bonus odor Societatis*) that after the Theatines, it was the Somaschi who proposed a merger. Ignatius refused with the same firmness as before. The benevolence of the Pope did not diminish. During the entire year, Julius III supported the plan to raise Borgia to the rank of cardinal and Ignatius failed in his attempts to help Borgia avoid this honor. On June 5, Ignatius wrote to Borgia, leaving the final decision up to him. This letter was very characteristic of the manner in which Ignatius proceeded in such delicate circumstances.[40] By the end of the year, the danger seemed to have been averted. On October 22, the Pope wrote the brief *Sacrae religionis* in which he granted new privileges to the Society, he accorded in general the favor, which was very rare, of conferring academic grades to students inside and outside the Society's universities.

Two very hard blows fell this year on the *primi Patres*: the death of Jay (August 6) in Vienna, and the death of Xavier on the Island of Sancian (December 2). Confirmation of this death did not reach Ignatius until two years later: during this time Ignatius had continued to write to Xavier.

---

[40] *Epist. ign.* 4, pp. 283–85, no. 2652.

In Rome, that year, besides the *ministeria assueta* two important events occurred:

First, at the Roman college (three hundred pupils and twenty-five students of the Society) the first solemn "Act" took place on October 28 in the church of St. Eustace. It was a novice, Dr. Martin Olave, who presided.[41] From this year on, the arts and theology began to be taught in addition to the "three languages". The second event to note is the creation of the German college: Cardinal Morone supported the project with fervor, and Julius III got much satisfaction from it. The material and financial organization was quickly disposed of: they expected one hundred young men, but at the beginning they admitted only thirty or forty. Almost all, to the great regret of Ignatius, were natives of northern Germany; on November 21, the first of eight pupils took their vows.

The novices were numerous at La Strada. There were candidates from Italy, France, Flanders and Germany, but also novices already admitted and already "tested" in regions like Spain and Sicily, which had regular novitiates. They had come to train under the personal supervision of Ignatius. The recruitment in certain regions concerned Ignatius: the need for men, especially for the colleges, caused haste and a lack of rigor which were contrary to the "general welfare" of the Society. In his correspondence Ignatius insisted on two apparently incompatible points: that they seek recruits, but that they be severe in their choice of candidates; he also asked that among those admitted, there be further selection for those being sent to La Strada. Finally, he announced, first for the Roman college, but also for the other cities, that no pupil of the day colleges would be admitted into the Society without the formal authorization of his parents.

Two of Ignatius' personal decisions should be remembered: in August he refused to attend the weddings of Lawrence of Loyola and of John, the second son of Francis Borgia at Loyola (Francis attended). From November 2 through 12, Ignatius went with Polanco to Alvito (on the border of the kingdom of Naples) to attempt a new reconciliation between Joan of Aragon and Ascanio Colonna. On this trip Ignatius preached, taught and heard confessions, as he had during his time in Venice; he worked as a missionary.

ITALY AND NAPLES: On June 11, Laynez, freed from the Council of Trent, was named provincial of upper Italy; in November-December,

---

[41] Martin Olave, chaplain of Charles V, had entered the Society two months previously. His participation in the Council of Trent did not pass unperceived. His entrance was announced as an important event to all the houses by letters from Ignatius-Polanco.

Viola, freed from Paris by the arrival of Broët, would be named "commissioner of Italy", working with Laynez.

In 1552, three new colleges were founded in Italy: Perugia requested one through Cardinal Fulvio della Corna and the local bishop. (A dozen companions under the direction of Everard Mercurian left Rome on foot in June, begging, preaching and hearing confessions. Before their departure, they received the blessing of Julius III.) Gubbio (at the request of the Cardinal of St. Croix, a colony of eight companions began courses on November 3); Modena (at the request of Cardinal Morone, Duke Ercole, the Bishop and friends, but also at the insistence of Father Sylvester Landini who had been a fervent missionary in the area for some time). At Padua, the companions began classes in September for day pupils. All these activities brought about transfers of personnel; moreover, Ignatius was obliged to transfer the excellent personnel from the regional colleges for the Roman and German colleges. When he recalled Frusius, for example, Laynez protested and Ignatius reacted, which resulted in admirable letters from both of them. In the name of Ignatius, Polanco wrote to Laynez: "The chaff is mixed with good grain, even in the Society. The Lord knows those who belong to him and those alone constitute the Society."

In Venice-Padua the situation was unchanged. In Ferrara, the departure for Paris on June 2 of Paschase Broët, who had worked there for twelve years, was sorely felt. In Bologna, the college prospered, but modestly. As for Florence, the college founded in 1551 was developing in extreme penury. Salmeron went there after the suspension of the Council of Trent; when Ignatius sent him to Naples, Laynez, already overwhelmed with work, took his place.

In Naples, the college (five professors, three hundred pupils) lived in great poverty. They had more to contend with than their poverty, however, because the division of authority between Bobadilla and Oviedo was badly defined. Finally, the crisis struck; it was even more serious because Bobadilla was considered undesirable by the authorities in Naples. The Duke of Monteleone invented an unusual solution; he proposed to Ignatius that Bobadilla go away for two months to do missionary work on his lands and then that Salmeron replace him later. Ignatius accepted this suggestion. After the two months of missionary work were up, Ignatius gave Bobadilla a free rein to go "anywhere he felt called, in the whole kingdom of Naples, provided that he not cross its borders". Salmeron and Oviedo quickly put things to rights at the college.

SICILY: Nadal left Sicily January 31. On February 1, Jerónimo Doménech, who was in Spain on family business, was named Provincial of Sicily. In fact, Doménech would not depart from Valencia for Rome until August 25, and he would not arrive in Sicily until the end of the year. It was Nadal who, after a two month stay in Rome where he made his profession on March 25, returned to Sicily, and it was not until the arrival of Doménech that he could finally begin to announce the *Constitutions*. Nadal would not leave the big island until very early in 1553. From this visit he would draw up a critical report on the *Constitutions* which would be completed before October 6, 1553.

The burning of Reggio by the Turkish fleet, the permanent threat of Islam which weighed upon Sicily and the southern Italian coasts, suggested an audacious plan to Ignatius: that Charles V should equip a fleet to annihilate the sea power of the Turks in the Mediterranean. Ignatius was anticipating the Battle of Lepanto by twenty years. Polanco sent this report to Nadal on August 6.

PORTUGAL: The Portuguese crisis would take up the whole year of 1552: a veritable imbroglio of orders and counter-orders, of letters which did not arrive, or arrived too late, of decisions and the failure to implement them, confused communication among Rodríguez, Miron, Torres and Borgia. An almost insoluble situation was created, which was complicated by the slowness of couriers and of travel. What was certain was that this time Ignatius was deeply upset: "Who is the provincial?" he wrote to Câmara on September 1, and "How was the change made?" The provincial of Portugal, or rather the visitor of Portugal, was definitely Michael de Torres, whom Ignatius had named on January 1. The province of Aragon which he had created and conferred upon Rodríguez still existed, but Rodríguez had not gone there; the companions of Portugal, especially the scholars of Coimbra, were greatly upset; the others, especially the missionaries, took the shock better. The friends of the Society were discountenanced; the rumor even circulated that the Society in Portugal was going to be dissolved. Fortunately, John III did not desert Ignatius. He even asked Câmara (who refused) and Miron (who managed to avoid it also) to be his confessor. Such a crisis could not go without departures or dismissals: the result was even more troubling in that those who "left" continued to work, and often to work well, in the area. The recall of Torres in November would bring back a little peace to their minds, but the crisis would continue into 1553.

INDIA: This year the missionary martyrology of the Society, begun by Criminali, would be increased by yet another name: Louis Mendez (at Comorin). At the end of December 1551 Xavier unexpectedly arrived at

Goa. He redesigned the whole missionary structure of India in light of the manpower which he had at his disposal and of their experience—taking into account those who had died as well as those who had been sent away.[42] Many companions asked to be sent to Japan and China, in the hope of martyrdom. The file of letters which he wrote to Europe or even in India, between April 6 and 14, upon the eve of his great departure, should be analyzed line by line if one wishes to know the mind and heart of Xavier, particularly the "instructions" which he left to Gaspard Barzée, whom he named Vice-Provincial and Rector of Goa (until Ignatius should decide). Gaspard Barzée, a magnificent type of missionary, began to work with such ardor that he fell ill and died, but as a result "things got moving in Goa".

The mission developed, but at the cost of what suffering! Hormuz was besieged by the Turkish fleet in September. Cochin and Cape Comorin with its sixty thousand Christians were spread out over fifty leagues of coast. Ceylon, far from the eyes of the Viceroy, was rife with misappropriation of public funds, depraved customs and injustices. Then there was Coromandel (São Tomé) where "outside the core of apostles there was nothing good". Malacca, the great cosmopolitan market place, was spied upon and coveted by powerful neighbors. Ternate, Amboina, and the Mauri Islands were full of captivity, tortures and the "miracles" of Juan de Beira. . . . This was an epic written by men whom no obstacle would stop. Opposite these heroes, the miseries of the others pale in comparison: they do not count.

In Japan, evangelization continued, apparently quietly but not without opposition. This relative calm was due to the benevolence of the King of Bungo and Amanguchi.

SANCIAN: After having regulated everything in Goa as if he would never return and having sent Father Andrew Fernandez with two Japanese (of whom one, Matthew, died in Goa before leaving, and the other, Bernard, would die in Europe before returning to India), Xavier left on April 17 for China. His voyage was reminiscent of those of St. Paul. At Sancian, he tried in vain to find merchants who would transport him to Canton. In October and November he wrote letters to Goa, Malacca, etc., which showed with what courage and what wisdom he carried the weight of India, Japan and China. On December 2, worn out, he died at Sancian, alone.

---

[42] No missionary was sent this year from Portugal. The fleet underwent formidable tempests: four ships out of six arrived in Goa.

BRAZIL: Nobrega's group had recourse to desperate activity: the schools showed themselves to be the only way to make progress in evangelization: even then the progress was precarious. The setting did not make perseverance easy.

THE CONGO: In 1550 the missionaries who had not been able to obtain authorization to preach the gospel had had to reembark for Portugal: it was a failure. But King John III was planning at the time to remove the deranged King and to confer the whole spiritual responsibility for this territory upon the Society. Two companions departed at the height of the Rodríguez crisis.

SPAIN: January 1, Ignatius divided the province of Spain: on one side, the province of Castile (with Araoz for Provincial), and on the other, the province of Aragon, to which were attached the kingdom of Valencia and the principality of Catalonia, which he conferred upon Simón Rodríguez. In fact, the two provinces would remain under the administration of Araoz for the whole year. Rodríguez actually did not return to his post, except for a brief period of time.

The opposition of Archbishop Siliceo increased. As early as January 1, Ignatius had believed it his duty to make an appeal to the Pope. In the course of the year, the Nuncio Poggio and the legate of the Pope in Spain tried to arrange things amiably in the local area. Ignatius wanted more: investigation and judgment in Rome. Villanova, the rector, tried to the best of his ability to get along with Siliceo, Poggio and Ignatius.

Borgia's home base was the hermitage of St. Madeleine, near Oñate, but he preached, heard confessions and gave the Spiritual Exercises in the whole region. His influence was very great. Then came the order which sent him to Portugal; Ignatius actually feared that the court and the nobility of Lisbon would take Rodríguez's side. Borgia departed as a pilgrim on March 19; actually, he did not reach Portugal and returned in summer to the province of Guipúzcoa.

The Society experienced rapid growth in Spain. Numerous candidates presented themselves, some of whom were of great worth. Anthony de Córdoba entered the Society officially, at the time when Julius III, at the request of Charles V, was preparing to name him a Cardinal. Salamanca, Medina del Campo, Valladolid, Burgos, Alcalá (whose rector at least during the first months was still not ordained as a priest), Valencia, Barcelona and Gandia—all these posts were developing. Saragossa, however, remained "weak"; the group there was small in number and, confronted with opposition, they even thought of withdrawing.

Provincial Araoz was a very active man despite his poor health. The Rodríguez affair, with the inevitable backwash that it created, even in

Spain, weighed upon Araoz. He did not understand the reasons for some of Ignatius' measures; the division of Spain into two provinces displeased him. His relations with Torres were not easy: Araoz reproached Torres for not having enough *modus procedendi Societatis*.

GERMANY AND EASTERN EUROPE: At *Ingolstadt*, Ignatius made a decisive move. Since Duke Albert had not consented to create a college for day students as Ignatius had requested, the latter, supported by the Pope's wishes and family relations which linked Duke Albert to the King of the Romans, decided to withdraw from Ingolstadt Canisius, Goudanus and the three novices from Louvain who had joined them. Ignatius sent them as reinforcements to Vienna. Their departure took place on February 28.

Vienna: The community was active and animated (after the arrival of the group from Ingolstadt, it was composed of twenty-five members); the companions were of different nationalities and could work effectively in this city with a cosmopolitan population: Hungarian refugees, Italian workers, French and Spanish soldiers and local Germans. However, here once again the division of authority (between Jay and the rector Lanoye) made the situation difficult. Canisius worked with ardor at the *Compendium theologiae* which Ignatius and the King of the Romans had requested from him: the work was not finished, but many already used it, read it in the courts, cited it and used it for sermons. On August 6, Jay died: Lanoye was elected in his place and Ignatius ratified the election. At the end of the year, plague ravaged the city: the companions remained there and devoted themselves to the service of the population: the ill, the soldiers and the prisoners. Vocations presented themselves "to be Jesuits" (it seems that it was at this time that the word was applied to the companions, at least in Germany).

Cologne: The situation was unchanged. However, in the course of the year, a crisis shook the little community. Kessel, called to profession, went to his own country to arrange family business. When he returned, he found his fold in revolution; he did not hesitate to dismiss nine of his fourteen companions. Evidently, the opening of the German college in Rome had raised high hopes in Cologne. However, neither the Archbishop nor the civil authorities officially recognized the Society.

PARIS: The group was small and poor: the hostility of the Parliament and of the faculty of theology bothered the companions very much and left them little hope of obtaining the ratification of royal authorization. Broët came to replace Viola, who seemed overwhelmed by the situation.

As the correspondence becomes more and more copious, it becomes ever more valuable. From this particular year date several very significant "instructions"—whether to groups leaving for colleges, to an individual companion entrusted with a delicate mission (Corsica), or to those making a voyage. More and more, the contrast in Ignatius between spiritual director and administrator reveals itself. In both, however, he was punctilious. Grandeur and minutiae! One fact that we should remember about 1552 is the similarity in the reactions of Ignatius and of Xavier in all that concerned obedience; despite the distances and the differences in the situations, their severity was the same.

It seems that there was at that time throughout the Society—more or less accentuated according to the regions—a diffuse crisis of obedience and poverty. The *faciano come potranno* of a letter of Ignatius to a companion[43] was perhaps more than a passing mood—and actually a private confidence!

1553

ROME: If one judges from the official correspondence, 1553 would seem to be an auspicious year for the Society; however, perils, persecutions, difficulties and even dissensions between some companions would not be lacking. Certainly, the mission of Nadal and that of Borgia in Portugal would finally reestablish a certain peace in the troubled province; but was the crisis resolved? Were the differences among Miron, Polanco, Borgia, Torres, Câmara, and even Ignatius resolved? In India, in addition to Xavier, three other companions of great worth had died and the members in Europe would not know of it until much later. Those who had been ousted by Xavier returned to Portugal and found there those who had left or been dismissed because of the Rodríguez affair. In northern Italy, the colleges for day pupils were having financial difficulties and sometimes sanitary problems which affected studies, health and even vocations. Cologne, Louvain and Paris did not obtain legal recognition, and in Paris the situation worsened because the Parliament sent back the file of the Society to the faculty of theology. To the attacks of Cano and Siliceo was added at the time a censure in Spain of the Exercises by the Dominican Thomas de Pedroche. (The Spiritual Exercises were the symbol of the formation of the apostolate of the companions.) The health of Ignatius underwent a severe crisis from April on. Ignatius knew all this, observed all this, but through all these obstacles, he went forward tenaciously.

[43] *Epist. ign.* 4, p. 528, n. 3052.

The work on the *Constitutions* changed form, but it continued: at this time, they corrected and improved the text of 1550–1551. The version which Nadal had used in Portugal already incorporated many amendments, and Ignatius, aided by Polanco, still consulted, annotated and worked: Nadal declared the *Constitutions* in Portugal, then in Spain. Many of Ignatius' letters to the rectors or superiors clarified obscure points. The famous letter on obedience, dated March 26, 1553, was sent to the students at Coimbra. It was a veritable blueprint on obedience, but one which must be placed in its context, if one is to give it its proper weight in relation to preceding and succeeding documents on the general doctrine of the *Constitutions*, the "praxis" of Ignatius, and the circumstances which provoked it.

According to a letter from Polanco to Xavier (of whose death the former did not know),[44] the Society then included nine hundred eighty members. Twenty had made their profession; in addition, there were the *primi Patres*. The figures indicated by this letter are differently interpreted by historians, but the size remains constant.

The year 1553 abounded in facts and documents which teach us about certain aspects of the Ignatian mentality: his penchant for increasing the number of responsible people when situations called for it (Portugal); or again, his sense of timing concerning professions: in Portugal he ordered Nadal to ordain, in the midst of the crisis, five or six professed whom he should choose from among the most solid and most faithful companions. He asked Xavier to leave behind him seven or eight professed because Ignatius had called Xavier back to Europe. Many of these measures and decisions were aimed at confirming or keeping the Society's original identity. Thus, he refused a new proposal of a merger with the Theatines. In the midst of great financial difficulties, he bought the house called the "Roscian Tower", and some other small houses around La Strada (worth six hundred gold pieces) intended primarily to endow the Roman society with a spacious and comfortable church, which at that time was indispensable for a religious order in Rome. The church, begun in 1550, was falling apart: a new plan was in progress.[45]

The Roman college was doing very well. Its public meetings enjoyed great success. The new courses in the arts and theology were being set up. Ignatius sought to make them a model (*specimen*) for other colleges and universities belonging to the Society. However, moves and construction expenses burdened him with debt and it was necessary to

---

[44] Letter of July 30, *Epist. ign.* 5, p. 269, n. 3604.
[45] *Chron.* 3, p. 13.

provide for the expenses of the teaching; Ignatius called the different sectors of the Society to his aid. The college in Germany was in the same straits. According to the agreements with Cardinal Morone and Cardinal von Truchsess, the Society did not have financial responsibility for the college, but what would happen if the eminent cardinals did not keep their promises? Moreover, the choice of first pupils was not always fortuitous: it was necessary to dismiss a few students.

The recruitment of the Society itself preoccupied Ignatius: one could enter the order and one could also leave too easily. He worked locally or by correspondence to sustain several shaky vocations. He also analyzed the motivations of those departing: the overload of the students in certain colleges, combined here or there with the too-temporary aspect of the installations and a too-heroic poverty were not unaccountable for this instability. Ignatius tried to improve the situation by establishing "the Rule of Fourteen" for the foundings of new colleges: that is to say, by rejecting all plans which did not include in its clauses a "sure income", assuring the upkeep of fourteen companions. It was a prudent rule, too prudent for a missionary order: Ignatius would be the first to depart from it.

On May 23, Luis Gonçalves da Câmara arrived in Rome from Portugal. He had been chosen to inform Ignatius of the real situation in the troubled province. At the end of August, he obtained Ignatius' permission to write about the latter's life; it was the beginning of the *Autobiography*; the "dictation" went on until September, not without resistance on Ignatius' part. The *Autobiography*, however, is perhaps the most precious and reliable document that we possess on his life and spiritual experiences.

ITALY AND NAPLES: 1553 was for the colleges of *Italy*, with rare exceptions (Ferrara for example, where Maria del Gesso increased her alms but monopolized Rector Pelletier), a difficult year as a result of poverty which bordered on abject misery; this excessive scarcity was no good for community life. Laynez, sick, overburdened with work and worry, and, it must be said, tired of observing the spiritual mediocrity of certain subjects whom Rome sent to him (who soon would have to leave the Society or be discharged from it), was driven to the point of asking Ignatius to relieve him of his duties as provincial. Ignatius refused and tried to lighten the burden of his faithful companion a little by giving him Viola as an assistant. However, Viola was also ill and it was necessary to relieve him of the assignment in December. Let us not, however, paint too gloomy a picture: many of the companions were doing very good work. Despite the difficulties caused by Duke Cosimo de Medici and the capricious Duchess of Florence, Laynez himself was able to resolve the matter concerning the college of Genoa. If Gubbio faded to the point that they thought of transferring the college to Montepulciano, Mercurian succeeded well at Perugia. At Padua and at Venice the companions worked successfully. At Bologna, where things had first gone well, everything deteriorated little by little, because Ignatius had too frequently changed the men in charge. At Ferrara, Pelletier was well thought of at the court—too well, thought Laynez and Ignatius—but his "favor" with the dukes facilitated many things. It was Modena which caused the most anxiety. Cesar de Aversa was an inadequate rector; moreover, a persecution was harshly afflicting the group; finally, the environment was so unhealthful that several companions fell ill and some died. Cesar de Aversa himself died in November. Ignatius had to threaten to withdraw the group if authorities did not put more healthful quarters at their disposal.

Naples: Salmeron enjoyed great personal prestige, but difficulties were not lacking: the vocation of Octavio Cesare, the son of the secretary of the Duke of Monteleone, particularly, created some disturbance: the affair went as far as the Pope. One companion, Father de la Goutte, fell into the hands of Moslems. Ignatius demanded that everything be done to liberate and to ransom him, but the captive died just at the moment when the negotiations were about to succeed. As for Bobadilla, he continued his unusual existence which gave him complete satisfaction, but worried others. Ignatius knew his man and did not overreact.[46]

SICILY: The benevolence of Juan de Vega did not diminish. Even the exchange of Nadal with Doménech (in March) was accepted by him with good grace. It is true that Ignatius proved generous toward Sicily: on two occasions he sent colonies of twelve or fourteen companions there. The novitiates of Messina and Palermo were flourishing; the colleges were well thought of: two of the sons of Juan de Vega studied at Messina. Other plans were again elaborated by Juan de Vega or by his daughter Elizabeth, who married the Count of Luna (Duke of Bivona). However, where would they find the money and men for all these enterprises? There was a question of a college in Majorca, and of another Arabic-speaking one in Malta.

PORTUGAL: The situation did not resolve itself except little by little under the influence of Miron and Torres, but especially under that of

---

[46] Cf., for example, *Epist. ign.* 6, pp. 13–14, n. 3956.

Borgia and Nadal. Nadal arrived in Portugal on July 11, Borgia on August 16. Nadal departed on December 23,[47] Borgia at the end of September.[48] Provincial Miron and the Visitor Torres were already in Portugal. That made a lot of authority in the same territory. Nadal declared the Constitutions, separated the house of the missionaries and the college at Lisbon, and the novitiate and the college of Coimbra. He organized and "stabilized" Evora, studied a project for a college at Compostella; and proceeded on October 1 to Lisbon for a solemn ceremony wherein the companions took or renewed their vows, each according to his status. All this activity on the part of Nadal clarified the situation and renewed confidence. The friends of the Society rejoiced; the demands for colleges and missions multiplied.

The balance sheet of the crises, departures and dismissals was not encouraging. In July, one hundred five companions remained in Portugal. The dissidents dreamed of founding a new Society. The King dissuaded them. For Ignatius, the refusals and equivocations of Simón Rodríguez were very painful: he was torn between his friendship for his former companion of the early days and what he thought to be his duty as Superior General. Should he expel Simón Rodríguez from the Society? Rodríguez finally arrived in Rome on October 10.

However, the crisis did not slow down the missionary zeal of the faithful companions: fourteen departed that year for India and Brazil. And then the preparations for the Ethiopian mission caught their imaginations. John Nuñez, the apostle of the Christian captives of "Mauritania" was chosen as patriarch, Andrés de Oviedo (Rector of Naples) and Melchior Carneiro as bishops and eventual successors of the Patriarch; Quadros was designated as the future Provincial of Ethiopia. This plan, however, would be inaugurated only in 1555 after the death of Julius III.

INDIA: Ignatius, believing Xavier was still alive, recalled him to Europe, with the permission of the Pope. Why this recall? Historians disagree about it. Ignatius wrote also to Barzée to ask him to prepare himself for the Ethiopian mission. Barzée too was dead. Two other excellent missionaries were also dead: Emmanuel de Morales (Comorin) and Christopher Ribero (Amboina).

"In the first months of the year", the body of Xavier was brought back to Malacca, but at that time there was no companion in the city.

---

[47] His departure was delayed one month by the revolt of Don Theotonio of Braganza, an ardent supporter of Rodríguez.

[48] Not without having invented for Princess Jean and the ladies of the court the "game of cards of virtue" which would have Ignatius' approval.

Accordingly, when the two companions sent to Europe by Xavier arrived in Lisbon in September, they themselves did not know of the death of Xavier. It was Melchior Nuñez who would learn the news on Cormorin and would write to Ignatius in 1554.

The mission continued with the same heroism and the same miseries.

JAPAN: Three companions departed on February 4 for Bungo. Despite the obstinate opposition of the local leaders, a community of Christians of seven hundred was born and continued to increase. At Amanguchi, the Christians were less numerous but the development continued. Hope was in the air.

THE CONGO: Of the three companions sent to the Congo, two died. Cornelio Gomez alone remained among unexpected difficulties: the King was a roué, if not a madman.

BRAZIL: Nobrega showed himself to be a great missionary. He adapted evangelization to the conditions of the country. His ideas on confession, pagan rites, integration of the popular traditions into Christian ceremonies, etc., were ahead of his time. Confronted with the scandals and injustices of the Portuguese colonists and soldiers, did he not go as far as dreaming of creating a purely native city, a sort of Brazilian "reservation" prior to those of Paraguay? He was not afraid to forge into the interior of the country to meet the tribes that were still not contaminated by Europeans. However, in all this, he ran up against the misunderstanding of the Bishop: the relations between them were extremely strained. In 1553, he received a reinforcement of seven companions. Although there were scarcely thirty missionaries, Ignatius raised Brazil to a province and named Nobrega (who was not yet professed) provincial.

SPAIN: The province of Castile included: Alcalá, Burgos, Medina del Campo, Salamanca and Valladolid; and the province of Aragon was comprised of Barcelona, Gandia, Oñate, Saragossa and Valencia. These "residences" were of different importance: if there were twenty-three companions at Medina, there were only six at Valladolid, and four at Barcelona. The year went well, despite Siliceo and Cano. The problems that year were at the level of the superiors: the Rodríguez affair could not help having repercussions in Spain, especially in the province of Castile. Araoz, the Provincial, who had the opportunity of meeting Rodríguez, was inclined to a certain indulgence toward him and a certain severity toward Torres. These were silent differences, but they displeased Ignatius: in October, Araoz, in a letter to Rome, had to reveal his precise feelings.[49]

At Medina, Borgia also met Rodríguez who was going to Rome and he begged Ignatius to welcome him *qua solitus est benignitate* (with his customary kindness).

Moreover, between Araoz and Borgia relations were delicate: both were well established at court; they were consulted about affairs of the kingdom, and Borgia begged for alms· for the indebted Roman houses. In addition, Ignatius willingly consulted him on the status of the Society in Spain. These difficulties between the two men became further complicated by the presence of Nadal who came in the role of a messenger to declare the *Constitutions*, and to whom, for this mission, Ignatius had given "full authority".

GERMANY AND EASTERN EUROPE: *Vienna* first: to open the college, the companions, on the advice of Ignatius, acted boldly: the university, greatly riddled with heresy including even the faculty of theology, fiercely opposed this plan and the royal council, intimidated, plotted. The Bishop of Laibach himself, previously so much in favor of the companions, began to hesitate. The companions went ahead. It was an immediate success.

The students came to class with "magnificent catechisms"—Lutheran ones. Canisius, whose influence continued to grow (as the usual homilist to the King, earmarked for a bishopric), hastily began to write his "abbreviated catechism": it was dictated in the classes even before it was finished, and the students took it home with them.

Canisius and Goudanus entered the professional corps of the faculty of theology: they felt ill at ease there. The King and many other people well understood the necessity of reforming the university, but they wondered how to accomplish it.

Duke Albert, however, gave new life to the plan for a college at Ingolstadt. To Ferdinand, who was upset about it, Ignatius promised that in any circumstances, he would not reassign anyone from Vienna to Ingolstadt. However, the Cardinal of Augsburg himself was asking that Canisius participate in the upcoming Diet at which Charles V would be present.

At *Cologne* that year there were war and plague. There were no courses at the university: the students were sent off to other academies. The companions remained there to care for the ill.

LOUVAIN: The Emperor and the Provincial Estates kept trying to foist off on each other the responsibility for refusal of naturalization.

[49] *Epist Mixt.* 3, pp. 567–569 and 594, n. 694 and 706.

PARIS: Broët was the only priest with some students. At the request of Guillaume du Prat, he went to do missionary work for some time in Auvergne. One event would have dire consequences: the Parliament of Paris relinquished the file on the Society of Jesus and transferred it to the faculty of theology, which was even more hostile to the Society than the Parliament. There were seven months of futile discussions. Finally, under the pretext of the plague, they gave the file to Broët. Before the group of companions had to disperse, Broët, with Claysson and Le Bas, left for Auvergne: Guillaume du Prat wanted a college at Billom.

Two large "missions" were conducted in Europe as they had been "in India": first, in Corsica, by Sylvester Landini and Emmanuel de Montemajor. They were "messengers of the Holy See". They were very badly received by a large part of the local clergy and a few Capuchins. Moreover, the Turkish fleet was incessantly threatening the island. To sustain them in these difficulties they had the support of Governor Don James de Matra, a man "who scared the Turks themselves". The religious situation of the island was totally deplorable. Thanks to their zeal (sometimes intemperate) the two missionaries effected a real religious and social transformation. They even ended a few vendettas. The other "mission" had been developing from the autumn of 1552, in Graubünden with Morbegno as the center. The Bishop, inclined to heresy, was obliged to leave the city "so as not to be killed by the Catholics". Andrew Galvanello corrected the situation as well as could be expected. But what would happen if he departed, as Ignatius asked? From postponement to postponement, he would remain in the area until the end of the year.

It was in 1553, under the pressure of Peter de Zarate, grand master of the Order of the Holy Sepulchre, that the founding of three colleges—at Jerusalem, Constantinople and Cyprus—was decided. This triple founding was very well accepted by the Holy See, and Ignatius supported it strongly. On March 8, 1554, the bull *Pastoralis officii* which founded the Archconfraternity of the Holy Sepulchre would be very solemnly promulgated at Santa Maria Sopra Minerva in the presence of twenty-four cardinals. However, the distance between the planning stages and their realization was great.

As the distances that separated the companions grew larger, the human aspect of their activities became more evident in their correspondence. Ignatius himself was caught in the middle, and he reacted characteristically. But over and above all these "affairs" he forced himself to maintain what Polanco called "the simplicity which the first Fathers used among themselves": their simplicity, that is to say, their unique passion for God and for souls, their zeal, worthy of any test, and their concern for the glory of God. Nothing, it seemed, could disconcert him, neither success nor failure, neither friendship nor opposition nor calumny. He remained incapable of being flustered. This steadfast man in his little house in La Strada seized events on the wing, which he took as signs of God, pushed his companions forward, sustained them in battles, sometimes even in hopeless ones. He was the soul of this immense missionary movement.

1554

ROME: The work on the Constitutions continued. The observations that Nadal had gathered in the course of his trips to Portugal and to Spain, after Sicily, were examined with close attention by Ignatius and Polanco. At the same time, Ignatius was constrained to face serious matters, some of which did not come within the normal purview of the Constitutions: the "trial" in Rome of Simón Rodríguez, the Ethiopian expedition with all its complex aspects, his own replacement when illness would prevent him from assuming the responsibilities of General (in April he instituted a "council" of four Fathers; in November, he proceeded to the election of a Vicar General, Nadal), the terrible Decree of the faculty of theology of Paris (December)[50], the designation of the newly professed to better balance the Society, a penury in the Roman missions which bordered on famine or bankruptcy, the attacks in Spain against the Spiritual Exercises, etc.

Nevertheless, Ignatius remained in touch with the affairs of the Church and the work of the companions everywhere in the world.

On January 7, he redesigned the map of the provinces of Spain: henceforth there would be three provinces: Castile (with Araoz as provincial), Aragon (Strada) and Betique (Michael de Torres). Borgia exercised his authority in the name of the General in the three provinces of Spain and in Portugal.

In May the approaching marriage of Philip II of Spain and Mary Tudor of England was announced. This union portended the return of England to the Roman Church; Ignatius hoped fervently that the Society would participate in this work of reconciliation; he insisted that one of the companions be admitted to the entourage of Philip II.

---

[50] Cf. the vicissitudes of the Rodríguez affair in *Scripta* 1, pp. 673 sq.; the condemnation of Rodríguez on February 7 by the tribunal of four judges (Miona, Olave, Polanco and Cogordan); his request to be exempted from all obedience having regard to Ignatius and the Society in order to live in a hermitage of his choice; the intervention of Cardinal Carpi. The story of this proceeding is recounted in the *Font. narr.* by Fr. Candido de Dalmases. Text of the Decree of Paris: *Chron.* 4, pp. 328 sq., n. 703.

In June, following a modification in urban planning, they had to renounce the plan of reconstructing the church of La Strada. The new plan, financed by the Cardinal of Cueva, was entrusted to Michelangelo. The work began on October 6 but there would be interruptions at the beginning of 1555, because of circumstances.

At the end of June, Ignatius was thinking of establishing a province in Northern Germany. He consulted the companions of Louvain and Cologne, who, in general, considered the plan premature. Ignatius postponed it until later.

On August 4, he enthusiastically supported the proposition of Ferdinand, King of the Romans, who wanted to create a Hungarian college on the order of the one in Germany.

On August 13, he sent Canisius a very well thought-out letter on the manner in which Ferdinand could and should defend the Catholic faith in his domain.[51]

October–November, Ignatius finally obtained from Julius III the gifts and support to save the Roman college; unfortunately, the Pope died on March 25, 1555, without having had the time to fulfill his promises. Debts and scarcity continued to burden Ignatius.

At the end of November, fourteen companions left to found a college at Loreto which would be very close to Ignatius' heart. He also undertook to found the college of Prague in September 1555.

On December 6, to relieve the ailing Laynez a little, Ignatius took back (under his own jurisdiction) the regions of Venice and Ferrara.

At the end of December, Ignatius bought a "vineyard" on the Small Aventine near the Antonine Baths of Caracalla, where the students would be able to go to relax and rest.

These examples suffice. Ignatius was decidedly a singularly active invalid; although his severe health problems increased, it was he who kept up the morale of his companions in Rome and outside of Rome. He encouraged Laynez, Canisius, Oviedo, Salmeron, etc. so that they would accomplish as soon as possible certain works which would serve the apostolate of all.

The number of companions, if one compares the commentary of Polanco and that of Luis Gonçalves da Câmara, oscillated between nine hundred and nine hundred fifty.

ITALY AND NAPLES: Laynez prepared at Genoa for the arrival of the companions who would come in September to found the college. This long absence kindled the anger of the Duchess of Florence. The team

[51] *Epist. ign.* 6, pp. 395–404, n. 4708 and 4709; cf. 12, pp. 254–56, n. 25.

chosen by Ignatius was remarkable: unfortunately, two deaths soon occurred. Genoa, whose port activity was intense, was consumed by a bad inner plague—usury; Laynez attacked it by "public lessons" on contracts, which provoked reflection and a certain amount of backwash among the Genovese merchants.

A colony of fourteen companions, of whom five were priests, founded the college of Loreto. Ignatius demanded that the trip from Rome to Loreto be made in an "apostolic manner" in the way in which the first Fathers had traveled.

Gubbio was decidedly a failure. Ignatius closed the college. On the other hand, at the request of the Duke of Ferrara, a college was opened at Argenta: but could it survive? Difficulties abounded.

Ferrara was a trouble spot in northern Italy. Its Duchess, Renée of France, was leaning toward heresy. Pelletier, in the name of the Duke and of Ignatius, and Dr. Ory, in the name of the King of France, brother of the Duchess, on one side, and a pastor in the name of Calvin on the other side confronted each other over the conscience of the Duchess (April). In September the Duchess finally chose Catholicism. Her conversion seemed sincere, but it would give way again in a few years. An analogous situation, but with less dramatic consequences, was created at Placenza: Doña Isabel de Brisegno also leaned toward the "new ideas". Dr. Olave, although very useful at the Roman college, was sent to her by Ignatius.

Venice, Perugia and Florence survived but not without risks and difficulties. At Venice, Rodríguez arrived in the course of the year:[52] he had the authorization of the Pope and of Ignatius to make a pilgrimage to the Holy Land; he prepared for this very expensive trip (Ignatius paid the bills and his expenses). He embarked, then returned to port, for the Turkish fleet was cruising in the vicinity. He wanted to stay in Rome; Ignatius refused and offered him a choice among Ancona, Padua and Bassano.

As for Bobadilla, he served as a missionary in the region of Ancona; after Easter he came to Rome because the Bishop of Malta wanted him in his diocese. This bishop did not press the matter, so Bobadilla, at the request of Cardinal Saint-Ange, went off to reform the Abbey of Tafa and the twenty-eight hamlets which were connected with it.

At Naples, Salmeron was the indispensable man without whom the

---

[52] Condemned not to reenter Portugal, deprived of the authorization which he had at first obtained from the grand penitentiary to live in a hermitage exempt from all obedience to Ignatius and the Society, Rodríguez began a very painful and errant life.

Viceroy and Governor could no longer manage. Ignatius had thought of sending him to free Laynez of the burden of Genoa; it was impossible! Ignatius could scarcely keep him in Rome for twenty days. A vocation of great value was in preparation in Naples: that of John de Mendoza, the son of the Marquis of la Valle Siciliana and the captain of Castel Neuf; but he had to have the authorization of Charles V. Rector Oviedo, having been named Bishop of Ethiopia, was replaced by Christopher de Mendoza.

SICILY: The euphoria continued: two new colleges were founded: Monreale in July and Bivona on May 21: the Duchess of Bivona (daughter of Juan de Vega)[53] wanted a magnificent college and worked to achieve it. An Islamic center was planned and the companions learned Arabic in preparation for missions in Africa. Still other plans were also being developed. But where could one find the men? Doménech sought them from Rome; Ignatius answered him that Sicily was already privileged among all the regions of the Society.

PORTUGAL: While the personal crisis of Rodríguez continued, the province of Portugal received its second wind: Nadal's work[54] produced its effect, the houses and the companions entered little by little into the spirit and practice of the *Constitutions*; Ignatius took great care that John III and the court be informed exactly of everything concerning Rodríguez (then in Italy).

However, there existed a certain malaise regarding those who had left the Society: the nuncio was of the opinion that he had the power to relieve them from their first vows; moreover, the King gave them assignments and benefices, as if nothing had happened. Finally, Theotonio de Braganza became upset and in turn upset many other people; he agreed, however, to leave for Rome; he was converted there . . . but not for long.

In fact, the problem in Portugal lay elsewhere: the companions who had remained faithful, had difficulty in coping with the apostolic work. There would have been a good solution: Spain refused candidates for lack of the resources to feed them; why not direct a few Spanish recruits to Portugal? However, that plan was stymied by the autocracy of King

[53] The count of Luna was elevated to the title of Duke of Bivona.

[54] At the request of Nadal himself, Ignatius asked several companions from Portugal for their criticism on the "visit" and the Visitor. The responses were laudatory: several even wished that Nadal be named Provincial of Portugal.

John who refused to allow Portuguese money to be used for non-Portuguese purposes.

This was so much the case that when the new Viceroy, Pedro de Mascarenhas, left for India on April 2, he took with him only two companions, a pair whom Nadal dared not trust to declare the *Constitutions* there.

Until autumn 1554, no one in Portugal suspected that Xavier was dead. The fleet which then returned from Goa finally brought a brief, vague letter from Melchior Nuñez and one of the captains recounted a story too strange to be believed.

In autumn, some companions destined for Ethiopia arrived in Portugal and revived the missionary fervor.

INDIA: Xavier, Barzeé, and Morales were dead, Urbano Fernandez, the Provincial sent the previous year by Ignatius, lost at sea; Melchior Nuñez acted as Provincial while waiting for Ignatius to designate one, as they had asked him to do. Little by little at Goa the circumstances of Xavier's death became better known; his body was returned from Malacca to Goa, not without great danger, on March 16. Soon, an inquiry was begun by the Vicar General (the Bishop was dead) into the life and miracles of Xavier. Noting the importance of the work being accomplished in Japan, Melchior Nuñez decided to leave and go there with a Father, four brothers, a merchant who was a candidate for the Society, and five Portuguese "orphans".

Father Balthasar Diaz succeeded him in his capacity as rector of Goa and performed the functions of provincial. Conditions were hard: the companions were overworked. The new Viceroy arrived September 23 and reduced the allocations to the missionaries, an action which put certain charitable works, houses and individuals in a difficult position. Diaz was a man of great faith who boosted the morale of his companions: it is in weakness, he reminded them, that God manifests his strength.

JAPAN: In Bungo as in Amanguchi, the atmosphere of the primitive Church prevailed. The conversion of a learned man who enjoyed great authority among his compatriots facilitated the missionaries' translations and adaptation of texts, ceremonies and Christian prayers.

THE CONGO: The King was without doubt a maniac. However, the Bishop and the few white priests who surrounded him were responsible for much of the degradation of Catholicism that surrounded him in the country. Cornelio Gomez desperately opposed this mess. There was only one hope that things might change: the recall of *all* white clergy and their replacement by five or six Jesuit priests.

BRAZIL: Rather than at Bahia São Salvador where the governor and the bishop resided, Nobrega, the provincial, chose to be installed at São Vicente, with five priests and a few brothers. This choice had an apostolic significance. Nobrega did not hope for big things from the Portuguese colonists nor even from the Brazilian populace which was in contact with them: but beyond the known lands when one penetrated the back country one met tribes that were called "savage"—especially Indian tribes—of whom some would be open to the gospel. This was precisely the case in the area of São Vicente and the phenomenon became even more apparent in proportion to the extent that one advanced in the direction of Peru. That year, a fifth post was established: Pinativy. The Nobregan group inscribed two names in the martyrology of the Society: Peter Correa, a former merchant, and Brother John de Sousa.

Despite the trials, disappointments, and failures, the companions held fast, invented missionary methods and acted with courage and tenacity.

SPAIN: Three events mark this year in the life of the companions in Spain: Nadal's visit during which he promulgated and launched the *Constitutions*, regularizing in particular the system of vows; the dividing of Spain into three provinces; the departure for Portugal at the end of the summer of the companions ultimately destined for Ethiopia.

The Province of Castile: The two large colleges (Alcalá and Salamanca) and the more modest houses (Medina del Campo, Burgos, Cuenca, Oñate) were going well. At Alcalá, Borgia stayed one week at the beginning of March, for the first time since his *mutatio vitae*: the university welcomed him with much solemnity. Everywhere there were vocations of great quality and a choice of vocations; the novitiate was pursued at Alcalá, under the authority of a master of novices and apart from the community of students. A few differences of opinion between Provincial Araoz and Ignatius arose, especially pertaining to the role that Araoz played at court. After the departure of Philip II for England, the Princess Juana (widow of the Prince of Portugal) ruled Spain. Araoz was very well considered at court and he accomplished a great deal of spiritual good there, but the Princess also consulted him on temporal affairs. From afar Ignatius fretted uneasily, but Araoz retorted that to be busy with affairs of state was also to work for the glory of God and the salvation of souls.[55] The attack against the Spiritual Exercises, unleashed

---

[55] This letter is important for it touches precisely upon a delicate point of apostolic

two years earlier, worsened to the point that Nadal thought it appropriate to draft a note on the contested points for the companions. That year there were also three nascent houses: Avila, Plasencia and the novitiate of Simancas.

The Province of Aragon: Gandia and Valencia had a single rector and he preached everywhere. Nadal put this situation in order. Once Borgia was commissioner, he wanted to install a true novitiate in Gandia, but the novices, because of the climate, would spend three or four months in the summer at Valencia. At Barcelona, the atmosphere around the companions was very reserved, if not hostile. Only Borgia, who had formerly been Viceroy of Catalonia, could perhaps improve it. Saragossa remained the trouble spot of the province: "More contradictions in this city than in all of Spain." Strada, the new provincial, fought courageously, supported by the Viceroy and by some local notables.

The Province of Andalusia (Bétique): Requests for colleges were not lacking, but only one was established: Córdoba. Nadal, who very much admired Anthony de Córdoba, named him rector for nine months (afterward Anthony would go to study theology). The great foundress and benefactress was the Marquise de Pliego, Anthony's mother. To her alms were added those of Don John de Córdoba, dean of the chapter. From its opening, the college experienced great success and Córdoba was a city spiritually inspired by Juan de Ávila. The terrible Siliceo, however, did not back down, and neither Nadal nor even Torres, who was Siliceo's friend, could succeed in appeasing him; Torres, the new provincial, arrived at Córdoba at Pentecost; the province then consisted of only thirty members.

Serious problems arose for Nadal and then, after his departure, for Borgia: the attacks against the Society, and especially against the Spiritual Exercises, which were the great instrument of the apostolate in Spain, alms collections for the Roman houses, where resources were lacking to the point that candidates were refused; the establishment of new provinces which a slight tension between the provincials did not facilitate (for example, regarding Salamanca); the insistent desire of Ignatius to send a companion to England in the retinue of Philip II; the

---

spirituality according to Ignatius: the use of "human means". Cf. *Epist. ign.* 4, p. 195, n. 813. On Princess Juana, see the article by Robert ROUQUETTE cited in the bibliography, and the remarkable study by Marcel BATAILLON, "Jeanne d'Autriche, princesse de Portugal", which appeared in the *Bulletin des études portugaises* (1939), and was reprinted by the author in *Etudes sur le Portugal au temps de l'humanisme* (University of Coimbra, 1952), pp. 257–83.

heavy weight of the confidence of Princess Juana, "governess" of Spain; and the responsibility for Queen Joanna the Mad whom Philip, before his departure for England, entrusted to Borgia. Moreover, Borgia had to bear the fault and exile of Duke Charles de Borgia and the renewed threat of being made a cardinal. Now, everyone, especially Borgia, sensed that the developments of the Society in Spain rested, in good part, on his shoulders.

GERMANY AND EASTERN EUROPE: Decidedly, the presence of the companions, and especially of Canisius in Vienna, was crucial. The religious situation of the city (among the local inhabitants and especially at the university) was deteriorating rapidly. Canisius was named to the "Archducal College of Vienna"; the King entrusted him (along with two doctors of law who finally abstained) with the reform of the colleges of Vienna. In the month of April, Canisius was named dean of the faculty of theology, a faculty which lacked theologians: the King decided then to create a commission *de collabenti religione*. Throughout that year loomed the question whether Canisius would be named Archbishop of Vienna: Ignatius refused, then accepted, out of sympathy for this people whose faith was in great danger, that Canisius assume the role of apostolic administrator for one year. Nevertheless, Canisius worked on his catechism (while Laynez, in Italy, tried to finish the theological work which Ferdinand had demanded.) The King wanted to print it and impose it on all the *ludi magistri* of the kingdom. So Canisius was the target of the Lutherans' attacks (pamphlets, songs, puns). The companions around Canisius and Lanoye worked fervently at missionary work, sometimes not without detriment to their studies. In an unusual case, the college opened a *convictus* (for six or seven boarding students at first). Novices presented themselves and Ignatius agreed that they be admitted at age fourteen (according to the *Constitutions*) and even before (but each case had to be submitted to Rome). The companions' move into an abandoned monastery of Carmes slightly improved their material situation, but it raised canonical difficulties and imposed other hardships.

The Duke of Bavaria insisted that the Society reassume the administration of the college of Ingolstadt, because many of the nobility were already becoming Lutherans. The time, however, was not propitious: a large part of Germany was armed.

At Cologne, Kessel's group was reduced to three or six companions. Vocations, when there were any, were sent to Vienna or to Rome.

Nijmegen was nineteen miles from Cologne and the Canis family were natives of this area. Some friends and the mother of Canisius offered all that was necessary for the founding of a college. The entrance into the Society of two canons (one of whom was a brother of Canisius) produced a feeling of sympathy for the order that was still almost unknown to the population.

LOUVAIN: Despite the intervention of very good friends, including the famous Louis de Blois, the Queen and the Chancellor remained distrustful of the Society. Peter de Soto, former confessor of Charles V, spoke successfully in its favor to the Emperor and Queen Mary. However, at that time, the Emperor was thinking of abdicating; it would be necessary to await the anticipated arrival of Prince Philip in Flanders. Cardinal Pole was passing through court; after his departure, he wrote a letter to all the bishops of northern Germany and recommended the Society to them. The letter was well received except by the Bishop of Cambrai; he nevertheless admitted three companions, natives of the country, to come to do missionary work in the area. Then he withdrew their permission to preach.

PARIS AND BILLOM: After three months spent in Auvergne, Broët returned to Paris with a small group of six companions which would increase to twelve by the end of the year. In Paris everyone opposed them. Nonetheless, Guillaume du Prat remained a faithful friend. Broët proposed to him that they create a university at Billom. Du Prat accepted without renouncing the plan for a college in Paris. Ignatius held the project in abeyance, since a war between Charles V and Henry II was in progress. Some friends pushed Broët to press the verdict of the faculty of theology in Paris: December 1 the Decree appeared. The companions were crushed. The document would furnish the adversaries of the Society with a redoubtable weapon for a long time. The faculty threatened, even if the Society appealed to the Pope, to ask him for a council on the subject.

CORSICA : On March 17, Ignatius recalled the two "commissioners"; he did not know that Sylvester Landini had been dead since March 3. Montemajor returned alone to Genoa where he did missionary work and studied philosophy.

CEUTA AND TÉTUAN: John Nuñez returned to Portugal with some "ransomed" Christians, and he sought alms to ransom others when he learned of his appointment as Patriarch of Ethiopia. His companion (not a priest) Brother Ignatius Bogado remained alone at Tétuan to continue the mission among the Moslems, who considered him "a saint".

ETHIOPIA: The mission to Ethiopia was briskly made ready that year. Organization went forward with the choice of twelve companions (eight of them priests) who would accompany the three bishops. Ignatius made sure that all of them were professed. Oviedo already was professed (February 9, 1549); Carneiro made his solemn profession at Rome into the hands of Bobadilla on June 24, 1554, and John Nuñez made his profession at Lisbon on September 8. Three of those leaving made their profession of three vows into the hands of Ignatius. Toward mid-September, the Roman group destined for Ethiopia departed for Portugal (via Lyon) and arrived, not without dangers, in Spain on November 9.

Beside the still far-off plan for colleges in Jerusalem, Cyprus and Constantinople, there was the seemingly more immediate project of a college at Malta which beguiled Ignatius. He always remained very eager to open missions in Islamic countries and encouraged companions whether in Sicily, Naples or Spain to prepare themselves by learning the language of the Koran.

POLAND: A plan for a college was in progress in April and there was even the question of a *concionator* at the court: Queen Catarina was the daughter of the King of the Romans. All these plans pleased Ignatius very much, for this mission seemed, according to his information, difficult and dangerous. In Poland, the companions saw a "northern India".

Other colleges were envisioned in northern Europe: Prussia, Bohemia, Hungary, Transylvania, Silesia; those which had the best chance of completion were those of Breslau and Prague. Canisius thought that, tactically, it would be better, first of all, to reinforce Vienna, take back Ingolstadt, then found Prague. There was even a plan for a college in the "Indies of Peru".[56]

There are more than a thousand of Ignatius' letters from this year. They are thrilling documents, but they make us even more regretful of the strange scarcity of letters from the companions to Rome (no letters from Bobadilla, or from Broët in Paris and only four from Rodríguez).

On the other hand, the "regulated" correspondence became better and better organized. The projects in progress gave the Society of Jesus a standing in the framework of Christianity. Thus, it was that much more moving to see Ignatius volunteer, despite his illness, to go himself to found a mission in northern Africa, in Islamic territory.

---

[56] Letters to Laynez. *Epist. ign.* 6, p. 299 (n. 4145) and 7, p. 28 (n. 4474).

1555

ROME: Julius III died on March 23. On April 9, Cardinal Cervini was elected Pope and took the name of Marcellus II. He was a great friend of Ignatius, but he died on May 1. On May 23, Cardinal Gian Pietro Carafa succeeded him under the name of Paul IV. Carafa was, of all the cardinals, the one whose election Ignatius could most dread. Even before the foundation of the Society of Jesus, Ignatius in 1537 had criticized the community of Theatines, of whom Carafa was the cofounder. Then, on at least two occasions, Ignatius had refused a merger between the Theatines and the Society. Recently, the two men had found themselves in conflict regarding the vocation of Octavio Cesari. Moreover, Carafa was fiercely anti-Spanish, and, finally, everyone knew that he was opposed to certain constitutions of the Society. However, he supported a bold reform of the church: and then by his election he had become "the Vicar of Christ on Earth". That was enough for Ignatius to put himself entirely at the Pope's service.

Carafa had at least two personal friends in the Society: Bobadilla (was that an advantage for Ignatius?) and Laynez. Paul IV had the latter come to Rome and even wanted him to live there, with some Theatines, in the Palace of the Vatican (Laynez spent a night there, to obey). The Pope thought of making him a cardinal; in any case, he liked to consult him. A curious coincidence occurred. Bobadilla and Laynez would be the two antagonists of the great crisis (1556–1558) which would shake the Society after the death of Ignatius.

These changes in the papacy had a material, but very painful, effect on the financial situation of the Roman and German colleges. Julius III had thought to help them and even to accord stable revenues to the Roman college; he died before carrying out his plan. Marcellus II took it up again. Paul IV, in turn, declared that he wished to intervene: in fact nothing would be accomplished.[57] Things would come to such a point that Ignatius, who had already asked rectors to receive students in their colleges, would soon have to send out of Rome more than a hundred companions (there were still one hundred fifty to feed in Rome). More serious still, Nadal stopped declaring the *Constitutions* and joined Borgia in Spain in order to beg alms for the Roman houses. His departure took place on October 23, but the travelers were held up for a long time in Genoa.

One of Ignatius' major preoccupations that year remained the work of the *Constitutions*: their promulgation by Nadal in Germany and in several

---

[57] The German college would decline until it was saved by Gregory XIII.

regions of northern Italy. Then, after Nadal's dispatch to Spain, their promulgation by Ribadeneyra in Flanders; their patient improvement in the light of experience and events[58]; their interpretation in this or that unusual case (for example the "vows" of Princess Juana).

The election of Paul IV also revived the campaign of calumnies and persecutions against the Society. People said that the new Pope was lukewarm toward the order. In Spain certain Dominicans preached openly against the Society and the interventions of their Father General did not suffice to appease them. Some thought of having the Dominicans' protector, Cardinal Morone, intervene, and Cardinal Carpi, protector of the Society, proposed handing the guilty preachers over to Rome. From Paris, the Decree of the faculty of theology had a considerable impact outside of France. Rather than initiate a judicial procedure, Ignatius preferred to take a calmer tack: he opposed the Decree with a series of "testimonies" from princes, cardinals, bishops and municipal authorities, who had seen the companions at work.

Nonetheless, La Strada, the Roman college, and the German college prospered. The novitiate flourished; the candidates waited for groups of companions to be sent elsewhere so that they could immediately take the free places.

Let us mention a few remarkable events.

At the beginning of January, Ignatius decided to go after Easter on pilgrimage to Loreto: the deaths of Julius III and Marcellus II prevented him from executing his plan. In August, the province of France (provincial: Paschase Broët) was created. On October 3, Laynez was named Commissioner General in northern Italy. When he left for Spain on October 23, Nadal took with him Gonçalves de Câmara and Theotonio of Braganza. Ribadeneyra, who departed the same day for Flanders, had two missions: to declare the *Constitutions* and to discuss with Philip II the official recognition of the Society. Between October 23 and 31, Ignatius entrusted to Father de Madrid the immediate administration of the house of La Strada and "to assist him", he named himself, Madrid, Polanco and Laynez. On November 13, Ignatius confirmed Borgia in his functions and powers as Commissioner General. On December 7, on the order of Paul IV, search took place at La Strada: people were saying that the Spanish party hid arms there. On December 12, Laynez, Olave, Polanco and Frusius began to argue with four "doctors of the Sorbonne" who had accompanied the Cardinal of Lorraine to Rome: two of these doctors were among the chief promoters of the Decree of the faculty of theology. In this regard, we should note Ignatius' "manner of proceeding" in

---

[58] *Epist. ign.* 8, pp. 484–85, n. 5212.

certain serious cases: he had the affair judged by a sort of commission or tribunal: he, himself, did not take part, but reserved the final decision to himself. He did this for Simón Rodríguez (and at the latter's request); he did it again in the affair of the "vows in the Society" of Princess Juana, and in the expulsion of Theotonio of Braganza.

Two documents of the most lively interest date from 1555. First, Ignatius finished dictating his autobiographical memoirs to Gonçalves da Câmara (March, then September–October): he had begun in August of 1553, but was interrupted during 1554. Moreover, Câmara, who was chaplain at La Strada, had been in daily contact with Ignatius since September, 1554, and noted on a day-to-day basis what he heard, saw, and observed from January 26, 1555 until his departure from Rome on October 23; these notes would become the precious *Memorial*.

ITALY AND NAPLES: The colleges of northern Italy had only a modest number of pupils. None had two hundred students, and some of them would always have fewer than one hundred. These statistics pose some problems, especially since that year several colleges lost some of their students as a result of the plague which dealt severely with the region. Everything depended very much on princes or benefactors, since the colleges had not been "founded" with stable revenues to support them. The gravest problems, in fact, were of another order. In Florence, it was the attachment of the Duchess to the person of Laynez. When Paul IV requested him to come back to Rome, the Duchess threatened to cut off the supplies to the companions. In Genoa, it was the conflict of the two succeeding rectors with Superintendent Viola. At Bologna the college collapsed. At Ferrara it was the "counseling" of the son of the Duke, Don Louis, who had been destined for an ecclesiastical career and who felt himself drawn to a secular life. At Modena, the college was nearing its end. Neither Ignatius nor the bishop wanted to maintain it, but Duke Ercole demanded the presence of the companions. Finally, the college was transformed into a missionary group. In Venice and Padua, Lippomani was still virtually starving the companions. At Argenta there were fifty pupils: Ignatius wanted to close the college, but Nadal saved it.

One strong point was Loreto. It must be noted that the number of companions in the course of the year went from eighteen to forty, thanks to the misfortune of the Roman houses. They did excellent work in preaching and in hearing confessions and at all the shrines frequented by pilgrims, but not without contradictions, difficulties and "attacks of the devil". It was impossible to open the college because there were no books! In the summer, Loreto was very unhealthful and consequently, many inhabitants left: only two or three companions remained, but the others did missionary work in the area.

Rodríguez wandered all over the country throughout the year; we cannot follow him in his aimless meanderings. It is necessary, however, to mention his encounter with Nadal in July in Bassano. We have a few letters which confirm this encounter. They clarify the disarray of Simón Rodríguez but they also constitute an excellent document on a too-much-forgotten point: while recognizing Ignatius' prerogatives as General, the *primi Patres* seriously considered themselves as cofounders of the Society of Jesus—Rodríguez as well as the others.

In Naples, everything had gone back to normal, but Salmeron came to preach during Lent in Rome, and twenty days later, Paul IV sent him with the legate, Bishop Louis Lippomani,[59] to Germany and to Poland. John de Mendoza was still waiting for the authorization of Charles V to enter the Society.

SICILY: Colleges, social works and ministers all prospered under the benevolence of Juan de Vega, of his sons, and of the Duchess of Bivona. This benevolence was not without risk for the future and aroused jealousies, at least secretly. The college of Syracuse began that year. An example of the kinds of initiatives which Juan de Vega made at the suggestion of Doménech was given when a great famine dealt severely with all Sicily: the Viceroy then created a *consilium* (or *officium*) *caritatis* which was centered in the college of Messina itself. The lay people worked there to help the poor; Juan de Vega and his daughter set the example.

PORTUGAL: Was the Rodríguez affair ended? One would not dare to say so. The wounds were healing slowly; a few companions remained or sought to remain in contact with the former "founder of the Society in Portugal". The expulsion of Theotonio de Braganza from the Society had threatened (for an instant) to begin the trouble all over again. All things considered, however, it seemed that Portugal had refound its equilibrium and its motivation.

Basically, the Rodríguez affair would never be finished. Simón would be a concern for Ignatius for the rest of his life, and afterward would be one for Ignatius' successors.

It was not until October 1555 that Ignatius considered Xavier's death certain. Until then, he had not wanted to believe it, but he finally had to accept the truth.

Of the two houses in Lisbon (St. Anthony and St. Roch), it suffices to note that they did very effective work. At Évora, the college developed

---

[59] Not to be confused with the Prior of Venice, Andrea Lippomani, brother of the bishop.

under the slightly draconian benevolence of the prince-cardinal. After the humanities, they inaugurated "the arts" and they prepared to begin courses in theology.

At Coimbra, the novitiate was flourishing and fervent. Everything would have gone well if the master of novices had not been sick so often. The college was appreciated, but at this point, the King transferred his own college called the Royal College (a thousand students and a boarding school) to the Society. Delicate problems arose like the fate of non-Jesuit professors, the financial management and the responsibility for boarders, etc. Borgia sent a few companions from Castile to help Évora.

ETHIOPIA: The King occupied himself personally and meticulously with the details of this departure. But the canonical questions dragged on longer than John Nuñez would have wished, owing to the double vacancy of the Apostolic See. A particular delay was caused because the apostolic letters which would permit the consecration of three bishops did not arrive. The fleet outfitted itself on April 1. John Nuñez and Oviedo remained in Portugal; Carneiro left alone with the twelve designated missionaries.

Ignatius wanted all fifteen missionaries to have professed either three or all four of the four vows. He even wanted them to be professed before embarking. However, they realized in time that if they had taken the solemn vow of poverty, they would not have been able to live in Goa on the revenues of the college. Finally, of the thirteen departing, two had taken all four vows (Carneiro and Quadros); two were professed in three vows; and the others would make their professions in India before departing for Ethiopia.

On April 5, the apostolic letters arrived in Portugal. On May 5, Nuñez and Oviedo were consecrated at Portalegro by the local bishop.

INDIA: After the deaths of Xavier, Barzée, Morales and Urbano Fernandez, India lacked men to take the post of provincial. Everyone in Portugal agreed to send Gonsalves de Silveira, the rector of St. Roch in Lisbon. However, Melchior Nuñez, lost on the routes of Japan and China, still considered himself the head of the province.

The thirteen missionaries destined for Ethiopia arrived at Goa on September 9, not without having undergone the usual storms, epidemics and even shipwrecks. Very wisely, Viceroy Mascarenhas decided to send two companions to Ethiopia to sound out the true intentions of the Negus. Gonzalo Rodriguez had left with a brother on February 7. On the seventeenth he arrived in the environs of the "King" of Ethiopia. After six months of discussion and theological arguments with the King or the Queen and of alternating hopes and disappointments, Rodríguez returned in November convinced that the Negus was playing both sides politically and that he sought only to protect himself from the "Saracens" and had no intention of being reconciled with Rome.

The Ethiopian missionaries brought the *Constitutions* and the Rules to India with them. They were declared that year and generously welcomed.

Before their departure from Portugal, the companions destined for Ethiopia had received the order not to leave Goa. However the scarcity of men in India was such that several of them were divided among certain posts in order to save the posts.

In fact, India had no Provincial. Things being what they were, Melchior Nuñez did not have the powers of a Provincial. Diaz, then, organized a regular election. At that time, among the missionaries of India, there was no one who had professed solemn vows. Among the "Ethiopian" missionaries, on the contrary, there were four (two who had taken four vows and two who had taken three vows), but could they be elected? In an emergency, they concluded in the affirmative. Quadros, the "designated" Provincial of Ethiopia, was "elected" Provincial of India. Wisely, he accepted only on the condition that they ask Ignatius himself to name a Provincial. Quadros would then cede the position to him.

At Hormuz, Baçaim, Tana, Cochin, Malacca and São Tomé, evangelization continued and, in certain places, took on an heroic character.

CEYLON AND COMORIN: In 1554, at Ceylon, 25,000 Christians had become apostates: the same thing had almost happened to 70,000 at Comorin. They had been held back by "God-fearing chiefs". In 1555, the young "King of Ceylon" (eight years old) took his classes at the college of Goa. The missionaries pinned great hopes on him for the future of the mission.

At Coulam, an admirable missionary named Nicholas Lancillotto was working. Ignatius knew him well and would have liked him to return to Europe to inform him of matters in India for the Lancillotto had some very accurate views of the mission,[60] and even on the future of the

---

[60] We have from him reports or responses to inquiries which are of remarkable lucidity. Therein, he describes with particular perspicacity the requisite qualities for a provincial of India.

Portuguese presence in those regions. Unfortunately, Lancillotto was old, worn out and sick. He was only able to continue his work by virtue of his extraordinary energy; two brothers lived with him.

At the beginning of 1555, Melchior Nuñez, the itinerant "provincial" was at Malacca with his group. There, he found an opportunity to go to Japan. Later, another opportunity presented itself to go from Japan to China (end of July–August). Actually, he succeeded in getting to Canton twice, the capital of one of the thirteen "regions" of China. Finally, he thought of returning to India. His mad enterprise almost succeeded because about this time, the Viceroy of India sent his nephew as a legate to the "King of China" and ordered his nephew to have Melchior Nuñez accompany him, if he found him in Malacca. Unfortunately, this legation never attained its destination.

JAPAN: At Amanguchi, there were more than two thousand Christians; at Bungo more than one thousand five hundred. Most of these people were poor, very much dependent on the rich and the *bonzes*. The *bonzes* were fiercely hostile to the new religion. The King, nevertheless, protected the missionaries, without, however, himself converting. The missionaries printed books in Japanese, but the evangelization by word of mouth proved itself to be more effective.

BRAZIL: Nobrega showed himself to be definitely a realist and a man of great lucidity: he sought out populations that "lived according to the natural law" to evangelize them and he reported that he met some of them. He required missionaries of steadfast virtue, and it did not matter if they were not too brilliant. Nobrega even discovered vocations locally and sent them to be trained at Coimbra; moreover, he reproached Portugal for having sent to Brazil a band of thieves who hindered evangelization. He pushed for the creation of a purely native college and would willingly locate it in the tribal area of São Vicente while in Paraguay (which depended upon Charles V) a college for Europeans would be founded. The great problem in Brazil was the same as in India: although the orders of King John III were favorable, and his financial sustenance quite sufficient, Brazil was so far from Portugal that administrators and local chiefs did not obey orders from the king except according to their whims, and hence, they often allocated not negligible subsidies to themselves.

The very active mission came up against great difficulties: the moral contamination of the local population by the Europeans was even more serious because the country disposed of very rich mineral and agricultural resources. The requests for baptisms were rather numerous, but experience had shown the companions that great prudence should be exercised: the milieu was not conducive to perseverance. John III ordered that a college be founded at Bahia São Salvador: it was necessary to transfer a companion from Porto Seguro.

THE CONGO: While the King, on the report of Cornelio Gomez, was preparing to send a team of secular priests and a group of companions to relieve the local priests, a dramatic event occurred: the King of the Congo expelled all of the whites, and Gomez returned to Lisbon. John III understood that there would be no point in having anything to do with the insane King. It was the end—for a time—of the Congo mission.

At Tétuan, Brother Bogado remained alone to help several hundred captive Christians. Ignatius had, however, given the order that a priest be sent to him to replace John Nuñez.

SPAIN:
The Province of Castile:

Salamanca: Even if Melchoir Cano did not back down in his attacks against the Society, peace was reestablished between the Dominicans and the Companions. The authorities of the city, the inhabitants, and the university held their work in very high esteem. The economic situation of the group depended upon the health of the Cardinal of Burgos, Francis de Mendoza.

Valladolid: Thirteen or fourteen companions lived there. Borgia and Araoz were often there, because Princess Juana resided at Valladolid. Many ministers of the court (and outside it) were there as well as a few ladies of the court, among whom the Princess herself had discreetly formed a kind of "religious community".

Simancas: At this time, there was no more at present than the novitiate and a flourishing, fervent one at that. Borgia called it *Gemma Societatis*. Medina, Burgos, Oñate, Cuenca, Ávila and Alcalá each worked according to its own pace and the opportunities that arose.

Province of Aragon:

The organization in this province was rather astonishing. Strada, the titular provincial, was completely taken up by his sermons and ministries. It was Barma, the rector of Valencia, who was responsible for the colleges of the province, without having the title of Provincial. When Barma was absent from Valencia, it was Cordeses, the rector of Gandia, who took his place, but without leaving Gandia. Moreover, since Strada had not finished his theological studies, they assigned Pinas to him as a companion to teach him theology "on the road". This unusual method of "giving oneself to the sacred sciences" proved very quickly too utopian to be practical.

The province, or more exactly Saragossa, was shaken that year by a violent storm of protest. When on January 3, Strada had left Saragossa for Barcelona, he believed that Archbishop Ferdinand of Aragon would leave the companions in peace. However, when a little later the companions wanted to start their church, the Archbishop, the tribunal called "Justice of Aragon", certain parish priests of the city, and the Augustinian monks, unleashed even more furor: posters, excommunications, interdictions. The Archbishop and Bishop of Huesca, who had taken the part of the companions, attacked each other with every means at their disposal. Princess Juana intervened. The Archbishop flouted her authority; then, sensing that things were deteriorating, he threw the responsibility for the disorder back upon the chapter of the cathedral. The election of Paul IV rekindled his audacity, but he quickly perceived that he had deluded himself: to save his episcopal see, he revoked all that he had said. On September 9, the companions, who had left Saragossa in the interest of peace, were recalled by the magistrates and the Senate and were returned to the city with the most solemn honors: the same crowds which had booed them a few months earlier gave them enthusiastic ovations.

Province of Betique:

Plasencia: Plasencia, "the oldest of the daughters of the Devil", as it had been called, was very welcoming to the companions: redoubtable factions were reconciled, the college got off to a good start; and understanding with the Dominicans and Franciscans was perfect. The Bishop helped the companions tremendously—so much so that Ignatius accorded him not only the title of "founder", but decided that each day a Mass would be celebrated for his intentions.

Seville: The fervor of Seville, and more especially of the port of Sanlucar, whence ships for the Spanish Indies departed, overwhelmed with joy the few companions that Borgia sent there. There was no college: the dukes of Medina Sidonia were greatly burdened by debts. Neither housing nor food was certain for the companions, but the population was generous and the companions lacked for nothing.

Granada: Besides the pleasantness of the site and the climate, Granada was a city where apostolic work was relatively easy. Since it had been reconquered from Islam, Granada had always had good archbishops at its head and Juan de Ávila had had an effect on the city. The university was flourishing, but there would still be room for a college of humanities there: plans were in progress.

As for Córdoba, the college there developed in full favor. By chance, a legal dispute arose between the bishop and the companions regarding school buildings but the Marchioness de Pliego, the Senate, Don John de Córdoba and the magistrates intervened.

When Michael de Torres was named provincial of Portugal, Bustamente replaced him as provincial of Bétique. Bustamente was a partisan of a strict selection process, of solid training and of well-supplied communities not burdened with excessive labor. He refused to create new colleges. Borgia, on the contrary, would be inclined to give way to innumerable friends who were asking him to create colleges. Between the Commissioner and the Provincial, conflicts could arise, but the two men had deep respect for each other and always ended by agreeing.

Palm Sunday of 1555, Joanna the Mad was dying at the castle of Tordesillas. Borgia, in accordance with the wish of Philip II, had been called to the Queen's bedside, and had been able to converse with her for a long time.

POLAND: In January, Julius III had designated Cardinal Morone as apostolic legate to the Diet of Augsburg and Laynez and Nadal were to accompany him there. However, the death of the Pope cancelled the departure. The plan was resumed in July by Paul IV but then it was the Bishop of Verona, Louis Lippomani, who was designated as legate to the Diet and simultaneously as nuncio to Poland. Salmeron accompanied him. From this trip, Salmeron came back sick and very pessimistic concerning religious affairs in Germany and in Poland.

AVIGNON: Cardinal Farnese thought of establishing a college there. For the moment, Cardinal Cervini (before his election to the sovereign pontificate) asked a companion to reform the monastery of La Celle: Cogordan was designated.

ENGLAND: Ignatius followed the religious progress in England with a good deal of attention. He remained in close contact with Cardinal Pole and always hoped that some companion would be able to rejoin the group of Catholic priests who had returned to England in the entourage of Philip II. In June he considered Tablares and then, Bernard Olivier. At the end of July, they learned that Philip II was going in person to

Flanders to meet Charles V there: the departure of Olivier was cancelled. In October, Ignatius sent Ribadeneyra into Flanders to promulgate the *Constitutions* (Nadal had already departed again for Spain) but also to discuss certain matters of the Society with the court. As early as January, Ignatius proposed welcoming young Englishmen at the German college.

The interesting quality of the events of 1555 makes us regret the scarcity of letters in the archives from some of Ignatius' important correspondents: nothing from Bobadilla, a single letter from Broët, and from Nadal himself we possess only nineteen. It is true that we have more than 1,000 of Ignatius' letters, more than a thousand *mixtae* letters and approximately one hundred fifty *quadrimestres*, but these do not recompense us for the lack of the former!

The correspondence of Ignatius himself shows him to be very oriented toward politico-religious problems of the time: England, Ethiopia, Germany, Islam and the Nordic countries: Poland and Bohemia, etc. Nonetheless, he did not neglect work on the *Constitutions*; he clarified the rules, and supervised everything which concerned the spirit of the order and its style of life. Certainly, it was urgent in his eyes to perfect the texts, but he hoped that they would be put into use as they were.

However, in Rome and elsewhere the companions were having financial difficulties: the traveling supplies for the companions who voyaged, the payment for books which the houses ordered in Rome, the clothing, food, lodging and garden all assumed a good deal of importance in this correspondence that one can only explain by realizing their extreme poverty. Nonetheless, at the same time, they built the new church of La Strada, but soon it would be necessary to interrupt the building. They also made rooms at the "Roscian Tower", a rest home in the Aventine vineyard.

Without really being restored, the health of Ignatius was less bad in 1555 than in 1554; but it was only a lull in the storm.

1556

In fact, on January 11, Ignatius was ill again: the pains and the fever resumed. If in February illness had eased a bit, it persisted nevertheless, and intensified again from June 11 on. "For several months", Polanco would say in a letter,[61] "our father could not celebrate holy Mass and contented himself with weekly Communion." However, despite his suffering, he continued to support the Society in its missionary zeal. He

---

[61] *Epist. ign.* 10, p. 656, n. 6181.

was aware of what was going on throughout the whole world, but he was also concerned with the humble details of the daily life of his companions.

ROME: Ignatius and Polanco busied themselves with gathering "testimonies" favorable to the Society so as to use them against the decree of the faculty of theology of Paris.[62] This matter necessitated a considerable amount of correspondence and was also a delicate operation because they risked giving the decree publicity in certain countries where it was unknown.

After Ribadeneyra's mission to Flanders, one could assume that the *Constitutions* were known throughout the whole Society. However, instituting the Rules, if not the *Constitutions* themselves, did not always proceed without some turmoil. To cite only one example, Ribadeneyra perceived that the Flemish did not have the same pace of living nor the same needs as the people of Rome, nor even as the Spanish. Ignatius was aware of the necessity of perfecting his text and he applied himself to it. "But," he said, "such as they [the *Constitutions*] are, let them be observed with holiness."

Did he feel that the end of his life was approaching? Nothing offers us any proof of this. However, he seemed worried that certain regions like India, Portugal and northern Italy did not have a sufficient proportion of priests who had professed their four solemn vows in relation to those who had not (this would indeed be in effect a difficulty for the first General Congregation). Another worry, more difficult to define, also cast a shadow over his administration in the last months: already for three years hc had maintained that the *Constitutions* should not be sent merely as a lifeless document, but should be declared in a vibrant manner by Nadal, Laynez or Ribadeneyra. But were such personal declarations sufficient for them to be put into practice—especially where particular difficulties presented themselves? A written text, like an order of obedience, is only worthwhile if it is received by a living person disposed to accept and practice it. Therefore, Ignatius had a tendency to depend more and more on the men who promulgated the *Constitutions*. The situation, which he would leave when he died, in Spain, in Portugal, in the Ethiopian group, in northern Germany and among his closest collaborators (Nadal, Polanco, his general assistants) bring up serious problems for the historian: how and why was such a situation established? Had

---

[62] At Christmas 1555, the Roman college had presented very brilliant academic sessions. In the auditorium, one saw the Cardinal of Lorraine and the four doctors of the Sorbonne with whom four companions had debated the Decree.

Ignatius wanted it? Had he consented to it? What did he do to strengthen it? to improve it? We shall have to try to clarify these obscure points.

This year, Ignatius created the province of northern Germany and that of southern Germany, despite the small number of houses and companions there.

Other decisions or directives—numerous ones—show us to what extent Ignatius' vibrant missionary spirit held sway and inspired the rest of the Society. At the time when he was forcing himself "to stabilize" the existing colleges and refusing to found new ones, if they could not assure the livelihood of fourteen companions from the outset, he launched (out of pure compassion) the college of Siena and (out of gratitude) the college of Cologne. He insisted that the companions, wherever they might be, and especially at La Strada, learn the "language of the country in which they lived", and approved that in Spain, Portugal and Sicily certain ones be initiated into "the language of the Koran" in view of their doing missionary work one day in the land of Islam. He pushed each province to have a regular novitiate. He favored the use of the Spiritual Exercises. He demanded that the "groups of missionaries" which departed to found Ingolstadt or Prague make the trip as apostles on foot, begging and preaching along the route. He had had translated into Ethiopian and printed in Rome a great number (*vis*) of New Testaments and sent them to India. He created, moreover, a printing house at the Roman college and busied himself with equipping it with the most beautiful print available—Venetian print.

The novitiate of La Strada was flourishing. Among the novices of 1556, was John de Mendoza, Captain of the Citadel of Castel Neuf in Naples, who for two years had awaited the authorization from Charles V and Philip II to consecrate himself to the service of Christ (he would die a novice on September 27, 1556). In May, more than seventy persons lived at La Strada. There were more than a hundred companions at the Roman and German colleges. Rome was then undergoing a grave famine. Prices were going up and it was necessary to feed everyone. Moreover, it became urgent to add on to the small house of La Strada, which was too small; and to buy or to rent a house for the Roman college which was expanding at a great rate. Nadal and Borgia begged in Spain, but how, in a full Hispano-papal war, were they to get these gifts to Rome? Laynez, just named Vicar General, would have to send many companions and pupils of the Roman and German colleges out of Rome: he could no longer feed them.

In January-February, Paul IV granted an exceptional favor to the Roman college: the right to confer university degrees on its own pupils.

Officially, relations between Paul IV and Ignatius were good. It was evident that Paul IV sought to avoid saddening Ignatius, in whatever concerned the latter's work—while he was still living. Paul IV confided in certain companions, particularly Laynez and Bobadilla. He. asked Laynez and Olave (Prefect of the Roman college) to collaborate in the reform of the Datary. He sent Salmeron with the nuncio, Louis Lippomani, to Poland; he also designated him, with another Father, to accompany his legates who were going to attempt to reconcile Philip II and Henry II (actually, Salmeron would not leave). Paul IV entrusted to Bobadilla the thorny reform of the Sylvestrians. However, everyone knew that the Pope was far from having renounced the idea of changing certain constitutions of the Society; Ignatius, to please Paul IV, reintroduced choral chant into the church of La Strada.

Toward June 11, the health of Ignatius provoked serious anxiety among the companions. Feeling that he could no longer assume, as he should, the administration of the Society, he relinquished a large portion of his powers to Polanco and to Cristóbal de Madrid.

On July 2, Ignatius withdrew into the house which he had just established in the Aventine vineyard; the walls were not yet dry; the doctor, however, permitted him to stay there. Meanwhile, Laynez fell ill at La Strada, to the extent that he received extreme unction on August 1.

Tuesday, July 28, Ignatius, feeling worse, went back to Rome.

Thursday, July 30: After the noon meal, Ignatius called Polanco, told him that he was going to die, begged him to go to the Vatican to ask the blessing of the Pope for himself and for the other sick members of the community. Polanco, who had often seen Ignatius in this state of extreme weakness, consulted Doctor Torres, who cared for Ignatius, and Doctor Alexander Petronius. With their agreement, he deferred the trip to the Pope until the following day. In the evening, as was his custom, Ignatius took a light meal with his associates. He inquired especially about the bargaining in progress for the purchase of the Colonna house, destined for the Roman college. Polanco and his doctors had a clear conscience: once again the patient seemed to have surmounted the crisis.

Friday, July 31: In the early morning someone entered Ignatius' bedroom and found him in the last agony. All those who could, ran to him. Polanco rushed to the Pope. Paul IV, much moved, gave the dying man the apostolic blessing and the plenary indulgence. However, when Polanco returned to La Strada, Ignatius was dead: it was about 5:30.

ITALY AND NAPLES: Loreto was evidently a place much visited by pilgrims, but it also constituted a very useful missionary center for all the surrounding areas. The college, however, was not thriving.

Perugia: Perugia developed under the intelligent motivation of Everard Mercurian, to the point that the city thought of entrusting its university to the Society (the plan failed). In the area, Bobadilla, though ill, actively lead in his straightforward way, the reform of the Sylvestrians.

Florence: Florence gave Ignatius only one worry, but it was a serious one: there were no stable revenues, hence no assured future. It was not that the money was lacking at the court: the Duchess, despite the misery of her people, spent scandalous sums in gaming.

Genoa: In Genoa, the college attained an enrollment of two hundred thirty pupils, a record number for the colleges of northern Italy at that time. There was much ardor for study and spiritual fervor among the pupils,. Genoa had a unique apostolic situation: it was the port which linked Spain and Italy. There, companions preached and heard confessions in Spanish, Italian and French. Moreover, as in all ports, they were busy with galley slaves. Two evils, however, undermined the city: games of cards (even among the poor) and usury practiced at unbelievable rates. Nadal and his group, departing for Spain in 1555, found themselves detained at Genoa for two months. This posed unsurmountable problems for this very poor community, especially in regard to food and lodging.

There were also very small colleges (with an enrollment under one hundred), or even houses without colleges—Bologna, Ferrara, Modena, Argenta, Venice, Padua, Parma—where the companions lived "like apostles"; poverty every day, sometimes the plague; and war throughout the entire region. Candidates presented themselves, but how could they accept them? They could scarcely think of sending them to the novitiate in Rome.

Simón Rodríguez came and went like a rolling stone, among Venice, Padua, Ferrara and Bassano. What memories Venice and Bassano held for him: his ordinations, his "primitive church" with the companions of Paris, and his serious illness, when Ignatius came to visit him and cured him. However, Simón did not overcome his distress and he wandered throughout the region. From Rome Ignatius could only pay the expenses of his trips and visits.

One event which occurred in northern Italy in 1556 is typical of Ignatian charity. The setting was the city of Siena which had been devastated by the Hispano-papal war: famines, ruins, perils, separations, deaths and abandoned children. Siena was overwhelmed by all the moral miseries which strike cities which pass from hand to hand. They asked Ignatius for a few companions to take charge of cloistered nuns and to visit prisons and hospitals. The Cardinal of Burgos who had jurisdiction over the city also wanted them to open a college. The time was hardly propitious for such a venture. The Cardinal offered the wherewithal to maintain four companions. Around April 20, Ignatius sent him eight. When they arrived, everything was lacking: no furniture and no books. They camped in "the manner of soldiers". However, two hundred pupils, both nobles and plebians, descended upon the college: avid for learning, but less disposed towards spirituality. Once the crisis was over, it was very probable that the college would close. What did it matter to Ignatius? For exceptional misery, he had provided an immediate remedy. The next day they would see what to do, according to the signs from God.

Naples: In Naples, the college would experience some rather happy days, but the city was in turmoil. John de Mendoza, the Captain of the Citadel, had left for the novitiate. Octavio Cesari, whose vocation had caused so much tumult (even as far as the pontifical court), left the Society of Jesus; whereas Vincent Cortesa entered it. Would it be necessary for Ignatius to dispatch Laynez himself to Naples to calm this tempest? The Neapolitans desired the return of Salmeron and he returned. The situation was not easy to deal with because the Duke and duchess of Alba, two friends of Melchoir Cano, spread the Decree of the Faculty of theology in Paris among the nobility and the clergy.

SICILY: Doménech appeared more and more like the "Apostle of Sicily". He had the confidence of the Viceroy and of everyone else. He supported the catechesis of the country and works of charity: for the poor and the ill abounded in this year of famine and plague. The evangelization came up against a great deal of magic, superstitution and pagan practices, especially in the countryside and along the coasts, but little by little a work of religious purification took place.

The colleges of Messina, Palermo, Monreale and Bivona prospered. The poor pupils, unfortunately, were often detained at home in order to work in the fields and to do domestic chores. As for Syracuse, the college there had some difficult times. Thanks to the protection of the governor, Suero de Vega (the son of the Viceroy), and thanks also to the examples of charity of the companions, hostility was allayed. In Catania, Ferdinand de Vega, another son of the Viceroy, and the Bishop asked for the opening of a college.

Although the support of high personages was indispensable, it was not without inconveniences: rumor had it that Juan de Vega was going to be recalled to Spain. Immediately, opinion again turned against the companions, especially the administrators: this change was evident, for example, in Palermo: The person in charge of the area once so eager to establish the college, was already talking of abolishing all the allocations accorded by the Viceroy. Two bits of news soon calmed this opposition: first, the nomination of Juan de Vega as president of the Royal Council, which was a very important promotion, and his staying in Sicily with his title and his powers, until January 1557.

Ignatius and Doménech wished that a printing house might be established at Messina; they could even add a paper factory to it. The Viceroy was in agreement except on the manner of how best to use this industry.

A delicate question arose: from a famished Rome, Ignatius, then Laynez, sent appeals to Sicily. However, Sicily herself was experiencing a serious famine. The Viceroy proposed a solution: that the companions sell in Sicily the wheat that was offered to them for Rome, and send the money to Rome. But what of the vow of poverty? Moreover, the attribution of the revenues "to stabilize" the colleges was hardly making any progress: the files were gathering dust at the imperial court, during this time of Charles V's abdication.

PORTUGAL: The situation in Portugal would be, this year, at the same time both brilliant and disturbing.

Disturbing, first because of the involvement of the authorities: Borgia was the commissioner (including India), Michael de Torres was the provincial, Luis Gonçalves da Câmara was the assistant to the provincial, but with "special powers". Finally, after the death of Ignatius, Ignatius de Azevedo, who was to exercise the functions of vice provincial while Torres was at the General Congregation, remained so after the delegates had turned back on the way to Rome. Moreover, at the court, after the demise of the heir apparent two years before, Prince Louis died. The King was getting old and left decisions in many areas to the Queen. The ministers profited from the situation by enlarging their personal authority at the expense of the all-powerful Queen. Matters took longer to regulate.

Coimbra, Évora (which the prince-cardinal more than ever considered as "his" college, since the royal college had been entrusted to the Society), and the two houses at Lisbon prospered. Cámara, who was nostalgic for the *societas romana* consoled himself by helping the communities to be in accord with life in Rome. He aided Torres effectively in transacting several delicate matters, like the departure of Don Theotonio de Braganza from the Society, the regularization of the "contracts", the "difference" with the University of Coimbra which feared that the court would divert some of its allocations in favor of the Society of Jesus and the status of the dormitory at Coimbra, etc.

Câmara stated that under a rather brilliant external appearance, the situation was no less disquieting. Portugal was burdened beyond her strength, a fact which had a disturbing effect on the studies of the scholars, on the number and the quality of the missionaries sent to India and Brazil and on the keeping of the rule. The situation appeared to be without resolution—at least immediately.

On March 28, John Nuñez and Andrés de Oviedo, who had finally been consecrated as bishops, embarked for India with a new Provincial named by Borgia: Gonzalo de Silveira. On the thirtieth, the ships took to sea.

INDIA, JAPAN, AND BRAZIL:

India: The Ethiopian group arrived September 6 at Goa. Quadros, who did a good job of reorganization "according to the *Constitutions* and the Rules" stepped aside before the new Provincial, Silveira, while Melchior Nuñez, who still thought himself Provincial, was returning to India. Everywhere, in all the posts, the missionary epic launched by Xavier continued with its joys and its sadnesses, its conversions and its apostasies. Deaths, illnesses and fatigue decimated the ranks of the workers, but many of these men were cut from heroic molds.

After having made contact with the different regions of India, Silveira and his assistant, Francis Rodriguez, were perplexed. Two points in particular demanded an immediate intervention: the Letters from India which had such a great repercussion in Europe propagated certain judgments not conforming to the reality; and the systematic profession for the "Ethiopian missionaries" was not a wise measure. They urgently requested a "Grand Provincial", and an excellent master of novices.

Japan: Amanguchi was destroyed in one hour by a palace revolution. Father Cosimo de Torres barely escaped from death and under the pressure of the Christians retreated to Bungo where the King remained favorable to the Society, but did not envisage becoming a convert himself.

Brazil: Despite the appeals of Nobrega, who would have wished them

---

[63] If one holds with Polanco (*Chron.* 6, pp. 40 and 256–58) one can not know whether Grana made profession of four or of three vows: on the one hand he does not appear on the list of the professed in 1556 (ibid. p. 40) unless he received the profession from Nobrega; elsewhere on p. 756, it is said that both made profession of four vows.

to send him at least the *Constitutions* and someone able to declare them, no one was sent to him from Portugal. In the absence of any bishop or any professed clergyman, Nobrega and Louis de Grana made their profession to each other on May 6 at São Vicente.[63] Some time later, Nobrega finally received the *Constitutions*. There was joy and fervor but a thousand problems arose regarding poverty: they found themselves in fact in Brazil in an economy of sales and exchanges not permitted by the Society. At Pinativy, the companions abandoned their agricultural cultivation and began to beg.

The apostolic effort came up against the manners and customs of Brazilians: the situation was without remedy except on a long-term basis. For the moment, they contented themselves with establishing personal contacts, devoting themselves to all the needy, organizing a basic technical course, and baptizing only the dying, children or old people.

SPAIN:

Province of Castile:
The eleven houses of the province worked effectively. The novitiate of Simancas was a model novitiate "in the Roman manner". The recruits there were numerous and of high quality. Not that there were no disappointments (at Burgos, the two Vittoria brothers, excellent apostolic workers, left the Society—no one knew why) or oppositions (a few everywhere, even at the court, spread the Parisian Decree). At Alcalá, after the epidemic of the previous year, there were numerous ill or long-term convalescents (where could they send them?). It was not until September that the community regrouped. One new school was founded at Montèrrey. Classes began toward mid-April and developed little by little as the provincial was able to send professors there. Truly, the province prospered. A cloud on the horizon was the war between the Pope and Philip II and the anti-Spanish attitude of Paul IV. What was Princess Juana going to do? Borgia and Araoz supported her in her fidelity to the Holy See.

Province of Aragon:
Valencia, Gandia and Barcelona developed despite a few local difficulties. At Saragossa, the tempest continued: since Princess Juana had taken a position in favor of the companions, one could hope that the conflict with the Bishop had had its final round. In fact, the attacks continued, more surreptitiously. The opponents of the Society whispered that it would soon be suppressed by the Pope, that the adversaries had cited it before the Roman tribunals and that it had been condemned. They

circulated the Parisian Decree. Then the Superior of the group, Francis de Rojas, a good preacher, but capricious, who had been eager to profess his four solemn vows, left the Society.[64] This blow hurt some of his companions, but far from discouraging them, it stimulated them: their work was admirable. Murcia finally had a lively year: Barma, the deputy of Strada, was chosen as companion-secretary by Borgia. Miron came to replace him; the college was constructed under the impetus and with the financial support of the Bishop, but the Bishop died. What would the future be? No one could say.

Province of Betique: At Córdoba, the house had been divided in two: on one side the college which succeeded well; on the other, the novitiate, fervent and filled. There were a few very fine vocations, like those of Doctors Ramirez and Madrid. At Granada the companions were very much a part of the city. Seville gave the impression of a "house of the professed" although six of the companions studied theology. At Sanlúcar de Barrameda, the port from which the ships headed for New Spain, two Fathers devoted themselves to good work among the population of sailors and merchants, but the Duchess, on whom the existence of the community depended, died suddenly. Bustamente, to everyone's regret, and particularly his own, abolished the post.

Bustamente was decidedly a very great Provincial. Borgia consulted him a great deal and finally appointed him as his companion-secretary.

In a Spain which was in the clutches of war with the Pope and in the political turmoil brought about by the abdication of Charles V, how could the situation of the Society be simple? There were too many major superiors to clarify the situation. On the other hand, when it was a matter of holding assemblies in one province or another and of sending delegates to the General Congregation, one could not find enough professed, at least in any one province.

GERMANY AND EASTERN EUROPE: In May Salmeron departed for Flanders. Ignatius entrusted him with the responsibility of naming Bernard Olivier first Provincial of northern Germany. On June 7, he created the province of southern Germany (first Provincial: Canisius).

Southern Germany: In Vienna, the college, the novitiate, and the ministries in the city and outside the city gave satisfaction and hope: Canisius' catechism proved to be such a successful apostolic instrument that the Lutherans edited a countercatechism. After the departures from Prague, thirty-

---

[64] Cf. *Chron.* 6, pp. 532 and 537 with references to volumes 3 and 5.

three companions remained in Vienna, of whom only five were priests; the others were still novices. Canisius was the heart of all this action; he remained responsible for the community despite all his courses at the University. The support of the King of the Romans and of the Queen was largely responsible for the results obtained by the group.

Prague: People called Prague the "Babylon of heretics" (Lutherans and Hussites). Few priests were in the region; all had been more or less contaminated by heresy. Approximately a seventh of the population remained faithful to Catholicism. Without the King of the Romans, all would have collapsed. At the end of February, Ignatius sent a colony of twelve companions to Prague. From Rome to Vienna they travelled "in the apostolic manner"; but from Vienna to Prague they used animals, at least for baggage and books. The group arrived at Prague on April 21. They received a warm welcome from the Catholics, but there was a distressing degree of poverty and they also faced the fury of the heretics: Canisius envisaged and hoped for martyrdom.

On May 15, before departing for Ingolstadt, where a college was going to open, Canisius sent Ignatius his "plan for recovery" of Bohemia: he insisted that they send there only some solid, well-trained companions who knew the language. Moreover, he pruned the group: of twelve, he would keep six. At the end of May or June, the companions finally entered the (empty) Dominican convent which the King had put at their disposal. On July 7, classes began: they had immediate success: the heretics themselves entrusted their sons to the newcomers.

Ingolstadt: All was ready in June to receive the companions. On June 8, a colony of eighteen or twenty left Rome. They travelled in "the apostolic manner". On the feast of St. Augustine, August 28, the college started classes; the buildings were extremely unhealthful and very quickly became too small.

In the middle of these crushing cares, Canisius found the time to write and to publish books.

Northern Germany: Olivier, the designated Provincial, died before assuming office. The death of Ignatius happened shortly afterward so the new province would remain without a Provincial that year.

At *Cologne*, Ignatius decided, out of sheer gratitude to the benefactors who for so many years had supported the companions, to send a reinforcement of three valuable fathers of whom one was a native of the country. They arrived on June 22, and Kessel remained Superior. At the end of the year the community numbered twenty-one companions. The

Carthusians dedicated their edition of the mystical theology of Hendrik Herp to Ignatius.

The group from Louvain kept Adriani at its head. On December 7, 1555, Ribadeneyra arrived in the city to try to obtain recognition of the Society in Flanders from Philip II. The court was very divided on this question. It was finally at Anvers that Philip II discussed it with Ribadeneyra.

On September 16, the licensing letters which authorized the legal opening of a college in Belgium were sent.

Between Ribadeneyra and Adriani, there was a great deal of misunderstanding regarding the *Constitutions* and the Rules. Adriani's argument with Ribadeneyra was that one could not live in Flanders as one lived in Rome. This was true to such an extent that Ribadeneyra renounced the plan of declaring them: they would be neither accepted nor observed. Ribadeneyra advised Ignatius to favor Olivier over Adriani as first Provincial of northern Germany.

Ignatius, however, pushed Ribadeneyra to go to England with Olivier. The death of Olivier, then that of Ignatius, relegated to another time this project which visibly annoyed certain friends of the Society.

At Tournai, the plague reduced to nothing the little group which, despite opposition, continued to work in the region. Of three companions, two died and the last barely escaped.

THE FRENCH PROVINCE:

Paris: Broët was busy trying to get the Decree of the faculty of theology rescinded. He distributed the "Responses" to the Decree which Ignatius had had drafted. When Cardinal Pole passed through Paris, he arranged (via diplomatic channels) to have an informative report elaborated in Rome and transmitted to the King. The theologians of Paris did not give in. The Cardinal of Lorraine, however, had high hopes: France, at that time, was engaged against Spain on the side of the papacy; this was even more diplomatic than military.

During this time, the companions worked everywhere where they were not forbidden to work: St. Germain des Prés, St. Côme, St. Gervais, St. Loup, St. Gilles. The studies of the companions, despite the difficulties of the times, were seriously pursued, but their health was poor.

Billom: Everything here began in holy disorder. Little by little, the eight companions, of whom five were priests, regrouped—a reorganization which allowed ministries and missions. While the plans for a "university" were still being studied, they opened the college. Five classes were begun "on the Feast of St. Madeleine" (there were seven hundred pupils). Canal was Rector of Billom and John Baptist Viola Superintendent of Paris. Guillaume du Prat approved everything and financed everything: but all depended on his generosity . . . and his good health.

A benefactor at Lyon proposed a college at Fourvière. Everything would have been perfect, if they had not been lacking in manpower. Ignatius refused.

The seven hundred letters which Ignatius had sent during the first seven months of 1556 are touching: they represent the supreme efforts of the founder to unify, consolidate and develop the Society of Jesus everywhere in the world.

How does Ignatius appear to us in this correspondence? Above all, as an indefatigable worker in the "vineyard of the Lord". This perpetually ill man undertook a labor which would have crushed a man in perfect health. He was very much aware of the world and very much a force in it: he followed his sons on all the routes where "the Vicar of Christ on earth" had sent them. Ignatius' admirable instructions to Gonçalves da Câmara leaving for Portugal, to the companions who were going to found Prague or Siena or Cologne or Ingolstadt, date from 1556: what a missionary!

The spiritual letters of these last months are worth remembering: the experience of a whole lifetime is expressed in them, and they show that the apostolic heart of the Society did not diminish. Ignatius followed the important affairs of the world and the Church with great interest while remaining a meticulous administrator especially punctilious in everything relating to poverty and the mode of life of the companions.

The letters of July 1556 are the most revealing of all: in the letters of July 3 and 20, Ignatius deals with the house to be bought or the constructions to be completed in Tivoli. In a letter of the fourth, he asked all those responsible for recruitment to be more discriminating in their choice of candidates; in a letter of the seventh, he specified the duration and the duties of those in the novitiate; in one on the eighteenth, he chose the characters for the new printing press of the Roman college; in a letter of the nineteenth, he settled a matter wherein the "good name" of the Society was involved; on the twenty-fourth, he wrote "a letter to be distributed around the world" for the "consolation of the companions". Thus, until his death, he shouldered the administration of the Society of Jesus before God. He inspired his sons with the spirit with which the Lord had filled him at Manresa, Jerusalem, Montmartre, Venice and finally Rome: he thrust his companions toward the most arduous and the most audacious missionary tasks. He inspired, he animated, he inflamed.

However, didn't this strength of action and his omnipresence with the companions relegate the legislative work which devolved upon the General of the new order to second place? His task was made that much more difficult by the dispersion of the *primi Patres* and also by deaths. From nearly the beginning the burden had fallen on him alone.

We must now turn our attention to the genesis of the *Constitutions*—a genesis which would not be completed in Ignatius' lifetime. He left the *Constitutions* in the state of an annotated, amended text, still in the form of a rough draft. How then did he work? Are these legislative texts authentically his? Through what editorial stages did they pass? All these questions, which are of the greatest interest, are crucial, if we are to grasp the mentality of Ignatius of Loyola and the character of his work.

CHAPTER II

THE CONSTITUTIONS:
AN APOSTOLIC PLAN?
AN ANTHOLOGY OF EXPERIENCES?
OR THE BLUEPRINT OF A "MISSION"?

The subject is complicated![1] In order not to embark on paths that lead nowhere, it is necessary to remember why and under what conditions Ignatius of Loyola found himself responsible for drafting the *Constitutions* of the Society of Jesus:

1. The original intention of the first Fathers was together to draft the principal constitutions of the new order—so far as it was possible—even before electing a Superior General. This was the circumstance that led Ignatius alone to be the master of the work. He still, however, took care to submit his version, as it progressed little by little, for the approval of the *primi Patres* and even for that of the new companions who seemed to him to share the *mens Societatis.*

2. The work on the *Constitutions* came after (and in a sense was independent of) the community's decision to go to do missionary work "everywhere in the world, wherever the Vicar of Christ would send them—whether "to the faithful or to the pagans". Their self-offering to the Pope (November 18–23, 1538) preceded by five months the "deliberation" (from mid–March through June 24, 1539). Thus, even if the Society of Jesus had not been founded as a religious order, the group of the *primi Patres* and of those who joined them, found themselves bound by a free decision (separate from any canonical vow) to live and to do missionary work "according to the will of the Vicar of Christ on earth".

3. It is necessary to raise, with all due respect, a personal question: was Ignatius prepared, or even designated as a result of his native skills, to

---

[1] This chapter has been adapted from numerous conversations with Fr. Antonio Maria de Aldama, one of the best current experts on the *Constitutions* and their genesis. Fr. de Aldama, who pursued his studies of the sources of the *Constitutions* presented the substance of his position on this very confused subject in a conference during the Ignatian Days for the CIS of Rome in 1971: "*La Composición de las Constituciones de la Compañia de Jesus*" (mimeographed CIS volume; forthcoming in *AHSI*). Of course, we bear sole responsibility for our presentation. See also the excellent chapters of T. VENTURI, op. cit., 3; we shall refer to them frequently. In the voluminous bibliography of the subject, one article seemed to us to present remarkable qualities: Manuel QUÉRA, "San Ignacio, legislador de la Compañia de Jesús", *Estudios ecclesiasticos*, vol. 30 (1956), pp. 363–90.

draft the constitutions? There are perhaps five aspects to this question—for in order to undertake such a work several superficially dissonant qualities would be required: one would need a great intuitive grasp of the kind of grand designs that can move the best of human energies; and Ignatius possessed this sense to a marvelous degree. One would also need a knowledge of canon law—in the highest sense of the word—that is, a knowledge of everything connected with the Church, experience with comparable institutions and ability with juridical language. Ill-possessed of this science, Ignatius was equally disinclined to achieve it, as a result of his temperament or his schooling. Yet another requisite ability was that of organization—the gift of creating an integrated whole in which all of the parts would work together harmoniously in proportion to each other and would constitute a strong unity with a well-defined goal in mind. Indisputably Ignatius possessed this gift. Still another prerequisite for this undertaking was a sense of spiritual values—a clear conception of the importance of even seemingly trifling details in daily life and of their influence on the general atmosphere of religious existence. As we shall see, Ignatius had this particular ability to a very high degree—to too high a degree for the taste of some. Finally, Ignatius enjoyed another advantage which is very valuable in these kinds of enterprises: he had behind him considerable spiritual, apostolic and human experience; he was a man of fifty, trained in the school of "hard knocks", which was both difficult and enriching for those schooled there. This experience would show on every page of his draft. However, would not his lack of canonical science hinder his success in the duty that his fellow companions had conferred on him?

I. THE STAGES OF THE LONG GENESIS

The First Stage: The primi Patres work together.

The *primi Patres* had barely decided to make themselves into a religious order (mid-April, 1539), when they defined the characteristic principles of their new organization. They tackled this effort together, not only as an abstract plan for perfection, but with the realism born of spiritual experience and of the call they had heard from God; "[We wanted to] treat together our vocation and the formulation of our way of life."[2] On May 4 and 25 and on June 11, the companions, after deliberating, decided to entitle their work "The Determinations of the Society" (which traditionally already was called the "constitutions"); but although eleven companions had signed the resolution concerning the vow of obedience

[2] *Const.* 1, p. 2.

on April 15, only seven had signed the deliberations. Broët and Rodríguez had, it seems, already left Rome;[3] Xavier was absent (ill or on a mission). Bobadilla refused to sign the document because it specified that the companions were obliged to teach children Christian doctrine during a forty-day period (an hour a day) and he did not think that this should be part of a vow.[4] These first "constitutions" were of major importance in understanding the later development of the order. Already we see in them that which will mark the spirit of the future texts: the *mens Societatis*; the obedience to the Pope and to the Superior General, the importance of missions, the teaching of Christian doctrine, the "ministries", and the basic formation, the principle of deliberating to arrive at communal decisions, and the admission of new recruits—we find all these things in the early constitutions—the Society's first clear and significant expression of a certain controlling spirit.

At the end of June 1539, the companions living in Rome continued to work together; they composed the "Five Chapters" or "Summary of the Institute"[5] that they submitted to the Pope as the fundamental rule of the order. These "Five Chapters" were very much a collective work—even though Ignatius enjoyed a considerable personal authority among the companions: if nothing else, Bobadilla's resistance would suffice, in the absence of other proofs, to testify that freedom of speech, of judgment, and hence, of making amendments, were the rule in these group meetings.

On September 3, 1539, Paul III approved and confirmed the "Five Chapters" *viva voce*. More than a year would go by before this verbal approval would be transformed into official approbation in the form of the bull *Regimini militantis* (September 27, 1540).[6] We have already recounted the difficulties which the new organization had confronted during this time.[7] The bull *Regimini* would reproduce almost word for word the "Five Chapters". One important change, however, stole into this first legislation concerning the Society of Jesus: in the "Five Chapters", it was foreseen that the Society itself would be able to possess permanent goods and revenues, with a view toward supporting the companions who were students in the universities (in sum, an economic system analogous to that of the first Fathers in Paris); in the bull another

---

[3] *Const.* I, p. XLVIII.
[4] *Const.*, p. 12. Cf. T. VENTURI 3, p. 180.
[5] *Const.* I, pp. 21–22.
[6] *Const.* I, p. 24.
[7] Cf. supra, pp. 107 sqq. See particularly T. VENTURI, *Storia*, 3, pp. 267–97 and SCHURHAMMER, *Franz Xaver*, I, pp. 447–58.

solution arose: that of creating for these students colleges to which the goods and revenues would belong and which the Society would merely supervise. This change indicates once more the collective character of the group's thought; for it seems likely that this idea was due to Laynez: it was Laynez, Ignatius insisted, who had "invented the colleges" and found the solution "for everything concerning poverty".[8] In any case, this was the point of view that was developed in the document ("To Establish a College") that has to be dated at the end of 1540 or January of 1541.[9]

Another document, which came shortly after the preceding one, dealt with how the problem of poverty was difficult to resolve in these first months of the order's existence; this work is entitled "The Establishment of a House".[10] Does this not mark a step backward in relation to the first legislation? Whereas the "Summary of the Institute" rejected all revenue (other than that destined for the college), the "Establishment of a House" allowed revenue for certain specific ends. On November 18, 1540, Codacio had obtained from Paul III the transfer to the Society of the church of Santa Maria de la Strada, which was a parish church and, as such, had certain revenues attached to it.[11] The companions groped their way forward concerning these questions of poverty which would determine their material existence as well as their apostolate. Later, we will see that Ignatius would react vigorously in favor of the strict poverty of the "sacristies" and would go back on all concessions.

On March 4, 1541, those first Fathers who could gathered in Rome. There were only six of them, but during the course of 1540, and at the beginning of 1541, those who had had to leave Rome had sent a delegation back to the gathered companions in order to "compose (the constitutions) as if all the Society were present".[12] Before proceeding with the election of a Superior General, Jay, Broët, Laynez, Codure, Ignatius and Salmeron once more wanted to regulate (by throwing open to a discussion and vote) a few points that had been omitted in 1539 or some which experience had demonstrated needed to be more intensely examined. One finds there, in more developed, precise form, the themes of the deliberation concerning the "Determinations" of 1539 and of the "Five Chapters". The procedure adopted for this common work was interesting. As early as March 10, the six companions delegated Ignatius

---

[8] *Font. narr.* I, p. 610.

[9] Cf. ALDAMA, op. cit., p. 2 and note no. 9.

[10] *Const.* I, pp. 61–65.

[11] *Const.* I, p. 71, n. 4.

[12] "Determinatio Societatis" of March 4, 1540. Votes of Fr. Favre of December 27, 1540, and January 23, 1541. *Const.* I, pp. 23–24 and 32–33.

and Codure to examine in the spirit of the "Five Chapters" and of the bull *Regimini militantis*, the points which called for closer examination, while Jay, Salmeron, Laynez and Broët would continue to do their missionary work in Rome. Ignatius and Codure would submit the result of their work to the approval of the four other companions. Once this was done, they would ask the Holy Father to correct the bull on these points—through his supreme authority. In fact, in this document of March, 1541, we find several important decisions concerning poverty,[13] the election of the Superior for life, the habit, the teaching of Christian doctrine to children, the scholasticates within the order (how to avoid them), the voting procedures (elections and decisions), and the admission to probationary candidacy, etc. One can easily see the interest of this long document,[14] but what should one call it? Father Codina calls it the "Constitutions of the Year 1541"; Nadal refers to it only as *bonae voluntatis et pii conatus*,[15] and his argument is not lacking in strength: it was on the Superior General himself, "in the opinion of the companions arrived at by a majority of the voters", that the bull *Regimini militantis* conferred the power to make the constitutions.[16] The name really does not matter very much. Besides its importance for its own sake, this document shows us a new spirit of close cooperation which existed during the work on the constitutions.[17]

At the beginning of April 1541, the document was completed and approved. It was only then that the six companions, taking account of the votes of those absent, proceeded to elect a Superior General. We have already mentioned the dramatic atmosphere in which Ignatius' election took place.

[13] We note that the conception of poverty which had appeared in the document "The Establishment of a House" is here repeated.

[14] *Const.* 1, pp. 33–48.

[15] *Font. narr.* 2, p. 99.

[16] *Const.* 1, p. 27.

[17] It is important virtually, to insist on this point. Even the marvelous historian Tacchi Venturi has a tendency to present Ignatius as the sole drafter of these first texts (cf. for example op. cit., 4, pp. 5 and 6), a fortiori the following ones. It is very certain that the opinion of Ignatius was particularly listened to and respected by the other companions; but it is no less certain that the first Fathers, and especially Ignatius, maintained that the constitutions were a common enterprise. To consider the constitutions, even at this primitive stage, the fruit of Ignatius' sole efforts, is to imagine a situation which would create pseudo-problems in the ensuing years, like the part of Polanco in the specific drafting of the constitutions, the "remarks" of the consulted Fathers, the corrections proposed by Nadal, the "noluit claudere Constitutiones". All this is simplified, on the other hand, if one admits that Ignatius was always considered, for the work of the constitutions, as the "delegate" of the entire Society, and that he *always* sought collaboration, criticism, corrections and experiences.

The Second Stage: 1541–47: Ignatius worked alone on the Constitutions.
The majority of the primi Patres ratified in advance what Ignatius decided,
and would decide, but he, according to the bull Regimini militantis, *tried to*
get their approval as much as possible.

This situation was significant in its complexity. As Superior General,
Ignatius had the authority to "create" the constitutions "with the counsel
of" and "in consultation with the opinion of his companions, according
to the majority vote"; nothing indicated that he had to draft these texts
himself, but in fact, it was upon him alone that this burden would fall: on
March 4, 1540, the "six companions" actually in Rome had delegated
"those who would be in Rome or who would be able to be convoked
there or who could send their written votes there" to "make" the
constitutions and even "to make decisions concerning them (*determinare*)".[18]
As a result of circumstances, and particularly because certain companions
had been sent on far-away missions, only Ignatius and Codure were left
in Rome after the election of the Superior General. By an act on May 14,
1541, "six companions" (Broët, Laynez, Salmeron, Ignatius, Codure and
Jay) decided once again "to confer on those who remained in Italy the
power of bringing to a fruitful conclusion the affairs of the Society".
These decisions would be made by plurality vote in Rome or by correspondence. A clarification: "the conclusions could not modify the
already-approved and undersigned constitutions unless there was unanimous agreement to do so."[19] Clearly, this document indicates that the
situation created on March 10, 1541 was continued. The burden of
drafting the constitutions fell on Ignatius and Codure, and Codure died
on August 29, 1541. Ignatius was the only one left to take the work in
hand; and he realized the extreme difficulty of reassembling some of the
first Fathers in Rome or of rapidly getting an opinion from them, and
thus, of getting their approval on the acts of the constitutions. Jay, for
example, would give his agreement in advance to "whatever Ignatius
and his brothers in Italy will decide in things concerning the Society";[20]
and even though this was in 1548, Ignatius had to interpret in the same
way the "vote of the four companions" (Laynez from Siena, Salmeron,
Broët from Bologna, and Jay) that gave Ignatius total approval concerning the future—for everything that he had or would obtain from the
Holy See, for the constitutions which he had already made, and for those
that he would make.[21] In other words, even when they were doing

---

[18] *Const.* I, pp. 23–24; 32–33.
[19] *Const.* I, p. 69.
[20] *Const.* I, p. 77.
[21] *Const.* I, pp. 244–46.

missionary work in Italy, it was not easy to get the "first Fathers" to come to Rome—nor to solicit their votes. Doubtless Jay had good reason to precede his signature on the document with these words: "I approve all that will seem well (or good? *al buon parecer*) to our Reverend Father Master Ignatius." This is a far cry from a crafty, authoritarian Ignatius finagling to impose his vision of the Society on his companions. We can see here what we have already seen in the history of the Society's apostolic developments: the Society and most of all Ignatius grew as they could, in accord with the realities and the events they faced.

This period from 1541 to 1547 appeared to many historians like a hollow time in the elaboration of the *Constitutions*. To cite some support for their thesis we have Nadal's observation that "Ignatius did not get to work on the constitutions seriously (*serio*) before 1546."[22] If we compare this period to the two preceding years and to the following years, we cannot deny that it seems less active. But how can we reproach Ignatius for a certain lack of free time to devote to this work which demanded reflection when the exigencies of everyday life devoured all of his attention? Moreover, despite appearances, quite a bit of progress with the legislation of the new organization was being made during this time.

In 1542, Ignatius obtained from Paul III the right for the Superior General to send companions on missions among the faithful; but the right to send them on missions among the pagans was still reserved for the Pope.[23]

The fragment that we possess of the *Spiritual Diary* (February 1544–February 1545) clearly shows Ignatius in the midst of reflections and prayer concerning the constitutions. In 1544, he made his dramatic deliberation on poverty; he daringly overturned on the decision unanimously made in 1541 by the companions and approved by Pope Paul III's second bull *Sacrosanctae Romanae Ecclesiae* (granting the possibility for the "*sacristie*" at La Strada to have revenues); without going into detail, it suffices to say that in the course of his long term, he never reopened this question except "for [his] part and for those who depended on (him)". He evinced this reserve in respecting the right of decision of each of the companions who had signed[24] the preceding constitutions. On March 12, he noted, "I have taken four days in which I have not examined a single point of the constitutions",[25] which implies that this hiatus was unusual. Finally, on March 17, 1544, he says, "Here, I started to get

---

[22] NADAL, "*Apologia contra censuram*", ch. 6, no. 115, *Font. narr.* 2, p. 100.
[23] *Scripta* 1, p. 550.
[24] *Const.* 1, p. 105.
[25] Ibid., p. 126.

ready to examine for the first time the question of missions."[26] It seems that this referred to the "Constitutions concerning the Missions" (1544–1545?)[27] which would later form the principal core of the seventh part of the *Constitutions*. Finally on Sunday, May 12, he remarks, "This Sunday, before Mass, I started and decided to continue with the constitutions:"[28] poverty, missions, other points of the constitutions—all of the serious problems envisaged before God and particularly according to "spiritual indications" that he had experienced before, during or after Mass. Without claiming, as does Father Zapico, the knowledgeable editor of the *Regulae S.J.*, that Ignatius began writing the *Constitutions* in 1541,[29] it seems difficult to consider this period from 1541–1547 as a vacuum. It would be better to believe Jerónimo Doménech who, at the beginning of 1544, wrote to the companions in Spain that among other very important activities, Master Ignatius was busy drafting (*adressar*) the constitutions.[30]

To these we must add still other documents, many of which date from 1546. The document "Against All Ambition" (a refusal of ecclesiastical honors) is a text which is illuminated by the circumstances: between 1543 and 1546, six of the first Fathers were threatened with being made bishops: Rodríguez (as early as 1543),[31] Laynez, Favre, Bobadilla, Jay, Broët; and, moreover, they began around 1546 to talk of the patriarchate of Ethiopia; the brief *Cum inter cunctas* (June 3, 1545) which enlarged the "powers" of the companions for apostolic action;[32] the brief *Exponi nobis* (June 5, 1546), which established the degrees of the spiritual and temporal coadjutors, suppressed all limitation in the number of professed, and introduced into the organization the subordinate levels (of officials, vicars, provincials, etc.);[33] the "ordinances" of the scholastics of Padua (1546);[34] the definition of certain impediments to admission into the Society (1546);[35] and a text on benefactors, etc.

Also dating probably from this period, we have one or two drafts of what would become, in the *Constitutions*, the "Examen" (of candidates). Even if, as is our case, one does not subscribe to the theory of François

---

[26] Ibid., p. 128.

[27] Ibid., pp. CXXI and 159.

[28] Ibid., p. 137.

[29] See the general preface of this edition.

[30] *Epist. ign.* 1, p. 290.

[31] T. VENTURI, op. cit., 4, p. 92.

[32] *Const.* 1, pp. 166–70.

[33] Ibid., pp. 170–73.

[34] *Mon. Paed.* 1, pp. 3–17.

[35] *Const.* 1, pp. 178–80.

Roustang and François Courel in the French edition of the *Constitutions*,[36] this first draft of the "Examen" is of extreme interest.

One document reveals the intensity of the work accomplished by Ignatius in these particular years. It is a kind of collection of approximately eighty-seven questions concerning the organization. It had already given rise to long discussions, and it does not seem that they had yet integrated all of the opinions on the author (or the authors), the dates (1544–1549), the meaning of the questions: and also this collection is perhaps the pivotal document between the period when Ignatius worked alone and the period when Polanco assisted him. We cannot enter into a technical study of the text; let us consider only three points, even though the editor of this text, Father Codina, has affixed a single title to this collection (*Constituta et annotata*).[37] First, it is truly a collection; it contains three texts of different meaning and dates. The first dates from 1547, and even from 1546: "Determinaciones antiguas" (Old Determinations), to which Ignatius added in his own hand the subtitle: "Determinaciones antiguas y nuevas" (Old and New Determinations): then a second text of 1548: "Determinaciones in Domino"; finally a third; "Notas para determinar", which would be from 1548 or 1549. In the second place we note on the manuscript that some entire chapters are written in Ignatius' own hand, and that there are many other evidences of his writing. Thirdly, we can state that almost all the answers to these questions are found incorporated in one way or another in the *Constitutions*, and that this collection served as the basis for the later work of Polanco. Such are the three points that one can affirm without risk of error. Numerous obscurities remain: Who asked these questions? Of whom were they asked? When were they asked? We agree with the position of Father de Aldama: it was Ignatius who asked himself the questions and he planned to respond to them in the process of the drafting of the constitutions. Knowing how Ignatius, in order to consult his companions, had, so to speak, to grab them "on the wing", on the occasion of brief stays in Rome, one can even formulate a hypothesis: it was of this collection that he made use for these consultations. Thus, we are certain that he submitted a question concerning the poverty of the church of La Strada to three Fathers [Don Jacques (Lhoost?), Polanco and a "third of their choice"]. In short, this collection would have served as an ever-present reminder to solicit the opinion of certain companions, as he felt obligated to do.[38]

[36] In the "Christus" collection of texts, preface to volume 2. On this text of the "Examen", see pp. 22–23.

[37] *Const.* 1, pp. 186–220 and CXXXIX–CLIII. Polanco even calls them "constitutions" (*Epist. ign.* 2, p. 760 dated July 6, 1549).

[38] *Const.* 1, p. 193 and n. 20. Cf. Joseph WICKI, *Pfarrseelsorge und Armut der Professhäuser*, in AHSI, vol. 12 (1942), pp. 71–72.

If our analysis is correct, it opens up to us very valuable perspectives on the manner in which Ignatius, in these years when he was alone, worked on the constitutions. These were active, effective years filled with business and with his numerous, personal ministries.

Under such conditions, was it possible for a man alone to plan, to sketch out an ideal architecture for "putting together" perfect constitutions? The whirlwind of worries, of meetings and visits permitted him at most to draft, on a specific problem which arose from daily life, a text which more resembled an informal, casual ruling than an article of canon law. However, who would disagree that it was time that the work be continued, under the inspiration of Ignatius, by a methodical, erudite secretary, competent in many disciplines and techniques into which Ignatius had never been initiated?

The Third Stage: The three decisive years: 1547–1550.
Ignatius with Polanco.

The man who was chosen by Ignatius to be second, to assist him in this enormous task, was Father Juan Alonso de Polanco: in March 1547, Ignatius called him to Rome in the capacity of secretary of the Society of Jesus.[39] He was to fill this position for a quarter of a century, to work with the three first generals of the order; at the death of Francis Borgia, he was elected vicar general; he would have been chosen general if his nationality had not been an obstacle. He was a man of exceptional scope.

He was born in Burgos on December 16, 1517, of a noble and powerful family, descendant according to the testimony of contemporaries from "new Christians", that is to say, converted Jews. After having completed his first studies at Burgos, he was sent, at the age of thirteen, to Paris: it was there that he received his literary and philosophical training; from France, he went to Italy, to Rome, probably around 1539. The Spanish then enjoyed great favor in the pontifical curia. Very quickly Polanco obtained important benefices, but first of all, he was named Apostolic Secretary, Count of the Sacred Palace and of the Lateran *aula*, and he bought (for one thousand ducats) the position of Notary of the Holy See, on March 20, 1541. This very honorable position carried with it ample privileges and introduced him into the

---

[39] Cf. supra, p. 140. A detailed monograph regarding the role and the person of Polanco is still much to be desired; it would certainly be vital for knowledge of the history of these first years of the Society of Jesus: cf. *Font. narr.* 1, p. 11, his brief but vigorous praise by Leturia, op. cit.; ASTRAIN, 1–3, *passim;* T. VENTURI, op. cit., 2, 2, pp. 114–16 and 266–67; Ludwig KOCH, *Jesuiten-Lexikon,* col. 1437–38 (a few errors of detail); and the notes of Jean-François GILMONT, *Les Ecrits spirituels des premiers Jesuites, passim,* especially pp. 196 sq.

pontifical nobility. In the course of the summer of 1541, however, Juan de Polanco, undoubtedly at the urging of his friend and compatriot, Francisco Torres, made the Spiritual Exercises under the direction of Laynez. Polanco rejoined the group of companions in the little house of the Astallis, to the great fury of his family who had high hopes for him; there, he received training from Ignatius. At the end of April, 1542, Polanco was sent to Padua to study theology, then to Pistoia to prepare for the establishment of one of the companions' schools in Tuscany; the matter was extremely delicate. For Polanco it was a difficult trial: a paper, undoubtedly not very diplomatic, drafted for Duchess Eleanor earned him a stinging reprimand from Ignatius accompanied by a penance.[40] This summons from Ignatius arrived just at the moment when young Polanco was undergoing fearful pressures from his family—specifically from his cousin, Ludovico, who was much in favor at the court of Duke Cosimo de Medici—to detach himself from the "reformed priests". Ignatius then energetically intervened with the Duke[41], and to protect the liberty of his son, he called him to Rome as Secretary of the Society; it seems unlikely that this persecution was the sole reason for the nomination, but there was here one of the favorable coincidences which typify the governing of Ignatius.

When he arrived in Rome as Secretary of the Society, Polanco was thirty years old (Ignatius was fifty-six). He had a vigorous personality, lucid intelligence in which reason and moral qualities predominated. His thinking was well organized, solidly structured, accompanied by a genius for organization. His mind was remarkably clear, precise, methodical, capable of long periods of concentration and deep reflection; he rapidly seized the circumstances of a case, of a situation, or of a text, and was as gifted at analysis as at synthesis. Polanco's style reveals the man to us: precision of expression, choice of terminology, internal organization of thoughts; he preferred clarity to brilliance; there was something of the perfectionist about him; among the first companions, he seems without doubt to the best writer: the *Chronicon*, his correspondence (personal and *ex commissione*) abounds in felicitous expressions and significant well-turned phrases. Sometimes he allows a smile to escape, an irony, a touch of humor, but in general he is "serious" (*serio* would be one of his preferred terms). With that, a deeply moral honesty,

---

[40] *Epist. ign.* I, pp. 457–60, n. 152.

[41] *Epist. ign.* I, pp. 467–72, n. 154 and 155; and *Chron.* I, p. 209, n. 168. What is it that one can derive from this account from the pens of certain historiographers? Would Polanco have been thrown into prison in Florence, would he have fled, etc.? Letter 154 seems to make of this account a legend.

a concern for absolute fidelity: a historian, Arcardo,[42] suggests that the overzealous disciple "sometimes went beyond the thought of his master", but he scarcely proved it; in fact, Polanco sought above all to "reflect" with the greatest possible exactitude the thought of Ignatius: even if it entailed questioning him, soliciting and receiving his corrections. Father Scaduto, in the preface of his study on the "Rules of the Secretary",[43] went so far as to speak of his "integrity of identification between the person and the institution". This combination of the intellectual and the moral, to which was added an inexhaustible good health (in addition to his work as Secretary General, as collaborator with Ignatius on the constitutions, as Procurator, Polanco did missionary work in Rome: he heard confessions, gave spiritual direction and gave the Exercises): this combination, I maintain, made Polanco the perfect example of the "outstanding administrator". For the position of administrator, he had received training in Paris, then in Rome (before his entry into Ignatius' group).

Such was the collaborator whom Ignatius proposed at present for the drafting of the constitutions.

His first work, it seems, was to undertake an in-depth study of the *Constituta et annotata*, the collection Ignatius had begun in 1544 and which he continued to develop: it was a matter of the Secretary's assimilating the true thought of the master of the work. He noted in writing everything which seemed to him obscure, unsatisfactory, or all that occurred to him on the subject of the organization, in order to talk to Ignatius about it. It was thus that we have from Polanco four series of *dubia* ("Doubts") that the editor of the *Constitutions* dates very exactly from 1547–1548.[44] Methodically, he inventoried the documents: the "Constitutions concerning the Missions", the "De Ambitu", the "Old and New Determinations" (first series of "Doubts"), and he sometimes noted the reaction of Ignatius; in the second series, he tore apart the legislation of other religious orders, extracted what seemed to him applicable to the Society, pointed out what, in his opinion, the Society ought to do as opposed to the way in which things were done in existing orders. Here again, a few of Ignatius' reactions were recorded.[45] In the

---

[42] Cf. *Comentario á las Constituciones de la Compañia de Jesús*, 6, p. 617.

[43] *"Uno scritto ignaziano inedito il 'Del officio del Secretario' del 1547"*. *AHSI* vol. 19 (1960), pp. 305–28.

[44] *Const.* 1, pp. 268–339 (hence the first four of the six "Series of Doubts").

[45] We find them perhaps in another document of 1549 (?) which Fr. Codina entitled "Capita quaedam Constitutionum" (*Const..* 1, pp. 261–66). A remarkable study of the work of Polanco on the Dominican documents has been done by Fr. Aloïs Hsu: "Dominican Presence in the Constitutions of the Society of Jesus", PUG Rome, 1971.

third series, Polanco systematically examined the pontifical documents which concerned the Society: the bulls *Regimini militantis* and *Injunctum nobis*, and the briefs *Exponi nobis* and *Inter cunctas*. He noted the doubts which they awoke in him and, in the margin, Ignatius' responses. As for the fourth series, it seemed to be a sort of summary of the three previous ones; it was written with more care. There, Polanco reassembled the questions of the preceding series with the answers furnished by Ignatius. In the margin, Ignatius, in his own hand, confirmed or corrected his earlier responses.[46] We are then seeing a recapitulated document, which marks the taking over of the work by Polanco: it was an important moment in the genesis of the *Consitutions*, there was no break with what was in the process of being developed. There were two at that moment present to accomplish the task, two men who worked in hierarchical collaboration. The "Rules of the Secretary" of 1547 admirably reveal their rapport and relationship to each other.[47]

Along with these collections of "Doubts", Polanco introduced another, no less delicate: he set up an index (*Indices*) of the "things" which are treated in the papers of "our Father" (Ignatius) and tried to classify them according to basic topics.[48] Above all, in 1548,[49] Polanco composed a document which would have a great influence on the definitive draft of the *Constitutions*; it was what was called his *"Means"*,[50] of which the entire title was "Here are twelve means by which the Society could be better helped to achieve its goal".[51] For the first time, a unified plan was designed according to which different documents, scarce up until then, would be presented: historians are agreed in their recognition of the common work of Ignatius and Polanco in the *"Means"*, some giving priority to the inspiration of Ignatius, others to Polanco; would it not be wiser to admit that in order to decide such a question, one would have had to be present at the conversations of the two collaborators?

At the same time, Polanco prepared the new pontifical bull which the

[46] Certain responses of Ignatius referred by prudence to high Roman authorities or others? "Let Puteo (Jaime del Pozzo) Dean of the Rota, see this point or someone who has experience. . . ." "Let it be as it will appear better to the members of the Curia. . . ." "If that does not seem contrary to the opinion of the officials"; whence the last two of the six series of Doubts (*Const.* I, pp. 346–55).

[47] Cf. supra, p. 241, n. 43. Although they especially concern the correspondence, these Rules define the general spirit of the position.

[48] *Const.* I, pp. 220 et sq.

[49] On this date, historians of the *Constitutions* are today in agreement, it seems.

[50] That is to say means.

[51] *Pol. comp.* 2, pp. 725–75. Cf. also on the date and their relation to the Constitutions: *Const.* 2, pp. CLXXVII–CLXXVIII.

experience of seven years of missionary existence rendered necessary. On October 18, 1549, Paul III produced the bull *Licet debitum* which singularly enlarged the privileges accorded to the Society. Scarcely elected, Julius III promulgated on June 21, 1550, the bull *Exposcit debitum*, which confirmed all that Paul III had accorded to the companions, even enlarging it. Two bulls within nine months! Without doubt the fact is explained by the change in the papacy; but we have perhaps not sufficiently noted the modifications, let us say the considerable progress, which distinguishes the first bull of 1540 from the bulls of 1549–50. The Society appears simultaneously the same and different: it takes on the look of canonical maturity. To such a point that a historian could say that it had been transformed more between 1540 and 1550 than between 1550 and 1950. Caprice rather than objective judgment: for through the transformation imposed by the apostolic experiences of the companions and the legislation of the Church, Ignatius vigorously maintained an identity of purpose and spirit. However, it remains true that the progress achieved in the ten years of legislation of the Society of Jesus seems considerable.

The Fourth Stage: The "threshold" of 1550–1551

Ignatius and Polanco worked with ferocity. 1550 was a Holy Year, and at least since 1546, Ignatius had wanted on this occasion to gather together the *primi Patres* and the other companions in whom he had confidence; he wanted, according to what the bulls of Paul III prescribed for him, to submit to them a coherent text of the *Constitutions* for approval, and especially for corrections, criticisms, suggestions. "For Ignatius", notes Nadal in his "Ephemerides" in 1550, "convoked the professed who could come without too many difficulties, and a few other Fathers *for a kind of general congregation*, in order to show the *Constitutions* to them so that they might make comments on what seemed good to them".[52] He particularly increased his letters and efforts so that all the surviving *primi Patres* could be there: he insisted, as we have already seen, to John III that Rodríguez and even Xavier come to Rome. All actually (except Xavier) would meet Ignatius either in 1550 or 1551; and several others also, like Borgia who remained officially the Duke of Gandia. All would be consulted, whether in small groups or individually. From this consultation, we have a witness in the "Observata Patrum" (Remarks of Fathers Laynez, Salmeron, Araoz, Bobadilla).[53]

What then was this text which was presented to the different guests of La Strada in the years 1550–1551? On the text which all the historians call

---

[52] *Nadal Mon.* 2, p. 4.
[53] *Const.* 1, pp. 390–96.

"text A" of the *Constitutions*, there is no disagreement. All also consider it the work of Ignatius, seconded by Polanco, according to the indications which we have given above: the only problem would be to assess the importance of this collaboration of Polanco; but no one would question that text A accurately and faithfully reflects the thought of Ignatius. One thesis was sustained for several years (in 1967) in the preface of volume two of the French translation of the *Constitutions*;[54] a serious thesis, which created much confusion in certain minds. This A text, regarding which the companions were called in 1550 to give their opinions and on which Ignatius and Polanco were going to work another six years, according to the criticisms of the companions and in light of their experiences, would not be a purely Ignatian text: it would have undergone transformations by Polanco who would have profoundly modified the point of view of which Ignatius, nor perhaps Polanco himself, had measured the importance. The wholly Ignatian text would be a text "a" edited for the first (and only) time by Father Arturo Codina in the MHSJ in 1936.[55]

"Everything transpired", wrote Father Roustang, regarding the texts on obedience, "as if Polanco had limited himself at first to writing under the dictation of Saint Ignatius [*this would be text* "*a*"—*Author*], but that little by little the freedom which had been left him would allow him to express himself in his own way without realizing that it was very far from that of the founder of the Society [*this would be text A, then text B—Author*]"[56] and farther on, regarding text B: "It is likely that [Ignatius] voluntarily accepted the diverse influences which came to bear on his work of elaboration. It was for him a way of not locking himself into a too personal vision which risked not being understood and therefore being ineffective. The symbiosis of his genius and the prevailing mentality of his era, particularly that of his collaborators, was necessary to the pursuit of his work."[57] Affirmations from which one can draw explosive conclusions . . . were not long in coming. Whoever wishes to know the *Constitutions* of Ignatian mentality must then, according to Father Roustang, refer to text "a" and not to text A.

The limitations of our study do not permit us to discuss François Roustang's preface in depth. In addition, such work would repeat the minute criticism which has been made of it by Father de Aldama in his

---

[54] By François Courel and François Roustang ("Christus" collection).

[55] *Const.* 2, pp. 127–57. The name "text a" is unfortunate; one must remember that it leads to confusion.

[56] *Constitutions* ("Christus" collection), vol. 2, p. 33.

[57] Ibid., pp. 34–35.

work: *La Composición de las Constituciones de la Compañía de Jesús*.[58] We shall say only this: the structural analysis of Ignatian thought which Roustang establishes (genetic structure, rational structure and dialectical structure) is interesting in itself; it projects onto the text a particular light; but like every method of stylistic analysis, it ought to be completed and controlled, so to speak, by other methods of textual criticism; it is, by itself, unilateral and systematic. Moreover, one cannot be surprised that Roustang in his study didn't take account of what we know of the way in which Ignatius carried on his work from the time of 1541, and especially from 1544 on. It was well before 1547 that Ignatius had renounced the idea "of locking himself into too personal a vision" of the Society, and this was not because that vision "risked being misunderstood and therefore being ineffective", but simply because Ignatius was a truly spiritual man who sought the will of God; gropingly like all the truly humble, he did not pretend to have a monopoly on the inspirations of the Holy Spirit and wanted to verify, control and complete his own thoughts through the thoughts of those whom God himself had given him as collaborators and cofounders. Finally, the thesis of Roustang does not stand up to direct examination of the manuscript of one hundred forty-five pages of text "a" which is preserved in the Roman archives of the Society of Jesus:[59] this examination and research of the sources for each part of these *Constitutions* proves by the evidence that one is dealing with "an artificial compilation of great variety and previous writings".[60]

A last point merits being pinpointed: the internal criticism of text "a", and the external criticism of his manuscript, strongly incline, if not oblige us, to fix as extreme dates of its printing the middle of 1549 (beginning) and the middle of 1550 (end). The text of the *Constitutions* which was submitted to examination and to the criticism of the companions, reunited in or passing through Rome, was text A. This text A was finished before the end of the summer of 1550. Between the end of the drafting of text "a" and the end of the drafting of text A, scarcely two months passed. That's little time for a text of Ignatian mentality to be transformed into a text of Polancian mentality. What to conclude? Text "a" was an attempt, or even a group of attempts, like those of which the archives possess several others, to elaborate this coherent text which Ignatius wished to present to the companions reassembled in Rome in 1550.

[58] Cf. supra, p. 216.

[59] (72 ff. and half, Inst. 7) Let us note in passing, without drawing any conclusion for or against the thesis of François Roustang, that of these 145 pages, 109 are written in the hand of Polanco.

[60] Antonio Maria DE ALDAMA, op. cit., p. 18.

Let us stop this discussion right here. To my mind, Ignatius and Polanco had continued, up to the point of finishing the text which would be submitted to the companions, their close collaboration, the latter making an effort to understand the thought of the former. Since it was his job to question, and Ignatius had invited him to do so, Polanco was not afraid to solicit specifics and finalizations, to suggest, to propose, to submit himself in total loyalty to the ultimate choice of Ignatius.

Let us hasten to return to La Strada, at the end of the summer of 1550. Ignatius began to receive the companions whom he wished to consult on the constitutions; on November 23, it was "the Duke of Gandia", Francis Borgia (privately professed in the order since February 2, 1548) who arrived with an entourage of twenty to twenty-five people; and this group lodged separately in the small house. Araoz, Strada, Miron, Andrés Oviedo, Francis de Rojas and Master Emmanuel de Sa[61] accompanied him. Borgia sojourned in Rome until February 4, 1551: two long months of conversations with Ignatius. In January, it was Salmeron who, after having preached during Advent in Verona, joined "Father Ignatius and the other Fathers reunited in Rome" to say there "what he thought of the constitutions".[62] Laynez was there; with Salmeron and Araoz, he drafted a certain number of "Observations":[63] simple, but frank; visibly this first draft did not fill them with enthusiasm, Salmeron declared: "the shorter and briefer the constitutions are, the better it will be: transfer many things into the declarations." They were not reunited to congratulate each other and to ratify a wholly completed text! On February 4, Borgia departed for Spain with the Fathers who had come from there only for this meeting and with a few others, in all thirty people; Laynez would travel with them as far as Genoa.[64] The Spanish group had hardly departed when, on February 8, who should arrive but Simón Rodríguez, whom John III of Portugal, after much equivocation, had finally allowed to leave for Rome;[65] he would stay there until June 1 and depart with Miron for Portugal. There were four months of conversations between Ignatius and that companion who presided over the development of the then most flourishing province, the province on which depended all the young Society's missions out of Europe. It was undoubtedly during this visit of Rodríguez at La Strada that Bobadilla turned up in Rome between two apostolic missions;[66] at least he had the

[61] *Chron.* 2, p. 10.
[62] Ibid., pp. 162–63 Cf. supra, pp. 155 sqq.
[63] *Const.* 1, pp. 391–95.
[64] *Chron.* 2, p. 164. *Epist. ign.* 3, pp. 338–39, n. 1601.
[65] *Chron.* 2, p. 165. *Epist. Mixt.* 2, p. 515.
[66] *Bobad. Mon.*, p. 624. n. 33.

chance to let a few arrows fly as was typical of his manner. "It seems to me that the same thing is repeated several times. It would be a good idea to make a brief resume of all these rules which would cover the essentials."[67]

One would like to be sure that the impetuous Bobadilla had taken the time to sit down to read the text which he criticized! In 1557, he would make even stronger remarks: he was not a man to enjoy the austere savor of canonical texts. Others came to Rome, the invitations which Ignatius sent them and which are preserved in the correspondence were not in vain, certainly; the list, however, is not contained in the accounts.[68] It was, then, to quote the words of Nadal, a "sort of first general congregation" that Ignatius held between the end of 1550 and the beginning of 1551. His responsibilities as general demanded it of him, according to the pontifical bulls; and his humility, or simply the wise position which he had taken, as early as Paris, of considering everything with his companions, required it as well. They would depend upon the opinions of all of the participants: the meeting was not just for show.

We hold, it seems, a proof of the importance which Ignatius attributed to this meeting. He tried to profit from it . . . to be relieved of the generalship. That happened on January 30, 1551, before the departure of Borgia and the Spanish group. We possess his act of resignation, in seven points,[69] which he offered to all the companions present.[70] Truly, he offered a good argument: the deterioration of his health. However, the letter was so beautiful that in itself, it would have sufficed to keep him in command. Evidently, the companions refused this resignation, having confidence in Providence that their fidelity would not turn into homicide. The scrupulous Oviedo alone accepted the proposal of Ignatius: "With an admirable ingenuity", says Nadal, "he said that Ignatius no longer appeared to him to be able to act in the post of General; because, since the holy man said so, it was necessary to believe it."[71] The gesture of Ignatius had at least this advantage: it signified that he would consider this reunion of the *priores Patres* to have marked a threshold in the work of the constitutions and that he had, as far as he was concerned, honored his mandate.

The Fifth Stage: 1551–1556. Ignatius and Polanco perfect text A of the Constitutions *in the light of the observations of the companions and of their*

---

[67] *Const.* 1, p. 396.
[68] *Nadal Mon.* 2, p. 5.
[69] *Epist. ign.* 3, pp. 303–304, n. 1554.
[70] *Chron.* 2, p. 15.
[71] *Nadal Mon.* 2, pp. 4 and 5.

experience. The Constitutions, *were nevertheless "declared" from then on in the different provinces and regions.*

Five facts characterize this new period: Ignatius and Polanco continued to correct text A of the *Constitutions* and drew from it text B. At the same time they drafted and put the Rules in order. They hoped to print the *Constitutions* and Rules, if one may believe Ignatius' letter about it; in any case, copies of it were completed. The *Constitutions* and Rules were declared. Putting them into practice did not occur without some difficulties here and there. There are five facts which we must presently study in order to understand the mentality according to which Ignatius worked.

One preliminary remark is essential: from 1553 on, Ignatius' health deteriorated. It would pass through crises increasingly frequent and serious, to the point that in April 1554, a "general council" was instituted "to consider particularly serious matters of the Society": the consultants were Olave, Frusius, and Gonçalves de Câmara; Polanco was its secretary; and in November of the same year, Ignatius ordered that all the priests present in Rome, of whom four were delegated from the scholasticates, should elect a vicar general to assist him in his administration of the Society. Nadal was chosen. The deterioration of Ignatius' health coincided with the considerable growth of the Society and the multiplication of his worries: the Rodríguez affair, the death of Xavier, the Ethiopian mission, the increase of colleges for day students, and later the election of Paul IV, among other things. It was in this atmosphere that the *Constitutions* were being perfected. Thanks to the indefatigable Polanco, Ignatius faced up to the situation.

1. *The work of the Constitutions.* We have said that it was the A text which had been presented to the Fathers united in Rome in 1550–1551. Now, the manuscript of this A text contained, in addition to the annotations of Polanco, more than two hundred twenty corrections or additions by Ignatius (more than one hundred forty in the constitutions themselves, more than forty in the declarations). Sometimes they are corrections of style, but often there are entire passages modified, replaced or added. It is important to specify whether these corrections were anterior or posterior to the consultation of the *priores Patres*. One very detailed study by Father Codina[72] proved that many of them were, in effect, posterior: they were the result of the Fathers' criticisms and of Ignatius' wish to take them into account.

It seems that at the beginning, Ignatius and Polanco had believed that it would suffice to correct text A itself: but they quickly perceived that it

---

[72] *Const.* 2, pp. CCXLVII–CCLV.

was necessary for them to make a new edition. It was the text that they labeled B that the first General Congregation in 1558 would baptize the "autograph of Father Ignatius";[73] not that the manuscript was written in Ignatius' hand, but to signify that it was the original text of the Ignatian constitutions. One can fix the drafting of this text B as 1552; Nadal, who had not participated in the reunion of 1550–1551, came then from Sicily to Rome to make his profession; he stayed there two months, then departed for Sicily with the mission to "declare"[74] the *Constitutions* there: the text that he carried away was still another copy of text A. But the following year, in April 1553, Nadal was named commissioner for Spain and Portugal, in order to accomplish the same mission there as in Sicily. He tells us himself that the copy of the text of the *Constitutions* which he would have had to take with him, was not finished;[75] it was sent to him later, to Portugal, and he received it in Lisbon, on September 8, upon his return from Evora. The Roman archives preserve this copy of Nadal's: it is an exact copy of the B text.[76]

The comparison between text A and text B makes clear the considerable work that Ignatius and Polanco undertook in order to perfect the constitutions. It is notable, for example, that several of the corrections seek to conform to the desires expressed by Salmeron and Bobadilla: to transfer to the declarations several passages of the constitutions. We note again that it was in text B that the much–celebrated preface appeared, the one that without doubt was inspired by the doctrine of St. Thomas and St. Augustine, on the primacy of the interior law of charity and of the necessity of exterior laws, but which corresponds profoundly to the Ignatian mentality; in itself, it would explain why Ignatius always put the work of the Society, that is to say, its missionary activity, ahead of the writing of the constitutions. It might also explain why, while unceasingly revising the text of the constitutions, he wanted not "to conclude" (*claudere*) them before his death. For up to the end, Ignatius was going to correct, amend and improve this B Text to the point that there could be no misunderstanding of it; they would date from 1556, although they had existed since 1552–1553; thus two important passages of Part IV[77] would not be inserted until after 1553.

Of these additions and corrections by Ignatius and Polanco in Text B,

[73] This manuscript B was published in phototype in 1908, on the order of Fr. Wernz, and the critical edition of it was given in 1936 by Fr. Codina in the MHSI.

[74] This "declaration", in canonical strictness, would not confer the force of law on the Constitutions.

[75] *Nadal Mon.* 1, p. 174; 2, pp. 16–17.

[76] *Const.* 2, pp. LXXXIII–LXXXVII.

[77] Chapter 7 (undoubtedly between mid-1553 and mid-1554), and chapters 11–17.

we have the list: it suffices to compare the text of 1556 with the copy which Nadal used in Portugal and in Spain and which is today preserved in the Roman archives. Everything that is in the former and not in the latter appears as modifications inserted after 1553; and the difference between the two is not negligible.

As far as Ignatius was concerned, the continuity of the life of the order and its primacy should precede the written text. It had always been thus for him. So as not to go back to the documents, "Foundation of Colleges," or "To Found a College," (1540 and 1541), "Against All Ambition," (1546); "Constitutions concerning the Missions" (1546), "The Constitutions of Scholastics" (1546), "On the Refusal of Granting Ministries to Women" (1546, owing to the failure of the troublesome Roser experience)[78]—all were texts which influenced the editing of text A and sometimes were even inserted into it—let us cite Part X of *Constitutions* B, which relates to the fifth vow of the professed (vow of listening to the Father General, in case a professed were elevated to some ecclesiastical office): this vow must have been added after the consultation which was held September 17, 1554, on the occasion of the nomination of the Patriarch and of the bishops[79] of Ethiopia. Ignatius continued thus to enrich and to improve the charter which he wished to transmit as a legacy to his companions. The best definition which we have of Ignatius' attitude (and that of Polanco) in this work on the constitutions was given to us by Polanco himself in a letter to Xavier in 1552: "We believe that, through the special providence of our Lord [the constitutions] will not be 'closed' until experience shows many things, as it has already, and until the Society has firmer roots in numerous regions."[80] This letter of Polanco clarifies the slow elaboration of the constitutions.

2. *The collection of the Rules.* This is doubtless one of the most confused questions in the history of Ignatian documents.[81] Some would say that there must have been in Ignatius' temperament something picky, even niggling, and who could deny it? It suffices to read his correspondence or the *Memorial* of Câmara to perceive this: although the big questions of the Church occupied and preoccupied him, although very grave difficulties rose as obstacles to his plans or to'those of his companions, this man was capable of interesting himself in the tiniest details of clothing, nourishment and domestic functions. Many of these details

[78] Almost all these texts were published in *Const.* 1.

[79] *Const.* 1, pp. 404–408.

[80] The letter of February 1, 1552 (*Epist. ign.* 4, p. 130, n. 2386). Polanco will use the word again in his letter of August 6, 1556 to the whole Society; the founder, he says, died without "*cerrar las constituciones*" (*Font. narr.* 1, p. 768).

[81] Cf. *Const.* 2, Proemio, art. 1 and 2, especially pp. 264–65.

have, we perceive in retrospect, a significant value, for example, for poverty [hence the *jumenta* or the functions (for the cook, the buyer, etc.)]. Even for those for which the meaning escapes us today, it is fitting to judge with prudence: to hear him declare to Laynez and Ribadeneyra about the "Rules of Modesty" (1555), "I assure you that these rules have cost me prayers, and tears at least seven times", invites caution. However, once this tendency is mentioned, it is a matter of seizing, so far as possible, the meaning and the scope of these Rules, in their essence, for each group had its own aim. This meaning is clear: Ignatius feared nothing so much, in spiritual, intellectual, apostolic or community life as good intentions which remained at the stage of good intentions; in everything, he sought efficacy, sincerity, honesty and the truth of life. The rules were, in his eyes, the least illusory means of self-control and to be controlled by those responsible for the religious life. Even more than the Constitutions, the Rules had no value or meaning unless the heart was moved by "the law of love and charity".[82] Writing to Father Bustamente in 1560, Laynez, then General, reproached him for having decreed for his province rules which were too severe and too picayune, "for", he said to him, "observance which is habitually useful would prevent in certain cases the greatest divine service, which is the purpose of all the Constitutions and Rules."[83] As paradoxical as this comment might appear in light of what we have said above, to regulate with too much meticulous detail went against the Ignatian spirit. Proof of this is that the Superior remained the arbiter in all situations: it was up to him to adapt the laws to persons and to circumstances.

Our plan is not to enumerate the Rules created in Ignatius' time and by Ignatius.[84] It is necessary, however, to clarify one point: in the *Chronicon* and the correspondence, we encounter frequently the double expression: "The Constitutions and Rules", particularly regarding the trip of Nadal in 1553 to Portugal and Spain. What then does this expression connote?

---

[82] The best statement in French of the complete Rules which we know, the most correct and complete, is that which Jean-François Gilmont gave in the *Ecrits spirituels*, pp. 82–93. Of course, one must refer to the volume of the MHSJ. *Const.* 4: *Regulae*. A group of rules typical of the style of Ignatius is, I think, document 39, pp. 146–77 of 1547 (?): "*Observanda sacerdotibus et aedituo*", which Fr. Zapico had the fortitude to reproduce photographically at the head of the work.

[83] *Lainii Mon.* 4, p. 650.

[84] A list and an analysis may be found in Jean-François GILMONT, *Les Ecrits spirituels*, pp. 82–93. Still it is not entirely exhaustive: besides the rules, there were the "rulings" which Ignatius liked to multiply; one finds examples of this in numerous "instructions" and even in some letters; it is also certain that from 1540, there were "rules of the house" at La Strada.

The best answer might be to try to inventory what Nadal took with him in his baggage.

On this voyage, as we have seen, Nadal the Commissioner carried the *Constitutions*; he also carried the "Rules in Use in Rome", with the widest powers to adapt them to the differing conditions of localities, and he had actually to use these powers at several stages.

Among the Rules, there was probably our present *Summary of the Constitutions* (for the first text of which we have the precise date of 1553). In fact, this *Summary* consists more or less of extracts from the *Constitutions*, and presents the fundamental "kernel" of the principles of religious life in the Society. Certain people have questioned, and not without reason, whether Ignatius had not drafted or ordered drafted this *Summary* precisely for Nadal's trip to Portugal.

There were also the "Rules in Use at Rome" composed by Polanco and based on earlier Ignatian documents, particularly taken from pre-scriptions addressed by Ignatius to various colleges. They started with a section which was subsequently called "common rules": it is a combination of prescriptions and counsels which express the Ignatian concept of community life; the text which Nadal took with him was changed a little and bore his personal mark.

Then came the "Rules concerning Offices", or rules especially for those responsible for the offices of the house: rector, procurator, porter, etc. The "Rules in Use at Rome" envisaged eleven office-holders: the rules carried by Nadal in 1552 included twenty-three. It was Polanco himself who was largely responsible for this multiplication. For that, he was inspired above all by the thinking of Ignatius, but also by the rules created by Simón Rodríguez in 1545, for the college of Coimbra;[85] but he did it with great freedom; to this enlarged draft, Nadal certainly added his own contribution. All in all, these "Rules concerning Offices", carried by Nadal, marked a progress in coherence and spiritual teaching in comparison with those used in Rome.

Did Nadal carry with him directives concerning the studies and the scholastics? The contrary would have been astonishing, as this question had much preoccupied Ignatius since 1540. The first constitutions concerning the colleges date from 1541; they were revised and improved by Ignatius in 1545. Of the directives which he undoubtedly gave to each college, we have kept several examples: the oldest which we have at our disposal are those of the colleges of Padua and of Bologna (1546–1547); they reveal a very realistic sense of situations (Padua, Coimbra, Gandia, Valencia, Louvain—all lived at different tempos). Ignatius tended thus to

---

[85] Jean-François GILMONT, *Ecrits spirituels*, pp. 82–83.

individualize the rules of each house: studies, spiritual life, community life were organized according to changing proportions. In 1547–1548, Polanco portioned out in advance among these different documents the common directives, in particular those concerning spiritual life:[86] a hasty compilation, but one that he would improve and complete in "Constitutions of the Colleges" (1549–1550). This document had a determining influence on Part IV of the *Constitutions of the Society of Jesus*;[87] this time it was a question of global synthesis wherein all aspects of the life of the scholastics and of the scholasticate were presented: the spiritual progress of students, their intellectual life, their health, the life of the community and recruitment for the Society. It was not yet a question of colleges for day students, but for the colleges within the order.

In 1549, the creation of the University of Gandia brought about the drafting of particular constitutions, soon followed by instructions for the Italian colleges for day students (these colleges with a skeletal teaching staff, we should remember). An important event occurred then: the foundation of the Roman college, which Ignatius dreamed of making the archetype of all the day-student colleges. For the Roman college, some rules were composed, very similar to the "Constitutions of the Colleges" of 1549–1550; and the *Constitutions* formally invited the other colleges to be inspired by the rules of the Roman college in creating their own rules.

A number of indications make us think that Nadal carried this legislative package in his luggage, in departing for Portugal;[88] its influence can be perceived in several rules which he promulgated in the course of his visit.

3. *When did Ignatius have the Constitutions printed?* This is a question which to my knowledge, historians do not ask, but which, however, merits clarification. It is generally understood among specialists in Ignatian bibliography that the *Constitutions* were printed for the first time on the printing press of the Society's houses in Rome (*in aedibus S.J.*) in 1558–1559:[89] it was this little duodecimo volume, composed of four portions completed successively. The edition was published after Ignatius' death; Laynez, elected General, was in charge of the first General Congregation. There would have been nothing here to indicate what interests us if a text of the *Chronicon* and a letter of Polanco to Câmara of August 9,

---

[86] *Mon Praed*, 1, pp. 38–45.

[87] Cf. LETURIA, *Estudios* 1, pp. 353–87, and Angelo MARTINI, "Gli studi di Giovanni de Polanco" *AHSI*, vol. 21 (1952), pp. 225–81.

[88] Cf. *Mon. Praed.* 1, pp. 185–210, and *Regulae*, pp. 493–507.

[89] Cf. Giuseppe CASTELLANI, "*La tipografia del collegio romano*", *AHSI*, vol. 2 (1933), p. 16.

1552, had not raised a problem. The *Chronicon*[90] let it be clearly understood that Ignatius had had, from this moment, the intent of "printing" the *Constitutions*: "Francis Borgia suggested [to him] that the *Constitutions* be put into practice (*exercerentur*) for two or three years before being printed, so that experience could better show what success they might have (*quomodo procederent*)." What attention Ignatius paid to this suggestion the *Chronicon* does not tell us. However, the letter of Polanco to Câmara informs us:

> Concerning what you say about the *Constitutions* that some people [perhaps Borgia had not spoken in only his own name?] think that they ought to be put into practice for a few years before being printed (*imprimirse*): although printed, they will be so only for the Society: they have been done in such a way that, as you will see, they can be introduced and adapted to some extent without any damage to their integrity: In short, one will see how this works out here where there are many colleges in which to test the experiment.[91]

The interest of these two texts evidently surpasses the simple anecdotal facts which they present. If this Ignatian project to print the *Constitutions* from 1552 is correct, it proves that he considered them from that time on as being sufficiently finished to be published, at least for internal use within the Society. Besides, the Portuguese reaction, like that of Borgia, tended to show that far from Rome and far from Italy, they preoccupied themselves with how the *Constitutions* would be "received" (*quomodo procederent* can be understood in several ways, all of which express a certain uncertainty, if not an anxiety). If one relies on the letter of August 9, one could think that Ignatius had decided to go beyond these objections or suggestions: as in fact the specialists do not indicate to us any printed edition of the *Constitutions* before 1559, it seems that he had renounced his project, and that they were content for the moment to "transcribe" this text by copyists.

4. *The declaration of the Constitutions and Rules*. Ignatius, in any case, perceived from the beginning that it would not suffice to expedite in the various regions of the Society a text, printed or transcribed, so that everyone could put it into practice. He gave to this declaration an animated, personal character, by his own direct contact with it. The companions in whom he had particular confidence would more or less take the *Constitutions* and Rules to each enclave from house to house in

---

[90] 2, p. 688.
[91] *Epist. ign.* 4, p. 365, n. 2786.

each province. The man in whom he placed his confidence for this mission was Jerónimo Nadal.

Nadal had not entered the Society until 1545. Ignatius marked him from the moment when they met at the University of Paris. He had even tried to win him as a companion, but Nadal was apprehensive of joining this still unformed spiritual group which appeared to him to be engaging in an adventure for which he scarcely felt any inclination. Finally, after knowing the companions in Rome better, he decided to join the Society; and in accord with his temperament, this gift of himself, certainly ripened over a long period, was a gift absolute, total, "with neither ifs nor buts": Nadal was the archetype of the faithful disciple who would never betray his commitment.

Ignatius's choice was a good one: Jerónimo Nadal possessed an intelligence that was lucid, penetrating and flexible, with a bit of stubbornness and obstinacy: but he had an understanding of men and of human problems, for he was endowed with a fine sensitivity which made him a good observer and an acute psychologist. In addition, he was of an irreproachable rectitude, having a horror of all which would sway or betray one from near or far. His physical resources, especially his nerves, were not inexhaustible, but his will supplemented his strength whenever his task, or the spiritual good of his neighbor, required it; he had just proved this in Sicily, where his apostolic dynamism had done wonders. He knew Ignatius as well as the latter could be known; for three years Nadal had been with Ignatius in Rome. Ignatius could be at ease: he would not slant the *Constitutions* and Rules either by over-interpreting or under-interpreting them. Nadal also had experience with the *Societas romana*. "It was he, more than any other," wrote Father de Guibert, "who contributed to establishing the traditional manner of understanding and practicing the *Constitutions*."[92] And this manner was discounting various nuances, according to different temperaments, the Ignatian manner. If he enriched the way of understanding the *Constitutions* with all the theological and spiritual knowledge that he had acquired before entering the Society, this knowledge did not deform the *Constitutions*; on the contrary, his promulgation made what were only buds burst into full flower.

It was in Sicily that an Ignatian order to return to Rome (December 19, 1552) reached Nadal.[93] The letter warned him that his return to Rome was not so that he could go to the Council of Trent with Laynez and

---

[92] Guibert, *La Spiritualité de la Compagnie de Jésus*, p. 192.
[93] *Epist. ign.* 4, pp. 44, n. 2286.

Salmeron, as it had been a question of his doing for two weeks.[94] Why then? Ignatius would not tell him except in Rome. Actually, he stayed there, not only one month as he had foreseen at first, but two, for he fell sick. On March 25, he made his solemn profession in the hands of Ignatius and soon was designated to declare the *Constitutions* in Sicily. Barely recovered, he departed nonetheless: for the declaration of the *Constitutions* was pressing and Doménech, named Provincial of Sicily on February 1, 1552, was retained in Spain.[95] Sicily was then a flourishing region: Viceroy Juan de Vega, his wife, his sons and his daughter favored all the efforts of the companions; the college of Messina prospered: men of worth—B. Palmio, John Philip Casini, Cornelius Wischaven, Ribadeneyra and still others—taught and did missionary work there. Novices were abundant. Nadal, who had already worked for four years (1548–1552) among them encountered (for his mission) only the difficult minors. In sum, this first experience was spent in a very encouraging manner; all was easily organized according to the *Constitutions*. There was a single dark cloud: Doménech was delayed in leaving Spain. Finally, he came back at the end of 1552. Nadal returned to Rome at the beginning of March 1553.

On April 10, Ignatius named him Commissioner of Portugal and Spain. His mission: he would declare the *Constitutions* and Rules; he would also regulate many pending situations. He soon departed from Rome for Geneva, fortified with very extensive powers and with diverse instructions for himself and with the General's "carte blanche" for certain cases which would ordinarily surpass his powers as commissioner.[96] On April 17, Nadal embarked from Genoa; on May 5 he reached Barcelona from where he soon got to Portugal, not without having visited en route two or three of the Spanish houses.

If Sicily in 1552 was the calmest province of the Society of Jesus, Portugal in 1553 was incontestably the most turbulent. From January of 1552 on, it had been deeply divided and in tumult: Ignatius had withdrawn the office of Provincial from Rodríguez who, along with Xavier, had established the Society in these regions as early as 1540, had developed it under the efficacious benevolence of King John III and had governed it for twelve years. Although Ignatius had soon named him Provincial of Aragon, this change had appeared in the eyes of the majority, companions or strangers, as a disavowal and as a sanction.

[94] Ibid. 4, p. 30, n. 2259.
[95] *Chron.* 2, p. 553.
[96] It was the custom of Ignatius to give his signature on a document to the men to whom he confided delicate missions. To inspire confidence in responsible people was one of the marks of his manner of governance.

There was soon a faction faithful to Rodríguez and one which sided with Ignatius: dismissals and departures increased.[97] Did not certain ones dream of creating a new "religious order" independent of Ignatius? The least one can say is that "Rome", and the "*Societas romana*" did not there enjoy esteem. Even the person of Ignatius was denigrated without shame. What welcome would be given his Commissioner?

On the part of John III, of the court, of the visitor Michael de Torres, of Miron, and of the majority of the companions, there seemed to be no major difficulty: John III, after the first astonishment had passed, had taken Ignatius' side. The contending parties remained, however: Nadal took charge of them with a firm good will. Above all, he restored a normal climate to the province of Portugal. In his way, he gathered the community around him in each house, read the *Constitutions* and commented on them; he received his companions, one by one, conversed with them at great length, listened to their questions, and strove to respond to them: by these informal conversations, he peacefully transmitted the spirit of Ignatius. Thanks to the action of Nadal, Miron and Torres, matters became tranquil again. However, at the moment that Nadal was prepared to leave Portugal for Córdoba, in November, he was again held back by an upheaval: the tragedy of Don Theotonio de Braganza. He did not return to Córdoba until December 23, 1553.[98]

Nadal's mission to Portugal testifies to the confusion which the absence of the *Constitutions* had allowed to become entrenched, at least in the regions distant from Rome, but also shows the effective work which the Commissioner accomplished. On Sunday, October 1, 1553, a ceremony which would astonish us today took place at St. Roch of Lisbon in the presence of the King and the Prince: three companions "who had lived ten years in the Society", Gonsalves de Silveira, Gonsalvus Vaz, and Anthony de Quadros, pronounced their solemn profession; then four others pronounced the vows of spiritual coadjutors (among them Father Juan de Beira who had just come back from India); four others pronounced the vows of temporal coadjutors; still others took the vows of scholastics. Nadal celebrated the Mass and received all these commitments; before the ceremony Borgia preached with a "spiritual vehemence" which greatly touched his listeners. No doubt this solemnity, though somewhat spectacular, was not useless: "The people of Lisbon", claimed Polanco, "began to understand something of the caliber of the persons in our Society." While the vows were being pronounced, Borgia

---

[97] Regarding the figures on these departures we have already said that Portuguese and Spanish historians do not agree; but neither group denies the gravity of the crisis.

[98] The letters of Nadal to Ignatius in the course of this Portuguese visit are particularly remarkable. Cf. *Nadal. Mon.* I, pp. 156–212.

remained near the King and explained the *"ratio votorum, quam ipse scriptam habuit"*. Another remark of Polanco's gives us more to think about: apart from the professed, the others who could have made their vows this day were "too numerous to be able to pronounce them"; it was necessary to arrange for the following day, in the same church of St. Roch, a ceremony for the overflow.[99] Lisbon would not be the only place to benefit from this administration of professions and vows; the ceremony would be repeated in many places and would constitute one of the most useful acts of Nadal's trips.

In December of 1553, Nadal arrived at Córdoba and undertook to declare the *Constitutions* there, and to regulate several affairs pending action. One of the most important was the project elaborated upon during the course of a consultation in which Araoz, Strada, Torres, Borgia, Bustamente and Villanova participated, to divide Spain into three provinces: Castile, Andalusia and Aragon, and to name Borgia Commissioner General of the four provinces of the Iberian peninsula: the decision, reserved to the General, came on January 7, 1554.[100] This visit of Nadal was well received by the companions of Spain, although certain difficulties arose in the following years, which necessitated his return to Spain in the fall of 1555, as we shall see.

It was in the course of 1554 that a significant fact occurred: this year, only two companions departed from Portugal for India. There, they very much wanted to receive the *Constitutions* and Rules. However, Nadal did not entrust them to the two departing companions. Why? "No one", Polanco tells us, "appeared qualified to declare them, and their dispatch was put off until the following year."[101] It was Anthony de Quadros, the designated Provincial for Ethiopia, who would carry them with him in 1556,[102] a professed member of the order.

On September 29, 1554, Nadal left Spain; he arrived in Rome on October 18. His mission was accomplished. He reported also to Ignatius a harvest of direct information of remarks on the *Constitutions* and Rules, of which the legislator would take account in his work. On November 1, Nadal was elected Vicar General by the companions in Rome. This choice was the one desired by Ignatius himself. The moral and spiritual authority of Nadal thus grew even more.

His sojourn in Rome would be brief. As early as February 18, 1555, Ignatius, feeling himself in better health, entrusted to Nadal a new

---

[99] *Chron.* 3, pp. 404 and 405.
[100] *Epist. ign.* 6, pp. 151–53, n. 4048.
[101] *Chron.* 4, p. 550; cf. ibid., p. 662.
[102] *Chron.*, p. 779.

mission, similar to the preceding ones: he would go to declare the *Constitutions* and handle pending matters "in northern Italy, Austria and other regions", for that, Ignatius named him Commissioner General with "full powers to resolve ongoing questions; however, he was not to make decisions except jointly with Laynez, unless they found themselves separated; in this case, each could decide by himself".[103]

Nadal and Laynez arrived at Augsburg on March 24, 1555. Soon Laynez had to leave again with Cardinal Morone. Nadal remained alone. In Austria, the companions were fewer in number and there was only one residential post: the college of Vienna. Prague and Ingolstadt were only in the planning stages. The "concerns", on the contrary, were multiple and serious. Scarcely arrived in Germany, Nadal became aware of the amplitude and virulence of Protestantism and very quickly devised an urgent plan to check its spread.[104] On the advice of Ignatius, he talked long and frequently with Canisius on whose shoulders had rested, since the death of Jay, the heaviest of the task, but who was fitted morally and spiritually to carry this burden: the meeting of the two men under such circumstances was extremely important to the near future of Catholicism in Germany and Eastern Europe. On May 1, Nadal visited the college of Vienna where the companions lived according to a few "customs", rather than under a real rule; he declared the *Constitutions* and Rules there, and began to put all in order according to the *formula instituti*. In Vienna on June 9, the ceremony of St. Roch, adapted to the local situation, took place but without the ostentation of Lisbon: Canisius, Lanoye and Goudanus were already professed, but they had not yet pronounced the four vows which companions henceforth were to take after profession: they did so; Nadal himself pronounced "the fourth supplementary vow" of the professed which he had not yet previously pronounced.[105] The other brothers renewed or pronounced for the first time, according to the individual's situation, the vows of the scholastics.

Nadal's plan was to stay in Vienna until the end of July. In fact, he anticipated his departure and went to upper Italy to visit the colleges there and to declare the *Constitutions*. Venice, Padua, Ferrara, Modena and Florence received him, but on September 17, 1555, Ignatius recalled him urgently to Rome (*quanto prima potera*).[106] He was to be returned to Spain. Polanco explains why: "It was to help Francis Borgia in whatever

---

[103] Again one of those pluralities of authority, familiar to Ignatius. Cf. *Epist. ign.* 8, pp. 436–37, n. 5196; and *Nadal Mon.* 1, pp. 279–82.

[104] Letter of March 30, written from Augsburg to Ignatius, *Nadal Mon.* 1, pp. 286–93, n. 73.

[105] On these vows which accompanied profession, cf. *Chron.* 5, p. 237, note 5.

[106] *Epist. ign.* 9, p. 627, n. 5737.

concerned putting the Constitutions into practice; the admission to vows, and the vigorous introduction of our rules to the colleges".[107] It was also in fact to stimulate almsgiving in favor of the impoverished, indebted Roman college. Who would finish organizing everything according to the institutes in northern Italy and more simply in Italy? Laynez was chosen by Ignatius. On October 3, the General named him Commissioner General for all Italy, Rome included: in the provinces of Italy *citra et ultra Romam* (hence also in the kingdom of Naples) *et in ipsa etiam Urbe*.[108] Even in Rome! It was the first time that Ignatius had entrusted to a companion, albeit one of the *primi Patres*, an effective authority over the Roman houses and that *cum omni nostra authoritate*. Perhaps the new situation created by the election of Paul IV and the friendship which linked the Pope with Laynez was not uninfluential in this decision: Ignatius tried to avoid a danger which he considered serious.

There remained the budding communities in France, Flanders and Cologne. In France it was Broët, Provincial in title since August, 1555, Provincial in fact since he had replaced John Baptist Viola in Paris, who introduced the *Constitutions* and the Rules. In Cologne, there was not much to do on this count, for one supposes that Salmeron handled the matter. As for Flanders, Ignatius sent Father de Ribadeneyra there.

Ribadeneyra was a faithful and filial disciple of Ignatius. However, he was far from having the human breadth of a Laynez or a Nadal. It is true that he went there to negotiate the legal recognition of the Society of Jesus at the court of Philip II and that, being Spanish, he enjoyed relations and friendships which facilitated his introduction to the Prince. As for the internal affairs of the Society, however, he came up against personalities stronger than his own and against a national temperament—the Flemish—of whose reactions he was not aware. Whatever it was,[109] Ribadeneyra did not succeed in getting himself accepted by the handful of companions living in Louvain. Between him and Adriani the conflict was severe: in his letters to Ignatius, Ribadeneyra was stern concerning the "administrator" of Louvain; he was perhaps a saint, he said, but "he has no talent for governing, and he does not know how to steer his ship on the waters of state (*en agura del regir*)"; there could be no question of naming him Provincial or Superior of these regions.[110] Worse still, he did

---

[107] *Chron.* 5, p. 30.

[108] *Epist. ign.* 9, pp. 684–95, n. 5781.

[109] Reciprocal responsibility in the conflict which would break out between Ribadeneyra and Adriani is difficult to pinpoint. Paul DUDON (*Saint Ignace*) favors Ribadeneyra. However, he cites only Ribadeneyra's letters! Polanco is a little more fair-minded.

[110] One of the missions of Ribadeneyra was to give his opinion on the future provincial of northern Germany.

not have "the mentality of Your Paternity nor the Society's manner of proceeding".[111] No more needed to be said to turn the possibility of his being nominated Provincial away from him. After many an upheaval, the Commissioner acknowledged himself discouraged and powerless to declare the *Constitutions*: "As for the *Constitutions*, my wings are broken, and also my heart, seeing how few in this country have the disposition to receive and observe them (as they ought to); it is still in Cologne that things are going best."[112]

As a crowning misfortune, Olivier, the Provincial named at the suggestion of Ribadeneyra, and then Ignatius, died. Ribadeneyra effected an honorable retreat to Rome.

The missions remained. We have said above what the situation was for India. The *Constitutions* were awaited there with impatience, for the missionaries feared that "under pretext of charity, they would be separated from inspiration of the rule and be given burdens very little in harmony with it".[113] So when Anthony de Quadros brought the *Constitutions* in his luggage in 1556, they were received "with joy and alacrity": still it was necessary that they be adapted to the missionary life outside Goa. In making his visit to different posts, Silveira, Quadros's successor, recognized that "in what concerns the establishment of the Society, he found missionaries *valde rudes et inexercitatos* (that is to say very ignorant and without training)."[114]

It was in Brazil perhaps that the reception of the *Constitutions* and the reaction of the missionaries was the most admirable. We have already said with what difficulties Nobrega and his companions had to come to grips. They too awaited with impatience for someone to come to declare the *Constitutions* to them in the name of Ignatius. When the *Constitutions* finally came to them, they confirmed that on many points—particularly on the matters of food, clothing, trips—because of local economic necessities they had taken steps which did not entirely conform with the principles of poverty of the institute. Courageously, they strove "to conform themselves to the *Constitutions*": Very fortunately, Polanco added: "as much as it can be done and so far as the region permits".[115]

Thus, one can say that when Ignatius died, on July 31, 1556, all the provinces and regions of the Society had received the *Constitutions* and the Rules. The text was doubtless the one of 1552–1553, that is to say, the text amended after the reactions of the Fathers reunited in Rome, or passing through Rome in 1550 and 1551. Except for Brazil, the declara-

---

[111] *Ribad. Mon.* 1, pp. 131–32, n. 24.
[112] Ibid. 1, p. 194, n. 65.
[113] *Chron.* 4, p. 662.
[114] *Chron.* 6, p. 833.
[115] Ibid. 6, pp. 758–60.

tion or promulgation of the *Constitutions* and the Rules had been done vocally: one companion had carried them to his companions.

5. *The reactions.* Apart from Flanders, one can affirm that the reception was generous and that everywhere the members strove to adapt themselves with more or less good humor to the orientations as well as to the exigencies of the *Constitutions* and the Rules. The prestige of Ignatius and of the *Societas romana* was particularly high everywhere.

The success was particularly remarkable there where, to prolong the work of the commissioner or of the visitor, he found himself a man, trained in the school of Ignatius, penetrated with the *mens* and the *modo del proceder* of the founder. Laynez in Italy, Canisius in Austria, Broët in France, Gonçalves da Câmara in Portugal; Câmara arrived there on February 12, 1556, after a voyage from Rome to Genoa, Alicante and Lisbon which had lasted close to four months. He arrived there in the capacity of an assistant to the Provincial, but he was a collaborator of an unusual character: he would not depend on his provincial, he would not be obliged to accompany him, he would be free to take care of the ministries of his choice. He was then enriched by a halo of the years spent in Rome in daily intimacy with Ignatius (May 23, 1553–October 23, 1555)[116] and especially by the autobiographical confidences he had received from Ignatius. Better still: he reported from Rome some very good testimonies of Ignatius himself. Such was the praise that Ignatius gave him in his letter of October 22, 1553:[117] "By reason of the confidence which we have in the charity and discernment that the Author of all good has given him, by reason of the intelligence he has of things in the Society, I have entrusted to him certain things to be announced orally: all that he will say or write on my behalf should be believed as from me." In fact, scarcely arrived in Portugal, his heart full of nostalgia for the *societas romana*[118] Câmara strove to introduce everywhere "the Roman way of doing things".[119]

It was not only with Portugal that Ignatius acted thus. To launch Billom in France, he sent Le Bas there who had seen how the Roman college operated.[120] They asked for people here and there, for example,

---

[116] More precisely: September 1554–October 23, 1555, the period during which Câmara was "minister" of the house of La Strada, a minister who was practically the local superior.

[117] *Epist. ign.* 10, pp. 21–22, n. 5837. See regarding Luis Gonçalves da Câmara the remarkable introduction that Roger TANDONNET drafted for his translation of the *Mémorial*, especially pages 15–22 ("Christus" collection).

[118] *Chron.* 6, p. 742.

[119] Cf. ibid. 6, pp. 720, 732–33 (praxis of the rules, recreations, etc.); 737, 741 (manner of proceeding); 739 (penances in the novitiate); 750 (statutes of the royal college); etc.

[120] Ibid. 5, p. 41.

the rectors who had been trained in Rome by Ignatius.[121] Already experienced masters of novices wanted to come to be trained with him.[122] Each felt that the *Constitutions* and the Rules risked remaining a written text, and therefore a dead text, if it was not animated by that imponderable *mens et modus* which alone could transmit the spirit of the Society, the mode of life of the Companion of Jesus Christ.

It was undoubtedly because of the living testimony that this trustworthy man gave to the Society that more or less serious difficulties did not occur: the most serious were perhaps those in Flanders.[123] However, Spain was not exempt: for example, at Córdoba in 1554, when "the good Father" Gonzalo Gonzales showed reluctance before "the eighty-some rules of the rector", as well as the minister and other office-holders; he would not have the time, he objected, to observe them or even to read them;[124] there were difficulties in other cities also, and we have said that difficulties of this nature prompted Nadal's new trip to Spain in 1555.[125]

Let us not, however, talk of the arguments which the opponents of the Society, like Melchoir Cano or "the doctors of Paris", could find in the *Constitutions* or of points which caused difficulty for certain of our friends like Dominique de Soto.

More interesting to recollect are certain dissatisfactions which several companions faithful to Ignatius manifested: Laynez,[126] Strada,[127] Bustamente,[128] Ribadeneyra himself and still others. At the moment of Ignatius' death, several were ready to demand this or that modification. The astonishing thing was that at the first General Congregation in 1558, perhaps under the effect of circumstances (Paul IV himself requested certain changes), everyone was agreed to respect to the utmost the complete text of Ignatius.[129] Bobadilla himself who, in one of those moods which were typical of him, had gone so far as to write to the Pope in 1557, "The *Constitutions* and the *Declarations* are a labyrinth of the most confused nature; they are so numerous that no one, neither inferior nor superior can arrive at knowing them, even less at observing them",[130] was not the last to condemn the integrity of the Ignatian text.[131]

---

[121] Ibid. 4, p. 598.
[122] Ibid. 6, p. 346.
[123] Ibid. 6, p. 434, 435, 445; cf. supra pp. 246 sqq.
[124] Ibid. 4, p. 460.
[125] Ibid. 6, p. 30.
[126] *Chron.* 6, p. 446.
[127] Ibid. 6, p. 634.
[128] Ibid. 6, pp. 701–702.
[129] Cf. the remarkable study of Mario SCADUTO: *L'Epoca*, 1, pp. 103–23.
[130] *Nadal Mon.* 4, p. 733, an echo of his position of 1549–1551, *Const.* 1, p. 396.
[131] Mario SCADUTO, op. cit., vol. 1, pp. 32–46, 102.

We must not be astonished by these reactions: they would be very
serious if Ignatius had considered the *Constitutions* as his personal
work—completed and untouchable. Once again we must state that this
was not at all the case. He wanted his text to be examined freely, even
critically, by his companions; he wanted even more that it pass the test of
"experience". It was not only "for form's sake" that he refused and
refused again to conclude (*clore*) the *Constitutions* and took care not to
give them the force of law before his death: only a General Congregation, representing the entire Society and freed from his presence, had, in
his eyes, the right to make the work a law in the full sense of the word.
This respect that Ignatius had for the Society, the Society reciprocated in
1558 by ratifying his work: but this should not falsify our point of view
concerning Ignatius' attitude in drafting or in declaring the *Constitutions*.

II.   THE COMPANY OF JESUS
SEEN THROUGH THE CONSTITUTIONS

Here it is not a question of presenting a detailed analysis or even a
summary of the *Constitutions*. Others have done so and in a remarkable
manner. To speak of only one of the companions in the Ignatian period
who could pride himself on knowing them in depth, we need only
mention Jerónimo Nadal.[132] As for the moderns, it suffices to mention
Joseph de Guibert, Pietro Tacchi Venturi, Paul Dudon, and above all,
José Manuel Aicardo,[133] and to renounce any new attempt at presenting
this material. So we shall insist on only three points: the place of the
Constitutions in the collection of the fundamental texts of the Society, the
characteristic "movement" of the total *Constitutions*, and the understanding of the "portraits".

The Constitutions *in the Collection of the Fundamental Texts of the Society.*
Their place is primary. But it is fitting:
—To accord a great importance to the bulls and briefs of the Roman
pontiffs who approved and confirmed the new Society. They were,
moreover, at the source of many a prescription or clarification of the
Constitutions.
—Never to lose sight of the decision to offer themselves to the Vicar of
Christ on earth for all missions anywhere in the universe preceded the

---

[132] Cf. different writings on the *Constitutions* in Jean-François GILMONT, *Ecrits spirituels*,
pp. 237–49.
[133] *Commentario á las Constituciones de la Compañia de Jésús*. This list is not exhaustive.

project of creating a religious order—hence the independence of the *Constitutions*. It belongs to the period of simple companionship. Moreover, it was because this decision concerned, as an immediate and inevitable consequence, the dispersion of the companions to all corners of the world, that it appeared "more useful" to unite itself into a "formal religion" and to give itself some constitutions. One might perhaps object that it was not just a matter of a simple "placement at the disposition" of the Pope for all missions. These are the facts. But at first this step was the equivalent for the companions of a pilgrimage to the Holy Land with what represented to their eyes, prayer, suffering and love of Christ; in departing for Jerusalem they put themselves at the service of the Vicar of Christ on earth as they would put themselves at the disposition of Christ, including martyrdom. Secondly, when they decided to make the vow of obedience to the Pope, no one hesitated to object that they were vowing that to which every Christian and especially all religious already are bound by Baptism and by faith; they did not persevere less in their decision: it was then, that, according to them, the vow created for them a special vow of obedience to the Vicar of Christ on earth.[134] As for distinguishing obedience for the mission and obedience to all that the Pope represented in the Church, there was there a subtlety which seems very strange: just as well to say that the Apostles could have followed Christ in his mission and, that being the case, not transmitted his teaching in its totality.

—Finally, to confirm the perfect harmony of tone, accent, spirit which link the *Constitutions*, from the spiritual point of view, with the major texts which preceded them, in spite of important canonical modifications (poverty, privilege, etc). In order to understand them it suffices to compare the *Summa Instituti* of 1554[135] and the bull *Regimini militantis* of September 1540[136] with Part X of the *Constitutions*, which is considered its resumé and the "pearl" (*gemma*). Here and there, the hand of God in the destiny of the Society of Jesus was recognized; here and there it was given the same primacy as in the *Dextera Excelsi*; the "power of God" was recognized in the efficacy of apostolic action, as was the value of "human means", utilized under the influence of divine grace; there was also the same affirmation of the irreplaceable role of poverty, of humility, of obedience and of the same counsels concerning physical and spiritual well-being: here and there, there is the same desire for unity and for charity among the companions. The *Constitutions* appear as the

---

[134] *Const.* I, p. 27.
[135] Ibid. I, pp. 14–21.
[136] Ibid. I, pp. 24–32.

flowering of the early budding of the *Summa*. The same "mentality" is
evident throughout the diverse language and structures.

The "Characteristic Thrust" of the Constitutions. One can say without
exaggerating that no "rule" of a religious institute was submitted to
closer scrutiny, analysis and research than the *Constitutions* of the Society.
Our plan is not to follow this route[137] but to try to grasp in its originality
the thrust of the Ignatian document; in such an interpretation we take
into account the subjective and therefore debatable elements. What
characterizes the *Constitutions* of the Society of Jesus is that they are,
rather than structural or architectural, essentially missionary (this has
often been emphasized) and that this missionary itinerary faithfully
reproduces the long experience of the group of the first companions. If
the words do not seem pedantic, we shall say that here the "ontogeny" of
each companion reproduced the "phylogeny" of the Society—that of a
missionary religious order.

The "General Examen", this important section, located before the
prologue of the Constitutions, apart from and prior to the legislation
proper within the order, what was this if not a picture—doubtlessly
more elaborate, but still real—of the conditions in which the early
Parisian group had been constituted? Does it not evoke, from the first
words "the total little community which from the moment of its founding has been called the Society of Jesus" (1,1)? Why group themselves
thus? For what reason? And this Society presents itself to the one who
desires to join it; it declares clearly to him what, from the beginning,
would prevent him from completing his plan. Then one makes even
further acquaintance, as artisans in a difficult undertaking speak loyally to
an eventual recruit: one hides nothing of the conditions of the ordinary
work and one helps him to examine himself to see whether he has the
strengths and resources for such a difficult task. Since the words are
always subject to illusion, one asks him to prove to himself and to his
eventual companions that he is truly capable of launching himself on this
evangelical adventure. It is what one calls, in technical terms, "probation" or an "experiment", but perhaps we should call them experiences.
There were six of them and it was here that a marvelous parallelism was
established between the history of Ignatius, his first companions and the
life of the candidate. Their first experience reproduced Manresa (Ignatius'
experience) and Paris (that of the other first Fathers): these were the

---

[137] We point out, however, certain more recent works: Hsu, Costa, Egaña, Olivares,
etc., and, obviously, the valuable introductions of Codina in *Const.* 1, 2, 3. A systematic
research of "sources" has been undertaken by Fr. de Aldama.

month-long Spiritual Exercises. The second stage reproduced the hospital service (Barcelona for Ignatius; for all, the period in Venice and in Upper Italy); the third experience, of primary importance, was that of the pilgrimage: a test of poverty, humility and confidence in God (the pilgrimage of Ignatius to Jerusalem and the voyages: Paris to Venice and Venice to Rome). The fourth stage consisted of practicing within the residence house "low and humble" works. The fifth experience would be that of teaching Christian doctrine to children or adults. The sixth was that of preaching and, for the priests, of acting as confessors. The order in which these experiences were accomplished is of little importance; one can even de-emphasize the pilgrimage and elongate the hospital service or vice-versa; the important thing is that they did them and that they were actually renewed and reinvigorated by doing them: these activities were fundamental and constituted, so to speak, the base of the apostolic life of each companion. A significant fact is that the behavior of the candidates during the course of these different trials was evaluated by those who supervised their work, whether or not they were members of the Society. Consequently, the evaluators were hospital directors or heads of departments, people who lived in the house or natives of the area, officials or individuals, and obviously, according to the case, other companions. It was, however, in an account of conscience between the Superior and the candidate that all these experiences and the totality of the "probation" had to be considered; a dialogue, animated by total charity and kindness, on the part of the Superior, and reflecting a manner of absolute honesty and guilelessness on the part of the candidate. So long as this period of experiences and tests was not completed, the candidate, even if he lived in the house with the companions, was not allowed to say that he was part of the Society. This phase corresponds actually to the phase of companionship of the first Fathers, *before* the deliberation of 1539. "To him who will feel", says the "Examen", "that for all that we have said, God our Lord gives us courage and strength and who will judge that his incorporation into this Society is for the greater glory of God and for as greater good for his conscience will be given to peruse the bulls, the *Constitutions*, and the other texts relative to the Society." Experiences, study and meditation on the documents of the Society would last for two years. Only then, if the candidate himself "is content, as well as the Society or the Superior of the house, he will be able to be received into the body of the Society".[138] The "body of the Society", that is the expression of the deliberation of the *Summa Instituti*

---

[138] Nos. 97 and 98.

of 1539. It was the threshold where the candidate became a companion.[139] Again, it is fitting, before crossing the threshold, that the candidate again place himself face to face with "our Creator and Lord", that he interrogate himself a last time: has he really the desire "to accept and embrace all that Christ has loved and embraced"? "the desire to resemble him"? "the desire to clothe himself with his clothing and his livery"? And if "by reason of his weakness and human misery, he does not experience these ardent desires", has he at least "some desire to experience them", "the desire to have these holy desires"? For without this total love for Christ our Lord, the most successful experiments, the most accomplished training risk being only illusion. Before all else, the companion must be the companion of Jesus Christ in his work of the redemption of the world.

It was necessary to insist on this examination as a *preamble to any agreement*, be it on the part of the candidate or on the part of the Society. For with Ignatius, the beginnings were always a very important and decisive phase: whether it was a matter of work, a budding community, a mission; whether it concerned a communal or a personal choice, it was necessary that there be an outlining of the file, a preliminary study, a weighing of the possibilities and risks, all in a very pure contact with God and in prayer. In whatever concerned the *Constitutions*, that did not begin to concern the candidate until after the "Examen".

The two years of the novitiate completed, the "probationary candidate" was advanced to pronounce his simple vows of poverty, chastity and perpetual obedience.[140] He became an "approved" scholastic (or coadjutor). For several years, the Society would help him to train

---

[139] To understand this fundamental transition, it was necessary to set aside the aspects that were not secondary but were the second stages of "probation". In the same way, it was necessary to neglect specific questions touching on different situations or aptitudes of the candidates: "instructed men", spiritual or temporal coadjutors, students, "indifferents". We have retained only the common basis for each "examen".

[140] The canonical legislation of the simple vows of the Society of Jesus is delicate; inasmuch as it has evolved in the course of centuries, in the function of the canon law of the church. The crucial point is this: the companion may be already "incorporated" into the Society of Jesus, be a "member" of the *corpus Societatis* and yet not be one "integrally"; there are progressive zones of belonging or of "interiorization"; text "a" of the *Constitutions* distinguishes several meanings, from the "most universal" (that is to say the widest) to the "most exact" in the expression "body of the Society". The current text prefers to speak of admission more and more "intrinsic" or more and more "interior" (*Const.* P.V., ch. I). It's of no consequence, the meaning is clear: the novice is already "incorporated" into the Society, the approved scholastic (or coadjutor) is more so, the professed (or the fully formed coadjutor) is completely so. Thus, it is explained that the approved scholastic can "promise to enter the Society of Jesus".

himself, both spiritually and intellectually;[141] he would give himself to
secular and sacred studies: he would prepare to become a "useful
worker" in the "vineyard of the Lord": it was the time which the
Constitutions call "the school (or the education) of the intelligence" and
which achieved for him a "final probation" called "the school of the
heart" (*Const.* P.V., ch. IV [text a] or ch. II [official text]).

In this period of formation, the approved scholastic relived in sum the
Parisian phase of the itinerary of the first Fathers (with, for the climax,
the vows of Montmartre), the Venetian phase (with, for a climax, the
sacerdotal ordination), and finally "the forty days in the desert" of
Vicenza (he again made the long Spiritual Exercises in the course of his
final probation); but he relived all of this in the context of the deliberation
of 1539; the Society of Jesus, in which he had consecrated himself to God
and made his obligation to the Vicar of Christ on earth, was no longer a
loosely-bound group; it was a "body" of which each member was freely
linked "to one of the companions by the vow of obedience".

Into this *corpus Societatis*, he had been "incorporated" from the time of
his admission to the novitiate; then in a more "internal" way by the
simple vows of an "approved scholastic", but not to the point, however,
that he did not have to add to these three vows the "promise of entering
into the Society". There remained to him one more step to take.

At the end of this long formation "of intelligence" and "of heart", the
companion was ready to make, on his own account, the act which the
first Fathers had made at St. Paul-outside-the-walls on April 22, 1541,
and to receive from the "Vicar of Christ" or, in his place, from the
scholastic's superiors, his "mission" in the "vineyard of the Lord"
(*Const.* parts III, IV, V). By his profession, or his formulated vows as a
coadjutor, he was from then on a part of the body of the Society, in the
most *precise* manner (text "a")—"in a manner most intrinsic . . . , most
internal" (official text).

Parts VIII and IX correspond to the years following the determination
of 1539, in the actual experience of the "*Corpus Societatis*"; it was the
codification, for illuminating the fact and realities of the "mission", of
the unity lived in the diversity of tasks and territories.

It was in the future—the unforeseeable future to be sure, but according to the precise conditions—that the *Constitutions* were achieved. The
Constitutions, for the life of the *corpus Societatis* did not end; it bloomed—
opening onto the future. "How the whole body would maintain itself

---

[141] We speak of approved scholastics; the transition to temporal coadjutor will be easily
accomplished. (*Const.* P.V. ch. IV, n. 544).

and develop in good health. . . ." All of the language is oriented toward the future as is the thought of the document.

This forward thrust of the *Constitutions* dates at least from the year 1548. For one finds it already clearly indicated in the first series of the "*Industria*", this document which one could consider as the very pure schema of the Ignatian project.[142] The document is entitled: *Here are twelve* Industria *with which the Society must aid itself to better achieve its purpose*. The attitude of this document is very dynamic; it corresponds to a story which unfolds: (1) to assemble men, (2) to choose men, not for them to make profession, but for them to enter the houses or colleges of the Society, (3) to retain those who have been chosen, (4) to help them make progress in their studies, (5) to make them grow in spirit and to receive them for profession, (6) to instruct them practically in the ways which the Society uses to serve God and to help souls, (7) to dispatch those who will have finished their studies there to a place where they may render the best service, (8) how, in this reassignment, they must unite themselves with the superior and how they can be guided, (9) how they can strive personally to bear many fruits; (10) how those who are outside Rome can be aided from Rome by the Superior, (11) of the Superior General; (12) to conserve and perpetuate the entire Society.

It would be necessary to go into the details of the various paragraphs, but already it is evident, if one judges from this schema, that the definitive document would be more a biogenesis than a code of canon law or a treaty on perfection. We should note, for example, the verbs of this document; they all express action, a deed or an act. One feels oneself closer to the basic thrust and source of energy of the "Meditation on the Two Standards" than of the *Rule of St. Benedict*; but let us not anticipate.

The Meaning of the "Portraits". The remarks which we are going to make at present are going to confirm the feeling of "apostolic dynamism" and of "missionary biogenesis" that we have just discovered in the *Constitutions*. In a movement, the type of man who is carried away and sustained by this movement and who in his turn animates it is of the greatest importance. The quality of the "movement" depends on that of the "movers". From the *Constitutions* one can distinguish successive "portraits" of the companion which are very indicative of the Ignatian ideal and of that of the *primi Patres*. The Society of Jesus was a grouping of persons, let us even say, of personalities; the value of the Society rested

---

[142] Cf. *Const.* 2, pp. CLXVII–CXCII; specified by Antonio Maria DE ALDAMA, *La Composición de las Constituciones*, p. 9 and note 60. It will be noted that there are twelve activities, whereas there are but ten parts in the *Constitutions*.

essentially on the value of the companions. Here it is not necessary to find contradictions. These personalities, as rich in humanity, culture and natural gifts as Ignatius wished, were first of all, Christian, evangelical, apostolic personalities. A very instructive little activity consists of detaching from the "General Examen" the portrait of the candidate, then from the first four parts of the *Constitutions*, the portrait of the scholastic, then from parts V, VI and VII the portrait of the professed or the coadjutor; and finally to confront them with the portrait of the General in chapter II of part IX; one would discover then the same visage—at different "ages", surely—but fundamentally the same, through a variety of temperaments, gifts of grace and personal histories.[143] The *Constitutions* are the story of a maturing companion, or better yet of a group of companions growing together. Not that all were, according to legend, "poured in the same mold", but they bore an air of spiritual relationship which designated them. Let us think of the group of the ten first Fathers: these men were as diverse as possible in race, culture and character: the "gentle" Favre and the impetuous Xavier, the even-tempered Laynez and the lyrical Salmeron; Bobadilla, the tempestuous companion and Broët the tranquil man, Ribadeneyra, an eternal adolescent, the sinusoidal Rodríguez, and Jay, Codure . . . and apart, the enigmatic Ignatius linking within himself the most contrasting traits. All, however, form a unity, are welded together, unified, "fraternize".[144] How? Why? One can discourse *ad infinitum*, as on the *mens Societatis* or the *modo del proceder*. It seems, however, that the first Fathers have given us the secret of what gathered them and unified them indissolubly in the prologue and in the first of the "Five Chapters": they "con-spired" in a "single will" (*in unam voluntatem conspirasse*), and this unique decision was to "renounce" under the guidance of the Holy Spirit even the legitimate joys of existence in the world, "to dedicate forever their life to the service of Jesus Christ our Lord and to his vicar on earth";[145] as for one who henceforth would wish to join the group, they would ask him as a fundamental condition that he wish (and this word had the sense of a strong, irrevocable decision) "to militate for God under the standard of the Cross and serve God alone and his vicar on earth".[146] Here, we turn

---

[143] It would be interesting to compare to these portraits of the *Constitutions*, certain portraits of the *Chronicon* or of the correspondences, such as: *Chron.* 3, p. 412; *Chron.* 5, p. 675; *Chron.* 6, p. 435, etc.

[144] Cf. The "portraits" in *Les Chroniques Saint Ignace de Loyola*, p. 305. This gallery of portraits can also be reconstituted at the end of the twelve "activities": the study is perhaps still clearer and more conclusive.

[145] *Const.* 1, p. 15.

[146] Ibid. 1, p. 16.

back again to the "Contemplation of the Two Standards": decidedly, it
was not an agreeable and comfortable harmony of temperaments which
assembled the companions; it was the same project, better, the same
love, the same Person; it was Jesus Christ. Like Peter and John, Matthew
and James, Andrew and Jude, the other Apostles, and before his ruin,
Judas Iscariot himself.

In beginning this chapter, we proposed three hypothetical formulas to
characterize the *Constitutions* of the Society of Jesus: an apostolic planning, a gathering of experiences and a guide for missions. May our
hesitation be lifted at present? Yes and no.

Of the gathering of experiences, the *Constitutions* certainly keep the
historic realistic, human flavor. First in their totality: the written text was
adapted in time to life. After all, the first constitutions by the first Fathers
before the election of the General, and the texts created or sketched by
Ignatius between 1541 and 1547 were inspired by events. They are
responses to questions which life posed: "The Establishment of House",
"To Establish a College", "Concerning Missions", "On the Refusal of
Ecclesiastical Dignities", "Constitutions of Scholastics", "Impediments
to Admission", "Ministries to Avoid", "Not to take the Responsibility
of Feminine Communities". Also the celebrated "Deliberation on Poverty", described in the *Spiritual Diary*, bears on a concrete case, a
situation which has actually been experienced: the revenues from the
sacristy of La Strada. And Ignatius would continue to work thus, even
after the arrival of Polanco in Rome in March of 1547. "On the renunciation of his goods in favor of the Society", "On the Manner in which the
Society Must Watch over the Superior General", "Of the Relations
between Provincial and the Collateral", "The Fifth Simple Vow of the
Professed":[147] all texts were drawn from circumstances.

One can even say that the patient research which Polanco conducted in
agreement with Ignatius, on the constitutions and rules of the great
orders that preceded the Society, were marked with this experimental
spirit. For, if Polanco executed this work, it was not to imitate the other
orders, but to confront the *modus Societatis* with the wisdom of the elders
and to better situate it in relation to a tradition which had been proven. It
was not a compilation, it was a reflection on experiences taken from his
own experiences, and election of the original path of the Society.

Reflection and prayer: they are, with experience, the key words of the
genesis of the *Constitutions* and the great secret of the vitality of the
Society for the future. On condition that one gives to the word "reflection"
its meaning both personal and communal—that one well understand

---

[147] One finds all these texts in *Const.* 1.

prayer in its profoundest Ignatian sense of total interrogation of God, by every means at human disposal, in order to discern the providential design.

On a date in 1548,[148] hence at a period when the work on the *Constitutions* was intense, Polanco noted in his *Chronicon*: "In those times, Father Ignatius devoted himself to creating (*conficere*) the constitutions and rules: and partly by prayer, partly by reflecting and partly also by experience, he fit together (*concinnabat*) little by little, one by one, the things which he subsequently promulgated concerning our institute." This affirmation comes from a direct witness, even better a daily collaborator: and it exactly translated the effort which Ignatius devoted to it. On his effort of prayer, the *Spiritual Diary* furnishes an immediate and moving document.[149]

Of his effort in reflection, an autograph of 1544, entitled by the editors of the *Monumenta Historica*: "Deliberation of Our Father Ignatius on Poverty",[150] gives us a typical example: this deliberation is presented as a balance sheet in three parts: first the disadvantages of having no income which are the advantages of possessing something totally or partially; then the disadvantages of possessing something, which are the advantages of possessing nothing; finally the thirteen advantages and reasons for not possessing any income. One grasps immediately the process of reflection; he supposed evidently that anyone who devoted himself to this analysis would have purified his spirit previously of all emotional inclinations: he would have set his conscience face to face with God. As for experience, it suffices to recall that we have said on the manner in which Ignatius had the *Constitutions* "declared", by soliciting a trial attempt on the part of the companions, isolated or in groups, and correcting the *Constitutions* according to the indications, criticisms and suggestions which were addressed to him.

Prayer, reflection, experience: if one consents to let oneself be led by these undoubtedly incomplete but sincere documents which we possess on the manner with which Ignatius worked on the *Constitutions of the Society of Jesus*—if one consents, in short, to place himself back in the historical movement of their genesis, one is forced to confirm that they are something other than a juridicial code, an apostolic plan, a gathering of experiences, a guide for the missions; they are the living fruit of a very deep experience of God, the response, on the human level, of a dramatic

---

[148] *Chron.* 1, p. 268, n. 230.
[149] In the Christus collection: the translation is preceded by a remarkable introduction by Fr. Maurice GIULIANI.
[150] *Const.* 1, pp. 78–81 and XCII–XCV.

interrogation on the design of God, Creator and Redeemer, the extreme effort of a group of companions who wanted to organize, among themselves, in the Church in such a way that they would collaborate as efficiently as possible in the divine work of the salvation of the world. What is the literary genre of such a document? Who can say? What one can say is certain is that in this plan the antinomies and difficulties which we have encountered in the course of this study can, it seems, be resolved: for example, were the *Constitutions* from Ignatius or Polanco? But what historian could maintain that Polanco had ever "carried" within him the *Constitutions* as Ignatius had "carried" them in his prayer before God?[151] The reproach of Bobadilla contained in its error more truth than Bobadilla thought: "Master Ignatius did them alone (the *Constitutions*) because he was a Father and an absolute leader and did all that he wished":[152] no companion would have been able to claim more than Ignatius the spiritual paternity of the *Constitutions*. Other authors have insinuated, with more or less insistence, that the *Constitutions*, at least in certain portions, were "inspired" in Ignatius by God:[153] the letter-prologue of the first Latin edition of the *Constitutions* affirms this almost explicitly. "During numerous years [Ignatius] asked of the Lord the serene light (*unctionem*) of the Holy Spirit, with tears, the most fervent prayers, with frequently offered Masses, to such an extent that under the inspiration and the guidance of the Spirit, he succeeded through divine grace at what would not have been possible through human wisdom."[154] What exactly does this mean: "Illo [Spiritu] inspiratore et duce"? A genuine "revelation"? An "inspiration" in the biblical sense of the word? A normal help from God to one who in all sincerity seeks him? According to the conclusion of Father de Aldama: "When it is a matter of interpreting this divine assistance, the decision is up to the theologians rather than to the historians."[155] What seems incontestable is that Ignatius, according to his own principles of obedience, brought all his genius, all the strength of his union with God, all his gifts of nature and grace to achieve the best possible work which the first companions and the pope himself had entrusted to him: he wrote the *Constitutions of the Society of Jesus* personally, dramatically, with holiness. The word of a

---

[151] See also the first paragraph of the 3rd activity of the Rules of the Secretary, Mario SCADUTO, *Uno scritto, art. cit.*, p. 316.

[152] *Nadal Mon.* 4, p. 733.

[153] Cf. T. VENTURI, op. cit., 4, pp. 120–21; the author cites known passages from Câmara (*Font. narr.* 1, p. 504, n. 100–101), Ribadeneyra (*Vita, Font. narr.* 4, pp. 738 sqq.).

[154] On the author of this letter prologue, see note 189 of the pamphlet of Antonio Maria DE ALDAMA, *La Composición de las Constituciones*, p. 61.

[155] Op. cit., p. 48.

Portuguese missionary, at the time of the crisis with Rodríguez, is without doubt the most exact that could be pronounced: "In hearing about all this disturbance, he protested by letter that he would never recognize any other Society than that of Ignatius, that which God had founded through the hard labors, vigils and prayer of Ignatius."[156]

It is doubtless fortunate that Ignatius had put so much time into elaborating the *Constitutions of the Society*. For among the "experiences" which influenced this long labor, there was in the first place, the experience of Ignatius himself: now, it appears certain that, the more he advanced in age, the more God presented himself to him, quite simply as the God who is Love, the more also that he insisted that the relations of the companions to each other and above all the relation of authority —obedience, be relations of love and that the entire society be, according to the words of Xavier, a "Society of love". Two facts, among others, support this view: it was only in text B (1552–1556) that the important prologue on the "law of love and charity" appeared, without which the most beautiful constitutions would remain a dead letter.[157] It was likewise in text B that a very characteristic modification was inserted: Polanco had noted, in his study of the Benedictine rule, a counsel of St. John Chrysostom concerning religious who merited punishment: it was necessary, said Chrysostom, to warn them with love, then humiliate them and make them ashamed, finally, punish them with rigor. Polanco presented this text to Ignatius in the second series of his "Doubts",[158] and in effect the text of Chrysostom was cited in text "a" (1549–50) of the *Constitutions*. Now, in text A (1550), Ignatius used the passage and corrected it, once adding the words: "with gentleness" and twice the words " with love". The text then became this one: "First, one admonishes with love and with gentleness those who have committed a sin; (2) with love and making them ashamed; (3) with love and an authority which makes itself feared." The correction went in its entirety into text B (1552–1556).

Such corrections retrospectively clarify more than all the critical analysis, the mentality of Ignatius in elaborating the *Constitutions*. Without abandoning oneself to any sentimentality, one can see in the *Constitutions*, rather than this or that detail, the word throbbing from the heart of Ignatius, in his intimacy of reflection and prayer with the Heart of Christ, Savior of the world and Lord, "for the glory of God the Father".

---

[156] *Chron.* 2, p. 717.

[157] This formula is borrowed from the doctrine of Saint Augustine and Saint Thomas, but the thought is traditional in the Church.

[158] *Const.* 1, 292, no. 25.

PART THREE

ASSESSMENT OF THE IGNATIAN YEARS
OF THE SOCIETY OF JESUS

POLANCO'S ASSESSMENT
AND CRITICAL ANALYSIS

I. THE ASSESSMENT OF POLANCO

There have certainly been many who have praised the administration of Ignatius Loyola. Aside from the process of beatification and of canonization whose literary genre inclines the historian toward prudence, praise poured forth from the pens of Ignatius' first biographers: the most famous are undoubtedly the *Roman Exhortations*[1] (1557) and the *Biographical Essays*[2] (1554–1567) by Jerónimo Nadal; *The Life of Ignatius Loyola*[3] (1567–1569) and *The Ignatian System*[4] (c. 1610) by Pedro Ribadeneyra; *The Life of Saint Ignatius*[5] (1579) by Jean-Pierre Maffei. But, of all those who knew Ignatius as the Superior General, the best-placed individual to assess the Society of Jesus as of July 31, 1556, was undoubtedly Juan Alonso de Polanco. He did not shirk his responsibility in this regard. In the sixth volume of the *Chronicon* in the chapter devoted to the death of Ignatius, Polanco erects a sort of diptych with startling contrasts: on one side the humility, the self-effacement, the silence of Ignatius' death, and on the other side, God's many blessings such that Polanco comments, lyrically "I know not if God gave equally great blessings to the founders of the other religious orders."

These favors are listed under seven headings:

1. The Society of Jesus was at the death of Ignatius not only instituted and approved by the apostolic authority but confirmed also by several pontiffs.

2. The Society of Jesus was endowed with the greatest of privileges, graces and powers, as much for the good of individuals as for the common good.

3. Ignatius brought forth the *Constitutions* from a mind which was

---

[1] *Font. narr.* 2, pp. 3–10.

[2] Ibid. 1 and 2, passim.

[3] Ibid. 4, which also contains censure of the work.

[4] Ibid. 3, pp. 606–34.

[5] *De vita et moribus Ignatii Loyolae*, Francesco Zannetti, Rome 1585; see the censure of the work by Ribadeneyra (1585) in *Font. narr.* 3, pp. 208–36, and the remarks of Candido de Dalmases.

profound and filled with great prudence. He established the rules and regulations for the proper administration of the Society and for the workings of its different offices. His laws were published and applied while he was living although he left the task of putting the finishing touches on them to the first General Congregation.

4. His institute included many members from different nations who stood out because of their birth, their knowledge or their prudence, and many more because of their virtue and their unusual gifts from God. Nonetheless, at the time, there were not many who made the four solemn vows: in fact, counting all nations only thirty-five of them were living. Among this number, there remained five of the ten first companions, four others having died before Ignatius.

5. Ignatius was able to witness the beneficial effect which the ministries and the example of the Society were producing widely throughout the Church. It was not only among Catholics but also among heretics and infidels that he saw the grace of God work many marvels for the glory of God and the universal good—the good for which he himself felt such a burning thirst.

6. He saw what authority and what respect the Society enjoyed, whether with the Sovereign Pontiff and the great dignitaries of the Church or with the secular princes, the city states and the various populations, because the good reputation of the Society had spread widely and its detractors were for the most part discomfited or repulsed by the truth.

7. He saw the Society established (stabilitam)[6] in different countries around the world where many houses and colleges had been founded. Among these colleges, many had assumed the painful but necessary responsibility of teaching. Some of these schools even had advanced faculties of philosophy and theology. Ignatius left all of these houses and schools divided into twelve provinces.

It is probably a good idea to stop our analysis here because we shall return to the above-mentioned list of the twelve provinces.

The record of achievement is brilliant. Furthermore, from Polanco's perspective (the "favors" given by God to Ignatius as Superior General) it is easily understood: Polanco does not at all aim to create a critical

---

[6] This word merits closer examination. For "to stabilize" has a very precise meaning in the Ignatian vocabulary, at least if it concerns colleges and universities; it signifies "to endow with fixed revenues". Is this what Polanco intends in this passage? If he does mean this, how many colleges and universities or missions had revenues consistent with the principles specified by Ignatius? Venice, Padua, Genoa, etc. of the "contracts" entered into by Borgia in Spain, of the "legal" situation of Paris, Louvain, Cologne, etc. come to mind. The majority of the houses and colleges were far from "stability", especially, if one considers that in addition to the financial and juridical stability it is necessary to take into account the religious "stability".

assessment of the situation of the Society of Jesus in July 1556. Moreover, he does not write his *Chronicon* until 1573–1574, a time when several of the problems up in the air in 1556, had already been resolved.

It is very necessary for us to adopt Polanco's point of view today, if we do not want to misread this balance sheet. The first, second and fifth "favors" are tangible and precise. The third, which involves the *Constitutions* and the Rules, had already acquired certain nuances—as we saw in our Part II. As for the fourth, sixth and seventh "favors", it is essential to make a critical commentary on them if we wish to measure the work of Ignatius as Superior General and to advance further in understanding his mentality.

II. THE REAL SITUATION

Consequently, we must study the statistics concerning the companions a little more closely, especially those regarding the members who took the four solemn vows; the statistics concerning the "authority of the Society" and its detractors; and, finally, the real situation in the "twelve provinces" as of 1556. This analysis will introduce us to the crisis which shook the Society between 1556 and 1558, and whose tremors were felt even by the Borgia and Aquaviva governments.

Statistics concerning the Members of the Society and Their Different "Degrees" of Their Belonging to the "Corpus Societatis"

First of all, a paradox: although the *Chronicon* and the *Correspondences* furnish us with numerous statistics, some of them very detailed, regarding different houses, especially the houses and colleges in Rome or Spain,[7] it is nonetheless impossible to determine the exact number of companions at the time of Ignatius' death, and even more difficult to follow the growth of the Society between 1539 and 1556. To what is this difficulty due? The causes are definitely many, but it seems that at the time in question there was a great deal of individual coming and going in many of the houses and schools which sheltered candidates not yet admitted to the order, the admitted candidates, people who were undergoing a probationary period (especially the Spiritual Exercises), students, etc.; as well as the regular members of the community. It is necessary to

---

[7] A few examples of "statistics": information about Xavier (*Epist. ign.* 5, p. 269, n. 3604); beginning of real catalogues (*Chron.* 3; p. 135); list of missionaries for Ethiopia (*Chron.* 4, pp. 577, 581, 582); list of the professors of Coimbra (1555) (*Chron.* 5, p. 595); in 1554, on order of Araoz, catalogues in the houses of his province (*Chron.* 4 between pp. 353 and 447).

realize that neither departures nor explusions were rare, nor were returns;[8] until formal rules gave a certain consistency, there was a "floating membership". In Portugal, even before the crisis of 1552, Ignatius asked King John III to intervene so that too-frequent transfers from one religious order to another would be stopped. Consequently, at the time of the crisis, how was it possible to determine exactly the number of faithful companions and the number of rebels or dissidents?[9] The four reference points worth keeping in mind would doubtless be the following: first, the letter from Polanco to Francis Xavier dated July 30, 1553 which would establish the number of members (not including The Indies) at about 550; the famous conversation between the archbishop of Toledo and Nadal in 1554[10] which would put the total number of companions at 1500, figures which Polanco confirms, realizing nonetheless that they represent a maximum; the testimony of Father Luis Gonçalves da Câmara (January 29, 1555) which declares that as of that date Ignatius set the number of companions at 900.[11] After having examined this information, the authors of *Fontes narrativi I*[12] think that it is feasible to set the figure of a thousand companions for July 1556. Since more precise information is lacking, let us adopt these figures.[13] Even while taking into account Polanco's often-repeated affirmation that candidates came in abundance but were obliged to wait at the door by the authorities because of the smallness of the residences or the lack of the necessary financial resources, we must recognize that the growth of the Society in twenty years or so had nothing of a tidal wave about it. The Society's development was indeed good, but its growth had nothing miraculous about it.

This is especially true if one considers the renown of some of the companions admitted: vocations like those of Polanco, Francis Borgia, Canisius, Doctor Olave, John de Mendoza (and how many others?) which were not unnoticed. The least that one can say is that they weren't hiding their light under a bushel. The *multos instituti nostri sectatores* of Polanco's assessment is perhaps a euphemism.

There is, however, nothing astonishing about that because Polanco

[8] Was it possible, for example, to set up a real catalogue of the companions living in communities like Louvain, Cologne or such missionary posts as India or Brazil?

[9] Even today, there still exists divergence in the interpretation of certain figures which we possess for this difficult period for Portugal: ASTRAIN (historian for the Assistancy of Spain) is not in agreement with RODRIGUES (the excellent historian for the Assistancy of Portugal), and the *Synopsis historiae Societatis Jesu* on the entrance of novices in Portugal from 1540 to 1556 results in still other figures.

[10] *Chron.* 4, pp. 476–77.

[11] *Font. narr.* I, p. 579, n. 87.

[12] Ibid., p. 63.

[13] Let us note, by way of comparison, that toward 1264, thirty-eight years after the

himself warns us of this by a discreet "although" ("although those who took the four solemn vows are few"). In fact, out of the thousand companions only thirty-five took the four vows. To this number may be added the five surviving first Fathers. Later we will analyze the names of those who took the vows. For the moment, however, one should remember the proportion that this number represents in relation to the total.[14] Even if one adds the eleven "members who took the three vows",[15] one gets one twenty-fifth (four percent) of the total membership of the Society.[16] This statistic gives rise to many questions. Let us only consider here the situation in which it places the Society upon the death of Ignatius. A General Congregation, whose task it would be to provide a successor to Ignatius and Constitutions for the whole order was to meet. According to the provisions in the constitutions written by Ignatius and conditionally approved by the principal companions during 1550–1551, the General Congregation was to be composed of three professed delegates from each province (the Provincial and two other elected members).[17] Three professed delegates? Some provinces, like France and Southern Germany, etc., did not have that many, whereas, India, because of the presence of the missionaries in Ethiopia, had many but was unable to send delegates to Europe because of the distance. Why did Ignatius, who was not unaware of the fragility of his state of health, and knew the importance of the future General Congregation, let such an imperfect situation come to pass? Undoubtedly, in Portugal and in Spain there were members who had been designated to take their vows, and who, according to the extant rules, were prevented because of Ignatius' death. Some thought that this rule should be disregarded but Laynez, the Vicar General, who was responsible for preparing the General Congregation, refused, for fear of creating a precedent. Moreover, neither Spain, nor especially Portugal, was among the poorest provinces. It was amid a certain amount of confusion concerning rights and powers that the Society began its first General Congregation.

---

death of St. Francis of Assisi, the Franciscan order numbered about 30,000 religious. The Capuchins, born from a separation, toward 1517, of the Observants and the Conventual Franciscans, had about 25,000 at the time of the death of Ignatius. As for the Dominicans, in 1256, that is to say about forty years after their founding, there were about 7,000.

[14] The editors of the *Chron.* (6, p. 40, note), counted 42; and the *Font. narr.* (1, pp. 63–66), 43.

[15] *Font. narr.* 1, p. 65.

[16] Let us remember that the first pontifical bull *Regimini militantis* (1540) had limited the number of professed to sixty: a limit which the bull *Injunctum nobis* (1544) had abolished.

[17] *Const.* 2, p. 628.

The "Authority" of the Society of Jesus in 1556 and Its "Detractors"

This authority, Polanco declares,[18] was at the time "not mediocre", the renown of the Society being "widely known" and its detractors being "confused" or "conquered by the truth" (*superatis ab ipsa veritate vel mitigatis*). Here again, it is fitting to examine the truth of the matter a little more closely. It is incontestable that the Society of Jesus was known, appreciated and loved in many Christian regions. But did not the heavy cares, indeed even serious threats, weigh upon the very existence of the order, or on what we would call today its identity? Gian Pietro Carafa then reigned over the Church under the name of Paul IV.[19] And despite official declarations of benevolence regarding the Society and of his friendship for Bobadilla and Laynez, he did not hide his plan of modifying certain points of the constitutions, already approved several times by Popes preceding him and which Ignatius and the *primi Patres* judged essential, like the election for life of the Superior General and the dispensing with choir in favor of apostolic work. Did he entirely abandon his idea of fusing the Society with his congregation of Theatines, an idea which Ignatius had twice rejected?[20] To prepare for this threat Ignatius even, a few months before his death, partially established liturgical chant in Rome.[21] Nor was anyone unaware of the anti-Spanish sentiments of Paul IV; raised to the sovereign pontificate at the age of forty-eight, this great old man, wry and irascible "all nerves and little flesh"[22] at first gave great hopes to all who wanted reform of the Church; but soon, under the pressure of his nephew, Charles Carafa, a greedy and proud adventurer whom he made a Cardinal on June 7, 1555, he let himself be drawn into the plan of reconquering the republic of Siena and driving the Spaniards from Italy. The story of these preparations for war and of the diplomatic maneuvers by which he cemented an alliance between the Pope and France is not part of our study; it interests us, however, because it had a bearing on the relations of Paul IV with Ignatius. Of Spain and of Spaniards in general, Paul had a very prejudiced opinion: "He never spoke of his Majesty [Charles V] and of the Spanish nation without calling them heretics, schismatics, cursed by God, offspring of Jews and louts, scum of the earth; he deplored the misery of Italy which was constrained to serve such abject and vile people." "He experienced", he said, "an immense displeasure that these

---

[18] *Chron.* 6, 41.
[19] Cf. The remarkable portrait of Paul IV in Mario SCADUTO, *L'Epoca*, I, pp. 10–15.
[20] *Chron.* 6, p. 53.
[21] *Chron.* 6, pp. 8 and 9.
[22] Bernard Navagero, in Mario SCADUTO (lib. cit., I, p. 11).

cooks and hustlers were in charge in Italy."[23] Now, for several months already, the community at La Strada had been the object of the suspicions of the belligerent and temperamental pontiff—undoubtedly the numerous relations of Ignatius and his entourage with the numerous Roman Spaniards sufficed to explain this malevolence—when suddenly, in the wake of an anonymous denunciation, Paul IV sent the governor of the city to La Strada with an escort of soldiers to requisition arms, which he had been told were hidden there for the use of Spaniards ready to revolt.[24] Friends of the Society were caught up in the fury of the Pope: the Colonnas were excommunicated, their goods confiscated. On July 19, 1556, Polanco had to notify the rector of Naples where the Colonnas lived, so that he could suspend any liturgical function if any one of the Colonnas appeared at one.[25] Then Paul IV had Antonio de Tassis, master of imperial posts, arrested along with two diplomatic agents.[26] With his typical lack of verbal restraint, he insulted Charles V, threatened him with being deposed. Signaling a forthcoming declaration of war, on September 1, 1556, the Spaniards crossed the pontifical frontiers. Ignatius had been dead a month; but these prospects of war had shadowed his last days: Paul IV, in his eyes, remained "the Vicar of Christ on earth"; the future of the Society was in his hands.

It was not only from Paul IV that there was danger of profound changes in the Society once Ignatius was gone. Several times, in different places, for example in Portugal and in Northern Italy, the rumor had been started that when Ignatius died, the Society would disappear. "Gossip", surely, and negligible! But from Paris had risen on December 1, 1554, a much more serious threat: the faculty of theology of the university had issued its decree[27] against the Society. It was a document without hope of recourse, since, if the Sovereign Pontiff defended the order, certain members of the assembly let it be known that they would call the Pope to the council. In this condemnation it was not only a matter of the legal recognition of the Society in France. Given the audience in the Catholic world which the faculty of theology of Paris enjoyed in fact, if not by right, the very work of Ignatius and his companions was endangered. Very quickly, the decree became known in Flanders, Spain, Sicily, and Portugal—and definitely in Rome. In Rome where, just at that time, Gian Pietro Carafa acceded to the sovereign Pontificate. No doubt, Ignatius began to assemble "testimonies" of

---

[23] Ibid., pp. 12 and 13.

[24] Chron. 5, pp. 47–49.

[25] Epist. ign. 12, p. 143, n. 6693.

[26] Mario SCADUTO, L'Epoca, 1, p. 15.

[27] Chron. 4, pp. 328–31.

princes, bishops, municipalities, universities in favor of the companions
and of the Society. No doubt he made them known to the Pope himself.
No doubt, also in December 1555, he received with much friendliness
four of the principal authors of the decree who came to Rome with the
Cardinal of Lorraine,[28] and by means of a face to face discussion and a
frank "putting the cards on the table" for one thing and with the help of
Polanco, Laynez, Frusius and Olave, he succeeded in seriously dissipat-
ing the hostility of the doctors. However, the opposition in Paris
continued nonetheless, and the decree spread more and more into the
Christian world: it would furnish to the "contradictores Societatis" the
best of their attacks for the whole course of history.

The "Twelve Provinces"[29]

It was in this part of his tableau that one feels most clearly that Polanco
drafted the Chronicon some seventeen years after the death of Ignatius. He
himself recognized that the province of Ethiopia never—or hardly—
existed except on paper: "These schismatic Kings do not obey the patriarch whom the Pope sent them." But could he not have made a
similar remark of the North German province, whose numbers were
then minimal despite three establishments and of which the designated
Provincial, Bernard Olivier, died before being "declared".[30] As for
France, Paris had had very few Jesuits and Billom only an inchoate
house; and the Society did not yet have a legal existence. The Indies, after
the death of Xavier (1552), then of Barzee (1553), went through some
great difficulties: happily, the arrival in 1555 and 1556 of the missionaries
destined for Ethiopia furnished a reinforcement in men (of whom some
had great value) who had become indispensable to them for survival.
The eight other provinces: Brazil, Portugal, Castile, Betique, Aragon,
Southern Germany, northern Italy and Sicily seemed like apostolic
groups in the best designed structures: the numbers, the types of establishments, the ways of life, the apostolic demands varied greatly from
one region to another. Rome itself is to be considered separately: with
Tivoli and Amerino, the city was under the authority of the General
himself.

The real problem of these "twelve" provinces was not a matter of
numbers. It was rather a matter of their spiritual and apostolic "maturity". Among these twelve provinces, what differences there were! Each
was developed in accordance with the circumstances, that is, according

---

[28] Chron. 1, pp. 11–13 and 320–23.
[29] Chron. 6, p. 41.
[30] Chron. 6, pp. 32–33.

to its opportunities and its men. Rome, with its Roman college, the Germanicum, its works, and Sicily, thanks to the exceptional protection of Viceroy Juan de Vega and to the valuable companions whom Ignatius sent seemed to have been the most favored. Portugal, with India, Brazil, the opening in the Congo, Japan, China and Ethiopia could have played— it even did play for a certain period—a typical role in the praxis of the young Society; but it was harshly hit by the crisis of December 1551; so, very quickly the "faithful" were resuscitated under the influence of Nadal, Borgia, Miron and even as in 1556 with the presence of Câmara, it became again a fervent province, the trauma remained: Ignatius himself had been, at the heart of the crisis, resisted, scoffed at, and the submission of Simón Rodríguez remained fragile, extravagant, unsettling. Spain, thanks to Borgia, Araoz and Bustamente was developing rapidly, especially after Princess Juana had succeeded Philip II as regent in the name of the Emperor: but the attacks of Siliceo and of Melchoir Cano were not without influence upon public opinion.

A simple analysis reveals many of these differences to us: analysis of the distribution of professed in different provinces aside from the Five surviving first Fathers, the professed of four vows were distributed among the provinces as follows: three in Rome, six in Spain (three provinces), Sicily, southern Germany (of whom two were at Prague), four among the missionaries to Ethiopia (of whom three were bishops), four in Portugal (Borgia was also the commissioner of Portugal), two in Flanders (one to Louvain, the other in Cologne), two in northern Italy; one in France (in Billom), one in the Indies (the new Provincial had recently arrived, but the "Ethiopians" there were in transit though they would remain longer than they expected), one in Naples, one in Brazil.[31] We shall apply this analysis to the following chapter and shall try to discern the principle by which Ignatius decided to call someone to solemn profession. But for the present one may note that in this distribution Ignatius had not at all paid attention to the representation of the provinces to the General Congregation, and that his concern had been the "mission" rather than the administration.

This fact is important: it supports the conclusion which will soon result from the anaylsis of the names of the professed. The more we advance into this study of the governing of Ignatius, the more we confirm that it will be necessary to seek the secret of his *ars gubernandi*

---

[31] We have followed the list of professed given by the edition of MHSJ (p. 40). Let us remember that to this list the editors of *Font. narr.* add the name of Riera (1, p. 65). As for us, we would add the name of Louis de Grana (*Chron.* 6, p. 756). Riera was then in Loreto, and Louis de Grana in Brazil.

elsewhere, rather than in a concern for planning, or even for organization.

Was this an advantage or a disadvantage? Who would dare say? For the moment, we are forced to confirm that the situation at the death of Ignatius would cause a grave crisis, for which the first General Congregation would find a definite solution, but which would nevertheless extend beyond 1558.

CHAPTER II

THE CRISIS OF 1556–1558

1556–1558:[1] These were two crucial years for the existence and the orientations of the Society of Jesus. For this crisis, the reasons are numerous: one of the strongest surely, and, of itself, independent of the Society, was a state of war, sometimes active, sometimes languishing, which opposed Paul IV and the France of Henry II to Philip II and Charles V; this Hispano-papal war had a great influence[2] in 1556–1557 on the disposition of the Pontiff and his reactions regarding the Society of Jesus, of which he had difficulty understanding problems which the General Congregation did not succeed in solving; the sequels extended into the year 1557–1558 (diplomatic, financial and economic difficulties remained in the hands of a conquered pontifical state).

However, one must realize that it was also, and perhaps principally, from inside the Society of Jesus, that the crisis arose. The interpretation of the facts is extremely delicate; we are without doubt at the heart of the Ignatian "enigma", at least in our opinion, which is undoubtedly open to discussion. We beg the reader, however, not to reject our thesis, without taking account of the preceding analyses and the detailed explanation of our Parts Four and Five. Above all, it is necessary to consider calmly the essential facts and the questions which they pose.

I. TWO VICARS GENERAL?

On August 4, 1556, the Society of Jesus found itself with two Vicars General at its head, but had at its disposal no clear and obligatory legislation on the election and the role of Vicar General.

In Rome, Laynez: a Laynez who had received extreme unction on the first of the month, and whose first gesture, after his election, had been to confirm Polanco and Madrid in their mission of "governing the Society", two Spaniards of whom one, Madrid, was not professed in the order;[3] with the restriction, however, that they would not exercise this

[1] One of the most objective studies of the serious events of 1556–1558 is assuredly book I of volume III of the *Storia della Compagnia de Gesù en Italia*, a volume written by Fr. Mario SCADUTO and entitled *L'Epoca di Giacomo Laynez*.

[2] It ended in August 1557 by the Treaty of Cava, "anticipating the Treaty of Cateau-Cambresis", cf. SCADUTO, op. cit., p. 45; NORES, *Storia della guerra*, pp. 215–21; PASTOR, *Histoire des papes*, 6, pp. 416–21.

[3] A mission which had been entrusted to them by Ignatius himself, on the preceding July 2. Cf. *Chron.* 6, p. 35, n. 94.

authority except in case of real necessity. Now, in Spain, there was another Vicar General, this one elected by all the companions residing in Rome since November 1, 1554 and endowed by Ignatius with full powers of the General: Jerónimo Nadal.[4] No doubt, in sending him to Spain toward the end of 1555, Ignatius, through consideration for Borgia, who was Commissioner in Spain and Portugal, with the same powers, had stipulated that there during his mission, Nadal "would have neither superior nor subject, but that he was to collaborate with Father Francis and the provincials".[5] This was a strange and uncomfortable position, but one from which Ignatius, very solicitous of collaboration and counting without doubt on the virtue of the men, scarcely retreated. Whatever the case might be, as soon as he knew of the death of Ignatius (in the first days of September), Nadal considered himself Vicar General and acted accordingly. After having consulted Borgia, Araoz, Strada and Bustamente, he wrote to the Fathers of Portugal and asked that some delegates to the General Congregation prepare themselves to depart from Rome. "A few days later", he recounted, "we received the letters of Father Polanco who announced the nomination of Father Laynez as Vicar which did not bother me at all."[6]

Undoubtedly, this serenity was admirable. However, the problem remained: who was the legitimate Vicar General? Laynez or Nadal? Many asked themselves that question. Nadal himself wondered if the death of the one who had named him (through selection) annulled his powers, and Laynez for his part wrote to Borgia, on August 6, a letter which showed a certain perplexity. "As for the authority of the companions, one can doubt [si e dubitato] whether it remains in effect. . . . Here we are inclined to think that every commissioner or provincial remains in charge inasmuch as their nomination depends on the General. . . . As for what concerns the entire Society, we have been unsure whether the authority of Father Nadal, named Commissioner General by Our Father and with all his powers, continued or ceased. Although he had been sent to Spain and his authority had been suspended during the time of his sojourn, he found it again in its entirety, on leaving Spain." Then was Nadal the Vicar General? No. Laynez gives an explanation in which it is difficult not to feel a certain embarrassment: "Here, Dr. Madrid and Master Polanco had been invested with total authority of our Father for matters concerning the governing of the Society, and they have exercised it, because of the illnesses of our Father. However, at present, we judge that this delegation of authority has no further need of existence: they

[4] *Epist. ign.* 8, pp. 42–43, n. 4951; 9, p. 430.
[5] Ibid. 10, pp. 16–18, n. 5834.
[6] *Nadal Mon.* 2, p. 48.

will only exercise it in case of real necessity, if the common welfare demands it."[7]

The wisdom and humility of Nadal preserved the Society from an internal conflict on this point. He withdrew before Laynez. There were others than he, we shall see, who would raise the question of the legitimacy of the election of Laynez. Further, it was at the suggestion of Nadal himself that the problems concerning the rights of the commissioner or of the vicar were determined by the First Congregation, at least concerning essentials.[8]

Here we must pose the crucial question: how and why did Ignatius let such a situation occur? He knew that he was ill; he knew the men, *his* men; he did not overlook their differences of temperament and tendencies, he could not have failed to foresee what tensions would arise among them after his death. Without completed constitutions, without hope of finding a firm and sure support in the Pope, everything happened *as if* he had refused to "*claudere*" not only the *Constitutions*, but his own work, leaving afterward to his sons after him, from generation to generation, the work of "making the Society of Jesus"; as if any companion, although he might have been the initiator and artisan of the foundation, were only a thread in the web which would greatly expand in space and time.

The question of the vicar was not ended with the voluntary resignation of Nadal. There was a third "actor", or rather a third group of "actors". And it was Bobadilla who raised the juridical question and at the same time unleashed the tempest.

II. BOBADILLA ENTERS THE SCENE

We have already met this personality. In the group of companions Bobadilla was the maverick; he represented in his excesses and his extremes, what could have been before, or even without, the Society: a powerful, dynamic radiating personality, free of all shackles and of all convention, totally devoted to Jesus Christ, to the Catholic Reform and to the "Vicar of Jesus Christ on earth" (provided that he be a reformer); Bobadilla was a force of nature and faith, a torrent which nothing could hold back or stop. "Another St. Paul", he said of himself with an

---

[7] *Lainii Mon.* 1, p. 288, n. 113. On the other hand Polanco does not seem to have had any hesitation on the merits of the election. As early as August 19, urging the companions of the Roman college, he invited them to see in the Vicar Laynez in Madrid, in Polanco himself, and in their Roman Rector , their superiors, the true fathers of their souls and their bodies (*Pol. Compl.* 2, pp. 588, 595).

[8] SCADUTO, op. cit., pp. 114–15.

ingenuousness often comical, but also disquieting. It was in the tempests, the fracases and the perils that he was entirely himself, that he breathed with ease; "a child, he was climbing on the highest towers or the sharpest rocks, to gather birds at the risk of breaking his bones".[9] Military chaplain in the Imperial Army during the war of Charles V against the League of Schmalkalden (he was then less than thirty), he caught the plague, got well, was taken prisoner, escaped, received the blow of a Protestant halberd on his head and escaped death thanks only to the thickness of his helmet.[10] He confronted Ferdinand, King of the Romans, without flinching. When Charles V, on June 30, 1548, proclaimed the *Interim*, Bobadilla, who was not at all in accord with conceding anything whatever to the Protestants, drafted two strident memoirs which circulated among the Catholic and Lutheran princes and which he put "under the nose of the Emperor."[11] What was supposed to happen happened: Charles had the "naive"[12] militant conducted to the border with a good strong interdiction against returning. Ignatius, who knew his man, far from censuring the exile, gave him the kingdom of Naples in which to express his fire freely, forbidding him nonetheless to cross its borders. Canisius, one day, would express what seems the most equitable judgment of Bobadilla: "Exceptional in the penetration of his mind, the power of dialectics and of jugment, simplicity of soul, the transparence of his manners and the charm of his affability with everyone."[13] As for the individual himself, there was no end to his self-praise: the night before being expelled from Germany, he wrote from Ratisbon to Michael de Torres:

> In short, at the court, they do not stop saying that if all the Society were like Bobadilla, it would be very fortuitous. They place me above everyone. . . . You know how much people are wrong in that, but I thank Christ, because I speak without acrimony, in such a way that my modesty and my soul are known by men. Ask Christ that he give me perseverance in everything, and patience to bear these harsh labors, especially those of war: it is quite another thing from being in a garden or in kitchen in the city of Rome.[14]

[9] SCADUTO, op. cit., I, pp. 32–33. For out preceding encounters with Bobadilla, cf. supra pp. 69–70 and 91–93.

[10] *Bobad. Mon.*, p. 107.

[11] SCADUTO, op. cit., I, p. 34, citing *Bobad. Mon.*, pp. 137–46.

[12] The word is from Bobadilla himself: *candidamente*; *Bobad. Mon.*, p. 146.

[13] *Can. Epist.* I, p. 159. The more one knows Bobadilla, the more one regrets that the life of this tempestuous companion was not written; but much humor and a serious knowledge of the heart of Ignatius would be required of that biographer.

[14] It is difficult not to see here a "low blow" against the hosts of La Strada, and especially against the "Reverend Father (*dominus*), Dr. Torres, a very worthy theologian, gentleman and dear friend" who was then in Rome. Were these emphatic remarks without irony? The "man in the front line" has always scorned the "man in the rear"!

Ask that I may be glorified in the cross of Christ, no less than any other might be. I have therefore no account to render to the companions of Trent [that is to say, to Laynez and to Salmeron] or elsewhere: it is Farnese who is my immediate superior. I write all this not to exalt myself but to humble myself to render thanks to God and to confound those who expect to find some evil in me; thus did St. Paul.[15]

Such was the man. Polanco felt that Bobadilla would definitely play a role in the situation created by the death of Ignatius. At that time, however, Bobadilla was in Tivoli. As early as July 31, the Secretary advised him of the event, asked him to return to Rome (he even sent him a mule for the trip) and, in case of obstacles, to designate in writing by the same messenger, the companion he would choose as Vicar General: it was good diplomacy to involve Bobadilla in this election. Impediment? Fatigue? Or simply a matter of whim? Bobadilla did not come to Rome; he abandoned his vote "to the choice of the secretary";[16] knowing the attitude which Bobadilla had taken in 1539–1540, regarding the rough drafts of the constitutions, one could legitimately think that he would not be more interested in the election of a Vicar General. He came, however, some time later, for northern Italy chose him among the three professed who were to represent it at the General Congregation (the two others were Rodríguez and Pelletier): at that time, Laynez hoped that this Congregation would be held in Rome, or if need be in Loreto or Genoa, in November 1556. The circumstances of the war prevented this, and the Congregation was postponed the first time to April of 1557.

Whatever may have been the date of his arrival, Bobadilla, as soon as he arrived at La Strada, sensed the atmosphere of incertitude in which the Vicar General and his entourage were struggling; meetings about which little leaked out were held among Laynez, Polanco, Madrid and Nadal (arrived in Rome December 2, alone of all the representatives from Spain). He had the feeling that the Spaniards were pressing for the Congregation to be held in Spain. This intuition was not unfounded. In the account of his departure from Spain, Nadal himself reported:

When I saw these Fathers (Borgia, Araoz, Strada, Bustamente) so little inclined to come to the General Congregation which moreover had been postponed, I asked them what they thought of my own departure. At the regular meeting, Bustamente, in the name of all, told me that they thought I

---

[15] *Bobad. Mon.*, p. 102, cited by SCADUTO, op cit., 1, p. 35. One understands that, in Trent, Laynez and Salmeron had been a little annoyed by the conduct of Bobadilla. *Epist. Salm.* 1, pp. 20–22.

[16] *Chron.* 6, p. 46.

ought not go to Rome, but remain in the province of Aragon until the opening of the Congregation. This opinion displeased me and I do not know what suspicion came to me that the matter was not treated with sincerity (*sincere rem non tractare*); then I thought that they were deluding themselves perhaps with the hope that the election would not take place in Rome, as they worked to obtain the following year.[17] So I do not dissimulate: I clearly scorned their opinion; I did not hide the fact that their plan shocked me, and I told them that I wished to depart the same day, which I did: actually the same day I came to Torquemada. Father Francis [Borgia] and the others were irritated (*succensuit*) by my freedom; but I conceded so little that, with adequate modesty (*modestius*), I declared to Father Francis, who seemed to insist, that I respect in him not the duke which he had been, but the companion which he was.[18]

In fact, in Rome, Nadal would change his mind and become one of the group of Laynez-Polanco-Madrid-Nadal a firm defender of the plan to hold the Congregation in Spain.[19]

Bobadilla then had perceived the elaboration of the Spanish plan. In the spring of 1557, the Hispano-papal war reached its critical point. And it was just at that moment that Laynez solicited from Paul IV a meeting wherein he would sound out the feelings of the Pope on an eventual Congregation in Spain; the reaction was what one would have expected: "Surely go to Spain if you wish!" Then the Pope added, "What will you do in Spain? Carry your support for schism and the heresy[20] of Philip?" "No, not that", answered the smiling Vicar.[21]

In any case, the General Congregation could not be held in this terrible April of 1557. Bobadilla, supported by Rodríguez, began the task of combatting, in his way, the plan for a Congregation in Spain. Incisive arguments, already decisive for the Pope, were numerous: they were recapitulated in the "Votum P. Nicolai Bobadilla" of April–June, 1557.[22] Bobadilla saw clearly in the majority of his observations; the subsequent events would show him right on more than one point: certain refusal of the Pope to allow the General Congregation to be held outside Rome,

---

[17] That is to say in 1557.

[18] *Nadal Mon.* 2, pp. 48–49.

[19] Ibid. 2, p. 12. That proves that this plan was justified: war, weighed by Paul IV, etc.

[20] On April 9, the Pope had solemnly recalled the nuncios accredited to the Emperor and to Philip II. "It is not fitting", he had declared, "that the Holy See maintain nuncios and representatives to a certain Philip who has become schismatic and to a certain Charles of whom it is not known whether he is living or dead" (letter of Pasino di Giusti, of April 10, 1557, to Cardinal Farnese, cited by ROMIER op. cit., 2, p. 158, and SCADUTO, op. cit., 1, p. 27).

[21] *Nadal Mon.* 2, p. 13. It is true that there is quite a gamut of "colors" possible for a smile!

[22] Ibid. 4, pp. 98–104.

desire of the Pope to see the Society revise certain points of the *Constitutions* of Ignatius; the risk for the Spaniards of being suspected of wanting to monopolize the heritage of Ignatius, etc. In his paper, a certain serious new tension appears: the questioning of the vicarate of Laynez; it was, Bobadilla said, up to the "founders", that is, the surviving "first Fathers", to govern after the death of Ignatius until the election of a new General. In several instances, implicitly or explicitly, Bobadilla suggested that the *Constitutions*, not yet having been examined and approved, could not be obligatory.

Laynez and his counselors went beyond the arguments of Bobadilla. Meanwhile, the Hispano-papal war had taken a disquieting turn for the pontifical armies. When Laynez returned to visit Paul IV, he found the Pontiff very deflated and conciliatory. The latter promised to respond to the Spanish plan in a short period of time. Laynez returned to La Strada, convinced that, contrary to the dire predictions of Bobadilla, the cause was won; the first General Congregation would be held in Spain.[23]

III. THE CHANGE OF PAUL IV, THREATS TO THE CONSTITUTIONS

To think this was not to know Paul IV or Bobadilla well. Long before Cardinal Gian Pietro Carafa was elevated to the sovereign Pontificate, he had granted total friendship to Bobadilla. Once elected Pope, he maintained the friendship. And, in the presence of the Pontiff, Bobadilla hid his feelings no more than he did in the presence of princes or of Charles V. So it was in the *Plan for the Reform of the Church* which he addressed to him around 1555, and wherein he blamed him for his nepotism. It is certain that he spoke freely before him about Ignatius and concerning the Society. Did he place before the eyes of the Pope his "Vow" and his "Paper" of 1557? We have no material proof of that. However, it is certain that these criticisms and requests could not be overlooked by Paul IV; for Bobadilla could not keep from him the themes of his "crusades", his indignation and his justifications: papers, speeches and reports circulated either overtly or *sub rosa*. Whoever wanted to could know what he thought of the vicarate of Laynez and of the *Constitutions* of his order. Paul IV would have had knowledge of the internal dissensions of the Society from all sources, but Bobadilla and Cogordan spared him the bother of an investigation; they themselves transmitted their report via

---

[23] However, according to the "Ephemerides" of Geeraerts (*Pol. Compl.* 2, pp. 596–97), the delegates to the assembly were already numerous in Rome: Viola, Canisius, Broët, Ribadeneyra, Kessel, Adriani, Goudanus, Lanoye, Simón Rodríguez, Doménech, Vinck, etc. Lacking were the Spanish (those in Spain) and the Portuguese.

Cardinals Scotti and Reuman.[24] Some of Bobadilla's ideas more than accorded with the Pope's own ideas; his recent benevolence regarding the Society of Jesus changed again to severity.

When, some days after the favorable audience with the Pope (early June 1557), Laynez presented himself again at the Vatican to obtain finally the permission to depart for Spain, he was not received. Several times he renewed his attempt in vain.[25] On June 18, according to the reports which Polanco and Nadal give of it, the Pope, without receiving him personally (although Laynez was well known to Paul IV), suggested the order to him, by Cardinals Scotti and Reuman, to remit to him within three days all the constitutions and bulls of the Society, as well as the list of companions who were located in Rome, and he forbade all to leave Rome without his personal permission. Scotti specified that the intention of His Holiness was to reexamine the manner of life of the order and that he had confided this work to him, as well as to Reuman: they would have to submit a report to him before he pronounced judgment. Laynez withdrew in consternation.

The following day, June 19, 1557, he called together the Fathers in Rome and informed them of what had happened the day before. He asked for prayers and penances from everyone: as early as the June 25, each day five companions flagellated themselves and recited together Litanies of the Saints to stave off the danger. These were hours of anguish, for they remembered what Paul IV had declared the previous year: "Don't depend upon your bulls, because what one Pope has done, another Pope can undo": would the spiritual heritage of Ignatius be ruined?

Who had been able to transform the feelings of the Pope in but a few days? They soon knew: "Ponce (Cogordan)", said Polanco dryly, "admitted his actions."[26] Their stupefaction was joined to their anguish when they discovered that behind Cogordan, the true author of the petition was Bobadilla.

On June 20,[27] Laynez had the required documents sent to the Pope:

---

[24] *Nadal Mon.* 2, p. 15. This report was in effect a petition: Bobadilla and Cogordan "implored" Paul IV not to authorize the trip to Spain: for, they said, the companions wished by it to escape the authority of the Holy See and to maintain certain intolerable things in the *Constitutions*; finally, to establish a general of their fashioning who would do only as he pleased (*pro libitu*).

[25] *Nadal Mon.* 2, p. 14. It seems, according to Nadal, that Laynez and the Fathers proposed to the Pope holding the Congregation in Portugal, if he did not accept holding it in Spain.

[26] *Pol. Compl.* 2, p. 598.

[27] We agree with SCADUTO that it was by mistake (op. cit., 1, p. 32, n. 6), that Nadal at first, and the editors of MHSJ subsequently, talked of July 20. Cf. the letter accompanying

bulls, *Constitutions*, Rules and the list of companions in Rome "with indications of their nationalities for greater clarity". As for the *Constitutions*, they indicated that they did not yet have definitive approval;[28] they even gave a Latin translation "made in haste, but accurate"; all the professed had been invited to present their remarks on the text, so that the General Congregation might decide about it: thus modified, the *Constitutions* could be submitted to the Holy See for definitive approval. "What His Holiness will urge, we shall rapidly integrate and will add the finishing details with the ripened judgment of the General Congregation. In all this may all be done in accordance with the will of His Holiness whom we shall always humbly obey, as his sons and servants, submissive to his person and to the Holy See." This accompanying letter was signed by the group of responsible companions; Laynez soon added to it a personal letter.[29]

The behavior of Bobadilla and Cogordan was assuredly serious. One can even add that it constituted an underhanded "blow" because they took this step *omnibus insciis* (*without the knowledge of any*).[30] Father Scaduto entitled his study of these events: "Il dissidio di Bobadilla",[31] which goes from disagreement to dissidence; let us say that something was broken among the companions; Ribadeneyra evoked Judas. . . . Polanco would not forgive Bobadilla and Cogordan and tried to obtain from the congregation an official and vigorous condemnation against them, which fortunately would not be obtained. Happily, for if the "manner" was indefensible, the "matter" of disagreement was not imaginary. As for Nadal, he undertook a refutation, in his methodical way, of the Bobadilla-Cogordan report:[32] the counterattack lacked neither force nor truth; but it was spoiled by excessive personal invectives; he accused Bobadilla of being motivated by worldliness, a frenzy for authority, unscrupulous ambition, resentment, etc.; it was "almost exactly on target", as St. Francis de Sales would have said; the faults of Bobadilla were sufficiently monumental that Nadal did not have to

---

the documents of deposition in *Nadal Mon.* 4, p. 123, n. 10, note 1. The corrections there in the hand of Polanco are especially interesting.

[28] The Society was governed then (in the strong sense of the word govern) according to the *Formula Instituti* and the papal bulls, with also a few rules which the legitimate superiors had imposed. The *Constitutions* were only "declared", that is to say revealed, introduced little by little, region by region.

[29] *Nadal Mon.* 4, pp. 125–26, n. 11.

[30] *Pol. Compl.* 2, p. 598.

[31] *Op. cit.*, 1, p. 31.

[32] *Nadal Mon.* 4, pp. 130–47. It is necessary to read the page which Nadal dedicated to Bobadilla in his "Ephemerides" of 1557. The least that one can say is that it does not do him any honor (*Nadal Mon.* 2, p. 53).

invent any on his own. Nadal was more accurate, if not less angry, when he accused Bobadilla, during a heated argument, saying, "You say that Laynez is not the Vicar? Very well! If he is not, I am, and I can show the papers signed by Ignatius."[33]

In the campaign (because one must call things by their name) led at that time by Bobadilla, there were two slightly different themes:

First, the legitimacy of a Vicar's governing the Society during a vacancy in the post of Superior General. In the absence of approved constitutions, maintained Bobadilla, the Society was ruled by pontifical bulls which do not mention vicars: only the surviving first Fathers, the "first founders", were sufficiently capable of governing the Society—according to him. Moreover, even if they were approved, the *Constitutions* (in the state of 1556) provided for that Vicar only one role: to call together the General Congregation. Let him govern, then, since he actually existed, but "more with the first *founders* than with the others". The others were Nadal, Polanco and Madrid (who, we should remember, was not yet professed).[34] For this part of the thesis Bobadilla had rallied Paschase Broët and, one guesses why, Rodríguez, badly scarred from his wounds: a total of three *primi Patres* of the four surviving were in agreement. With them were J. B. Viola who had a bone to pick with Laynez, Adriani, an honest man but one who had recently come up against Ribadeneyra, and evidently Ponce Cogordan, for whom the fact of being professed of only three vows had caused an incurable state of trauma.[35]

The other theme which ran through Bobadilla's protest was the juridical value of the *Constitutions* as Ignatius had bequeathed them. Let us say immediately that on this point Broët, Viola, Adriani and even Rodríguez refused to follow him: only Cogordan remained blindly faithful. Around 1540, Bobadilla had revealed a certain distaste for juridical texts and canonical obligations. When, in 1540, Ignatius had recalled him from Bisignano to decide on the first constitutions, "There will be time later on", he had said "to think of that and to compose them."[36] In 1551, his remarks on text A of the *Constitutions* were not

---

[33] Ibid. 2, p. 59.

[34] *Nadal Mon.* 4, pp. 103–23, n. 3 to 10.

[35] It is necessary to read in ibid. 4, pp. 15 and 16, his invective against Cogordan: "We all knew that he had been profoundly wounded, in the last years, in his desire for profession of the four vows." Ignatius, to console him, named him professed of three vows, and Laynez minister of La Strada. "They could not lessen his desire: he himself was so obsessed, it seemed, that he was heard to declare that if he was not professed, he would prefer to go away elsewhere so as not to see the General Congregation." The fact that Nadal let himself be so carried away as to make such confidences, shows us to what degree the pitch had mounted! One likes to believe that it was but a flash of anger.

[36] *Bobad. Mon.*, p. 619; *Const.* 1, LIII.

without a vested interest: "They repeat the same thing several times", he said without giving details or perceiving that the very motivation of the Ignatian text required these revisions at different levels.[37] And if he failed in beginning of the college of Naples in 1552, it was, according to witnesses, even lay people, because he had installed there a climate of excessive "liberty".[38] His criticism of the *Constitutions*, as he presented it to Paul IV, bore on numerous points: he wanted in particular that the passages which attacked the doctors of the faculty of theology in Paris be revised—and he enumerated, without prejudice, the decisions to be made, a whole list of serious questions on which it was important to shed full light. A precise and concentrated light, for, he repeated, "the Constitutions are a prolix labyrinth".[39]

The weakness of this kind of quarrel is that what there can be of truth in each of the positions is smothered under the excesses of language.[40] Neither Bobadilla nor Nadal nor Polanco was entirely wrong, nor entirely right. And in their combat both had at heart the wish to safeguard the integrity of Ignatius' plan. In a memo to Cardinal Carpi,[41] Bobadilla showed that he had "scored important points" against his adversaries: "Since they [Nadal and his group] had so magnified the Constitutions and their authority, they now recognized that the Constitutions were *in fieri* and had no legal value", as he had written to the Most Reverend Cardinals charged with informing the Pope, an obvious allusion to the letter which accompanied, on June 20, 1557, the dispatch of the documents demanded by the Pope.

Such was the debate and such were the stakes. The Roman summer was "hot" for the Society. It was even more so for Rome and for the Pope. The pontifical armies were beaten, pontifical diplomacy with France had failed, the treaty of Cave was signed in haste and established the hegemony of the Spanish power in Italy. These reverses and this defeat were accompanied, as usual, with grave economic difficulties; for the Roman college and the German college it was almost abject poverty; it was necessary to disperse the students everywhere that the war allowed; in the territories occupied by the armies, there was also famine. To that was added the arrival of a flood of unaccustomed magnitude (the night of September 14 to 15), which swamped the low quarters of Rome where the Roman college was situated.[42]

[37] *Const.* I, LXXXII, LXXXIII, p. 396.

[38] *Chron.* 2, p. 522; SACCHINI, *Historia Societatis Jesu*, bk. I, p. 74.

[39] *Nadal Mon.* 4, pp. 101–2; cf. ibid. pp. 104–106, 112–17, 732–33.

[40] See for example the "Ephemerides" of Geerarts in *Pol. Compl.* 2, pp. 602–3.

[41] Attribution and date are given as uncertain by the MHSJ, *Nadal. Mon.* 4, pp. 729–34; but from the context, at least the date can be pinpointed.

[42] An excellent account of the situation in SCADUTO, op. cit. 1, pp. 43–59.

IV. THE ARBITRATION OF CARDINAL CARPI
AND THE DEFEAT OF BOBADILLA

Bobadilla asked that the question of the vicar be submitted to the judgment of Cardinal Carpi, the protector of the order. Laynez accepted.

The confrontation took place on August 9, 1557.[43] The Cardinal first ordered that the meetings of the Fathers be held as they habitually were, without any of the professed being excluded from them; but that Laynez be accorded rank and authority as Superior: first, because he had been legitimately elected according to the provisions of the Constitutions; also because subsequently his election had been considered legitimate and had been approved by all of the assembled Fathers; finally because Spain, Portugal, Sicily, Germany, Italy and France—in short all the regions of the Society—recognized him in their correspondence as the true Superior. According to Nadal it was, however, recommended to Laynez not to take any administrative steps without having convoked the first Fathers and the other companions.[44]

Bobadilla kept silent, but everyone was afraid that, where parts of Carpi's judgment contradicted his own, he would appeal to the Pope: in fact, he had threatened the Cardinal with doing so! Also, on the advice of some Fathers, Laynez hurried to see Paul IV and asked him to study this affair raised by Bobadilla and Cogordan and to help the Society surmount this impasse.[45] With benevolence the Pope listened to Laynez; he promised him that he would do nothing that would not favor the Society's interests; that Laynez should give him the name of a cardinal through whom the Pope could be kept current concerning all the news. "Whomever Your Holiness designates will be our representative", responded Laynez. The Pope chose Cardinal Ghislieri. He was a great supporter of the Society.[46] He began by forbidding Bobadilla and Cogordan to speak henceforth of this affair with anyone except himself. Then he wished to talk with all the Fathers, and, so that these conversations would be more useful, he decided not to have them come to him at St. Peter's, but to visit them in their quarters.[47] It was on September 7 that Ghislieri talked with Bobadilla; according to a statement, made by Polanco and countersigned by Laynez, of the minutes of the conversation

---

[43] The date comes from the "Ephemerides" of Geerarts, *Pol. Compl.* 2, p. 602, where the interview is summarized on August 10.

[44] According to the context, it seems that it concerned only the professed delegated to the Congregation.

[45] *Nadal. Mon.* 2, p. 56.

[46] The future Pius V, a man of stern rectitude.

[47] *Nadal. Mon.* 2, pp. 56–57.

drafted by Bobadilla[48] himself, the latter repeated to the Cardinal what he had said and written many times; he was asking in closing that, until the election of the General, Laynez govern, not with the agreement of all the professed (for that would create great confusion), especially during the General Chapter, but with the first founders rather than with the others; however if they had need of one Father or another, he could be called upon for consultation but not for decision-making! It was there, he said, a question of honesty and it was not difficult, provided that everything was done with justice, charity and for the edification of the Society.

Nadal contends that, from all these conversations, the Cardinal concluded that a "profane and seditious" action (*prophane et seditiose egisse*) had been perpetrated by Bobadilla and Cogordan, and that they were guilty of ambition and intrigue.[49] We are not obliged to believe that. In any case, Nadal avows that the Cardinal kept the secret: his role was not to pass judgment, but to refer it all to Paul IV. Whatever happened, Bobadilla felt that the affair had turned out badly for him; inasmuch as Cardinals Scotti and Reuman themselves seemed to drop him, as well as Cogordan.[50] Cardinal Guido Sforza of Santafiore insisted specifically then that Bobadilla undertake the reform of the Sylvestrians; Bobadilla put himself at the disposal of the Cardinal and left Rome for the area of Foligno and Perugia. Nadal adds, "Then everything became easier."[51] This sigh of relief did him no honor. As for Cogordan, he still tried to fight after Bobadilla's departure, but soon, he too left Rome for Assisi: the leaders responsible for two charitable groups and the Senate of the city had asked Laynez to send them a "good spiritual father of the Society . . . of a fitting age"[52] to help them in their work with prisoners and indigents. In this fief reserved for the sons and daughters of St. Francis, the "other religious" were not easily introduced; Cogordan knew how to make himself effective, without offending anyone or departing from his role: he heard confessions, celebrated Mass, occupied himself with the two charitable groups; briefly, he quite simply led the life of a companion in the manner of the first Fathers so well that his mission, which was to have been temporary, ended in a request for a college.

What were the feelings of these two "seditious" Fathers after their departure from Rome? Quite simply, it seems, the feelings of faithful

[48] Ibid. 4, pp. 109–112.
[49] *Nadal Mon.* 2, p. 57.
[50] Ibid. 4, p. 116, n. 1.
[51] 2, p. 57.
[52] Cf. *Lainii Mon.* 2, pp. 533–34, cited by SCADUTO, op. cit., 1, p. 87.

companions of Jesus Christ . . . each according to his temperament, his
grace and his crisis!

As for Bobadilla, he remained convinced of the justice of the views
which he had held in Rome. However, he held no rancor against those
who had fought with him and who, finally, had won over him with the
Pope; he wrote to them as if nothing had happened, fraternally, light-
heartedly. On October 26, 1557, he wrote to Laynez, gave him news
(brilliant as usual) of his mission of reforming the Sylvestrians thoroughly,
and then he added:

> Last Sunday, the legate Carafa passed by here and I went out of the abbey to
> meet him on the road. He embraced me with great joy. . . . Tell Master
> Polanco to inform me at length about the affairs of the Society, have him tell
> me how they are going, and ask him to have my valise brought to me: I left
> it at Master Romulo's, auditor of the Most Reverend Camerlingo; he will
> send it to me: I have great need of it, for in Foligno they insist that I give
> lessons and that I preach. Master Paschase [Broët] is very highly regarded in
> this city. . . . I commend myself to the prayers of Your Reverence and of all
> the Fathers. . . . I shall send you news from time to time. Au revoir.[53]

What a superb ability to forget and to bounce back. Enough to take
away Polanco's breath!

Cogordan was not of this mettle. While doing his best as a missionary,
he thought about his misfortunes, was heartsick and fell ill because of it.
Bobadilla, having learned of it, took advantage of Cogordan's visit in
Foligno to meet with him. Bobadilla even sent him a horse for the trip.

> He was so ill that he seemed half dead; today he departed. I consoled him; I
> gave him letters, dispatches and answers. . . . I uplifted his body and soul. I
> told him to be joyous, that there was little time before the General Congre-
> gation, which I hoped would be convoked, and that he must make sure that
> he would be in good health, etc.

For himself, all was going well: Foligno was thrilled with his return;
he counted on the prayer of the city as well as on that of the Society and
of all the house of La Strada *in genere et in specie*.[54] To whom did
Bobadilla write this letter? To Polanco, on January 25, 1558. One almost
thinks that one must be dreaming when one reads it!

As for Polanco, he was far from forgetting the events of the autumn.
On the topic of Bobadilla and Cogordan, "he let fall, in a very studied
manner, a thick curtain of silence."[55] He strove to keep them far from

---

[53] *Bobad. Mon.*, pp. 186–87, n. 112.
[54] Ibid., pp. 199–200, n. 122.
[55] SCADUTO, op. cit., I, p. 84.

Rome, controlled them discreetly, "kept track of them, awaited them at the threshold of the General Congregation for the punishment which would serve as an example". For the moment, he was not uncovering his artillery, and "sending them in various places for honest motives", he sought to prevent them from "infecting the corps".[56] Foligno was, in his eyes, "an enforced residence" for Bobadilla, and Assisi was the same for Cogordan. Father Scaduto is right: implacable and tenacious harshness is astonishing in Polanco, but it is hardly disputable. His correspondence gives it credence: let one read, for example, the letters which he wrote to the Rector of Perugia on October 20, 1557 and January 1, 1558: in them Bobadilla is presented as a man "who spreads his venom everywhere, even when the occasion does not arise", a man whom one must not let go anywhere or speak to anyone, a man "who is no longer united with the head or the body of the Society".[57]

The excuse of these men, all desirous of safeguarding the inheritance of Ignatius (one cannot too much emphasize this) was the climate of this fall and winter of 1557—a climate of anguish, despite the rather comforting conversations with Ghislieri, but as the documents submitted to the Pope on June 20, were not judged, approved and given back, a return of anger was always possible on the part of Paul IV; and they knew from experience that Bobadilla was capable of provoking such about-faces in Paul IV, as abrupt as they were formidable. Moreover, were all the faults on the side of Bobadilla? Could not certain measures arouse the suspicion that a "tendency" in the Pope's character sought to embroil Bobadilla in this conflict? Beyond Polanco and Bobadilla, is one sure that the "reading", as one would say today, of the documents left by Ignatius, was the same in the eyes of Laynez and of Bröet, of Borgia and Canisius, of Rodríguez and Câmara?

Did not the unanimity against Bobadilla veil in fact a diversity of interpretations and even of criticisms? The *Constitutions* remained "opened" or rather "not closed". Laynez rejoiced in that fact; but how would one close them? The whole problem lay therein, and it is a pity that one could not record on the spot certain conversations between the responsible leaders, once Bobadilla and Cogordan were sent "on assignment".

At La Strada, they waited to know what Paul IV would do about the *Constitutions* and Rules which had been remitted to Scotti and Reuman on June 20. They had asked the Father Vicar to send them someone who

[56] Ibid., which refers to the file of the archives for the quotation *Ital.* 61 (Epistolae generalium 1557–1559), 20v-21r.

[57] *Bobad. Mon.*, p. 185, n. 112 and p. 196, n. 119. The unfortunate Viola who nevertheless called himself "repentant" was no better treated by Polanco?

would read the texts to them and who could respond to their requests for clarifications. Laynez chose Nadal, but soon Scotti no longer supported "the liberty of Nadal or even his importunities"[58] and got rid of the reader. "We were calm, but not without anxiety." And then, one day, the Pope sent back the pontifical documents and the writings which he had demanded in order to examine them. He condemned nothing: it would be necessary, perhaps, insinuated Scotti, to rework the choir question. "For Bobadilla, Cogordan and the others, there was no sanction, as if the Pope wished that they be treated rather with benevolence and charity and that we might be inspired more with good than with evil."[59] The Pope's gesture was interpreted by the Fathers as a "vigorous approbation".[60] This was perhaps a little over-optimistic.

Meanwhile, the Pope had signed the peace with Philip II and had granted the Fathers, contrary to his attitude of June 20, the authorization to leave Rome: he even provided them with a hundred ducats for their trips. Thus, Adriani departed for Flanders (of which Mercurian had been named Commissioner), Canisius and Goudanus for Germany, Lanoye for Vienna, Vinck for Perugia and Doménech for Sicily. The others awaited in Rome the convocation of the General Congregation which was at present scheduled for the month of May 1558.

V. THE GENERAL CONGREGATION OF MAY 1558

Who Would Be Electors?

If the way was cleared, it remained no less filled with bitterness: real difficulties, interior to the order, pertaining to the legislative situation, had not been resolved by the defeat of Bobadilla, nor even by the fact that the Vatican had sent back "intact" the documents for June 20, 1557.

One primary question arose: who would participate in the assembly? Of the forty-two professed whom the order numbered in 1556, seven were in India or Brazil and two, Olave and Frusius, were dead; there remained only thirty-three who could participate in the meeting. Now, if one replaced the numbers with the names behind them, one would perceive that the professed who spoke Spanish were decidedly the most numerous: the problem of the universal representatives of the Society was also raised. Would they convoke "all the professed"? That would be to the advantage of the Spaniards. Or would they convoke, in accordance with the *Constitutions*: "The Provincial and two other members

---

[58] It was Nadal himself who spoke thus: *Nadal. Mon.* 2, p. 58.

[59] Ibid., pp. 58–59.

[60] NADAL, "Scholia" in *Institutum Societatus Jesu* (1883), 2, p. 271.

elected by the province?" But many of these provinces lacked professed . . . and the Indian, Brazilian and Ethiopian groups would not be able to send their representatives. Such were the alternatives. Two solutions were considered.

The first consisted of having a certain number of Fathers, who had been "designated" by Ignatius, before his death, make their profession. This solution in fact resolved nothing, because these "designated professed" belonged primarily to Spain and Portugal. As early as August 1556, Laynez, still very ill, had, through the offices of Polanco, rejected this plan. He did not go back on his decision, even if he authorized Borgia, one month before the Congregation of 1558, to promote to profession Father John Plazza, the master of novices of Andalusia, so that the latter might replace, and represent, him at the Congregation.[61]

The second solution was to authorize each province to name delegates from the nonprofessed and those elected, once they had arrived in Rome, would be admitted to profession by the Congregation. However, was this not falling into the very situation which Laynez wanted to avoid in refusing the first solution: i.e., to create a precedent?

On January 25, 1558, Laynez, Nadal and Polanco submitted the difficulty to the Pope: the verbal response allowed for doubt in interpretation. But Cardinal Ghislieri clarified the meaning: "How many must come according to the *Constitutions*?" he asked. "The Provincial and two others, elected from each province." "That suffices," said the Cardinal. "And thus", said Polanco, "we had the interpretation of the thinking of His Holiness from the one whom he had designated to us."[62]

Laynez could, from that moment, announce to all provinces the date of the first General Congregation (May 19, 1558) and indicate the method of election of the participants.

Who Was Chosen as Elector?

From Portugal, Provincial Torres, Vice-provincial Gonsalvus Vaz, and Luis Gonçalves da Câmara, then Rector of Coimbra, were chosen. Two "procurators" were added to them: Manuel Godinho and Jorge Serrano. They were the first to arrive in Rome. Canisius came from Augsburg in the south German province, Lanoye arrived from Vienna and Goysson traveled from Prague: they were all three in Rome by the end of June.

Of the two representatives from France, only Broët who had not departed from Rome was there at the opening of the Congregation and participated in the election of the General. Viola, after the "dissidio" of

---

[61] *Chron.* 6, pp. 51–52; *Lainii Mon.* 1, pp. 285–86; 2, p. 67; 3, pp. 195, 259, 491.
[62] *Nadal Mon.* 4, p. 148.

Bobadilla, had been sent to Verona, and the letter announcing the convocation sent on May 21, did not reach him. Notified by a second letter, he arrived at the end of July and was able to participate in the discussions on the *Constitutions*.

From Sicily, Provincial Doménech and Anthony Vinck arrived on May 9. The third delegate, Ugoletti, was detained in Palermo by sickness.

From North Germany Commissioner Everard Mercurian came; Adriani and Kessel, both ill, withdrew before the trip. The same was true for Goudanus. Salmeron, who was in Brussels as a theologian to Cardinal Charles Carafa, was able to accompany Mercurian.

Borgia, who was ill, had himself represented by Plazza, professed at the last minute. Bustamente from Andalusia and Strada from Aragon were also ill. Araoz, by a series of unexplained circumstances, and undoubtedly for diplomatic reasons, returned soon to Valladolid, after having attempted, or having pretended to attempt, the trip by land. Had he had wind of the wish of Borgia that he be named Assistant General, so that, remaining in Rome, he would be far from the court? Upon his return, he put himself at the disposal of Princess Juana. "As long as he remains here," wrote Borgia, "this college of Valladolid will be a chancellery rather than a religious house: the Father is unceasingly plunged into secular matters, foreign to our institution."[63] The other delegates from Spain were Miron, Cordeses, Avellaneda, then Barma. They arrived in time for the election of the General.

Also present were Simón Rodríguez, Bobadilla, and the Romans, Laynez, Polanco and Nadal.

In the order that the delegates arrived, Laynez had them provided with a kind of instruction in twelve chapters, which contained regulations for assuring the "sincerity" of the election of the General and preventing any maneuver based on intrigue or on personal ambition. Nadal called attention to what was not a good example: a vicar was to prescribe only what was in the *Constitutions* or what was approved by the majority of the Congregation.[64]

The first General Congregation of the Society of Jesus could finally begin its labors.

Election of the Superior General[65]

The delegates began by establishing and declaring that the meeting

---

[63] *Lainii Mon.* 3, p. 296; ASTRAIN, op. cit., 2, p. 481. It would begin again in 1565, for the second General Congregation.

[64] *Nadal Mon.* 2, pp. 59–60.

[65] We shall follow very closely the report which Nadal gives us of it in his "Ephemerides": *Nadal Mon.* 4, pp. 60–62. Fr. SCADUTO, op. et loc. cit., offers many useful details.

was "legitimate and fully represented", taking account of the imminent arrival of Barma, the Vice-provincial of Aragon. Before a meeting could be held, which might precede the election, they dispatched Laynez and Salmeron to the Pope to apprise him of everything.

Paul IV received the two Fathers on June 20. The reception was very benevolent. "I have already aided this Society blessed by God", he said, making allusion to the frequent support and favors which he had bestowed on the Society since the beginning of his pontificate; it was true: in spite of the fears and anguish that his whims had caused the companions, Paul IV had often and greatly aided them, for example in their difficulties with the University of Paris, in Germany and even in Flanders. This recall of the past indicated his present and future attitude; it was a promise. Their Cardinal-protector Carpi being absent from Rome at that time, the Pope indicated that, for these decisive days, Cardinal Pacheco would replace him with the Fathers for the election. He insisted that the group act with full liberty. He touched also, in passing, the question of the choir; he praised Mary Magdalen, whom according to legend, the angels themselves came to awaken so that she might recite, without ever missing the hours of the canonical Office. Finally, he expressed a desire to know the procedure of the election of the General. He blessed the Fathers, regularized the *defectus* which could have occurred up to that point, etc. Laynez and Salmeron returned to La Strada praising God.

To satisfy the desire of the Pope, Nadal formalized the instruction on the election which Laynez had distribued to the delegates upon their arrival in Rome. This was a simple matter: for aware of the criticism of Nadal on the regularity of his action, Laynez had already asked Nadal for a revision of the document, then had submitted it for the approval of the group. Certain minor improvements sufficed. A few days after the request of the Pope, Laynez took him the *De ratione electionis praepositi*. The Pope had it read to him, and expressed his agreement; he wished, however, that it be examined by Cardinals Ghislieri, Reuman, Scotti and Rebiba; they returned it after having deleted the censures which attacked the "ambitious". In any case, the document was not a part of the *Constitutions*, and it was only a standard, not a law: it forecast in particular that the election would take place in the room where Ignatius had died on July 31, 1556.

On June 21, the meetings resumed. Would they begin with the election of the General or with the examination and the approval of the *Constitutions*? Bobadilla had raised the problem in 1557; in fact, in this phase of the genesis of the order, the question was not farfetched: in 1539, had not the first Fathers wanted to draft together all that they could of the *Constitutions*, before proceeding to the election of the General? The delegates decided then to reverse the order of work; they chose first of all to elect the General by a majority of votes.

A week passed in tasks preliminary to the election and in personal reciprocal consultations. The delegates were not to leave the house or to be active except among themselves. One more point was submitted to the arbitration of the Pope: the votes that those delegates who were chosen but prevented from coming had sent by those who had come, should they be taken into consideration either for the election or for the *Constitutions*? The Pope, at the suggestion of Laynez, responded negatively: in order not to jeopardize the future of the general congregations. This was wise.

Having accomplished the two days of prayer and penance prescribed by the *Constitutions*, the delegates were ready to vote. The election took place, on July 2, the Feast of the Visitation of the Virgin. The twenty electors[66] gathered together in the presence of Cardinal Pacheco, in the little room sanctified by the works and death of Ignatius. Canisius was assigned to address the group. They then prayed for an hour. Pacheco departed, not without having reminded them to elect a companion *"probatae vitae et sanae doctrinae"*; he added that the Pope wished the General to reside in Rome unless he was presented with the necessity of visiting the Society; he insisted again that the group act in full liberty.[67]

On the first ballot, Laynez got thirteen votes; Nadal four; Broët, Lanoye and Borgia (absent) one each. Broët, in the role of the longest professed, proclaimed Laynez the Superior General of the Society of Jesus.

Regarding this day, we possess two reports which agree in several minute details: a letter from Polanco to Oliverio Manareo dated July 16,[68] and an account, still unpublished, kept in the archives of the Gregorian University in Rome.[69] Let us read the account in Polanco's letter:

> Upon a gesture of the General, everyone went forward, beginning with the secretary, and each kneeling, kissed his hand. Immediately, the ballots of the vote were burned. One full hour had not passed, when the Cardinal reentered the room. Thus ended the matter of the election, not only in community accord, but in the spiritual joy and consolation of all: the Cardinal was greatly edified. When the secretary left to announce the election to the people who were waiting at the door, there were so many

[66] Twenty, that is to say ten Spanish, four Flemish, one Dutch, two French, three Portuguese.

[67] *Nadal Mon.* 2, pp. 61–62.

[68] *Lainii Mon.* 3, pp. 394–98.

[69] Archives of the Gregorian University, MS 119, pp. 302–22.

people, companions and foreigners, curious to know the result of the election, that the house was full of them. Among the important and the unimportant, the joy was universal. We returned to the church singing the psalm "Benedictus Dominus Deus Israel"; then in the church the "Te Deum", with tremendous joy. . . . Upon return to the house, everyone presented his respects to the new General. The good Cardinal, who had had a meal prepared for us, went to announce the election to the Holy Father: Paul IV seemed very satisfied and edified. Only the Father General hardly showed any joy, but patient and good, he put his confidence in the Lord our God.

The event was celebrated by "public meetings" for six days (July 3–9); the attendance was such that it was necessary to move to the Pantheon. Everything ended with an "appropriate"[70] theatrical presentation.

On July 6, Laynez and the Fathers of the Congregation were received by the Pope, surrounded by Scotti, Ghislieri and Alphonso Carafa. Paul IV signalled the Fathers to approach him and spoke in a tone of confidence and with such a spiritual familiarity that the listeners were astounded and overwhelmed. "Remember", he said to them among other things,

that you have not been called and that you are not destined for tranquility and comfort, but for fatigue and for the Cross: take as your example our Lord and Savior. . . . If you do not yet have an awareness of the critical situation in which we find ourselves it will be revealed to you by this world in full disarray (in scompiglio) where the Church is so cruelly treated, goaded and attacked on all sides. And its persecutors are not only the impious, the infidels, the barbarous and those who in the new continents attack all that bears the name of Christ, but also those who are sanctified by the same baptism, who benefit from the same sacraments. . . . Cling to your vocation, banish fear and human respect, venerate the name of the Lord with intrepidity before men with your face uncovered and with your head held high. Consecrate yourselves totally to the defense of the Holy Church, so that you may be an offering acceptable to God.[71]

The Pope then confirmed the election and also all the favors and privileges that he and his predecessor had granted to the Society. "If there is need of other favors and privileges, we are ready to grant them. We wish to be for you not only the communal Father, but the special Father of your Society. . . . You can come to us at any time; our door will always be open to you."

The letters or accounts of witnesses reflect an immense joy: "It seemed", wrote Doménech to the Rector of Messina, "that the Holy Spirit spoke from his mouth. . . . The joy, the consolation, and the

[70] Lainii Mon. 3, p. 397; VILLOSLADA, Storia del Collegio Romano, p. 50.
[71] Text of the address in Lainii Mon. 8, pp. 665–69.

jubilation which the Lord gave us in this 'Visitation'[72] are inexpressible."[73] Polanco, the modest Polanco who always hid his feelings so well, was no less lyrical: "[This discourse] was pronounced by Paul IV with so much force and feeling that he seemed to want to bare his heart and one might have said that it was Christ who spoke through him, consoling us and inspiring us marvelously."[74]

Bobadilla himself had acknowledged his errors. Cogordan had asked pardon, weeping. Unanimity was renewed around Laynez. Scotti had returned the *Constitutions* without criticism. The clouds of tempests had dissipated. It was in euphoria, a euphoria which did not obliterate the recent anguish, that the Fathers were going to examine the *Constitutions*.

The Examination and Approval of the Constitutions

Who would have the right of discussion and vote? There were the twenty electors, at first, evidently, but at the beginning of the month of August, Pelletier and Canisius had to ask permission to return to their apostolic sector. On the other hand, six new delegates were admitted to participate in the work and in the votes: Godinho from Portugal, Serrano from Brazil, Cordeses from the province of Aragon, Guzman from Italy, Avellaneda from the province of Bétique and finally Viola who had not received the first invitation and had not been able to set out to arrive on time for the election. The Spanish-speaking element was thus found to be singularly reinforced. Upon these twenty-four men a very heavy task fell. On August 10, the day when the labors began, they were so aware of this that some of them proposed that they content themselves for the time being with naming a commission to study the *Constitutions* more at leisure and that they put off discussions and votes until later. Once bitten, twice shy! No one wanted to risk another crisis. They decided then not to separate before having made some definitive decisions. The Congregation would last from June 10 until September 10, 1558. This decision, simple and uncomplicated as it appears, was not without ambiguity in its individual motivations: knowing the men who made it, one cannot help wondering whether the motivations were not in fact very divergent: unconditional respect for the thinking of the Founder, fear of raising explosive problems in these circumstances of an unstable pontificate and internal tension, desire to have finally an authoritative law from which, as in the time of Genesis, "the waters could be separated from the earth", etc.[75]

---

[72] The election had taken place on the day of the Feast of the Visitation.
[73] Manuscript *Ital.* 112, p. 310.
[74] *Lainii Mon.* 8, p. 399.
[75] Fr. SCADUTO discreetly indicates these diverse motivations: op. cit. 1, p. 109.

The initial decision of the Fathers imposed not only a time schedule for work—they could not dally—but also an attitude, a method of work, indeed a spirit: it was unthinkable to undertake matters *ab ovo*.

And indeed one primary question arose from the outset: was it fitting to introduce modifications into the *Constitutions*? The group responded that, "it was necessary to respect and observe them inasmuch as they appeared in the original text of our Father Ignatius"[76] and that "neither in their entirety nor in their particulars should the substantial sections of the *Constitutions* be submitted to discussion." However, we are certain from the correspondence that several of the members of the group had "observations" to present on the Ignatian text: Borgia (through his representative), Canisius, Salmeron, Bobadilla, Bustamente, etc., and Laynez himself, not to mention Ribadeneyra who must have been bored to death from not participating in the debates. Did certain ones nevertheless try to make themselves heard?

A decree, the seventy-first, seems to indicate as much in its brevity: "Other propositions were advanced concerning the *Constitutions*, but as it had been decided after deliberation that no innovations would be added, we shall not transcribe them here."[77] In the absence of the actions of this first Congregation, it is impossible to specify what these "innovations" were; it is already very much to know that there were true innovations.

The Contributions of the First Congregation

Even taking into account this initial position, it is difficult to affirm, as one often reads, that the First Congregation was content to correct certain printing errors which had slipped into the Spanish text of the *Constitutions* left by Ignatius, or to introduce therein paragraphs or chapters that Ignatius had already proposed. Its contribution was important.

1. First, because it approved and gave the value of law to the Ignatian texts that it had examined; in September 1558, the Society finally had a set of laws. This was a considerable gain. Each and every one had a "mental image", an ideal according to which, in all conscience, alone or in community, they could judge themselves. This was a significant change because formerly, each of the companions had measured himself, had assessed himself or had sought to recognize the others according to the "personality" of the first Fathers—sometimes not exempt from legend—or according to a "prototype" which was not without some

---

[76] *Institutum Societatis Jesu*, 2, p. 161, decree 15.
[77] Ibid., p. 162, decree 16.

ambiguity: the "Society of Rome" (*Societas romana*),[78] sometimes even according to the still more or less mysterious "portrait", of Ignatius himself. For the "spirit" the "letter" was lacking: the approved *Constitutions* furnished it for them.

2. The Congregation—which worked on the Spanish text, called the "autograph"[79]—introduced a few slight modifications: for example, it suppressed a few "Declarations" of the "Examen", or another "Declaration" of part VI which permitted the solemn professed to accept legacies or inheritances for pious purposes, with the permission of the Holy See. It examined whether it was fitting to insert in the body of the *Constitutions* a few texts which did not yet appear there and about which one wondered whether they had been reviewed by Ignatius. For example, it accepted the constitution which forbade receiving any reimbursement for ministries; it transposed, on the contrary, into a simple rule the constitution concerning "the table of the General"; it accepted, but for a time only (until 1563), the text declaring that no new college would be accepted for which the founders did not guarantee the maintenance of a community of fourteen persons and would not offer sufficient scholarly locations and a church for the free exercise of worship, but, by reason of this provisory character, it did not judge it useful to insert it into the body of the *Constitutions*; it finalized the thorny text (and revolutionary in the juridical context of the times) which reserved to the General the power of making contracts.[80] Finally, it examined the variants in the text, introduced by the secretaries or copyists, notably by Polanco, to authenticate them: for it was not always certain that Ignatius had reviewed or approved them.

3. The Congregation had to interpret certain points of the *Constitutions*—some very grave points—and it was not the least concern of its work, even after it had decided to maintain the objectivity of the text and of the Ignatian "praxis". It is easy to recognize among the points examined those which had been the most criticized, whether by adversaries, or even by friends of the Society, or which had brought about the most internal difficulties.

[78] Cf. our *Chroniques saint Ignace de Loyola*, p. 297.

[79] Let us remember that this word does not have its usual meaning: the text is called an "autograph" not because it was written by the hand of Ignatius, but because it was the one on which Ignatius himself was still working even up to his last days, the one which he discussed, on which he noted his comments, and about which he prayed. "*Original*" or "*originel*" would have been more exact. On this point the historians are in agreement.

[80] A very delicate text, because the other contracting party did not consider itself sufficiently "protected": it will be necessary to wait for the bull *Ex debito* of Gregory XIII (August 5, 1582) for the problem to be resolved.

First the nature of the vows. In the Ignatian system, the "solemnity" of vows was no longer required to establish the religous state; this view of Ignatius constituted a very important innovation in the canonical legislation of the period. In that time, religious orders consisted only of novices and of those professed in solemn vows; and here, Ignatius was introducing between these two categories, religious of simple yet permanent vows (scholastics and approved coadjutors). Without entering into the labyrinth of this wholly new legislation, it is easy to perceive that it raised problems; and that the involved "cases" had not been lacking as early as in Ignatius' time. What if scholastics left the order irregularly and married? This marriage was valid, although illegitimate. Moreover, after their departure, or dismissal, whether regular or irregular, others demanded the alms which they themselves or their families had given to such-and-such a college or such-and-such a house. What should they do except to make reimbursement, when no longer responsible for their debts?[81] The complications were so real that the procurators of Spain proposed that the solemn profession of the three vows be made at the completion of the novitiate, whether by the scholastics or by the coadjutors, allowing, however, the Society the right to dispense a subject (who might reveal himself as not suited to the order) from his vows and hence from their effects. This proposition had the support of Borgia: "If one does not find a remedy for these concerns," he wrote, "I fear that we may be constrained to confer the sub-diaconate after the novitiate to candidates whose vocation is fragile. The recitation of the breviary will be a hindrance to their studies."[82] The Congregation rejected the request. The Second Congregation of 1565 rejected an analogous proposal. Gregory XIII would later bring a partial solution in declaring that marriages by religious of simple vows who were "fugitives", that is to say, who had left the order without approval of the General, were invalid.[83]

The Spaniards, always with the support of Borgia, proposed again some other important modifications on the subject of the daily time of personal prayer, of required penances and even of the choral Office. It is necessary to say in their defense that the freedom of initiative that the *Constitutions* left in these areas did not coincide with the mentality of the spiritual Spaniards of the period: such as those of Luis de Granada, or St. Peter of Alcántara. The echoes of reproaches which were addressed to the

[81] Cf. the difficulties with the family of Don Theotonio de Braganza, and this was not the only case.

[82] *Borgiae Mon.* 3, p. 349, quoted by SCADUTO, op. cit., p. 110.

[83] The declaration conforms to the other declaration of Gregory XIII that scholastics and coadjutors, were, by virtue of their simple vows, *"vere et proprie religiosi"*.

Society on this subject, resound in the accusations of Melchoir Cano and, outside Spain, in the Decree of the faculty of theology of Paris: the innovations of the Society, in this "claustral" aspect of the religious life, appeared to its adversaries as a sort of criticism or challenge. On several occasions, Ignatius had to intervene to prevent monastic tendencies from infiltrating the houses of the order: one remembers his directive letters to men like Borgia, Oviedo, Barma and Rodríguez himself, and the discussions on the time of prayer for the scholastics. In his report to Laynez,[84] Borgia proposed that the time of prayer be prolonged, that chanting at vespers and solemn high Masses be reintroduced, that periods and days of penance be fixed (for example, during Advent and Lent): the Spanish delegates presented all these requests, even before the report of Borgia reached the General. They were rejected.

Rejected also was the proposal of including the solemn profession in a spectacular ceremony, as had sometimes been done in Portugal, Spain and Flanders; it was decided to maintain henceforth the sober rite which the *Constitutions* suggested. On one point, however, the Congregation introduced a novelty: it specified the formula—as yet undecided and diverse—of the five simple vows of profession and of the four solemn vows; and these specifications seemed so important that, on the afternoon of August 25, all the professed Fathers pronounced anew their five simple vows before the General, according to the formula approved by the Congregation.[85]

Other questions were also decided according to the lessons of experience: like suspension, by entrance into the Society, of all vows previously pronounced, the adoption of the Roman rite for celebration of the Mass, the freedom of teaching given to certain companions in the universities, and especially the way of establishing new provinces.

For other questions which it judged less urgent, less ripe or minor, the Congregation delegated its powers to the General. It asked him also to draft various "Directories" to provide a certain unity in the ministries, and also the special Rules.[86]

4. Among the most important labors of the First Congregation, one must count the establishment or the better organization of certain machinery of the central government of the Society, regarding which the intention of Ignatius had remained vague, and his *praxis* experimental. Harassed by events, he had resolved problems to the best of his power with the men at his disposal.

---

[84] *Borgiae Mon.* 3, pp. 345–53.

[85] One may even wonder if some, even among the first Fathers (Bobadilla, Rodríguez) had ever uttered them previously.

[86] Cf. for details on these points, SCADUTO, op. cit., I, pp. 112–15.

First, concerning the assistants of the General: it was foreseen as early as the drafts of the *Constitutions* of 1550–1551, that the General would be surrounded by "a few men who would shine in their knowledge and in their character; they would be charged with watching over the universal problems of the Society with particular care and they could divide up the task better to get to the heart of things; one, for example, would follow the affairs of the Indies, another those of Spain and Portugal, another those of Germany and France, another those of Italy and Sicily."[87] But where to find men of this caliber, who would be close enough to Rome and could spend enough time? It had first been in the time of Ignatius a question of three *primi Patres*: Laynez, Salmeron and Bobadilla; three men already overcommitted, scattered, and little acquainted with the problems of regions other than Italy or Germany. Later it was a matter of Polanco, Nadal, Madrid, Olave and Frusius. In fact, assistants did not exist. In 1552 or 1553, Polanco indicated to Ignatius the urgency of establishing an administrative structure which was very important to the order.[88] In 1554, Polanco was insistent, for Ignatius was very ill.[89] He proposed the names of Olave, Frusius, Câmara and Madrid, with, as Secretary, Polanco himself. Did Ignatius finally decide? It is probable, but not certain.

During the summer of 1558, the Congregation regularly named four assistants:[90] Nadal for the German provinces, Flanders and France (he also retained superintendance of the Roman college), Madrid for Italy and Sicily (he remained the minister of the professed house, that is, to say, practically its superior), Gonçalves da Câmara for Portugal, India and Brazil (with the superintendance of the German college) and finally Polanco (who remained Secretary of the Society and was named "Admonitor" to the General). The Assistancies were then redesigned as permitted by the *Constitutions* of 1550–1551. At the same time, the Congregation decided that the assistants should exercise their functions until the elec-

---

[87] *Const.*: text a: P. IX, C. VII, § 2 (French edition: vol. 2, p. 277); definitive text: P. IX, C. VI, § 10, n. 803 (French edition: vol. 1, p. 250).

[88] This report of Polanco (*Pol. Compl.* 1, pp. 81–87) is extremely interesting: it shows effectively to what point the Secretary had become aware of the gaps in the current organization. (For that concerning assistants, see p. 83, n. 6.) He was not alone in wishing for the establishment of this structure.

[89] This new report, as significant of the situation as the preceding one is in *Pol. Compl.* 1, pp. 97–115; cf. for the assistants p. 101. *Font Narr.* 1, does not quote Madrid (p. 54); one does not know why: is it because he was not professed? But the *Constitutions* predicted that it would be the professed "as much as possible" (*Const.* 2, pp. 688–89). Cf. also *Epist. ign.* 1, p. 79 and *Nadal Mon.* 1, p. 342.

[90] Let us remember that Olave and Frusius had died during the summer of 1556, a few weeks after Ignatius.

tion of the new General in the event of a vacancy, and that they would have the right to vote in that election.

The prickly problem of the commissioners remained. Ignatius had very much used this manner of government in difficult regions and cases: Nadal, Laynez, Ribadeneyra and Salmeron had been commissioners; Borgia was still one. This personage, to whom the General delegated for an indeterminate time or a particular mission, a part or even the full extent of his own powers, had no "status" in the Constitutions.[91] It was necessary at least to define what would happen to him upon the death of the General. Was he an "ordinary" superior? Then his functions continued. Was he an "extraordinary" superior? Then his functions ceased. The Congregation decided that he was to be considered an extraordinary superior. By right, however, he could participate in the provincial congregation of the province in which he exercised his functions and could be eligible through this province for the General Congregation.

It was believed advisable also, on the suggestion of Nadal (and one can guess why), to specify the texts of the *Constitutions* which concerned the Vicar General, the modalities of his nomination, and the jurisdiction with which he was invested. It was clearly decided that the Vicar had not only the functions of convoking the General Congregation but also of governing the Society effectively during the absence of the General. They even wanted to draft the rules of this primary function: time was lacking, and the matter was postponed until later.

The Fathers felt that the *Constitutions* called for a kind of commentary, to clarify the interpretation of certain difficult points. They conferred this work upon Polanco and Nadal: in fact, it was Nadal who completed the *Scholia in Constitutiones*. The Second Congregation (1565) would confer an indicative but not normative value upon them.[92]

5. Edition of the *Constitutions*. The *Constitutions* of 1550–1551 were drafted in Spanish and the text on which Ignatius and Polanco worked between 1551 and 1556 was also a Spanish text. It became evident very quickly that only a Latin text would be accessible to all the companions. As early as 1553, Polanco made himself the proponent of this need;[93] already however, fragments of varying lengths had been translated and began to circulate.

Polanco,[94] seconded at certain times by a fine Latinist of the Roman

---

[91] Cf. *Const.* p. IX, ch. III, n. 765.

[92] *Institutum Societatis Jesu*, 2, p. 204 (Dec. 42) and p. 208 (Dec 57). The "Scholia" of Nadal remained in manuscript form until their printing in 1893 by Fathers Altini and Boero.

[93] *Pol. Compl.* 2, p. 81; *Const.* 3, p. LXI, n. 1.

[94] A discussion had been raised in the nineteenth century on the drafter of this

college, Father Fulvio Cardulo, completed a translation at the end of autumn of 1556. Towards the middle of 1557 it was ready to be submitted for the examination of Cardinals Scotti and Reuman. It was minutely compared against the Spanish text during the Congregation of 1558 and recognized as the official version. Included therein were additions and corrections made on the "autographic" text of Ignatius. Warning was given to anyone who printed another translation. Orders were given to print the one which had been approved. On September 10, 1558, in fact, the day of the closing of the Congregation, the Latin text of the *Constitutions* had already been in the hands of the press of the Roman college for several days.[95]

6. The last hurdle of the crisis. The principal Latin edition of the *Constitutions* appeared under the name of Ignatius of Loyola around the end of 1558. It carried the date of 1558 or 1559;[96] a glance at certain examples of this edition will reveal to us the last act of the drama, the ultimate scene of the crisis: at the library of the cultural center of Fontaines in Chantilly, there are two of these examples in existence;[97] in one, page 159 is replaced by a blank page; the other has kept page 159; and what do we read? The choral Office is (partially) reestablished and the generalship would be for three years; this is declared according to the text of the *Constitutions* which ends with page 158.[98]

What, then, had happened? The very text of page 159 shows us:

On September 8, 1558, the Most Reverend Cardinal of Naples, in the name of His Holiness Pope Paul IV, addressed all the members of the General Congregation, presented the two provisions to them and ordered them to insert them in the *Constitutions*. Our Congregation declared itself ready to obey in the two matters: that is why they were introduced here. The first point is that at the will of His Holiness, the Superior General of our Society, was elected for three years and not for life; with the possibility always of his being confirmed in his post, at the end of the three years. The second, that our Society say the canonical hours in choir, as do other religious orders, always with the modifications that the Superior General would judge fitting.

---

translation. Without explicit proof, everything points to Polanco: cf. SCADUTO, op. cit., I, p. 107.

[95] This was one of the first works printed at the Roman college. Cf. Giuseppe CASTELLANI, *La tipografia del collegio romano*, in AHSI, vol. 2 (1933), p. 16.

[96] Cf. *Const.* 3, pp. CXXIX-CXXI; SOMMERVOGEL, *Bibliothèque*, 5, col. 75.

[97] The two copies are actually sides N. 250–9; the one that lacks page 159 contains numerous manuscript notes in Latin and Spanish; it would be interesting to study them to identify the handwriting.

[98] More precisely, the last eight lines of the *Constitutions* are still lacking.

The blow which Ignatius had feared since 1555 had indeed fallen on the *Constitutions*. Even more difficult was the fact that the General Congregation had conducted the work in the euphoria of recovered unanimity and pontifical benevolence. At least, the Fathers could or wished to believe so.[99] Until the last days of the session, Paul IV, for his part, had hoped that the Congregation had grasped his verbal allusions and would have itself included these two modifications which were dear to his heart.

Since August 24 in reality, the Fathers had been uneasy. On August 24, Cardinal Scotti had presented himself to the Congregation on behalf of the Pope and had invited the participants to reexamine the length of the generalship. They discussed it that same day and in the ensuing days in a climate that one may imagine. The dilemma was crucial; fidelity to the thought of Ignatius obliged them to sustain the office of General for life and obedience to the Pope demanded acceptance of the generalship for three years. A letter was drafted to the Pope: in very respectful terms, it indicated to the Pope that the decree instituting the generalship had been taken "in unanimity",[100] but the Society could not disobey an order of the Sovereign Pontiff, if he imposed the change; the Congregation confirmed that it did not want anyone to think that it was through its own will that the institution of the Society had been modified.[101] This letter was signed by all the members of the Congregation, except for Laynez who was to write a personal letter to the Pope. He did not have the time.

In taking recognition of the letter from the Congregation, Paul IV reexperienced all his former fury toward the Society.

On Tuesday, September 6, Laynez and Salmeron were received in audience. Paul IV entered immediately into the heart of the subject; he muttered in barely audible terms *sotto voce*, but not so much so that the two Fathers did not get the gist of his diatribe: the government of Ignatius, he said, had been a tyranny; it was only in the present that one could talk of election of a General; and since it was a matter of a first choice, he, Paul, judged it more opportune that the term of Generalship be three years, even if it entailed renewing the term for three additional years, as it was done elsewhere. The old man was getting overheated and when immediately afterward, he approached the question of the choir, it

---

[99] The personal allusion to Bobadilla that we read on p. 306 in the response of Laynez to Paul IV, at the time of the audience of September 6, gives an indication that unanimity was less total than one was willing to say.

[100] *Institutum Societatis Jesu*, 2, p. 167, decree 47.

[101] Ibid. 2, p. 167. For all this last squall we follow closely the documents left by Nadal and Laynez. Through a prudence which the reader will easily understand, we base our account on the one made by Fr. SCADUTO (op. cit., 1, pp. 117–20).

was really with frenzy: the Jesuits, he said in plain speech, were rebels, because they had not accepted the recitation of the Office in choir, and in acting thus they were carrying water to the mill of the heretics; he feared that some day a new Satan would rise from their ranks: the choral Office was essential and basic to religious life, and even to divine law (*jure divino*). As for him, he was resolved to suppress a patent abuse. "I urge", he added, "that you recite the Office in choir; if not, you will end as heretics. You must do it—even if it costs you a great deal; and woe unto you, if you do not do it."

While he was talking, the face of the Pope reflected intense irritation, his eyes, filled with menace, shifting back and forth from Laynez to Salmeron, from Salmeron to Laynez. He again accused the companions of accepting too many young men from too many nations who could not be trained in such a mediocre Society. The most devastating epithets fell thickly on the Fathers: certain ones came straigth from the Gospel (*Si vos cum mali sitis* . . .). "This verbal violence was accompanied by insults and threats."[102]

Does this account, drafted by Laynez, exaggerate the facts? They are so astonishing that, at the bottom of his report, Laynez thought it best to sign and certify it, "ita est"; and Salmeron countersigned it, "*Ita est.* . . . This is what His Holiness said to us."[103]

Laynez let the storm pass. Then he humbly asked authorization to speak; the Pope acquiesced. "By the grace of God," said Laynez,

> I had no ambition for the generalship and I did even less to have myself elected. If it were a question that concerned only me, not only would I be satisfied with a generalship lasting only three years, but I would even be happy if Your Holiness would free me of it on the spot, for I know well that I am not prepared to bear such a responsibility. As for the election itself, we thought we were acting in accordance with Your Holiness' wishes, as conveyed to us by Cardinal Pacheco, whether it concerned the residence of the General in Rome or the duration of his term of office.

The Pope here interrupted Laynez: he refused his offer of resignation; it would be an evasion of the work to be done; had he not said that after the elapse of three years, the General would be confirmed in his post?

On the subject of the choir, Laynez raised the question of rebellion: he could not see how there could be rebellion since there had never been a formal order. Did the companions not faithfully recite their Office— although not in choir?

Favor the heretics? It was just the opposite: in combating them the

---

[102] Jerónimo NADAL, "Scholia", in *Institutum Societatis Jesu*, 2, p. 273.
[103] *Lainii Mon.* 8, pp. 673–75.

companions had drawn their hate and their persecutions and were treated as papists. "Your Holiness", concluded Laynez, "ought rather to sustain our courage, embrace us and infuse us with the hope that his aid will never be lacking to us."

As for the candidates, continued the General, the Society was rather reluctant to welcome them and even more to admit them to profession. The pontifical bull against apostates had never been used in the Ignatian family.

In response to Laynez, Paul IV abruptly changed humor: he asked the General if he had favors to ask. The latter asked for two: that he might finally be allowed to build the church of La Strada, and that no one—not even Bobadilla[104]—be sustained by the Pontiff against the authority of the General. The Pope granted them to him. Before taking leave of the two Fathers, he notified them that he would soon send his nephew Carafa to the House of the professed, to make known to the members of the Congregation his will on the subject of the generalship and the choir.

Two days after this dramatic interview, on Thursday, September 8, Cardinal Carafa presented himself, as we have said above. The Congregation accepted the act of pontifical injunction with a very admirable discipline.[105]

It remained for the companions to determine the import of the order which had been given to them. They consulted Cardinal Pozzo, one of the best canonists of that time. He responded that this injunction of the Pontiff had only the value of a personal order, that is, that it would cease, in good jurisprudence, upon the death of the one who gave it. "Comforted by this hope," commented Nadal, "we are tranquil in the Lord."[106]

The printing of the Constitutions had been going along well since the month of August. The "additions of Paul IV" were inserted after the text of the Constitutions, that is to say, after the text of part X; a page which could be suppressed when Paul IV should die.

To make a judgment on this authoritarian intervention of Paul IV, it is necessary to situate it in its historical and canonical context. Paul IV, certainly, granted great favors to the Society of Jesus; he changed nothing in the bulls and privileges which his predecessors had granted to the order; even for the triennial generalship and the choir, he contented himself with an order transmitted viva voce, not being unaware that such

---

[104] This specification is heavy with meaning.

[105] It is in the correspondence that one can perceive something of the bitterness of the Fathers.

[106] NADAL, "Scholia", in op. cit. 2, p. 273.

an order had neither the same value nor the same import as a written act. What should we conclude about it? It is certain that the Pope would have like the Congregation itself to modify the *Constitutions* on the two disputed points; since it had not done so, he followed a mitigated procedure: an order, but an order which did not hold beyond his pontificate: this is only a hypothesis, but a hypothesis that does harmonize with the facts.

On September 10, 1558, the Congregation declared itself dissolved, not without having affirmed one more time the Society's fidelity to the thinking of Master Ignatius. By a decree, it authenticated the Spanish text of the *Constitutions* "transcribed from the autographical text of Father Ignatius and compared against it, comprising therein the additions and affixed corrections, whether in the margins or between the lines, added by order of the Congregation".[107] Immediately after this solemn act, they voted the decree of dissolution.[108]

[107] *Institutum Societatis Jesu*, 2, decree 78; *Const.* 2, pp. 123, 726.
[108] Ibid. 2, decree 148.

CHAPTER III

THE MEANING OF THE CRISIS OF 1556–1558

The crisis of 1556–1558, and especially the attitudes of Paul IV in the course of those decisive years, have been differently interpreted by Jesuit and non-Jesuit historians. It is not our plan to enter into this debate. It seems interesting to us, however, to review briefly in the light of the crisis the events of 1541–1556, the labors of the Society during the years 1556–1558, and the subsequent history of the Society of Jesus. In short, to cast a glance at yesterday, today and the days following the crisis. A very rapid glance, but an instructive one.

I. THE CRISIS AND THE DIRECTION OF IGNATIUS FROM 1541–1556

Let us imagine for an instant that before the death of Ignatius, the *Constitutions* had been completed and solemnly approved by a General Congregation which he would have called together himself. The problems which were posed after his death and which so deeply divided the companions would not have existed: the legitimacy of the Vicar, the "rights" of the first Fathers, and the legislative value of the *Constitutions*. Paul IV would undoubtedly have intervened on the principle of the generalship for life and on the choir Office: but in what way this would have occurred, one could not say for certain.

A series of questions arises however: why and how did Ignatius allow such a dangerous situation to occur? Was he aware of it or not? If he was not aware of it, the situation is serious; moreover, that seems rather unlikely on the part of a man who felt so keenly the events, chances and inherent risks. If he was aware of them, why did he not thwart them while he was alive? Could the explanation be fatigue and illness? Did he allow himself to be surprised by death? Was it profound humility, voluntary abasement before "the entire Society" (*tota Societas*)? Was it desire to allow the companions to remodel the Society according to their apostolic experiences? But how, why, then, had he not at least specified in a clear and precise manner the conditions of assuring a serene, peaceful preparation for the future Congregation: the establishment of the assistants of the Father General, who would elect a Vicar, the representation of the provinces, the precise function of Nadal in the order, etc.? These questions and still others which one could pose, leave us, truthfully, without a satisfactory response.

At the stage where we have arrived in our analysis, we have the feeling that we do not yet hold the key to the Ignatian way of acting and that it is necessary for us to search further. It may be suggested that behind this state of affairs, if not wished, at last consented to by Ignatius, there is a certain way of conceiving the existence of a missionary order, of a Society which bears the name of Jesus and not that of a man. This will be the theme of the following chapters.

Therefore, it is fitting to look beyond the house of La Strada: while the fate of the Society was being played out dramatically between Paul IV and about twenty companions, what was becoming of it? What were the few thousand companions around the world doing? Just as during the sixteen years when Ignatius worked with slow deliberation on the legislative text of the *Constitutions*, piece by piece, the companions were rendering around the world a dynamic action, new, sometimes heroic, in the service of Jesus Christ and of his Church, with the unforseen hazards, sometimes the mistakes and the sufferings of the apostolic existence, in short a missionary life. The overwhelming activity of the missions brimmed over and carried along these thousand men like a torrent but also confirmed and justified the labor of the General Congregation, and conferred upon it its fullness of meaning.

II. THE LABORS OF THE COMPANIONS DURING THE YEARS 1556–1558

One simple statement characterizes this story: "*Life* continues", an ardent, enthusiastic life. One could almost say with a bit of humor: as if nothing serious threatened the existence, or at least the Ignatian authenticity, of the order; the correspondence of the period corroborates it. This active peace was not due solely to the orders of silence which had been given several times by Laynez to the Fathers in Rome,[1] but rather to a certain manner of seeing the things which Ignatius had bequeathed to his own: important and necessary as the legislative labors might be, the "law of love and of charity" is still more urgent: the spirit surpasses the letter; the life, especially apostolic life, is superior to the law.

Of this ardent life of the majority of the companions we have incontestable evidence.

1. First, the Indian province experienced a resurgence of vitality with the presence of the Ethiopian missionaries and the arrival in 1556 of a

---

[1] For example on September 26, 1556: the "Ephemerides" of Geeraerts on this day (*Pol. Compl.* 2, p. 590); and especially the step taken on August 10, 1557. "It was decided, in order to avoid any danger of corruption, that no one, for so long as the crisis lasted, would go to the professed house, except in a case of major importance, and that no one would converse with any of the hosts of the professed house" (*Pol. Compl.* 2, p. 603).

Portuguese group, whose Provincial was Gonsalves de Silveira: without doubt, difficulties existed, but the men, for the most part, were courageous and sincere; if they disagreed among themselves on their conception of the mission, of the methods of teaching, the love of Jesus Christ and the apostolic zeal vanquished all differences: the letters which departed from there in 1557 (some of which were still addressed to Ignatius) give testimony of it.[2] The extraordinary personality of Xavier continued to illuminate this missionary land: to the extent that the inquiry regarding his beatification developed, his marvelous sanctity radiated. From Brazil also the news was such as to cause enthusiasm and to attract the youth of the order: the death of the two martyr-companions, Peter Carrera and John de Sousa, had been known in Europe since the beginning of March 1556[3] and had marked for all time this dangerous and heroic mission.[4]

The letters from the German province, that land "which was killing itself" (because nine-tenths of the population was already touched by Lutheranism or other heresies, and because religious dissensions were politically tearing apart the empire), were at the same time desolate and stimulating.[5] This was even more so since Canisius, then visiting in Rome, communicated orally a thousand details which were not in the correspondence and involved his auditors in the activity of his struggle; when he left Rome, for example, in June 1557, everyone knew that, in a few days, he would be plunged again into the politico-religious furnace, where the fate of the Church was being partially played out. All is lost there, all can be saved therein. These alternations in his letters and the personal conversations with this missionary, on whose shoulders rested the Catholic future of Austria, Bohemia and Poland, had a singularly urgent effect on minds and hearts.

This enormous work which the missionary Society accomplished while twenty companions were leading, in their own way, a difficult battle to establish the Constitutions of the order, offers a contrast which it is necessary to grasp. We can do so, thanks to a quasi-providential document: the "Ephemerides" of the scholastic Dirk Geeraerts. He lived a few hundred meters from the house of La Strada; he studied at the Roman college. This young man, of an exceptional spiritual depth, a "major" at the age of twenty years, in 1551, of the doctors of philosophy of Louvain, had entered the Society in 1553; Ignatius identified in him a

---

[2] *Mon. Ind.* 3, pp. 607–811, n, 100–120.

[3] "Ephemerides" of Geeraerts, *Pol. Compl.* 2, p, 583.

[4] *Mon. Brasil.* 2, p. 263 *ad finem*, see especially the interesting "Dialogue du P. de Nobrega sur la conversion des païens", pp. 317–45.

[5] *Can. Epist.* 2, p. 183.

companion such as he desired: "A seasoned man. . . . In his soul, fear and love of God. . . . Endowed with a character so tenacious that no 'return to Egypt' is to be feared, no more so than a deviation under inducements or threats."[6] Canisius, moreover, was not mistaken in him: Dirk was one of the hopes of Germany. At the Roman college, he maintained his diary, almost day by day. On the advice first of Canisius, then of Laynez himself, he noted everything that appeared interesting to him; but the anecdotes were intertwined with personal reflections, so much so that this diary provides at once a journal and a confidence, the history of a soul and a newspaper. The accounts of the moving of the Roman college (Nadal in charge); the inundations of the Tiber, or of the grape harvest, alternate in it with the summaries of meetings, exhortations, conversations made by the most notable companions present or passing through Rome. Through him, one knows the effect of the letters arriving from India, Brazil, Germany, France and other regions of the Society. All this, seen in the view of a scholastic who had but four or five years of life in the Society; one perceives in the "Ephemerides" the atmosphere which then reigned at the Roman college, a realistic atmosphere wherein the lack of restraint,[7] the mournings, the sadnesses mingled with the joys and the enthusiasms.

Thanks to the "Ephemerides" of Geeraerts, we have the echo not only of the letters which arrived from distant regions, but also the repercussions provoked by the Hispano-papal war in Italy. Evidently, it is about Rome that Dirk furnishes us with the most valuable information; he makes us breathe the atmosphere of these years 1556–1558: inside the house, fervor for studies and the spiritual life, but also hunger, penury and illnesses; on the outside apostolic labors which were necessitated by the economic and political situation: the presence of the companions in the pontifical prisons, the spiritual assistance for those condemned to death, action among the Jews, the Moorish and Turkish slaves, and the enormous misery of the people whom the companions were forced to help by their alms, their begging and their personal devotion.

2. Among these "labors" of the Society in the years 1556–1558, it is fitting to emphasize certain points which seem very characteristic of the Ignatian spirit: these are the "missions" which the "enfants terribles" of the crisis successfully directed: let us not even speak of Paschase Broët, of Adriani, and the nostalgic Rodríguez. The three others, Bobadilla,

---

[6] *Epist. ign.* 6, n. 4290, p. 500.

[7] Geeraerts does not fear specific detail: on August 8, 1557, he notes for example that two novices departed during the night and that one other, on August 3, "leaped over the wall" (*conscendens murum*) and fled; he adds with a touch of sadness: "*conterraneus meus*" (*Pol. Compl.* 2, p. 602).

Cogordan and Viola, had the opportunity to show that despite the canonical discussions and the diplomatic lack of skill, they did not belong, as Polanco and Nadal asserted, to the "camp of Satan", but "to the camp of Jesus Christ our Lord." And that, through missions where the desire to distance them from Rome intervened as much as the concerns to respond to the episcopal requests.

Viola worked for a certain time in the region of Bologna and Ferrara: it was about this time that he declared one day to Pelletier that he had "repented".[8] Then he returned to France: the young college of Billom had developed in a satisfactory manner under his leadership. He returned to Rome for the General Congregation of June 1558. He arrived there after the election of Laynez, but in time for the deliberations on the *Constitutions*. Nothing lets us suspect that he played any role whatever of opposition in the Congregation; his repentance was, it seems, sincere.

Cogordan himself had been sent to Assisi, as we have said, to satisfy the request of the Senate of the town and of the leaders of two important organizations of charity. From his adventure and his "exile" he certainly remained wounded. However, this trauma did not keep him from working silently at the task which had been assigned to him. The letters which he sent to Laynez testify in themselves the quality and efficacy of his activity; one could certainly believe them nothing but edifying even if certain communications from Assisi, meant to preserve this apostolic worker, had not come to confirm the merits of the case. "On last November 16", the magistrates of Assisi wrote to Laynez,

> we received the letter of Your Reverence and that of the Reverend Master Ponzio. We have not yet responded to them. Now that we have seen and appreciated what he has achieved in these seven months during which he lead, in the paths of God, not only the Confraternity of Charity, but a good part of the city as well, we thank Your Reverence for having consoled and helped us through this priest whose virtue, doctrine and exemplary life render him dear to our spiritual leaders and universally to all the city where he has launched many pious works to the praise of God our Lord. So we beg Your Reverence not to deprive us of this spiritual joy, and to leave us under the leadership of this father; with the grace of the Holy Spirit, he enlightens our hearts.[9]

The success of Cogordan was such that Assisi contemplated endowing a college of the Society: the time was not yet favorable for the creation of new colleges. Laynez, on September 13, 1558, declined the offer of the city and recalled Cogordan to send him to France with Bröet and Viola

---

[8] Manuscript *Ital.* 109, p. 257, letter of Pelletier of 11–5–57.
[9] *Lainii Mon.* 3, p. 292.

who were returning from Rome after the General Congregation. The separation was hard on all sides. Assisi was dismayed; as for Cogordan, he wrote a letter to Laynez which must in justice be cited:

> I leave willingly because I know that it is the Lord God, I am certain of it, who has ordained it. I willingly accept holy obedience in which it has always been agreeable to me to live, and I hope, through the grace of God, to persevere until death; never has my soul had other dispositions. Change nothing in your order. Father Paschase told me that if I behave well, Your Reverence will do this, that . . . and all kindness in my behalf. It is not for this motive that I shall leave for France, but I wish that it be only through the obligation which links me to the Lord our God, to our Society and to Your Reverence; therein lies the sole motive which makes me act; and no other.[10]

Decidedly, these "rebels" had nobility!

With Bobadilla, this Ignatian "nobility" is still more striking because the man was hardly bothered by psychological complexes. He departed for Foligno and the reform of the Sylvestrians, his heart as light as his body. Repentant? How could he have been since he did not feel the least bit guilty? To speak again at random of the Roman conflicts, mixing criticism with praise: prudence, dear to Ignatius, was not his strong point. However, he was an indefatigable worker, and that, in the Ignatian manner. Although ill, he visited all the convents of the Silvestrians; and these canonical visits did not hinder him from preaching, hearing confessions, reconciling people, holding meetings concerning "matters of conscience"; nor even from creating a new monastery.[11] His letters when he had the time to write, were reports of victory. "I am so busy making peace among the inhabitants", he wrote to Polanco from Foligno on November 30, 1557, "that they leave me no time to breathe; it is still necessary to help the impecunious; there are some girls to be married, and others to be put in convents: I see from the evidence that it is God who works and gives so much fruit, in Foligno as with the monks and at the abbey." Moreover, Bobadilla asked Polanco for his news as well as news of the others *imperno Avisatimi*.[12] Polanco could have thought that Bobadilla was exaggerating, but his companion, Antonio Gaetano, confirmed this success; and at the same time, Archbishop of Ragusa, a Franciscan, insisted to Laynez that he send him "Dr. Bobadilla, or a Father of the same type (*o un simile de vostri*)".[13] However, Bobadilla was supposed to participate in the General Congregation; Laynez refused.

---

[10] Ibid., 3, pp. 526–27, quoted by SCADUTO, op. cit. 1, p. 90.
[11] "Autobiography" in *Bobad. Mon.*, p. 626, n. 40.
[12] Ibid., p. 189, n. 115.
[13] Ibid., p. 197, n. 120.

Viola, Cogordan, Bobadilla; these three cases are significant. Rough, painful temperaments, but ones which Ignatius had borne with patience and from which he drew much for "the vineyard of the Lord". They had temperaments which created difficulties for the successors of Ignatius, but souls marked deeply by a mystique, a spirit, which allowed them to surpass their crises, to develop into "reformed priests", into disciples of Jesus Christ, with a true sense of the Church.

This vitality of the companions in the crisis which affected the institution of the Society, this vitality of the "rebels" in crisis after crisis which they set off is one of the most characteristic givens of the Society of Jesus which Ignatius bequeathed to us. We are going to find this again, as a constant, through the four-hundred-year history of the order.

III. THE PRESENCE OF THE CRISIS OF 1556–1558 IN THE HISTORY OF THE SOCIETY

There can be no question of covering the four centuries of this history, even "by hitting the high spots".[14] We would like merely to offer a few reflections based on certain facts.

First, this one, which can appear rather insignificant, and which would be, in effect, if these men had not exercised, for the most part, very great responsibilities in the order after 1558: the great protagonists of the Society from 1556–1558 continued, at least some of them, for many long years, to live and to be active. Now, if sufficient unanimity had been reestablished to conclude the Congregation of 1558 successfully, the temperaments and especially the mentalities, would remain what they had been and, with the help of age, the divergences would become even more pronounced. This was so since each pretended, with good reason, "to have known Ignatius well",[15] and took advantage of that to support his own views.

Laynez lived until 1565: seven years of generalship, but during which he had to absent himself (for two years) to accompany the papal legate to the colloquium of Poissy, then to present himself for the third time to the Council of Trent (1561–1563). Salmeron lived until February of 1585; he was "the man of Naples": Provincial of Naples from 1558 to 1576, he then resided in Naples until his death. Bobadilla lived to be more than an octogenarian; he did not die until 1590: after having served as a missionary in Valteline (1558–1559) and in Dalmatia (1559–1561), he traversed

---

[14] Cf. my article "Jésuites" in the *Grande Encyclopédie Larousse*, 1972.

[15] Let us not talk of the conflict in the "portraits" of Ignatius (cf. DUDON, *Saint Ignace de Loyola*, p. 647) and the biographies of RIBADENEYRA and of MAFFEI.

Italy in every direction; under the generalship of Aquaviva (the fourth General of the Society after Ignatius) he visited all the colleges of the order in Italy.[16] Simón Rodríguez led his languishing life until 1579: first in Italy, until 1562; then in Spain until 1573: it was then that Father Everard Mercurian (third General of the order) authorized him to return to Portugal; the last years were painful for him and for his associates.[17] Thus, it was with Bobadilla, in 1590, the group of first Fathers died out.

Juan Alonso de Polanco, elected assistant for Spain in 1558, remained so until the death of Laynez in 1565, but he still remained Secretary under Borgia; in all, he was secretary of the Society for a quarter of a century. At Borgia's death, he was elected Vicar General: only an order of the Pope forbidding the naming of a fourth general of Spanish nationality prevented his becoming General. From 1573 to 1575, he busied himself with putting his historical notes in order; but Father Mercurian soon sent him, in the role of visitor to Sicily; he returned, exhausted, from his mission and died in Rome on December 21, 1576. Peter Canisius was the admirable apostle to Germany, as we all know: Austria, Bavaria, Bohemia, the Rhineland, Poland, Switzerland and the Coucil of Trent. He did not die until 1597, after several years of partial paralysis, during which he continued to work, to preach and to write: he marked the Society of Jesus in Germany with his spirit—a typically Ignatian spirit. Jerónimo Nadal was assistant for the nothern regions (Germany, France, Austria, Bohemia and Poland), Visitor (1560–1562) of Spain, Portugal, Flanders and Germany, then (in 1566–1568) "worker" in Germany, and assistant for Spain in 1568–1573. In 1574 he withdrew to the Tyrol to complete the numerous writings which he had drafted, but he returned to Rome in 1577; he died there in 1580. Pedro de Ribadeneyra also played a not negligible role among these Ignatian "familiars" and "men of confidence": after his profession in 1560, he was successively Provincial, Visitor, Superintendent, in several regions of Italy; and finally Assistant for Spain and Portugal; but in 1573, he returned to Spain and began a writing career; he died in 1611, aged 84, the last "witness" of the Ignatian era.

To this early group, it is fitting to add Antonio Araoz, by reason of the importance of his role in Spain and his effect on the entire Society. He lived until 1573, not without having given much anxiety to Laynez, then to Borgia. Nadal had named him commissioner after his visitation to Spain. He managed not to attend the first two general congregations; and when the Second General Congregation named him assistant for Spain,

[16] *Bobad. Mon.*, pp. 628–29.
[17] Cf. two unpublished documents in *Eph. Lusitaniae* 1577–1584. Arch. Lusit. 68, new ff. 48-49 (letter of December 16, 1578) and 71–72 (letter of January 25, 1579).

he wished to remain at Valladolid where his friends, particularly Philip II, wanted to keep him; he died in Madrid in 1573.

Through their assignments, but especially through their memories and their writings, these few men would greatly influence the "style" which the post-Ignatian Society would assume. Incontestably divergent tendencies would manifest themselves gradually: they would erupt during the government of Francis Borgia. Difficulties of living in a group according to the strict poverty which Ignatius desired for his followers, principles and methods for the formation of novices and scholastics, tensions between missionary fervor and fidelity to rule, delicate questions concerning apostolic spirituality, constant temptation to lean toward contemplation, or toward the action to say nothing of political influence (for example, the position of Araoz at the court of Madrid, or of Gonçalves da Câmara at the court of Portugal), conflict between the demands of organization and individual availability (the serious question of the colleges). Cares were not lacking to the leaders of the order, whether at the level of general, or that of assistants, visitors or provincials. It was in this environment that one must situate the government of Francis Borgia (1565–1572), if one wishes to judge equitably.[18] However, this goes beyond our subject.

What is totally remarkable is the fact that, despite all these difficulties, the vitality of the Society of Jesus established itself with a prodigious dynamism. One must say more: these difficulties themselves revealed, whipped up, this vitality. While "problems", administrative and structural, presented themselves, and often in an acute way, an apostolic, ardent and generous work was accomplished. Sometimes in zeal on the worldly scene; sometimes also, more often perhaps, in the humility, and silence of the *ministeria assueta*, dear to the heart of Ignatius: prisons, hospitals, college classes, help to the poor, seminars and catechisms, confessions and retreats. Certainly, among these apostolic "workers", these missionaries, the differences of temperament, grace and spiritual gifts, were great; but some common bond united them without standardizing them: a certain manner of "being with Christ" and of "helping men".

This contrast between the problems or even the tensions, and the "apostolic" work seems indeed one of the existential laws of the Society of Jesus. It would be easy to rediscover it in the different periods of the history of the order, especially at the moment of great crises: the attacks

---

[18] Cf. the suggestive study of Mario SCADUTO, "Il governo di san Francesco Borgia 1565–1572", AHSI, vol. 4 (1972), pp. 136–75, and our "Bulletin d'études ignatiennes", *Christus*, vol. 20 (1973), pp. 506–10. The government of Borgia will be the subject of the fifth volume of the history of the Assistancy of Italy.

of Mariana, supported by Philip II, against the *Constitutions* in the time of Aquaviva, the matter of the Chinese and Malabar rites (in the middle of the seventeenth century), the "reductions" of Paraguay, the matter of Peter Claver and the black slaves of America, the Jansenist and Gallican crisis in France in the eighteenth century, the quarrel between probabilism and the generalship of Thyrsus Gonzáles, the suppression of the Society, first in the countries of the "most Christian Kings", and then in the universal Church (the bull of Clement XIV on July 21, 1773), or even closer to us, the whole question of modernism, etc. Agitated epochs, eras of crisis? Certainly, and humanly speaking, one might sometimes have believed that the Society of Jesus would perish in them. But always, in the same times and sometimes in the same places where the tempest was raging, there were companions to continue humbly, with tenacity and often with creativity, the tasks of corporal and spiritual charity which Ignatius had one day established "for the better service of Christ our Lord" to the glory of the Father.

The personal mystery of Ignatius is hence doubled at this point in our reflection of the mystery of the Society of Jesus: but one feels indeed that the latter depends closely upon the former, as a river on its source. It is the personal mystery of Ignatius which must be penetrated; this research will be the goal of Parts IV and V of this study.

PART FOUR

THE "ARS GUBERNANDI"
OF IGNATIUS OF LOYOLA

A long association with Ignatius in his daily life has convinced us that there is no "grid", properly speaking, by which to read him, because just as he was so open to the Spirit of God and to the appeals of men, so much so was he unpredictable in his reactions and conduct. However, it is sure from this existence that a spirit, a style and an art evolved: how to encompass it?

If we wish to raise, at least partially, the mystery in which this strange and fascinating personality is enclosed, one method is indispensable: as objective a reading as possible of the facts.

This is what we are going to attempt, holding more than ever to the gifts of the *Chronicon* of Polanco and the *Correspondences* of the period.

Strong indications, it seems to us, unimpeachable points, stand out in the course of this story. They are significant; and we shall see whether they are sufficiently numerous to constitute a coherent network from which, with the utmost prudence, one might extract a meaning.

CHAPTER I

THE UNION WITH GOD

Ignatius the Superior General was a man who deliberately plunged himself and the whole Society into the universe of God as Jesus Christ revealed it to us by his work, his life, his death, and his Resurrection. His companion is essentially someone who "follows Jesus Christ", who does the work of Jesus Christ in the world and who works as Jesus Christ did, through Jesus Christ, and with Jesus Christ, for an always greater glory of God; he is a missionary in the manner of the apostles, in intimacy with Jesus Christ.

What the companions sent by Ignatius on the routes of Europe, to India, Brazil and Ethopia, sought to establish or to restore was the "kingdom of God", a breath of the gospel permeated the accounts of their acts: they worked "in the vineyard of the Lord", in the "field of the Lord". The populations which they evangelized were not deceived: in Portugal,[1] in India,[2] in Syracuse,[3] elsewhere also, they called them "apostles", "apostolic fathers", "apostles of Christ"—or also "priests of Christ", "reformed priests", "holy Roman priests", "companions of the Holy Spirit". . . . Their identity, at least when they worked as true disciples of Ignatius, is well established.

I. "THE PRIMITIVE CHURCH" AND THE "VERBI DEI ENERGIA"

Such was the atmosphere in which Ignatius made his spiritual sons develop, the experience which he wanted them to know. Actually, they felt and projected the feeling that God, using them, was restoring the atmosphere of the primitive church. The Bishop of Palencia, writing to Ignatius, congratulated him on what he strove to do: "to restore the sacerdotal order to the primitive type of Blessed Apostle Peter through the example of his perfection and his poverty",[4] and the Dominican Luis de Granada, one of the spiritual masters of Spain, declared in a sermon of 1551 that the vocation of the Society was to "lead men back to primitive sanctity".[5] The groups of Christians who gathered in the mission coun-

---

[1] *Chron.* 4, p. 557.
[2] Ibid. 2, pp. 321, 324 and 465.
[3] Ibid. 6, pp. 210, 211.
[4] *Chron.* 1, pp. 248–49.
[5] Ibid. 2, p. 378.

tries, especially, around certain companions, presented the "aspect" (*species*) or the "visage" (*vultus*) of the primitive Church:[6] thus it was in cosmopolitan Ormuz where races and religions mingled,[7] and it was the same in Corsica.[8] What the reports sometimes a little prematurely called miracles contributed to this feeling; even taking into account an undeniable tendency in the companions to see in certain events, especially natural ones (tempests, floods, etc.) an exceptional intervention from God,[9] there remained quite enough marvelous facts to justify the enthusiasm of witnesses—as for example around the body of Xavier in the Orient.[10] It was, moreover, in the matter of conversions, reconciliation and fervors that the companions liked to recognize the blessing of God. "The Lord did many other marvels in this Church, as in the primitive Church, and it was rather clear that his arm was not shortened."[11] Thus ends the Chronicle of 1554 of India and Japan.

The arm of God—the Dextera Excelsi, or the *Verbi Dei energia* to use the language of Polanco—was perceptible to the whole generation of companions. They had a very strong feeling of disproportion between acts and effects, especially the spiritual effects of their acts: between what they did and the results of what they did, the power of God intervened. A very apostolic, very Pauline feeling: it was in weakness that the force of the spirit was revealed. In Portugal (1548) the reconcilations and the conversions were so copious that they "manifested externally the 'energeia' of the Word of God which worked on souls internally".[12] So this intervention was all the more remarkable when the "instruments", which were the apostolic workers, were more "mediocre": in such situations the "Divina Bonitas" appeared more clearly.[13] It was thus, for example, that in 1555 it was confirmed that Messina, "refuge of brigands", had become, through the care of the companions, *sancta Messana*.[14] This conviction was firmly anchored in the heart of the sons of Ignatius: one of the most touching accounts of the *Chronicon* on this subject comes to us from a missionary to India: in 1554, the Portuguese

---

[6] *Religionis faciem* (ibid. 4, p. 298); *quasi nova facies* (ibid. 5, p. 311).

[7] Ibid. 2, p. 156.

[8] Ibid. 3, p. 84.

[9] One of the most typical: Hormuz (ibid. 2, p. 732). It is essential here to talk of the intense devotion of Ignatius to "relics of the Saints" and to "blessed objects". The head of one of the eleven thousand virgin martyrs which he sent to Goa produced miracles (ibid. 2, p. 742).

[10] Ibid. 2, pp. 784–85.

[11] Ibid. 2, p. 677.

[12] *Chron.* 1, p. 322. Cf. ibid. pp. 222, 231, 256; 5, pp. 468, etc.

[13] Ibid. 6, pp. 90, 134.

[14] Ibid. 5, p. 182.

ships which approached Goa had on board only an absurdly small reinforcement when the mission had a great scarcity of men; and so the missionaries were concerned. From Portugal, they said, they sent us only those people whom they judged the least fit for use. Father Balthasar Diaz, then rector of the college, strove to build up the courage of his men: "It is", he said, "through the ministry of rather weak workers that the Lord has until now worked marvels."[15] This conviction sustained and animated the companions, who, in certain posts or certain tasks, found themselves confronting the impossible: they offered their sufferings and their failures, even came to desire the supreme sacrifice of blood, persuaded that their death would have more spiritual efficacy than their deeds.[16]

It appears, moreover, that certain companions participated more than others in this "*Verbi Dei energia*". Among them the "power of God" manifested itself even more. This was so with Laynez, the most frequently ill and an indefatigable worker, like Ignatius himself. The case was rather frequent enough in isolated missionary posts where the companion, agonizing perpetually, accomplished a task well beyond his strength: such was the admirable Lancillotto in India,[17] or Henriquez also in India[18] or Louis de Grana in Brazil,[19] and many others. One recalls that this surprising fecundity of their humble labors had been for the first Fathers in 1539 a sign that the benediction of the Lord was upon them and that he wanted their group to be perpetuated in the Church by becoming a religious order. And this blessing seemed to remain on the whole Society. From there, to believe that because they were blessed, they were privileged was a tempting step to take: one senses, perhaps too often among certain companions, a concern to have it noted that they had succeeded where all the other priests or religious had failed.[20] Let us pardon them this modest pride.

II. THE SPIRITUALITY OF THE "INSTRUMENTUM DEI"

It is from these perspectives that one must understand the word which reappears several times in the *Constitutions* and rather often in the correspondence: the companion, according to Ignatius, was an "instrument" of

[15] Ibid. 6, p. 662.
[16] Ibid. 3, p. 213
[17] *Chron.* 5, pp. 675–76 and 6, p. 796.
[18] Ibid. 5, pp. 680–82 and 798.
[19] *Chron.* 6, p. 769.
[20] Ibid. 2, pp. 770–71; 6, pp. 502 and 505–6.

God. From the moment that he received his vocation and mission from the Pope or from Superior, he could count on the power of God—whatever might be the difficulties of the task. This conviction of faith explains the courage, sometimes the boldness, which characterized the majority of the companions. It was not by enticing them with promises of apostolic harvests that Xavier in the Orient, Canisius in the German province and Nobrega in Brazil helped to motivate the novices and scholastics of Coimbra, Rome and elsewhere; it was by presenting to them in all its harshness and its dangers the life which awaited them. It was for the hazardous mission that their hearts showed a preference.[21] For example, Ignatius took a poll, first among the companions of Rome,[22] then among those of Spain, Portugal and Italy,[23] to know whether they would accept assignment to the mission of Ethiopia which promised to be very harsh and where there was the risk of dying. The Yes was almost unanimous: "Almost all declared not only that they were totally available, but eager and much drawn to this mission." It sufficed that a mission in Europe—such as a city suburb where the poor, Moslems and Jews were in profusion, or a region like Poland and Bohemia—merited the name of the "Indies of Spain", or "Indies of the North" for the volunteers to offer themselves. This *promptitudo* for the old desolate lands or for the new worlds delighted the heart of Ignatius: he recognized therein the *Verbi Dei energia*. These who were willing to risk all for God would be good workers in the *vinea* of the Lord, because they leaned on a force which was not their own.

That was the important point for Ignatius. One is not the instrument of the Lord, unless one is authentically poor, detached for all ambition and pretense, and stripped of all personal desire. This was an even greater necessity when the subject was rich in human and natural gifts. His manner of proceeding, before designating some companion for such-and-such a work or such-and-such a mission, very well characterized his spirit . Luis Gonçalves da Câmara tells us in his *Memorial*:[24] he "made him say prayers or the Mass" and tested his "indifference". "Assuming that he possesses obedience and abnegation, I find myself very willing to follow his inclinations." Provided that he did have those qualities, Ignatius still preferred the total availability of the *instrumentum*. Basically, it

---

[21] In the great majority, for there were also some fainthearted: such a Father for example who left the order because he was appointed for India. In everything we say in these chapters, let us not forget that in the first years of the order there were departures, dismissals and even some swindlers. Cf. our index in the *Chroniques saint Ignace de Loyola*.

[22] *Chron.* 3, pp. 15–16.

[23] Ibid. 4, p. 575.

[24] *Mémorial* ("Christus" collection), p. 112, n. 117.

was perhaps therein that was hidden the key to the incredible patience Ignatius showed in regard to Bobadilla: the intrepidity, the impetuosity of the apostle rested on a total availability for the will of the Lord and for the missions of the Vicar of Christ: his self-encomiums amuse us or even annoy us; but from these victories, he finally made all the glory rise to "the one who sent him".

III. UNIVERSAL PRAYER

The ten companions of Paris-Venice-Rome did not disperse to all the corners of the world without feeling pain as a result of the sacrifice of relished and deep fraternal friendship. We should remember that it was to affirm and safeguard their unity that they had accepted the vow of obedience "to one among us"; that they also had inaugurated this frequent correspondence, thanks to which each would inform the others of his own labors and would be informed of the works of the others; information which changed into fraternal prayers, in a spiritual responsibility by each one before God for the trials, difficulties and success of all. In proportion to the passing of time and the spreading out of the distance each could fear that the interest might lessen and that there could arise an apostolic self-sufficiency in each region of the Society. Ignatius tried to avoid this fragmentation and to maintain the spirit of love of the *tota Societatis*. Through his *tour d'horizon* letters, he strove to inform all the companions on the state of the Society; better still, he commended the labors of each to the prayers of all. On certain occasions, one sees a veritable mobilization of supplication and penance in the entire order for the profit of the universal Church.

Thus it was that when the Turkish peril threatened close to Sicily or Italy in 1551,[25] or when the Pope ordered jubilees (there were four of them during the generalship of Ignatius). Were certain countries more threatened by heresy or rupture with Rome? Ignatius asked all to participate actively in an immense crusade of prayer: England, especially when the accession of Mary Tudor and her marriage to Philip II gave an indication of the eventuality of a rapprochement with Rome; Germany, for whom Favre (as early as March 1546) asked Ignatius to have all the companions pray,[26] (and Ignatius accepted Canisius' recommendation that all the priests be ordered to celebrate one Mass each month);[27]

---

[25] *Epist. ign.* 3, pp. 551–552, n. 1903, 1906. Cf. for the mission of Ribadeneyra to Philip II in Flanders: *Chron.* 6, p. 440.

[26] *Fabri Mon.* pp. 296–297.

[27] *Chron.* 3, p. 250.

[28] Cf. *Epist. ign.* 5, 220–2, 279, 281, 291, n. 3578, 3609, 3610, 3615, etc.

northern Europe. . . .[28] In these difficult cases of conversion and reconciliation, the "apostolic workers" solicited spiritual help from the entire
region, the entire house.[29] The "prayer for the intentions of benefactors"
was not a hollow expression, a formality: all the companions began
prayer for John III of Portugal and his family on whom depended the
labors of the companions in Portugal, India, Brazil and the Congo.[30]
Scarcely had Silveira, the new Provincial of India in 1556, become aware
of the state of this mission, when he asked Ignatius that they pray
everywhere for it as well as for Germany.[31] Those who were disturbed to
see the Society renounce the choral Office and accused it of "not praying
more than the laity" would have been reassured: each companion, at least
if he was faithful to Ignatius' instructions, kept the entire world unceasingly in his prayers; the entire Society was immersed in a permanent
union of the most urgent intentions for the glory of God in the world of
men.

IV. THE PRAYER OF IGNATIUS THE GENERAL
AND THE PRAYER OF THE COMPANION

We shall consider more lengthily the personal prayer of Ignatius in the
fifth part of our study. Here we wish only to insist that in his prayer as
General and in the type of prayer he wished to see developed in each
companion, he evidently took into account the temperaments and inclinations of each. In many passages of the *Chronicon*, in the *Memorial* of
Câmara, and in many of the letters one sees the real quality of Ignatius'
prayer as General. No decision, one may say, was made except before
God, or better, in God; it was preceded, "enveloped", prolonged by
prayer. Briefly, for it is necessary to consider certain nuances of this
statement, Ignatius applied in his administration all that he said of the
election in the *Spiritual Exercises*. We have a typical example of this when
it was a matter of deciding the revenues of the sacristy of the church of La
Strada:[32] the question was an important one; but even in minor matters,
Ignatius consulted God, sought the will of God, "considered" matters in
God,[33] treated them in the manner of God, then, after the fact, weighed
them in the light of God.

It is thus, it seems, that we must understand the numerous testimonies

---

[29] Ibid. 5, pp. 142–144; *Chron.* 5, p. 219 (condemned to death); ibid. 6, p. 12.
[30] Ibid. 3, p. 409.
[31] Ibid. 6, p. 882.
[32] Cf. the *Spiritual Diary*.
[33] Cf. the emphasis of the *Constitutions* on "consideration"; see this Ignatian word in the
index of the French translation of the *Constitutions*, vol. 1, p. 268.

pertaining to the continual prayer of Ignatius. One of the best known is that of Câmara: "His facility of uniting himself to God through prayer is a very remarkable thing. I must recall how many times I found him, enclosed in his chapel [adjacent to his room] in such devotion that one could be sure of nothing except the facial expression—without forgetting, it seems to me, that that could continually be seen."[34] The same witness of Ignatius' daily life shows him to us offering prayer or asking others to pray before many a decision. Contemplative prayer or active prayer? These words perhaps no longer have meaning, since we oppose one to the other. It seems that Ignatius' prayer combined the two: everything for him was seen in God. One expression can indicate to us the meaning of this prayer: "The Father is accustomed to offer prayer each day for the Pope."[35]

As for Ignatius' attitude in regard to the prayer of his spiritual sons, significant testimony abounds: his moderation, for example, concerning the time of prayer for the scholastics in relation to studies;[36] or again his directives to Borgia, Oviedo, and still others. What does that signify? It is certain that in the eyes of Ignatius, a Society without union with God was emptied of its vigor, the companion without union with God was a *putridum membrum*, something pestilential, noxious, which would spoil the entire body. But what union with God? Ignatius' thinking on this was expressed frequently, forcibly and without ambiguity: it is a union with God which takes the entire being to its most existential depths. "When the Father speaks of prayer", said Câmara

he always seems to presuppose that the passions are truly subdued, mortified, and that is what he greatly esteems. I remember, one day, as I spoke to him of a good religious whom he knew, telling him that the former was a man of deep prayer, the Father corrected me and said, "He is a man of great mortification" and that is what one can see clearly in all the Father's manner of proceeding.[37]

Let not these words and their austere reverberations hide the spiritual reality from us: abnegation, mortification and domination of the passions signify no more than total opening to the Spirit, a total availability to its action. From this interior "nudity" the Ignatian prayer proceeds and in return is nourished and reinforced: it's a matter, in the last analysis, of the companions' immersing themselves with total Christian liberty in the love of God our Lord and in devotion to men.

[34] Mémorial, n. 175.
[35] Ibid., n. 301.
[36] Ibid., n. 256.
[37] Ibid., n. 195. Cf. also n. 256.

CHAPTER II

FOR THE WILL OF GOD

In this world of grace where Ignatius lived and acted, where he made the Society live and act, the task of the Superior General was delicate; it was necessary every minute that he himself be certain, as far as possible, of the actual intention of God for the entire order and for each of its members. What does the Lord wish for me, for us? Such was the question that he had to ask himself constantly, the quest that he had to conduct without respite. This question he posed in prayer, as we have said, and he finally received the response in prayer. However, between the question and the definitive response, there was a whole series of possible mediations of which we shall study the principal kinds, without pretending to exhaust the riches.

I. A FUNDAMENTAL OBSERVATION

It was neither Ignatius nor the first Fathers who chose the places, the countries or the areas where the companions would serve as missionaries and would establish the Society; no more was it they who most often chose the most important "missions" which they accomplished and which were going to open unforeseen paths to the destiny of the Society of Jesus. The beginnings of the presence of the Society in Portugal and the East Indies are significant to this study, especially when one recalls that this was the first "mission" which the first companions achieved outside of Europe; that Portugal was the first province of the Society, and for a long time the most flourishing; that the East Indies, Brazil, the Congo and "Mauritania" depended on Portugal; and that it was through the diplomacy of John III that the plan of the Ethiopian mission was conceived and put into execution. Aside from Rome, no other region of Christianity played a more decisive role than Portugal in the early developments of the Society of Jesus. Now, who took the initiative in contacts between Ignatius and King John III? Not Ignatius. Dr. Gouvea,[1] who had known the first companions in Paris, suggested that John III ask the Pope about them through the intermediary of his ambassador in Rome, Pedro de Mascarenhas; Paul III accepted the request and gave an order to Ignatius, who for several reasons would have preferred to direct his companions toward the West Indies which depended on Spain. The

---

[1] SCHURHAMMER, *Franz Xaver*, I, p. 526.

Pope gave Ignatius the task of assigning two missionaries: he chose
Rodríguez and Bobadilla; Bobadilla having fallen ill, it was necessary at
the last minute to replace him with Xavier.[2] Thus the departure of
Xavier for the East Indies on March 16, 1540, was not as a result of
Ignatius' choice but because of Bobadilla's fever, through an accident of
chance which we may call by its right name, God's Providence. Moreover, Rodríguez, like Xavier, was to depart for the Indies. Now in a
few weeks these two "reformed priests" affected the entire religious life
of Lisbon and its surrounding area. John III enthusiastically planned to
keep them in Portugal. He presented his new request to the Pope and the
Pope referred the matter to the General; Ignatius proposed that one
remain in Portugal and that the other depart for the Indies. Thus,
without Ignatius' having foreseen it, the province of Portugal and the
mission to the East Indies began. The case is typical of the manner in
which the Society of Jesus was inserted into the *vinea Domini* and
developed therein.[3]

It was not Ignatius, obviously, who took the initiative in naming
Broët and Salmeron as nuncios to "Hibernia". The first contact of the
Society with Germany was only a coincidence. Favre was designated to
accompany Dr. Ortiz en route to Spain, but his route went via Worms.[4]

It was not Ignatius who chose to send Laynez and Salmeron to the
Council of Trent; and again, they departed thence not as theologians of
the Pope, but as "reformed priests". These contacts with princes and
bishops of Christianity were to be determinants of the fate of the Society;
it was from these that a great number of requests for missions and
establishments came to Ignatius; from these contacts strong friendships
were cemented. To cite only this case, it was at Trent that Guillaume du
Prat, Bishop of Clermont, met the spiritual sons of Ignatius for the first
time, formulated the plan for two colleges, one in Paris, the other in
Auvergne, and conceived for the Society of Jesus an admiration that was
never to diminish during the impending tempests.

One last symbolic example: the entrance of the Society into Sicily, this
land where the Society in the time of Ignatius knew without doubt its
most rapid, most brilliant development. Everything began in 1546
through a request of Cardinal Carpi, protector of the Society: it was a
matter of a companion—Father Lhoost—accompanying the Vicar of
Agrigento on his diocesan visit. In 1547 another companion, Father
Jerónimo Doménech, was sent to Sicily. Who was behind this call? Juan

[2] *Epist. Xav.* I, pp. 36–44, n. 6. Cf. supra p. 100.
[3] *Chron.* I, pp. 86–87.
[4] *Lainii Mon.* I, p. 11, n. 4; *Fabri. Mon.* pp. 43–44, n. 19–20.

de Vega: he had been Charles V's ambassador in Rome until 1546, and had known Ignatius there. The vagaries of his personal career determined that he be named Viceroy of Sicily, and he did not stop until he had installed the Society of Jesus there: teaching, writing catechisms, colleges, "works" of all kinds, and even chaplaincies to the armies on expedition, what ministry was not practiced by the companions in Sicily? Furthermore, it was not only the Viceroy who used the companions for all charitable ventures but his wife, his daughter and his sons as well.[5]

Louvain, Cologne, Ethiopia, etc., would provide similar examples.

One might observe that Ignatius' method of operation was in accordance with the nature of the bond of obedience to the Pope: was it not up to the Pontiff to "send" the companions where he judged best? Also, from the beginning, had the companions not agreed among themselves that none would make any demands of the Pope to be sent on a mission in one country as opposed to another? That is entirely true. However, the fact is nonetheless remarkable; it was not by virtue of some strategy, or apostolic planning or diplomatic project, that the Society of Jesus spread throughout the world; it was "by the will of God".

Even when developments through the order of the Pope gave the General himself the right to send the companions on a mission, at least to the interior of the "ancient world", Ignatius' method remained the same: he responded to the calls of cardinals, bishops, princes responsible for states and former benefactors to whom the Society owed gratitude. If he happened to have the initiative of "choice", it was according to other calls also that he decided: calls of spiritual or human misery such as the college of Siena,[6] of Ingolstadt or Prague in 1556. The voice of misery was for him the Voice of God.

One other fact reinforces this observation: there is no doubt that the first Society had partially owed its renown and its development to the vocation of certain important personages. The case of Francis Borgia is the most striking: and the Archbishop of Toledo clearly harbored hate when he accused Ignatius of having flaunted the former Duke of Gandia throughout Spain *tamquam lupi caput*. However, the vocations of men like Canisius, already famous in the university world before his entrance into the Society, or that of Dr. Olave, procurator and theologian of Cardinal Otto Truchsess in Trent, or that of John de Mendoza, Governor of Castel Neuf in the kingdom of Naples, did not go unperceived. Without counting other vocations, of which the effect was undoubtedly

[5] *Chron.* 1, pp. 210 sqq.
[6] Ibid. 6, p. 122.

more regional, more local; such as that of Anthony de Córdoba or of those students, "flower of the university", of Alcalá, Gandia and Coimbra. One cannot truly say that these very personal decisions, however (also very "useful" to the development of the Society), were made by Ignatius.

With a touch of paradoxical spirit, one could easily sustain the opposite thesis: the apostolic desires dearest to Ignatius' heart, the projects for which he took the initiative or which he supported with the greatest enthusiasm, failed or at least encountered obstacles which delayed their realization for a long time.

Paris represents the most astonishing case. Scarcely General, Ignatius sent a group of candidates there under the guidance of Diego de Eguía to do their studies; he had approved of the methods and teaching of this famous university. Moreover, Paris was the first home of the companions; there was Montmartre and the first vows, a sort of "hearth" for the Ignatian family. Nonetheless, in fifteen years of effort, Ignatius did not succeed in legally establishing the Society in France; furthermore, it was from Paris that there came the most cutting blow that the Society received: the Decree of the Faculty of theology.

England is another example. As soon as the marriage of Philip II and Mary Tudor was known, Ignatius increased his efforts to have a companion accompany the prince to London so that the society might be able to show there the face of the "Catholic Reformation". He failed. At the most the Prince had promised that once he had arrived in England, he would call for a companion.

A last example: Ignatius never renounced, it seems, the idea of sending companions to the Holy Land. So he accepted unreservedly and supported with all his moral authority the plan of Peter de Zarate: this knight[7] of the Holy Sepulcher, enterprising and persuasive, had founded an "archconfraternity of the Holy Sepulcher" to which the Sovereign Pontiff and the elite of the cardinals had "given their name"[8] and "of which the purpose was the veneration" of the Holy Sepulcher and, if feasible, the recovery of the Holy Land and war against the infidels.[9] Now, the plan contained a paragraph which directly concerned the Society of Jesus. It was said therein that three colleges would be founded, one in Jerusalem, another in Constantinople and a third on the island of Cyprus. These colleges were erected only on paper—Polanco could have called them, like those which Bobadilla imagined, *collegia mathematica*.[10]

---

[7] Polanco even calls him: *"praeceptor vel commendatarius"* of the order. *Chron.* 3, p. 5.

[8] Were the Apostolic Letters ever dispatched? It is not certain: cf. ibid. 4, p. 130, n. 3.

[9] Ibid. 4, p. 130.

[10] Ibid. 4, p. 253 and n. 4.

Ignatius had accepted them;[11] in any case, he acted on all occasions as if the plan attracted him: would it not provide the opportunity of realizing in an unexpected fashion the old desire of the companions to go to the Holy Land and work for the glory of God in the same places where God our Lord had lived? This was a desire which he had never entirely renounced. Well, the Society, in its developments, did not penetrate the Holy Land, at least in Ignatius' time.

It is necessary to state that contrary to a certain legend, contrary to what Bobadilla reproached him for, Ignatius scarcely appears as "absolute despot who does only what he wants" who drew his plans from his own solitary reflections or from his ambitions, however holy they may have been. Ignatius asked God and read His responses in what today we are accustomed to calling "the signs of God".

II. THE "SIGNS OF GOD"

1. The first sign of God for Ignatius, actually the only incontestable one, the only one which presented no ambiguity for him, was *the "mission" indicated by the "Vicar of Christ on earth"*. Let us divest these two words from all the clinging nuances in which a certain literature has enveloped them; let us give them all of their evangelical vigor, hard and pure. When the Pope formally assigned a task to the Society or to a companion, he made again the gesture of Jesus Christ sending his apostles or his disciples on a "mission"; his order proceeded from the toil of the Spirit to the work in the world, from the "mission" even of the Word Incarnate among men. One easily recognizes there the spirit of the "Meditation on Two Standards". So, well before the *Constitutions* were drafted, the Spirit which animated the companions was already clearly affirmed. To put oneself at the disposition of the Vicar of Christ was not, in the perspective of the vow of Montmartre, a last resort which would console them for not having been able to depart for Jerusalem; it was, on the contrary, an enlargement to the extent that the living resurrected person of Christ was present throughout the universe: in any case, if they had returned from their pilgrimage, they would have presented themselves in Rome and put themselves at the disposal of the Pope. Favre declared it soberly, but clearly, in the name of all on November 23, 1538, in a letter to Diego de Gouvea:

> We, such as we are, who have bound ourselves to one another in this Society, have dedicated our persons to the Sovereign Pontiff, inasmuch as he is the master of the vineyard of Christ. . . . Why are we subjected by

[11] Ibid. 3, p. 6, n. 1.

such a link to the judgment and will of the Pope? It is because we are convinced that he has a better knowledge of what befits universal Christianity.[12]

Majorem congnitionem, a simple comparative: the Pope is not infallible in his apostolic choices, but he is best placed for his choices, to be more just, more wise, more opportune. And that sufficed in the eyes of the companions to justify their offering. This attitude would become crystallized in the *Constitutions*.[13]

2. *The events.* Except for the pontifical missions, events were the great response of God to the questions of Ignatius as General. These events could assume many voices: there were the calls of the bishops, princes and benefactors, but there were also, even on a daily basis, situations, facts, circumstances, successes, reverses, oppositions, friendships, all of which created the fabric of human existence in general and the existence of the Society in particular. On each day, at each minute, Ignatius had to be attentive to God, expressing God's will by his actions.

This listening was not passive. On the contrary, it was necessary in each event, always ambiguous, to test, "to discern", what God meant. Of Ignatian "discernment", all that can be said, has, it seems, been said. Perhaps it would be interesting to cite a few specific facts as an example: we shall review three aspects of his "manner of proceeding" in relation to different situations which seem very typical: the state of society at the time, failures and persecutions, and debts. There would be many more situations that would be as significant.

a) *The state of society at the time.* The gravity of the question escapes no one. First, to stick to indisputable facts, the society of the time was a monarchical one where everything depended on the good will of the prince and his representatives, a society which in its entirety declared itself Catholic, or at least Christian, but which was destroying itself and was reduced to game playing and monstrous alliances (the support of France for the German Lutheran princes, the alliance of the Most Christian King with the Turks, the Hispano–Franco–papal battles for hegemony in Italy, etc.) a society which was reduced by the very dynamism of its institutions to utilizing methods so little evangelical as the Inquisition, prison or even condemnation to death for offensive opinions, etc. What attitude was Ignatius to adopt in the face of such a state of things?[14]

---

[12] *Fabri Mon.* p. 132, n. 16. One would find analogous testimony among Ignatius, Laynez, Salermon and Xavier. See also the account of the "Deliberation of the first Companions" and the *Summa Instituti*.

[13] In 1538, it still concerned only an offering.

[14] We analyze this attitude outside any reference to our time, certainly. We reaffirm that any allusive or projective intention is foreign to our study.

He took it as it was. Like Paul, like Peter, announcing the gospel to the heart of paganism, he discerned in all of that what could be the forces of evangelization, redemption, and he rejected the rest; he even took care to distinguish what was political and what was religious: he did not allow himself to fall into the trap of considering "the Turk" solely as the agent of a religion opposed to that of Christ, but he also perceived him as the warrior who threatened to submerge Europe. And what of the Protestant princes? Behind the religious quarrel, he revealed their intention of dismembering the empire and of appropriating for themselves the tremendous holdings of the Church. What interested him was that in Europe, as it appeared to his eyes, nothing could work—even evangelization itself—without the accord or the support of these omnipotent monarchs: to enjoy their esteem and their benevolence was indispensable; he strove then, not to alienate them; but, and this was essential, he attempted at the same time to convert their hearts, to make them into just heads of state, concerned for the common good; for example: his relations with John III of Portugal, Philip II of Spain, Princess Juana (whom he admitted, against the advice of Borgia, to the vows of the Society), and Juan de Vega were representative of his rapport with heads of state. If he ordered certain companions (Laynez, Salmeron, Miron, Câmara), despite their personal repugnance, to be confessors of kings or princes, it was not ambition, but a sense of service to the Church and concern for their sanctification which motivated him. To take a position is dangerous and it lends itself to malicious interpretations. After weighing it all, Ignatius decided to run the risk. At the same time, he sent his sons to labor among the *plebeii*, he took over the miseries of the common people, he directed the companions to show greater interest and love for the social scourges (pauperism, abandoned children, prisons, convict ships, the sick and dying, famines, plagues, the intemperate, invasions, prostitution): in these public calamities, his companions had to be ready to give of themselves, to seek and procure remedies which would be the most efficacious. Always without forgetting that the love of God and of others must remain the primary concern: reconciliation with God through confession, with others through mutual pardon, solidarity through all the forms of charity, always held first place. No matter how confused or how terrible a situation might be, it remained in his eyes "the time to exercise love": but how difficult it was to plunge his sons into the heart of worldly misery—social, economic, human—his sons for whom he wished, as Christ wished for his disciples, that they be not "of the world"; between temptations of power and despair concerning salvation, how unstable was apostolic equilibrium, how necessary was spiritual "discernment" in analyzing events.

b) *Failures and persecutions*. The reactions of Ignatius to all that contradicted, undermined and ruined the apostolate of the Society are particularly significant. Failure in itself is more ambiguous than any other event. By it, does God mean to imply that it is necessary to abandon the plan or enterprise? Or, on the contrary, does he urge that one persevere, but with more courage, more purity, more generosity? Therein lies a very delicate language to interpret for one who seeks the authentic divine intention. Polanco is very quick in the *Chronicon* to attribute to Satan and his devils every obstacle which arose against the companions: *diabolus ex machina*, one might say. Ignatius was more prudent, more sagacious: he sought to distinguish what was from God, what was from men (he knew that his companions were not infallible), and what was from Satan; and he rectified the situation by means of discernment. One of the most typical cases concerned the expulsion of Bobadilla by Charles V after the affair of the *Interim*: Ignatius did not protest in any way against the imperial order; he made no judgment on the merits of Bobadilla's protest although he evidently blamed the manner in which the latter had proceeded; but far from "breaking" his man, Ignatius sent him to do missionary work in southern Italy. In the face of other "failures", Ignatius set aside his plans: after the unfortunate experience of Salmeron and Broët as nuncios in Ireland in 1541, he salvaged his two companions and assigned them other tasks according to the wishes of the Pope; the college of Gubbio was stagnant; didn't the population want it? Ignatius closed it;[15] Modena would have suffered the same fate; but Duke Ercole d'Este was against it:[16] Ignatius kept it; if the prior of the Trinity, Andrea Lippomani, whose charitable projects exceeded his means, caused the companions to live in a penury which hindered their studies and the vocations of certain young Fathers, Ignatius, after weighing all the circumstances, asked the companions to hold firm and without transgressing the laws of religious poverty. What if the first mission to the Congo failed through the fault of a crazy king? Well, then the missionaries would come back to Portugal but they would return later to that cursed land.[17] It is necessary to read all the correspondence of the Rodríguez crisis in order to appreciate Ignatius' art of discernment: did he at times make mistakes? Was he the victim of insufficient information? This is not the place to determine that; but what is quite certain is that he strove at each step of this sad affair, to act in all things according to the intention of God, whatever that might be.

---

[15] *Chron.* 4, pp. 51–55; *Epist. ign.* 6, pp. 246, 283–84, 629, n. 4100, 4133, 4387, etc.
[16] *Chron.* 4, pp. 99–108; *Epist. ign.* 7, p. 560–61, n. 4811; *Chron.* 5, pp. 148–51.
[17] Ibid. pp. 601–10.

The reactions of Ignatius in regard to persecutions, calumnies and false rumors reveals more clearly still what value of divine signs he attributed to events. His attitude in the face of the Decree of the faculty of theology in Paris was even more significant—Ignatius did not hesitate before certain accusations (especially those which concerned the *bonus odor Societatis*, the reputation of the Society), to resort to the judgment of law courts. In the case of the Decree of Paris, although the companions or friends pushed him to institute a lawsuit, Ignatius opted for a slower method and one which seemed to him more in conformity with God's intentions: to the infamy of the Decree he would oppose a series of favorable "testimonials" which he solicited from princes, towns, universities and dioceses where the companions had worked. In effect these would say, "Observe what they are, what they do and what God does through them." Moreover, he did not miss the opportunity which was given him on December 1555 to receive at La Strada and at the Roman college, four of the Parisian doctors (and among them the most relentless).[18] This way of retorting to calumnies through testimonials Ignatius used on other occasions: it was the sign of his spiritual realism, of the preference he accorded facts instead of quibbling, disputes and condemnations, in order to show the judgment of God.

c) *Debts*. If there is one aspect of Ignatius' administration that offers choice arguments to critics and disconcerts friends, it was his financial management. He swam in debts and money difficulties and cruelly experienced that poverty, if liberating when experienced alone on a pilgrimage, becomes a permanent concern when one lives in community, as part of a society.[19] The number of houses (the house of La Strada), or the colleges (the Roman and German ones), that had no stable revenue but were sustained by oral pledges of cardinals, bishops or princes, and might be in financial difficulties would astonish only those who are unaware of the risks of pious works and the worries of those responsible for them. That the financial fate of La Strada depended entirely on the life of Pietro Codacio, so much so that his death in December 1549 could bring about a veritable temporal disaster for these houses: this is a matter which leaves one perplexed.[20] Other problems arrived immediately, independent, certainly, of Ignatius' wishes: the Roman college, opened in January 1551, thanks to the support of Borgia, then Duke of Gandia, had its existence assured as long as Borgia main-

[18] *Epist. ign.* 10, pp. 313, 447–48, 453–54, n. 6001, 6067, 6079, etc.

[19] It would be interesting to compare this Ignatian experience with that of Francis of Assisi and of the Franciscan order in its infancy.

[20] However Codacio was a good procurator. Ignatius, in recognition of his gifts and his administration, recognized him as a "benefactor".

tained his fortune; then it would rest in great part on a pledge of the new Duke of Gandia, but unfortunately the young Duke did not keep his promises; the burden of the heavily indebted college then was added to that of La Strada. In 1552, the German College was founded in its turn, and its expenses had to be assumed by the King of the Romans and by the cardinals, but they disregarded their promises. Julius III understood the danger in which the two colleges stood and promised to help, but he died in 1555. Paul IV took up these promises in his turn and even wanted to enlarge the amounts, but the concerns of the Hispano-papal war prevented his accomplishing his benevolent plans. One may say that from 1551 to 1556, Ignatius did not cease begging and having others beg for the Roman houses in every country where the Society was established, particularly in Spain: the financial situation was truly catastrophic.

It was in this extremely serious crisis that he raised with the support, it is true, of Borgia and the Cardinal de la Cueva, the plan for a new church of Our Lady of the Way (La Strada): the blueprint was conceived by Michelangelo; the first stone was solemnly placed, but the work was soon interrupted: famine then raged in Rome and furious neighbors vandalized the construction site.[21]

What is also comprehensible concerning the church of the Society in Rome is that the place of worship which, in the context of the time, had to assure it apostolic liberty and which was financed to the knowledge of all by gifts, becomes more astonishing when it is a matter of other expenses: at the height of the financial crisis of La Strada and even of Rome, Ignatius bought, in December 1553, the "Red Tower and some other houses to enlarge the house of the professed"[22] and, in the course of 1554, a property (*vinea et domus ampla*) on Mount Aventine near the Antonine baths "for a place of rest and relaxation for the students". Polanco felt that this decision risked disapproval, so he thought it wise to add: "although life was then expensive, Ignatius thought that nothing should be spared in procuring a house for convalescents and the sick."[23] This explanation of Polanco gives us the key to the attitudes of Ignatius, it seems: when, before God, he judged a plan useful and the opportunity presented itself for realizing it, he went ahead, without bothering himself too much about the human wisdom of his bursars.

---

[21] The work would be resumed fifteen years later under the generalship of Borgia, and thanks to the generosity of Cardinal Alexander Farnese: this would be the current Gesù. In comparison with the Gesù, Tacchi Venturi terms the Michelangelo blueprint as one of "a church of medium grandeur". See these projects and blueprints, T. VENTURI, *Storia*, pp. 545–59.

[22] *Chron.* 4, p. 10: *Epist. ign.* 6, pp. 466–540, n. 4265 and 4319.

[23] *Chron.* 5, p. 22 and *Epist. ign.* 8, pp. 277–78, n. 5097.

Other examples lead us to the same conclusion: Ignatius "planned" little, but he decided according to a certain idea which he revised every instant according to the context of the circumstances, the situations, and of the intention of God.

III. EXPERIENCE, THE MISTRESS OF LIFE

Experience played a primordial role in the *ars gubernandi* of Ignatius of Loyola. There is nothing astonishing in this when one recalls a little of how he governed himself when he was alone or recruited his first companions. Experience, for him, was a sign from God and one could have inscribed the preceding paragraph with this title, but it is even more the training from God, *probatio*, trial and test, the mistress of life. It is through experience that the Holy Spirit gives to each one or to the body of the Society, the "shape" the carriage, the bearing, the style—that he wishes; it is through his reaction to experience that the Society or the companion becomes aware of what it is or what he is and manifests it.

"Experience has taught us": this statement returns like a leitmotif in the *Chronicon* of Polanco and also in the correspondence. Whether it is a question of missions, colleges, vocations in peril, relations with certain personages, dangers of too-little-controlled acceptances, crooks, money, promises, health, etc., experience is there, as a "source of revelation" to say what one must or must not do, how it must be done, what such a companion can bear and withstand, what exceeds the strengths of another, how one must take it all into account in order to evangelize one region and how, another. Briefly, every individual and collective existence is dependent upon experience.

There is a stylistic rapprochement of terms that is characteristic: the quasi-synonymy of the words *experiencias* and *probaciones* in the *Constitutions* and the frequent coupling of the two words.[24] These "experiences", "probations" and "experiments" we know well: they are the month-long Spiritual Exercises, pilgrimage, service in hospitals, menial functions, *sancta mendicitas*. In these experiences to which Ignatius attributed strength and the seriousness of veritable tests, trials as much as "proofs", the candidate revealed to himself and to others his potential natural and supernatural strength. And these "probations" made up the ultimate "probation", that is, they helped the candidate achieve his deep personal vocation.

So it was with the entire Society.

There was audacity in this Ignatian viewpoint, but it conformed to his

---

[24] For example in the "General Examen", ch. 1, n. 9.

idea of the basis of the apostolic life. The true spiritual resilience of man is magnanimity and generosity: a companion of Jesus Christ is always, in one way or another, a zealot. And who can say in advance what God reserves for him in the way of help and sustenance? The point is that he knows and that his superiors know how far he can go in his "unabated love" without tempting God. This knowledge is given in neither conversations nor psychological nor sociological analyses, nor can intuition indicate it to him. Only experience, spiritual and apostolic experience, reveals it without illusion. Let us take a simple example: Ignatius would have liked the entire community to reflect the universality and cosmopolitanism of the Society, for it to regroup Italians, French, Spanish, Flemish, Portuguese and Germans in the image of the group of the first Fathers.[25] The idea did not lack audacity, especially in regard to day students and teaching masters. What was meant to happen did happen. . . . "*Experientia docuit!*" "Lessons of experience" were also necessary in order to put in order the regime of rest and labor, the establishing of dwellings, the uses of horses and mules to carry baggage on trips, indeed, even the situation of the scholastics in the colleges,[26] and other more or less serious questions such as the readmission into the order of men who had left it or had been sent away. The Society did not cope well with certain emotional situations in which simple common sense would have sufficed to avoid more or less disastrous experiences.[27] At least it is fitting to affirm that Ignatius was not deterred by these lessons of experience and that he hastened to remedy difficulties which his orders had provoked.[28] We should acknowledge that he needed some time to realize that not all candidates for the Society of Jesus had his strength of character nor the dynamism of his grace. To the extent that one can discern an evolution in his *ars gubernandi* it is toward a more indulgent appreciation of human fragility, of "the weakness of many" which takes place. Was it without a certain regret of thus seeing the idea devalued which he was creating of the "companion of Jesus Christ"? Must we not necessarily perceive a certain disenchantment in this avowal offered at the end of his life: "If he wished", reports Polanco, "to live longer, it would be to prove himself more severe in admissions into the Society".[29]

---

[25] *Const.* 1, pp. 2, 15 and 25.

[26] *Chron.* 3, pp. 138 and 239.

[27] An example of such a young "cultivated" man is the one who was left for four months "in the kitchen", at the college of Naples, with no one having any responsibility for his formation and he left the Society. Ibid. 2, p. 528.

[28] Ibid. 4, pp. 28–29.

[29] *Pol. Compl.* 2, p. 772; *Scripta* 1, p. 434.

IV. TESTING, DEVELOPMENT AND EXECUTION OF THE "SIGNS OF GOD"

Signs of God are difficult to pin down, to decipher: even pontifical orders of "mission" require a precise, attentive reading so that the executor may enter into the heart of the "Vicar of Christ on earth". A fortiori, the events, whatever they may be, need to be carefully scrutinized.

Ignatius, who made use of a technique for decisions depending on signs from God, proposes it to us. He reveals it in the *Spiritual Exercises* and also in the various correspondences, but above all in the *Constitutions*.

Evidently, the flashing, stunning inspiration with which the Holy Spirit overwhelmed Saint Paul is always possible. The Spirit blows where it will.[30] However, even in this "supranormal" case, Ignatius, by his advice or his example, encourages us to verify or even to test the authenticity of the phenomenon by an ordinary method. It is a simple method, but one of great human and spiritual prudence.

According to Ignatius, there are *three preliminary steps* to the interpreting of a sign of God which result in an authentically spiritual decision: to have authority or responsibility for making the decision or participating in it, to pray to God to bestow his light, and to be inwardly free of all preference and of all personal passion.

The Decision-making passes through five major phases:

1. *The information phase*: the person responsible and his ordinary counselors become acquainted with the "dossier" of the matter, which must have been assembled in the most complete manner possible—a dossier which can be illuminated also by consultations with competent persons.

2. *The deliberation phase*: the responsible parties examine the advantages and disadvantages of adopting or rejecting the plan.

3. *The interrogation of God in prayer phase*: the one responsible and each of his advisers pray again and strive to perceive with total interior purity and personal disinterest whatever solution the Holy Spirit indicates to them.

4. *The decision phase*: the counselors give their opinion. The one responsible receives them, confronts them with his own opinion, weighs them again before God, and regardless of whatever may be the majority of the counselors' votes, makes his decision before God and his own conscience.

5. One last time, the one who has made the *decision offers it to God in*

---

[30] He foresaw the possibility of such an inspiration even for the election of the General. Cf. *Const.* 2, pp. 642–45.

prayer, and, whether it be by interior indications or simply by a feeling of peace he has that he has sought God's will to the utmost, God approves this decision.

A decision made in this manner then became for Ignatius the will of God. Unless there were obviously contrary signs, he carried it out regardless of cost. His contemporaries and, after them, his historians, have noted his tenacity and his perseverance in accomplishing his plans. Faithfulness to himself was assuredly a part of his character; but it was only secondary—a kind of servant—in relation to his convictions that a decision made in this manner, with the guidance of the Holy Spirit, was a divine wish. To execute this order, it was then a matter of bringing to bear all the resources of his human and spiritual personality on it.

Gonçalves da Câmara notes with accuracy: "Our Father [Ignatius] is accustomed to being so firm in things which he undertakes, that this steadfastness amazes everyone. Here are the reasons that come to my mind. The first is that he carefully considers each matter before deciding it. Second, he prays very much on this subject and is illuminated by God. Third, he makes no particular decision without hearing the opinion of those who are competent in the matter, and he asks them for the majority of circumstances with the sole exception of those of which he has full cognizance. He was accustomed also, very often, when he did not have full knowledge of the matter, to postpone it and to let some general opinions on the topic suffice for the moment."[31]

We possess, by chance and doubtless by Ignatius' wish, a model of his decisions. From the heavy notebooks in which he wrote practically every day about his relations with God,[32] the pages remain (February 2, 1544–February 27, 1545) which correspond to his decison to propose a stricter poverty for the Society. To grasp properly the original value of the document, one must remember that in the meetings prior to the election of the General, the companions and Ignatius himself had made a contrary decision; and, moreover, the *Constitutions*, where it is inscribed that the new position taken by Ignatius would not have the force of law until after receiving the approbation of the First General Congregation: this "election" of Ignatius in 1544, was then only a step in the definitive decision. No group of documents better allows us to grasp vividly the exact nature of the Ignatian decision, personal or collective.

---

[31] *Mémorial* ("Christus" collection), p. 205, n. 282 b; see also pp. 56–57, n. 15–16, and 59, n. 20; Fr. Tandonnet is right to refer, by a note, to *Const.* P. II, ch. III, § 2–4 (n. 220–22).

[32] *Autobiograpie*, no. 100, cf. supra, p. 222.

CHAPTER III

RELATIONS WITH PEOPLE

I. THE PRIMACY OF PERSONAL RELATIONS OVER STRUCTURES

If one considers the activity of Ignatius of Loyola, General of the Society in its entirety, one can affirm that he was more concerned with people than with structures.[1] Through conversations and through correspondences, he always sought person-to-person contact, one to one, where Superior and companions strove every minute to discover the will of God together. That was very much one of the aspects of the Ignatian mentality which at first sight disconcerts the modern mind: but let us have confidence in the spiritual wisdom which governed this view. Yes, Ignatius appreciated rich and powerful individuals; he sought them as recruits and he wished, by their training, to develop to the maximum in each one his original resources, his possibilities. But what was for him a strong personality? Everything was involved therein. It was a personality rich in spiritual gifts, as well as in natural gifts, a complete Christian personality, the saint who was at the same time a man. But if someone had not attained this plenitude of spiritual development, Ignatius infinitely preferred that natural (rather than spiritual) gifts be lacking. He knew, from having confirmed it, that a saint deprived of natural gifts could be splendidly useful to the "mission", and that the opposite was not true. What he feared was the Christian who was neither saint nor man, the "lukewarm" in the language of Revelation.

Of this conviction, Ignatius himself, by his own existence, gave proof: when he began to study Latin, then philosophy and theology in his thirties, when he worked to obtain the degree of master of arts, it was from a desire to make himself more the *instrumentum Dei*. If he chose his first companions from among the student youth, it was not only because he lived in a university; if he advised Borgia, still the Duke of Gandia, to take his doctorate in theology and if he insisted that his new companions continue their studies to receive degrees, it was very much because he saw in science, and even in diplomas, a truly apostolic value. The risk of pride and of possessiveness did not escape him; but Ignatius never capitulated before danger when the desired benefit seemed to him,

---

[1] It is a matter of Ignatius as General of a religious and missionary order. As for the structures of the Church, Ignatius took them as they had been established by Jesus Christ and the Apostles: he interiorized them, personalized them, wanted them "pure"; he wished reform for them but accepted them with docility and spiritual simplicity.

everything considered, to warrant it; spiritual equilibrium, in his eyes, neither sought nor found itself in flight before difficulties, but in a reinforcement of the values of grace: the development of natural gifts must be accompanied by "solid and perfect virtues", and these virtues are called abnegation, renunciation, mortification, detachment and obedience—the wherewithal to eradicate the temptations of pride. Nothing is more significant than this "constitution" of 1539 (one of the first) which demands all the companions by vow—and all then held masters of arts degrees—to teach catechism for forty days per year[2] and Bobadilla, who loved far-flung apostolates of great magnitude, certainly understood it: he refused to put his signature on the document;[3] this "determination" of the first Fathers passed into the *Constitutions*, and well before they were finalized, Ignatius many a time reminded the professed of the order—provincials, rectors and others—of their obligation of conscience to teach catechism to children.

Undoubtedly, there were times when Ignatius insisted upon the importance of certain natural gifts like nobility of blood, titles, fortune, the quality of one's friends or relatives, and the responsibilities fulfilled before entering the Society. About these "exterior" gifts, let us not deceive ourselves, Ignatius thought what he thought of science and of academic grades: they were useful, but not indispensable. The essential was elsewhere. He affirmed that in many passages of his letters or of the *Constitutions*. One of the undoubtedly most characteristic can be read in the portrait of the Superior General: "The exterior gifts" are delineated in the sixth position (and we know that the General's gifts are presented in descending order; we are then at the last echelon of the hierarchy). These exterior gifts, are "those which in such a context aid the edification and service of God, our Lord. They ordinarily consist of credit, good reputation and that which, among the rest, is an aid to authority among people within and outside";[4] and it is directly specified in the "declaration": "Exterior gifts are nobility, fortune previously possessed in the world, honor, etc. These gifts, *all other things being equal,*[5] are of consideration but there are others of *more importance*, which, if the former are lacking, would suffice for election".[6] These gifts "which would suffice" for the Father General, Ignatius enumerated in the following paragraph: "a great goodness [bonté],[7] and a great love for the Society, as well as

---

[2] *Const.* I, p. 11.

[3] *Const.* I, p. 12, n. 12.

[4] *Const.* P. IX, ch. II, n. 733.

[5] The emphasis is ours: for this interpolated clause controls the whole meaning.

[6] *Const.* P. IX, ch. II, n. 734.

[7] For the meaning of this word, see infra, p. 470.

good judgment added to good education": we are far from the "cult of personality".

This admiration for strong personalities, which in Ignatius' case had come from a sense of "apostolic mission", was also from a certain specific theological view: the Society, as a body—and each companion—was in the service of God our *Creator* and Lord. Natural gifts are creatures, and like every creature they had two faces, one of grace and one of sin. Utilized by a man united to God and matured by charity, they were means of "aiding one's neighbor", if not, they were, or risked being, in effect, sources of sin.

It seems incontestable that this primacy which Ignatius accorded to persons over structures proceeded from his realism. He knew that beautiful writings are but dead letters, if there is no man to assume them, animate them and give them substance and life. Perhaps even (this is only a hypothesis) he scorned documents that were too perfect, and the prologue of the *Constitutions*, even though a late insertion, partakes no less of the spirit which presided at their drafting. Whatever it might have been, oblation (then the vow of obedience) to the "Vicar of Christ", the generalship for life, could well have come from this importance which Ignatius attached to the human personality.

In any case, giving precedence to man over documents was not facilitating the task of the founder: his Society would depend for its value and its destiny on the quality of the companions more than on the perfection of legislative texts, on the "law of love which the Holy Spirit alone inscribed in the hearts" more than on the "exterior Constitutions". As valuable as the companions would be in each era, in each region, so would the Society be valuable. Four centuries of history have proved the strength and the audacity of the plan, but also its risks: it was a gamble!

To go into more detail, we shall briefly analyze the relations of Ignatius with the *primi Patres*, the "professed" of the order, the companions, and finally with laymen.

II. IGNATIUS' MAJOR RELATIONSHIPS AS GENERAL

The Primi Patres

Ignatius' relations with the *primi Patres*, i.e., with the group of companions of Montmartre and Venice, of the oblation to the Pope and of the first period in Rome *before* the deliberation of 1539, were totally novel: Ignatius, as General, had always, until his death, considered these men as cofounders, as those responsible with him for the foundation of the Society of Jesus. Everything happened *as if* this handful of men, which had submitted to him as General, remained in some measure his equals, having a right to his respect: In his relations with them Ignatius had respect for the role that they had played in God's story.

One first verfication is essential. It involves those upon whom Ignatius conferred every time he could, the great responsibility of the emerging order. When as he did not have other valuable recruits, that is understandable: whom could he have sent to the Indies and Portugal in 1540? to Germany and Spain in 1540? to Ireland in 1541? However, later when men like Araoz, Doménech, Borgia, etc., were integrated into the order, Ignatius continued to use the first Fathers for his big assignments: he shifted certain ones with an astonishing rapidity and, I was about to say, lack of constraint. Favre traveled the routes of Europe, from Germany to Spain and Portugal, from Spain and Portugal to Germany: he acknowledged in his *Memoirs* that he suffered from it and he even died from it. Laynez and Salmeron: how many miles they traveled in order to accomplish the pontifical missions assigned to them by Ignatius! Let us not speak of Bobadilaa, that vagabond of God, nor of Xavier. If matters deteriorated in France, it was Broët whom Ignatius sent to Paris. Still more than the trips which he imposed on them, it was the confidence he accorded them which was remarkable: once they were sent in a certain direction, Ignatius gave them free rein, confident that they would immediately renew the marvelous experience which the group had known before the founding of the Society, that they would bring to it the same "spirit", the same *modo del proceder*: when soon he became concerned about the turn things were taking in Portugal, he sent Favre to observe objectively what was happening, he waited patiently and hopefully until the spiritual problem became apparent to him.

As for creating the provinces, it was to the first Fathers that he assigned them, if they were available: Rodríguez to Portugal (1546), Xavier to the Indies (1549); Broët was his first candidate to the patriarchy of Ethiopia, before John III demanded the nomination of a Portuguese, and he became the first provincial of northern Italy (1552); then, when Ignatius sent him to France (with the powers of provincial, first without the title, then with the title) he replaced him by Laynez; Jay was also provincial without title to Vienna, but he died before upper Germany was elevated to a province. This even extended to Bobadilla to whom, in order to console him, Ignatius indicated that he was "quasi-provincial" of the kingdom of Naples and that, if he was not given the title, it was because the Society had only one house there. Bobadilla, a provincial—that would have been the last straw! When he was found undesirable in Naples, it was Salmeron that Ignatius sent there to replace him, with the same powers, so that he would be the first provincial from 1558 until 1576. Not to mention the Council of Trent, where Ignatius, to whom the Pope left the duty of choosing men, assigned Laynez, Salmeron and Favre the responsibility of representing the young Society. These were, with a few rare others who little by little were added to them, Ignatius' "men of confidence". It was truly through them and with them that Ignatius founded the Society of Jesus.

So they enjoyed everywhere great prestige: they were, in the eyes of all and especially in the eyes of Ignatius, the companions of the "early hours", those on whom the Holy Spirit had breathed, those who had lived a unique, novel adventure, the ideal of Paris, Venice and Rome. At Parma, in 1541, they remembered these reformed priests who had preached, heard confessions, lived as apostles in 1537–1538 and they asked for them again.[8] At Alcalá in 1553, Rodríguez stayed a few days at the college: the Portuguese crisis had already erupted, but it brought to the companions "much consolation because they greatly wished to see (*videre*) one of the first Fathers of the Society".[9] If there was a crisis somewhere, as in Venice and Padua in 1555, our friends advised Ignatius to send one of the first Fathers to it, "like Laynez or Salmeron, or someone similar *ei similes*".[10] And Ignatius, very far from taking umbrage at this prestige of the first Fathers, sustained it.

This explains the drama that took place within him when his duty as general obliged him to deal severely with one of these men who were for him, in a certain respect, sacred. With Bobadilla, it was an easy matter: for this terrible companion was resilient. But with Rodríguez, who passed so abruptly through phases of depression? It would be necessary to analyze, piece by piece, document by document, the crisis of 1552–1556: from this study, it emerges that Ignatius did all that he could to treat the rebel as a true companion, as much as he could, each time that he could; on this point at least, Rodríguez praised Ignatius.

The Professed

We touch here a point which we should know was a sore point, even a traumatic one, from the very beginning of the order:[11] it has been said and repeated that Ignatius' thought on the choice and hence the identity

---

[8] *Chron.* 1, p. 174.

[9] Ibid. 3, p. 322.

[10] Ibid. 5, p. 167.

[11] We repeat again on this subject that our study is historical and objective and that we have neither the right nor the plan to influence through it in any way whatsoever the modern changes which the General Congregations can bring in our days to the Institute. Regarding this problem of "degrees" in the Society we refer to Ladislas LUKACS, "De graduum diversitate inter sacerdotes in Societas Jesu", AHSI, vol. 37 (1968) and to the study of Gervais DUMEIGE, *De mente sancti Ignatii et posteriore evolutione historica in questione de*

of the "professed" was not clear. It seems, however, that one can, by a close analysis, extricate certain important elements of his *ars gubernandi* in this regard. If the texts themselves appear obscure to some, the Ignatian *praxis* seems helpful in pointing out the meaning.

We should recall, before entering into the analysis itself, that two of the first Fathers aroused in Ignatius some concerns regarding their solemn profession. On April 22, 1541, at St. Paul Outside the Walls, there were only five companions around Ignatius to pronounce their solemn vows: Broët, Codure, Jay, Laynez and Salmeron. Four companions were missing: they were already on a pontifical mission. While Favre[12] and Xavier[13] were hastening to make their professions as soon as circumstances would permit and they would insist on using the formula used at St. Paul Outside the Walls, Bobadilla, passing through Rome in October 1541, declined at first, then, after an arbitration by Doctors Michael de Torres, Iñigo Lopez and Licentiate Christophe Madrid, decided to make his profession into the hands of Ignatius in December, before leaving for Germany.[14] As for Simón Rodríguez, he waited until December 25, 1544, and still did not decide except at Ignatius' request: it was in Evora on Christmas night when he decided to follow a formula of his own invention[15] for this profession.

These beginnings of the solemn profession did not augur well. Actually, as early as the Ignatian years, there were a few cases which resembled the quarrel of the pulpit more than the spread of evangelical feeling. To mention only two fathers yearning for solemn profession, Cogordan managed by dint of sadness that Ignatius admit him in 1553 to the profession of three vows,[16] a consolation which traumatized him; and Françis de Rojas came near to leaving the order because Ignatius demanded that he complete his regular studies before admitting him to solemn profession: it took nothing less than Borgia's intervention to restore—temporarily—the young superior of Saragossa[17] to his equilibrium. On the contrary, Ignatius should have recognized his spirit in this response of his former confessor in Venice and Rome, Diego de Eguía: when Diego was dying in June 1556, Ignatius sent to tell him that "if

---

gradibus in Societate Jesu (out of print, Rome, 1969). The 31st General Congregation assigned to a commission the responsibility of studying the question of degrees.

[12] Ratisbon, July 9, 1541. *Fabri Mon.*, p. 117, n. 39.

[13] In Goa, in December 1543, cf. *Epist. Xav.* 2, pp. 575–81; SCHURHAMMER *Franz Xaver*, 3 pp. 579–80.

[14] *Bobad. Mon.*, p. 620, n. 21; *Chron.* 1, p. 97.

[15] *Epist. Broëti*, p. 535.

[16] *Chron.* 3, p. 367; *Epist. ign.* 5, pp. 324–25, n. 3639.

[17] *Chron.* 3, pp. 347–48, 367. He ended by leaving the Society: ibid. 5, p. 537.

there would be consolation for him in it, he could declare his solemn profession". Diego responded, "Now is not the time, and it does not interest me in my present state; moreover, I feel very intimately united to the body of the Society."[18]

One cannot deny that, as early as the first years of the order, the profession of four vows did not seem like a rewarding choice, with the advantages and disadvantages that each distinction brought in its wake. As early as 1551, Ignatius had to fight against a custom which tended to infiltrate, especially in the provinces of Spain: that of incorporating the title of "professed" in the addresses of letters,[19] just as one uses the titles doctor and master of arts. When Borgia asked[20] Ignatius to let Bustamente, who had not entered the order until 1552, make his solemn profession as early as 1553 "by reason of his age, his eminent learning and his virtue", it was necessary that the ceremony take place—almost in secret—in the chapel of the hospital of Tordesillas: Ignatius had so ordered it because "there were other companions older [in the order] whose profession had been deferred".[21] When in 1547 four missionaries to the Indies were called by Ignatius to pronounce the vows of spiritual coadjutors, Polanco, in announcing this news, took care to remind them that this call in no way insured a subsequent call to solemn profession of the four vows; and cited to them the cases of Jerónimo Doménech and André Frusius as exemplary.[22]

It is in this context that one must place the following analysis. At the death of Ignatius, as we have said, there were in the order "thirty-five professed of the four vows, among whom were five surviving first Fathers".[23] The editor of the *Monumenta* corrected this figure:[24] he counted thirty-seven in addition to the five first Fathers. Father Zapico, in his turn, found thirty-eight.[25] Let us not quibble: it is the proportion which counts: there were thirty-five, thirty-seven, or thirty-eight

---

[18] Ibid. 6, pp. 48–49; Diego was a spiritual coadjutor, although Ignatius had accepted him into the group of companions of Venice, 1537–1538; then he had departed for Spain to set his affairs in order.

[19] Several letters, for example *Epist. ign.* 3, 514; 7, 69; 8, 341, etc. Ignatius had to battle against the use of honorary titles like Reverend, Fatherhood, etc, Cf. index of the *Chroniques saint Ignace*, under the heading: "Titres honorifiques".

[20] "Genibus flexis supplicavit": *Chron.* 3, p. 343.

[21] Ibid. 4, pp. 585–86.

[22] Ibid. 1, pp. 346–47; *Epist. ign.* 1, p. 639, n. 225. Polanco, if he had been a prophet, would have been able to cite to them the case of the future General, Everard Mercurian, who was at first only spiritual coadjutor.

[23] *Chron.* 6, pp. 39–40.

[24] Ibid., note 1.

[25] *Font. narr.* 1, p. 63.

professed out of a thousand companions, that is the interesting point—a fact of which Ignatius had to be aware.[26]

Obviously, these thirty-eight companions (four per cent of the actual total) benefited from a choice. Can one from then on disclose what criteria determined this choice? It is imperative to consider the names and dates, companion by companion; and here are the results: Let us set aside four cases wherein Ignatius proceeded, through personal initiative, beyond every formulated "rule": Araoz (1542), Ignatius' nephew, who joined the group of companions in Rome as early as 1539 and whom Ignatius sent to establish the Society in Spain; Borgia (1548), who took "the vow of the Society" in 1546, but in secret, and who still remained the Duke of Gandia; Bustamente of whom we spoke above; and finally Dr. Martin Olave, this truly remarkable vocation, whom Ignatius admitted to the Society in 1552 and called to profession as early as 1553.

It is important to note one fact here which is not without interest: except for Araoz (1542) and Borgia (1548), Ignatius admitted no one to profession before 1549, i.e., for eight years, and this first class was submitted to the four first Fathers before being announced to those concerned. The class consisted of ten men.[27]

Except Araoz, Borgia, Bustamente and Olave, the other professed constituted four rather different groups:

One compact group (about twenty-three) which exercised major responsibilities (Polanco, 1549) or important assignments (provincials, rectors of universitites or scholasticates, or—rarely—colleges of day students, visitors, commissioners, superintendents). We shall see farther on that these important duties were essentially, in Ignatius' eyes, "missions" much more than administrative responsibilities. One case is rather striking: Lanoye, Polanco tells us, was called to profession "when he was the superior of the professed".[28] Does "when" mean "because"?

From these twenty-three, a very significant group emerges: Viola, Superior of the community in Paris (1551), Adriani, Superior of the community in Louvain (1551), and Kessel, Superior of the community in Cologne (1553). It is probable that these three companions, or at least two of them,[29] would not have been called to profession if they had not been responsible for informal communities, isolated and still legally

---

[26] Fr. Zapico, loc. cit., also enumerates 11 professed of three vows, 5 spiritual coadjutors and 13 temporal coadjutors.

[27] *Const.* 1, pp. 244–46.

[28] *Chron.* 2, p. 581.

[29] One remembers with what relentlessness Ribadeneyra, in 1556, opposed the nomination of Adriani as provincial of Northern Germany: he had not, he said, the spirit of the Society either in his administration or in his ministries. Cf. supra, p. 246.

unrecognized by the authorities in the countries where they worked; but civil legislation of the time required, in order that a religious order might carry out "judicial actions", such as donations, funding of revenues, contracts of sale or purchase, etc., that the religious guarantor be "professed" in the order. And the distinction of degrees and vows that the Society had set up still escaped the common language of the legal writers.[30] It was not necessary that a question of vocabulary also come to complicate the judicial imbroglio. The simplest solution was therefore that the companion responsible for business and other procedures be able to declare himself professed so as to achieve legal recognition. It was thus that Viola in 1550 was called by Ignatius to solemn profession:[31] "Some people would have liked to donate income for a college," said Polanco,

> but, because there was no companion who had pronounced his vows in the Society, because the Society did not as yet have its *naturalization* rights, as they say (for it was not yet recognized and provided with this privilege), those pious desires could not be realized. What was essential to promote one to profession, Father Ignatius finally provided. He sent his legal documents of profession to Viola.

The same reasons seems to have decided Ignatius to admit Adriani to profession.[32]

A group of four or five companions scarcely seems to have been moved forward to profession, solely on the basis of the original criteria: *eruditio solidior quam quae possit ad multos se extendere*[33]—Canisius (1549), Goudanus (1550), Frusius (1550), Olave (1553), Couvillon (1556).

Finally comes the group which perhaps best exemplifies the spirit of Ignatius: the group of missionaries designated for particularly perilous regions, missions which involved the risk of martyrdom—let us say, to speak more precisely, missions which strongly resembled the pilgrimage to Jerusalem which Ignatius and the first Fathers had hoped would furnish them with the opportunity to shed their blood for Christ our Lord. First, there were the missionaries of Ethiopia. It certainly seems that the patriarch, John Nuñez and one of the coadjutor bishops, Melchior Carneiro, were called the profession only because of the Ethiopian mission: for Ignatius had decided that all those departing for Ethiopia

---

[30] This common language recognized only the distinction between novice and professed. Already the Society made a distinction among novice, approved scholastic or coadjutor, spiritual coadjutor (and temporal), professed of three vows and professed of four solemn vows: jurists and canonists unfamiliar with the Society could not make head or tail of it (cf. the spectacular Lisbon ceremony: *Chron.* 3, p. 402).

[31] *Chron.* 2, pp. 88–89.

[32] Ibid. 2, p. 284.

[33] Ibid. 1, p. 169.

would make either profession of the four vows or profession of the three vows;[34] and, if their names did not appear in 1556 on the list of professed, it was because they realized in time, that in the Indies, through which they would pass, the solemn vow of poverty would prevent them from living on the revenue of the college of Goa. Nonetheless, they would make their profession before leaving the Indies for Ethiopia.[35] Christopher de Mendoza, destined for Africa, also made his profession into the hands of Laynez on his passage to Sicily.[36] Goysson and Brogelmans, because they were destined for the Bohemian mission (Prague, 1556), one as rector, the other as professor,[37] Nobrega because he was at first the one responsible, then the Provincial, of the perilous mission of Brazil.

To complete this analysis, it is necessary to cite a fact which casts an important light on the Ignatian mentality. Five times, to our knowledge, he insisted in different regions that those responsible for the missions propose companions to be called to profession, and three times at least his requests corresponded to a more or less dramatic situation. In 1549, he asked Rodríguez to designate "three or four" companions from Portugal and the Indies;[38] in 1553, he ordered Xavier (whose death was not known in Europe) to return to the Indies, but "he entreated him to leave there five or six professed (of whom Father Gaspard Barzée was also dead), and even more, if he judged it opportune;"[39] in June 1553, he gave the order with firmness and in detail, to Diego Miron "to call five or six companions (or more) to profession".[40] Now, Portugal was then in the midst of a full-blown crisis; in 1554, it was to Nadal, Commissioner in Spain, that he sent a similar order for all Spain and without limiting the number (*algunos professos*)[41] he himself specially designated two or three fathers by name; and it was Nadal, in agreement with

[34] *Chron.* 4, pp. 8–9. The professed of three vows were: Jean Boukyan (or Bochiu), Belgian; Michel Barul, from Valencia; Thomas Passitano. Cf. also *Epist. ign.* 7, 533–34, n. 4792.

[35] *Chron.* 5, p. 608. Actually, this promotion of Ethiopian missionaries would raise many difficulties; the Provincial of the Indies, Silveira, Francis Rodriguez and a few other Fathers responsible for the mission would firmly state that this initiative was neither to renew nor establish principle. (*Chron.* 6, p. 836).

[36] Ibid. 4, pp. 8–9; 186–87.

[37] Ibid. 6, p. 23. The case of Goysson is interesting, for he was rector of the German College and it was not until the moment of his leaving for Prague that he was called to profession.

[38] *Epist. ign.* 2, p. 418, n. 693.

[39] *Chron.* 3, p. 498.

[40] *Epist. ign.* 5, pp. 127–28, 138–39, n. 3473 and 3489; this last letter is particularly precise and emphatic.

[41] *Chron.* 4, 386.

Borgia and Araoz, who restrained and spaced the nominations;[42] finally, in 1556, he ordered Doménech "to arrange the profession of six persons from his province" (Sicily) of whom he gave the names.

When one considers these different facts and puts situations and faces behind the names, certain constants of Ignatius' conduct in this important sector of his administration became clear:

1. The professed, in his eyes, was essentially a "man of mission". The orders which he sent to Xavier, Nadal, etc., giving them the responsibility of choosing the professed, were accompanied in general by this refrain: those designated must be "more mature in life and doctrine which is fitting for our Society";[43] "más"—again the comparative dear to Ignatius; concretely, it signifies here that the designated companions must be those in whom the first Fathers, especially Ignatius, would better recognize themselves and on whom the Society of Jesus would be able to establish itself and be supported in its development and its activity, especially in serious situations.

2. As we shall see below, the provincials, the rectors of important colleges, they too, they especially, were "missionaries". They were men of apostolic radiance: their selection was very characteristic.[44] Characteristic also was the list of "professors" called professed: they were truly men who had "such wisdom as would not be the case for most people".[45]

3. Ignatius wanted to install or multiply this type of man in sectors where he thought that there might be a more or less incipient crisis. The Indies, Portugal, Spain, Sicily (where he had a presentiment that the recall of Juan de Vega to Spain risked opening a period of crisis): they would be there as pillars on which the least strong, the least "mature", would lean. So, apart from exceptions, he asked the provincials or commissioners on the spot in contact with the persons, to designate them to him.

4. But among all these missionaries, one place apart, one exceptional place was reserved by Ignatius for those who were designated to open to the Church new ways of evangelization—at the peril of their lives, those had a sort of right to consider themselves the privileged sons of the missionary order which was the Society of Jesus: a generous and beautiful idea, without doubt a little too generous and too beautiful, but one which exalted, more than it diminished, the apostolic generosity of Ignatius.

[42] Ibid. 6, 640.

[43] Example: *Epist. ign.* 5, pp. 127–28, n. 3473.

[44] This analysis must begin with the *life* of each one; it is very conclusive. The clearest case is that of Strada; we shall return to that.

[45] *Chron.* 1, pp. 169–70.

Decidedly, in the face of such an Ignatian view, how could one still doubt that his desire was to make the Society a "corpus" of persons, united in the same spirit, in the same enthusiasm, more than a perfectly structured organization? One, moreover, in his plan, is not incompatible with the other: he would bring the same heart to draft the *Constitutions* that pervaded the entire Society: "the law of love and charity".

The Companions

Whoever wished to know the heart of Ignatius must try to perceive the quality of his relationships with his companions, be they the most humble or the most strained. We have had the opportunity, in the two preceding paragraphs, to give examples of this. However, one must read the entire correspondence or the direct testimonials which Câmara preserved for us in his *Memorial*.

One expects here a study on the fundamental authority—obedience realtionship, and rightly so; it has seemed to us that it would be better situated in the following chapter concerning structures. We must, however, note that fundamental and essential as it may be, it is second—but we do not say secondary—in regard to one other aspect of unity: that of friendship or, to avoid all sentimental misinterpretation of that word, that of companionship. The Society of Jesus, in Ignatius' eyes, was a *corpus, corpus Societatis*, before being an organization. Organic, without being organized. A *corpus vivens*, of which the members, the cells, were linked together by the same Blood, caressed by the same living breath, nourished by the same Word and by the same Bread, called together by the same Voice, and hence jointly responsible for each other, through the mediation of the same leader, Jesus Christ or his "Vicar on earth". Companionship, in the Society of Jesus, is not a coincidence, a matter of fortuitous encounter; it has a profound unity, founded on the same grace. Simón Rodríguez stated that before even being acquainted, the seven students of the Paris days had heard—each in the depth of his freedom—the same call: personal reform through absolute poverty and pilgrimage to Jerusalem with the possibility of dying for Christ; even if Rodríguez, aging and dying, overestimated his former feelings, his affirmation contains a bit truth: prior to a communal life, a communion of soul is necessary. The serious candidate in the Society was one who, prior to this decision, "wished under the standard of the Cross to fight for God and for God alone and to serve his Vicar on earth".[46] Such companionship surpasses by far the coincidences of friendship and its demands and vulnerabilities. . . . It was in unity with Christ that the

[46] *Const.* I, p. 16.

companions were united. According to Nadal, the Society constituted a *corpus mysticum* within the *Corpus Christi*. The correspondence, the visits, the witnessing of the most spiritual friendship—what would these be, how would they endure between missionaries, without this unity impervious to time and distance that is charity in Christ?

Whatever may have been the mentality of Ignatius, in his governing, one may find the proof of it, it seems, in his relationship with three types of companions: those whose vocations were in peril, those who had committed some transgression, and finally, "those who left us": sent away or departed on their own initiative.[47]

a) *Vocations in peril*—Whether this peril came from the subjects themselves, or from their relatives, or from external circumstances, Ignatius' great principle, his unique principle, one could say, was the freedom of the individual. Companionship with Jesus Christ, under the particular form of the Society of Jesus, was chosen freely and was not imposed; if it was proposed, it was by the example of life, the "appeal" of an ideal, the witnessing of a love; and if it was chosen, especially at the moment of candidacy, it had to be chosen for one's entire life. Ignatius protected this freedom, defended it as much as possible: it was only after a long and patient "Examen" that the candidate, on his side, the order on the other, mutually committed themselves; once the candidate was admitted to the novitiate, Ignatius helped him to remain faithful to his choice, but always respecting his freedom; if the novice was tempted, he helped him through prayer, through long, personal conversations, through counselors whom Ignatius procured for him, by all these spiritual ways which permitted the soul to make its own decision.[48] One case reported by Câmara illustrated Ignatius' manner of proceeding; a Flemish scholastic, who had been at La Strada for several months was experiencing violent "homesickness". "Neither the Exercises nor any other remedy had succeeded" in comforting him; the consulted Fathers were of the opinion that he should be made to leave; Ignatius, after having prayed, concluded otherwise:

> That we advise him to go to Loreto, telling him that if he first wishes to be relieved of his vows here, we shall relieve him of them but that we advise him to present himself to Our Lady and decide before her whether or not to remain in our religious group; and if he decides not to remain, from that moment his vows shall cease to bind him. Let him remain here eight days to rest, whether or not the decision to leave has been made clear to him or simply in order to reflect further.

[47] It is clear that this list is not exhaustive.

[48] See for example the *Mémorial* of Luis GONÇALVES DA CÂMARA, n. 43, 48, 78, 128, 342, 348.

This stance, which consisted of entrusting to one's soul one's personal liberty, is typically Ignatian. We keep finding it, in different contexts, in many a matter of vocation: for the number of letters devoted wholly or in part by Ignatius to sustain wavering vocations is considerable. We shall bring up only one well-known and frequently studied case, which summarizes, it seems, all the steps which Ignatius took in similar circumstances: Octavio Cesari, the son of the secretary of the Duke of Monteleone: to preserve Octavio's freedom of vocation, Ignatius battled against the tears and intrigues of his mother, dared to oppose cardinals and even Paul IV, and tried to organize harmoniously all the facilities which appeared to him still compatible with a religious commitment.[49]

b) *Those "who committed some transgression"*—This is one of the dark parts of Ignatius' portrait. That he himself, in the first times after his conversion, was given to excesses of humiliating penances will hardly startle anyone who knows the zeal of the newly converted, and many of his subsequent directives offer evidence on this point, which, as on the matter of times of prayer, experience permitted him to regain the equilibrium which apostolic life demands.[50]

Then, how and why all this atmosphere of penance and humiliations which emanate from the *Memorial* of Câmara[51] and from the correspondence (because Ignatius inflicted penances even by letter)? Why this severity of tone in the reproach which bordered on harshness and risked wounding? The facts are what they are; at the most we can confirm that, as early as Ignatius' time, this system of penances and humiliations was not universally practiced. If Portugal hastened to imitate Roman penances,[52] Viola did not wish to introduce them at Genoa,[53] and Adriani made it known in Rome that they were hardly compatible with the nordic temperament; Jay and Lanoye thought the same for Germany. The fact remains that Ignatius thought them valuable and put them into use. Without pretending to clarify this mystery,[54] it is necessary to present certain facts for the case for the defense.

First this one: these penances (of which Câmara, then minister of La Strada, tells us) were carried out inside the house and were not compara-

---

[49] Regarding this matter about thirty letters were sent or received from different people, from April 1553 to the end of May 1556. Cf. in *Epist. Mixt.* 4, pp. 365–71, n. 867; finally Octavio left the order.

[50] Cf. the letter to Borgia, *Chron.* 1, pp. 316–17; *Epist. ign.* 2, pp. 233–7, n. 466 (September 20, 1548); see also ibid. (2, 136; 5, 316–17) etc.

[51] Numerous examples, cf. n. 217, 218, 242, 243, 250–51, 267, 328, 351.

[52] *Chron.* 2, p. 374; 739.

[53] Ibid. 1, p. 113.

[54] Cf. however our study of the "character" of Ignatius in Part V, pp. 393 sqq.

ble to public penance out on the street (like the processions of flagellants which were practiced in Portugal, the Indies, Spain, southern Italy, and which were little favored by Ignatius).[55]

It is worth noting that usually when the guilty party showed signs of real repentance Ignatius lightened or even cancelled the penance.

It was not on just any companion that Ignatius thus inflicted penances; the most famous, if one can so speak, remain the reprimands which he addressed by correspondence to Polanco, whom he was going to attach to Rome as Secretary of the Society,[56] to Lanoye[57] and especially to Laynez: the spiritual reaction of the last is worth, in itself, all the commentaries and attempts at justification of the Ignatian *praxis*.[58]

The case of Laynez shows the complexity of the feelings of Ignatius' followers, who were basically as disconcerted by and attracted to him as we ourselves can be. Câmara expressed this feeling well when he thus described "our Father Ignatius":

> One totally remarkable fact is the way with which our Father, in matters which seem identical, uses totally opposite methods, like great severity with one and great gentleness with another; and one sees immediately by the result that the remedy he used was the best, though we had not previously recognized that. However, he was always rather inclined toward love; even more, it seems total love and through that he was universally loved by all and one will find no one in the Society who does not have a very great love for him and does not consider himself much loved by him.[59]

Does this mean that Ignatius was a "dual" being—two-faced? He has been accused of this but wrongly so. It suffices to step outside this ambience of personal love which Ignatius created around him and of which the incontestable sign was "joy and taste"[60] in order to grasp certain less likeable aspects of his character which had, in his union with God, taken on a new meaning.[61]

c) *Those who were dismissed from the order or who departed on their own initiative*—Again a blemish on these Ignatian times of the Society of Jesus: there was then a rather astonishing coming and going of entrances and departures and even of returns of those who had just left. It is fitting first to situate this phenomenon in the context of the times: this instability, especially at the level of nonprofessed religious, was customary. The

---

[55] Example: *Chron.* 2, pp. 87–88.
[56] *Epist. ign.* I, p. 457–59, n. 152.
[57] *Chron.* 4, p. 261.
[58] Ibid. 3, p. 61.
[59] *Mémorial*, n. 86–87.
[60] Ibid. 87.
[61] Cf. our Part V.

Constitutions of the Society of Jesus forbade accepting candidates into the order who "have taken the habit" in another order, that is to say, those who have made even a simple attempt at religious life under some form—whatever it may be;[62] and Ignatius in 1548, had to have Rodríguez ask John III of Portugal to forbid companions from "passing to other religious orders".[63]

The motivations behind these departures were varied. The ambiguity of the canonical status of vows[64] was the reason for many. Some left from lack of education,[65] especially if candidates were placed or admitted into colleges which were too small and too burdened with hard work,[66] because some did not wish to depart for the Congo where they had been assigned.[67] Some left because of an excess of freedom;[68] others because they wanted to study elsewhere, in Paris, for example;[69] still others for having been "too much nourished on the milk of hermits".[70] Then there were those who left for family reasons,[71] because they were *inter nostros, sed non ex nostris*,[72] because it was painful to live with people who "whether you wish it or not want to make you a saint"[73] without reason and to the stupefaction of the people around you.[74] The crisis of Portugal provoked many[75] departures, to the point that the dissidents thought for a while of creating a new Society.[76] Among these departures there were a good many who took "French leave" (*hospite insalutato*), as Polanco jokingly said, among whom there evidently were "crooks".[77] Therein lies a story which has not yet been sufficiently explored for the purpose of understanding the mentality of the first generation of the Society.[78]

---

[62] *Constitutions*, "General Examen", n. 27.

[63] *Epist. ign.* 12, p. 229, n. 10.

[64] Cf. index of the *Chroniques saint Ignace*, pp. 291 and 302.

[65] *Chron.* 2, p. 528; 3, p. 131.

[66] Ignatius would draft, on the occasion of sending companions to Sicily, an instruction: "How to treat young companions sent to the colleges" (*Chron.* 3, p. 239).

[67] Ibid. 2, p. 698.

[68] Ibid. 2, p. 251.

[69] Ibid. 6, 181–84.

[70] Ibid. 3, 116.

[71] Ibid. 3, pp. 188–89.

[72] Ibid. 3, p. 393.

[73] Ibid. 3, p. 415.

[74] Ibid. 1, p. 248; 6, 585.

[75] Our formula remains purposely vague so as not to take part here in the debates which still divide the historians; what is certain is that there were numerous departures.

[76] *Chron.* 3, pp. 436–37.

[77] Cf. index of the *Chroniques saint Ignace*, p. 275.

[78] Cf. A curious document, preserved in the library of Lyon (MS n. 1277): Pedro de RIBADENEYRA, *Dialogues. Où sont rapportés les exemples de quelques-uns qui, pour être sortis de la*

Whatever the situation, we have seen with what "love" Ignatius tried to help the vocations in peril.

More delicate was his attitude towards the dismissed. A systematic study permits the classification of the motivations for departure into three large categories, aside from those dismissed for their unsuitability: the most numerous group included cases of disobedience or lack of detachment;[79] a second group included cases of swindling or fraud;[80] and a third fuzzier group contains those who "contaminated" the communities or even "diverted others from the Society".[81] The problem, here again, consists of a certain contrast in Ignatius' conduct. Câmara himself admits that often Ignatius was quick to issue dismissals; he reports several cases where Ignatius dismissed a subject during the night; and he even reports this statement of Ignatius' "that he would not spend a single night under the same roof with someone from the Society that he knew to be in mortal sin".[82] However, in certain other cases, he knew how to wait patiently, to give opportunities for repentance to the guilty, sending them, for example, on a pilgrimage or to service in the hospitals;[83] in any case, he wanted these dismissals to be done "with love", and "through love".[84] Above all, he who decided that "there were not enough dismissals", accepted returnees! Thus, he asked the rebels of Portugal to come to him in Rome;[85] he called Anthony Gomez, the former rector of Goa whom Francis Xavier sent from the Indies, with some others (neither did Xavier have a gentle hand in cases of dismissals);[86] in fact, this indulgence of Ignatius' succeeded only rarely, and experience advised against it.[87]

In these actions of Ignatius it would be vain to seek a logical principle; it was the individual case which determined his attitude. The last word here belongs to the *Constitutions*.[88] "Three things will be observed: first [the one who dismisses] must pray and order others to pray in the house; must consult several persons; must rid himself of all attachment, keeping

---

Compagnie de Jésus, ont esté chatiez severement par la main toute-puissante de Dieu. . . . Escrits en espagnol par le R.P. Pierre de Ribadeneyra. Et mis en français par un N. de la mesme Compagnie (The dialogue takes place "among Pierre, Cyprien and François").

[79] *Mémorial*, n. 115; *Epist. ign.* 2, p. 710; 6, p. 560 (n. 1109 and 4333), for example.

[80] Two fine cases: *Chron.* 3, pp. 192–93, and 447–49. Cf. *Mémorial*, n. 352.

[81] *Mémorial*, n. 46, 277.

[82] *Mémorial*, n. 396; cf. n. 46 and 277.

[83] Ibid., n. 61, 384, 283.

[84] Ibid., n. 61, 348.

[85] *Chron.* 3, p. 440; *Epist. ign.* 5, p. 28, n. 3338.

[86] *Chron.* 2, pp. 766–67; 776; *Epist. ign.* 6, pp. 89–90, n. 4012.

[87] *Chron.* 3, p. 415.

[88] Part II, ch. III. "The method of dismissal". Let us note that this text was already almost the same in text "a" of the *Constitutions* (1549–1550).

before his eyes the greatest divine glory, the common good, and so far as possible, the good of the subject, he must weigh the pros and cons, then make a decision." And the "Examen" in the *Constitutions* adds other, very significant, prescriptions:

> One must arrange things so that the one departing may have the greatest possible love and charity for the house and the greatest possible consolation in our Lord. . . . One will try to direct him so that he may take another good way of serving in religion or outside endeavors, according to what will best conform to the divine will, and one will aid him by advice, prayers and whatever, in charity, will appear preferable. . . . So far as possible, one must not remain without affection for him, nor keep a bad opinion of him. On the contrary, one must have pity for him, love him in Christ and recommend him in prayer to the divine Majesty.

This chapter three of the "Examen" is one of the most beautiful documents which Ignatius has left us.

The Laity

Tradition demands that we stress the "aid" that every companion had to give to men, "to his neighbor": that is correct. However, we must not forget this prodigious effort (and, moreover, far from being unheard of in the Church of the sixteenth century) that made Ignatius, and, under his prodding, the companions to lead and stimulate the laity to create, organize and conduct "charitable works". One recalls the passage of Ignatius at Azpeitia in the spring of 1535: leaving his little village two months after his arrival, he left a work so well organized to aid of the poor of the country that it would last for centuries. From the first years of his generalship in Rome, he created different programs or houses to assist catechumens, converted "fallen women", the poor, the ill, prisoners, "orphans" and "young girls in danger": a concern characterized these programs, that of engaging men and women who not only financed these projects but who also devoted themselves personally to them, directed them, organized them and bore responsibility for them. When the companions still participated in them, it was for spiritual service of one kind or another and sometimes to beg when resources were lacking. When there were plagues, famines or perils, the companions had to be in the front lines of charity; by their example, they were to encourage self-sacrifice from others among the Christian population. Everywhere the companions did the same: the action of Doménech in Sicily was, in this regard, extremely Ignatian.

To reduce this "method of proceeding" to a necessity imposed by a multiplicity of crises and a too-small number of companions would be a very poor interpretation of the Ignatian mentality. To understand his plan, it is necessary to refer neither more nor less to his view of the action of the Church of Christ in the world, such as he discloses it in the "Meditation on the Two Standards". There, we touch upon a primary point: the Society of Jesus was indeed without any doubt this handful of companions which grouped themselves little by little around Ignatius; but it was also the immense crowd of men and women which fought with Christ for the coming of the royal kingdom of God, "under the standard of the cross": Ignatius did not deny it, Ignatius did not forget it, Ignatius entered fully into the divine project for the salvation of the world through charity. What were the "degrees" of vows among the companions in comparison with this essential hierarchy of charity as he had glimpsed it in the "Two Standards"? Composed of some "distinguished individuals" and some "reasonable",[89] some hearts which refused the call of Christ, this hierarchy existed in all the professions, in all the social milieus, even in the prisons, the galleys, among children and adults, the married and the celibate; undoubtedly, it even existed in the order which he had founded. Everywhere there were those who "wished to love more and to distinguish themselves in the service of their universal Lord", those who, through judgment and reason, voluntarily offered themselves to the task and those who evaded it. Everywhere grace confronted sin; and it was the free choice of man to decide regarding this combat.

It was perhaps this desire to involve the laity, each according to his grace and his vocation, in the labor of the *vinea Domini*, which best illuminates the genesis of the Society of Jesus, the opinion of Ignatius about "degrees", "the priesthood" and vows. When he created the "coadjutors", spiritual or temporal, he did not have the feeling of constituting marginal categories of religious, or what is worse, inferior categories: a coadjutor for Ignatius was, according to the etymology of the word, a companion of apostolic work, a full companion in the order of charity. For Ignatius, there were not the professed and "the others"; there were only companions, enamored of Jesus Christ and desirous of helping souls; and among them, a group to whom he believed he could entrust more particularly the fidelity of all to the fundamental "spirit" of the order and its destiny.

---

[89] One recognizes here the terms which Ignatius used in the meditation on the Call of the King.

CHAPTER IV

THE STRUCTURES

In the preceding chapters, and particularly in chapter three, our study constantly skirted the problem of structures. To govern, according "to the will of God" and the thread of unforeseable events, to govern in accordance with the love of the people while seeking to understand and to help each one in his particular situation, these goals were scarcely favorable to the creation of structures, in the rigid meaning of the word. Ignatius accepted the idea of structures, wanted them, and instituted them because they were indispensable to the work of the mission; but we must expect them to bear the mark of his temperament and his personal grace, even though he was aided in this work by certain companions.

To bring this study to a successful conclusion without its getting out of proportion, it is helpful to begin with an established fact: the day in 1538-1539 that Ignatius with his ten first companions seemed to leave the route of the pilgrim in order to found a religious order at the disposition of the Vicar of Christ on earth, he agreed to reintegrate himself and the Society of Jesus into the structures of a society with which he had pretended to quarrel openly, by formerly leaving Loyola for Jerusalem and by exchanging his gentleman's clothes for the worn garments of the pilgrim. After pure and exalting years of poverty, freedom and companionship, these men found themselves at grips with the harrowing paradox of every disciple of Christ, and especially of the apostle: to be and to work in the world without being of the world.

I. IGNATIUS IS CONSTRAINED TO REINTEGRATE HIMSELF INTO THE SOCIAL STRUCTURES OF HIS TIME

The social structures of the period can be classified according to three types: the power structure, the money structure, and the intellectual structure. The names of Machiavelli (the *Prince*), Fugger (banks) or those of the Medicis, Copernicus (his scientific revolution): these names evoke in themselves the forces which were molding old Europe and making it, in some way, be "reborn"; the word "Renaissance" says it all.[1] We have already analyzed these forces.

[1] To deal with this chapter correctly, it would have been necessary to spell out the meaning of the word "Renaissance", or again the word "Reform". We can only refer to the authors whom we cite in our bibliography, such as Renaudet, Imbart de la Tour, Febvre,

In the fervor of his conversion, in 1521, Ignatius, like all neophytes, had broken—not without fanfare—with all these structures. In leaving for Jerusalem he opposed the power structure with humiliations, rebuffs and derision: people considered him "crazy"; to the money structure, he opposed the *sancta mendicitas*, the uncertainty of daily bread, a place to sleep, hospital work and penances; to the scientific structure, he opposed ignorance, lack of cultivation and rusticity. Henceforth, he would belong to that anonymous world which society definitely rejected.

What took place in the course of his pilgrimage to the holy places? How did his thoughts progress? We do not know, but the fact remains that when he again set foot on Spanish soil, his decision had been made: he would study; and soon he would realize that these studies had to be pursued with great seriousness, under penalty of being foiled by the Inquisition in his conversations and especially in the Spiritual Exercises which he considered from that time on to be his privileged way of aiding souls. Was he aware of the significance of this decision? He would discover, in any case, that science has two faces, that it can serve faith in Christ as well as attacking and destroying it. The day that he began to learn Latin grammar, Ignatius would reintegrate himself into the social structure of knowledge.

Soon, in Paris, he would complete the experiment. Obliged to support himself and his friends, he would have to beg first, then receive money from the letters of exchange of "rich Spanish merchants" living in Flanders. The vows of Montmartre themselves would take account of this social conditioning; the companions, in effect, vowed themselves to the strictest "evangelical poverty", but qualified it with two clauses: this vow would not be in total effect until the end of their studies, and it would not prevent them, contrary to the conduct of Ignatius in 1523, from accepting the necessary funds for the trip to the Holy Land.

In Rome, from 1539 on, it was finally necessary that Ignatius and the companions realize the situation: in any kind of society, but especially in that concrete society in which they lived, it was necessary for them, whether they liked it or not, to be reintegrated into the power structure. Science, money and power—society inexorably imposed these conditions of existence and action upon them. A group, a "society" could not live in the world without accepting, or at least submitting to, civilization.

Ignatius did not rebel against this law of life. How could he have done so? The Church herself is, in one of her aspects, a human, political and financial society, a society in which theological science had to be up to

---

etc. And in this article, we would have had to stress the great currents which swept through the University of Paris about 1530–1537.

the level of contemporary humanism. A society which is simultaneously holy and sinful. In deciding that the Society of Jesus—a group of a few companions—would become a Society of Jesus—a religious missionary order—Ignatius accepted the fact that the Society risked carrying in itself, like all of society, like the Church itself, the triple sin of pride: the pride of knowledge, of money and of power.

Henceforth, the preliminary documents to the *Constitutions*, then the *Constitutions* themselves, and especially the correspondences, would be filled and sometimes almost encumbered by questions of relations with the great, benefactors, revenues, inheritances, solicitations by begging and problems raised by studies and diplomas. As early as the *Summa Instituti* of 1539, they appeared, and the two first documents which would be entered into the *Constitutions* concerned the "foundations" of colleges or houses. Where was the evangelical freedom of Monserrat, Manresa, Paris and Venice?

II. IGNATIUS' PERFORMANCE

Ignatius' performance in taking risks, the importance of which he measured carefully, would be totally original, and even exemplary for the companions who would come after him; since he had to cede something on "methods", he insisted on the final and unique goal: God. Although enmeshed in money matters, he maintained absolute, total poverty as an economic rule for the professed Society—note his *Spiritual Diary* and his deliberation on poverty. Here he was constrained by the very service of God to involve the companions in advanced studies, degrees and even in honorary titles of the universities; without delay he proposed to them, as an ideal, the humble Christ, laden with opprobrium in the course of his Passion, and he required of them, even of the most learned, especially the most learned, that they be involved by vow in teaching catechism and elementary prayers to little children. Here he was at the head of a powerful Society well thought of at court, endowed with privileges and favors, charged with responsibilities for the most honorable missions; he established obedience as the primary structure of the order: everywhere at each moment the companion was to consider himself "*missus*" by the "Vicar of Christ on earth" as Christ himself had been "*missus*" by his Father; the true companion would not wish to be at the heart of his most resounding apostolic success, he would be aware of being only an *instrumentum* in the hands of God our Lord. Briefly, in these conditions of existence and action, Ignatius tried to maintain, in all its rigorous beauty, the ideal of the "pilgrim". The *corpus Societatis*, like each companion, would be essentially a pilgrim of Christ; only this separation from the world, instead of being exterior and spectacular, would become intimate detachment. Hence an inevitable tension existed between this detachment and the indispensable attachment to action: the drama of the apostle affected his personality at a more profound level than the wanderings of the simple pilgrim. The true missionary, according to Ignatius, was one who in the very heart of action maintained within himself the intransigence of evangelical poverty, a feeling of nothingness and of his basic radical weakness in the order of grace, and humility concerning the obedience of the Spirit: this was so of Xavier, Favre, Laynez, as well as others less illustrious and scarcely known—all men who had firmly planted within themselves "the law of love and charity", by the action of the Holy Spirit. This first sentence of the prologue of the *Constitutions* was not a platonic declaration; it alone gave meaning, value and efficacy to the institutional structures. The companion was first a man enamored of Jesus Christ, "enflamed by God", said Ignatius.

The audacity of Ignatius was to suppose the problem resolved, that is to consider it an established fact that the men who "would wish to imitate this way",[2] which he and the first Fathers followed, would be by the grace of God, of the same spiritual generosity as themselves, and nothing would lessen for them the ideal of Manresa and of Paris. They, the first Fathers, knew from experience (*experti sumus*), that this way was strewn "with numerous and great difficulties",[3] but also that no life was "more rewarding, more pure and more apt to help one's neighbor".[4] Their plan? It depended entirely on their hope, that is, on their conviction, a fervent conviction (*de reliquo in Dominum jactare omnes cogitatus nostros*), that "God who is good and generous never refuses his spirit (*spiritum bonum*) to whoever asks it of him with simplicity and humility of heart"; moreover, that "he who gives it to all in abudance and without keeping account of faults, not only would not refuse it to them, but would give it to them, according to his benevolence, more abundantly than was asked of him and more than they could understand."[5]

The tenth part of *Constitutions*[6] would coincide perfectly with all these first documents:

The Society which was not established by human means cannot maintain

---

[2] "Prima Instituti Summa": *Const.* I, p. 20.
[3] Ibid., p. 20.
[4] Ibid., p. 19.
[5] "Deliberatio primorum Patrum" (1539): *Const.* pp. 2–3.
[6] Title: "How the whole body of the Society can be preserved and developed in its well-being".

itself nor develop itself by them, but by the *all-powerful* hand of Christ our Lord and God. It is therefore necessary to *"hope in him alone"* that he will maintain and successfully complete what he deigned to begin for his service and glory and for the aid of souls. Since such is our *hope....*[7]

An experiment and a hope: in the throes of labors and difficulties undertaken for the love of God our Lord, that is what Ignatius delivered to his companions to inspire them. In short, the transformation of the Society of companions into a religious order of strict structures was on the part of the first Fathers grouped around Ignatius an act of faith, a wager on the bounty and power of God.

All the *ars gubernandi* of Ignatius were founded on the fidelity of God to himself, on this initial act of faith. We shall cite a few examples chosen from among many others.

The Constitutions and Occasional Documents

One characteristic was common to all of them: it was the place that charity holds, under whatever name it is called: love, service, bounty—and if it concerns neighbors—help. Let us not be blinded by the complexity of canonical prescriptions, the banality of business and administrative considerations, the minutiae of details or a certain solemnity of style; all this life is bathed in an intense atmosphere of charity: let us take care always to give to this vocabulary of charity, the meaning which Ignatius gave it; it was not a matter of sentimental love, but a virile gift, in faith, of all his being to the being of Christ and to his brothers—men.

Nonetheless one always notes a few differences; these were not divergences, far from it, but diversities of tone owing in general to the literary genres of the documents: the *Constitutions* are more "official", a little academic, if you wish; the other documents are more direct, more personal, more circumstantial, and give us a better, more vivid picture of the Ignatian mentality. Let us keep one fact in mind: the *Constitutions* were "declared" only in the last years of Ignatius' life and still had not the force of law since no General Congregation had approved them. On what basis then was the unity of the companions founded? Laynez, Nadal, Polanco, etc. said repeatedly in the crisis of 1556–1558: on the pontifical bulls and especially on the first bull of Paul III, *Regimini militantis*, which was merely a transcription of the *Summa Instituti*; to which were added "a few regulations". In fact, the great method which Ignatius used then to form the companions and the one he would use throughout life to give them common spirit, was the *instructions*, those exact, detailed documents, directives which he gave to a companion

[7] *Const.*, P. X, n. 812.

or to a group departing for some mission. In them Ignatius allowed his apostolic heart to speak, communicated to his companions his ardor and his fire: all therein burned with the love of God and neighbor: Whatever instruction the reader may choose, the breath of charity flows through it: (1546) "To the Fathers sent to Trent"[8] or that of 1549 "To the Fathers sent to Germany",[9] or that of 1554 "To Oliverio Manareo and to the companions sent to Loreto",[10] or that of 1556 "To the companions who are going to establish the college of Prague":[11] what inspired charity!

> For the greatest glory of God our Lord, our chief objective in this trip to Trent . . . , each according to the talent which he has, we shall motivate those whom we can to devotion and prayer, so that all may ask God our Lord with us that the divine Majesty deign to spread his spirit in all those who have to consider the questions affecting such a high gathering. Thus, the Holy Spirit will descend upon this council in greater abundance with his gifts and graces.[12]

Or again to the companions of Germany:

> Their works will prove that their love is true. They will render service to a great number of souls, whether aiding them spiritually, or in giving themselves to works of corporal charity. It is necessary that one grasp that they do not seek their personal interests, but those of Jesus Christ, that is, his glory and the salvation of souls.[13]

Let us end these quotations. This period predates the administrative structures, but the society was already at the point where the "mission" was being organized and regulated: and charity pervaded every part of it.

The Foreign Provinces

Is not the province the most impersonal administrative unit, an arbitrary but commodious practical division of evangelized territories? Undoubtedly. However, for Ignatius it was much more. Let us look at the picture of the provinces in July of 1556. There were a dozen outside Rome, Polanco tells us.[14] At that time one did not yet exist, and would not for a long time: Ethiopia, Brazil, France, Northern Germany, Southern Germany, a total of five provinces counting only a handful of

---

[8] SAINT IGNACE, *Lettres* (translation by Gervais DUMEIGE), pp. 109–13.
[9] Ibid., pp. 199–207.
[10] *Epist. ign.* 8, pp. 89–92.
[11] Ibid. 10, pp. 689–97, n. 6205.
[12] *Lettres* (DUMEIGE translation), p. 111.
[13] Ibid., p. 201.
[14] *Chron.* 6, p. 41.

men (between 15 and 30), two "houses" for certain provinces, scarcely more for the others and as yet amorphous. But, even more, it was a unity of action, a "corpus" of men harnessed to the same task, having comparable apostolic problems, confronting common difficulties. What then was a province for Ignatius? An administrative unit? Certainly. What does arithmetic matter? It is missionary experience that counts and for that, the communion of hearts and spirits, which can be obtained only by the presence of a companion in whom the essential quality is "to have always present the mentality of Father Ignatius" and to act according to his "way of proceeding".[15] One fact is significant: before any companion had set foot on the soil of England, before even anyone was so designated, Ignatius dreamed of establishing the "province of England":[16] the problems there would be novel and totally different from those of France, Italy and Germany.

Comparable to the Ignatian idea of a province was his idea of a provincial. We have already indicated that the first Fathers had all been chosen by Ignatius as provincials or as those made responsible for regions; even Bobadilla had performed these functions in Naples, although without the title. But the others, the newly arrived? How were they chosen? One little sentence by Polanco could well furnish us with an answer: Miron, Provincial of Portugal, he tells us, gave in the course of his visits, *exemplum professi Societatis nostrae* (the very prototype of the professed of the Society), and he made the same impression on the people as Xavier did in the Indies.[17] What is significant, especially if one compares this passage with others analogous to it, is that a provincial was to reproduce in his person and in his life something of the missionary ideal. That was not always without inconvenience: Ignatius had had to remind Xavier, the Provincial of the Indies, that he was to reside in his province, rather than enter Japan and China; and was not the crisis of the Indies between 1553 and 1556 partly attributable to the fact that the successors of Xavier, and Melchior Nuñez in particular, were missionaries of wide-ranging itineraries? On the contrary, Nobrega, in Brazil, better balanced his administrative responsibilities and his missionary fervor. Was not Ignatius himself inclined, in Europe, to give priority to missionary activity over administrative responsibilities? The case of Strada, the Provincial of Aragon, is revealing. François de Strada, born at Valladolid, joined the group of companions at scarcely twenty years of

---

[15] *Chron.* 6, p. 435.

[16] *Epist. ign.* 6, p. 713, n. 4455.

[17] *Chron.* 3, p. 412. This whole page describes the different qualities of the Provincial and ranks them in order of importance.

age, as early as 1539. Ignatius soon sent him to Siena as a companion of Broët and Rodríguez: the young man revealed exceptional talents for preaching; and he actually became one of the most celebrated "orators" of the Society of Jesus. Portugal, Spain and Italy quarrelled over him, and when it was a matter of gaining the sympathy of a prince or of a city or of appeasing the antipathies of a bishop, like Siliceo, Strada was the perfect choice for the mission. When in 1554, Ignatius at the suggestion of Nadal, divided Spain into three provinces, he named Strada Provincial of Aragon. A Provincial who had to "complete his studies in theology"[18] and who was traveling from city to city and even from region to region, in order to preach. Nadal was hardly in favor of this choice; Ignatius ignored the opposition. He expected to ward off the difficulties of this nomination by giving Strada first an assistant (John Baptist Barma) who would be in charge of the administration of the province and visits to the houses, then a travelling companion, selected from the theologians of Gandia, who would give him private theology lessons on the road. Barma, in this situation, felt rather ill-at-ease and Borgia believed it wise to warn him that he was to take charge of the province as "if he had to render account of it before God".[19] As for the private tutor of theology, he soon ceased giving his lessons; Strada was too busy "to apply himself seriously to his scholastic studies" and the assigned theologian, Father Balthasar Pignas, was too "necessary for confessions at Saragossa".[20] The case of Strada is very indicative. Once again, we surprise Ignatius paying more attention to the man than to the structure. For him, Strada was someone who had participated in the beginning and in the first deliberations of the Society of Jesus, had been with the first Fathers at the time when they chose their way and defined their spirit, before the great missionary dispersion; Ignatius knew Strada, Strada knew Ignatius; he had the *mens et modus Societatis*, moreover, he represented an apostolic "force" of the first order through his gifts of eloquence, his charisma, his accomplishments and activities. Let him have the title of Provincial, with the provision that he have an assistant who could assume the administrative work.

This manner of envisaging the relationship between men and jobs was

---

[18] Strada had pursued theological studies somewhat chaotically: first in Paris, in 1541; from there the war between the King of France and Charles V chased him to Louvain; finally, he went to Portugal where he completed his studies and was ordained a priest: the "completion of theological studies" after the priesthood, was frequent, even if one did not aspire to the degree of doctor of theology. Let's note that Strada had been professed since 1551.

[19] *Chron.* 4, pp. 482 and 596.

[20] *Chron.* 5, p. 379.

to lead Ignatius, when a situation became entangled in one location, to count more on people than on structures to untangle it. From this came the system of commissioners, visitors, superintendents, assistants and this strange plurality of offices and authority in the same place: we have given examples of it. Experience revealed that the procedure seemed to result more in inconveniences than in efficiency: undoubtedly, Ignatius credited his trusted men with more flexibility and virtues than human weakness possesses. Moreover, to certain of these commissioners or visitors he gave back the totality of his power, and even gave his signature as General on blank documents so as to legalize measures which they would take; that certainly casts a strong light on Ignatius' *ars gubernandi*.

The Authority–Obedience Relationship

Whatever might be the fundamental relationship, the essential structure of the Society of Jesus as a religious order, no one, provided he read the texts honestly, could be uncertain about.

Nor can it be denied that the companions of Paris-Venice had not accepted this structure with spontaneous enthusiasm, but evidently from a necessity to maintain unity of the *corpus Societatis*: it suffices to reveal the "Deliberation of the First Fathers" of 1539: they spent several weeks in deciding "to obey one among us".[21] They hesitated, and minutely weighed the pros and cons. Without difficulty, one understands this hesitation, not to say the repugnance, on the part of men who had tasted the fraternal appeal of free companionship, and the spiritual power of evangelical poverty. Love, poverty and freedom—what was to become of these precious qualities if obedience henceforth ruled their mutual relationships? Obedience had to appear to them in its turn as the guarantee, indeed, the new source of their union, in the missionary situation on all horizons which would henceforth be theirs, for them to renounce their marvelous experiences.[22] Once this change was effected, the companions respected their commitment.

[21] *Const.* 1, pp. 4–8.

[22] Ibid. pp. 6 and 7. This hesitation will manifest itself later, in 1549–1550, when it would be a matter of drafting the text of the *Constitutions*. It has been noticed with reason that between text "a" and text A there has often been a transposition in the order of presenting obedience and poverty, to the benefit of obedience. This change is especially perceptible in the chapters of part VI. One has wished to see therein the substitution of the canonical schema of the three vows for the genetic activity of Ignatian thought, a substitution for which Polanco would be responsible (French translation of the *Constitutions*, vol. 2, pp. 84–85). That would be to forget that it was the first Fathers and Ignatius himself, when Polanco was not in the Society, who agreed to put obedience as the basis of the mutual relations of the order.

When one considers the authority–obedience structure in the Society of Jesus, it is necessary to keep oneself from putting on the same plane the authority of the "Vicar of Christ on earth", with the obedience which is due him, and the authority–obedience within the order. One cannot insist enough on the fact that the former preceded the latter, that the companions decided to place themselves and were placed at the total disposition of the Pope *before* making themselves into a religious order by the vow of obedience "to one among us", that they considered obedience to the Pope as part of their *personal* reform, because it was imposed upon each baptized Christian, and especially on each cleric.[23] The Society of Jesus, if it had remained at the companionship level, would have had as law for its apostolic activity total and unconditional availability for pontifical missions. Obedience "to one among us" has a totally different meaning; one can even maintain that it has as its purpose the avoidance of the inconveniences (dispersions and rupture of companionship) that obedience to the Pope involved. The religious evolution of the companions in the course of the deliberations of 1539 is very important, in order to grasp the meaning of this authority–obedience structure.

From this interior obedience to the Society of Jesus, as a religious order, the first Fathers gave us a perfectly clear formula in the report of their deliberation:

> After numerous days had passed in hesitation regarding the resolution of our doubt, in weighing reasons which would seem more conclusive and more efficacious,[24] in fulfilling the usual exercises of prayer, meditation and reflection, we finally decided (*conclusimus*), with the help of God, not by majority of votes, but in unanimity: for us[25] it is more advantageous and more necessary to obey one among us, in order that we may better and more effectively achieve *our first desires* to accomplish in all things, the will of God, in order also that the integrity of the Society be better protected and finally, so that all that concerns us personally, spiritually as well as temporally, may be correctly regulated.

---

[23] From such proofs Cardinal Guidiccioni drew the argument for demonstrating the futility of founding the Society of Jesus. The echo of his objection is found again in the "Summa Instituti" (*Const.* 1, p. 17).

[24] *Gravioris momenti et efficaciores* . . . [and farther on] *expendientius, magis necessarium, melius et exactius* . . . *tutius*: all these comparatives signify a preferential, and hence free, choice; they correspond to the famous *magis* which characterizes the Ignatian mentality. The contrary choice was possible; it was in full conscience and freedom that the solution was achieved. Let us note that in the very beautiful doctrine of Vatican II on religious consecration this little sign "+" characterizes the religious life in contrast with the condition of the baptized. Cf. *Const.* 1, p. 7–8.

[25] The companions did not claim in any way that their choice be imposed on others: new witness of their total freedom of commitment.

They have obviously deliberated at length on each word in the text.

All the nuances of this choice would resound, whether in the correspondence of Ignatius, or in the *Constitutions*, or in the *ars gubernandi* of Ignatius: firmness certainly—rigorous firmness—of principle and structure;[26] but beyond obedience, penetrating it and transfiguring it there would have to be in the superior who gave the order and the inferior who received it, a common love of Jesus Christ, a reciprocal love among the companions: the act of authority and the act of obedience, according to Ignatius, were both acts of faith and of charity.

a) In the *Constitutions*—a single observation will explain the role of "the Superior" in adapting rules and regulations to the particular case of each companion, while mindful of the apostolic purpose and the communal bond of the group.[27] Ignatius saw in this role of the Superior more than a simple, human and spiritual wisdom: as early as the text "a" from 1549–1550, indicating "what can help to unite the companions spread throughout the world with their head"[28] Ignatius stated,

> The essential bond, simultaneously uniting the members among themselves and with their head, is the love of God our Lord. The Superior and the inferiors, in effect, if they are united[29] to the divine and sovereign Good, will be very easily united among themselves thanks to the unique love[30] which will expand and spread to one's neighbor and particularly *to the body of the Society*. It was thus that charity and in general every goodness[31] helped this mutual union, just as did total scorn for worldly interests which are often an occasion of distress for love of self, the principal enemy of this union[32].

Would it not suffice in this text, to substitute for the words "Superior" and "inferior" the word "companions", as a means to indicate the atmosphere of the Society of Jesus before and after 1539?

Moreover, when one speaks of the authority–obedience structure, it is indispensable to equate the words with the exact meaning they represent.

---

[26] To attribute this firmness to Polanco, this *primat* of obedience in the *corpus Societatis*, is to ignore the history of the Society prior to March 1547 (example: *Epist. ign.* 1, pp. 228–29, 687–93; 2, pp. 54–65, n. 52, 243, 295, etc.); it is to scorn the *ars gubernandi* of Xavier who never knew Polanco (cf. the return from the Indies of Anthony Gomez, Rector of Goa).

[27] *Mémorial* p. 272:

[28] *Const.*, VIII P.: in the French translation, vol. 2, p. 254 (text a) and vol. 1, p. 213 (definitive text).

[29] Definitive text: *very* united.

[30] Definitive text: (love) *which will descend from it* (and will spread).

[31] Definitive text: (goodness) and *every virtue which makes us walk in fidelity to the spirit* (they will help).

[32] Definitive text: (of the union) *and of universal good*.

If the obedience of a companion must be absolute, unconditional and extend on occasion as far as obedience despite objections, and if the *promptitudo oboedientiae*[33] was the mark of an authentic vocation of the Society of Jesus, to the point that disobeying members were considered as *membra putrida* of the *corpus Societatis*,[34] the relation was profoundly specified by the manner with which the *Constitutions* present authority. Authority has demanding obligations: the obligation of total information; the obligation of consultation and discussion not only with the customary counselors but with every person competent in the matter to be settled, the obligation of conversation—an in-depth spiritual conversation, which may be an exchange between consciences—with the concerned individual, in order to adjust as much as possible the order to his temperament and to his level of grace; the obligation to hold in deep regard, as an important sign of God, the opinion of the majority; and finally the obligation of prayer and choice in relation to conscience and to God. It is only if he respects these obligations that the superior can decide and legitimately give orders. The exercise of authority stipulated by the *Constitutions* is a highly spiritual act, as well as one of extreme human prudence: it is different from a purely administrative act.[35]

So much so that Ignatius dared place it at the level of Christ. He asked the one who obeyed to "keep before his eyes God our Creator and Lord, for whom one obeys, and to strive to act with a spirit of love and not with the disquiet which is born of fear".[36] But the one who orders, be it even the cook, he asks to command without false fear and in so doing to "show that he speaks as Christ to a man".[37] The act of authority, like the act of obedience, is justified only on the level of faith: that is to say with the firmness, but also with the prudence and the mutual respect for persons that they both demand.

b) In the Ignatian *praxis*—this *praxis* offers the same contrasts between firmness of principle and the flexibility for adaptations to persons. A statement of Câmara gives evidence that in the immediate entourage of Ignatius an atmosphere of obedience—blind obedience—reigned, and that was well known outside Rome: one of the motifs which pushed him to desire to come to Rome, he tells us, was that "I hoped to arrive at

---

[33] *Chron.* 3, p. 116.

[34] Ibid., 2, p. 430.

[35] An analysis of the legislation of the General Congregation would be, from this point of view, very enlightening: cf. all of part VIII of the *Constitutions*; and also numerous other passages which concern the powers of "the entire Society reunited in the General Congregation", according to the expression in use: n. 206, 554, 743, 779.

[36] *Constitutions*, P. VI, ch. I, n. 547.

[37] *Constitutions*, "General Examen", n. 85.

obedience from understanding, about which I heard so much said in the Society".[38] He was entirely satisfied, whether by his own experience or by the experience of others. Thanks to him, the daily *praxis* of Ignatius is well known to us: "Our Father strongly deplored and punished the lack of obedience not only in essential matters, . . . but also in every other matter;"[39] such was his constant attitude. And here are the nuances of it:

> Our Father was accustomed, in all that he could have others do with gentleness and without recourse to obedience, not to let obedience intervene; on the contrary, when he could have someone do something, not because the person had seen the wish of His Reverence, but because the individual did it of his own free will—that pleased Ignatius much more than if the individual did something because he had realized Ignatius' wish but without anyone's telling him to do so—that pleased him more than to have to give the order, finally, for the same reason, [it pleased Ignatius more] when the matter was ordered without its being under pain of obedience.[40]

With Ignatius, it was always fitting to seek, beyond the action itself, the spiritual view which caused it: "Our Father said one day: I very much desire general indifference, etc., in all; and thus, assuming that obedience and abnegation exist on the part of the subordinate, I am very willing to follow his inclinations":[41] those particular ones Ignatius considered as "his children and the true children of the Society".[42] There lies one of the keys for grasping the differences which we are going to establish in the behavior of Ignatius.

For he had some disconcerting behavior. When he designated someone for profession or the priesthood, he often allowed the interested party the responsibility for exercising this authorization immediately or waiting to choose the date and place and (if it concerned profession) the style of the ceremony, with the exception of the formula itself.[43] In 1545, he wrote to Simón Rodríguez of his great desire to see him in Rome, "but I will, for my part, leave it to your conscience": it was up to Rodríguez to judge the situation.[43] In 1548, Ribadeneyra was to study philosophy. Ignatius allowed him to choose among Valencia, Gandia, Sicily, Bologna, or even, if he wished, Padua.[44] In 1549, he proposed three mission areas to Bobadilla: *que haga á su plazer*.[45] Guzmán and Loarte entered the Society

---

[38] *Memorial*, n. 3.
[39] Ibid., n. 78–79.
[40] *Memorial*, n. 262.
[41] Ibid., n. 117.
[42] Ibid., n. 115.
[43] *Epist. ign.* 3. p. 85, n. 1236.
[44] *Epist. ign.* 2, p. 93, n. 322.
[45] "That he may do at his convenience", ibid. 2, p. 377, n. 634.

in 1552: he allowed them the choice of location: either Rome or Spain.[46] Examples abound of these cases in which Ignatius left the final decision to the "choice" of a subject whose obedience and total profound "indifference" he knew. This did not prevent him one bit from giving formal orders *ex virtute oboedientiae* to these same "trusted men", when he considered it advisable. He would do this, for example, with Borgia, on several occasions, notably in the matter of the vows (*vota Societatis*) of Princess Juana.[47] This art of giving alternate orders, counsels or freedom of choice, according to the circumstances and the spiritual condition of the subject, breaks down in the Rodríguez affair. Rest assured: this was not a Machiavellian game of "carrot-and-stick", it was a matter of leading each companion, at each instant, according to his actual dispositions of interior freedom.[48]

One chapter of the *Constitutions* summarizes all that can be said on the authority–obedience structure, as it was conceived by Ignatius: Chapter 3 of part VII, "Freedom in Displacements". The shortest, it is one of the most remarkable of the *Constitutions*.

> Those who live under obedience to the Society are not to intervene, either directly or indirectly, in the missions assigned them, whether they are sent by the Holy Father or by their Superior in the name of Christ our Lord. Nevertheless, when one is sent into an extensive country such as the Indies or other provinces, and no particular field of action is specifically assigned, one may remain more or less in one place or in another, and when, one has *considered* everything, and when the will is *indifferent* and one has offered *prayer*, to go wherever one judges it *most useful* for the glory of God our Lord.
>
> It stands to reason that, without prejudice of primary and sovereign obedience due to the Holy Father, the Superior in these kinds of missions will be able to direct the subject on one point more than on another as he will feel the opportunity in the Lord.
>
> Wherever he finds himself, if no procedure has been assigned him, for example, teaching or preaching, the subject will be able to utilize that which he deems *the most advisable among those methods used by the Society*, and which have been indicated in the fourth principal part and will be in the following chapter. Similarly, he will avoid what is prescribed to be avoided, for a greater divine service.[49]

---

[46] *Chron.* 2, pp. 420–21.

[47] Ibid., 5, p. 47.

[48] A passage of Câmara on the "freedom" which Ignatius wanted the immediate "Superiors" to enjoy in conjunction with indirect Superior is so significant that it appears a major item in the authority–obedience dossier. Cf. *Mémorial*, n. 269, 270, 271; and supra pp. 87 sqq.

[49] *Constitutions* ("Christus" collection), vol. 1, pp. 201–2. It is almost a repetition of the

The text, in itself, constitutes an abbreviated chart of the mission and presents the authority–obedience–initiative structure in its spiritual truth.

The Defense Tactic: Testimonies

From its beginning the Society of Jesus knew opposition and criticism; it was attacked and often calumniated. What was the defense tactic utilized by Ignatius in these circumstances? He hardly counted on the tribunals for doing this, unless he was denounced or some companion was denounced by the Inquisition. No more did he like regular litigation, and he did not resort to wrangling when he could do otherwise. His tactic in such situations was still of a providential, and hence supernatural, order: he strove—with great diligence and meticulousness—to gather "testimonies": from princes and bishops with whom the companions worked or had worked, he asked not pleading arguments, nor petitions to passion, but factual reports: here is what we have seen, this is what we have confirmed, this is what the companions have done in the area, through the power of God (the "Verbi Dei energia", the "Dextera Excelsi"). Such an attitude goes along with Ignatius' conviction that all the good which the Society did it owed to the Lord and that it was also up to the Lord if he judged it appropriate to make the persecution cease or be prolonged: while he thus gathered testimony, Ignatius had the Society offer prayers.

It was through this defense tactic that as early as 1540, Ignatius had warded off an unfavorable arbitration by Cardinal Guidiccioni, which risked stopping the bull founding the Society of Jesus.

It is the same tactic which he used in 1554 to counterbalance in the mind of the viceroy of Aragon the attacks of the Archbishop of Toledo,[50] and especially, in the matter of the decree which the Parisian faculty of theology submitted against the Institute of the Society, on December 1, 1554.[51] Two counterstrokes were open to Ignatius: the first, recourse to the Pope, was direct but would not fail to open a painful conflict; it was that much more tempting because the decree, through the Society, questioned the very authority of the Apostolic See;[52] some friends of

---

text "a" of 1549–1550, ibid., vol. 2, p. 246. From our point of view, the original text was even more sober and terse; above all it contained one sentence which serves our purpose: in place of the second paragraph of the definitive text, one reads: "To discern that, one will use the means that the Superior will have sanctioned to send one individual to this place or that duty rather than to another." The flow of the text was more continuous and more in conformity with the outpouring of the thought. The emphasis is ours.

[50] Chron. 4, pp. 369–70.
[51] Ibid. 4, pp. 324–30.
[52] Chron. 4, pp. 324–30.

Broët himself, the one responsible for the Parisian group, strongly advised this procedure. Ignatius, on the contrary, preferred the second, much longer, more risky, but more respectful of God's initiatives and the dignity of the Faculty of theology; he would gather favorable testimonies from all the regions of the world where the companions had worked and send them to those responsible for the decree, to the Archbishop of Paris, and to the King himself.[53] Dr. Olave and Polanco also drafted a response.[54] This affair, which would have an inauspicious influence on the history of the Society, at least had the merit of focusing light on an important aspect of the *ars gubernandi* of Ignatius of Loyola.

This attitude of Ignatius went beyond the cases where he had to defend himself or defend the Society. It became associated with whatever was more general and more essential in Ignatius' apostolic activity: to act as an apostle, and companion of Christ, that was first and above all other activity, to manifest the power and goodness of God our Lord. The place, the situation, the case was of little importance! It was to create around oneself a certain atmosphere of grace, to spread everywhere the *bonus odor Christi*. Ignatius has often been reproached, as has the first generation of Jesuits, for their sense of "publicity": for example, the "publicity letters" or "edifying letters" or certain spectacular ceremonies or public meetings with many invitations; it is difficult to clear certain of Ignatius' companions from this reproach—Bobadilla to name but one. It seems that "a good reputation", primarily spiritual but also human, was for Ignatius a basic condition for working among men, helping them to be converted, to be saved, and to lead them in the pursuit of Christ. A basic way, but not an indispensable one. Persecution, calumnies, condemnations occurred: in them also "the instrument of God" could bear witness,[55] that of patience, courage, humility and faith.

---

[53] More than fifty of these testimonies are preserved. Cf. *Epist. ign.* 12, pp. 525–614. Some princes or cities refused to draft their testimonies, for fear of making the Parisian Decree known in their area.

[54] Ibid. 12, pp. 614–29; the correspondence of the time very often calls to mind this affair.

[55] 2 Cor 6: 4–11.

CHAPTER V

THE IMMOBILE MISSIONARY

It will be wise, no doubt, at the end of this study—both too long and too brief—of the ars gubernandi of Ignatius of Loyola, to transport ourselves mentally into those little rooms of the house of La Strada, and to surprise the Superior General of the Society of Jesus in the act of living one of his days.

The contrast is striking: in Rome and outside of Rome, an explosion of life, the vitality of the companions, expansion and conquest; here, in this tiny apartment, a man who seldom leaves the house, at least in the last years, and who nevertheless gives life to this vast movement of evangelization: The immobile missionary.

It would suffice to follow the portrait of the General as sketched in the *Constitutions*[1] in order to picture Ignatius governing the Society of Jesus. Let us rather make a sort of cross-section in this existence to grasp the different levels of occupations and concerns.

It is a simple man who lives here; there is a tiny room where he works and sleeps; he takes his meals in a neighboring room, very often he has as guests a few companions from whom he likes to get advice on current concerns, or, more rarely, "people from outside"; whoever the guests may be, the meal is frugal;[2] a third room serves him as a chapel: here he celebrates Mass or merely attends, according to the physician's orders;[3] in the fourth room sleeps the Brother who is at his service.[4] A modest life, poor without outward glamor, without pretense, and monotonous.

What then fills the days of this companion upon whose failing body the companions have imposed the heavy burden of presiding over the destiny of the young and still chaotic Society of Jesus?

I. THE PRAYER OF SPIRITUAL GOVERNMENT

First and foremost, he *prays*. This prayer one could call the prayer of spiritual government. He literally carries before God the *Corpus Societatis*; he considers himself a "mediator" between the "Source of all good" and the entire order.

---

[1] P. IX, ch. II.

[2] See the picturesque description of the meals and menus in the *Mémorial*, n. 184–194.

[3] Ibid., n. 179, 183, 194.

[4] Regarding the distribution of these little rooms, see our *Chroniques saint Ignace de Loyola*, p. 262.

The first of the qualities which one must expect from the Superior General is a close union with God our Lord, and a great familiarity with Him in prayer and in all activities, so that, from God, as the Source of all good, he obtains so much the better an abundant participation in his gifts and his graces for all the body of the Society, as well as great value and efficacy for all the methods which are used to help souls.[5]

This prescription of the *Constitutions* is merely the projection of the *praxis* of Ignatius. Of the intensity of his personal prayer, of the continuity of his union with God, testimonies abound. "It is a remarkable thing", notes Câmara, "his facility for uniting himself to God through prayer. I must recall how many times I found him in his chapel in such devotion that one could see it simply by his face." In his chapel? Not only in his chapel, "it is continually that this expression can be seen on his face".[6] And Câmara remarks, "The interior devotion of our Father was manifested and continually made itself recognized through great peace, tranquility and the external expression of his face."[7]

What did it mean for Ignatius "to carry the Society before God in his prayer"? Can we pierce his secret? It seems that this prayer concerned the most important missionary preoccupations, as well as the most specific cases of the companions. When he mobilized the prayer of all the Society for this or that serious intention of the Church, for example, as we have seen: the conversion of Germany, the reconversion of England, or the evangelization of the Indies, Brazil, or the Congo, there is no doubt that he was the first to enter into this immense activity of supplication. However, one can be even more precise: The Vicar of Christ on earth, the Pope, was for Ignatius not only the one who sent people on missions, he was also the one who carried on earth the heavy responsibility of the Church: "The Father has the custom of praying every day for the Pope; now that this one [Julius III] is ill, he does so twice daily, and always with tears."[8] When Julius III died, Ignatius prayed for the election of his successor, and, when Marcellus II himself became very ill, Ignatius decided that two Fathers should depart on pilgrimage, on foot and begging, to Loreto, and had them chosen by the community. He would have sent more of them if the physician, "fearing that they would fall ill from the great heat", had not opposed the idea: and Ignatius "commuted these pilgrimages to stations and visits at the *Scala Santa*."[9] In this prayer for the Pope, the reform of the Church held the first place. As for

[5] *Const.*, P. IX ch. II, n. 723.
[6] *Mémorial*, n. 175. See also n. 179.
[7] Ibid., n. 180.
[8] Ibid., n. 301.
[9] Ibid., n. 339.

Ignatius' prayer for the companions, it takes all the forms that concrete circumstance demand: correspondence and the *Memorial* of Câmara furnish the proof of that: temptations of the companions, decisions on vocations, expulsions, departures, labors, illnesses and captivities; nothing happened to anyone that the Father, if he learned of it, did not make the object of a prayer.

Through his own prayer Ignatius prayed for the Society itself about which he was concerned. Not that he wished to impose a uniform prayer on all: he knew too well how varied are the calls to God. However, he was concerned that this diversity not become a deformation or a deviation. Borgia and Oviedo were not the only ones to sense within themselves a propensity for long prayers and excess penances which did not to him seem suitable for the life of a companion; opposed to them, there were those who neglected prayer in preference for study or action. Throughout his own spiritual experience, Ignatius strove to find and maintain the difficult balance which is expressed in the *Constitutions*. Nadal, upon his return from Spain in 1554, learned this at his own expense: at the time of his visit, he had heard some of the companions complain of the little time that was allotted in the Society for prayer (one hour each day), he let himself "be swayed that this request was valid" and proposed it to Ignatius. "Our Father was confined to his bed," reports Câmara, "and I found myself alone with both. He responded on this point with an expression and words showing such displeasure and such extraordinarily strong feeling that I was nonplussed by it." The unfortunate visitor received a "strong penance". Ignatius concluded: "A man truly mortified would find a quarter of an hour sufficient to unite himself to God in prayer."[10] This was because he feared nothing so much as the "illusions" which often accompany "long prayers".[11]

Nonetheless, the same man who manifested "such displeasure", when Nadal proposed to him to extend the time of prayer to an hour and one-half, counseled and required, as an essential condition of the apostolic life and its success, a "continual union with God".

II. "ONE AMONG US WHOM THE OTHERS WILL OBEY"

Ignatius was aware of being the personal and living link of the *corpus Societatis*, from the deliberation of 1539, and he remained aware that, if the companions were resolved to bind themselves together by the vow of obedience, it was in order to remain united despite dispersion so as to

[10] *Mémorial*, n. 196.
[11] Ibid. and n. 256.

"realize better and more efficaciously their first desires, which were to accomplish the will of God in all things" so that "the Society might more surely remain faithful to itself" and "in order to provide wisely for the spiritual and temporal needs of all the companions". In these tasks Ignatius did not fail; he gave himself entirely to them, but without forgetting the time prior to 1539, when all among the companions was friendship, unanimity and profound agreement of hearts and souls. That "spirit" which then animated the companions, he strove to direct into the *"corpus Societatis"*, to keep it alive and intact from day to day, through the hazards of the new conditions of life. His great concern was to safeguard and develop in all this undefinable and, at the same time, demanding reality: *Mens et modus Societatis*.

Mens et modus Societatis; this expression encompasses the entire existence of the companions. There was a certain way of dressing, eating or even of traveling (as pilgrims and mendicants), but there was also a choice of ministries[12] (the *ministeria assueta*), a way of organizing a college,[13] a way of establishing oneself in a city or region (the *humble beginnings*), a way of enduring trials and surmounting obstacles, a way of acting with *nobiles* and *plebeii*, a way of welcoming brothers in transit, of governing a house and even of participating in a session of the Council of Trent,[14] or of pronouncing one's vows. It was a form of life (*forma vivendi*)[15] which was defined as much by what it affirmed as by what it rejected;[16] it was an original *modo del proceder*, a certain style which had to be maintained despite the diversity of temperaments and occupations in the houses and in the missions, whether one lived alone or in community.

To create or maintain this *mens et modus Societatis* correspondence was obviously very useful; in some seven thousand letters, one perceived how Ignatius took things, treated them in each case and resolved the problems. Likewise, with the first Fathers; actually, their *mens* coincided with the *mens Ignatii*: all was to be done *juxta mentem Ignatii*.[17]

Specifically, because of the vague intangibility of the formula, the least detail of life became significant: the *jumenta* of the trips, the "corrector" of the colleges, the way of begging for the poor and for oneself, the habit, the beard, the gait and the facial expression. All this minutiae which we discover in the letters and regulations of Ignatius, not without

---

[12] Even on mission: *Chron.* 4, p. 661.

[13] Ibid. 3, p. 111.

[14] *Epist. Salm.* 1, pp. 22 to 30, n. 8, 9, 10.

[15] *Epist. ign.* 1, pp. 451–52, n. 149.

[16] For example, "the hermitage" of Borgia (*Chron.* 5, p. 528), or even certain matters: *Epist. ign.* 6, p. 245, n. 4109.

[17] *Chron.* 6, p. 661; 6, pp. 737 and 741; 4, p. 598; 2, p. 586; 6, p. 346; 4, p. 381.

some amazement, and which sometimes can be disconcerting, have their explanation in a very spiritual concern: they were for him the sign of poverty, prudence, humility, or other interior virtues of the true companion.

Thus, more and more, the *Societas romana*, i.e., practically the Roman community of La Strada, took on, in the eyes of other provinces, exemplary value. Everyone wanted to come there to be trained, to see it function and to live there, and to welcome rectors or Provincials who knew it well. Ignatius liked to send into the houses which were being founded someone who had lived in Rome, even if he was not to be a superior there.[18] When Câmara, after his years spent at La Strada, returned to Portugal, he experienced nostalgia for the *Societas romana*,[19] but he consoled himself by introducing everywhere the *romanae consuetudines* (Roman customs).[20] Here or there some resistance was undoubtedly manifested, for example in Flanders,[21] where they wanted more unity than uniformity; but poor Adriani, who thus dared to free himself, was formally excluded from the provincial's post by Ribadeneyra: the commissioner said that he did not govern, that he did not even do missionary work *juxta mentem Societatis*.

As early as 1553 the formula was created: "Nothing new must be done nor anything foreign to the Society's manner of doing things" (*nihil novum aut inusitatum Societati faciendum*).[22]

It is undeniable that, viewed from the distance of time, this fervor, with its negative side and a certain rigorous quality, astounds us. It is again Câmara who helps us place ourselves in the exact context. When he confides to us the two motives which prodded him: "from [his] entrance into the Society" to "enjoyment of the view and conversation of our Father Ignatius of Loyola, whom our Lord gave us as an exemplar and leader of this mystical body of which we are all members". He wrote: "The second motive was the sovereign opinion which I had conceived of the personal sanctity of the Father, not only from all that those who had conversed with him had told us, but also from that great perfection which one had noted at that time in the Society and in his whole manner of proceeding."[23]

It was Ignatius in those years who made the unity of the Society of Jesus visible. In electing him General, the first Fathers had sought him

[18] *Chron.* 5, p. 41.
[19] Ibid. 6, p. 742.
[20] Ibid. 6, pp. 582, 641, 720, 732, 737, 739, 741, 750, etc.
[21] Ibid. 6, pp. 434–35.
[22] Ibid. 3, p. 165.
[23] *Mémorial*, n. 3.

and had wanted him. Let us recall the explanations of Salmeron, Codure and Xavier at the moment of the election of the General.[24]

Through the authority which he had in his capacity as General, Ignatius only continued the work of spiritual formation which he had previously achieved among the companions of Paris and Venice.

III. ONE AMONG US CHARGED WITH DRAFTING THE CONSTITUTIONS

In this long and difficult work, Ignatius considered himself "charged with the mission" by the Pope, and "delegated" by the companions. The "rooms" of La Strada were the location for numerous prayers, reflections, conversations and discussions among Ignatius, Polanco and still others. However, in addition to this intellectual and spiritual work, the *Memorial* of Câmara lets us perceive a more familiar and at the same time more intimate aspect of this creative effort which Ignatius put forth: to establish at the house of La Strada (on the inside or outside in Rome) this *Societas romana* which could serve as an example, a prototype for the *tota Societas*. "I remember my astonishment, the first time that I read the *Constitutions* a little before departing for Portugal," notes Câmara, "for it seemed to me in reading them, that I found there nothing more than a painting of our Fathers".[25]

IV. THE MASTER OF NOVICES AT LA STRADA

Among the occupations of Ignatius, not the least heavy was the training of novices. The *Memorial* of Câmara is filled with this Ignatian activity: if in the last years Ignatius had sought help in this duty,[26] he nevertheless kept the prime responsibility. The novitiate did not diminish: in addition to the novices from all over Italy, he received also the majority of those from the whole Society, since novitiates were not established in the provinces; and even then, many, after having their novitiate locally, went off to "perfect" their training near "Father Ignatius".[27] So much so that there were always candidates waiting and

---

[24] Cf. the above mentioned, pp. 147–48 and *Epist. Salm.* 1, p. 1; *Epist. Broëti*, p. 418, n. 4; *Epist. Xav.* 1, p. 26.

[25] Mémorial, n. 98. This note is precious: even before reading them, Câmara *lived* the *Constitutions* by seeing how Ignatius lived. This "experience" confirms again this link between the life of the Society and the letter of the *Constitutions*, which seems to us one of the most characteristic aspects of the *meaning* of the *Constitutions*.

[26] *Mémorial*, n. 82–83; Fr. Cornelius Wischaven, a Fleming.

[27] See the index of the *Chroniques saint Ignace de Loyola*, under the entries "Novice" and "Noviciate".

when a "colony" departed for some college, the places were soon taken by other novices. Ignatius even had to forbid everyone from sending anyone to the novitiate of Rome without his previous authorization.[28] If it is correct that the sojourn of novices at La Strada did not always last two years (especially in the first years), in order to measure the burden of Ignatius it is necessary to remember that, from the beginning, *the* probation included several probations, among which were the Spiritual Exercises: even if Ignatius was assisted by some trusted Father, he assumed the greatest part of this ministry himself.

V. THE COMPANION AMONG COMPANIONS

A remarkable trait in Ignatius' personality as General of the Society, was that he "did missionary work" in Rome just as the other companions did missionary work elsewhere. "Missionary work" is the appropriate expression: in Ignatius' eyes, it was very much a question of a pontifical "mission". As early as May of 1538, the companions had received permission from Cardinal John Vincent Carafa, governor of the Papal States, to preach and hear confessions.[29] and they had worked effectively in the different churches of Rome. However, after the "oblation" of November 1538, it was the Pope himself who had assigned Rome to them as the first field of missionary activity: they were to preach and hear confessions there, but also to teach catechism to children. The companions soon dispersed into other areas of Christianity; Ignatius saw that the "Roman mission" continued: Rome, more than any other place, had need of conversion and reform. Ignatius set himself rigorously to the job, with the companions who had not yet departed, and the recruits who were awaiting admission into the order or who, little by little, were becoming absorbed into it. The house of La Strada very quickly became a veritable apostolic center.

Certainly, the companions were not alone working in the *vinea romana*. For a quarter of a century, there were "The Oratory of Divine Love" of Ettore Vernaza, the founder of so many hospitals in Italy, the Theatines of Gian Pietro Carafa and Cajetan de Thiene, the confraternity of the Blessed Sacrament of Minerva, the Mount of Piety of Brother Giovanni da Calvi, the works of Philip Neri and still other efforts—all of which gave evidence of this surge of Christian souls in the face of religious misery in the metropolis of the Catholic world. Ignatius modestly took his place in the enormous effort of reform and charity.

[28] Example: *Epist. ign.* 1, p. 625, n. 211; or *Chron.* 3, pp. 198 and 215.
[29] The Pope was then in Nice to attempt a reconciliation between the King of France and the Emperor.

The first work which benefited from his apostolic zeal was the help to abandoned children: they were numerous, boys and girls, left in the streets of Rome, victims of wars, epidemics and famines which ravaged the states of the Church during the pontificate of Clement VII. The companions were not yet in Rome, when charitable hearts, like Gian Pietro Carafa's, had attempted to save these miserable children. As soon as Ignatius arrived in Rome, he became interested in this undertaking; he strove to create a stable organization to develop this charitable movement: on February 7, 1541, Paul III published the bull *Altitudo*, which confirmed the confraternity for orphans; Ignatius was no stranger to this pontifical act.[30]

His interest very soon focused on the problem of Jews living in Rome: they were relegated to their ghettoes and generally scorned: people were hardly concerned with their dignity as men and as sons of Israel. Ignatius did not see things in this way: he did not fear to state, Ribadeneyra tells us, his respect for the race which Christ had chosen for his temporal birth; did not Jesus even declare that he had considered it a special grace to belong to it by blood?[31] So from the first months of 1541, and perhaps before that, he worked actively with catechumens and neophytes who were Jews. The time was favorable: Paul III had just modified the attitude of the Holy See regarding the Jews of Rome, but nothing definite had yet been done. In the little house of La Strada, Ignatius began to welcome Jews desiring to become better acquainted with Christianity: he received them there, welcomed them, instructed them himself or had them instructed by one of his own members, until they were ready for baptism, if their study lead them to desire it. He wished to do more: it was necessary that a sort of statute of conversion be instituted, so that, for example, new Christians would no longer be obliged to renounce their patrimony, and Ignatius obtained from the Pope the brief *Cupientes judaeos* (March 21, 1542) which he uses himself in Rome and sent to the companions who worked throughout Italy. The new legislation stimulated and facilitated conversions; soon the house of La Strada, where novices gathered from all over, became too small. Thanks to Margaret of Austria and some other benefactors, a house was rented for the catechumens (1542). On February 19, 1543, was published the bull *Illius qui pro dominici*, which created a double hospice—one for men, the other for women—for Jews and other infidels (especially the Moslems) of no

[30] Cf. the letter from Laynez, in *Font. narr.* 1, p. 127.
[31] Pedro RIBADENEYRA, "Dichos y hechos de N.P. Ignacio" (*Scripta* 1, pp. 398–399) and "De prognatis genere hebraeorum Societatis aditu non excludendis" (cf. *Ribad. Mon.* 2, p. 375).

matter what nation, who were desirous of embracing the Catholic faith: this house of catechumens was called the hospice of St. Jean-del-Mercato from the church of its site; Ignatius continued to occupy himself on the spiritual level with the work and begged alms for it. This apostolate later caused him a few problems,[32] but it also brought about numerous similar works in the big cities of Italy.

While busying himself with Jewish or Moslem catechumens, Ignatius participated actively with his companions in the battle against prostitution. This "blight of the metropolis of the Catholic world"[33] was an apostolic problem but also a social problem. The prostitutes, whether they were "honored courtesans" or "fallen women", converged on Rome from all the cities of Italy, France, Germany, England, Spain, Greece, etc. Their attempts at or desires of conversion always ran into the near impossibility of subsequently finding lodgings and the wherewithal to live. There existed many monasteries of "converted women", but not all envisaged the religious life. Then what marriage could be arranged without dowry and without property? What shelter should be established for them? Ignatius attacked the problem head-on: he procured a shelter for prostitutes who were disposed to end their unfortunate way of life, whether they were free or married, and whether or not they had any intention of entering the religious life. Moreover, their social reclassification would be provided in the best way possible. Such was the origin of the "House of St. Martha": Ignatius assembled, without too much difficulty, some people to sponsor the new work. However, alms did not flow in: it was then that he made a spectacular gesture: he ordered Codacio, his agent, to sell some marble antiques[34] which had been discovered in the excavation of the soil for the future church of La Strada and he devoted these one hundred gold pieces to the burgeoning work. "There was no one who wanted to be the first. Let them follow me and I shall be the first." Poor Codacio: the community was then in great need of money. A confraternity was established, in accordance with the custom of the times; by the papal bull of February 16, 1543, it took the name of the "Society of St. Mary of Grace"; in fact, it was spoken of more familiarly as the "House of St. Martha". Its statutes were a model of the type and served for other foundations, even outside Italy. For the good progress of the work, Ignatius and his best

---

[32] Cf. T. VENTURI, *Storia*, 4, pp. 157–58. For the history of these first works of Ignatius in Rome, Tacchi Venturi remains the best guide, vol. 4, chapters 5 and 6: writing the story of the Assistancy of Italy, the author enters into the details of all these foundations.

[33] T. VENTURI, op. cit., 4, p. 161.

[34] There were elements of the celebrated portico *Hecatostylon* of Pompei: cf. ibid. 4, p. 164 and n. 3.

companions in Rome brought to it not only their spiritual assistance but also material aid which weighed heavily on the indebtedness of the house of the professed.

Like the houses of the catechumens, St. Martha's House brought Ignatius and the companions calumnies and persecutions. One of the most important members of the confraternity, the Francisan Doctor Valentino Barbaran changed one fine day from a friend into a violent enemy (1546), and let Ignatius know that he would have all the religious of the Society who existed from Perpignan to Seville burned alive. Ignatius had the reply sent to him, "and as for me, I desire that he and all his friends and acquaintances, not only between Seville and Perpignan, but in the entire world, be burned with the fire of the Holy Spirit."[35] The attack of Barbaran was cut short. However, in the same year another affair obliged Ignatius to demand a judgment in good and due form, for the honor of the Society was involved: Mathias Gerardo de San Cassiano, Master General and Commissioner of pontifical posts, was known as a great friend of the companions. Nevertheless, one day his mistress, with whom he was madly in love, was converted. Mathias, enraged, allowed himself to indulge in the vilest insults and calumnies against the companions and particularly against Ignatius, who had aided the sinner in changing the way she lived; the Fathers no longer dared show themselves in public or exercise their ministry. Paul III was made aware of the matter; but Mathias had solid support within and around the Vatican. A legal proceeding was, however, undertaken; Mathias tried at first to beg off, then to lessen the consequences of his condemnation. Ignatius held fast, he demanded that the judgment be made public, as was the custom in such cases. Let us add to the credit of the Master of posts, that a few years later he recognized his errors and strove to recapture Ignatius' friendship.

In addition to the work of Saint Martha, one must consider another which was dear to Ignatius. The name of it is almost untranslatable: it concerned the *Compagnia delle Virgini Miserabili de Santa Catarina della Rosa di Roma*: in the houses of courtesans lived little girls who, very young, were given their turn at prostitution. From 1546, Ignatius worked at finding a solution to this social scourge. His plan consisted of withdrawing these children from the surroundings where they lived and rearing them in houses created for them by the Pope: the monastery of Santa Catarina della Rosa was the prototype, and a confraternity of laity was provided to sponsor and direct it. The bull did not appear until after the death of Ignatius; but without waiting, Ignatius and his companions

[35] Ibid. 4, pp. 176–77.

devoted themselves to this work which seemed "fundamental" to them. Through vicissitudes and inevitable changes, it still exists in our day, after having served as a model for other foundations.

In 1547, the charity of Ignatius prodded him to establish, in Rome, a type of association, which, in truth, already existed in certain other Italian cities. It was concerned with saving people from indigence with both discretion and delicacy. These were people who had previously known good fortune, but who, for diverse reasons, had fallen into a poverty which they dared not admit. For these "ashamed poor" Ignatius created the Archconfraternity of the Twelve Apostles (from the name of the church where it was located). The work prospered and still exists after four centuries.

In Ignatius' fervor for works of charity, one must seek without doubt the explanation, and, rather than excuse it, the justification for the debts which weighed, during his life, on the finances of La Strada.

Two "works" to which Ignatius attached himself with his customary tenacity are disconcerting to our present-day mentality. He caused the celebrated decretal *Cum infirmitas* of Innocent III[36] to be put back into effect: it obliged physicians first to provide for the spiritual health of the ill at the bedside to which they were called, before caring for them: if a sick person refused confession, the physician was to refuse him services. It was inevitable that such a decree would encounter resistance on the part of practitioners and in effect, it was hardly ever observed. Ignatius did everything to have it put back in force; the physicians protested. Ignatius asked that the question be submitted to a certain number of ecclesiastics of incontestable knowledge and virtue: some answers suggested a mitigation of the decretal, but all approved the Ignatian initiative. It remained to obtain the ordinance of the Sacred Penitentiary: Ignatius worked ardently, close to the Pope; it appeared on May 30, 1543.[37] Without making a judgment here on this Ignatian behavior, let us at least place it in context of its long history: promulgated in 1215, this decretal was still a means of excommunication in 1725, under Benedict XIII; and in the interim, several popes insisted that it be applied.

Another stand taken by Ignatius surprises us still more: it concerned his active adherence to the establishment of the Inquisition in Rome and in the Pontifical States. He was certainly not the instigator of the bull *Licet ab initio* of July 21, 1542, but he was pleased with it.[38] Let us not

---

[36] Canon 22 of the Fourth Lateran Council.

[37] Cf. *Epist. ign.* 1, pp. 263–69, n. 67 *bis*, 68, 69; cf. "Sumarium hispanicum Polanci", n. 81 and "Summarium italianum Polanci", n. 22 (*Font. narr.* 1, pp. 199 and 273).

[38] *Epist. ign.* 1, pp. 216–20, n. 48, letter of July 28, 1542 to Rodríguez, seven days after the publication of the bull.

conclude too quickly from this Ignatian conduct that he approved of the Inquisition without reservations, whatever its form: when in 1554–1555, King John III proposed to entrust the Portuguese Inquisition to the Society, Ignatius blamed the companions of Portugal for being too inclined to take on this responsibility, ordered them to put off a decision until he had made his own decision known, assembled a commission of six Fathers to study the question, and resolved, only with reservations, to accept the proposal of John III; again it seems that the difficulties of the Society with the Inquisition in Spain were not unrelated to this acceptance.[39] Ignatius shared, in fact, the opinion of Laynez: he did not contest this establishment of the Church of the times; he was aware of it and without doubt regretted the necessity for it in the objective context of the Reformation. That did not mean that he approved of all the methods, and he remained firm in whatever concerned the vocation of the Society itself: "this vocation is to help souls through the way of humility and hence it did not seem good to him that the Inquisition be accepted."[40]

Thus, while doing missionary work in Rome, Ignatius was heedful of what was happening to other areas of the Church. He had a very strong feeling that what he was creating in Rome and the *modus et mens* which he used to do so were having their repercussions in the provinces of the Society: that it was a matter of the atmosphere which reigned at La Strada, of the Roman and German Colleges, of the training of novices, of the prison apostolates, of the activities for the poor, of the *ministeria assueta*, confessions, communions, sermons, catechesis; everything, whether he wished it or not, assumed a value of example for the entire Society. Ignatius was aware that what was done "to reform" Rome would have influence on the reform of the universal Church.

From Rome, this "immobile missionary" went out, to our knowledge, five times: between 1538 and 1552; and these trips are symbolic: the first time, it was during Easter of 1538 to give the Spiritual Exercises at Monte Cassino, to Dr. Ortiz. The second, in August of 1538, occurred when he was welcomed by Paul III at Frascati and pleaded with the Pontiff the cause of the companions who were being persecuted and calumniated in Rome. The third time, in September, 1545, he went to Montefiascone to discuss with the Pope the serious matters of the Inquisition's introduction into Portugal. The fourth time, in October, 1548, he went to Tivoli to arbitrate the disagreement between the city and the Castel Madama. Finally, the fifth time, in November 1552, he went to Alvito to attempt the reconciliation of Joan of Aragon and her

---

[39] *Mémorial*, n. 354, 368, 380, 382.
[40] Ibid., n. 368. Cf. the position of Laynez, n. 382.

husband Ascanio Colonna. On the way, he usually did missionary work, preached, heard confessions, catechised . . . and it was on foot that he traveled. To complete this picture we should note that he "volunteered" three times to leave Rome: when in 1546 John III asked the Society to take charge of the Ethiopian mission, Ignatius volunteered himself, should the other companions decline;[41] in 1554, he envisaged departing for Africa and ending his life "among the barbarous nations";[42] finally, in January of 1555, he planned to go to Loreto as a pilgrim, on foot and begging: the death of Julius III, then that of Marcellus II, prevented his doing so.[43]

Such are the most significant aspects of Ignatius' *ars gubernandi*: the examples we have chosen do not exhaust the immense subject. At least they throw light on the prodigious activity of this man who was beyond his fifties, and whom illness frequently kept in his room. A fire devoured him, a power emanated from him and spread among the companions first and then into all those who had dealings with him. He was a great motivator of men; a pioneer ready to become enthusiastic about every generous idea and every bold project, for even the smallest cause, if God our Lord was concerned. In him the tremendous misery and generosity of his time were blended. The man was of a human and spiritual dimension which surpassed the common measure: he was born for the missions.

Thus, the question which always arises with the passage of an exceptional being, and particularly of a saint among men, arises even more acutely regarding Ignatius—and today more disturbingly than ever. From this light which dazzled our earth for a short time, would there not remain a bit of golden dust which in the course of centuries might dissolve, then fade, and one day finally vanish? Does God retain the prerogative to give each age the saint which befits it? Or do certain ones have the privilege of carrying to the world a message which endures?

---

[41] *Chron.* 1, p. 171; and *Epist. ign.* 1, p. 429, n. 140.
[42] *Epist. ign.* 6, p. 189, n. 4073.
[43] Ibid. 8, p. 616, n. 5304.

PART FIVE

MENTALITY, MYSTIQUE, MISSION, MESSAGE

CHAPTER I

THE MENTALITY OF IGNATIUS OF LOYOLA

In striving to penetrate the mentality of Ignatius of Loyola, Superior General of the Society of Jesus, have we not darkened, rather than lightened, the mystery with which this strange personality is enveloped? Throughout these sixteen years during which we have attempted to follow him, has he not appeared still more disconcerting to us than during the years of Manresa, Jerusalem, Alcalá, Paris and Venice? This is the moment of trying to recreate the unity of his personality. In the account of his life which he gave to Gonçalves da Câmara, he called himself "the pilgrim". Let us enter into his way of thinking in order to pose the fundamental question of this chapter: between the "pilgrim" and the "General of the Society of Jesus", was there continuity or discontinuity? Was it really the same man who here roamed at random, asking on the "Way" the thrill of long prayers, the joy of providential encounters, and then immobilized himself into a punctilious adminis-trator—the same man who asserted himself on every occasion, enamored of total Christian freedom and then legislated, created rules and even minutely detailed regulations, and distributed penances—also the same man who formerly quarreled openly with money, its property, its litigation, its security, and then changed into a man of business, filled his correspondence with requests, questions of inheritance, of "stable re-venues" to assure the colleges? One could multiply the contrasts, if not the contradictions. Is it necessary to pronounce the decisive *quantum mutatus ab illo*? Must one choose between the poetry of the Poverello of the pilgrim and the slightly hieratic gravity of the General? Such is the problem. One must take into account the stakes.

To escape this imbroglio, a single way is open to us: to return to the center, to the point of origin, to the source of the personality of Ignatius, to try to reunite in this "Saint of Saints", in him, in this "fine point of the soul", to this "heart of hearts",[1] where man meets God, where the initiatives of God and the free responses of man interplay and weld together. In other words, to attempt an analysis of the act of freedom and its history in the personality of Ignatius.

This project will appear audacious. However, we present it only as an attempt, an approach to the secret of Ignatius' personality. An attempt

---

[1] All these expressions come from chapters of the *Treatise on the Love of God*, wherein Saint Francis de Sales endeavors to express the mysterious encounter, within man, between the calls of the Holy Spirit and our freedom.

which will take account of the numerous and remarkable attempts which have preceded it, which will remain as close as possible to the facts and the documents and finally, not to impose itself, but to offer itself for discussion.

One point strikes us. Precisely because Ignatius is more "mysterious" than the majority of founders of religious institutions, it is incumbent upon us to formulate with much more rigor the problem which is at the heart of our research since Vatican II has asked religious to renew themselves according to "the charism of their founder": What rapport links the natural temperament and the mystical gifts of a man, of a woman, with his or her mission and with his or her message? What can, what must survive from him or her, after his or her passage, however resplendent it may have been among us?

I. THE BACKGROUND, THE FAMILY, THE CHILDHOOD OF INIGO

The mentality of Ignatius of Loyola was, it seems, rather well defined. It is regrettable that the *Autobiography* begins only with the affair of Pamplona (1521), but we are not, however, deprived of all significant information on the childhood of Inigo. He was not only the youngest but the last of eleven legitimate children, born of the marriage of Beltran Ibañez de Loyola and Maria Sanchez de Licona. Among those eleven children, seven were boys and four girls (however, Sancha was perhaps a bastard). Maria Sanchez de Licona died before Inigo had reached the age of seven; it was the young wife of Martin Garcia de Oñaz, the second of the children, that is to say Madeleine de Araoz, who then became "the lady of the casa solar". To this young sister-in-law the child became strongly attached: for seven years, that is until the death of his father, Madeleine de Araoz, pious and charming, exercised a profound influence on him.[2]

In what atmosphere did these sons of Beltran de Loyola grow up? If we do not set out numerous statistics here, at least we will state what we know. The oldest, Juan Perez de Loyola, made his will in Naples on June 21, 1496: he was not married, but he left two bastards by two different women. The third died likewise in Naples before 1527. The fifth, Hernando, departed for America in 1510; any further trace of him was lost. The sixth, Pedro Lopez de Oñaz, was "of the Church", and rector of Azpeitia: at his death, which occurred in 1529 in Barcelona, he left two bastards. These three last existences characterize rather well the destiny

---

[2] His second son, Emilien, would enter the Society of Jesus in 1541 and die there in 1547.

of the younger sons of noble families of the time, when the chief of the line had, as was the case with the Loyolas, come of age and inherited almost everything:[3] they sought their fortune in adventure, or if their title permitted them, in marriage; some were "of the Church", without vocation, but in order to enjoy certain benefices. Inigo himself was tonsured.[4]

Faith was, moreover, a matter of background and family honor. Here one was Catholic through heredity, which does not necessarily mean without sincere faith. A faith which existed less through dogmas than from certain customs: pilgrimages, pious works, testamentary bequests, patronage accorded to hermitages or "basilicas" which were established in the environs of the strong houses or chateaux. As a child, Inigo was steeped in this atmosphere: his personal devotion to St. Peter (who intervened in his conversion) could well have come to him from the hermitages of St. Peter of Loyola or from St. Peter of Elormendi, two of the nine or ten rustic sanctuaries which rose on the slopes of the neighboring mountains of Loyola.

This faith accommodated itself rather well to certain laxities. The example came from above: Alexander VI (Borgia), who occupied the throne of St. Peter, Ferdinand the Catholic and Charles V had similar familial situations. "Far from the courts, in the solitary valley of Iraurgui, the Loyolas had in their manor a tradition of sin; testaments offer evidence of it. Such as the milieu in which Ignatius grew up. Faith was ineradicable; pride, honor and bravery were a tradition, education did not count, the idle life filled itself as best as it could, at the risk of circumstances."[5] In Ignatius' own family there were two bastards, a boy, Juan Beltran, and Maria Beltran, who would actually be a *"fleira"* (nun) in one of the neighboring hermitages of Loyola, San Miguel.

II. THE PAGE AND THE SOLDIER

Inigo was about fourteen years old when his father died. Then he was an orphan, without father or mother, and he could scarcely count on his brothers and sisters to aid him in shaping his destiny as the baby of the family. He became a page of the "contado major" (that is, of the minister

[3] Fr. Candido de Dalmases found the document showing the family successesion (while Ignatius was living). With his kindly authorization, we have reproduced the authentic Loyola family coat of arms which appears at the top of the document: see our *Chroniques saint Ignace de Loyola.*

[4] This is an established fact: in the permit to pass into Palestine, which has been rediscovered, he designated as *clerus Pampelonensis* (AHSI, vol. 25 [1956], 49, p. 26).

[5] DUDON, *Saint Ignace*, pp. 25–26.

of finances of the King of Castile), Juna Velasquez de Cuellar. Was it to the friendship which linked Juan Velasquez and Beltran Ibañez de Oñaz, or to some cousinhood that Ignatius owed this opportunity? It matters little. There he was transplanted from the somewhat uncouth life of Loyola to the life of the court of Castile. He spent eleven years there, at the age when the orientation of a man is decided, especially if he is an orphan. Now, if the home environment of the Velasquezes seems to have been rather close to that of the Loyolas, the employment of Juan obliged him to follow the prince; and in the capacity of page of the grand treasurer, Inigo discovered this prestigious world of the court of Castile. The historians assure us that the deceased Queen Isabella and Cardinal Cisneros had reformed its manners. However, Germaine de Foix had replaced Isabella beside Ferdinand, and this young queen who was, it seems, *pinguis et bene pota* (heavy in flesh and a heavy drinker)[6] loved orgies; and Maria de Velasco, the wife of Juan Velasquez, was the grand organizer of the pleasures of the Queen.[7] In this ambience, what became of Inigo? Documents are scarce. However, they have already told us much about the mentality of the adolescent: he threw himself, wholeheartedly, into the merry life of the pages of the court. He dreamed only of "being a soldier" and of accomplishing exploits which would prove him to be one; lacking countries to conquer, he sought gallant adventures and succeeded in them, even if it entailed fighting duels with his rivals.

Ribadeneyra, his first biographer, depicts him to us as "an elegant youth, fond of laughter, a great lover of handsome clothes and the good life", a "wild and vain solder": he was very proud of his light hair; he cared for his nails, his doublets and his cap. He was the young hidalgo in all his arrogance and his cockiness! Already, he had to have heroes with whom to compete: He found them in the novels of chivalry which were then enjoying great popularity. Amadis of Gaul was his teacher of courage, but also of gallantry: there crept, however, into his heart a feeling of romantic love for an imaginary lady of his dreams. Here, we begin to enter into the direct confidences of the *Autobiography*:

> [He[8] thought] of things of the world of which he had previously been in the habit of thinking. And among the numerous vanities which offered them-

---

[6] LETURIA, *El Gentilhombre*, p. 66, citing Peter Martyr.

[7] Regarding the atmosphere of this period it is essential to mention as evidence the success of a "comedy", which enjoyed a "popularity comparable only to that of *Don Quixote*": the *Comedia de Calisto y Melibea*, better known under the name of *La Célestine*. It was still famous in the nineteenth century. Cf. *Encyclopedia universalis*, vol. 1, and Marcel BATAILLON, *La Célestine selon Fernando de Rojas* (Paris: M. Didier, 1961).

[8] In the *Autobiography*, Ignatius speaks himself in the third person: he calls himself "the pilgrim".

selves to him, one held his heart in its possession to such an extent that he was absorbed, sometimes, in reflecting on it for two or three or four hours without counting, imagining what he had to do in the service of a certain lady, the means which he would take to be able to go to the land where she was, the bits of verse, the words which he would say to her, the deeds of arms that he would accomplish in her service. He was so conceited about this project that he did not see how impossible it was for him to bring it to fruition; because this lady was not of the common nobility: neither countess nor duchess, but her condition was higher still.[9]

The dreams of the wounded soldier of Pamplona clarify retrospectively the mentality of the page of Arévalo.

The young gentleman was not satisfied with dreams. In 1515, he made a trip to Loyola. Concerning this visit we have the complaints of the corregidor of Azpeitia who accused Ignatius and his brother Pedro Lopez, the chaplain, of having committed "very enormous crimes" there: "nocturnal excesses, characteristic and serious misdemeanors . . . deliberately and with perfidy". This official document, to tell the truth the only one which has been saved for us, explains for us the statement of Ribadeneyra that Ignatius was then particularly given to gaming, to women and to duels and weapons.[10]

After the death of Ferdinand of Aragon (1516), Juan Velasquez de Cuellar was suddenly disgraced by the new King of Spain; he died on August 12, 1517.[11] Inigo then entered the service of the Duke of Nájera, Viceroy of Navarre, Antonio Manrique. It seems that, unlike three of his brothers, he wanted to realize his dreams of glory and love in Spain itself, in the shadow of one of the greatest personages of the kingdom. The Duke introduced him, moreover, into a post of confidence; Inigo became a part of his *gente de caballo*, that is, of his personal guard; half-gentleman and half-soldier. In 1520, Inigo participated in the recapture of Nájera by the troops of the Duke and refused to give up his share of the booty; but in 1521, it was a more diplomatic mission that he was charged with by

---

[9] *Autobiog. A.G.*, op. cit. p. 46. The historians have not neglected to ask the identity of this lady. One tends today to identify her with Princess Catalina, sister of Charles V, who lived then as a recluse at Tordesillas with Joanna the Mad, and who would later marry John III of Portugal. Ignatius had seen her when he accompanied the court to Tordesillas on the occasion of Charles V's visits to his mother. Some historians prefer to identify her with Germaine de Foix, widow of King Ferdinand, or with another sister of Charles V and Catalina, Eleanor, Queen of Portugal from 1519 and whose husband had just died.

[10] *Font. narr.* 1, p. 154.

[11] DUDON (op. cit., p. 32) places the death of Juan Velasquez in 1518. We prefer here to follow LETURIA (*El Gentilhombre*, pp. 91 sq.). It is Fr. Leonard Cros who discovered this important information: the Cros archives (province of Toulouse) contain other treasures.

his lord: he was going to establish peace between the factions which were tearing apart Guipúzcoa, and he succeeded.

It was then that the incident of Pamplona occurred. A matter which, without Ignatius, would scarcely have left a trace in history, because it was so insignificant. A minor episode of a major political crisis, a notable one which had aroused all Spain: the movement of the *Comuneros* against the young Charles V: this insurrection of the nobles against the King was intensified as a result of a popular revolt against the nobles. It was at this moment that Francis I deemed it opportune to reestablish in Navarre the authority of the Albrets, allies of France, whom Ferdinand of Aragon had recently evicted. In fact, the people of Navarre had never, for the most part, accepted this transfer of their country to the crown of Spain, and the approach of French troop, commanded by André de Foix filled them with hope. For the French, the expedition turned into a "military parade": no resistance; and here was Pamplona itself, the capital of Navarre, negotiating with the victor: on Monday, May 20, 1521, André de Foix made his solemn entrance into the city. Only the fortress resisted. Herrera, the alcalde of the city, commanded it, but the soul of the combat—was Ignatius of Loyola. An unequal combat, of which the issue was not in doubt by either of the adversaries, and which would last only nine hours. The "campaign" of Ignatius lasted two days. He left the battle wounded: a cannon ball broke one of his legs and tore apart the other. The French—or the people of Navarre, according to a recent hypothesis—took him back to Loyola in a litter. The convalescence, which would lead Inigo to conversion, began.

First, it is fitting to pause. Slim as the historical importance of Pamplona may be, it reveals clearly, for the first time, certain major traits in Inigo's character.

First, his sense of honor and glory. The Duke himself entered into negotiations with the French;[12] with the provision that his properties, those of his vassals, and of all Castilians be respected; he accepted the surrender of Pamplona; such a proposal did not satisfy Ignatius: he bolstered the slight inclination for resistance of the alcalde Herrera and reanimated the courage of the officers who commanded the little garrison of the citadel. Did he believe the time had come for one of those brilliant feats of arms of which he had dreamed since his adolescence? Perhaps; but perspicaciously, he nourished no illusions as to the outcome of this "fight of honor".

Another trait appeared, which we shall often find in him: a lucid obstinacy, the *ego contra omnes* in desperate situations. When all judged

---

[12] DUDON, *Saint Ignace*, pp. 47–49.

resistance vain, he resisted all. The word "capitulate" had for him no meaning, it had no hold over him. "Impossible" meant nothing: a great-hearted man always attempted the impossible; he must. His strength of will was extraordinary, his tenacity and his fidelity to himself likewise, because he feared neither physical suffering nor death.

This force of will was contagious; it swept along and awakened energies; it rallied around him the desperate and the discouraged. With Inigo wounded, the combat ended, and by the most cowardly surrender of the defenders. "The alcalde", the admiral of Castile would write to Charles V, "committed the greatest treason in the world; and not only have we not cut his throat but we have supported him and the others, like good servants. . . . The favors which these people deserve—are that one should cut off their heads." Some were so eager to capitulate that they went so far to tear out the locks of the doors of the castle. It's enough to indicate what energy Ignatius radiated to galvanize such cowards into action for few hours.

One last trait merits mention: the faith of this mediocre Christian. Before the combat, Inigo confessed his sins, in the absence of a priest, to one of his companions in arms. He knew the great danger which he risked in this assault of the French and he, a sinner, wished to present himself absolved to the judgment of God.

III. THE HIDALGO WITH THE BROKEN LEG

There traits we shall find again in the wounded Inigo. We are deprived of important lights on his mentality as a gentleman by passing too quickly over these days, these weeks, which preceded conversion. Three times it was necessary to operate on him to mend the leg fracture. At Pamplona, the French surgeon attempted it: "After twelve or fifteen days", they thought that the wounded man was capable of withstanding the trip to Loyola. Let us leave the description to him, not without reminding ourselves that he gave this account some thirty years after the event.[13]

> As things were going very badly, they called all the doctors and surgeons from all sides. They decided that it was necessary to break the leg again and reset the bones in place. For having been badly set the first time, they said, or for having been disturbed during the trip, they were not in their place

[13] The text is taken from the *Récit du Pèlerin*, pp. 46 sq. Our quotations will be most often borrowed from the translation done by André Thiry (*Autob.* R.P.). Sometimes we shall prefer the more literal translation of Alain Guillermon (*Autob.* A.G.). Sometimes also we shall give the translation which has willingly been done for us by a specialist in the Spanish language.

and under these conditions healing was not possible. They recommended therefore this butchery (*carneceria*). During the operation, as in the course of all those which he had already undergone and those he would subsequently undergo, never did he say a word or give any sign of pain other than to clench his fists firmly.

This testimony of resistance to suffering was given by Ignatius himself. And here he is again face to face with death:

However, the condition was getting steadily worse: he could no longer eat, and already the other symptoms which ordinarily precede death were appearing. At the approach of the feast of St. John, as the doctors had very little hope, they advised him to confess his sins. He received the last rites on the vigil of the Apostles St. Peter and Paul. The doctors declared that if he did not feel better by midnight, they could consider him doomed. The sick man had always had devotion to St. Peter, and it was in the middle of this same night that our Lord allowed him to find himself better; the improvement was so rapid that at the end of a few days he was judged to be out of danger.

Ignatius was far from proclaiming it a miracle. He did not even say that he had solicited a cure from St. Peter: he noted simply that he had always had a devotion to St. Peter. On the other hand, he indicated that, as at Pamplona, he had put his life in order, like any good Christian, in order to appear before God.

One important trait of his character would escape us without the extremely important admission which the third operation involved: this man who bore all suffering without saying a word "by firmly clenching his fists", this sick person who faced death with serenity, for him there was, however, a wound which he could not tolerate: that of "ugliness", that which might taint his beauty and elegance. Rather than "suffer it", he preferred to endure "martyrdom". We must be present at this episode and hear Ignatius recount the operation to us:

Already the bones had begun to knit together but under the knee, one bone overlapped another, which shortened the leg. Not being able to stand it, because he was determined to follow the world and estimated that he would be deformed, he inquired of the surgeons regarding the possibilities of cutting it (the bone). They told him that it was possible, but that the suffering would surpass anything that he had ever experienced, for it was already healed and the operation would take some time. Nevertheless, he resolved to undertake this martyrdom of his own free will (*martirizarse por su proprio gusto*, literally " to martyr himself for his own pleasure"); and despite his oldest brother who was afraid and said that he himself would not dare face such pain. The wounded man bore the pain with his habitual endurance (*con la sólita paciencia*). They made an incision in the flesh, cut the protruding bone and used all possible means so that the leg would not remain so short; they applied quantities of salves and continually pulled the leg with instruments that martyred him for many days.[14]

What concern for keeping intact his appeal, his appearance, his "physique" for preventing the deterioration of his seductive appeal which helped him to conquer the hearts of women! For he had abandoned nothing of his gallant dream. Into such assaults one does not throw oneself limping!

Priceless confidences from Inigo on his heroic and amorous youth. The affair of Pamplona and the "butcheries" of the surgeons of Loyola tell us much about the character of our hidalgo.

IV. THE HUMAN SIDE OF IGNATIUS OF LOYOLA

However, it is necessary to try to pinpoint again these "natural and cosmic" roots of the Ignatian mentality; if we wish to understand later the penitent of Montserrat, the pilgrim of Jerusalem, the missionary and the mystic and even the Superior General of the Society of Jesus. The human personality of Ignatius is too strong, too characteristic not to intervene in these roles, even the most spiritual of them. Let us investigate the paintings of Jacopino del Conte[15] or of Coello[16] which we are sure resemble the model or the mortuary mask preserved in the archives of Rome.[17] Let us analyze by the techniques of modern psychology, the handwriting[18] and the style of the authentic writings of Ignatius. Here, at least in the traits which seem the least contestable, is the psychological profile which emerges from these confrontations.

The will dominated the temperament, a powerful will, unswerving, all of a piece, which fixed itself and its purposes and pursued them against winds and tides. Far from overcoming it, contradiction and difficulties even stimulated it. There, where all others hesitated, faltered, capitulated, Ignatius held firm: he exulted, he was exalted in attempting

[14] *Autob.* R.P., pp. 47–48, n. 4 and 5. Let us remember that anaesthesia had not yet been invented.

[15] The celebrated Florentine painter was a renowned portrait painter, and was a penitent of Ignatius. The same day as the saint's death, the Fathers of La Strada asked him to do a portrait of Ignatius. This painting is preserved in the apartment of the Generals of the order.

[16] Alonso Sanchez Coello, the great painter of Philip II, painted this canvas at the end of the sixteenth century, from a mask taken from the plaster mask preserved in Rome. He was aided in his work by Ribadeneyra and by Gaspard de Guiroga, Archbishop of Toledo, who had known Ignatius well in Rome. This portrait was very much circulated: Coello himself drew sixteen copies from it.

[17] Cf. our *Chroniques saint Ignace de Loyola*, pp. 256–257.

[18] Ibid., pp. 306–307.

what was presented to him as impossible. He was tenacious to the point of obstinacy, even to risking his life if necessary. Ignatius was hyperactive, a "beast of action", served by considerable vital resources, an exceptional resistance to fatigue, to suffering, with a physical courage which was intoxicated by danger.

Very fortunately, he had at the same time a measureless pride, a sharp sense of his honor and glory, an imperious need to surpass himself, "to do something big" with his life. No goal seemed to him beyond his grasp, and he was eager to forge his destiny himself. "He was so sure of this project that he did not see how impossible it was for him to bring it to fruition": it was he who spoke thus of himself. What he said of his love for the lady of his thoughts, he could also have said of his battle of Pamplona and many another project.

Not that he did not bear within himself a strong sensibility, even a demanding sensuality. Powerful desires agitated him. To serve them, he spent himself; life for him had to have savor. However, he mastered these intimate demons when they threatened to spoil his glory. Then he majestically rejected, controlled, them. Gallantry suggested exploits to him and exploits in turn competed with gallantry. It is important moreover to distinguish in the young gentleman—and in this he appears typical of the nobility of his time—three attitudes in regard to women: there was the wife whom one chose or whom one could choose for love, but also more or less for social reasons which have nothing to do with love (in 1552 the marriage of his niece Lorenza would reveal to us an Ignatius, even converted, even sanctified, in the clutches of the "principles" of the society of his time). Then there was gallant love, and by his own avowal, Inigo was not without filling his leisure with this game. Finally there was the ideal woman, the "lady" to whom one would vow a "courtly love", a chivalrous, dream love: would she one day be wife or mistress? Adventure or chance would decide. Whatever it might be, in the flower of his youth, the young clerk of Pamplona had long since renounced celibacy. He knew success in the world of women: for such a conquest, he was not afraid to draw the sword or dagger and to do battle. Free, before the combat, to commend his soul to God!—And who could ever tell us with what secret scar his heart was wounded, when, still a child, he lost his mother?[19]

He seemed moreover to have a refined, meticulous concern about his person. Small of stature, he compensated for his unimpressive size by the care of his long, curly, fair hair, of his hands, his nails, by the dash of his doublet, his breeches and his cap. To make himself elegant, he exercised

[19] Cf. Louis BEIRNAERT, "L'expérience fondamentale d'Ignace de Loyola et l'expérience psychologique", Expérience chrétienne et psychologie, Epi edition (Paris, 1964).

a feminine attention to detail; he neglected nothing: untidiness was repugnant to him, as was dirtiness. This hero in battle wished himself at court to be the perfect, attractive knight. In everything, he surveyed himself, controlled himself, and verified the impression he produced. Was he really artistic? Perhaps: we are assured that he composed some "motes", that is, kinds of "legends" addressed to women, in truth certain cantilenas, and even a poem in honor of St. Peter; he was incontestably fond of music. Nothing, however, offers proof that he enjoyed, in this domain, any original gifts; at least we know enough about it not to make of this fighter a barbarian. A corner of his soul which could have escaped us is revealed: a delicate sensibility which thrilled to something besides honor and love. His dream did not scorn to cling to the stars of a night sky.

This fiery temperament did not leave his followers indifferent: they liked him, at least they either admired him or he annoyed them. Eventually, they feared him—as with all strong personalities. French and Navarrans, after the combat of Pamplona, honored him, but other people of Navarre who were ashamed of his bold fidelity detested him. There was never unanimity about him personally—even when he had become a saint—and even less about his work than about him personally. It is the mark of his force of character. People of this stamp are not "easy to live with". On the contrary, he exercised a certain fascination for some which could eliminate all structural authority. He was a born leader around whom people rallied spontaneously. A leader by natural charisma, a "mover of men" who had no need to command to be listened to: one followed him more than one obeyed him. He magnetized, he radiated, he was the strongest. To those companions who accepted sharing his dream or his fight, he attached himself indissolubly: he stimulated them and helped them to achieve, like himself, the height of their potentialities; in return, they became for him beings who were almost sacred. He was as faithful to them as to himself; which is saying not a little.

So much physical and moral vigor, however, did not make of Ignatius an invulnerable being: he carried within himself an anguish which allowed him no rest. It is hard to define it other than to call it the anguish of death. For he did not fear death, he scorned it. This was rather the anguish of the lack of meaning of banal existence. Nothing would cost him more than to see in an honest mirror what St. James calls "the visage of his birth":[20] he needed the mirror to reflect an enlarged image of himself, embellished, idealized, glorious. Life had no meaning for Ignatius except in the combat which he encountered in the service of a

---

[20] Jn 1:23.

cause—glory or love—which went beyond him; once this goal vanished, life became absurd, an absolute void, nothing. His courageous decision to have his badly set leg broken again and to undergo a third "butchery", worse than the first two, undoubtedly hid a desperation: what would his life be if he were henceforth no more than a cripple, an ugly man? With his mentality, then, would life be worth living? This anguish with Ignatius was more profound than it first appears: in the dark hours through which the convalescent of Loyola would pass it would provoke in him doubts, oscillations, scruples and strong temptations of self-destruction. For the moment that is of no concern to us: the will suffices to master instinctive impulses and to free from all shackles the vital forces of the temperament.

One must wonder then what role religion played in the moral life of Inigo. He prayed before fighting in a duel, as today a champion of the Tour de France makes the sign of the cross at the moment of departure. He made his confession before a battle or when the doctors offered him little hope of life. He had some devotion to St. Peter. He had faith, but what faith? It did not seem, in any case, to restrain him in his pride or his manners. His virtues bore very human names: loyalty, honesty, fidelity and sincerity. He certainly had devotions; however one is less sure that he was devout. But who knows the secret thoughts of a heart?

Ignatius' character points out his traits and points them out from the beginning as much as his intellectual activity escapes us. It is true that until his university days, one would not know how to talk of culture in relation to him. At Loyola, he learned (doubtlessly) to read and to write; he spoke Basque and until the end of his life, his correspondence would remain strewn with idiomatic expressions. At court and in the milieu of Juan Velasquez, he polished his language, he read novels of chivalry, he even composed some small bits of verse; but how far did he progress? We know that he never had facile speech and that he never actually spoke any language in its literary purity, not Spanish, French, Latin or Italian; the correspondence gives evidence of that: prolific as he was as a letter writer, he was never a stylist. However, intelligence is something other than culture. With Ignatius, intelligence was less cerebral than practical; less extensive than penetrating. He proceeded by sight; he "saw" situations, men, connections between facts and the play of causes and effects with a "sharpness", a lightning insight; he went directly to the heart of the matter. These affirmations were so moderate that they sometimes appeared to be excessively meager, but they compelled recognition through their force of truth. The *Spiritual Exercises* would represent the unique example of an unclassifiable literary genre: illegible as simple reading, it can metamorphose one's existence, if one "does" the

Exercises, that is, if one "lives" them. The structure of the thought is strong but more organic than organized; it espoused the growth or at least the movement, of reality. It used a vocabulary which concerns action rather than abstract ideas. One can, without risk of error, see in this realism of the intelligence the consequence of the belated studies of Ignatius, but it is also the mark of a temperament entirely oriented toward action. Here a parallel asserts itself between Ignatius' intelligence and his imagination: his imagination is powerful, capable of creating vast frescoes, of an unforgettable symbolism; and it lacks colors, expressions, picturesqueness; it is visionary more than visual. When he would confide the mystical graces—rare and deep—which he received from the Lord, the bareness of the narrative would filter, sometimes to the point of veiling the splendor of the experience.

We have in this analysis run over a little into the worldly life of Ignatius. Let us now return to Loyola, to the convalescent Inigo. The operation this time succeeded: the limp would be so slight that according to a contemporary it would pass unnoticed unless one had been warned to watch for it.[21] If he slipped a heel-piece into his shoe, it would become imperceptible. Here he was, then, with new freedom. Free to pursue his dream. Free to make his destiny by force of will. Free? With what freedom? St. Francis de Sales notes very fairly that if "the will has domination over love . . . love in its turn, dominates the will", colors it, gives it its quality.

> The will is mistress of the loves, as is a young lady of the lovers who seek her, from among whom she can choose the one she wishes. However, as after the marriage she loses her freedom and from mistress becomes subject to the power of her husband, a captive of the one whom she had captivated, in the same way the will which chooses love to its liking, after it has embraced someone, lives enslaved under him.[22]

So it was with Inigo; his liberty was illusory: in fact, his will chose its master; it was himself whom he loved, his glory, his honor, and he loved himself to the point of passion, for his temperament was fiery. All his natural strengths, regrouped, stimulated, sustained by the vigor of his will, were once again directed toward a dream Inigo. He "imagined" what he had "to do in the service of a certain lady. . . . neither countess nor duchess, but of even higher standing": a love which must lead him to a wordly glory and joy. He asked that in anticipation of this conquest, he asked that he might be brought "books . . . which one ordinarily calls books of chivalry".

[21] LANCICIUS in Scripta 1, p. 490. Cf. LETURIA, El gentilhombre, p. 133.
[22] Traité de l'Amour de Dieu, bk. I, ch. IV; in our Pleiade edition, p. 363.

CHAPTER II

IGNATIUS THE MYSTIC

A long mystical adventure was to begin for Ignatius, an adventure in which the rarest of divine interventions would abound, actions, visions and words. Let us admit it: what we know about it—and we don't know all—disconcerts even historians and psychologists most aware of the phenomena of the mystical life. Speaking of the enigmatic *loquela* of the *Spiritual Diary*, Louis Cognet writes, for example: "These passages have greatly disconcerted the commentators, and one must acknowledge that they are rather strange."[1] Ignatius, far from resisting, like a John of the Cross, these exceptional movements of the Spirit, seems to have been pleased with them, and even, in certain "choices", to have solicited them and almost required them as indispensable signs for his decisions.[2] From these obscurities divergent interpretations were born, as is usually the case. We hold, for our part, that the analysis left us by Father de Guibert is one of the most objective and the wisest.[3] Our intention is not, moreover, to enter into the conflict of specialists on supernatural phenomena of divine union, but to follow as closely as possible the story of Ignatius' freedom, that is to say, his more and more absolute clinging to the Mystery of God.[4]

I. A FEW PRINCIPLES OF THE CHRISTIAN MYSTIC

To clarify our procedure we recall the first six principles which seem to be fundamental:

1. In Christian life, the Mystery is more important than the mystical just as essential reality is more important than an experience which, however precious it might be, is not indispensable. The Mystery, the "kerygma hidden in God from the beginning" is the adoption of man by God in Christ, born of the Virgin, dead and resurrected, that is to say, man's participation in the life of the Trinity through faith, hope and charity. The entire spiritual destiny of man is based on this reality.

---

[1] Cf. the penetrating pages of Louis COGNET: *Histoire de la spiritualité chrétienne*, vol. 3, pp. 16–23.

[2] Cf. the "elections" of the *Spiritual Diary*.

[3] *La Spiritualité de la Compagnie de Jesus*, pp. 3–58.

[4] Cf. the introduction of Henri DE LUBAC and our chapter "Vie humaine et vie divine dans la mystique chrétienne", in our collaborative work: *La Mystique et les mystiques*, (Paris: Desclée De Brouwer, 1965).

2. The progress of a soul is therefore not measured—if such can be measured—by the abundance or rarity of supernatural gifts which God grants but by the development of faith, hope and charity.

3. The perceptible sign of this progress in faith, hope and charity is not the feeling that we can experience for God, but the firmness of our decision to unite our will profoundly to the will of God so that we recognize it *hic et nunc* after having loyally and sincerely sought it. In that is the only "ecstasy" which is without risk of illusion: for, said St. Francis de Sales, "to give the true ecstacy of the will by which it attaches itself uniquely and powerfully to the divine goodness, that belongs only to the sovereign *Spirit* through which *the charity of God is expanded within our hearts.*"[5]

4. Christian freedom consists of "loving God above all things", according to the Great Commandment and to love others as we love ourselves, for the love of God. This freedom is not a nondependence, it is a submission, but a filial submission and accepted as such. St. Paul dared to use the expression *servus Christi*, "slave of Christ", of the man liberated from sin by Christ. It is "the freedom of glory of the children of God": the love of the Father in Christ takes precedence for the Christian over all other love and especially over all love which would alienate him from divine love.

5. The love of God in us has varying degrees of intensity; it radiates into our sensibility, our imagination, our instinctive urges. These degrees of love are degrees of the mystical life. The love of God is always "grace, gift" on the part of God; but when it attains a specific force, when, more than offering itself, it imposes itself upon the soul, it is at such a juncture that one considers it "exceptional", "preternatural". Nonetheless, even in such a case, it does not "render" perfect the Christian who is favored by it: at the very heart of this wave of love that submerges him, the mystic retains his temperament, his natural mentality and his faults which he must ameliorate by the appropriate ascetic effort. Peter himself gives us the proof of this: the lavish gift of primacy among the Apostles, the grace of a prestigious love made him neither prudent nor unshakeably faithful to his Master: he denied Christ.

6. The exceptional "mystical graces", no more than normal grace, do not inhibit the natural temperament, or supplant it or "constrain" it:[6] they help it, they sustain it, they rectify its deepest orientation. Moreover, the true "freedom" of the Christian is neither acquired nor perfected on earth: it is created; it is always "threatened"; it is conquered day

---

[5] *Traité de l'Amour de Dieu*, bk. VII, ch. VII, p. 681.

[6] The phenomenon called the "binding of powers" does not go against this principle.

after day through actions and sometimes revolts of the personal nature.

These elementary principles of Christian mysticism must be kept in mind if one does not wish to lose oneself in the labyrinth of the mystical manifestations of Ignatius and of his behavior: Ignatius received, definitely, the gift of an exceptional love for Jesus Christ; nonetheless, with the exception of his faults, he remained the man Ignatius. Actually, his good points and his defects assumed a new meaning under the Love which called him and to which he gave himself.

Moreover this "conversion" was not accomplished in one fell swoop, but by stages.

II. THE STAGES OF CONVERSION

First stage: Loyola (August–September, 1521)

The liberty of Ignatius oscillated for a long time between two loves. The people in the house where he was recuperating could not furnish the convalescent who still dreamed only of his lady with the novels of chivalry with which he wanted to nourish his dream. "In the house, not a single one of them could be found . . . ; they brought him therefore a 'Life of Christ' and a book in Spanish on the lives of the saints."[7] Now he said, he experienced a "certain attraction for the stories recounted therein". Divine attraction, doubtless. But here is the interpretation Inigo gave to it because of his temperament:

> In reading the life of our Lord and of the saints, he began to think and to say inwardly to himself: "And what if I were to do what St. Francis and St. Dominic did?" He dreamed also of many things which appeared good to him and he constantly envisaged difficult and painful undertakings. In proposing them to himself, he had the feeling that it would be easy to accomplish them. All his reflections came back to say to him: "St. Dominic did this, therefore I have to do it; St. Francis did this, therefore I have to do it."

The divine compulsion changed into a heroic dream in which sudden appearance, absolute necessity and disdain for every obstacle were very much in the character of the gentleman.

Two loves presented themselves to him, both noble, both worthy of his pride. He dreamed of rivaling the saints, in exactly the same way that he dreamed of conquering his lady. And he "dreamed two, or three or

---

[7] The *Vita Christi* of Ludoph the Carthusian, translated into Castilian by Ambrosio Montesino (Alcalá, 1502–1503); and the *Légende dorée* of Jacques de Voragine, presented in Castilian by the Cistercian Gauberto M. Vagad (1493 and 1511).

four hours without being aware of it". He balanced the two, up until the day when he recognized in joy the sign of the "Spirit of God" and in sadness, the "sign of the demon". A simple and elementary criterion about which one should not generalize too quickly. This discovery led him to consider his past life and to recognize therein the presence of sin and to perceive the necessity for doing penance. "It was then", he said, "that the desire to imitate the saints came to him." And this imitation took the form of a pilgrimage to Jerusalem, which he would accomplish by doing "with the grace of God, all that they had done . . ., offering himself to as many voluntary constraints and abstinences as a generous spirit enflamed by God is accustomed to hope for."

This confidence of Ignatius can lend itself to several interpretations: Was it love of Christ or love of self? It seems to us, however, that up to this point of his spiritual evolution, the freedom of Ignatius remained the slave of his dream of adventure: it was himself basically that he sought and whom he loved in this plan of making a pilgrimage to the Holy Land.[8] To imitate the "generous hearts inflamed by God" was stronger in him than "to be inflamed by God". His motivation remained human more than spiritual. It was only successive thresholds that he would experience authentic spiritual freedom.

Second Stage: The Eruption of Exceptional Phenomena and the Interior Change in Inigo

Inigo had not yet chosen and yet had already received a vision. "He had seen clearly a picture of Our Lady with the Holy Child Jesus." The fact is noteworthy: for it marked the beginning of "visions" which would multiply during Ignatius' life: at Manresa, when he totally abstained from meat, "he saw meat all ready to be eaten";[9] he saw "the Trinity, in the image of three keys of the keyboard";[10] then "how God had created the world";[11] then "the humanity of Christ", "Our Lady";[12] during the voyage from Jerusalem "Our Lord appeared often to him";[13] on the way to Rome, at La Storta.[14] In Rome, while he drafted the *Constitutions*,[15] or around that time, "he saw sometimes God the Father,

---

[8] Fr. de Guibert aptly notes that, in his prologue to the *Flos Sanctorum*, Brother Gauberto Vargad presented Christ as the incomparable leader whose "caballeros de Dios", (knights of God) followed "the always victorious standard", "the eternal Prince, Jesus Christ".

[9] *Autob. R.P.*, p. 70.

[10] Ibid., p. 71.

[11] Ibid., p. 73.

[12] Ibid., p. 73.

[13] Ibid., p. 85.

[14] Ibid., p. 134.

[15] Cf. the *Spiritual Diary*.

sometimes the three Persons of the Trinity, as well as sometimes the Madonna."[16] Each of these visions had its own particular meaning, but there was among them a common basis which the first vision at Loyola has already permitted us to define. Inigo considered it first as a "confirmation" of what then happened within him: it was not detached from his intimate questions, it entered into the very movement of his soul as it was developing at that moment. Secondly, he noted of it that "he received during a notable period of time extreme consolation". Above all, he stated that it produced a "decisive" spiritual transformation in him: "He kept from it such a distaste for his whole past life, especially for things of the flesh, that it seemed to him that all the *images* (*las especies*) that had been *engraved* upon it had been *erased* from his soul. Thus, from this day until when these things were written in August 1553, he never more gave the least consent to them." This interior transformation was such that it did not escape his brother "or other persons of the house". A last characteristic trait: the prudence of Ignatius in his statement: "One can judge from this effect (of transformation) that the vision came from God although one would not dare to so decide and would state nothing more than the preceding." What is the meaning of this formula? For Ignatius, there was the fact even of the vision; it was a thing; but from whom did it come? That was another question. It could come from his dreamer's temperament, from his active imagination, stimulated by his sensibility; it could come from Satan (like the astonishing vision of the "serpent with many points which shone like eyes but were not"[17]); finally, it could come from God. And the proof that it came from God was its *lasting* effect of *conversion*, that is to say an increase of faith, hope and charity and also progress in the profound attachment of his being to God, finally of his interior freedom. Here it was from the sins of his past life "especially of things of the flesh" that he found himself freed. "Confirmation", profound transformation of his spiritual being, real and persistent progress in the "freedom of sons of God"—we shall find all these characteristics in the innumerable visions that Ignatius will authenticate as coming from God, particularly in the visions of Cardoner and La Storta.

Regarding this time at Loyola, it is necessary to stress also three major confidences: from then on he did not keep to himself his progress in the love of God; he let all his followers profit from it.[18] It was the beginning of his "spiritual colloquies", of his "familiar conversations" which would be to the end one of his most efficacious apostolates. The second is

[16] *Autob.* R.P., pp. 138, 139.
[17] *Autob.* R.P., p. 64.
[18] Ibid., p. 54.

that the first lines of the *Spiritual Exercises* date from Loyola: "As he liked very much these books, the idea came to him to extract from them, in the form of summary, the most important things from the life of Christ and the saints. He began to write a book with much care."[19] The meticulousness that he had formerly put into caring for his person, he presently transferred to his spiritual notebook. Did he already note movements of the spirits in his soul? He did not say, but what is sure, is that he kept the remembrance of them in his memory. Finally, the third trait was that he conceived "a hate against himself" (*el odio que contra si tenia concebido*)[20] to the point that he feared not being able "to give himself free rein" if upon his return from Jerusalem, he entered the Carthusians. He had not yet left Loyola when the battle between the two loves in him had terminated. But even if he had "exterminated" the worldly thoughts, it seems that God had not yet taken his true place in the depth of Ignatius' being. At heart, Inigo remained a captive of the image which he had created of himself: "His soul [was] still blind, although animated by a great desire to serve [Our Lord] in accordance with all the illumination that that could have."[21] The attitude of Inigo on the way to Montserrat (February–March 1522), proves it: his strange way of interrogating God in the Moorish affair,[22] as well as his armed vigil the night of the Annunciation before the Black Madonna of the Abbey; these remain more the actions of a knight than of a man truly "taken" with God. "Just as he had filled his mind with stories of Amadis of Gaul and with other books of the same kind, the idea came to him to imitate them. It is thus that he resolved to make an armed watch for one entire night."[23]

Third stage: "The New Man" of Manresa (March 1522–February 1523)

Despite the little time he was at Montserrat, he made there "a general confession which lasted three days": we understand that he made a three-day retreat during which he prepared and then made his confession. To aid the retreatants, the monks utilized a little book composed by the abbot who had reformed the abbey, Garcia de Cisneros, nephew of the celebrated Cardinal Ximenes: *L'Exercitatoire de la vie spirituelle*. This little book is an anthology of methodical meditations which insists

[19] *Autob*. R.P., p. 54. This notebook represented three hundred pages in quarto (*Font. narr*. I, pp. 376–377).

[20] *Autob*. R.P., p. 55.

[21] Ibid., p. 57.

[22] Ibid., p. 57–59.

[23] Ibid., p. 60. The words "imitate" and "imitation" will be key words of Ignatian spirituality.

strongly, as it should, on contrition; it had a certain influence on the pilgrim; Inigo would borrow from it for the *Spiritual Exercises* the meditation called "on the triple sin", the contemplation of hell and the colloquy of the sinner with Christ on the Cross. This was the first initiation of Inigo into the technique of the spiritual life, so to speak; but especially the beginning of the transformation which he would know at Manresa.

Ignatius' biographers have described at length his stay at Manresa; he wanted to stay only a few days before going to Barcelona and beginning his pilgrimage to Jerusalem, but he stayed more than a year: his health, the plague which quarantined Barcelona, the delay of Adrian VI in returning to Rome, such are the reasons that are given to explain this change of plan. It is undoubtedly necessary to add to it the most intimate spiritual motivations. Whatever the reason, surely Manresa was for Ignatius the place of radical spiritual transformation. He who was accustomed to conduct himself as he wished and tasted "extreme joy" in doing so, but now, "he began to know a great instability" (*a tener grandes variedades en su alma*), to the point that he asked himself: "What is this new life which we are now beginning?"[25] Then there was the tempest of scruples, so violent that he was assailed by "frequent temptations" to commit suicide, a "supreme disgust for the life which he was leading, and strong desires to abandon it". A sudden peace came over him. "The Lord permitted him to awake from these feelings as from a dream." One will recognize without difficulty in this plan the typical itinerary by which God conducts souls whom he wishes to sanctify greatly with nonetheless this mark of excess that typifies all that happened to Ignatius.

After the tempest (perhaps already in the tempest itself) there were for Ignatius "great lights and consolations". Frequently, the only grace one remembers of these graces is the one called "the vision of the Cardoner": the *Autobiography* inclines us to a much richer view of these graces. "During this period," said Ignatius, "God treated him exactly as a schoolmaster treats a child: he instructed him."[26] It is necessary to see the point of departure: Ignatius at this moment knew of his religion only what he had learned at the school of Azpeitia, that is to say, very little: he was "untutored and ignorant", and had not had, and did not have, anyone to teach him. Now, here, according to his own avowals, is what he learned from God at Manresa; he had knowledge[27] (1) of the mystery

---

[24] *Autob.* R.P., p. 60. This general confession spread out over several days was, and long remained, a Christian custom.

[25] *Autob.* R.P., p. 65.

[26] For this and the following quotations, see ibid., pp. 70–75.

[27] It was Ignatius who thus numbered the enlightenments received at Manresa.

of the Holy Trinity; (2) of the manner in which God created the world; (3) of the manner in which Jesus Christ Our Lord exists in the Holy Eucharist; (4) of the humanity of Christ, and of Our Lady; (5) of "many things, as much of the spiritual order as of the domain of faith and of *letters*" (that is, the "illumination" of the Cardoner). All these things by means of (simple, summary, almost childlike) "visions", except specifically the fifth where no visual support was part of the illumination. And these "teachings" which he received were not simple enlightenment but transforming illuminations. Of the first, he said "throughout his life, this impression remained with him of feeling a great devotion when praying to the Most Holy Trinity"; of the fourth: "These visions confirmed him and *gave him so much assurance in faith* that very often he told himself that if there had been no Scriptures to teach us these truths of faith, he would have been ready to die for them, solely because of what he had seen at that time." It was especially in regard to the teaching received near the Cardoner that Ignatius is most categorical: "That [happened] in such a light that everything appeared *new* to him." And Câmara added more in the margin concerning this memory of Ignatius: "That happened in a manner to leave him such enlightenment of mind that he seemed to himself to be *another man* and to possess another intelligence than the one which he had previously had."

This time, we are really faced with a radical phenomenon of conversion, the metamorphosis of the carnal being into the spiritual being, to use the words of St. Paul. *Homo Novus*, that is what Ignatius became. And it was in the most intimate part of his personality that this transformation took place. Henceforth, his "union" with the Triune God would be constant, and would take precedence over all his loves. He was introduced into the freedom of the sons of God.

Three points should also be noted: first, the appearance of exceptional phenomena, notably "the tears and even the sobs": these were evidently the physiological after-effects of his profound change. And for my part,[28] I am inclined to believe that the "visions" "the three keys of the keyboard" for the Holy Trinity; the "white thing from which radiated a few rays" for the Creation; the "white body, neither large nor small and without distinct members" of the humanity of Christ and, a fortiori, "the thing which was so beautiful and had a great number of eyes" were nothing more than psychological reactions to his deep emotion: they were of a sobriety which corresponds too much to the natural imagination of Ignatius. And the fact that the *teachings* of the Cardoner were done

---

[28] So many interpretations have been given of these phenomena, and by highly competent authorities, that I propose this interpretation only with timidity.

by illumination, not "by vision", without shaking so violently his sensibility, appears very much to confirm our hypothesis. No matter, the essential is not there: the essential thing is that Ignatius, thirty years after the event, when he had know other graces and other visions, could date his "interior renewal" from this time at Manresa.[29]

The second point to remember is that the exceptional graces received at Manresa, like those of Loyola, were linked to "familiar conversations", as those of Loyola were linked to "spiritual colloquies" with his followers.[30] This "new soldier of Christ", as he called himself, kept his natural radiance. These conversations provided aid for his listeners: "Beyond his seven hours of prayer, he busied himself with helping friends who came to seek him in their spiritual life."[31] Finally, this decision, the suddenness of which was much in the style of Ignatius: "After the divine consolations had begun and he saw the success which he had in treating souls, he abandoned the excesses to which he had previously devoted himself. From then on, he cut his nails and hair",[32] that "beautiful hair of his" which he had not tended after his conversion.

Here we touch on a very important point, and one which will continue to develop in Ignatius' conduct, what one could call the concessions of the mystic to a more efficacious apostolate. From its very weight, the love of God, when it has pervaded a soul, inclines it to scorn the "things of the world", and even to react excessively to what was formerly an occasion of sin. That is what the pilgrim did at first; but his break with his past, his surroundings, his worldly life and his family was radical, total; and here was the first gesture by which he relaxed his stringent requirements: he cut his nails and his hair. . . . Soon it would be studies, and for the studies, the acceptance of money; later, human relations and politeness. His ascetic requirements would give way each time that a better apostolate would solicit him—but to the extent that all these things were in themselves "indifferent".

He was really a "convert", a free man, who departed from Manresa for Jerusalem in February of 1522.

Fourth Stage: The Jerusalem Pilgrimage (February 1523–Lent 1524); The Spiritual Experience of the Way

---

[29] The attribution of the vision of the serpent to Satan, by Ignatius himself (*Autob.* R.P. p. 75) does not go against our hypothesis: Satan, according to spiritual authors, can act on the imagination.

[30] *Autob.* R.P., p. 65.

[31] Ibid., p. 69. But he recognized moreover that he himself also found help in so doing: cf. ibid., p. 80.

[32] Ibid., pp. 72–73.

Inigo would finally realize his great dream of rivaling the saints and of making his own adventure in the service of his leader, Christ Our Lord. But it was with a new soul that he was going to accomplish it: the love of his Lord and no longer the love of himself.

It is, however, noteworthy that this love, of which he was henceforth possessed rather than possessing, had not as yet transformed his natural temperament. One could, without forcing the text, place in parallel or superimpose the pilgrimage to Jerusalem and the Pamplona affair. His rapidity and strength of decision, his obstinacy in fidelity to the ideal of which he dreamed, his strength of spiritual influence, his scorn of all obstacles and all objections were, here and there, the same; but all had taken on a new meaning: previously it was confidence in himself, here it was confidence in God, faith, hope and charity; there, it was the desire for his own glory, here it was the "fear of vainglory" and desire for "the greater glory of God".[33]

The Road to Jerusalem would mark Ignatius deeply. It was the route to true companionship with Christ in his historical reality, his Incarnation, his suffering as a man, his resurrection; it was the plunge into the event of Pentecost and the mystery of the Church. This Road to Jerusalem was a unique fundamental experience of the mystical life. It was an experience henceforth unforgettable: all his life Inigo would remain "the pilgrim", even when he would be closeted in Rome by his functions as General; the "roads of the world" would not for him be equivalent to the Road to Jerusalem, divinely prolonged by the exaltation of Jesus Christ.

Inigo departed for Jerusalem with a well-fixed idea: "His well-fixed plan was to remain in Jerusalem to visit constantly the holy places there. He had also, beyond this devotion, the plan of helping souls." This plan was previous to the embarcation, since "to this end he carried letters of recommendation for the guardians [the Franciscans]". This trip and this sojourn he had well decided to accomplish in absolute, radical poverty, to the point of risking his life, his health, and one might say, to force God into a miracle. "Although certain ones offered to accompany him, he wanted to travel without companions, for the essential thing for him was to have God as his only refuge."

Having established this purpose, nothing could deter him from it. He knew neither Italian nor Latin; he would need an interpreter. "He answered that even if it were a matter of a son or brother of the Duke of Cardona, he would not go in his company. He desired in effect to practice three virtues: charity, faith and hope." No provisions, no money; if he accepted them, he reproached himself for it quickly as a

---

[33] *Autob.* R.P., pp. 78–94.

weakness, he experienced "scruples" for it; he redistributed them to other poor people. He even refused to comply with certain formalities: no certificate of good health (although the plague was in Venice); he did not "take any special pains to know or seek how to make the trip". The Turks had taken Rhodes and held the Mediterranean; many people who wanted to depart for Jerusalem gave up on taking the voyage. Ignatius was one of those who persisted; he finally embarked sick, despite the contrary opinion of the physicians. "If it were to be buried in Jerusalem, he could well embark." At Cyprus a change of boat "brought him no other provisions than his hope in God". This would have been cause to put God to the test if the pilgrim had not been filled with the "conviction": "in his soul, he was absolutely certain that God would not fail to provide the means of going to Jerusalem for him, and that gave him so much assurance that all the arguments and all the fears with which he was confronted could not make him doubt." Decidedly, this road to Jerusalem was really, in its way, a mystical experience.

However, in Jerusalem it was necessary that the pilgrim capitulate, but not without fighting which he sustained to the end when he declared to the guardian of the Franciscans that his intention "to stay there because of devotion"; the latter confronted him with the extreme poverty of the convent. "The pilgrim answered that he expected nothing from the house, except that someone hear his confession from time to time." The guardian then submitted the decision to the Provincial; the latter refused: "Many in effect had had the same desire, but one such had been captured and another was dead. Consequently, he must prepare to depart as early as the next day." The pilgrim was stubborn: "He responded to this that his resolution was well fixed and that he saw no reason to give it up for anything in the world; he gave him politely to understand that, despite the Provincial's unfavorable opinion, no fear would make him abandon his resolution, except to hold to it under pain of mortal sin." The Provincial then threatened him with bulls from the Apostolic See which gave him power to excommunicate anyone who refused to obey him. The pilgrim capitulated. Let us note this first capitulation of Ignatius; if he did give in, it was only before a decision of the Church: but then his action was clear, frank and immediate. The next day he reembarked for Cyprus.

The spiritual progress realized by Inigo during this pilgrimage was considerable. Nothing, without doubt, could be superior to what he experienced at Manresa; but at the heart of this experience composed of illuminations or inner revelations, the contact with the land where the Lord was born, lived, died and came back to life, created a sort of realistic "reverie". Jerusalem laundered, so to speak, Inigo's devotion of all vestiges of dreams and abstractions. Not that he had not again been favored with exceptional phenomena and even with numerous "visions", but one will note that, in those which he reported, there was nothing that concerned the Trinity nor the divine Essence. All concerned the historical person of the Incarnate Word.[34] Lacking that lost letter wherein he recounted his trip,[35] we have at least the account of his last day as a pilgrim.[36] "This [his departure] being taken care of, as he was returning, an active desire came to him to visit one more time the Mount of Olives before his departure." Why? "There was at the Mount of Olives a stone from which Our Lord mounted to the skies and one could still see there the imprint of his feet: it was that which he wanted to see again." However, "those who went there without a Turk to guide them, ran a great risk." No matter. Ignatius ventured forth alone: giving the guards the little penknife from his desk, he was granted permission to enter the sanctuary. He prayed and departed: suddenly, he remembered that "he had not looked at which side was the right foot and which side the left." He retraced his steps, and divesting himself this time of his scissors, he could enter anew. At the convent of Mt. Zion where he stayed, his absence was noted and they sent to seek him a "Christian of the belt", that is to say, a Syrian, half-servant, half-soldier, who grabbed him vigorously and threatened him with his staff. "As Inigo was making his trip, he seemed to see Christ continually around him, and this consolation lasted with unceasing intensity right up until his arrival at the monastery." This experience sheds light on some interesting perspectives for us: the detailed realism of Ignatius' devotion, his scorn of prudential instructions, the link between his "visions" (even if, as it seems may be the case, it was a matter of merely natural imagination) and his emotions, his "consolations", the primacy of the Christ-like visions over the trinitarian visions on this pilgrimage to Jerusalem—all is gathered together here. And, during this solitary escapade to the Mount of Olives, Inigo experienced "intense consolations": several times previously, he had experienced such feelings. It was "in joy" that he accomplished all of this pilgrimage: an intense joy which overwhelmed,

[34] *Autob.* R.P., p. 85, and always with the same poverty of images.

[35] No doubt this letter of which Ribadeneyra speaks (*Font. narr.* 1, pp. 1–4). The "journals along the way" of two of his companions on the pilgrimage, Pierre Füssli from Zurich and Philip Hagen from Strasbourg, with which biographers console themselves for the loss, obviously tell us nothing about the personal feelings of Ignatius.

[36] *Autob.* R.P., p. 88. One will note that the "Mount of Olives" is at the same time the place of the Agony of the Lord and of his Ascension, of his "rising in glory": the curiosity of Ignatius was not without spiritual significance.

absorbed, his entire being, a joy which was at the same time "consolation and strength" (*mucha consolación y esfuerzo*). He inhaled in deep breaths, the freedom of the Way of Christ. Nothing in his life would surpass this experience; on the contrary, this experience would return again and again, like a secret source, in all that he would henceforth achieve. He was definitely "the pilgrim of Christ".

The refusal to the Franciscans to let him stay in Jerusalem posed an urgent problem for him, *Quid agendum*? What should he do now? Become a Carthusian? No, decidedly that was not his way: he certainly appreciated the life of the Carthusians "hidden in Jesus Christ for God", the simplicity and the severity, the fasts and the austerities; but the solitude was not to his liking, he had the instinct and had fostered the desire for "aiding souls". In this direction, he oriented his life according to the signs of God. He decided "to go thus throughout the world", moved by his permanent desire always "to forge ahead", he took stock of his poverty, catechetical so to speak, and wanted to improve it: the "schoolmaster", who had so much illuminated him at Manresa was not a professor of theology. The fervor of the soul, experience of the ways of God, even vigor of faith, did not confer competence, nor supply his lack of "culture". It was necessary for him "to study": to study when he was over thirty? What did it matter? He would return, then, to Barcelona.

The decision was a serious one. For several months, Inigo had again taken care of his hair and nails, because "to help souls" seemed to him to demand it. Now, the same reason led him to surrender on another point: study. Did he measure the risk that he was taking? For the moment he retraveled the road to Jerusalem in reverse, not without adventures: from Ferrara to Genoa, the country was occupied by troops of Charles V and of Francis I; from Genoa to Barcelona, the sea was held by Admiral Andrea Doria. What did that matter to him? He went his way, dressed in rags: "The pilgrim wore no other clothing than breeches of thick canvas which went down to his knees, leaving his legs bare, shoes, a doublet of black material torn at the shoulders and a hooded cape—short and worn." Unwelcome were those who gave him advice of simple prudence. "He did not follow their advice."

Fifth Stage: The Time of His Studies: Barcelona, Alcalá, Salamanca, Paris (1524–1535) or the Withdrawal of the Mystic

Let us not give the word "withdrawal" the least significance of abandonment; it signifies merely that the mystic would have "to deal" during this period with other cares. We could have borrowed from Ignatius his own word, such as we find in a confidence to Laynez: "at the time when he was *distracted* by his studies (*en el tiempo de la distración de su estudio*)".[37] However, the expression appeared to us even more ambiguous than the word "withdrawal".

First, one fact is certain: in undertaking his studies, Inigo did not realize immediately that they could not be reconciled with poverty, prayer, mortifications and the apostolate of the pilgrim.

Once more "experience" taught him. It was truly difficult to be a "pilgrim" and a student at the same time. From the first day of his studies with Master Ardevol at Barcelona, he became aware of it: certainly, he threw himself into the rudiments of Latin grammar "with a great deal of zeal". However, "when he wanted to learn by heart, as is often necessary in the beginning of grammar, a new illumination overcame him, with a renewed taste for spiritual things. This was to such extent that he could not memorize; it was in vain to deny it; he could not drive these illuminations away." However, a promise made "with much firmness" before Master Ardevol sufficed, this time to liberate Inigo's spirit for the demands of grammar. "He had great repugnance to study", reports Laynez, "because it was a matter of grammar and of human things, insipid in comparison with celestial ones."[38]

Grammar was not alone responsible. The same difficulty arose again in Paris, when, after the failures of Alcalá and Salamanca, he came to enroll in the course of arts (that is to say, philosophy): "From the time that he began to take lessons from the faculty, the same temptations which had overcome him when he studied grammar at Barcelona began again to assail him. During the course, he could not fix his attention because of numerous pious thoughts which overcame him." And he renewed his performance at Barcelona. "Seeing that in this manner he was making little progress in letters, he went to find his master and promised him never to miss class, so long as he could find bread and water for his own existence. This promise made, all the devotions which had come to him at inopportune times left him and he progressed tranquilly in his studies". If one can believe Ribadeneyra, the sacrifice of Inigo went ever further: the two roommates of Sainte Barbe, Inigo and Pierre Favre, made a pact not to talk of things relating to God because "once they began, they forgot all about Aristotle and his logic."[39] It was the same with everyone: Inigo renounced—momentarily and not without exception—"speaking of things relating to God. However, after the course, we shall resume our custom."

The first limitation of the myticism by studies would be accompanied by others which were more profound. Would Inigo take his degrees—

[37] *Scripta* I, p. 127; *Font. narr.* I, p. 140, cited by GUIBERT, *La Spiritualité*, p. 16.

[38] Diego LAYNEZ, letter of 1547, *Font. narr.* I, pp. 90–92, n. 22.

[39] RIBADENEYRA, "De Actis, Patris Nostri Ignatio", ibid., 2, p. 385.

and degrees which then were so expensive? He opted for the bachelor's degree, the licentiate, then the master of arts: despite the fact that these titles involved risk of vain-glory. And then, to live one must have money. To beg, that was the end of studies! Should he go back to benefactors who with a single gift would liberate him from all financial care for a year at least? So be it, but it was necessary to go begging in Flanders or even in England, to the rich Spanish merchants. Moreover, soon Ignatius no longer begged for himself alone but for his companions as well. Light though the wallet might be, it was no longer the beautiful "hope in God" of the Jerusalem pilgrimage!

Without doubt, Inigo profited from all the opportunities which arose to satisfy his thirst for sufferings and humiliations, and the jails of Alcalá and Salamanca on this point gratified him. To one of his judges who was astonished that he did not escape one day like the other prisoners, he answered, "For me, there are not so many bars and chains at Salamanca that I do not desire even more for the love of God." Undoubtedly, he would again take to the road with joy when it was necessary and there, he would find again his dear penances, mortifications and his fasts: the trip which he made to Rouen, to encounter the swindler who had divested him of his first money, was accomplished "without drinking or eating, and barefoot". Doubtless, he still bravely faced repugnances so far as to carry to his mouth the hand of a plague-stricken invalid. All these actions, wherein we find the neophyte who wanted to rival the saints, did not resolve the problem which posed itself to him henceforth: one did not live in the university world without accepting the required structures, honors, money and health. How to reconcile what seemed irreconcilable? Ribadeneyra bears witness, for example, that while Inigo was studying he contented himself with serving Mass and making a short prayer.[40] As for Father de Guibert, he wrote,

> Neither is there any reason to think that in his prayer there was an interruption of infused graces and a return to a prayer simply discursive or imaginative, even to one highly simplified. His manner of union with God must have kept the character of passivity which Divine Providence, it seems, usually does not withdraw from souls who are truly faithful, once this gift has been given to them. Ignatius, then, remained under the guidance of a special and very strong grace, which caused the essential elements of infused union to persist in him. But the more conspicious and extraordinary manifestations of this divine activity in him are no longer what they were at Manresa. Neither are they yet what they will be when they will come anew in Italy and at Rome.[41]

[40] "Dicta et facta Patris Nostri Ignatii", *Scripta* I, p. 395. n. 10.
[41] *La Spiritualité*, pp. 17–18.

It may well be, but we would like to know how in his soul and conscience Inigo the student succeeded in balancing his mystical desire and the conditions of his existence. One solution would stand out if we were sure that from this time in Paris the "Principle and Foundation", with its rule of *tantum quantum* for the use of created goods, already occupied in the *Exercises* (hence in the spiritual thought of Inigo) the place which it occupied there in the definitive draft, but on this point specialists are not in accord.[42] If, as Father de Guilbert thinks, the draft and the placement of this essential text date from the time in Paris, that would signify that his spiritual difficulties aroused in Inigo a profound reflection, and softened the absolutes of the pilgrim. Unfortunately, here we can only conjecture.[43] These years of study reveal to us another important development of the mysticism of the pilgrim. A development and not a transformation, for it was in the logic of his apostolic plan: in Barcelona, Alcalá, Salamanca and Paris, Inigo attracted companions. In Barcelona, Calixto de Sa, Juan de Arteaga and Lope de Cáceres, then later Jean Raynal. In Paris, Peralta, Castro, Amador, but especially those who remained faithful to him: Pierre Favre, Francis Xavier de Jassu, Laynez, Salmeron, Simón Rodríguez and Bobadilla. What is the significance of this companionship? If we believe Ignatius himself in his *Autobiography* his desire was contemporary with his decision to study in order "to do good for souls". "In Salamanca, at the time of his imprisonment, he had not lost these desires . . . of reuniting a few men animated with the same ideal and to keep the companions which he already had."[44] Polanco, in 1548, added an enlightening statement: " [In Alcala] he began to have a desire to add a few people to his *society* to follow from that time on the plan that he had to help reform, the flaws which he saw in the divine service and who would be like the trumpets of Jesus Christ, and he had four companions."[45]

In short, from these thirteen years of Inigo's studies, we have but a fragmentary, rather disparate view of his mystical life. In the same way,

---

[42] Cf. José CALVERAS and Candido de DALMASES, *Exercitia spiritualia* . . ., in MHSJ, vol. 100, pp. 31–32; and GUIBERT, *La Spiritualité*, pp. 107–108.

[43] What were the *Spiritual Exercises* in the time of Paris? We can only conjecture. All that we can affirm is that they were still presented in the form of a personal notebook of Ignatius: it was the notebook which he had shown to the Bachelor of Arts Frías of Salamanca (*Autob.* R.P., p. 107), then to the Inquisitor of Paris (ibid., p. 124). The latter, after having become acquainted with it, "praised it highly and begged the pilgrim to give him a copy of it: this was done". It no doubt concerned the notebook begun in Loyola and continued thereafter. But what were the contents of it? That is the real problem: we shall speak of it further on.

[44] *Autob.* R.P., p. 110.

[45] "Summarium hispanicum", *Font. narr.* 1, pp. 170, 35.

we do not know—and it's really too bad that we don't—too many things about the theological training which he received in Paris, which must have had some influence on his prayer. Even if we can establish that during the three years when he took courses of arts (October 1529–October 1532) he was principally nourished by Aristotle and that he very honourably passed his exams, we are less informed regarding what he learned of theology during the eighteen months that he devoted to the sacred science. Again, these "eighteen months" which are attested to in his diploma for the master of arts degree can be but an administrative formula: it was the schooling required in order to obtain the master's degree. Perhaps Inigo devoted, in fact, more time to theology: perhaps also he gave less, taking into account his trips, his illnesses and his apostolate. To what extent was he informed of the movements of ideas which agitated the university world of Paris at that time—Humanism, Reform, Protestantism—and what attitude did he take toward these "novelties"? We must say that we know very little about this and that we are driven back to rather problematic reconstructions. From his advice to Bobadilla to apply himself to theology with the Dominicans and Franciscans, rather than study Hebraic languages,[46] one cannot, it seems, draw any conclusion. It is a matter of personal affinity more than of principle. Moreover, as often happen, the conversations among the students must have exerted an influence at least as decisive on their doctrinal formation as the magisterial courses which they took: for everything was oriented toward helping souls. Whatever the case, it seems that his studies neither profoundly modified the "catechism" of Inigo, nor notably enriched his mystical life.

However, during this Parisian period a decisive event occurred: the vows of Montmartre.[47] This commitment, of a spiritual depth and marvelous theological sense, reassures us, if that is needful: Inigo always lived and made his six companions live in the atmosphere of Manresa and of his pilgrimage to the Holy Land. Was the time of studies a withdrawal of the mysticism of Inigo? Perhaps, if it concerned exceptional phenomena.

---

[46] We have already pointed out the existence of an enormous notebook of about a thousand pages, in which Bobadilla noted his extracts from reading and his personal reflections during the Parisian years (Opp. NN 52 in the Roman archives of the Society). There is also a quarto notebook of 343 folios in the archives of the province of Southern Germany; it represents the class notes of Jay. These are, in the current state of our knowledge, the only documents coming from the first Fathers which give us some idea of the atmosphere of the theological studies of the group. But further research on the side of the masters who were then teaching theology would be necessary.

[47] POLANCO, "Summarium hispanicum", *Font. narr.* 1, pp. 185, 57.

Certainly not, if it concerned his veritable, profound spiritual freedom. He can only turn back momentarily to expand soon and copiously into a priesthood entirely oriented toward the "service and praise" of God our Lord.

Sixth Stage: The Fullness of Christian Freedom (Azpeitia, Venice, Rome, 1535–1539)

In 1535, Inigo, emerging from a painful bout with illness, left his companions in Paris and took the road to Azpeitia. "The physicians said that only his native air was capable of curing him";[48] and then, after their vow of poverty, it was necessary to resolve the affairs of the companions in Spain. We shall return farther on to the effect of his actions in Azpeitia. Having visited the families of a few companions, he embarked at Valencia for Genoa although he had been told that Barbarossa cruised in the region "with many galleys". Having disembarked at Genoa, he took the road to Bologna on which he suffered much. Let us say in passing that it was in the course of this trip that he experienced the only "great fear" of which the *Autobiography* takes note.[49] From Bologna, he went to Venice: did he again study the theology interrupted in Paris? In any case, if he studied, he studied alone, and scarcely deprived himself of "devoting himself to giving the Spiritual Exercises and other spiritual conversations". The Paris companions (there were nine at present) rejoined him at the beginning of 1537, after an odyssey which must have made the heart of the pilgrim rejoice. Two or three months later, all save Ignatius departed for Rome in order to receive a papal blessing for the trip to Jerusalem and to obtain authorization to have themselves ordained. To go and to return "on foot and begging" in little groups of three. Upon return to Venice, all those who were not priests were ordained in June of 1537, "with the title of voluntary poverty and of sufficient scholarly preparation".[50] Then, while awaiting the opportunity "to go to Jerusalem" they departed again in small groups into cells in the environs of Venice, in order to prepare themselves to celebrate their first Mass:[51] "They thus passed forty days, doing nothing but praying."

During the first days of September, all reunited around Ignatius at San Pietro-in-Vivarolo and the new priests, except Ignatius and Rodríguez,

[48] *Autob.* R.P., p. 122.

[49] *Autob.* R.P., p. 128.

[50] It was by favor that they were ordained "to the title of poverty" for that normally supposed that the one ordained belonged to a religious community which took him in charge. As for the ordination "to the title of adequate knowledge", that was for the companions a certificate of orthodoxy and of studies rather than hope, as is the usual case, to obtain through it some fat sinecure.

[51] Cf. supra, pp. 26 sqq.

celebrated their first Masses. Two months more they lived together in Vicenza, combining their prayers with spiritual conversations and a some public preaching.

About his mystical life in Venice and in Vicenza Ignatius informs us soberly, in his manner, but magnificently:

> During his sojourn at Vicenza, it was the reverse of what had happened in Paris, the pilgrim had many spiritual visions, numerous and almost continuous consolations. During all these trips, and especially at Venice, when he got ready to receive priestly ordination and prepared himself to say Mass, he received great supernatural visits, similar to those which he had constantly had at Manresa.

Manresa! This evocation signifies it all. Manresa, but Manresa enriched by the priesthood of Christ. This time it was total eruption of the mystical life which unfurled in the soul of Ignatius; it was the plenitude of love, the summit of Christian freedom according to St. Paul. From this time of Venice and Vicenza, Ignatius would keep not nostalgia—for the grace would remain—but the presence, like that of supreme joy, that a man could taste here below. Something of these intimate feelings appeared in the letter which he wrote in August 1537 to his friend Peter Contarini:

> we experience more each day the verity of these words, *"having nothing and possessing everything"* (2 Cor 6:10). I can say that we have all that the Lord has promised to give in abundance to those who seek first the kingdom of God and his justice. If everything is given in abundance to those who seek the kingdom of God and his justice, can anything be lacking to those who seek only the justice of the kingdom and the kingdom itself? . . . Those, I say, who are not divided: *those who fix their eyes on celestial good?*[52]

It is not surprising, if at the end of a long deliberation, before separating themselves, the companions decided to respond to those who asked their name, "We are of the Society of Jesus."[53] This was not pride, as later they would often be accused; it was the fullness of love and of spiritual freedom.

In November, "both eyes fixed on celestial goods", that is to say, on Jesus Christ, Ignatius took the road to Rome with Laynez and Favre. On the way, near the place called La Storta, some fourteen kilometers from Rome, he experienced the mystical grace which is generally mentioned as the "vision of La Storta".

Have not certain hagiographers too much isolated this vision from the rest of Ignatius' mystical life? And in so doing, have they not

---

[52] SAINT IGNACE, *Lettres* ("Christus" collection), pp. 63–64.

[53] *Summarium hispanicum, Font. narr.* I, pp. 203–4; cf. supra, p. 28.

fundamentally harmed the latter? In fact, what is called *the vision* of La
Storta should be called the *visions* of La Storta. If one refers to the most
certain non-Ignatian source of this event,[54] that is, to Laynez's report to
all the Fathers in Rome in 1559, calling to mind the *recent* confidences of
Ignatius, it is necessary to distinguish at least two successive times in this
revelation. First, during several days, an interior *word* of the Father
which *imprinted itself in the heart* of Ignatius, in the course of the Mass: "I
shall be favorable to you in Rome" [you in the plural]; and another time
(*poi un altra voce*), it was undoubtedly the episode of La Storta "it seemed
to him that he saw", said Laynez "Christ with his Cross, on his shoulder
and near him the Eternal Father who was saying, 'I want you to take this
one as your servant.' And thus Jesus took him and said; 'I want you to
serve us.'" This time the words (you in the singular) and the gestures
concerned only Ignatius. This testimony by itself thus leads us not to talk
as if it all took place in the chapel of La Storta at one single time.

But why not hold to the restrained confidence Ignatius makes in the
Autobiography?[55] It agrees with all that we have discovered up to the
present of the extraordinary phenomenon of "vision", as experienced by
Ignatius.

"He had decided", the *Autobiography* tells us, "to remain one year
without saying Mass, preparing himself and asking the Madonna to be
willing to unite to him her Son." A longtime desire which dated from
June 1537, and about which he had frequently besought the Virgin.[56]
"And one day when he found himself in the church saying prayers—it
was a few miles before arriving in Rome—he felt such a change in his
soul and he saw so clearly that God the Father was uniting him with
Christ his Son, that he would never dare doubt that God the Father had
united him with his Son." Then there was first, a transforming illumination which provoked in him a profound emotional shock. This illumination was accompanied, without being a part of it, by a "vision": Ignatius
did not specify whether it was an "exterior" or an "intellectual" vision:
he did not speak of "words" exchanged before him between the Father
and the Son.

---

[54] The other principal accounts, which have been exploited by biographers, are: Nadal
(4 accounts), Polanco, Ribadeneyra (2 accounts) and Canisius: the comparison of these
different accounts is very interesting. Note that in 1601, Oliverio Manareo, former rector
of the Roman college, former assistant of Mercurian, and Vicar General of the Society upon
the death of Mercurian, acknowledges not knowing where the vision took place. *Scripta* 1,
p. 507.
[55] One could legitimately wonder if this *desire* did not prolong the choice, made after
long deliberation, of the name of the Society of Jesus.
[56] *Autob.* R.P., pp. 132–133.

Seventh Stage: Ignatius in Rome (1537–1556)

Father de Guibert, who was, and still remains, one of the best analysts of the mystical life of Ignatius[57] entitles his study of this nineteen-year period, "the summit". He is right, provided, however, that this summit is not considered as a solitary mountain peak jutting out over the country-side, but as the purest and most elevated point of a chain of continuing mountains. On this mystical life of Ignatius, testimonies of contempora-ries abound. But none is so valuable as the memories of Ignatius himself. Ignatius himself.

At the end of the *Autobiography*, which ends practically with the Mainardi affair (1538), Câmara was able to add a few last confidences of Ignatius on the manner in which he composed the *Spiritual Exercises* and the *Constitutions*: in fact, Ignatius, in his brief notations, half-opened for us the treasures of his mystical life during his years of administration: "He had, he said, much offended our Lord from the moment when he had begun to serve Him, but he had never consented to any mortal sin. On the contrary, he believed (*crescendo*) always devotedly, that is to say, in the easiness of finding God, and now more than ever;[58] at any time, when he wanted to find God, he found him."[59]

A little overwhelmed by the number of exceptional phenomena which surrounded Ignatius' life and still envelops it, we like to set down the pertinent confidences which render it more intelligible for us; we find there the fundamental experience of the saints: the very strong feeling of their past sins and of their present negligence, joined to a parallel feeling of the presence of the action of God in themselves. Ignatius, by his expression, specifies for us that this sentiment, although it was gratu-itous, was permanent, that it awakened him to his clear conscience as soon as he communed with himself. Here we are, in what we call the ordinary of the extraordinary, in the highest and purest states of union with God often described by the mystics. Ignatius even joined to this a nuance of which certain ones of those favored by God tell us nothing: "He grew in devotion"; not all note that they experience this feeling of growing in the ease of finding God.

Was this state superior to the illuminations of Manresa? If we hold to the "five points" which Ignatius memorized after these illuminations: the Trinity, the Creation, the presence of the Body of the Lord in his Eucharist, the humanity of Christ (and Our Lady), the "numerous things as much of a spiritual order as of the domain of faith *and* of letters";

---

[57] *La Spiritualité*, pp. 22–57.
[58] This is in October 1555, a few months before the death of Ignatius.
[59] *Autob.* R.P., p. 137.

enlightened by the light of the Cardoner we have the impression that Manresa and Rome were two very diffirent mystical states. It was the feeling of "growing" which it would be necessary perhaps to analyze in order to answer well: what is an "increase" of faith, hope and charity? It is up to the theologian to tell us. It is at least certain that this growth is not of the order of the content of faith but of the profound union, of the attachment of a being to the Being; what is certain is that in Rome the "debates" of Ignatius with God, if we believe the *Spiritual Diary* (it is the only text with the direct notations), take on in Rome a violence of "feelings"—joy or anguish, consolations and tears—rarely attained by a human being: "Tranquility and extraordinary lightness," he noted on February 19, 1544, "to the point of feeling my intense love which I felt for the Most Holy Trinity."[60]

Whatever it was, the exceptional phenomena appeared more than ever as a repercussion of the intimate grace of love (*agape*) in an unusual temperament.[61] It sufices to open the precious and very enigmatic *Spiritual Diary* to convince us of it. On each page Ignatius avows himself "covered with tears and love",[62] "very excessive love directed to the divine Majesty and covered with intense tears".[63] Among these habitual phenomena appeared that interior or exterior *loquela*, which so disconcerted the commentators: "It seemed to me", he wrote for example on May 22, "that I took too much delight in the tone of the *loquela* as to its sound, without paying enough attention to the significance of the words of the *loquela*". Words and music, such are then the constituent elements of the phenomenon. St. Teresa, St. Francis de Sales and other mystics also tell us of interior and exterior "words"; the musical element is peculiar to Ignatius. Here, as when he saw the Trinity under the guise of "the three keys of the keyboard",[64] or in other musical visions, it is difficult not to recognize the projection of feeling in the sensibility of a man for whom music or "a chanted office" suffices to "transport him totally beyond himself", and to whom they "do good not only to the soul but also to the health of the body".[65] In the same way, all the visions of "Christ as a sun"[66] call attention to an imagination which had, since

---

[60] *Journal spirituel*, pp. 60, 68, 71.
[61] How interpret otherwise the trinitarian representation of February 19, 1544? (ibid., p. 66).
[62] Ibid., p. 76.
[63] Ibid., p. 83.
[64] *Autob.* R.P., p. 71.
[65] *Mémorial*, nn. 177, 178.
[66] *Autob.* R.P., p. 138.

Manresa, taken pleasure in "looking frequently and at length at the sky and stars"[67] and which at moments of "very great humility" could not "even look at the sky any more".[68] The astonishing thing is surely the importance that Ignatius attached to these phenomena, concerning his personal life, whereas in numerous letters, he denounced their ambiguity and declared that they were not necessary.

It may seem paradoxical to affirm that, in the middle of this unfolding of visions, tears, "motions" and *loquelae*, Ignatius in these years of administration appeared more and more "reasonable". Father de Guibert himself believed it necessary to note:

> At first, what dominated everything was an enthusiastic drive to attach himself to Christ whom he passionately loved, and to serve him on a magnificent scale. But little by little the difficulties, the repulses, the reflections, and study itself developed in Ignatius' soul his strong supernaturalized power of reasoning, that judgment so firmly guided by the faith. This power of reason and judgment did not in any way diminish his enthusiasm and docility to divine guidance. Instead, it united itself with the enthusiasm. The result was a harmonious union between Ignatius' driving love and his strong power of reasoning, and this combination was devoted to the service of Christ. That balanced union of the intellectual and volitional powers is perhaps the most characteristic trait in Ignatius' spiritual personality.[69]

To this statement, Ignatius himself bears witness: in his last confidences to Câmara, when he spoke to him about these visions in which Christ appeared to him "as a sun", he added: "It happened to him often when he was dealing with important things and [the visions] came to him *in confirmatione* [as a confirmation]".[70] Among these "important things" there was first of all the *Constitutions*: so "the very thick bundle of notes" that he showed to Câmara "concerned for the most part the visions which he had had in *confirmation* of some point of the *Constitutions*. He sometimes saw God the Father, sometimes the three Persons of the Trinity, and sometimes the Madonna who interceded [for him] and other times gave him confirmation." Between the drafting of a text and its confirmation, the step was enormous. It seems that although Ignatius had governed and created the *Constitutions* using his reason enlightened by faith, in working, consulting and reflecting before God, all he had asked from visions, tears and other exceptional phenomena was *confirmation*

---

[67] Ibid., p. 54.
[68] *Journal spirituel*, p. 92.
[69] *La Spiritualité*, pp. 56–57.
[70] *Autob.* R.P., p. 138.

of what he had decided or drafted.[71] This manner of Ignatius' working, if it was correct, would throw an extraordinary light on the "times of election" of the *Spiritual Exercises*; it would endow the "third time" (the time when the natural faculties functioned normally and peacefully) an importance, a value which the commentators did not always attribute to it; it would draw together the personal election with communal deliberation. All perspectives which would be more in conformity with the usual manifestation of divine grace and human liberty.[72]

We must regret that we cannot date exactly this confidence of Laynez to Nadal: "Ignatius is a very intimate and special friend of God *Deo familiarissimus selectissime*, for he has passed beyond all the visions, [like seeing present Christ, the Virgin, etc.,] so realistic that by images and subjective displays he lives in a state (*versatur*) of pure interior knowledge in unity with God (*in unitate Dei*)."[73] It very clearly tells us what the too-rare direct documents suggest to us: whatever importance Ignatius gives to them at certain moments, the true mystical life of Ignatius must be situated beyond the exceptional phenomena; it is "unity with God", beatifying participation in his trinitarian life, active illumination of the mind by the Holy Spirit, total interior freedom; it is personal grace and particularly intense faith, hope and charity. The rest is second, if not secondary; a matter of temperament and sometimes weakness of body. At the end of this analysis, it appears to us indispensable to relegate to second place, in the mystical life of Ignatius, the visions, words, tears, etc., whether it is a question of authentic charisms of the Holy Spirit or of projections, reactions of an exceptional fervor on the human temperament—and to consider as essential, first, this "love of the Father", of which St. John speaks to us: "If anyone loves me he will keep my word, and my Father will love him, and we shall come to him and make our home with him":[74] it is in the secret development of this Infinite Love in him that the incessant "conversion" of Ignatius consists.

---

[71] Cf. his prayer: "Eternal Father, confirm me; Eternal Son, confirm me, Eternal Holy Spirit confirm me; Holy Trinity confirm me; my God who is the only God, confirm me" (*Journal spirituel*, pp. 63, 65, etc.).

[72] One could show here how the notion of "mediator" (Christ, the Virgin), which Ignatius introduced in such an insistent manner in his *Spiritual Diary* balanced his theological universe. At the same time, however, when this notion, so theologically correct, is projected into a vision, it creates an imagery for which all the subtlety of the commentators could not succeed in bestowing the strictness of orthodoxy: such, among others, was this vision of February 27, 1544: "The feeling, *or more exactly the vision*, outside natural forces, of the Holy Trinity and of Jesus who presented me, or placed me, or served me as intercessor to the Most Holy Trinity" (*Journal spirituel*, p. 76).

[73] Jerome NADAL, "Patrum dicta aliquot", *Font. narr.* 2, p. 315, n. 10.

[74] Jn 14:23.

CHAPTER III

THE MISSION ACCORDING TO IGNATIUS

Ignatius of Loyola was a convert, and a convert who sought all his life to remain faithful to this first grace in truth, to develop it in himself and to expand all its riches.

It is from that point that one must set forth, if one wishes to understand his personal apostolic style, his evangelical action: this convert wanted to help others to respond to the permanent interior call, to conversion itself and to an ever greater conversion.

The great lines of force of his apostolic action he drew from his own spiritual experience. Every man who is converted certainly does not live this experience with the same intensity; but all happened just as if Ignatius was persuaded that what he himself had experienced was found again, at least basically, in every conversion.

I. THE ELEMENTS OF CONVERSION

1. A conversion has always *God's initiative* as its origin. It is, like faith, a free gift of God. In the conscience of each man, be he an unbeliever or be he a sinner, the Holy Spirit makes the call heard. A call which is specified by the event, the opportunity, the interior motivation, or by a combination of all these means. A call which imposes itself spontaneously, or launches a long debate in the heart of the man or which slowly mounts from the unconscious depths of the being up to a clear awareness. Ignatius knew this, from personal experience, at different stages of his life; he codified it in the rules regarding discernment of the spirits and selection in the *Spiritual Exercises* and he referred to it in numerous spiritual letters. God always has the initiative.

2. A conversion always reveals upon analysis a disproportion between motivations and decision. It is because the acquiescence (like the call, although under a different form) is a free gift of God: all spiritual "resurrection" operates "through the effect of the Holy Spirit". Ignatius was entirely aware of this. Manresa was, in his eyes, "his primitive church",[1] that is to say, a time of Pentecost, of charism, of disproportion. So he himself counted more on his union with God than on his own words, efforts or acts to effect a conversion. And he convinced his companions of it, if there was need of that: they themselves, when they

---

[1] Cited by GUIBERT, *La Spiritualité*, p. 16.

did missionary work, obtained spiritual results—Polanco notes this emphatically—which one can only attribute to the *Dextera Excelsi* or to the *Verbi Dei energia*. Thus the contradictions, the trials, the failures, the calumnies and the abuse were just as much opportunities for God to change hearts as were successes and supportive human friendships. The words with which Ignatius defined the true apostle *Instrumentum conjunctissimum Deo* finds here its meaning and its justification.

3. Under a (more or less pure and more or less uncertain) form, the convert, if he is faithful to the first grace, aspires to grow "in faith, hope and charity". This is what happened to Ignatius after Manresa: "He desired to practice faith, hope and charity."[2] The three *theological* virtues are the result and the sign of authentic conversion. This is true even if the baptismal life received or recovered still includes many defects because of temperament, even if it is accompanied by numerous temptations and weaknesses. It is the essential reference point that nothing can replace, not tears, or consolations, or long prayers, or penances.

4. This progress requires that the convert "henceforth order his life": one recognizes the saying from the *Spiritual Exercises*, and one knows what it signifies: it is a matter of "conquering oneself" and of "not making up one's mind through any disordered attachment". Asceticism is necessary to perseverance, and perseverance to spiritual progress. However, as a realist, Ignatius had always perceived that certain conversions could not be accomplished unless new conditions of life were created for the convert: he was always attentive to this favorable environment for a lived faith. Many of his "pious works" bear the mark of this concern.

5. Unconsciously perhaps, but really, the convert belongs to a new universe; not always by a radical, external break with the world, but by an internal one, by "intention". Now he participates in the universe of Redemption, to this body of which Christ is the head and at the same time the model, a life by the grace of baptism, nourished by the Eucharist. Through Christ, he learns to say "Our Father", to practice the love of neighbor and particularly the love of the poor and the ill, of all those who suffer. As Ignatius himself had experienced, the convert undergoes more or less profoundly, more or less rapidly, a "transformation of his being": Christ, suffering his Passion and resurrection from the dead, becomes the life of his life, mysteriously but efficaciously. He desires to know him by reading the Gospel and, if possible, walking in Christ's footsteps in the land of Jerusalem.

6. The authentic convert becomes a member of the Church. Not

---

[2] *Autob.* R.P., p. 78.

necessarily a clergyman, cleric or monk, but a man of the Church. He listens with respect to its counsels, practices its rites, and enters into its liturgy. He seeks the *company* of those who share the faith and hold to its unity. He desires its integrity and hence its reform—an incessant reform. He defends it and respects it. For its visible chief, because he is the successor of Peter and hence the Vicar of Christ on earth, he has devotion and fidelity: despite the faults of the Pope, if there are any, he recognizes in him a providential function. The growth of the Church through its missions, its peace, its unity, its honor, he holds close to his heart: if not, he is not really "Catholic".

Such is the true convert. Such was Ignatius. Such he desired that all men be in this tumultuous society of the sixteenth century, in this Church with its image marred by money, sensuality and power. One word summarizes the whole experience and all the desire of Ignatius in his apostolate: Reform.

It was for this that one day he set out en route "to help souls".

II. IGNATIUS OF LOYOLA, APOSTLE OF "CONVERSION"

It has often been said that Ignatius had practiced a mystical apostolate. It is necessary to understand this saying. From the moment that he centered his apostolate on the very act by which human liberty is converted under the action of God, Ignatius was to lean on divine forces of conversion, such as we have revealed above. Ignatius, in his connection with men, went right to the essential of the mystery of grace: in this sense, his apostolate was mystical. However, it was at the same time a practical apostolate aware of carnal realities: he knew from experience that grace passes through temperaments, situations and social conditioning: his apostolate was, in this sense, very human.

For more clarity, we shall distinguish five phases in the personal apostolate of Ignatius of Loyola, with the reservation of not erecting too rigid border lines among them.

First Phase: From Loyola to the "Time of Studies": The "Familiar Conversations"

It is notable that the first apostolate of Ignatius was, so to speak, an involuntary one. It was at Loyola and he was barely emerging from his own conversion. "He devoted all the time that he was passing among his people, to speaking of the things of God, thus doing good to their souls." An unsought, spontaneous effect gushing forth from what he had become—it was as simple as that! At the same time that he discovered in himself the interplay of spirits, and noticed alternations in his behavior, he discovered the efficacy of the "familiar conversations" wherein one "spoke of the things of God".[3]

This apostolate he soon practiced on the road. Thus with the Moor who "rejoined him on the way", he "struck up conversation and came to speak to him of Our Lady"—a conversation which almost ended in a stab wound!

At Manresa, at the very time that he knew his desert of purification, he conversed sometimes with spiritual persons who gave him confidence and sought his conversation; for "although he had no knowledge of spiritual things, he always showed great fervor in his manner of speaking and a great wish to advance in the service of God."[4] It was then less from doctrinal content than from their spiritual dynamism that these conversations of Ignatius did good to souls. But in return, whether at Montserrat or at Manresa, especially at the time of his scruples, Ignatius sought for his own profit the conversations "of spiritual men".[5] One incident is significant: at Manresa, he almost died.

> At this moment a thought came to him which told him that he was a righteous man. . . . When he recovered from his fever and was no longer on the point of death, he began to call loudly upon some women who had come to visit him; for the love of God, if they saw him again at the point of death, they should cry out with all their strength that he was a sinner and that he should remember the offenses which he had done to God.[6]

And his confidences on this time at Manresa end thus: "At this period, he had been for a long time very avid for spiritual conversations and to find people capable of them." This type of speaker is rare. "Before his departure, while he was still at Barcelona, he sought, according to his custom, spiritual persons, even if they lived as hermits far from the city, in order to converse with them. But neither at Barcelona nor at Manresa, during all the time that he spent there, did he find anyone who could help him as much as he wished."[7] Only one woman seemed to him "to go further into spiritual matters. So, after his departure from Barcelona, he totally lost this concern for finding spiritual people."

In these conversations, there was nothing affected or academic: just relaxed spontaneity. "From the time of Manresa on, the pilgrim had made it a habit, when he ate with others, never to talk at table; except to

---

[3] *Autob.* R.P., p. 58.
[4] Ibid., pp. 66, 69, 72.
[5] *Autob.* R.P., pp. 66, 68.
[6] Ibid., pp. 75–76.
[7] Ibid., p. 80.

answer; but he listened to what was said, gathering certain things from which he would be able to take the opportunity to talk of God, and that is what he would do after the meal."[8] Thirty years later, Câmara would give us examples of the very lively traits which characterized Ignatius' conversations and perhaps were the secret of their efficacy. Such was this portrait which would have charmed La Bruyère:

> The Father has great skill for recognizing the feelings and inclinations of each; for example, he talks of general things and while waiting until the one who is speaking to him comes to the point where he manifests what he has in his soul. In these conversations, he is so much the master of himself and of the person to whom he speaks that, even with a Polanco,[9] he seems to dominate him, as a wise man surpasses a child. I must recall a few details on this point, for certainly it is something quite admirable to see how the Father regards the face [of the one who speaks to him], although it is very rarely; how at times he is silent; finally, how he uses such great prudence and divine skills that from the first time that he converses with someone, he knows him immediately from head to toe.[10]

Happily, Ignatius was especially interested in "spiritual things": if not, what a godsend for those who saw in him a Machiavelli!

> One very surprising thing to see was with what patience he listened to the useless discourse of those from outside or of those from the house, long conversations which could be abridged, and how he concluded them; in such a way that one sees clearly that he held his thoughts to one side, putting the conversation in relation to some spiritual object to which he was obviously in the process of adapting it.[11]

In the "speaker" (if one may say so) one recognizes the manner of the writer:

> The Father's way of speaking consists in saying things uniquely in very few words. . . . What he puts there of art is restricted to this, he touches all the essential points which can produce persuasion and leaves aside all that does nothing for the situation according to what he judges expedient. And his manner of conversing is accompanied by so many gifts of God that it is very difficult to describe it.[12]

All those who have practiced the Exercises will recognize Ignatius in these traits.

[8] Ibid., p. 84.

[9] This incidental reference tells us more about Polanco than all the psychological analyses!

[10] *Mémorial* n. 199.

[11] Ibid., n. 202.

[12] Ibid., pp. 171, 172, n. 227.

Second Phase. The Time of Studies: The Familiar Conversations, the Spiritual Exercises, the Catechism

It is in recounting his life at Alcalá that Ignatius makes two new aspects of his apostolate appear. "He was also occupied there giving the Spiritual Exercises[13] and explaining the catechism." And he was aware of the disproportion between his poor words and the "fruit which contributes to the glory of God": "Many people arrived at a great knowledge and a very active taste for spiritual things. . . . A great crowd of people came forth everywhere that he gave the catechism."[14] Now, this catechism was very rudimentary: it contained the simplest truths of Christian doctrine. As for the "Spiritual Exercises", we are still far from the structures which they would present a few years later; one must give to the word "exercises" its most ordinary meaning; what Inigo taught to the people were fundamental prayers like the Our Father, the Hail Mary, and also the Commandments of God and twice-daily examination of conscience; even more, he encouraged them to confess and to take communion, as often as daily. To this he added, in accordance with the persons's level of culture, "the three powers" (which is to say: meditation on sins through the three powers of the soul), "the five senses" (meaning the *primus orandi modus*). All was supported by advice for discerning in oneself the interplay of joys (consolations) and sadnesses (desolations) such as they would later be formulated in the "Rules for Discernment of Spirits" of the "First Week" of the *Spiritual Exercises*: these are the fundamentals of the "conversion" from sin to the state of grace, or sometimes from good to better. Were other exercises already added to these? "If we wish", writes Father de Guibert, "to try to specify this *substance* of the Exercises established at Manresa (but who tells us that Ignatius had not introduced into them some elements drawn from his pilgrimage to Jerusalem?), the question becomes very delicate and opinions vary among the most competent historians."[15] What *seems* certain is that Ignatius did not exceed then, especially for people in the world, the perspectives of the first week. Did he push farther ahead with some people who desired to offer themselves "to show the service of God"? It is not impossible, since he tells us himself that the Exercises lasted sometimes "a whole month".[16] In any case, long or short, they were

[13] It is here that we find for the first time, subject to error, the expression "give the Spiritual Exercises": Cf. *Autob.* R.P., p. 97.

[14] Ibid.

[15] Cf. GUIBERT, *La Spiritualité*, p. 104. We shall take good care not to add a new hypothesis for so many interpretations. Cf. the minute and quasi-exhaustive study of the subject in *Exerc. sp.*, passim, notably pp. 30–32.

[16] Cf. *Scripta* 1, p. 611 (documents regarding the trial of Alcalá of 1527).

already producing strong impressions on the nerves of certain female auditors: the inquiry of the trial at Alcalá tells us of crises, weaknesses and fainting, . . . that Ignatius immediately attributed to the devil.[17]

Thrown into the prison of Alcalá, Ignatius received many visits. "Many people came to visit him. He explained the catechism and gave the Exercises as when he was free."[18]

The confidences of the *Autobiography* on the difficulties Ignatius and his companions encountered at Salamanca will furnish us with important lights on their apostolate.

To the assistant prior of the Dominicans who asked him: "What do you preach?" the pilgrim answered, "We don't preach; we content ourselves with talking familiarly about things of God, for example, after the meal, with the few people who have invited us."

"What are these things of God of which you speak?" insisted the monk.

"We speak", said the pilgrim, "sometimes of one virtue, sometimes of another, praising it; sometimes of one vice, sometimes of another, condemning it."[19] As the monk raised his voice little by little, Inigo cut short the conversation and retreated into silence. They cloistered him with Calixto de Sa, at the time of denouncing them to the judges. "Their room was almost always full of religious who came to see them. And always the pilgrim spoke of the subjects which were habitual with him."[20] At the end of three days, they put the two in prison, chained together. "Many people came to visit them and the pilgrim continued his conversations on God, etc. Frías, who had a bachelor's degree, came to interrogate them, each one separately. The pilgrim gave him all his papers, that is to say, the *Exercises*, to examine." His four judges read his notebook, came to ask Inigo "a host of questions, not only on the *Exercises*, but on theology" even on canon law.[21] In the answers of the pilgrim "they had nothing to challenge". Then "they made him explain the First Commandment. He began to do so, stayed on it so long and said so many things about it that they had no desire to ask him any more questions." Ignatius had to smile in reporting this victory to Câmara.

The judges "insisted *very much*", continued Ignatius, "on this single point: 'when is a thought a venial sin and when is it a mortal sin?'" It was in their eyes the sore point in the pilgrim's doctrine. And when, finally,

---

[17] Ignatius hardly doubted the existence and activity of Satan: his demonology is closely allied to that of the Middle Ages.

[18] *Autob.* R.P., p. 100.

[19] Ibid., p. 104.

[20] Ibid., p. 106.

[21] *Autob.* R.P., p. 107.

they gave a favorable judgment ("they could teach catechism and speak
of the things of God"), they made only one reservation: "on condition
that they never made any determination as to whether any act was a
venial or a mortal sin, until they had studied for four more years."[22]
Now in this simple restriction, Ignatius, who took exception to the
judgment but promised to respect it, saw the ruin of everything that he
was doing "in order to help souls": "To forbid him to define what was
mortal or venial sin, was, in his eyes, to close the door of his apostolate
to him."[23] This distinction between mortal sin and venial sin was part of
the "general examination of conscience in order to purify oneself and to
make a better confession": the importance that Ignatius attributed to the
sentence of his judges clearly indicates that his apostolate aimed at
"conversion" above all else.

He decided to go to Paris to pursue his studies. There, for seven years,
he was more reserved in his apostolate: from fear of new difficulties with
the Inquisitors? lack of time? primacy of studies? All of these motives
were doubtless combined. However, the matter of Peralta, Castro and
Amador showed that, at certain periods at least,[24] he "devoted more time
to spiritual conversations and he even gave the Exercises". Moreover,
we are certain that he gave the Exercises to each of his six companions,
beginning in January, 1534: but which Exercises? They were certainly no
longer the Exercises of Alcalá and Salamanca. Were they already the
Exercises of Rome? One may conclude that Ignatius, who from then on
had in his possession a text very close to the definitive text, varied it,
adapted it, lengthened it or shortened it according to persons and
situations: did he, for example, give the Exercises in the same manner to
Bobadilla and Favre, to Xavier and Laynez? That seems hardly likely.

Third Phase. Azpeitia (April-August 1535)

Episodic as this phase may appear, it was crucial for grasping the idea
that Inigo had of the apostolate. He was still not a cleric, nor even a
religious (in the canonical sense of the word: the vows of Montmartre
were "private" vows); moreover, the Eucharist and penance excepted,
here was someone who consecrated himself entirely to the "mission":
and that mission was essentially that of reform.

After the interval in Paris, he first resumed the customary forms of his
apostolic action: "In that hospital [where he lived] he conversed with
numerous persons who came to visit him about the things of God and
through his grace, he realized much fruit. From this arrival, he made a

---

[22] Ibid., pp. 108, 109.
[23] Ibid., p. 109.
[24] *Autob. R.P.*, p. 113.

resolution to teach the catechism each day to children." His brother objected to him that no one would come. "He answered that a single child would suffice for him." In fact, "from the beginning many people came to hear him" . . . including his brother. "Beyond the catechism, he also preached on Sundays and feast days so as to be useful to the souls that came from several miles away to hear him and in order to help them."[25] What did he preach? According to testimony of the trial of 1595, he elaborated upon the Commandments of God, commented on the Creed, taught how to pray; he explained what an "enormity" sin was. Polanco[26] adds that he also spoke of the Holy Trinity: the Our Father, the Creed, and the First Commandment provided him with the opportunity. Perhaps, in this large audience, it was necessary to satisfy some curiosity. . . . The good people of the region had not forgotten the elegant caballero, the hero rescued from Pamplona. However, the effect of these sermons was incontestably charismatic. It was "by the grace of God", "with the help of God", that all this good was brought about. Inigo was the first to be aware of this.

Up to the point there was absolutely nothing new in the apostolate of Inigo: but here he attacked the social evils which ravaged the country, and to do so, he did not fear to have recourse to the secular arm: "Thus regarding gambling, he managed to get it prohibited efficaciously, after having persuaded those who rendered justice to accept his views." Another scourge: concubines, especially those of priests;[27] and these liaisons were so commonly accepted that these concubines wore the veil, with which women did not cover their heads except after their marriage. "The pilgrim persuaded the governor to enact a law: every woman who covered her head for a man to whom she was not espoused would be punished by law." The poor, especially "the ashamed poor"—and they were numerous—were not forgotten: "He had an ordinance passed so that their needs would be regularly and officially provided for." To recall in the future all this action and its value, they would sound "the Angelus three times, morning, noon and night so that the people could pray as in Rome".[28]

---

[25] *Autob.* R.P., p. 126. Cf. *Epist. Mixt.* I, p. 46 and POLANCO, "Summarium hispanicum", *Font. narr.* I, p. 243. All that Ignatius says here is largely confirmed by the "survivors" who testified at the trial of 1595.

[26] "Summarium hispanicum", *Font. narr.* I, p. 186.

[27] In 1535, in Azpeitia (4,000 inhabitants) there was a rector, eight beneficed clergymen and fourteen chaplains who "were almost all leading a scandalous life" (José DE ARTECHE, *San Ignacio de Loyola* [Barcelona: Herder, 1941], p. 204. Cf. *Scripta* 2, p. 209).

[28] *Autob.* R.P., p. 128. It was only in 1540 that Ignatius asked his compatriots to institute, following the example of Rome, a confraternity of the Blessed Sacrament of which the purpose was to develop the practice of frequent communion.

Ignatius' apostolic action was already taking form in what he achieved in Azpeitia: the most elementary catechism, even if only for a single child, moral reform which attacked the social evils of society and was based (so that it would endure) upon legislation or at least solid regulation; these activities combined mysticism and realism. All that Ignatius accomplished in Azpeitia, he did alone, in scarcely three months, without any companion, while still a "layman", before priesthood and before he embraced the canonically religious life.

Fourth Phase, Venice: The Contribution of the Priesthood in the Apostolate of Ignatius

The place of the priesthood in the Society of Jesus is a question which is posed today: to respond to it would exceed the scope of this study. Perhaps, to clarify this debate, it would be useful to look closely at the situation of Ignatius and of his companions in these years, 1536–1537. Before tying the facts together, it is fitting to state them very objectively.

Familiar conversations, catechism, spiritual exercises, sermons of the preceding years, all aimed first at a general confession, then at regular weekly confessions. Penance and the Eucharist were at the heart of this apostolic action of Ignatius while he was still a "layman".

According to the plan of the companions in Paris, all were to receive Holy Orders. All prepared for it, all received them. Later, in the Society of Jesus which had become a religious order, temporal coadjutors were appointed to relieve the priests or scholastics preparing for priesthood of *officia domestica*, especially those which demanded a great deal of time, like cooking, gatehouse tending and shopping. This did not prevent these same *fratres laici* from pursuing, on occasion, the "ministries" which all laymen could legitimately exercise, nor stop priests and scholastics from being, on occasion, according to their abilities, coadjutors of the coadjutors.

Why then, if the priesthood held so central a place in the apostolic vision of the companions did they wait such a long time—forty days, Ignatius himself, more than a year—to celebrate their first Mass? Why does one not see them rushing "to aid souls" through penance and the Eucharist? Why, all their lives, did they no say their Mass every day? To understand it, it is necessary to consider the customs of the times and more seriously to examine the idea then held of the priesthood: the priesthood as such is at the service of souls. We do not doubt that if Venice, then Rome (in the first months when the companions stayed there) had lacked priests for confession and "distributing the Eucharist", Ignatius would have been the first to hasten to "utilize" his priestly ordination. In addition to service of souls, priesthood also appears as an exceptional grace for the priest; he is the object of devotion and a personal source of holiness: if the companions ordained in Venice waited forty days before celebrating their first Mass, it was to prepare themselves there in penance and prayer, in the purification of the "desert"; if Ignatius waited longer still, it was from hope of going to the Holy Land and celebrating his first Mass in Bethlehem surrounded by the mystery of the Incarnate Word; and if later he could not celebrate Mass every day, it was that in that celebration he received such an emotional shock that his health, especially his eyes, were affected by it. In other words, it is especially important to put oneself back into the climate of the sixteenth century and to distinguish clearly three aspects of the problem: the Eucharist, which is not separated from penance in the perspective of conversion; the priesthood which is located at the summit of missionary activity of the "*corpus Societatis*" and which thus characterizes the companion, whether he be priest or layman; the ordination of one or another companion, according to his personal vocation and the call of the superiors representing the Church.

It is in this light only that one can understand in what spirit (in Venice he was alone and still a 'layman'), the pilgrim "devoted himself to giving the Exercises and to other spiritual conversations".[29] This spirit which animated him in this work and in which he wished always to work in the future, he clearly defined in a letter of February 12, 1536, to one of his friends from Barcelona, James Cazador: "I would like, as a man of little importance, to preach on accessible and humble subjects, hoping from God our Lord that, if I am this humble conduit, he will give us the grace of being able to progress in the praise and service which are due to him." Where would this be? He did not know. "It will be, in any case, to preach in poverty and not with the cares and the impediments that I now have during my studies."[30] It was the period when he signed his letters adding to his name, *de bondad pobre*, poor in goodness, poor in that fundamental "goodness" that God the All-Good puts in the heart of man. He was, more than ever, in prospect of authentic spiritual efficiency: God alone gives fruit; it is up to us to acknowledge our radical poverty and to give ourselves up in all generosity to the humble tasks which the Lord indicates to us.

Thus he would continue to live—except for the time of the desert—after his ordinations, while Favre, Hozes and the other companions also, once they were priests, from time to time heard confessions. A little

[29] *Autob.* R.P., p. 128.
[30] *Lettres* ("Christus" collection), p. 46.

scenario, wherein one must perceive a touch of malice, permits us to imagine these first ministries of the new priests. Ignatius passed his "forty days in the desert" at St. Pietro-in-Vivarolo with Laynez and Favre.

> At the end of forty days, Master Jean Codure arrived and all decided to start preaching. All four went to different places, where the same day at that same time they began their preaching, crying very loudly in the beginning and calling the people on their own authority. These sermons caused a lot of reaction in the city; numerous people were touched with devotion, and the necessary material help came to them in great abundance.[31]

These were opportunities for practicing humility rather than preaching in the sense we give to that term, for, besides their clothing, their language was laughable. They jabbered a language in which they mixed fragments of Italian, Latin and French. Ignatius, they said, began his first sermon thus: "*Hojuordi [aujourd'hui] sancta mater Ecclesia . . .*"[32] However, people listened to them, and these droll "sermons" produced "fruits"!

In fact, this Venetian year unfolded in an atmosphere of expectancy: would a *navis peregrina* depart from Jerusalem or would it not? The companions watched for the least sign of departure. Their hearts were all turned toward Jerusalem, in the hope of working there, as priests of Christ, among the faithful and the infidels alike. A very special apostolate, evidently, which for the moment they did not wonder what it would be, once the occasion should arise, in some or other countries. They knew only that, if they could work in Jerusalem, this work would be an extraordinarily arduous apostolate, difficult in the extreme—Ignatius remembered his first pilgrimage—riddled with the daily risk of martyrdom. Martyrdom, a grace which, in the order of union with Christ, prevails over the priesthood itself.

The foreseen delay for the anticipation having expired, the companions divided themselves among the university cities of northern Italy. Ignatius, Laynez and Favre took the route to Rome. To anyone who asked their name, they would answer: "We are of the Society of Jesus", a title which they would not have dared to choose if they had not been priests.

Fifth Phase: Rome Before April 1541

On the route from Venice to Rome, Ignatius, who since his ordination had prayed to Our Lady asking her "to unite him with her Son", had his

---

[31] *Autob.* R.P., p. 131.
[32] NADAL, "Apologia contra censuram", *Font. narr.* 2, p. 84.

desire fulfilled: at La Storta he perceived that the Father asked the Son "that he take him with him".[33]

The apostolate of the companions in Rome, once they were all reassembled, was varied: they taught, preached, heard confessions or taught catechism to children, while Ignatius "gave the Spiritual Exercises to several persons in a group"[34] or individually, as to Dr. Ortiz, to Tolomei, Ambassador of Siena, or to Cardinal Peter Contarini. Two series of events occurred which marked the apostolate of the group with a frankly mystical note. They were, at first contradictory, i.e., the persecution which they underwent, "the most productive we ever underwent in all our lives"[35] and which risked leading them to the galleys or to be burned at the stake for heresy.[36] Then a little later, the famine which ravaged Rome (winter 1538-1539): the group then began a systematic apostolate among the poor, the beggars and the dying who, in case of public calamity, no authentic companion deserted or ever would desert.

Between November 18 and 23, 1538, the companions went "to offer themselves to the Pope".[37] Their action had not only administrative significance. From the circumstances—and especially from the past of Paul III which recalled to them that the Pope could be only a sinful man, although he was the "Vicar of Christ on earth", and Rome but "an ungrateful and desolate land"—their "oblation for all missions" was affirmed as a gesture of pure faith and evangelical hope. A few months later, on transforming this simple community oblation into a personal vow of obedience, they would cause what was only the promise of November 1538 to blossom: they gave to their availability its full evangelical meaning and its total spiritual value.

The first official "mission" that the Pope conferred on them in the universal Church was to teach catechism to the children of the schools in Rome. However, one can on cross-checking several documents derive some idea of other ministries that the companions exercised before the serious decisions of the spring of 1539 and the dispersion of the companions which followed. They received from the Pope the "powers of apostolic preachers",[38] and in effect they preached in the churches of Rome, perhaps also in public places;[39] Ignatius himself preached in

---

[33] Cf. supra, p. 425.

[34] Autob. R.P. p. 135.

[35] Font. narr. 1, p. 16.

[36] This is the Mainardi affair, already mentioned (cf. supra, p. 25); complicated by the Mudara and Barreda affair. Cf. Autob. R.P., pp. 135–36.

[37] Cf. supra, p. 31.

[38] Scripta 1, pp. 548–49.

[39] Bobad. Mon., p. 616; Epist. Broëti, p. 499.

Spanish in the church of Sancta Maria-in-Monserrato; the others in Italian:[40] they all preached, Ignatius admitted, "without elegance and style", and on very elementary themes; one easily believes this, at least for him who was never an orator. Laynez specified that these sermons were, especially for them, an exercise of mortification.[41] For them? And doubtless also for their audiences, but something got through to souls nonetheless.[42] They also taught catechism to children, and not, it seems, without a certain success, even though the urchins of Rome, malicious and unruly, did not hold back their jeers. However, at that time, it was the ministry of confessions which devoured their days and a part of their nights. In the *Deliberatio primorum patrum* of 1539,[43] the group declared that during this time of important decisions, they would continue, by day, to work "so as not to interrupt the great fruit which we are obtaining in confessions, sermons and other spiritual exercises; a fruit so great that if we were four times more numerous we would be far from satisfying all". Thus, their apostolic action took its priestly rhythm and as formerly they confirmed its charismatic character: there was a disproportion between what they did and "the fruit" which they produced.

Sixth Phase: Rome after the Election of April 1541

We have said that Ignatius as General continued to do "missionary" work personally; in him there reappeared the reformer of Azpeitia, but at present he was fortified with the powers of the priesthood. He continued his habitual preaching, spiritual conversations, Spiritual Exercises, indeed, even teaching catechism, and he added confessions to all that. Immediately, he took on sensitive projects which most concerned the reform of the Church, and in particular the reform of Rome: these burning issues we have already discussed; they were the conversions of catechumens, especially Jews; the reconciliation of Paul III and John III of Portugal; help to the "poor" of the City, aid to the "serious scourge" of "errant women" and young girls in danger; the spiritual care of the ill, etc. To all these evils, he strove to effect a solution which was both efficacious and lasting, a solution which might, on occasion, serve as a prototype for other souls dedicated to Catholic Reform. The missionary lived on in the General.

Two times at least—during the Ethiopian project and the project for North Africa—he dreamed of volunteering for perilous missions himself. Before all, his great care was to maintain and develop in the *corpus*

---

[40] *Epist. ign.* 1, pp. 137–44, n. 18. To Isabelle Roser, Dec. 19, 1538.

[41] *Font. narr.* 1, p. 124.

[42] Let us remember the sermons of the Curé of Ars.

[43] *Const.* 1, p. 5.

Societatis the spirit, the apostolic *mens et modus* with which he had imbued each of his first companions: the spirit that he drew him from his close union with Jesus Christ.

III. THE MYSTICAL ÉLAN OF THE "CORPUS SOCIETATIS"

One could not overestimate the spiritual value—the scriptural value—of the word by which the Society of Jesus was designated in its *Constitutions*: a "*corpus*". If nothing proves to us—to my knowledge—that in choosing this word, the companions had dreamed of the *corpus Ecclesiae*,[44] everything happened as if the mystical reality of the latter had inspired them: in any case, it is difficult to deny that they had sought to create among themselves such a link of unity, of charity and of spiritual communication, that their group thus testified to the unity of the Church. Only the Holy Spirit can permit men of nations, cultures, ages and temperaments all so different, working in conditions so diverse, to "form a single body", to "have but a single heart and a single soul", to obey but a single chief, to feel themselves members under a single Head. To show the unity of the Church was ipso facto to testify to its sanctity.

To maintain this unity, to reinforce it, to give it all its human and spiritual force, Ignatius worked with tenacity, whether through his *ars gubernandi* or through the drafting of the *Constitutions*.

Toward his *corpus Societatis* he strove to preserve the apostolic dynamism which had animated the companions before the foundation of the order.

It suffices to read the *Constitutions*, notably the "General Examen" and the seventh part which regulates "relations with one's neighbors", to see the continuity of the original spirit. The primacy of efficiency always belongs to union, "to good example of perfect honesty and Christian virtue", to "desires in the presence of the Lord our God", to "prayers for the entire Church", to "Masses and other forms of the Divine Office", to "administration of the sacraments, especially through confessions and Holy Communion", to the divine word sermons, courses, the teaching of Christian doctrine even in the city squares or elsewhere finally to the "spiritual conversations with individuals, giving counsel and encouragement to act well and to give the Spiritual Exercises".[45]

> To the extent that they will permit the *spiritual works which are most important* and to the extent that they will have enough strength, each will employ himself also in works of corporal mercy, for example, to carry aid to the ill,

[44] It was only later that Nadal would speak of the *corpus mysticum* regarding the *corpus societatis*.

[45] *Const.* part VII, chap. IV.

especially in the hospitals, in making visits and in sending a few people there to serve them and to settle disagreements; or again to act as much as they could personally and to get others to act on behalf of the poor and those detained in prisons.[46]

One could believe, in reading these texts, that nothing had changed in the apostolate of the first companions.

However, some serious problems presented themselves with the insertion of the group as a *corpus* into ecclesiastical society and into society as a whole. We have already seen that "to study", even if it were for the greater glory of God, Ignatius had had to sacrifice something of the *sancta mendicitas* for the demands of books, stays in the university, diplomas and degrees. At present with the development of houses and works, questions of money became more urgent and more thorny: without assured financial resources one does not project works like orphanages, St. Martha houses, Roman and German colleges, colleges for day students, or indeed, missions in India, Brazil and the Congo. All this activity demanded relations with the powerful of the world, rich and influential personages, princes ecclesiastical or temporal, municipalities, etc. From the mystical, one does not go to the political without some compromise nor even some compromising of principle. One can even fear that things will deteriorate in direct relation to the success and the size of the Society. Where are the "purity", the integrity, the *bonus odor Societatis*, so precious to Ignatius' heart?

The art of counterbalancing (or of counterpoint) did not suffice to prevent difficulty. Should one impose on the recruits a first training of the style of "Manresa" or of "Jerusalem" before starting them on their studies, on prestigious missions or those of great human influence, in important works? Indeed, should they even recommend that they combine, as much as possible, these brilliant ministries with purely spiritual ministries? What illusions were possible for oneself and for others since these mininstries were side by side rather than interwoven! And they intermingled only if the political became mystical and if the mystical in some way demanded the political. The integrity of Christian life assumed, required, the integration of human values.

It was to the credit of Ignatius not to enclose himself forever in the spirituality of the "pilgrim", not to wish to safeguard for himself or for some chosen companions the pure freedom of the Way, but to know how to rediscover this freedom even in servitude and the most human conditions, in every situation, to be at the same time very detached and very attached. Conversion is not fundamentally an incident in a story,

---

[46] Ibid., n. 650.

even if one can date the first manifestation of it to a clear conscience; it is, according to the words of Ignatius himself, "profound transformation of the being", as if the convert were "a new man"; he remains himself but is turned around internally, that is, he is turned toward another Love. From this transformation, incessant because always uncertain, Ignatius made a spirituality.

To this spirituality different names were given in the course of time: "contemplative in action", "service and praise of God our Lord", "for the greater glory of God", "with Jesus Christ, to serve", "*miles Christi*"; "spirituality of the *magis*", "*third degree of humility*". It is certain that each of these formulas, on the condition that it be understood with intelligence and not isolated, expresses a very important aspect, if not an essential one, of Ignatian spirituality.

In fact, if one applies one or the other of these formulas as "grids" to the *total* reality of the Christian life such as Ignatius understood it, one is compelled to state that one runs the risk of complicating what is simple, of containing what is effervescent, an incessant outpouring of systematizing what is personal invention, and especially of "encasing" in too human limits what is the divine measure of Creation and Redemption. Let us not seek to capture in human words, even if they are lifted from the texts of Ignatius, that which he himself wished to leave in simplicity, the savor, the love, and, above all the mystery of a Name: Jesus our Creator and Lord. The title, Society of Jesus, leaves far behind it all formulation, all "mottoes": it says everything, it excludes nothing.

Jesus! We have not always sufficiently noticed that he was present in the total fullness—plenitude, Saint Paul would have said—of his personality as early as the illuminations of Manresa: in his trinitarian reality and his role in Creation; in his historic and Eucharistic reality; in his *actual* life of Christ recapitulated; in his function as mediator. It is Ignatius who tells us this.[47] And he added, speaking of the Cardoner, "[The pilgrim] understood and knew many things of the spiritual order as well as of the domain of faith and of *letters*." Let us not neglect this small confidence: it signifies that already the human was integrated for him in the divine; and that the spiritual, that is to say, the action of God in souls—faith, that is to say, the revealed truths; letters, that is to say, human knowledge—all that for him was one with Jesus Christ. "Teaching" which enlightened "the eyes of understanding" but with such "light that all appeared new". Direct experience of the "Divine Mystery" *seen* in the person of Christ in such a way that "had there not been any scriptures to teach us" all that "he would be ready to die" for these realities "solely for what he had seen

---

[47] *Autob*. R.P., pp. 71–74.

then". This universe is that of St. John but John had seen and understood the Word of Life; it was also the universe of St. Paul, who, like Ignatius, had known only the resurrected Christ. Through the sobriety, the "rusticity", and the poverty of the Ignatian vocabulary, all the richness of the "Mystery" of Jesus[48] unfolds. Ignatius tells us again, by his life and by his work, the words of St. Peter confronting the Sanhedrin: "It is by the name of Jesus Christ the Nazarene, the one you crucified, whom God raised from the dead, it is by his name and by no other that this man[49] presents himself cured before you. . . . For of all the names in the world given to men this is the only one by which we can be saved." For Ignatius, Jesus was "God our Creator and Lord": Lord, the name "above all other names" by which the Father "exalted" the Risen Christ "so that all beings in the heavens, on earth and in the underworld should bend the knee", the name that "every tongue should acclaim . . . to the glory of God the Father".[50] Every human word fails before the Name that Ignatius gave to his Society and by which once and for all he defined its spirit.

[48] Col 1: 26–27.

[49] The sick of the "Beautiful Gate" of Jerusalem whom Peter and John had cured; cf. Acts 4: 10–12.

[50] Phil 2: 9–11.

CHAPTER IV

IGNATIUS' MESSAGE

A saint, even if he founds an order or a religious congregation, can be but an ephemeral witness, no matter how magnificent, of the all-powerful, all-bountiful, all-merciful God. The mystical spirit which animates him can have value only for a time, a region, an "epoch", because he is linked to a very characteristic mentality. How many congregations were thus born in the Church which were finally extinguished after having certainly illuminated and rekindled it splendidly? A few saints only have had the privilege, after having shone during their lives, to leave beyond them their personal mission, a universal mission, a source where generations may come, one after the other, to draw the living water.

One could have thought—some even think it today, wrongly, we think, and to the great detriment of themselves and others—that Ignatius of Loyola "has had his day", and that he will be surpassed in his turn. Has it not been said enough that he belonged in many aspects of his spirituality and his work to the Middle Ages? Or again, that his thought was "linked to the the theology of the Council of Trent"? Absolute fidelity to the Pope, blind obedience, abnegation, single-minded devotion to the Cross, penance; "poverty of the beggar", all these expressions, and still others, that have been taken from the Ignatian vocabulary to make of it—rightly or wrongly—characteristics of his spirit; who dares to pronounce them without surrounding them immediately with secular and secularizing commentaries? Have not we ourselves in this book lent a hand to this objection, recognizing in Ignatius a strength of exceptional will, rare extraordinary phenomena, an energy, a tenacity, a resistance to suffering which made him a being apart? What is there in common between this superman, hero and saint all in one, and the "ordinary Christian"? What can the humble baptized person draw from this monumental experience in encounters with his own difficulties, mediocrities and familiar conditioning?

It is the contrary which is true, The personality and the work of Ignatius continue to fascinate modern man, in the quest for truth in human existence, for sincerity with himself, with others and with God, authentic spiritual freedom, prayer and evangelical action. They fascinate and, if man's quest is accompanied by the virtue—both human and supernatural—that Ignatius himself called "generosity", they generally give to him the answer he expects; and this response is clear, firm and practical; it "changes his life".

In this contrast consists and has consisted from the beginning all the Ignatian mystery. On one hand, he appeared like a being whom nature and supernatural gifts had set apart from common humanity; on the other hand, this man touches in us the heart of our personality, the existential source of authentic freedom, the "inner recess of the soul" where we can neither use evasions with God nor lie to ourselves. We would like, in ending this long study, to outline an explanation from this contrast.

A saint, his life and his mission accomplished, leaves no message behind him unless he has succeeded in one way or another in "pouring out", so to speak, his own spiritual experience and rendering it capable of assimilation by the ordinary Christian, neither cleric nor religious, but engaged in the life of the world. It is the uncontested success, to cite but one illustrious example, of a St. Francis de Sales, with the *Introduction to the Devout Life*. "My intention", he says, "is to instruct those who live in cities, in households, at court and who by their condition are obliged to make a community life at least on the exterior."[1] And, in effect, his writings reached all social and religious environments, even among the Protestants; Philothea, each recognizes himself in her; moreover, Francis de Sales was himself a highly developed mystic. Ignatius has succeeded in his outpouring before Francis de Sales and without the magic of his style.[2] He left behind him to those who live "a community life at least on the exterior" an essential spiritual message. This message one can characterize in one word, on which we shall elaborate: it is the spirituality of "conversion". None better than he can teach a human being the art of converting himself to God or aid him more effectively to enter and progress in "faith, hope and charity".

I. IGNATIUS HIMSELF

This message consists, first of all, of Ignatius himself. To pretend that this is not so is to deal in paradox. No one should try to contradict this. We maintain that if one considers traits of his character and certain phenomena of his mystic life, he can disconcert, discourage and even rebuff certain people: Xavier himself or Nadal, at the time in Paris, Hozes at the time in Venice, were slow to let themselves be "won over" by this strange companion. During all of his life Ignatius knew personal

---

[1] Cf. our edition of *Oeuvres* in the Pléiade collection, p. 23.

[2] To say in passing, Francis de Sales, whether at the college of the "Gentlemen of Clermont" in Paris or whether in the course of his retreats, had recognized, practiced and assimilated Ignatian spirituality.

enemies and detractors; his force of will, his rigorous asceticism, his attention to detail sometimes separated him from certain souls. However, if one believes Câmara in his *Memorial*, Ignatius strove with all his strength to render himself agreeable and "attractive" to all. "He was always rather inclined toward love; moreover, he seemed all love, and because of that he was universally loved by all and there was no one in the Society who did not have great love for him and did not consider himself much loved by him." What was the source of this "love" with which the "subordinates" surrounded Ignatius? His "great affability; the great care which he took for the health of all"; and even in those charitable tricks wherein dour minds could see a bit of "Jesuitism": "The Father acted so that anything which might distress the inferior was never imposed by himself, but by another, without the subordinate's being able to think that the Father had any part in it; and on the contrary, for whatever might please the subordinate, the Father made himself the source." However, this was not a weakness; when he had business with vigorous souls of whom he was sure, Ignatius used an iron fist: "His circumspection was extraordinary in dealing with whatever person it might be, if it was not a Nadal or a Polanco, because he treated them without consideration, even rather harshly and with rigorous reprimands." Laynez perceived this, sometimes at his own expense: one day when he was dealing with Ignatius about an important matter, as he "insisted a little bit", he drew forth this response: "Very well! Take charge of the Society and run it." "With that", says Câmara, Laynez "had his breath taken away, and didn't add another word".[3]

If we have chosen these examples, it is because they manifest the work of self on self that Ignatius knew how to accomplish from the moment of his internal transformation at Loyola, but this transformed Ignatius who continued without ceasing to transform himself—do we know him well enough? Do we not prefer the Ignatius of myth and legend? One could multiply examples on other points.

There is one of them, however, in which Ignatius showed even more this progressive stripping away of the self for the profit of God. We have already said that pride dominated the natural temperament of the young hidalgo, a pride served by a vigorous will. Could one not fear that, converted, Ignatius would only transfer this willpower from "the things of the world" to "the things of God"? Indeed, this is what happened at first: at Loyola, at Montserrat, and even in the beginnings at Manresa, it seemed indeed that he had dreamed of being the knight of God, in flamboyant actions, "rivaling" those of St. Dominic and St. Francis of

---

[3] The quotations in this passage are borrowed from the *Mémorial*, pp. 96–104.

Assisi. However, without forcing the text, one confirms a transformation of this pride into peaceable and truly Christian humility. "The
Father told me", reports Câmara, "how he had been plagued, for two
whole years, by this temptation [of vainglory]. Thus, when he embarked
at Barcelona, he dared not tell anyone that he was embarking for
Jerusalem and the same occurred *on other occasions of the same kind*. He
added how much since then he had felt peace in his soul on this point."[4]
Peace, but a constantly threatened peace and one which demanded a
constant watchfulness; for his trip to Azpeitia, in 1535, there were several
motives, but was not one of them to prove to the six companions that
they could get along without him and to put Pierre Favre in the forefront
of the group, in his stead and place? At Venice, did he not do everything
to efface himself before Jesus Christ and to avoid having the group bear
his name? Let us recall his efforts to escape the generalship after the
election of 1541, his resignation of 1551, his plans to depart to Ethiopia
or Africa. And his concern not to "close" the *Constitutions*—did this not
come from a desire to submit what could be considered his work to the
criticism and recasting of the companions? Thus all his life he sought to
efface himself, "to become small", in the words of John the Baptist,
before the person of Jesus humbled, but without subtle detours, without
falsehood, without denying the good being accomplished, but making
all glory ascend to God alone: As a remedy for vainglory, Câmara also
said, "The Father advised me to report often all things to God, to strive
to offer all that there was of good in me, recognizing it as his and
rendering thanks to him for it."[5] Thus all was put back in its order with
rectitude and simplicity: the conversion of Ignatius, and conversion
according to Ignatius, was a return to the truth of being and of existence
in the love of Christ.

II. THE MESSAGE OF IGNATIUS' CORRESPONDENCE

This outpouring of his personal experience for "helping one's neighbor" manifests itself admirably in the spiritual letters of Ignatius. One
day (March 2, 1955), he told Câmara that "there could not be, in his
opinion, greater error in spiritual matters than to wish to govern others
according to oneself".[6] All his spiritual correspondence illustrates this
declaration. Two points, among several others from which we could

[4] *Autob.* R.P., p. 37.
[5] Ibid., p. 37.
[6] *Mémorial*, p. 189, n. 256.

have chosen examples,[7] are particularly significant: tears, as a sign of interior activity of the Holy Spirit, and prayer.

First, the tears. They played a very important role in Ignatius' personal relations with God. It suffices to open the *Autobiography* or the *Spiritual Diary* to realize this. Tears of contrition, tears provoked by contemplation of the mysteries of Christ (especially the sorrowful mysteries), tears of joy linked to the most vivid, intense consolations, tears of love (especially for the Eucharist): of what spiritual activity were they not for Ignatius the expression and the sign? Moreover, they appeared under several forms: "a deluge of tears" which covered the face[8] or "slow tears, *interior*, sweet without sound"[9] or even "tears accompanied by cries and great sobs".[10] Ignatius asked for these tears as a grace, awaited them as a revelation, and sadly bore the deprivation of them: for it seemed to him then that God had left him. "Our Father", said Câmara, "had such a gift of tears that, when he did not cry three times during Mass, he considered himself deprived of consolation."[11] From it, he would be sick for the whole day. So much so at first that he had to give up saying Mass every day and to accept not celebrating it "except on Sundays and feast days"; then "the physician prescribed that he not cry and he submitted through obedience." Truly, we are advancing in a "strange" world,[12] whatever might be the explanation which we could give for this phenomenon; and one is permitted to be astonished with this phenomenon in such a virile man, so much the master of himself, or even shocked if one is unaware of or neglects the confidences of other great saints.

Now, in 1553, Father Nicolas Goudanus wrote from Ingolstadt to Ignatius and confided to him the desire that he had for the gift of tears. Ignatius was then ill; it was Polanco who answered Goudanus on November 22;[13] but not without having previously "spoken to our Father Master Ignatius". "The gift of tears", he told Goudanus, "must not be asked for without some reserve, for it is not necessary nor always good and convenient for everyone." Why? "To those who have the will and the profound desire to have pity for the suffering of their neighbors, to help them with all their strength and who devote themselves effectively by using all means at their disposal, no other tears are necessary

---

[7] In like manner the penances, health, work, domestic offices, etc.

[8] *Journal* (Mar. 4, 1544), p. 82, n. 105.

[9] Ibid. (May 11, 1544), p. 114, n. 222.

[10] Ibid., p. 8, n. 105.

[11] *Mémorial*, n. 183.

[12] Fr. de Guibert who in his turn attempted an explanation of this phenomenon recognized that, in any case, "the thing remains obscure" and that "the act [is] strange and characteristic" (*La Spiritualité*, p. 48).

[13] According to SAINT IGNACE, *Lettres* ("Christus" collection), p. 326, our emphasis.

nor are other tendernesses of heart." Above all do not confuse tears with charity:

> Certain people cry, because their nature is such that the feelings of the superior portion of the soul easily overflows the inferior, or even because God our Lord judges that it is useful for them thus to dissolve in tears. They do not, however, because of it have *a greater charity*, they are not better apostles than others who do not have these tears and who have just as strong feelings in the superior part of their souls, let us say an equally powerful and efficacious will for the service of God and the welfare of souls as those who have tears in abundance. Now, that is *the real act of charity*. I shall acknowledge to you that even if it were in my power to give to certain people the gift of tears, I would guard myself from doing so because they do not help at all and they bring trouble to the body and the head, and henceforth prevent all *exercise of charity*.

This letter admirably blends the experience of Ignatius and his advice; and, with one stroke of the pen, it puts all spiritual matters in the right perspective: the unique and primary importance of charity, the love of God and the love of men.

This lucid firmness of doctrine we shall find again in another area of Ignatius' spiritual direction. This time it was not a matter of Goudanus, of a nervous, fragile temperament, but of Borgia, and of Nadal himself, one could even say with the whole tendency of Spanish and Portuguese spiritual men: it was a question of the time and the meaning of prayer. At Manresa, the pilgrim "was faithful to his seven hours of prayer each day"; if he had to lessen this time during the period of his studies, he had at Vicenza resumed "long prayers"; and Câmara tells us that at the house of La Strada "after the Mass Ignatius remained in mental prayer during a period of two hours."[14] To this prayer it would be necessary to add the frequent recourse to the illuminations of God to which Ignatius had recourse in his administrative days. It is useless to insist: no one questions that Ignatius had himself devoted much time each day to prayer, as the essential source of his personal life, of his administration, of his apostolate. Now, on September 20, 1548, he had to moderate the taste for long prayers and violent penances of Francis Borgia, still Duke of Gandia but for seven months a professed member of the Society. This was a very delicate operation, for Francis was, from all the evidence, in the grip of very great divine favors of which he should not be deprived; and then, Ignatius had not yet met Francis; finally Rome was far from Gandia: so, there, Francis sought spiritual direction from his former confessor Fray Juan de Texada, a Franciscan of deep spirituality and a very austere life,

---

[14] *Mémorial*, n. 179.

and Andrés Oviedo, the scrupulous Rector of the college of Gandia, who specifically the previous year had asked Ignatius' permission to go to live for seven years with Father Onfroy in the most eremitical and desert-like solitude. This was not the ideal situation to appease Borgia's appetite for the life of the hermit! One must first read the letter which Ignatius had Polanco write to Oviedo on March 27, 1548;[15] it preceded the letter of September 20, 1548, to Francis Borgia; the latter was without doubt one of the most detailed that Ignatius ever wrote.[16] He advises the Duke first to reduce by half the time "which he allotted to his interior and exterior exercises":

> I would prefer that one-half of the time be converted into study. . . . Utilize this time to govern your State, for spiritual conversations, trying to keep your soul calm, peaceful, disposed for the moment when our Lord will want to work in it. Without a doubt, there is for it a greater virtue and a greater grace to be able to enjoy its Lord in various activities and various places than in one. To achieve this, we must, in his divine bounty, make every effort.

And after judicious advice on the "corporal macerations in our Lord", Ignatius then came to those "most holy gifts" by which we must let ourselves "be surrounded and permeated".

> By these gifts, I mean those which it is not in our power to make come "at our wish", but which are purely granted by the powerful Giver of all good. Such are, in placing oneself in the perspective of the divine majesty, *a faith, a hope and a very active charity*, "joy and spiritual repose", tears, intense consolation, elevation of the spirit, divine impressions and illuminations and all other tastes and spiritual feelings regarding such gifts, humility and reverence toward our Holy Mother the Church and those who have the mission of governing her and teaching therein.

Corporal penance is but one way to obtain these gifts; let it thus be "judicious": "thus not only the soul will be healthy, but a *healthy spirit animating a healthy body*, all will become more healthful and more conducive to the greatest service of God." Health and sanctity: is it indeed the same man who gives such balanced advice and who himself practices asceticism to the point of making himself sick? Everyone will have noticed that the primacy among these "gifts" of the Lord belongs to "faith, hope and a very active charity". A year later (July 1549), Ignatius was again obliged to write a long letter to Borgia about "prophecies" regarding the Church and the Society which were circulating in the

---

[15] *Lettres* ("Christus" collection), pp. 155–59.
[16] Ibid., pp. 168–72.

Oviedo-Onfray-Texada milieu.[17] Let us consider these remarks.

> To say that a prayer of one or two hours' duration is no longer a prayer and that it is necessary to have more time is a bad doctrine, contrary to the sentiment and practice of saints: (1) The example of Christ shows it. If he sometimes spent the night in prayer, he remained at it for less time on other occasions, as with the prayer of the Last Supper or the three prayers he made in the Garden. . . . We have the prayer which he taught us. Since Christ called it a prayer, even if it is brief. . . , one must not deny that it is one. . . . (5) *If prayer is the request to God for what is fitting*, and if, more generally defined, it *is a movement of piety and humility which lifts the soul toward God*, which can be accomplished in less than two hours, indeed in less than half an hour, how can one refuse the name of real prayer to those which do not exceed one or two hours? (6) Ejaculatory prayers, so recommended by St. Augustine and by the saints, would they not be prayers? (7) . . . There are moments in which God is served by other things more than by prayer; if it pleases him then that one stop praying in order to offer oneself to these activities, all the more reason to abridge it.[18]

That suffices. Ignatius, we see, knew how to distinguish between exceptional favors in prayer which God granted to him and the ordinary treatment of souls by God. There existed, in his eyes, only one valuable and sure reference: the ardor of faith, hope and charity; all the rest was second and sometimes secondary, in relation to this divine reality. "A man truly mortified will have enough time in a quarter of an hour to unite himself to God in prayer", Ignatius had told Nadal in the conversation of November 22, 1554.[19] It even seems that Ignatius was afraid of "illusions"[20] in praying souls, of "great difficulties, especially the harshness of understanding".[21] Mortification and abnegation—those were the things that Ignatius considered as "the great foundation of all things in the Society of Jesus".[22] Well, one knows that under these austere words, the visage of a great love was silhouetted for him, the love of Jesus Crucified.

III. THE MESSAGE OF IGNATIUS IN "THE EXERCISES"

The *Spiritual Exercises* of St. Ignatius have been the object of innumerable studies. Their essential purpose, their spiritual doctrine, the manner of "giving" them or of "making" them: such are the questions which

[17] Long letter. Ibid., pp. 186–99, which would merit being studied in detail.
[18] *Lettres*, pp. 197–99.
[19] *Mémorial*, n. 196.
[20] Ibid.
[21] *Mémorial*, n. 256.
[22] Ibid.

have been raised for four centuries by some works which are of remarkable profundity.[23] Who could be astonished that there is not perfect agreement on all points among the specialists? The *Exercises* do not propose a ready-made spiritual experience but an experience to be undergone by each person: the *Exercises* are a guide which establishes a common language between the indispensable "director" and the retreatant. Each director to a certain extent rewrites the *Exercises* according to his own mentality, and each retreatant projects into it his own experience as well. It is not our purpose to enter into these scholarly debates but to answer this question which is rather simple in appearance but in reality already very thorny: Ignatius, who had drawn from his personal experience "of the things of God" the substance of the *Exercises*, had he known sufficiently how to pare down this experience to "help souls" according to his plan?

For in fact the question arises. In respect to Ignatius himself, there existed, there had existed from the beginning in regard to the *Exercises*, a reticence, sometimes even an aversion. This little book, so precious for many, remains for some—I do not speak only of those who, erroneously, take it for a book of cursory reading—a sealed book, or hermetic, or confused, or even an irritating one. Why cover our eyes? This phenomenon of rejection occurs for all spiritualities and for all the saints. The point is to see if, *in its own class*, this little book brings to *a certain family of souls* a message which is still relevant.

To answer this question, it is fitting to know first, and to know it from Ignatius himself,[24] what the purposes were that he was proposing in elaborating, stratum by stratum, the text of the *Exercises* as he utilized them himself; finally in what measure he confided to others the care of "giving" them. We shall ascertain then with what prudence he utilized his own experience for the profit of souls.

The Purposes Which Ignatius Proposed and the Slow Elaboration of the Text, Stratum by Stratum

One must return to the time of Loyola to find the origin of the Exercises: he read the *Vita Christi* and the *Flos Sanctorum*; this reading

---

[23] See the bibliography set up by SOMMERVOGEL. Closer to our times, cf. Jean-François GILMONT, *Les Ecrits spirituels des premiers Jésuites*, pp. 47–73, especially the bibliographical note, p. 49. Or Jean-François GILMONT and Paul DAMAN, *Bibliographie ignatienne* (1894–1957), pp. 77–180. To these it is fitting to add at the very least these among the works which have appeared since 1957: SAN IGNACIO DE LOYOLA, *Exercitia spiritualia* by José CALVERAS and Candido de DALMASES (MHSJ), wherein can be found an abundant bibliography.

[24] We deliberately set aside here the testimonies of Laynez, Polanco, Nadal, Ribadeneyra and Manareo: not that they are not very important, but because they do not always agree, and especially because they are less concerned with our specific question.

provoked in him the states of soul which we know, and "he spoke of things of God", that is to say, given his total lack of spiritual culture, from what he read and from what he experienced. "As he sampled many of these readings, the idea came to him to extract from them, in resumé form, the most important things from the life of Christ and of the saints. He began to write a book with much care."[25] The words of Christ in red, those of our Lady in blue; the paper was "glossy and lined", the entire thing "ornamentally written": a book of three hundred pages, which he carried in his bag on leaving the *casa solar*.

Montserrat: on leaving the monastery, after his few days of "general confession", he went toward Manresa. "He wanted also to note certain things in his book which he kept with great care and carried away with much consolation."

Manresa: There was the great test of troubles and scruples, even to the temptation of suicide, but also prodigious illuminations and intense spiritual consolations. Also there were his "conversations" with "spiritual persons", wherein he utilized his experiences, since, from his own avowal, he "had no knowledge of spiritual things".[26] Already this rhythm, so important for understanding the *Exercises*, was being created: an Ignatian experience—a group of "spiritual persons" with whom he talked—the utilization of his experience in those personal conversations, *in the ignorance in which he found himself of every other spirituality*.

At this point the debate among historians begins. On October 20, 1555, Ignatius confided to Câmara the manner in which he had drafted the *Exercises*. "He told me that he had not composed all the *Exercises* at one single time. However, when he had observed in himself things which had been useful to him, he had made note of them by writing *what appeared to him as being useful to others (gli pareva che potrebbero anche essere utili ad altri)*.[27] Such, for example, was the examination of conscience with the help of lines, etc. He told me in particular that the Elections (*in the plural in the original text*) had been drawn from this diversity of spirit and thoughts which he had known at Loyola, when he was still suffering from his leg."[28]

---

[25] *Autob.* R.P., p. 54.

[26] *Autob.* R.P., p. 65.

[27] The statement of Câmara is difficult to translate. We have preferred the Latin interpretation of Fr. de Coudret (undoubtedly 1559–1561), *Font. narr.* I, p. 505, to the French translations of the *Autobiographie* (A.G.) and the *Récit du Pèlerin* which do not seem to us to render the important nuance of the original *senonche*.

[28] *Autob.* R.P., p. 136.

What then was the earliest core of the *Exercises* after Loyola, Montser-rat and Manresa? If we follow the most certain and recent specialists, the balance sheet can be established as follows: the meditations and contem-plations for four weeks[29] (in particular those of the "Kingdom of Christ" and of the "Two Standards") and their methods (three powers of the soul, application of the senses, contemplation of persons, words and actions), particular examination, general examination with its rules for discerning mortal and venial sin, the three methods of prayer, at least a few of the rules for discernment of spirits of the First Week, and the rules of election. It does not seem that the "Foundation" was already part of the ensemble.[30] In any case, these elements of the *Exercises* were subse-quently adapted, improved and especially redrafted.

From Barcelona, after his return from Jerusalem, we know only one thing from Ignatius concerning the *Exercises*: "He sought out, as was his habit, spiritual people even if they lived as hermits far from the city, to converse with them."[31] Up until the time that he went to Alcalá, Ignatius in his *Autobiography* never used the term "Spiritual Exercises": it is only then that we find in his account the expression "to give the Exercises",[32] but it is not yet specified that the text of them had been written, at least in a structured and fixed form. On the contrary, at Salamanca, "the pilgrim sent back to Frías who had a bachelor's degree all his papers, that is to say, the *Exercises* for his examination." However, in this whole period, which extended from February 1523 until February 1528, nothing allows us to suppose that the *Exercises* were enriched with new additions.

Paradoxically, it was during Ignatius' stay in Paris, that is to say, in a period when he had cut down the "spiritual conversations", that a rather considerable development of the text of the *Exercises* was accomplished. Under what influences? His studies, without doubt, had much to do with it, his reaction to the intellectual and spiritual milieu, conversations with the first companions, and especially Ignatius' progressive experience.[33] It was in Paris that the *Exercises* were enriched by these documents: the "Annotations" which concern the dispositions of the retreatant,[34] the

---

[29] Let us not force this figure: it is not sure that structure in "four" weeks ever existed: cf. on this point, GUIBERT, *La Spiritualité*, p. 106. Regarding all that we analyze here, consultation of GUIBERT, pp. 98 to 110, is indispensable, all the more since his work is posterior to the works of Codina.

[30] José Calveras and Candido de Dalmases think the contrary, but with a strong reservation: "*Saltem imperfectiore seu simpliciore redactione*" (*Exerc. sp.*, pp. 31–32).

[31] *Autob.* R.P., p. 80, n. 37.

[32] Ibid., p. 97, n. 57 and p. 100, n. 60.

[33] Cf. George BOTTEREAU, "Le Role de 'l'indifference' dans la spiritualité ignatienne", *Revue d'Ascétique et de mystique*, vol. 45 (1969), pp. 395–408.

[34] Annot. 3, 5, 11, 12, 13, 16, 20.

"Presupposition", the "Foundation", the "Three *binaries*", the "Three Modes of Humility", the "Contemplation to Obtain the Love of God", the "Declaratory Notes", the "Additions" (except the fourteenth); and a few new rules (3, 4, and 5) in the Discernment of Spirits of the First Week. It was of this improved text that Ignatius left a copy for the Inquisitor Valentin Lévin, before leaving Paris; a copy of which there unfortunately remains no trace, no more than of the "notebook" of Loyola, or of the "papers" submitted to the ecclesiastical tribunals of Salamanca.

At Azpeitia, Ignatius does not seem to have utilized the *Exercises* and yet we know to what extent his apostolic action was exemplary. However, from the end of his studies in upper Italy, he "devoted himself to giving the Exercises and *other* spiritual conversations (*in dare gli exercitii et altre conversationi spirituali*)". After his priestly ordination, he contented himself with preaching like the other companions. The contributions of this time in upper Italy to the text of the *Exercises* was not less appreciable: thirteen annotations which, for the most part, concerned the role of the director of the retreat, the "Mysteries of Christ" added to the end of the booklet, the Rules of Temperance, the first and second rule of Discernment of Spirits of the first week and some other fragments.

When Ignatius arrived in Rome in December of 1537, the *Spiritual Exercises* were neither finished nor definitely structured, and yet he "gave" them to illustrious personages, like Dr. Ortiz. It is certain that the text of the *Exercises* underwent developments and experienced notable transformations. One can affirm that from this time date supplementary rules concerning the discernment of spirits for the first week, the rules of discernment for the second week, the rules for alms-seeking, scruples, and especially the celebrated "Rules for Thinking with the Church" (on this point agreement reigns among the specialists).

Having said this, numerous problems still remain. For we have from this period three texts of the *Exercises*:[35] the first of these texts is the manuscript called "autograph", in Spanish; in fact, this copy is in the hand of a scribe, but it bears some corrections in Ignatius' handwriting; according to Calveras, the scribe would have been Bartolomé Ferrâo, the manuscript would date, then, from 1544, before the approval of the text by the pontifical censors (1547); Ignatius introduced into his text forty-seven more corrections: some are in his handwriting, others in the handwriting of Father Broët, or in that of the copyist. The second text, called "*versio prima*", is in Latin: it appears as a translation of the original

---

[35] If one wishes to study this problem a bit seriously, it is indispensable today to have recourse to the studies of Fr. Calveras; their main point has been taken up again in the work already pointed out *Exercitia spiritualia*, elaborated upon by Fathers Calveras and de Dalmases (MHSJ).

Spanish. The essential part of this translation was done by Ignatius himself on his Spanish text, a little after his arrival in Paris in 1528. Then Favre improved the "hesitant Latin of Ignatius' attempt, too colored by Spanish expressions".[36] This work was accomplished, according to Calveras, before May-June 1539. The Salmeron revised the translation of Favre and translated some new additions of Ignatius; it bore as a title, in the handwriting of Ignatius, "*Todos exercicios breviter en latin*". Finally, in 1547, this text was reviewed still another time before being submitted for the approval of the pontifical censors and this clarification included new corrections of which some were written in Polanco's handwriting. A third text, also in Latin, is called the "vulgate version" (1546-1547): it was by order of Ignatius that Father Frusius, an eminent Latinist, completed the new translation. It seems that he utilized for this work a Latin text (different from the *versio prima*) and the Spanish autograph text: Polanco revised this translation once again, then in 1548, 500 copies were printed. After all these corrections and translations, does the text of the vulgate appear different from the text of the autograph? The experts disagree. Let us remember the judgment of Polanco, who was one of the architects of the work: "The *Exercises*", he wrote in the preface to the edition of 1548, "were translated from Spanish into Latin in two ways: the first rendered not only the meaning, but almost every word; the other, which was believed the preferable work, translated only the meaning, but with fidelity."

All this work finally proves two things: first, that Ignatius truly considered that the *Exercises* in 1548 had attained their point of maturity, since he desired that the companions and the friends of the order have henceforth at their disposal an impeccable text as to detail; but it should be noted that in order to arrive at a satisfactory text of the *Exercises*, Ignatius proceeded as he did for the text of the *Constitutions*: slowly, in the light of experience and experiments, while soliciting criticism, advice and fraternal cooperation.

How Did Ignatius Give the Spiritual Exercises?

He gave them an extremely varied fashion, according to the point of development of the text, but also according to the social and spiritual situation of the retreatant. According to the state of the text; it is clear that during a certain period, the *Exercises*, when they lasted for several days or even a month, as at Barcelona, belonged very much more to the "spiritual conversations" or even to the catechism than to what we call today the Spiritual Exercises. In the *Autobiography* Ignatius himself

---

[36] The expression is Jean-François Gilmont's.

willingly links these different forms of his "help for souls"; he does not distinguish between their fruits and their effects.[37]

According to the situation and the spiritual activity of the retreatant: the simplest form was "the Exercises of the first week" with or without some instructions concerning prayer. They lasted eight days, with or without election. Ignatius sometimes prolonged them so that one could clarify what he then added. It seems in any case that in the beginning, Ignatius had reserved these longer Exercises (one month?) for the religious men or women (especially the men) or for candidates for the religious life; and that he had not begun to give them to others until experience, led by prudence, had proved to him that priests or laymen, and indeed women, could profit from them. At least that was what emerged from his advice to the companions who gave the Spiritual Exercises. In any case, one must be very cautious when one reads in the *Autobiography* or in the other documents that Ignatius gave someone "the Spiritual Exercises". What exactly does that expression include? What were the Exercises he gave to Peralta, Castro and Amador in Paris, which so changed their lives that there ensued "great movements in the University"?[38] Did he give the same Exercises to Favre[39] in the clutches of his hesitations and reckless generosity, then to Laynez and Salmeron who made them at the same time, to Rodríguez and finally to Xavier "who was one of the most outstanding jumpers of the île de Paris", and later Hozes in Venice? A text of the *Memorial* shows us something of these Ignatian accommodations:

> The Father [Ignatius] in discussing with me the exercises of the Abbot [Martinengo] told me the following: 'In the first place, that they were no longer rigorous, that is [in comparison] to the rigor with which they were given in the beginning; that at that time no one made them without remaining a few days without eating [without any pressure to do so][40] and that now he would not dare to permit it for more than a day for a vigorous subject, although in the past he had not been troubled by any scruples. All the first Fathers made them with exactitude and on retreat, and the one who kept the least abstinence remained three days without eating or drinking anything whatever, with the exception of Simón [Rodríguez], who, so as not to put aside his studies and because he was not in good health, did not leave his lodgings and did not give himself over to any of these rigors, the Father simply giving him meditations, etc.[41]

Although this confidence concerns one particular point of the retreat,

---

[37] Cf. for example *Autob.* R.P., pp. 97–128.
[38] Ibid., p. 114.
[39] *Mémorial*, p. 216.
[40] In Latin in the text.
[41] *Mémorial*, n. 305.

one already sees clearly, in regard to Rodríguez and others after him, that Ignatius knew how to adapt these Exercises to the conditions of life, health and the spiritual state of the retreatant.[42]

To What Extent Did Ignatius Delegate to Others the Burden of Giving the Spiritual Exercises?

To a great but prudent extent. Just as certain persons, even very spiritual ones, can be averse to the Exercises, so not every priest, not every companion even if he is a good spiritual director is suited (idoneus) to giving the Exercises, at least in their entirety. Even among the first Fathers: "Speaking of the Exercises [Ignatius] said, [do not forget that we are talking about 1555] of all those he knew in the Society giving them, the first place went to Pierre Favre, the second to Salmeron, then he placed Francis de Villanova and then Jerónimo Doménech. He also said that Strada[43] gave those of the First Week well."[44]

Was it through the Spiritual Exercises, as Dudon affirms,[45] that Pierre Favre, during Ignatius' trip to Azpeitia, won over Jay, Codure and Broët to the group of companions? It is not certain: the text of Simón Rodríguez on which he depends says: "They had for a guide in the Spiritual Exercises (exercitationibus) Pierre Favre", can be interpreted to mean "of their spiritual life". Whatever the case, Ignatius had certainly very great confidence in the spiritual judgment of Pierre Favre. Two bits of evidence remain to assure us of that. In 1543 or 1544 Ignatius authorized him to communicate to his Carthusian friends in Cologne the text of the Exercises which Favre himself had used: from the manuscript preserved in the archives of the city of Cologne, one notices that it is not the integral and original text of the Exercises but an "accommodation" for a retreat of one month. This adaptation, according to Father Calveras, would be the work of Salmeron. The second bit of evidence is that Favre gave the Exercises in collaboration with Strada at Louvain in 1548: this time, the retreat lasted eight days and the text corresponds to the Exercises of the First Week.

This variety is found again in the manner with which certain companions,

---

[42] One will find other types of adaptations in José CALVERAS, "Estudios sobre la redacción de los textos latinos de los Ejercicios anteriores a la Vulgata", AHSI, vol. 31 (1962), pp. 3–99. The manuscript of the young English humanist John Helyar, who undoubtedly made the Exercises in Paris in 1535, under the direction of Ignatius or Favre, corresponds in the First Week with brief extensions for the three others.

[43] This reserve, though veiled, is significant: for Strada was one of the most popular orators of the first generation of Jesuits, and he had seen Ignatius himself give the Exercises to Dr. Ortiz at Monte Cassino in 1538. In 1555, he was Provincial of Aragon.

[44] Mémorial, p. 226.

[45] Saint Ignace de Loyola, p. 250.

with Ignatius' approval, soon gave the Exercises. In many of the houses or colleges, a few rooms were reserved for retreatants; and the candidates sometimes had to wait a long time at the door before obtaining a place.[46] On the other hand, there were some regions or cities, or even certain of our friends who showed themselves to be allergic to the Spiritual Exercises[47] to the point that Ignatius was obliged to order the companions to be more persuasive in proposing that retreatants make the Exercises among them.[48] In any case, the *Spiritual Exercises* became, especially after they were printed in 1548 and approved by the Pope one of the major ministries of the Society; in Paris, for example, where the action of the companions was undermined by the hostility of the Archbishop and of the faculty of theology, the *Exercises* were almost the only ministry which they were allowed to practice.[49] Solitary retreats, group retreats up to seven or eight persons,[50] retreats reduced by a third—all these forms existed. Often one restricted oneself to the First Week as a result of lack of time or the spiritual quality of the retreatant, but the result was already very appreciable;[51] it brought about such a change of life that, even if these retreats were held secretly, those of the house "who had a nose for it" (*nasutiores*), guessed.[52] However, certain of the companions were already giving the Exercises in an "incorrect" fashion;[53] even some rectors did.[54]

When Archbishop Silice and Melchoir Cano let loose their attack against the little book, Ignatius at first remained calm, but Araoz, Borgia and Nadal, who were on the spot, became incensed; Nadal, then commissioner, even sent to all the superiors in Spain interpretive directives concerning the incriminating passages: so much did it seem to them to attack the very heart of their apostolate.[55] Araoz even permitted himself to correct the vulgate Latin edition approved by Paul III: Ignatius showed himself very displeased with what he considered a lack of respect regarding pontifical authority.[56] This assemblage of facts shows us today, in a rather chaotic way, indeed an enigmatic one, that for Ignatius the

---

[46] Examples: *Chron.* 2, pp. 122, 641–42; 4, pp. 410–12 (Alcalá) 5, pp. 414–15 (Salamanca); 5, p. 585 (Coimbra); 6, p. 93 (Loreto), etc.

[47] Ibid. 4, p. 160 (Florence); 4, p. 198 (Sicily); 6, p. 275.

[48] Ibid. 4, pp. 95–211.

[49] Ibid. 4, pp. 318–22; 5, pp. 323–24.

[50] Ibid. 1, p. 241; 5, p. 67.

[51] Ibid. 4, pp. 540, 545–46 (The Princess Isabel and the Queen of Portugal).

[52] Ibid. 4, p. 410.

[53] Ibid. 6, pp. 172, 180.

[54] Ibid. 6, p. 228.

[55] Ibid. 4, pp. 473–74, 493; *Epist. ign.* 6, p. 598–99, n. 4360.

[56] *Mémorial*, n. 321.

Spiritual Exercises had to some extent grown out of his personal experience and had become common property of all the companions, an instrument of evangelical labor. Must one regret that he had not been able to complete the *Directory* of which he dreamed around 1555?[57] Doubtless this lacuna left the field wide open for the flowering of "directories" of which it is not certain that all reflect his authentic spirit, but in other respects the *Spiritual Exercises* remained more what he wished they were: a guide—more than a method—which "would help souls", each according to his personal way of life, to enter into the "freedom of the sons of God", that is, into authentic Love.

What Should One Conclude, without Imprudence, from This Analysis?

First this: between "the papers" of Ignatius of Loyola/Manresa/Alcalá and the *Spiritual Exercises*, printed in 1548 and approved by Paul III on July 31 of that same year, the differences are doubtless as considerable as between the first rough draft of a book and the completed volume: differences in style, but probably also in content.

Secondly, it is necessary to affirm that the text of the *Exercises* is but a guide: in the beginning, it was only destined for the director of the retreat, and not for the retreatant; each retreat demanded an original effort of presentation, adaptation and leadership. It is only by extrapolation, legitimate, moreover, but not indispensable, that one speaks of the "doctrine" of the *Spiritual Exercises*. It was a matter above all of a spiritual step: it is incontestable that concealed within this writing one might discern elements of doctrine, but the systemization of these elements will remain always the projection of a philosophy, a theology or a particular mentality. The *Exercises*, by virtue of their very history and by virtue of Ignatius' manner, resemble more a diversified collection of counsels, rules, experiences and above all, "views" of faith, than a system: this in no way diminishes their immense value, but on the contrary renders them accessible, available to all the souls of good will who truly seek to convert themselves constantly and more sincerely to God.

For there is therein a very important point for Ignatius: the *Spiritual Exercises* are not an esoteric manual, reserved for the initiated. They must be and remain—at least in their major and most essential portion—a sort of spiritual catechism which, as the dogmatic catechism leads to faith, to hope and to charity, leads one to live always more in faith, hope and charity in the steps of Jesus Christ. It is not by chance that so many "sermons" of Ignatius or his companions, so many "catechisms" in the

---

[57] Cf. *Mémorial*, n. 313, and *Direct.*, pp. 70–78.

churches or in public places—indeed even certain "familiar conversations"—in fact consisted of nothing more than utilizing and paraphrasing the *Exercises* of the First Week or certain meditations of other weeks. All that simplified the *Exercises* and drew them closer to the average Christian, as Ignatius intended; all that complicated them, rationalized them *to excess*, did them a disservice and could even falsify them.[58] For Ignatius, the *Spiritual Exercises* must be available to *all* "spiritual persons", the humblest and the highest, the "untaught" and the cultivated; it was up to the director to adapt them to his retreatant, to choose, to develop or to eliminate.

It is significant that nowhere in the *Exercises* does one find anything which appears reserved to the highest states of mysticism (have not people spoken of the "anti-mysticism" in the *Exercises*?) but which may nevertheless serve in the highest mystical states. Conversations, contemplations, the method of applying the senses, offerings, diverse rules, three ways of prayer, can "aid souls" of all levels, provided that they are generous.

Is anything simpler than looking at evangelical scenes than "conversations with God as from friend to friend", than the prayers which Ignatius proposed to the retreatant, the Our Father, the Hail Mary, the Anima Christi? The *Exercises* are a guide for every soul in search of a true love of God. The more they are simplified the more they are placed within the reach of the ordinary people of God, the more also is there the opportunity of sharing in Ignatius' intention.

If these views are correct, they could possibly bring a solution to a difficulty which is sometimes raised today: are the *Spiritual Exercises* still readable for modern man? Is their "literary genre" not out of date? In the *Exercises* several levels can in effect be distinguished: The fundamental truths of the faith, the methods of prayer, the psychology which underlies the principles of spiritual life, theology. It is evident that, since the *Exercises* must be adapted to the mentality of each retreatant, they can be adapted a fortiori to the current developments of psychology, philosophy and theology. The hard and lasting core remains the verities of

---

[58] Speaking of the graces which he received from God at Manresa, Ignatius confided this to Câmara: "he [the pilgrim] had great devotion to the Most Holy Trinity; so each day he prayed to each of the three Persons, and as he prayed also to the Most Trinity, it occurred to him to wonder how he could say four prayers to the Trinity. But this thought hardly bothered him, as a matter of minor importance" (*Autob.* R.P., p. 71). Father Fessard humorously takes up this comment of Ignatius' in his discussion at the end of his admirable study on the *Dialectique des Exercices spirituels* (Paris: Aubier, 1956, p. 21). This "touch of irony" of Thomas More in Ignatius is not displeasing. It is often found among authentic mystics!

faith, but why should they not take account of the progress of exegesis, theological research or even of liturgical renewal? As for methods of prayer, why would they not be enriched by all the experiences of contemplation, by all forms of meditation which can be found in other religions, on condition that they do not carry any religious philosophy harmful to faith and that they safeguard the supernatural, gratuitous character of divine union? Why would certain principles of spiritual life, like rules for discerning spirits or the direction of scrupulous persons not benefit from deepening by contemporary psychology, provided that God's freedom of action is respected?

Are not the *Exercises* more "spirit" than "letter"? One can certainly "give" them according to the rigidity of the text, but it is not illegitimate to transpose them into a language more accessible to our contemporaries. The spiritual ways are diverse: the purpose is unique, conversion, returning human liberty to the total disposition of God, that is to say, in the order of charity: whether it may be a matter of the conversion from sin to the state of grace, or the conversion of the good to better through spiritual progress. It is striking that from the *Exercises* there have come— even from the time of Ignatius—contemplatives, especially the Carthusians, missionary priests, religious and laymen; that the *Exercises* have inspired great works and humble devotions contributing to the reform of monasteries as well as of dioceses or parishes. What explanation can we give to this phenomenon, except that far from enclosing souls in his own experience, high as that might have been, Ignatius knew through personal self-effacement, how to put the riches of that experience at the disposition of whoever sincerely wished to know, to love and to follow "God our Lord"?

IV. THE MESSAGE OF IGNATIUS IN "THE CONSTITUTIONS"[59]

To pour out his experience of God for the benefit of his companions comprised for Ignatius an even more delicate operation. For he addressed himself this time to men who, like himself, had decided to "follow Christ" in chastity and evangelical poverty and to remain united by "obedience to one among" them. Their gift to Christ, in its call and its

[59] Regarding the *Constitutions*, the bibliography, less detailed than for the *Spiritual Exercises*, is still considerable. Cf. SOMMERVOGEL; Jean-François GILMONT: *Les Ecrits spirituels*, pp. 73–93; Jean François GILMONT and Paul DAMAN: *Bibliographie ignatienne* (1894–1957), pp. 180–90. Since 1967, the monographs and theses multiplied, by reason of the aggiornamento of the religious orders and the changes in religious life. We can only refer to the specialized bibliographies like those of AHSI, from the Institute of Spirituality of the Gregorian University and from the Center of Ignatian Spirituality (CIS).

answer, was absolute, like his own. Consequently, would he not be tempted to restrict his choice to a spiritual elite, marked like him by an exceptional grace of union with God and of apostolic fervor? More especially as the experience of free companionship, whether in Paris or Venice-Vicenza, had overwhelmed him, one could fear that his demands might be excessive. A handful of men decided to sacrifice all, like him, to the service of God our Lord. Would that not be more efficacious than a crowd, of which the weight would inevitably make itself felt on the fervor and zeal of the group? Number always entails difficulties. . . . Already when there were only nine or ten of them, had not the companions experienced fundamental differences of opinion on their spiritual life and actions, *aliqualis pluritas sententiarum?*[60] Had they not known defections and even treason? In their deliberation of 1539 they passed beyond these risks, and that under the thrust of their apostolic fervor: the more numerous they would be to work "for the harvest of the Lord" the more they could hope that the fruit would be abundant; so much the worse if human weakness (*infirmitas et fragilitas hominum*) resulted in disappointments! These risks, to tell the truth, scarcely led them to diminish either the vigor or the rigor of their ideal; in the first documents of the foundation of the Society there is a breath of the absolute, one could say a holy madness, that nothing has toned down.[61] A long time after 1539, in April 1555, Ignatius would recall, not without nostalgia, the first heroic days when Favre, doing the Exercises, "abstained from food for six days, slept in his shirt on the logs which had been brought to him for making a fire and meditated in a little courtyard covered with snow", and when Xavier, undoubtedly to expiate his vanities as a high-jump champion, "bound his legs and whole body very tightly with a rope" while he meditated;[62] how could the *Constitutions*, drafted by such a founder, be suited to men who were not heroes or saints and yet were souls of good will?

In fact, there developed in Ignatius little by little, with the passage of time and the accumulation of experiences, what one could call his founder's conscience. And these *Constitutions*, which are a spiritual document as much as a legislative text, represent a marvel of wisdom and prudence: without lessening his ideal, he succeeded in equilibrating it in such a way that men who were endowed with neither vigor of personality nor the fervor of the first companions, could accomplish through it

---

[60] *Const.* 1, p. 2.

[61] The examples of this would be numerous. For example: "nobis qui versamur in assiduis et jugibus laboribus, tam spiritualibus quam temporalibus" in the "Deliberation" of 1539 (§7), and all §3 (2nd) of the *Summa Instituti* ("huic oneri . . . hujus vocationis pondus . . ., diu noctuque succincti lumbos . . .", etc.).

[62] *Mémorial*, n. 305.

their desire of a total gift to Christ and to souls. About this balance we shall reiterate here four principal aspects which seem to us the most significant.

First, the Type of Apostolic Man That the Constitutions *Describes.* This man takes account of health, of physical strength which he needs for studies and for "divine service": an entire chapter of part III is devoted to "the preservation of the body".[63] This is a man who is guided by "reason" and possesses "good judgment"; who enjoys gifts of intelligence, memory, will, the art of "eloquence", and even gifts more "exterior", like "nobility, fame and the rest"[64] which could "aid in the edification" by the very oblation made in the service of God.

He must especially be endowed with all sorts of moral qualities: honesty[65] which is reflected in his appearance, conscience, prudence, rectitude, simplicity, firmness, constancy, courtesy and affability, "tranquility"—all of which make him "respected" by his neighbors, render him immediately likable and earn for him a good reputation (*bonus odor*) and "authority" and permit him to live without too many quarrels in a community. Many of the "true and solid virtues" which Ignatius favored insistently were merely human virtues which reinforce the grace of God. Among the impediments which rendered a candidate "less apt for the Society", almost all derived from the body or the character[66]—while natural gifts play an important role in the distribution of tasks among the companions.[67]

Briefly, it was a man who enjoyed by nature "human gifts", useful to the "apostolic community" with which he desired to affiliate, and who would develop them by his training and his concern with progress. "To admit very difficult candidates or those useless to the community, even if the admission were not useless for them, that, we are persuaded in our Lord, would not be fitting for his greatest service and his greatest praise."[68]

Saying this, Ignatius was far from reducing whatever might be his spiritual ideal. On the contrary, in recognizing the natural and human

---

[63] The solicitude of Ignatius for the ill continued to increase until the end of his life; not without his attributing to his companions over a long period of time physical resistance to fever and suffering for which he himself, Laynez, Bobadilla and Xavier were endowed by nature. One picturesque anecdote regarding Ignatius' principles of hygiene: a walk "in the fresh air of Rome before sunrise", to acclimate the new arrivals: *Mémorial*, n. 109.

[64] Cf. *Constitutions* ("Christus" collection), vol. 1, pp. 62–63, n. 153–61; it is useless to say what the "more exterior gifts" which Ignatius pointed out were worth for the society of the sixteenth century and how they could be varied according to mentalities.

[65] *Const.* P. I, ch. II, n. 3 and 10.

[66] Ibid., P. I, ch. III, n. 8–16.

[67] Ibid., P. VII, ch. II, declaration F.

[68] Ibid., P. I, ch. II, n. 4.

gifts as values which could be utilized in apostolic action, he was lead to insist on the radical condition of their real efficacy: the union of the apostle with the only source of grace.

> One must act in such a way that all the members of the Society give themselves to solid and perfect virtues and to spiritual things to which it is necessary to attach more importance than to science and to the other natural and human gifts. These are, in effect, those interior gifts which must give to the external gifts their efficacy in relation to the pursued goal.[69]

The companion, according to Ignatius, was truly a man who, in the manner of St. Paul, could boast, as much as anyone, of his gifts and of his talents, but who was convinced that all this human richness in the end is not spiritually efficacious except "by the grace of God". The greater these natural gifts, the more total must be the love for Jesus Christ: Ignatius wished and sought, this contrast, this tension between the human gifts and a total love of God, for the most authentic of his companions.

The Lesson of the Two Portraits of the Superior General in the Constitutions

In part IX of the *Constitutions*, in chapter two, there are two portraits of the Superior General. Sometimes the second is omitted to the benefit of the first. Nevertheless, their juxtaposition singularly reveals the thought of Ignatius.

The first portrait, the more detailed, is "ideal": united to God and familiar with him in all his actions, the General is a source of graces for the entire body of the Society; exemplary of all virtues, he aids "the rest of the Society"; in him particularly must shine charity for his neighbor and for the Society, as well as true humility which, to God and to men, renders him totally appealing; being free of all passions, nothing troubles the judgment of his reason and he remains, on all occasions, master of himself and "moderate in his speech"; he unites rectitude and indispensable severity to benignity and gentleness; he has magnanimity and strength of soul to bear the weaknesses of many and to undertake great things, and to persevere with constancy without losing courage in the face of contradictions; "he dominates events, neither letting himself be exalted by success nor cast down by adversity"; he must "be endowed with great intelligence and judgment to such an extent that such a gift not be lacking to him either in speculative questions or in practical questions"; in doctrine, he still joins "prudence and experience of spiritual, interior things in order to discern spirits"; in all activity he must be

---

[69] Ibid., P. X, n. 3.

"vigilant and active to undertake matters and energetic to see them through to perfection"; he must have good physical health, "dignity and authority"; "exterior gifts" (an honorable past and position before his entrance into the Society) are not negligible in giving him credit "with persons both within and without". If it is true, as Câmara says, and as others have repeated after him, that Ignatius "seems to be depicting himself" in this chapter,[70] any other general, however perfect he might be, would recognize without difficulty that he could only approach such an ideal.

Now in four lines at the end of this comprehensive chapter, Ignatius traces another portrait of which it is necessary to weigh all the prerequisites. "If a few of the qualities enumerated above are lacking [in the General] at least let him not be lacking in a great goodness and a great love for the Society, as well as good judgment and good training." Four words suffice; and these gifts are all human gifts, or at least can be merely human gifts. And they are only qualified in the most temperate way: no longer the superlatives, but this estimable "ordinariness" in which common mortals participate!

The contrast between the two portraits is striking. However, the lesson is made still more enlightening if we give to this word "goodness" at the head of this portrait, that meaning which the study of the texts and philology demand. Let us compare the diverse forms which this word has taken in the different drafting stages of the Constitutions. In text "a" which we have described earlier, we read "bondad";[71] but in text A (1550), text B (1556) and text D (1594) we read "el credito" (the credit)[72] finally, in the Latin version, approved by the Fourth General Congregation (1581), we read "probitas". The French translation of the Constitutions restores—appropriately, we believe—the word of text "a": "goodness". What is the significance of these vacillations? Unless the word "bondad" in the Ignatian language enjoyed a richness of sense and harmonics which surpassed the ordinary meaning of our word "goodness", or, in other words, that the quality which Ignatius wished to designate had no human word which expressed it perfectly. An explanation may clarify it for us: at a certain period of his life (1532–1543 approximately), Ignatius had the habit of following his signature with this mysterious expression: de bondad pobre. Of what goodness was he acknowledging himself poor? Of the goodness which flows into man from the All-Good, of the goodness which is in man the image of God,

[70] Mémorial, n. 226.
[71] Constitutions 2, p. 240.
[72] Ibid. 2, pp. 666 and 667.

which so many of the great mystics call *"Bonitas"*. Ignatius recognized himself as poor in love, in virtue, in truth, a poverty of being and of grace. An admission of his nothingness and of his sins in the presence of the All of God. In the portrait of the Superior General, the meaning is analogous. The goodness he mentions is simultaneously concerned with natural goodness and with supernatural goodness, created goodness and noncreated goodness, basic honesty, fundamental purity, humility, charity. All these nuances resound in the word: to be good, for man, is to resemble God by nature and by grace. "As soon as man thinks attentively of the Divinity," said St. Francis de Sales,

> he feels a certain gentle emotion in his heart which testifies that *God is God of the human heart*. . . . This pleasure, this confidence which the human heart *naturally* takes in God, can certainly come from the conformity that exists between this divine Goodness and our soul: great but secret conformity. . . . We are created in the image and likeness of God.[73]

This goodness is of the order of the Creation as much as of the Redemption: the word, like the word "virtue" to which Ignatius links it sometimes,[74] encompasses natural and supernatural gifts, which gave "credit" (as the Spanish texts A, B and D of the *Constitutions* translate it) with God and with men. He evokes the text of Paul to the Philippians: "Fill your minds with everything that is true, everything that is noble, everything that is good and pure, everything that we love and honor and everything that can be thought virtuous or worthy of praise." Here one uncovers the transformation which the spiritual thought of Ignatius underwent from the time of Loyola.

The Institution of Spiritual and Temporal Coadjutors

For having been suggested to him, if not imposed, by apostolic necessities, this institution does not less reveal, in its way, a profound evolution of Ignatius' mentality as Superior General. To tell the truth, since the first constitutions of 1539, the companions had envisioned adding to their group persons "less humanly endowed" (*minus sufficientes*) who would be "moved by the same spirit" (*eodem spiritu*) "and would take the vow of obeying the Sovereign Pontiff that he might send them to the infidels, even if they could not render other service than to say that Christ is the Savior, or to the faithful, provided that they could at least teach in public or in private the Our Father, the Commandments of God, etc.":[75] there we recognize Ignatius for whom nothing was little or

---

[73] *Traité de l'Amour de Dieu*, l.I, ch. V (*Pleiade* edition), p. 396.

[74] Examples: *Const.* P. VIII, ch. I, n. 8; P. X, n.2; and note 1 to p. 253 of the French edition, vol. 1.

[75] *Const.* 1, p. 10.

negligible, when the heart was united to God. However, it was in the brief *Exponi nobis* of 1546[76] that the idea of persons who would help the Society of Jesus "in spiritual things or the domestic offices" was born and assumed an authentically religious form. What are these *coadjutores*? Priests or laymen, who for one reason or another, do not wish, or cannot be admitted to, a solemn profession and who can, however, "serve God and souls" usefully: if they desire it, they will receive the same training, will make vows of chastity, poverty and obedience, and will participate in all the benefits, privileges and merits of the order. Whatever may have been the motivations of Ignatius in inventing this new form of religious life in the Society of Jesus, it testifies at least to his will not to reserve spiritual fervor and apostolic dynamism for those who would appear to be in an elite group, but to gather into the *corpus Societatis* any man who should be animated with his spirit. It is difficult not to see in this motivation a desire of Ignatius to bypass "canonicity" to the profit of charity. "They [the coadjutors as much spiritual as temporal] knew that, before our Creator and Lord, those deserve more who, with the greatest charity, give themselves to the aid and service of all, through love of his Divine Majesty, whether in matters of the greatest importance, or those lower and more humble."[77] Formulas of this kind recur from the pen of Ignatius each time that he talks of the coadjutors: for him, the only hierarchy which is important before God is the hierarchy of charity.[78]

The Superior

The authority–obedience structure plays several roles in the *corpus Societatis*, as we have already noted. Not one of the least important of these is the "tailoring function" of the Ignatian ideal to each particular case, to the concrete situation, to the current strengths of each companion. The *superior* is rather a *mediator* between the flexibility, the ever-surging novelty of the "law of love and charity, which the Holy Spirit engraves in hearts" and the rigidity, the fixity, of the written rule: such was really one of the advantages which the first Fathers recognized in "obeying one among them" in their deliberation of 1539. "He will look after, as is fitting, the affairs, as much spiritual as temporal, of each one."[79] This statement is found, intact, in the definitive *Constitutions*: "To consider the things in our Lord, it has seemed to us of the greatest importance, in his Divine Majesty, that the Superiors have a total knowledge of their subordinates, in order better to direct and to govern

[76] Ibid. 1, pp. 170–74.
[77] *Constitutions*, "General Examen", vol. 1, n. 13.
[78] *Mémorial*, n. 158.
[79] *Const.* 1, p. 7.

them, and, *keeping in mind what they are*, better to lead them in the way of the Lord."[80] Between the deliberation of 1539 and the *Constitutions* of 1558 are intercalated all the *praxis* and examples of Ignatius himself:[81] even in the severities imposed by the common good of the *corpus Societatis*, he always had the respect of the person or the companion: "One totally remarkable thing", confirms Câmara, "was the way in which our Father, in matters which seemed identical, used totally different means, like great severity with one, great gentleness with another; and one sees immediately, by the result, that the remedy that he used was the best, although formerly one did not see it. But he was always inclined toward love."[82]

"Always inclined toward love", so does Ignatius of Loyola appear to us at the conclusion of this study. A being enamored of God and of the action of God in the hearts of men. A being who dreamed of making others participate fully in that love in which he had let himself be totally enveloped, but who agreed to go to great lengths with each one, in order that he might finally consent to this radical conversion of his freedom to charity.

The man Ignatius had his excesses, even his faults: we have not hidden them. He was not unaware of them himself: in the course of his life and above all during his years of administration, he strove—and largely succeeded—in distilling from his personality the message for which he had the mission and desire to deliver to others. One can be un-Ignatian, either in temperament or in the attraction of grace, but one can also be Ignatian without being Ignatius: and that is considerable. The Society is not the Society of Ignatius; it is the Society of Jesus.

To "follow" Jesus Christ, that is to say to know, to imitate, to glorify and to love him. The "mystery" of Ignatius came undoubtedly from his desire to efface himself, to "diminish" to the point of self-annihilation before Jesus Christ. Humility was essentially for him a type of love. People have evoked, on his behalf, the personality of St. John or St. Paul. This is not without very good reasons. It is certain that Ignatius knew something of divine intimacies and of the flame of love of the two apostles. But he himself points us toward a more modest rapprochement:

---

[80] "General Examen", ch. IV, n. 34; in the French edition ("Christus" collection), vol. I, p. 39. Cf. the remarkable notes 271 and 272 of the *Mémorial* of Câmara.

[81] It was partially, in our opinion, this concern to adapt authority to each companion which inspired in Ignatius the idea of the famous and short-lived "collateral" of the Superior, of which one of the tasks was specifically "to promote accord among the subordinates and with their immediate superior, going among them as an angel of peace". Const. p. VIII, ch. 1, decl. D and the note on p. 209, vol. I, of the French edition.

[82] *Mémorial*, n. 86.

he was always a devotee of the "little book" which at the time was attributed to Gerson: *The Imitation of Christ*. "He told me", reports Câmara,

> that at Manresa he had read for the first time the little Gerson and that after that he had never wished to read another book of devotion; and he recommended it to all those who were associated with him, and each day he read one chapter after another. . . . He was so familiar with this book that it seemed to me, when I knew him in Rome, that I saw and found written in his conversation all that I had read in this book.[83]

Does the citing of this text serve to "demythologize" Ignatius? Then, we would have had predecessors, even among his companions. To the "apologies" of Ignatius one can legitimately prefer this exhortation, full of charm and smiling allusions, that Peter Canisius addressed to the community of Fribourg on July 31, 1587: "There are many things in our Father Ignatius which we cannot imitate": his revelations, his ecstasies, his extraordinary wisdom, his gift of discernment, his tears, his miracles, etc. "There are even many things in him which we do not have to imitate": his war years, his excessive penances, his illnesses and the foundation of a religious order.

> And there are finally things in which it is extremely important that we imitate him: his patience in trials, his love for the Cross of Jesus Christ, his piety, his familiarity with the source of all good, his confidence in God, his natural and supernatural prudence, his faith, his zeal for souls, his apostolic activities, his obedience to the point of blindness, the rectitude and purity of his plan.

And Canisius, in closing, recalled to his listeners that the Founder of the Society was Jesus, "who gave us Ignatius as leader and patriarch. . . . Let us ask him [Ignatius]", he concluded, "that he may always further purify the '*corpus Societatis*', enlighten it and propagate it and that he may unceasingly develop in us the *spirit which he himself had received*."[84]

Such is exactly our position at the end of our research. In the "spiritual conversations" inaugurated at Loyola, in his correspondence, in the *Spiritual Exercises* as in the *Constitutions*, Ignatius of Loyola did not impose on souls an experience of God; he helped each soul to make its own personal experience. He did not propose for it a "ready-made"

---

[83] *Mémorial*, n. 97–98. In *AHSI*, vol. 41 (1972), pp. 357–73. Father Ignacio IPARRA-GUIRRE presents his rescension of the recent works on Saint Ignatius under the title *Desmitificación de san Ignacio*.

[84] From this exhortation of Canisius, Otto BRAUNSBERGER (*Canis. Epist.* 8, p. 761) gives only extracts; to be completed by Georges SCHLOSSER, *Exhortationes domesticae Canisii*, J. J. Romen et fils, Roermond, 1876, pp. 255–60.

experience, but the way of doing something for the service and praise of God, better, of making itself in the image of God and with his grace.

Because for him, the spiritual world was like a sea of coral; one can surely map out the depths by confronting the experiences of the great friends of God; but this map is never anything but provisory, incomplete: an inner secret life unceasingly transforms the reefs and modifies the linking of the channels. It is up to each sailor to discover for himself his route, and to follow it.

CONCLUSION

AND WHAT IF THE SOCIETY OF JESUS WERE TO DISAPPEAR?

Well! The Church would continue.

But why speak of this possibility? Several times in history, in certain regions, the Society of Jesus has been suppressed or the companions exiled. For example, in 1760, Pombal chased them from Portugal; in 1762–1764, Louis XV and the Parliament of Paris suppressed the order in France; in 1767, Charles III imitated in Spain what the Bourbons had done in France; in 1773, Pope Clement XIV issued the bull *Dominus ac Redemptor* against the Society. Furthermore, everyone knows what is happening today in certain countries. Suppressions and exiles were certainly harsh blows; but even harsher were those periods—and indeed there were some—where in one region or another, the Society of Jesus experienced a sort of degeneracy from within and risked destroying itself.

But in all these crises Ignatius left an example to those of his sons who would wish to be faithful whatever the price might be. "Everybody knows", said Câmara,

> what little affection Pope Paul IV had for the Society and for Father Ignatius, both before and after his election to the cardinalate. Now, finding myself on the day of the Ascension, which was May 23, 1555, in the same room with the Father, he leaning on the edge of the window and I seated on a chair, we heard the bell give the signal of the election of the new Pope, and soon after the message arrived that the elected one was the same Theatine Cardinal who was called Paul IV; at this news, the Father experienced a notable agitation and his face altered, and, as I knew later, either from him or from older Fathers to whom he recounted it, he felt shaken to the depths of his body. He got up without saying a word and entered the chapel to pray; and shortly afterward, he came out as joyous and content as if the election had been totally in accordance with his desire.[1]

What was this prayer? Ignatius never said. Was he remembering what he wrote in July 1540 to Borgia: "It is not likely that the Pope will persecute the Society which is so much his own and given to his service

---

[1] *Mémorial*, n. 93.

even though in itself it might be possible."[2] Did he have a revelation that after a period of crisis Paul IV "toward the end of his life" would become "a great friend and benefactor of the Society, saying that he regarded nothing more highly than it"?[3]

Perhaps, more simply, Ignatius placed the event, as was his custom, in a global view of the world of Redemption. Whether the Society of Jesus existed or didn't exist, God existed; Redemption was ongoing through the Passion and the resurrection of Christ; the Church with the Vicar of Christ on earth at its head was spreading in the universe, with the passage of time, Christ's work of sanctification, the Holy Spirit was at work in the heart of each man to help him liberate himself from sin and to become, little by little, a son of God in Jesus Christ. The great frescoes of the "Meditation on the Two Standards", with what they imply of evangelical reality, remained the true vision of the Christian existence: hearts of men who refused the call of Christ, others who followed him "through judgment and reason", finally others "who wished to love more and to distinguish themselves in the total service of their eternal King and universal Lord". For Ignatius, the stages of his life proved that one can be a companion of Jesus without being of the Society of Jesus; better still, the Society of Jesus overflows the canonical limits of a religious order.

Ignatius founded the Society of Jesus only because he first, and several companions with him, Favre, Laynez, Xavier, Borgia, etc., had, at the call of Christ and through his grace, "wished to love more and to distinguish themselves in the total service of this eternal King and universal Lord", Jesus Christ. In founding a religious order on this framework, Ignatius was taking a fearful risk: the Society of Jesus, at each moment of its history, would be worth no more than were the companions. Would they give to the call of the "King of the Kingdom" the response which Ignatius and his authentic sons would give? Everything depends on that: upon the fidelity of each companion, at each minute, in each place, depends the fidelity of the *corpus Societatis* to its vocation in the Church "to the service of God our Lord", and for the greater glory of God the Father.

---

[2] *Lettres* (French translation, "Christus" collection), p. 192.
[3] *Mémorial*, n. 93.

BIBLIOGRAPHY

The bibliography of our subject is considerable; it is not possible to reproduce it here. We refer to the bibliographies of the specialized works cited *infra*, and particularly to that of Pietro TACCHI VENTURI and Mario SCADUTO, *Storia della Compagnia di Gesù*; of Georg SCHURHAMMER, *Franz Xaver*. Three works have been invaluable guides for us: 1. Jean-Francois GILMONT and Paul DAMAN, *Bibliographie ignatienne* (1894–1957) (Desclée De Brouwer), to which it is fitting to add Ignacio IPARRAGUIRRE: *Orientaciones bibliográficas sobre San Ignacio de Loyola* (IHSI, second edition, 1965); 2. Jean-François GILMONT: *Les Ecrits spirituels des premiers jesuites, inventaire commenté*, IHSI, Rome, 1961; 3. Carlos SOMMERVOGEL: *Bibliothèque de la Compagnie de Jésus*, Schepens, Brussels, 1890–1909, with the addenda by Ernest-M. RIVIÈRE: *Corrections et additions à la bibliothèque de la Compagnie de Jèsus*, Revue d'Ascétique et de Mystique, Toulouse, 1911–1930; 4. Finally, to get the most out of *Monumenta Historica Societatis Jesu*, our principal source, see Felix de ZUBILLAGA and Walter HANISCH, *La Guia Manual*, IHSI, Rome, 1971.

We shall content ourselves here with indicating to our readers the works which we have actually used in our work. So as not to burden our presentation unduly, we shall omit, however, certain books or articles cited occasionally, allowing ourselves to indicate their use in a footnote. On the other hand, for the works listed here, we shall not repeat in text the information relating to the edition that we have assembled in the following pages. On the left, we indicate the abbreviations used in the notes, either the title of the work or the name of the author.

I. ARCHIVES

ARSI: *Archivum Romanum Societatis Jesu*, General Curia of the Society of Jesus, Rome. We have been able to consult the original documents there.

II. MONUMENTA HISTORICA SOCIETATIS IESU (MHSI)

This collection (105 volumes, published in Madrid from 1894 and in Rome since 1932) was our principal source, whether for the texts themselves or for analyses, chronology and even history. The volumes cited here are those which have been the most frequently used; the number or numbers follow the title, and eventually the name of the author, refer to the *Guia Manual*, pp. 1–10, cited in the introduction to the Bibliography.

Chron. = *Chronicon, Vita Ignatii Loiolae et rerum Societatis Jesu historia*, by Juan-Alphonso de POLANCO (1, 3, 5, 7, 9, 11), Madrid, 1894–1898, 6 vol.

Const. = *Sancti Ignatii de Loyola Constitutiones Societatis Jesu* (63–65), Rome 1934–1938, 3 vol.

Regulae = *Regulae Societatis Jesu* (1540–1556) (71), Rome, 1948.

Epist. ign. = *Sancti Ignatii de Loyola, Societatis Jesu fundatoris, Epistolae et Instructiones* (22, 26, 28, 29, 31, 33, 34, 36, 37, 39, 40, 42), Madrid, 1903–1911, 12 vol.

Exerc. sp. = *Sancti Ignatii de Loyola Exercitia spiritualia*, new edition of the earliest texts (100), Rome, 1969, replaces the edition of 1919 (57).

Direct. = *Directoria* (1540–1599) (76), Rome, 1955.

Bobad. Mon. = *Bobadillae monumenta. Nicolaii Alphonsi de Bobadilla sacerdotis e Societate Jesu gesta et scripta* (46), Madrid, 1913.

Epist. Broëti = *Epistolae Patrum Paschasii Broëti, Claudii Jaii, Joannis Codurii et Simonis Roderici Societatis Jesu* (24), Madrid, 1903.

Fabri Mon. = *Beati Petri Fabri primi sacerdotis et Societatis Jesu epistolae, Memoriale et processus* (48), Madrid, 1914.

Lainii Mon. = *Lainii monumenta. Epistolae et acta Patris Jacobi Lainii secundi praepositi generalis Societatis Jesu* (44, 45, 47, 49–51, 53, 55), Madrid, 1912–1917, 8 vol.

Epist. Salm. = *Epistolae Patris Alphonsi Salmeronis Societatis Jesu* (30, 32), Madrid, 1906–1907, 2 vol.

Epist. Xav. = *Epistolae sancti Francisci Xaverii aliaque ejus scripta* (67, 68), Rome, 1944–1945, 2 vol. This new edition replaces the *Monumenta Xaveriana* (16, 43), Madrid, 1899–1912, 2 vol.

Epist. Mixt = *Epistolae Mixtae ex variis Europae locis ab anno 1537 ad 1556 scriptae* (12, 14, 17, 18, 20), Madrid, 1898–1901, 5 vol.

Epist. Quadr. = *Litterae Quadrimestres ex universis praeter Indiam et Brasiliam locis in quibus aliqui de Societate Jesu versabantur Romam missae* (4, 6, 8, 10, 59, 61, 62), Madrid, 1894–1932, 7 vol.

Borgiae Mon. = *Sanctus Franciscus Borgia, quartus Gandiae dux et Societatis Jesu praepositus generalis tertius* (2, 23, 35, 38, 41), Madrid, 1894–1911, 5 vol.

Mon. Paed. = *Monumenta paedagogica Societatis Jesus* (92), Rome, 1965, 1 vol. This edition replaces that of Madrid, 1901 (19).

Mon. Bras. = *Monumenta Brasiliae* (79–81, 87) Rome, 1956–1960, 4 vol. (et un 5ᵉ vol. de *Complementa Azevediana* (99, 1968). The first two volumes are pertinent for our study.

Doc. Ind. = *Documenta Indica* (70, 72, 74, 78, 83, 86, 89), Rome, 1948–1962, 7 vol. The first three volumes are pertinent for our study.

Mon. Jap. = *Monumenta Historica Japoniae*, Rome, in preparation.

Nadal Mon. = *Epistolae Patris Hieronymi Nadal Societatis Jesu* (13, 15, 21, 27, 90, 90a), Madrid-Rome, 1898–1964, 6 vol. Several of Nadal's writings have been published in other volumes of the MHSI, in particular the "Apologia contra censuram Facultatis Theologia Parisiensis" and the "Scholia in Constitutiones et Declarationes sancti Patris Ignatii", which were published separately in the *Institutum Societatis Jesu* (Prati, 1883).

Pol. Compl. = *Polanci complementa. Epistolae et commentaria Patris Iohannis Alphonsi de Polanco e Societate Jesu addenda caeteris ejusdem scriptis dispersis in his monumentis* (52, 54), Madrid, 1916–1917, 2 vol.

Font. narr. = *Fontes narrativi de sancto Ignatio de Loyola et de Societatis Jesu initiis* (66, 73, 85, 93), Rome, 1943–1965, 4 vol.

Ribad, Mon. = *Patris Petri Ridadeneyra Societatis Jesus Confessiones, Epistolae aliaque scripta inedita* (58, 60), Madrid, 1920–1926, 2 vol. *Vita Ignatii Loyolae*: it is volume 4 of *Font. narr.* (93).

Scripta = *Scripta de sancto Ignatio de Loyola* (25, 26), Madrid, 1904–1918, 2 vol.

AHSI = *Archivum Historicum Societatis Iesu*, semi-annual review published by the editors of MHSI; useful book reviews and bibliographies.

IHSI = *Institutum Historicum Societatis Iesu*, among which the *Bibliotheca* contains numerous fundamental studies on our subject.

AASS = *Acta Apostolica Sanctae Sedis*, periodical publication of pontifical texts concerning the Society of Jesus, etc. General curia, Rome.

III. HISTORY OF THE ASSISTANCIES

ASTRAIN, Antonio, *Historica de la Compañia de Jesus en la asistencia de España*, Razon y Fe, Madrid, 1912–1925, 7 vol.

DÜHR, Bernhard, *Geschichte der Jesuiten in den Ländern deutscher Zunge*, Herder, Fribourg, 1907–1928, 6 vol.

FOUQUERAY, Henri, *Histoire de la Compagnie de Jésus en France, des origines à la suppression (1528–1762)*, Picard, Paris, 1910–1925, 5 vol.

KROESS, Alois, *Geschichte der böhmischen Provinz der Gesellschaft Jesu*, Vienna, 1910–1938, 3 vol.

LEITE, Serafim, *Historia da Companhia de Jesus no Brasil*, Lisbon–Rio de Janeiro, 1938–1950, 10 vol.

PONCELET, Albert, *Histoire de la Compagnie de Jésus dans les anciens Pays-Bas*, Hayez, Brussells, 1927, 2 vol.

RODRIGUES, Francisco, *Historia da Companhia de Jesus na assistência de Portugal*, Apostolado da Imprensa, Porto, 1931–1950.

T. VENTURI = Pietro TACCHI-VENTURI, *Storia della Compagnia di Gesû in Italia*, Civiltà cattolica, Rome, 1910–1951, 4 vol.

SCADUTO, Mario, *L'Epoca di Giacomo Laynez*, Civiltà cattolica, Rome, 1964–1974, 2 vol.
These two last works are particularly interesting for our study both because of their subject matter and the value of their information.

AGUILERA, Emmanuel, *Provinciae Siculae Societatis Jesu ortus et res gestae*, Palerme, 1737–1740, 2 vol.

IV. OTHER REFERENCE WORKS

A) From the Collection *Christus*.

Collection de textes Christus (Desclée De Brouwer, Paris, from 1959).
In particular, we have cited from the following translations in this collection:

SAINT IGNACE, *Journal spirituel* (edited by M. Giuliani), 1959.

SAINT IGNACE, *Lettres* (édité par G. Dumeige), 1959. Selected letters, to which should be added the letters translated by P. Dudon, M. Bouix (Concordance for the latter: *Epist. ign.* 12, p. 731), H. Rahner (*op. cit. infra*).

Fabri Mem. = Bienheureux Pierre FAVRE, *Mémorial* (edited by M. de Certeau), 1959.

Exerc. = *SAINT IGNACE, Exercices spirituels* (edited by F. Courel), 1963.

RAHNER, Hugo, *Ignace de Loyola et les femmes de son temps*, 2 vol., 1964.

MÉMORIAL = Louis GONÇALVEZ DA CÂMARA, *Mémorial* (edited by R. Tandonnet), 1966.

SAINT IGNACE, *Constitutions de la Compagnie de Jésus* (edited by F. Courel, I.; F. Roustang and F. Courel, II), 2 vol.

B) Studies

ALDAMA, Antonio-Maria DE, *Vestigia sanctorum Societatis Jesu in Urbe Roma*, Rome (Borgo Santo Spirito), 1953 (French translation). *La Composicion de las Constituciones de la Compañia de Jésus*, C.I.S., Rome, 1972.

Autob. A.G., Autob. R.P. = *SAINT IGNACE, Autobiographie* (dictée à Gonçalves da Câmara). *A.G.* = French translation by A. Guillermou (Le Seuil, 1962); *R.P.*: French translation by A. Thiry (under the title: *Récit du Pèlerin*, Museum Lessianum, Desclée De Brouwer, Bruges, 1956, 3rd éd.). English edition: *St. Ignatius' Own Story*, as told to Luis Gonzales de Câmara, with a sampling of his letters, translated by William J. Young, S.J., Chicago: Loyola University Press, 1980.

AICARDO, José-Manuel, *Comentario a las Constituciones de la Compañia de Jesus*, Blass, Madrid, 1919–1932, 6 vol.

BATAILLON, Marcel, *Erasme et l'Espagne. Recherches sur l'histoire spirituelle du XVIe siècle*, E. Droz, Paris, 1937.

BROU, Alexandre, *Saint François Xavier*, Beauchesne, Paris, 1922.

Canis, épist. = *Beati Petri Canisii Societatis Jesu epistulae et acta* (edited by O. Braunsberger), Herder, Freiburg im Breisgau, 1896–1923, 8 vol.

COGNET, Louis, *La Spiritualité moderne* vol. 3 of *Histoire de la spiritualité chrétienne*), Aubier, Paris, 1966.

CODINA MIR, Gabriel, *Aux sources de la pédagogie des Jésuites: le «modus parisiensis»*, IHSI, Rome, 1968.

CONC. TRID. = *Concilium Tridentinum. Diariorum, epistolarum, tractatuum nova collectio*, Societas Gorresiana, Herder, Freiburg im Breisgau, from 1901 on.

CREVIER, Jean-Baptiste, *Histoire de l'université de Paris, depuis son origine jusqu'en l'année 1600*, Desaint, Paris, 1761.

CROS, Léonard, *Saint François Xavier, son pays, sa famille, sa vie*, Dourriol, Paris, 1903. *Saint François Xavier, sa vie et ses lettres*, Privat-Retaux, Toulouse-Paris, 1900, 2 vol.

DAINVILLE, François de, *La Naissance de l'humanisme moderne*, Beauchesne, Paris, 1940.

DELUMEAU, Jean, *La Civilisation de la Renaissance* (collection «Les grandes civilisations»), Arthaud, Paris, 1967. *Naissance et affirmation de la Réforme* (Nouvelle Clio), PUF, Paris, 1965.

DHÔTEL, Jean-Claude, *Les Origines du catéchisme moderne d'après les premiers manuels imprimés en France* (coll. «Théologie»), Aubier, Paris, 1967.

DOUMERGUE, Emile, *Jean Calvin, les hommes et les choses de son temps*, Payot-Edition de la Cause, Lausanne-Neuilly, 1899–1927, 7 vol.

DUDON, Paul, *Saint Ignace de Loyola*, Beauchesne, Paris, 1934.

EGANA, François-Xavier, *Origines de la congregacion general en la Compañia de Jesus*, IHSI, Rome, 1972.

FEBVRE, Lucien, *Le Problème de l'incroyance au XVIᵉ siècle*, Albin Michel, Paris, 1942. *Un destin : Martin Luther*, PUF, Paris, 1945. Lucien FEBVRE and Henri-Jean MARTIN, *L'Apparition du livre*, Albin Michel, Paris, 1957.

FÉRET, Pierre, *La Faculté de théologie de Paris et ses docteurs les plus célèbres*, A. Picard and Son, Paris, 1900–1910, 7 vol.

FLICHE, Augustin, et Victor MARTIN, *Histoire générale de l'Eglise* (continued by Jean-Baptiste Duroselle and Eugène Jarry), Bloud et Gay, Paris.

GUIBERT, Joseph de, *La Spiritualité de la Compagnie de Jésus, esquisse historique*, IHSI, Rome, 1953.

GUILLERMOU, Alain, *La Vie de saint Ignace de Loyola*, Le Seuil, Paris, 1956.

HAMY, Alfred, *Essai sur l'iconographie de la Compagnie de Jésus*, Rapilly, Paris, 1875.

HERMAN, Jean-Baptiste, *La Pédagogie des Jésuites au XVIᵉ siècle, ses sources, ses caractéristiques*, University of Louvain, 1914.

Hist. Miss. = *Histoire universelle des Missions catholiques* (especially vol. 2), Nouvelle Librairie de France, Paris, 1957.

IMBART = Pierre IMBART DE LA TOUR, *Les Origines de la Réforme*, 2nd edition, Librairie d'Argences, Melun, 1946–1948.

JANSSEN, Jean, *L'Allemagne et la Réforme* (translated by E. Paris for the 14th edition), Plon, Paris, 1887–1914, 8 volumes and 1 of tables.

JIMENEZ ONATE, Antonio, *El Origen de la Compañia de Jesus : carisma fundacional y genesis historica*, IHSI, Rome, 1966.

LAFONTAINE, Albert, *Jehan Gerson* (1363–1429), Poussielgue, Paris, 1906.

LECLERC, Joseph, *Histoire de la tolérance au siècle de la Réforme* (Collection «Théologie»), Aubier, Paris, 1955, 2 vol. *Le Pape ou le concile*, Le Chalet, Paris, 1973.

LETURIA, Pietro, *El Gentilhombre Iñigo Lopez de Loyola en su patria y en su siglo*, Mosca, Montevideo, 1938. *Estudios Ignacianos* : I. Estudios biograficos; II. Estudios espirituales (revised by Ignacio Iparraguirre), IHSI, Rome, 1957.

LEWIS, Jacques *Le Gouvernement spirituel selon saint Ignace de Loyola*, Desclée De Brouwer, Bruges, 1961.

MANARE, Olivier, *De Rebus Societatis Jesu commentarius*, Ricci, Florence, 1886.

NICOLAU, Michel, *Jeronimo Nadal (1507–1580). Obras y doctrinas espirituales*, Instituto Francisco Suarez, Madrid, 1949.

NORES, Pietro, *Storia della guerra di Paolo IV sommo Pontefice contro gli Spagnuoli* (Archivio storico italiano, vol. 12). G.P. Vieusseux, Florence, 1847.

OLIVARES, Estanislao, *Los Votos de los escolares de la Compañia de Jesus*, IHSI, Rome, 1961.

ORLANDINI, Nicolo, *Historiae Societatis Jesu pars prima sive Ignatius*, Bartolomeo Zanetto, Rome, 1614.

PASTOR, Louis, *Histoire des papes à partir de la fin du Moyen Age*, Plon, afterward Librairie d'Argences, Paris, 1888–1962, 22 vol.

PLATTARD, Jean, *Guillaume Budé (1468–1540) et les origines de l'humanisme français*, Les Belles Lettres, Paris, 1923.

PRÉVOST, André, *Thomas More et la crise de la pensée européenne*, Mame, Tours, 1969.

QUICHERAT, Jules, *Histoire de Sainte-Barbe. Collège, communauté, institution*, Hachette, Paris, 1860–1864, 3 vol.

RAHNER, Hugo, *Ignatius von Loyola als Mensch und Theologe*, Herder, Freiburg im Breisgau, 1964. *Ignatius von Loyola, Briefwechsel mit Frauen*, Herder, Freiburg im Breisgau, 1956 (translated in the collection *Christus*).

RAVIER, André, *Les Chroniques saint Ignace de Loyola*, Nouvelle Librairie de France, Paris, 1973. *La Mystique et les mystiques* (en collaboration), Desclée De Brouwer, Paris, 1965. *Saint François de Sales. Œuvres* (L◦ Pléiade), NRF, Paris, 1970.

RENAUDET AND HAUSER = Augustin RENAUDET et Henri HAUSER, *Les Débuts de l'âge moderne: la Renaissance et la Réforme* (Peuples et civilisations, vol. 8), PUF, Paris, 1946.

RENAUDET = *Préréforme et humanisme à Paris pendant les premières guerres d'Italie* (1494–1517), Librairie d'Argences, Paris, 1953. *Erasme, sa pensée religieuse et son action d'après sa correspondance* (1518–1521), Alcan, Paris, 1926, *Etudes érasmiennes,* Droz, Paris, 1939.

RICARD, Robert, and Roger AUBENAS, *L'Eglise et la Renaissance (1449–1517),* «Histoire de l'Eglise» (directed by A. Fliche and V. Martin), Bloud et Gay, Paris, 1939.

ROMIER, Lucien, *Les Origines politiques des guerres de religion,* Perrin, Paris, 1913–1914, 2 vol.

ROUQUETTE, Robert, «Essai critique sur les sources relatant la vision de saint Ignace de Loyola à la Storta (Octobre 1537)'', *Revue d'Ascétique et de Mystique,* t. 33 (1957), pp. 34–61, 150–170. Handwritten notes for a spiritual biography of St. Ignatius of Loyola (archives of Etudes). «Une Jésuitesse secrète au xviᵉ siècle», *Etudes,* vol. 316 (March 1957), pp. 355–373.

SACCHINI, François, *Historia Societatis Jesu,* Nutius, Anvers, pius Manelfius, Varesius, Rome, 1620–1652, 5 vol.

SCADUTO, Mario, *L'Epoca di Giacomo Lainez,* see above III, history of the assistancies. *Catalogo dei Gesuiti d'Italia* (1540–1565), IHSI, Rome, 1968. «Uno scritto ignaziano inedito: il 'Del officio del secretario' del 1547», *AHSI,* vol. 29 (1960), p. 305–328.

SCHRÖTELER, Joseph, *Die Erziehung in den Jesuiteninternaten des sechzehnten Jahrhunderts,* Herder, Freiburg im Breisgau, 1940.

SCHURHAMMER, Georg, *Franz Xaver, sein Leben und seine Zeit,* Herder, Friburg im Breisgau, 1955–1973, 4 vol. *Die Zeitgenössischen Quellen zur Geschichte portugiesisch-Asiens und seiner Nachbarländer zur Zeit des heiligen Franz Xaver (1538–1552),* IHSI, Rome, 1962.

STROHL, Henri, *Luther jusqu'en 1520,* PUF, Paris, 1962.

SUAU: Pierre SUAU, *Histoire de saint François de Borgia (1510–1572),* Beauchesne, Paris, 1905, 2 vol.

T. VENTURI = Pietro, TACCHI-VENTURI, «Le Case abitate in Roma da S. Ignazio di Loyola», *Studi e documenti di storia e diritto,* t. 20 (1899), pp. 287–356. *Storia della Compagnia di Gesù,* see above, III, history of the assistancies.

THIBAUDET, Albert, *Montaigne,* Gallimard, Paris, 1963.

THOMASSIN, Louis, *Vetus et nova Ecclesiae disciplina circa beneficia et beneficiarios,* F. Muguet, Paris, 1688, 3 vol.

URIZZA, Juan, *La Preclara Facultad de Artes y Filosofia de la Universidad de Alcala de Henares en el siglo de oro (1509–1621),* Editorial Consejo superior de investigaciones cientificas, Madrid, 1942.

VALIGNANO, Alexandre, *Historia del principio y progresso de la Compañia de Jesus en las Indias Orientales (1542–1564)* (edited by J. Wicki), IHSI, Rome, 1944.

VILLOSLADA, Ricardo G., *Storia del collegio romano dal suo inizio (1551) alla suppressione della Compagnia di Gesù (1773),* Gregorian University Press, Rome, 1954.

VOOGHT, Paul De, *L'Hérésie de Jean Huss* and his appendix volume of articles, *Hussiana,* Bibliothèque de la Revue d'Histoire ecclésiastique, Louvain, 1960.

WICKI Joseph, (cf. VALIGNO et *Epist. Xav.*), *Documenta Indica,* MHSI, 12 volumes have been published (vols. I, II, and III are pertinent to our subject). «Die Chiffre in der Ordenskorrespondenz der Gessellschaft Jesu von Ignatius bis General Oliva (ca. 1554–1676)», *AHSI,* vol. 32 (1963), pp. 133–178. «Zwei Briefe des Simon Rodriguez, s.j., an Johann III von Portugal», *AHSI,* vol. 24 (1955), pp. 327–335.

INDEX